Educational
Psychology

Educational Psychology

John F. Travers

BOSTON COLLEGE

Harper & Row, Publishers

New York   Hagerstown   Philadelphia   San Francisco   London

Sponsoring Editor: George A. Middendorf
Project Editor: Claudia Kohner
Designer: Robert Sugar
Production Manager: Marion A. Palen
Photo Researcher: Myra Schachne
Compositor: P & M Typesetting, Inc.
Printer and Binder: Halliday Lithograph Corporation
Art Studio: Vantage Art Inc.
Cover Photo: Burri, Magnum

Chapter 3, "Early Experience and Intellectual Development"
is adapted from the chapter "Early Experience and Intelligence" in John F. Travers, *The New Children: The First 6
Years*. Stamford, Connecticut: Greylock Publishers, 1976.
With permission of Greylock Publishers.

Appendix: Introduction to Statistical Methods in Psychology
by Foster Lloyd Brown. Copyright © 1973 by Harper & Row,
Publishers, Inc.

Figures 6.6, 9.3, and 14.1 from John F. Travers, *Learning:
Analysis and Application*. Second Edition. New York:
McKay, 1972.

The cartoon on page 656 is used by permission of Walter
Hagedorn.

Educational Psychology

Library of Congress Cataloging in Publication Data

Travers, John F
  Educational psychology.

  Bibliography: p.
  Includes index.
  1. Educational psychology.   I. Title.
LB1051.T669   370.15   78–27526
ISBN 0–06–046655–3

To My Mother
and the Memory
of My Father

v

Contents

vii

Part Four
The Learner and Individual Differences

Preface

Times and the concerns of educational psychologists change. Busing, teacher strikes, school vandalism, Supreme Court decisions, and mainstreaming handicapped children add new dimensions to teaching and learning. These issues, because of their impact on pupils and teachers and the psychological consequences of this impact, demand attention.

They demand attention not only because they are controversial and critical but also because they have become part of a national public policy: judicial and legislative mandates lead to action, and action affects both pupils and teachers. Programs for the handicapped necessitate a psychological as well as a physical atmosphere that insures warmth and support for all youngsters. English is a second language for some youngsters; no longer can a pupil's cultural background be a barrier to classroom learning. Add busing, teachers' legal status, children's rights, and intervention programs, among other concerns, and suddenly the conclusion is inescapable: many of the questions addressed to educational psychology reflect issues of public policy.

There are, however, constant issues that have traditionally distinguished educational psychology and have contributed to its status as a unique discipline. Of these, teaching, learning, and development are the most prominent. The more that teachers know about learners, their growth patterns and the outstanding characteristics of the various stages through which they pass, the better they can adapt their teaching to meet the individual needs of learners.

Consequently, the learner is the focus of this text. Educational psychology is now such a vast subject that some unifying theme is necessary to coordinate its many parts. By relating everything to the learner—the *learner* and development, the *learner* and learning, the *learner* and individual differences, the *learner* and instruction— you can organize educational and psychological data into meaningful models of teaching-learning interaction. Since teaching is a singularly personal act, using the learner as your focus will enable you to construct *your* model of successful teaching. Your personality, your experiences, your current study, should coalesce to help you develop this model.

Educational psychology, however, is no abstract exercise in theory construction. It is a vital, living subject, one that helps a variety of people to work better with others. Its connection to teaching and classroom learning is obvious, but parents and future parents will also benefit from discussions of human development and the meaning of a stimulating environment. Those working with adults in adult education programs, family support programs, prisons, or business seminars can profit from studying educational psychology. Considerable teaching occurs outside the classroom in sports activities, camps, clubs, and playgrounds, for example, and the principles of educational psychology apply there as well as in schools.

Times and the concerns of students also change, but for any author one theme remains constant: to exhort the reader to read carefully, to comprehend, but also to enjoy. Educational psychology is an exciting, relevant subject that sheds light on many contemporary issues. Tables, charts, and research studies come alive when applied to the burning issues facing modern society.

You will find study aids incorporated into the text that should help your reading and understanding. Each chapter has an identical format: a detailed chapter outline that tells you precisely what the chapter includes, marginal notations that call your attention to major topics, boxed materials that present research or comments on important subjects, discussion questions the answers for which will provide constant feedback concerning your understanding of the preceding section, a "some concluding thoughts" section that should suggest new dimensions to the chapter, a summary of the chapter's highlights, and, finally, a concise list of suggested readings. Before you begin serious reading, try to grasp the book's structure; thumb through several chapters and identify the features just mentioned. You will find that knowing how to use a book substantially improves comprehension.

Any author is bowed by the weight of indebtedness to others, but one, among many, deserves special recognition. My wife, Barbara, who typed the manuscript and aided in much of the research, has unfailingly throughout the years offered support and encouragement. Thanks alone are insufficient.

Part One

Introduction

1

Educational Psychology: Teaching, Learning, Developing

(continues)

Introduction

The philosopher Alfred North Whitehead has said that with good discipline it is always possible to pump into the minds of a class a certain quantity of inert knowledge. You simply take a textbook and make them learn it. But what good does this do? The mind is a restless, probing thing that requires stimulation and activity. The theoretical ideas found within a text must have practical application so that restless minds can test, recombine, perhaps even reject them. Otherwise students carry a burden of inert ideas. As Whitehead notes, a merely well-informed person is the most useless bore on God's earth.

Whitehead's beliefs, found in his classic work *The Aims of Education* (1949; originally published 1929), provide the guidelines for this book. Educational psychology books are treasures of information. If you want facts about human development, theories of learning, or the latest educational programs, try an educational psychology text. Their encyclopedic nature, however, poses some of the problems that troubled Whitehead, since the search for facts often obscures the reasons for seeking them. There must be appli-

The Aims of Education

Alfred North Whitehead was one of the most stimulating minds of the twentieth century. Philosopher, mathematician, and educator, in *The Aims of Education* (1949) he gives a penetrating insight into what education should be, and also what an educational text should be. Arguing forcefully against inert or dead ideas, Whitehead believes that the function of a university is to enable you to shed details in favor of principles. Only then can education produce individuals who possess both culture and some special expert knowledge.

Whitehead's meaning is clear: Education should impart a love of ideas, an appreciation of the structure of knowledge, thus developing the cultured mind. Joined with a particular expertise, that is, some specialized knowledge, there emerges an educated individual who *uses* these ideas in both a philosophical and practical manner. To produce such a graduate is the goal of a university— through its faculty, courses, texts, and gen-

eral atmosphere. As Whitehead notes, the proper function of a university is the imaginative acquisition of knowledge, both general principles and technical knowledge.

There is a perceptive theme in Whitehead's writing that is particularly pertinent for educational psychology. Of all the courses in teacher education, none combines the cultural and technical, the theoretical and practical, as does educational psychology. Theoretically, educational psychology delves deeply into human development, theories of learning and personality, and mathematical computations. But it must then *apply* these ideas: How does personality theory help me to understand pupils? Here is the great value of educational psychology; it contributes both to cultural attainment and technical expertise.

Whitehead's work is difficult but well worth the effort. If you are interested, *The Aims of Education* is available in paperback.

cation, and throughout this work you will discern an obvious effort to unite theory and practice, thus avoiding that ghastly label: "a useless bore."

A NEED TO UNDERSTAND

Students take an educational psychology course for a variety of reasons. You may intend to teach and want answers to such questions as:

1. When are youngsters ready for certain experiences? For example, are there developmental data that offer clues about the ideal time to begin reading instruction?
2. Are there different teaching techniques that are better with one child than others? Do some youngsters learn more with teaching machines than with the freedom of an open classroom?

3. Does a knowledge of learning theory help in the classroom? For example, does understanding the fundamentals of memory enable teachers to help pupils retain their learning and transfer it to other subjects?

4. Does knowing the details of test construction really matter? For example, if we understand the theory behind test making, does it help us to be more certain about the extent and quality of a youngster's learning?
5. What does the latest research say about discipline? Here is a question that usually is the first asked by student and beginning teachers. Children need a happy blend of firmness and freedom. But how do we arrive at this happy medium?

These are practical questions that have direct classroom application. They should also set the tone for your work. To answer them requires a combination of theoretical expertise, sound fact, and classroom experience. It is through the blend of theory, fact, and application that you will benefit from reading this text. When you complete your reading, if you are a beginning teacher, you should face that first day with more confidence. If you are an experienced teacher you should have new ideas to test, new techniques to try.

If you are interested in educational psychology for itself, as a discipline worthy of study, you should acquire a better understanding of our schools, the pupils who are in them, the teachers who instruct these pupils, and the administrators who are in charge.

Whether in undergraduate or graduate school, adult or continuing education, whether as a parent or concerned citizen, educational psychology offers insights into some of the most critical contemporary issues. Here are a few examples.

Busing

The vast majority of Americans state that they oppose racial segregation and favor integrated schools. Integrated schools, however, necessitate assigning youngsters—on a racial basis—to predetermined schools. This policy may force youngsters to travel a considerable distance, thus requiring busing.

For example, if you were the parent of a kindergarten youngster and realized that your child would travel many miles from home to school—even if there is a nearby neighborhood school—would your commitment to integrated schools remain firm?

Educational psychology can help you to weigh your child's maturity and health; consider the educational atmosphere of the new school; and evaluate the learning facilities your child may require. These are only a few suggestions, but your knowledge of educa-

tional psychology encourages you to ponder developmental and learning issues.

Back to basics

One of the most intense of the recent educational controversies is the back-to-basics movement. Concerned parents are raising a national clamor about students' inability to spell, write, read, and do simple mathematical calculations. While one community may focus on reading and writing, another may be outraged by discipline problems, and yet another may insist on a traditional marking system (A, B, C, or 100, 90, 80).

For example, your school system has an open-seat policy (any child may go to any school in the community provided there is a vacancy), but there is a school just around the corner. The principal has announced a no-nonsense discipline code and the removal of all "frills." You want your youngster to receive a sound linguistic and mathematical foundation but you also believe in the importance of sex- and drug-education programs in the elementary school. Would you send your child to the local school?

Your knowledge of educational psychology poses several questions that will help you to decide. Will your child be psychologi-

cally secure in new surroundings? Can you offset any weakness in
the new school's reading program by your familiarity with reading
readiness, educational materials, and teaching techniques? Do developmental considerations such as peer pressure and community
values dictate the necessity for your youngster enrolling in drug-
and/or sex-education programs?

Discipline

Student behavior, in and out of school, has aroused considerable
anxiety among teachers and parents. While some believe that
youth frequently reacts against society's rigid control, a growing
majority is convinced that today's permissiveness, both at home
and at school, has produced a disciplinary breakdown.

For example, you are among those who believe that schools
need firm control, an orderly atmosphere, and student respect for
authority. Yet the principal of your children's school has announced that as a result of the recent Supreme Court decision permitting corporal punishment, teachers have this right and will be
encouraged to exercise it. What is your reaction?

It is a difficult question and a knowledge of educational psychology can perhaps only help you to weigh alternatives. Does
your recognition of punishment's effects offset any possible advantages? What will be the emotional consequences of such an educational atmosphere?

These are only a few of the educational issues attracting attention. Others include the role of technology in schools, the dangers
of sexual stereotyping, the nature and role of testing, and the demand for a return to the self-contained classroom. Youngsters
caught in the resulting controversies react as individuals, and one
of educational psychology's great values is that it enables teachers
and parents to understand better the reasons for pupils' behavior.

WHAT IS EDUCATIONAL PSYCHOLOGY?

On the surface this is a deceptively simple question that should be
answered briefly and directly. Upon closer examination, however,
it is remarkably complex. Whenever a discussion centers upon human behavior, disagreement and controversy inevitably arise, with
the result that a tradition of critical examination has provided educational psychology with a rich legacy. Instruction proceeds more
efficiently and learning occurs more effectively because of continuing research that is a response to the challenge of inquiring
minds.

A Working Definition   Educational psychology remains difficult to define. Perhaps it is
best described as the systematic study of pupils, learning, and

teaching. Students, the learning process, and teaching are related and interactive aspects of education. To teach effectively requires extensive knowledge about human beings, the means by which they learn, and methods of communication. If comprehension of any of these aspects of the teaching-learning process is deficient, then classroom performance will undoubtedly suffer.

The Art of Teaching

Gilbert Highet has written a classic about teachers and teaching. Called *The Art of Teaching* (1950), it presents a thoughtful and witty commentary on teaching. Highet begins by noting what he designates as the three great rewards of teaching—leisure, useful and challenging work, and happiness in a constructive task. For example, teachers are not bound to a nine-to-five job; there is the joy of a free summer (most likely to work at something else), and the freedom to do routine chores at their own discretion. Leisure is a valuable commodity. Teachers use their minds on valuable subjects; there is no numbing, repetitive task that dulls mental activity. Rather, their work is both useful and challenging and leads to the third reward: happiness. Teachers do not merely insert facts into something else. They take a living mind and mold it. To have a student argue with you, using the facts and rationale you provided, is to achieve the satisfaction of an artist creating a picture on blank canvas.

Highet classifies the various forces acting on the teacher by sorting them into such categories as the qualities of a good teacher, the abilities of a good teacher, and teaching methods, and then relating these to some of history's great teachers. It is refreshing to pause and consider some of Highet's criteria of good teachers.

They must know their subject, which implies that teachers grasp not only the material that they are currently presenting in class, but also the core of the subject, and what research is discovering at the frontiers of the discipline. In an age devoted to empirical research, the expansion of knowledge necessitates constant independent study by a teacher to prevent personal obsolescence.

Teachers will avoid such work unless they like their subject and enjoy youth. To devote hours of study beyond the demands of duty requires a commitment to a discipline and the company of the young, both of which can be provocative masters. If a love of study and pleasure in working with youth is lacking, then one should shun a teaching career, whatever the temptation.

In addition to these qualities, Highet notes that teachers should possess certain abilities: memory, willpower, and kindness. Note how the combination of personal characteristics plus capacity will ultimately determine both teaching techniques and teachers' success in communicating knowledge through a particular method to students. Know your subject; know your pupils; know how to relate one to another—an age-old cry that still occupies our attention. You would enjoy reading Highet.

EDUCATIONAL PSYCHOLOGY AND STUDENTS

If educational psychology is to have a direct influence upon class-room practice, teachers need information about the pupils they teach. While detailed examination of youngsters — their physical, mental, and emotional attributes — will come later, there are many revealing demographic characteristics of the school population.

A greater proportion of Americans than ever before is going to school.

They are starting school at an earlier age and staying in school longer.

For the first time, the average American adult has completed high school.

People who live in urban areas have a higher level of education than those in rural areas.

MEDFORD, MASS. DAILY MERCURY

Although a higher percentage of whites than of blacks or those of Spanish ancestry finish high school, these minorities are closing the gap.

There is a definite relationship between level of education and the kinds of job people hold, and how much they are paid.

The 1970 census also indicates that there were nearly 60 million students in some kind of school. Of this number, 51.2 million were white, 7.4 million black, and 3.2 million shared a Spanish heritage. The numbers by grade level are as shown in Table 1.1.

The figures are fascinating. For example, the kind of community in which individuals live makes a difference. People who live in rural areas have completed less schooling than those in urban areas. The 1970 census shows that adults in urban areas had one more year of schooling than the average adult in rural areas. In 1970 men first equaled women in median years of school attended. The 1950 and 1960 census showed that women had about a half-year more schooling on the average than men. In 1970 both sexes had completed a median of 12.1 years. The accompanying map (Figure 1.1) is a graphic illustration of schooling completed by men and women in each state.

There are several other interesting characteristics of our school population.

1. *Minority groups.* In 1940 nonwhite minorities had an average of 5.8 years of school. By 1970 the average was up to 10.0 years, a gain of 4.2 years. For the same 30-year period, whites gained only 3.4 years (from 8.7 to 12.1 years). As younger members replace the older, the minorities will steadily narrow the gap. For example, 55 percent of blacks of 18 to 24 years have a high school diploma,

TABLE 1.1
1970 School Enrollment

Level	White	Black	Spanish Heritage
Nursery	805,000	128,000	51,000
Kindergarten	2.6 million	356,000	189,000
Elementary	28.2 "	4.6 million	2.0 million
High School	12.5 "	1.8 "	699,000
College	6.4 "	431,000	223,000

Source: U.S. Bureau of the Census, Department of Commerce, 1970 Census of Population: General Social and Economic Characteristics.

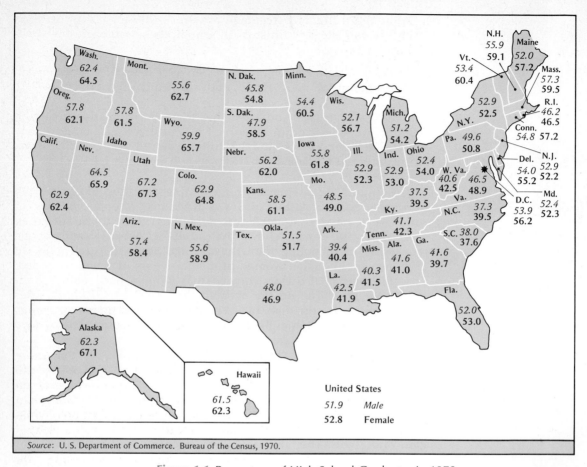

Source: U. S. Department of Commerce. Bureau of the Census, 1970.

Figure 1.1 Percentage of High School Graduates in 1970

compared with 31 percent of all blacks. In 1970 the median school-ing completed by those of Spanish heritage was 9.6 years. The cen-sus figures also reveal that for all minorities, the percentages of 16- and 17-year-olds attending school approximate the national aver-age.

2. *Illiteracy.* The illiteracy problem constantly appears in any discussion of schooling. You are probably aware of today's grow-ing concern that a high proportion of our high school graduates have reading and mathematical problems, which is not what is meant by illiteracy. Illiteracy as used here refers to a person's in-ability to read or write *at all.* The 1840 census showed that one of every five persons was illiterate. Today's findings indicate that while the percentage of people unable to read or write is small, the

BOSTON, SUMMERTHING

total number is large. Estimates are that one percent of the population over 14 is illiterate—about 1.4 million persons. The elderly comprise the largest illiterate group.

3. *Dropouts.* Surprisingly, the 1970 census indicates that more dropouts come from rural than from urban areas. Nationally, 15 percent of 16–21-year-old males are not in school—1.3 million whites, 345,000 blacks, and 139,000 of Spanish descent. More than twice as many minorities than whites had left high school. While rural dropouts are most numerous, the dropout rate in the central cities was 16 percent, compared with 11 percent in the suburbs.

4. *Types of school.* The pattern of American schooling has changed noticeably in the last 30 years. In 1940 there were more than 194,000 elementary schools. A majority of these (108,000) had only one teacher. By 1970 the number of elementary schools had dropped to 81,000, and of these only 2,100 had one teacher. During this same period the number of high schools increased from 29,000 to 30,000.

Most children go to public schools. Between 1960 and 1970, the proportion of youngsters attending private kindergartens increased, but declined for private elementary and high school (see Table 1.2)

The general description of the school population emphasizes the importance of education in a modern society while simultaneously identifying several national problems, particularly illiteracy and dropouts. As you read this description you probably wondered about your personal role, what you can hope to accomplish, and how you can help your pupils. If you are a beginning teacher, the

TABLE 1.2
1970 Percentage Enrollment by Type of School

Level	Public	Parochial	Other Private
Nursery	32	5	63
Kindergarten	84	5	11
Elementary	89	10	1
High School	90	7	3
College	66	34	

Source: U.S Bureau of the Census, Department of Commerce, 1970 Census of Population: General Social and Economic Characteristics.

letter shown in the box on page 15 will allay many fears and offer substantial encouragement. If you are an experienced teacher, it may rekindle the optimism and enthusiasm with which you commenced teaching.

Discussion Questions

1. Give an example of what Whitehead means by "inert ideas." Have you ever had inert ideas presented to you in any of your classes? Share with the group your experience by explaining what type of class (math, English, social studies), the kinds of teaching, and your evaluation of the teacher's personality.

2. If you intend to teach, can you think of other questions that you would like educational psychology to answer? How do they relate to the definition of educational psychology? Will they help you to understand better the teaching-learning process? How?

3. How would you answer the questions on busing, back-to-basics, and discipline? Although they were intended to illustrate educational psychology's disciplinary value, they are grimly realistic for many people. Can you suggest other insights educational psychology can offer?

4. Why are you studying educational psychology? What do you hope to gain from it? Do you agree with the assumption that educational psychology's value is not confined to education? Justify your answer.

Some contributions of educational psychologists

Many outstanding thinkers have contributed to the emergence of educational psychology as a distinct discipline, but several have made such significant contributions that they deserve separate consideration: Edward Lee Thorndike, John Dewey, Alfred Binet, Lewis Terman, and Ivan Pavlov.

Letter to a Fledgling Teacher

You ask for advice to carry with you to your first teaching assignment and, of course, I'm glad to give it. But, every teacher develops her own unique methods, and so will you. All I can do is tell you about those attitudes and feelings that mean most to me.

First, remember that children are *children*. The world is new to them. Their senses aren't dulled by high prices, government scandals and what might, or might not happen tomorrow. Children live in The Now, and their problems are almost always immediate and clear cut: "Will mother meet the school bus?" "What'll teacher say about the spilled paint?" "Why is Billy so mean to me?"

To a child, each day is a bright, new penny in the pocket. It is in the spending of it—as wise or woeful as that firsthand experience may turn out to be—that he learns. Never, ever get in the way of that learning. Even though you'll be under lots of pressure—from principal, parents, *everybody*—resist the temptation to hurry your kids. Let them savor each experience. Let their minds spread out. Let them find out for themselves if something does, or doesn't work. To let a child make his own mistakes may be the hardest lesson *you* have to learn, but such is the restraint of a good teacher.

Maybe your school will be tight and traditional, your classroom girded with rigid walls. Never mind. Architecture has little to do with whether a classroom is full of cobwebs or a place where sunbeams dance. Even if your room isn't open-spaced, you can make it open-hearted.

For starters, you can child-center it—let everything flow from the child out, and not from teacher to the child. It will be up to you, of course, to supply the props for learning—as many experiences and materials as you possibly can. But, if you listen to your children and take your cues from them, you'll make it *their* learning, *their* classroom. And that's what open-hearted is all about.

It helps, too, to perfume the classroom with the sweet smell of success. Be kind to your kids. Show joy at even their small achievements. Sprinkle each day with praise—sincere praise that can withstand a child's window-pane vision of the adult heart. Accent the positive—the good try; the perhaps slow but steady progress—rather than poor work on a task. Do all that and the waltzing sunbeams will crowd failure out the door.

One of the most important responsibilities of an open-hearted teacher, I think, is keeping her children tuned in to all kinds of beauty. There is beauty, for example, in order, and even an open-hearted teacher doesn't let her children run wild. Show your kids you care by disciplining them. Teach them concern for others, and how to take care of their classroom.

There is beauty, too, in people. Help your children see it in older people, as well as in their peers. Invite parents to work with you in the classroom and, if you can, adopt a grandparent or two, too.

And, of course, there is beauty in shadows playing tag with the sunshine, in the chirp of a cricket, in the grit-on-velvet feel of chalkdust between the fingers—*everywhere*. Remember the night you sat with me in the boat and the water was smooth as waxed paper and the moon was full and you could see all the way to the bottom? Remember the calls of the loons and the bat that flew across the moon? Wasn't that as important and as lasting an experience as learning to tie your shoes?

Give your children the same kind of glittering souvenirs. Keep their senses awake. Take them on walks and encourage them to look . . . listen . . . touch. And wouldn't it be wonderful, if some sparkling fall Saturday, you could take them camping or hiking? Wonderful, yes, for the kids. But think, too, what insights you could gain. Could it be that the children who shine in the classroom fade back as new leaders emerge in this natural setting?

Which brings up the specialness of each child. Not only does every child have unique gifts and attributes, but the same child sometimes seems to be several different children—or at least several different ages—in the same day. But, then, adults are like that, too. Don't you feel much more mature in some situations than others? I do. And, when I'm not feeling well, I just know I'm tiny and positively helpless.

One of the more obvious differences in children is in language. A child's talk is a reflection of his environment and experiences. Don't slam down on him if he uses expressions like "ain't" and "I is. . . ." Don't even tell him they're wrong. (How can they be wrong if father or sister uses them?) You have to learn to live with the language until the child discovers there are other ways to talk. And learn, he will, in an open-hearted classroom.

And Jody, please don't ever take it for granted that a child knows what *you're* talking about. I remember doing remedial work with Larry, one of a family of 12 that lived on an isolated farm. I was floored to find a 12-year-old who didn't understand the word *pair*. Well, Larry finally learned the concept and, in the process, he taught me a valuable lesson, too.

Like all young teachers, you're full of ideas, Jody, and I know for a fact that you're adventurous enough to try them. But, go easy. If, for example, you want to open your classroom, do it gradually. No doubt, some of your kids will be ready and raring to go. But how about the others? Perhaps they have enough coming down on them, without the added responsibilities that go with independent learning. Ease them into your new ways of doing things.

Anyway, thank you, Jody, for giving me this opportunity to dust off and polish up my ideals (all teachers need ideals). I'm looking forward to hearing about your first weeks of teaching. Mine, I know, were full of frazzle. And, later, when I told my kids that, like them, I had been nervous and worried about the new situation, they couldn't believe it. Well, at least I let them know I'm human. I hope I let them know, too, that I cared about them. For caring, as I'm sure you've guessed, is what this letter is all about.

Source: "Letter to a Fledgling Teacher," by Dorothy Marsh. Reprinted with permission of the publisher, Allen Raymond, Inc., Darien, Conn. 06820. From the September 1975 issue of *Early Years* Magazine.

EDWARD LEE THORNDIKE (1874–1949)

Often called the founder of Connectionism (a theory that states that all learning results from the connection between a stimulus and response), Thorndike, after initially rejecting psychology, succumbed to the charm of William James' writing. Studying animal learning, Thorndike became convinced that learning follows three major laws:

1. Readiness, which means that children must be prepared to meet new learning experiences.
2. Exercise, which means that the more we do something meaningful, the better we become at it.
3. Effect, which means that success increases the strength of an act, while punishment weakens it (Travers, 1977, pg. 275).

Thorndike's work, as scientific as the times permitted, stands as a monument in any discussion of the history of educational psychology.

JOHN DEWEY (1859–1952)

Dewey, perhaps America's greatest educational philosopher, has influenced American education since he first went to the University of Chicago in 1894. His emphasis on "learning by doing" revolutionized classrooms, since he advocated children's activity and participation in the learning process. They were not to be passive recipients of knowledge.

Learning, in his view, should not be just a matter of disciplining the mind or committing facts to rote memory. Thinking is problem solving, the application of the scientific method to all types of problems. Children must learn to define a problem, observe the conditions surrounding the problem, formulate hypotheses (tentative solutions), decide which solution is best, and, finally, test it. Such a procedure should be at the heart of schooling. Teachers should present children with meaningful problems, help them to identify the specific nature of the problem, obtain the necessary information, pose several explanations, and test the final solution. Throughout the procedure the children are to be active, and will learn to think if they are genuinely involved in the solution of pertinent problems (Butts and Cremin, 1953).

Dewey's ideas are as vital today as they were when he first proposed them. Student activity, involvement, and freedom to explore are today's terms, but they could have come from the pages of Dewey's books. In his enduring *Democracy and Education* (1916) he argues that the word "pupil" implies one who is *not* engaged in fruitful experiences but who absorbs knowledge directly:

> Something which is called mind or consciousness is severed from the physical organs of activity. The former is then thought to be purely intellectual and cognitive; the latter to be an irrelevant and intruding factor. The intimate union of activity and undergoing its consequences

which leads to recognition of meaning is broken; instead we have two fragments; weakly bodily action on one side, and meaning directly grasped by "spiritual" activity on the other. (pp. 164–165)

ALFRED BINET (1857–1911)

Examining some of the outstanding psychological research that has aided the advancement of education, the close relationship between education and psychology becomes more evident. For example, one of the basic tools of the educator has been the test, particularly the intelligence test that attempts to provide an insight into a student's capacity and thus enables the school to weigh actual achievement against potential ability to achieve. It had its origin in the search by the French Ministry of Public Instruction in 1904 for some means of detecting the truly feeble-minded child. In response to this need, Alfred Binet, with Theophile Simon, published in 1905 a mental-age scale for measuring general intelligence, which he revised in 1908, and again in 1911 just before his death.

The Binet scale today, having sustained numerous revisions and translations, is the standard against which all other intelligence tests are measured. Although recent evidence has damaged the claim of any intelligence test to measure a child's capacity, Binet's pioneering efforts have left the impression of genius. From this test have come such phrases as "mental age" used by Binet, and "intelligence quotient" (IQ) devised by William Stern and used by Lewis Terman in his 1916 revision of the Binet scale. As a result of Binet's work, educators became more aware of the distribution of intelligence that they can expect in school, of the great advantages that a child from a higher socioeconomic-status home possesses, and of the fluctuating nature of any index of capacity. Teachers are now less inclined to accept classroom performance as the sole criterion of intelligence, especially when we recall that both Charles Darwin and Thomas Edison were considered dull in school.

Binet knew that intellectual performance increased with age, so he had to obtain norms for different ages. For each correct item in Binet's test an individual is awarded a certain number of months, with the total number of months representing a person's mental age. This permitted the calculation of the famous IQ, as follows:

$$IQ = \frac{MA \text{ (mental age)}}{CA \text{ (chronological age)}} \times 100$$

For example, if a 10-year-old child has a mental age of 10 on Binet's test, the resulting IQ would be 100.

$$IQ = \frac{10 \text{ years } (MA)}{10 \text{ years } (CA)}$$

$$IQ = \frac{120 \text{ months}}{120 \text{ months}}$$

$$IQ = 1 \times 100$$

$$IQ = 100$$

The great psychological historian Edwin Boring (1950) has said that the 1900s "were Binet's" for his contribution to mental testing.

IVAN PAVLOV (1849–1936)

Another outstanding theme in the development of educational psychology has been the role played by conditioning. With its emphasis upon stimulus and response, it appeared to offer unlimited possibilities for manipulating the classroom. Pavlov's work, called *classical conditioning*, involved animal experimentation. Studying the digestive process in dogs, he was startled to see the animals anticipate food. The flow of saliva in an animal's mouth normally occurs when food is actually given to the dog; this is a typical and automatic reflex to a stimulus like food. Yet Pavlov discovered his dogs' mouths watering *before* food was given to them. The sight of the attendants, or the sounds they made, were sufficient to produce saliva.

Some stimulus, neither natural nor original, was eliciting a response as the natural stimulus (food) did. We can represent the change as follows:

A) $US \rightarrow UR$

B) $CS - US \rightarrow UR$

C) $CS \rightarrow CR$

where US = food
UR = saliva
CS = sight of attendant
CR = conditioned response (saliva)

The ability to elicit the response has shifted from US to CS. This is the famed conditioned reflex also called classicial conditioning. In some manner the dog formed a bond or link between a new stimulus and the original response, or, put more simply, the animal has "learned." The implications for education are enormous and educators have long recognized the possibilities of the conditioned reflex. If a student fears a teacher, that fear is liable to spread to other teachers and to anything educational until the pupil dreads going to school. Different school stimuli now have the ability to cause the same response—fear.

A) $US \rightarrow UR$ US = teacher who originally caused fear

B) $CS - US \rightarrow UR$ UR = fear

C) $CS \rightarrow CR$ CS = other teachers, counselors, even classrooms

                           CR = generalized fear of school

Other famous individuals, including Hermann Ebbinghaus, William James, John Watson, Edwin Guthrie, and Kurt Lewin, have contributed significantly to the advancement of educational psychology. Contemporary theorists, such as B. F. Skinner, Jerome Bruner, and Jean Piaget, continue the tradition, and their work will be examined in coming chapters.

The function of educational psychology

Since the interests of educational psychologists are so varied, and since the discipline of educational psychology encompasses so many extensive subdivisions, you may well ask what should educational psychology do. While there are many possible answers, a detailed list of specific functions will vary according to the individual who formulates it. Consequently, it is more logical to state general objectives, which then may be used as a guide for individual preferences. Regardless of the variations that are possible, educational psychology must: (1) apply the findings of general psychology to education; and (2) initiate and use experimentation that is designed solely for educational purposes.

General psychology, as used here, includes the findings from social psychology, experimental psychology, animal psychology, industrial psychology, and any other branch that may supply valuable information for education. Experiments should answer specific questions in an attempt to solve specific educational problems. Otherwise, crucial decisions about curriculum, methods, and instructional devices will depend upon pure speculation.

APPLICATION TO TEACHING

Whatever the source of data, conclusions should advance *both* teaching and learning. The results of carefully designed and con-

Students' Views of Educational Psychology

What do students think of educational psychology? Feldhusen (1970) argues strongly that educational psychologists must overcome limitations in students' ability to understand theories and to use them in the classroom. To determine how educational psychology could better serve students and to discover what students envisioned as the ideal educational psychology course, Feldhusen administered a questionnaire to 188 students at Wisconsin, Illinois, and Purdue universities. You can evaluate the results by using three categories:

The Ideal Course	Ideal Experiences in Educational Psychology	Ideal Content in Educational Psychology
Practical	Practical	Learning Theory
Relevant	Experiences	Discipline
Current	Group Work	Problem Solving
Considerable	Discussion	Creativity
Discussion		Individual
and		Differences
Participation		Testing

Students also had their expectations of the ideal instructor: good personal qualities and the ability to teach well, thus setting a good example. These responses were prominent at all three universities, especially those concerning practicality and application. These students may or may not be familiar with Alfred North Whitehead, but they share his opinion of inert ideas. There is a warning here to educational psychology teachers, authors, and students. You cannot afford to become too abstract and theoretical if you wish to help students and also make educational psychology meaningful to them.

Feldhusen concludes that if instructors are worried about their goals and methods, a good source of evaluation is the student. What are student needs, perceptions, and conclusions about educational psychology that are helpful in planning a course or writing a text? While these topics offer guidelines to those concerned with improving our discipline, they also mean greater responsibility for *you*.

To participate fully in an educational psychology course implies that you cannot be a mere passive receptor—you must constantly evaluate. Is the material helpful for me as a person, as a teacher? Where does it fit in the classroom? Can I use it? Answering these questions is difficult, requiring a thoughtfulness and maturity that enable you to recognize vital topics—those that contribute both to your self-fulfillment as an educated person and your professional expertise as a skilled teacher.

trolled studies are in themselves invaluable as an addition to knowledge of the behavioral sciences. Yet, for the educational psychologist, these findings are designed to insure better understanding of teaching, of learning, and of the interaction between them. Educational psychology helps the teacher to become a better teacher, and the learner to become a better learner. In the education of teachers, the discipline becomes a scientific tool, a precision instrument by which teachers clarify goals, increase their perspective of the learning process, and learn to evaluate not only pupils but themselves.

Educational Psychology Is Vital to Teaching

Educational psychology is as crucial to teacher education as physics is to engineering or anatomy is to medicine. Although anatomy offers no suggestions about surgical techniques, imagine the consequences if a surgeon operated without a sound knowledge of anatomy. There is the same relationship between educational psychology and teaching. In educational psychology you will find advocacy not of one particular teaching method or learning theory, but a variety of choices that will help you understand student behavior and thus improve your teaching techniques.

Consider pupils who enter the first grade and quickly become behavior problems. They may be bored and restless; they antagonize teachers and disturb the learning atmosphere of their classrooms. Teachers who have some experience with educational psychology realize that the problem is one of motivation—but how to solve it? An analysis of the records indicates that these youngsters come from homes that undoubtedly were stimulating and enabled them to become familiar with words and numbers before they entered school.

In the first weeks of class these youngsters discovered that there was nothing new; there was nothing to seize their attention. There was no feeling of self-actualization, the drive in all humans that makes us want to do what we are capable of doing. Once teachers determine the source of the problem they can challenge these children with provocative and exciting materials. These teachers have

Theory and Practice

united theory and practice to insure that instruction is sufficiently flexible to meet the needs of all pupils.

LOCATING, UNDERSTANDING, AND USING RESEARCH DATA

For teachers to act both competently and confidently in meeting problems such as those described, they have the right to expect that conclusions offered and suggestions proffered in an educational psychology text and course be practical, reliable, and verifiable. What are the means by which you can secure information, and how can you interpret it and decide if it is applicable to your particular interests?

Usually a person seeks published information to satisfy a course requirement or some personal need. Initially, the question becomes one of familiarity with pertinent sources. If the issue is essentially psychological, to what books and journals should you turn?

Basic References

Perhaps the most logical step would be to discover what the latest educational psychology texts offer about some topic. For example, the texts listed as references for this book might provide adequate information. They also enable you to determine what other authors who have examined the topic recommend. Since the typical educational psychology textbook must be general rather

than specific in its presentation of any subject, you may wish to determine if any books are available that are devoted solely to the topic under consideration.

An excellent reference tool would be the *Cumulative Book Index*, which is found in most libraries, as are the *Library of Congress Catalog* and *Subject Guide to Books in Print*. A quick check of the *Book Review Digest* may uncover valuable information.

Two outstanding handbooks are available with which you should be familiar. The first is the *Encyclopedia of Educational Research*, which is published at approximately ten-year intervals. The other reference is the *Handbook of Research on Teaching*, a project of the American Educational Research Association.

You should also be aware of the latest periodical literature. The best method of obtaining the latest material about a certain topic is to go to sources that afford contemporary bibliographies. Some of these will offer more germane data than others, depending upon your topic. All, however, present a remarkable coverage of a variety of topics.

The Review of Educational Research is particularly valuable. It is published five times a year by the American Educational Research Association, and each issue is devoted to pertinent and critical studies of contemporary issues. Each edition contains an index with specific page references to topics that the *Review* has explored during the same year.

The Annual Review of Psychology is especially helpful since, by its organization, it illustrates the nature of the research on any topic. Subjects are investigated every one or two years, depending upon the extent and importance of the research. For a thorough check of pertinent information, you should scrutinize the table of contents by year. For example, you will find chapters that yield valuable knowledge in such related disciplines as learning, developmental psychology, statistics, motor skills, concept formation, and educational psychology.

Psychological Abstracts is another helpful tool for locating information about a particular subject. It is published every two months and gives summaries of articles that appeared in other journals. Although it *does not* provide extensive bibliographical entries, the annual bound volume furnishes a subject index that is almost indispensable for both the theorist and consumer.

Specific Topics

If you know the precise topic about which you need information, you may disregard lists of articles about the general topic and search for an article that discusses a particular problem. Then you would need some reference to specific studies. *The Reader's Guide to Periodical Literature* is a useful beginning, but may not be sufficiently selective for you. You should locate the latest copy of the *Educational Index* that is convenient and scan the index for the name of your topic, but also consider synonyms. Many readers fail to utilize fully these reference tools because they ignore synonymous listings.

You will find that many of the references of a psychological nature will be to such journals as the *Journal of Educational Psychology, Journal of Educational Research, Journal of Experimental Educa-*

ERIC

If you search the educational literature, using the numerous sources possible, you will face a staggering task because of its mass. ERIC (Educational Resources Information Center) was founded to help bring order to the literature. Its headquarters is now in the National Institute of Education, with 16 clearinghouses around the country. Each clearinghouse is responsible for gathering information. For example, the ERIC clearinghouse on early childhood education is at the University of Illinois College of Education; the clearinghouse on teacher education is at the American Association of Colleges for Teachers Education.

Brandhorst (1977) states that the clearinghouses collect and process the pertinent literature and then distribute it. A central computer facility combines the data from the 16 clearinghouses and announces them in the monthly catalog, *Resources in Education* (RIE), which provides information about reports, papers, and curriculum materials. Brandhorst describes RIE as giving the reader access to the "fugitive literature." Another contractor publishes a monthly catalog *Current Index to Journals in Education (CIJE),* which summarizes the journal article literature. ERIC also makes uncopyrighted documents available to users through the ERIC Document Reproduction Service (EDRS).

Through its various processes, ERIC offers entry into a staggering amount of information. Brandhorst has furnished the following excellent summary of ERIC (Brandhorst, 1977: 629):

ERIC CRIB SHEET

1. Acronym.   ERIC

2. Name.   Educational Resources Information Center

3. Sponsor.   National Institute of Education (NIE) (Office of Education—1966–1972)

4. Subject coverage.   Education, in its broadest sense.

5. Purposes.   Bibliographic control over the literature and materials of education ("educational resources") and dissemination of bibliographic information to help achieve the objectives of educational change, renewal, and innovation.

6. Monthly catalog.   Resources in Education (RIE) and Current Index to Journals in Education (CIJE)

7. Coverage.   RIE covers reports, presentations, curriculum materials, etc., the so-called "fugitive" literature; CIJE covers the journal article literature.

8. Total size of
collection
(through 1976).   RIE—120,367 records and growing at the rate of 15,000 items per year; CIJE—142,252 records and growing at the rate of 20,000 items per year.

9. System components.   —Central ERIC, NIE, Washington, D.C. 20208

—Clearinghouses (16 decentralized), each with responsibility for gathering, processing, and analyzing materials for a given area of the field of education.

—ERIC Processing and Reference Facility
4833 Rugby Ave., Suite 303
Bethesda, MD 20014
(central editorial processing center, computer facility, and data base manager)

Provides magnetic tapes for both RIE, and CIJE. Note: The ERIC facility makes available a Survey of ERIC Data Base Search Services listing more than 200 locations where computer searches may be obtained and a Directory of ERIC Microfiche Collections listing more than 600 locations where ERIC microfiche may be consulted. Both major national vendors of on-line bibliographic search services (Lockheed and System Development Corporation) provide access to the ERIC data base.

—ERIC Document Reproduction Service (EDRS)
Computer Microfilm International Corp. (CMIC)
P.O. Box 190, Arlington, VA 22210
(document delivery service)

Provides microfiche and/or hardcopy for over 85 percent of the announced material. Alternative sources of availability are cited for the remainder (usually copyrighted material).
—CIJE Publisher, Macmillan Information,
866 Third Ave., New York, NY 10022.

—RIE Publisher, U.S. Government Printing Office,
Washington, D.C. 20402.

Source: Used by permission of the Phi Delta Kappan, © April, 1977. Ted Brandhorst, "ERIC: Reminders of How It Can Help You."

tion, Education, Journal of General Psychology, and *American Psychologist.* You will appreciate the value of knowing what journal is most suitable for your topic. Proper use of the reference tools will save you much time and enable you to formulate a more searching paper, or to acquire the latest thinking about some classroom problem.

CRITERIA OF GOOD RESEARCH STUDIES

If these studies are to help you, the aid must come from the data upon which authors base their conclusions. Consequently, the published studies should be as precise as possible. Berelson and Steiner (1964) state that any investigation claiming to be scientific must meet certain demands. These would include:

1. *The techniques and results are available to all.* A careful description of exactly how the study was conducted, what precautions were included, which statistical devices (if any) were utilized, and whether the statistics selected were faithful to the conditions in which they *should* be utilized are all necessary components of a satisfactory study. The details of the study should enable an investigation in another part of the world to duplicate the steps and compare results.

2. *The terms are specific.* A characteristic of any truly scientific discipline is its precision of expression. If terms are vague and ambiguous, the significance and applicability of any kind of research are limited, if not worthless. For example, the term "delinquent" is used rather loosely in many texts and studies. Exactly what is a delinquent? What are the age delimitations? There is a vast difference from state to state in the ages at which a youth may be designated a delinquent. A boy of 16 differs markedly from a youth of 21. Yet the age range is this great among the 50 states.

Consider also the offense that youngsters must commit before being delinquent. This varies tremendously from state to state. Two boys commit the same crime in different states, and both are apprehended. One state says that the crime is worthy of the court's attention, while the other state handles the youth in a more social than legal manner. Should one boy be called a delinquent while the other escapes this label? Terms must be defined in as accurate and explicit a manner as possible to remove a study from the charge of being "subjective."

3. *The entire process is scrupulously objective.* There can be no manipulation of data. Whether or not the results confirm the investigators' hypothesis, the conclusions are reported fairly and without bias. Otherwise the work becomes a mockery and may retard the progress of this discipline.

4. *The purposes are directed toward distinct goals, and ultimately toward theory construction.* By a series of calculated and verifiable steps investigators steadily enlarge their vision to establish a theoretical system that may well explain a fundamental problem of any discipline.

Endeavoring to study these criteria, investigators employ methods or research designs that seem most appropriate to a particular problem. Kerlinger (1973) states that social-scientific research can be divided into four major categories: survey research, field studies, field experiments, and laboratory experiments. Here is a summary of his description of each.

Survey research

The survey studies large and small populations by selecting and studying samples drawn from that population. The survey researchers want to assess the characteristics of an entire population: How many voters are Democratic? What do citizens think of their schools? They infer these characteristics from the sample they have drawn, thus the sample must reflect the total population as accurately as possible. Data are usually collected by personal interviews, mail questionnaires, panel interviews, telephone sampling, and controlled observation. Of these, the personal interview is the most powerful technique.

The Annual Gallup Poll of the Public Attitudes Toward the Public Schools is an excellent example of research using the personal interview technique. (The results of the Eighth Annual Educational Gallup Poll are discussed in Chapter 16.) The first two sentences stating the study's purpose illustrate the nature of a survey.

> The eighth annual survey of the series has attempted to measure the attitudes of Americans toward their public schools. Each year great care is taken to include new issues of concern to both educators and the public, as well as trend questions which have ongoing impact in the educational world. (Gallup, 1976)

Kerlinger believes that survey research can be a valuable tool for educational fact finding, especially for studies of integration and their impact on a community.

Field studies

Field studies attempt to study the relations and interactions among sociological, psychological, and educational variables in real social structures (Kerlinger, 1973, pg. 405). Investigators select some social institution such as the school and study the relations among attitudes, values, perception, and behavior of the individuals in that setting.

Field studies are an example of ex post facto research, that is, the investigators study results that have already occurred; they themselves do not manipulate variables to produce a result. Stating that the strengths of field studies are their realism, significance, theory orientation, and heuristic quality, Kerlinger also notes their weaknesses.

> Statements of relations are weaker than they are in experimental research. To complicate matters further, the field situation almost always has a plethora of variables and variances. Think of the many possible independent variables that we might think of as determinants of school achievement. (Kerlinger, 1973, pg. 408)

The experiment

Kerlinger states that the difference between laboratory and field experiments is not sharp. Both techniques try to exercise as much control as possible over any variables that could influence the results, thus clouding any conclusions. Most educational experiments are field experiments: a research study in a realistic setting in which one or more independent variables are manipulated by the investigation under carefully controlled conditions.

Although survey methods and field studies have made unique contributions to education and psychology, investigators prefer experimental methods whenever possible. The greater control that experimenters exercise over the conditions of the study encourages objectivity and strengthens the results. In experimentation, researchers deliberately manipulate some variable (the independent or antecedent variable) and measure the changes that arise in some other behavioral characteristic (the dependent or consequent variable).

By deliberately altering the independent variable, investigators know (if the experiment is properly designed) that such modification of experimental conditions produces certain results. That is, they attempt to establish cause-and-effect relationships that may have broad application to similar populations. The possibilities of error are many, and thus experimenters are constantly searching for more acceptable research designs.

The pretest-posttest control-group design or, as Berelson and Steiner (1964) refer to it, "the classical experiment," employs equivalent groups, one of which (the experimental group) has the independent variable changed. For example, two randomly divided groups of students are to be taught a pyschology course, one in the traditional classroom setting, the other by means of a programmed text and a weekly 20-minute meeting with instructor. This represents manipulation of the independent variable—the

COURTESY OF THE CHILDREN'S TELEVISION WORKSHOP

teaching method. The achievement of both groups—the dependent variable—will be measured by the same test. The design is:

$$E_b \: X \: E_a$$
$$C_B \quad C_a$$

where E is the experimental group, C is the control group, X is the change in the independent variable, b is before the experiment, a is after the experiment. If all possible conditions have been controlled, then any difference between E_a and C_a can only be attributed to X.

The Experiment — An Example

Wittrock, Marks, and Doctorow (1975) designed a reading experiment that is an excellent illustration of the experimental method. They hypothesized that familiar stories, as opposed to unfamiliar stories, aid pupils' search for meaning of low-frequency, undefined words. The subjects were 485 10- to 12-year old children who constituted the entire sixth-grade population of four Los Angeles elementary schools.

The students were given reading placement tests to determine their reading level. The authors then modified five stories by substituting words that created either high- or low-word frequency versions of the stories. The stories' syntactical characteristics remained constant.

On the experiment's first day all of the pupils took the placement tests. Each student was then randomly assigned (within sex and reading-ability level) to a high- or low-word frequency group. On the second day the familiar and the unfamiliar stories were given to the pupils. Immediately after reading or listening the students were administered a multiple-choice vocabulary test devised by the authors. One week later, on the experiment's third day, another reading test was given to the pupils.

The authors' hypothesis was confirmed: familiar stories aided the learning and retention of new vocabulary words. While the results themselves are fascinating, the technique itself is of primary concern here. Note the attempt to control: sixth graders, similar backgrounds, careful reading placement, consideration of sex difference in reading, and deliberate manipulation of an independent variable (high- and low-frequency words).

Here is an example of a carefully designed field experiment the techniques of which you could attempt to duplicate and on whose results you could rely.

The role of objectives in teaching and instruction

Throughout this chapter we have mentioned that teachers "should" or pupils "should," which introduces the issue of objectives. It is almost a cliché to say that without objectives, schools, teachers, and students have difficulty in determining how, why, and what they are doing. In earlier times the lack of definite statements detailing specific behavioral changes caused uncertainty as to what schools, teachers, and students should accomplish. Today's emphasis upon performance, competency, and accountability has removed much uncertainty.

School objectives are essentially general and, hence, vague. They should provide general guidelines, however, within which specific statements are possible. For example, the State of Massachusetts offers the following statement of educational goals:

1. *Physical and emotional well-being.* Education should contribute to the learner's physical and emotional well-being, especially to a sense of personal worth.
2. *Basic communication skills.* Education should provide the learner with the basic skills necessary for communication, perception, conceptualization, and evaluation.
3. *Effective uses of knowledge.* Education should provide each learner with access to man's cultural heritage and stimulate intellectual curiosity.
4. *Capacity and desire for lifelong learning.* Education should encourage the desire for lifelong learning and provide the skills to fulfill that desire.
5. *Citizenship in a democratic society.* Education should provide each learner with a knowledge and understanding of how our society functions and foster a commitment to exercise the rights and responsibilities of citizenship.
6. *Respect for the community of man.* Education should furnish the learner the knowledge and experience that advances mutual respect for humanity and for the dignity of the individual.
7. *Occupational competence.* Education should provide each learner with the skills, experience, and attitudes, and guidance for job placement.
8. *Understanding of the environment.* Education should provide the learner with knowledge and understanding of the social, physical, and biological worlds, leading to intelligent use of the environment.
9. *Individual values and attitudes.* Education should expand and advance the humane dimensions of all learners, especially by helping them to identify and cultivate their spiritual, moral, and ethical values and attitudes.
10. *Creative interests and talents.* Education should provide each learner with opportunities to nurture interests and to develop natural talents.

Obviously these are broad guidelines that the state hopes local communities will use to establish their own goals. There is no guarantee that this will occur, nor is there a guarantee that local communities, within the state's guidelines, will assign any priorities to these goals. They are no more than they claim to be: idealistic statements about what should be.

Students' Objectives

Students' objectives are just the opposite of state and community goals. They are highly specific and personal. For example, three students register for an educational psychology course. One desires to use the course as an aid to understanding children and how they learn; the second wants examples of practical application that will help in the classroom; another needs a good grade and believes that this instructor is easy. Three students in the same course with three different objectives. Will the course help each of them equally? Obviously not. Should there be three sections of the course? Again, obviously not. What is apparent from this example is the student's place in goal formulation. Teachers, authors, and curriculum makers need to know what students want in a course so that their objectives can be incorporated.

But it is the teacher who is the main architect of instructional goals and their attainment. As Bloom, Hastings, and Madaus (1971, pg. 8) state, there is no doubt that determination of the objectives of instruction rests largely with the teacher. These authors believe that teachers should immediately clarify, for themselves and their students, what changes are expected as a result of the course. Teachers can then consciously select content, material, and teaching techniques to achieve the stated objectives. Teachers should not simply borrow the aims and objectives of books, curriculum guides, and other teachers.

These authors note that a single teacher has limited objectives, which may be realized within the classroom, but other goals extend beyond any one classroom. It may be possible for several teachers of related courses to join in the formation of more extensive objectives, thus producing a more powerful cumulative effect than would be possible in any one course. This is especially true for any discussion of attitudes and values. But remember, in combining objectives, not all students will attain any one objective. Age, level of schooling, and previous learning are all significant.

PREPARING EDUCATIONAL OBJECTIVES

Robert Mager (1975) offers some excellent practical examples of instructional objectives and how to formulate them. He defines an objective as a description of a performance you want learners to be able to exhibit. Objectives describe the results of instruction, not the process of instruction, thus they help in the design and selection of instructional materials, content, and methods. Precisely defined objectives also aid teachers in constructing tests and students in organizing their efforts to accomplish discernible objectives.

Clear objectives improve each part of your teaching—preparation, instruction, and evaluation—so careful statements about what you hope to achieve are worth the time and effort they require. But, as Mager notes (1975, pg. 20), meaningfully stated objectives require work, and a major obstacle to accurate formulation is the "slippery word": know, understand, appreciate, enjoy. What do you mean when you want students "to understand"? Do you want them to memorize, to repeat, to use, or to solve problems? Objectives using these words cannot specify what students should do.

Teachers' Objectives

To help you state usable objectives, Mager urges a format that includes three characteristics:

1. *Performance,* which tells you what the learner is expected to do (be able to sing "America, the Beautiful").
2. *Conditions,* which tell you the significant circumstances surrounding performance (without the use of a book).
3. *Criterion,* which tells you how well students must perform (the first two stanzas without mistake).

The complete objective now reads: Without using your book, be able to sing without mistakes the first two stanzas of "America, the Beautiful." Performance, conditions, and criterion are included, and both teacher and pupils know exactly what is expected.

To test *your* ability to write clear objectives, Mager (1975, pg. 107) asks his readers to decide if performance, conditions, and criterion are present in the following objectives. Are all three, or any, of the suggested characteristics in these statements?

1. Given a list of descriptions of human behavior, be able to differentiate (sort) between those that are normal and those that are psychotic.
2. Without regard to subject matter or grade level, be able to describe ten examples of school practices that promote learning and ten examples of school practices that retard or interfere with learning.

In the first example, performance and conditions are given, but no criterion is stated. The second example meets all requirements: performance (describing), conditions (any subject and grade level), criterion (ten examples of each). Mager's suggestions are helpful and practical and deserve your attention. Try to devise several statements that incorporate the three characteristics of a good objective and ask the class if you succeeded.

SOURCES OF OBJECTIVES

When you face your class at the beginning of the year, you can visualize a model of what you want to accomplish. The overall model may still be rather vague, but you are undoubtedly aware of many particulars within the model, that is, many of the specific accomplishments you want. Bloom, Hastings, and Madaus (1971, pg. 14) state that today there is considerable emphasis on specifying the behavior students should exhibit if they have attained the objectives. To illustrate the relationship between content and objectives, the authors have devised the scheme shown in Figure 1.2.

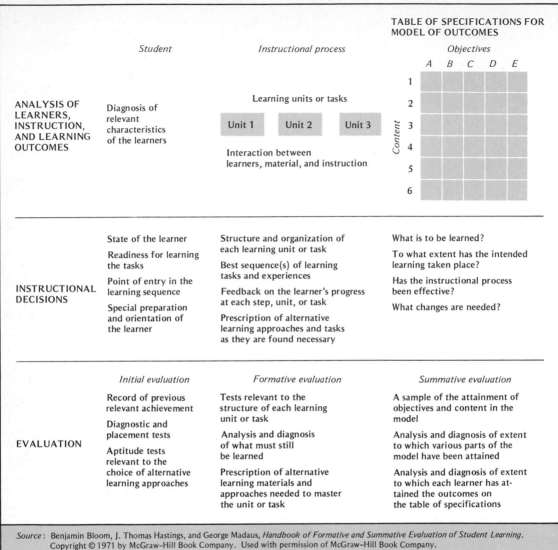

Figure 1.2 The Relation Among Evaluation, Instructional Decisions, and the Analysis of Learners, Instruction, and Learning Outcomes

If you examine Figure 1.2, you can see that the model relates to four questions posed by Ralph Tyler (1950). To analyze a school's curriculum and instructional procedures, Tyler devised a rationale based upon four questions:

1. What educational purposes should the school seek to attain?
2. What are the learning experiences that will help pupils attain these purposes?
3. How can a school organize these experiences effectively?

4. How can we determine whether the school has attained these purposes?

The Tyler Rationale

These questions force students, teachers, and administrators to consider objectives, learning, curriculum, techniques, and evaluation. To specify the objectives of instruction, Tyler urged that we study the learners themselves as a source of educational objectives: What do students need physically, socially, and intellectually to enable them to adjust? He stressed that the school should look beyond the classroom to find worthy objectives. We must also probe our contemporary society for objectives that will aid a pupil's adjustment. Another source of objectives is the expert in any subject, who can tell what a subject can contribute to a youth's education.

But these sources will usually lead to more objectives than a school can attain adequately. So Tyler suggests that the school filter them through a philosophical and psychological screen, That is, every school is committed to a belief in a particular philsophy of education and psychology of learning, thus automatically eliminating many objectives. For example, the desirability of a sex-education program will not pass through some schools' philsophy of education screen. Finally, as early as 1950 Tyler suggested that we must state objectives in as clear and helpful a manner as possible, thus leading to today's emphasis on behavioral objectives.

CBE

A popular current technique for stating and achieving educational objectives is termed Competency- or Performance-Based Education (CBE). As Houston and Jones (1974) note, the concepts underlying any form of competency-based education are relatively straightforward. Precise statements are made as to what learners must demonstrate for successful completion of the program. The primary emphasis is upon performance, that is, greater importance is placed upon what learners can *do* than upon what they supposedly *know*. A learner's progress is then contingent upon demonstrating the desired competencies.

It is impossible to overemphasize the role of objectives in education. Unless schools, teachers, and students know what they are attempting to achieve and why, instruction may be futile. Perhaps no one has expressed the importance of needs as well as Robert Mager (1975) when he states that if you give each learner a copy of your objectives, you may not have much else to do.

Discussion Questions

1. Can you think of any samples of classical conditioning that affected you in the classroom, involving either physical or cognitive learning? Give a specific example.

2. Dewey was a forerunner of many current educational beliefs. Specify some classroom practices that reflect his ideas about schooling.

3. Summarize the value of carefully designed research. What would you look for in a study? Why was the Wittrock study given as an example of a good experiment?

4. From your reading of this chapter, list the objectives that you would like to achieve in this course. What do you hope to gain from using this text? How do your objectives compare with those of the students in Feldhusen's study? If they differ, to what do you attribute the difference?

5. Objectives played a major role in this chapter. As an example of how they are helpful, return to the first page of this chapter. Using the chapter outline as a basis, formulate your objectives by expressing each of the highlights by behavior and content, for example, "to interpret census figures for their educational implications." You described a behavior—interpreting statistical data—and content—administrative policy for school planning. Do this for each topic in the outline.

6. Do you think CBE adds precision to the statement of objectives? If so, explain how it differs from more traditional statements. If not, support your answer by showing similarities.

Some Concluding Thoughts

This first chapter has attempted to indicate for parents, citizens, and future teachers what educational psychology is and how it functions in an academic and applied discipline. A major theme was the need for educational psychology courses to furnish students with practical examples of its principles, that is, how this subject actually helps teachers. Such a combination of theory and practice necessitates a model of educational psychology that permits instructors and students to relate application both to theory and research. Consequently, you will note that this text has the *learner* as its focus.

There are six major sections:

1. *Introduction.* The chapter you have just read is intended to present an overview of the field.

2. *The Learner and Development.* This section emphasizes the development of the child—physical, intellectual, linguistic, personality, and the effects of early experience. Given adequate care, both physical and psychological, how does the average child develop, and what does this imply for education?

3. *The Learner and Learning.* Knowledge of learning—cognitive, psychomotor, and affective—will enable you to identify certain kinds of learning and how pupils react to different circumstances. What motivational devices are particularly effective? Learning implies change, so you must assess your achievement of objectives to determine the degree of success or failure.

4. *The Learner and Individual Differences.* Today teachers are more sensitive to those children who suffer a handicap that restricts their learning. So you must know as much as possible about the slow learner, the mentally retarded, and the emotionally disturbed. There are those pupils, however, at the other extreme—the gifted. You must also provide for their uniqueness. Currently, the schools have received a challenging but welcome mandate—mainstreaming handicapped children, which demands considerable attention.

5. *The Learner and Instruction.* Finally, your work will culminate in the discussion of teaching and learning. With all that is known about development and learning, how can you best communicate with students and encourage their learning and adjustment by applying techniques that are best suited for *these* youngsters at *this* level and in *this* setting?

6. *Statistical Appendix.* Since so much of educational psychology's data involves the use of statistics, you should know and understand the basic statistical techniques. *Introduction to Statistical Methods in Psychology* by Foster Lloyd Brown is an excellent summary, one that should help you to interpret more meaningfully the many studies you will meet.

As you continue to read, read with one thought in mind: How can this theory or this study help me in the classroom?

Summary

- Educational psychology's major task is to combine theory and practice, thus producing a more efficient teacher.

- Statistical data about teachers and pupils reveal many qualities that help to promote better teaching and learning.

- An understanding of educational psychology's methods and techniques helps you to interpret and apply research findings.

- Without a capable teacher, the best-formulated goals remain unattainable and students' classroom behavior deteriorates.

- Teaching is reaching, communicating meaningfully with pupils in a process that actually involves both teacher and pupil.

- Historically, educational psychology has provided the classroom teacher with an array of valuable techniques, such as greater information about conditioning procedures, increasingly sophisticated tests, and the discovery method.

- Precise objectives, specifying both content and behavior, furnish teachers with definite guidelines that help in deciding what material is needed, what instructional procedures will be most productive, what learning experiences students will require, and what evaluation measures are appropriate.

● One method of specifying objectives is to use some form of Competency- or Performance-Based Education (CBE).

Suggested Readings

NOTE: Students often overlook chapter and even book bibliographies when lengthy lists appear. To avoid this possibility, only those references will appear at chapter ends that are most pertinent because of content, applicability, or humor. There will be only a few, so do not ignore them.

Highet, Gilbert. *The Art of Teaching*. New York: Knopf, 1950. A wise, witty, warm, well-written book by a renowned scholar who betrays his love of teaching here.

Stephens, J. M. *The Process of Schooling*. New York: Holt, Rinehart and Winston, 1967. A unique look at the forces and processes basic to education by a respected educational psychologist. It is here that Stephens stresses the significance of the teacher—without his or her cooperation even the most ambitious projects are doomed to failure.

Tyler, Ralph. *Basic Principles of Curriculum and Instruction*. University of Chicago Press, 1950. One of the great discussions of objectives that has been the foundation upon which all recent work rests. If you are ever engaged in curriculum construction, or even if you want to improve your own classroom performance and provide a more constructive classroom atmosphere, read this brief pamphlet.

Part Two

The Learner and Development

2

Aspects of Development

Introduction

Numbers are fascinating. Most of us are intrigued to know that over 3 million teachers instruct over 60 million students. Teacher-student ratios captivate us; we believe that knowing there are twenty students for every teacher affords insight into the educational process.

Such figures are helpful: they provide an educational overview that would otherwise be lacking. But you, walking into a second or sixth grade, or a high school history class, also need specialized information about the students in your class. What is the typical age range? Are there physical characteristics, such as the adolescent growth spurt, that could affect behavior? Are there typical emotional problems for students of this age?

The answers to these specific questions should provide practical help because the more that teachers know about the students they teach, the more effective they will be. In this chapter children of different ages are described: infancy (0–2), early childhood (2–6), middle childhood (6–12), and adolescence. The ages for each period are approximations; different children grow at different rates, and their ages offer rough guidelines for different developmental periods. Children of these ages possess characteristics that help us to better understand them.

It is necessary to include infancy since the latest research suggests the importance of proper stimulation during the first two years, and also the changing nature of society compels an examination of day-care centers. Finally, to make developmental facts practical and meaningful, each period is divided into four sections: an overview of the period, the outstanding physical, mental, and personality characteristics of the children, the major developmental tasks of the period, and the classroom implications of this knowledge.

Principles of development

Before analyzing the characteristics of each age level, there are several basic developmental ideas that deserve consideration. Knobloch and Pasamanick (1974) provide a rationale for studying development in educational psychology when they state that as a child's body grows, behavior also grows. Children come by "mind" as they do by body—through the developmental process. As the nervous system differentiates, behavior also changes and each behavioral pattern indicates a definite stage of maturity. Behavioral patterns are not quirks of fate; the human fetus becomes the human infant, the human child, the human adult.

A RATIONALE FOR DEVELOPMENTAL ANALYSIS

To simplify developmental analysis, Knobloch and Pasamanick (1974) propose five behavioral fields:

1. *Adaptive behavior*, which they consider most important, represents the child's ability to organize stimuli into meaningful perceptual relationships; for example, the development of hand-eye coordination.

2. *Gross motor behavior,* which includes sitting, standing, creeping, walking.
3. *Fine motor behavior,* such as the coordination of fingers to solve practical problems.
4. *Language behavior,* which includes all visible and audible forms of communication, such as facial expression, gestures, words, phrases, and sentences.
5. *Personal-social behavior,* which comprises the child's personal reactions to society and encompasses activities ranging from toilet training, through feelings of independence, to cooperation and responsiveness in social situations.

These five categories form the basis of the entire behavioral repertoire and they assume characteristic patterns as they develop. For example, if you examine Figure 2.1, you can follow the developmental sequence for the first five years. During these preschool years a child develops the foundation—physical, mental, personality, social—that helps to determine educational success and adjustment. Notice the importance of eye control at 4 weeks, the ability to manipulate objects at 28 weeks, and the use of words and phrases at 18 months.

The progress at these key ages represents normal development and is of considerable importance to both parents and teachers. If a child shows a marked deviancy from these norms parents should

FISHER-PRICE TOYS

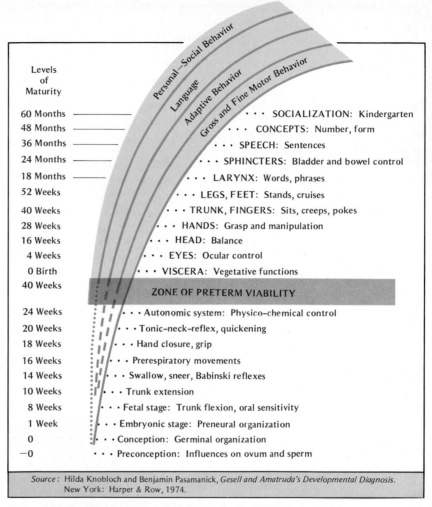

Figure 2.1 The Development of Behavior in the Five Major Fields

consider some form of developmental diagnosis as a precaution. Since educational institutions, such as day-care centers, serve ever younger children, teachers and staff members need some index of normality as a guide.

Physical and motor development is a good, reliable indication of a child's progress. J. M. Tanner (1970) states that all of a child's skills, attitudes, and emotions are rooted in the bodily structure. Learning depends upon brain growth, and social interaction depends upon body image; these are only two examples that illustrate how physical growth affects a youngster's feelings and behavior. If a youngster shows typical developmental characteristics,

The Invulnerable Child

There is growing concern that psychologists have too long focused upon pathology. Pines (1975) gives the example of a 10-year-old boy who had numerous negative influences: extreme poverty, an ex-convict, dying father, an illiterate mother who abused him, and two mentally retarded siblings. Yet the boy did well at school, was popular with peers and teachers, and was a natural leader.

How can we explain this "invulnerability"? Too little is known about normal development in the face of adversity and too little effort has been made to understand the sources that produce such invulnerability. Until these sources are understood, efforts at preventing developmental problems will remain limited.

Considerable credit for this new interest is given to Lois Murphy who, in 1962, wrote that it is a paradox that a nation which exults in its achievements has developed a "problem childhood" literature. While no one disputes that social disorganization, broken homes, poor prenatal care, and birth defects produce enormous burdens, there is no guarantee that some kind of disability will result. Competence may arise from disadvantage, incompetence from affluence.

Who are these invulnerable children? Investigators define them as children from disadvantaged homes who achieve well in school, but who also play well, work well, and love well—they have acquired a sense of their own power. They resemble competent children from affluent homes rather than the incompetents of their own class.

What causes such resiliency no one yet knows for sure. But one conspicuous feature of these children is their attention. If attention falters, is weak, or is uncontrolled, children may manifest incompetency. They become vulnerable to physical and mental disturbances. There are innumerable examples of invulnerability; the task now is to understand the reasons for success.

---

such as those in Figure 2.1, parents and teachers may feel confident about continuing progress.

COMMON GROWTH CHARACTERISTICS

Figure 2.1 reflects typical development, that is, most children show these behavioral changes. From this and similar figures, certain characteristics, or principles, or laws of the growth process follow.

1. *The developmental process is the result of the interaction of heredity and environment.* If either is disturbed (birth defect, injury, disease, malnutrition), the developmental sequence undergoes change, but change may be positive providing the environment presents particularly invigorating stimuli.

2. *Development is continuous, regular, and orderly.* Change occurs steadily in humans and happens in a fairly predictable sequence: children creep before running, babble before talking in intelligible sentences. Continuous, orderly change emerges in an established, regular fashion; there is a steady refinement in the developmental pattern. Awkward movements become smooth; hesitating, fumbling speech becomes precise expression of thought; uncontrolled outbursts become a search to avoid frustration.

3. *The rate of development varies for individuals.* While the developmental process is the same for all children, an individual child may vary noticeably from the usual standard. Adolescents undergo a height spurt, but one youngster may spurt at 13 years whereas another youngster evidences a similar increase at 16.

4. *The developmental process is a complicated, interrelated procedure.* At any time a youth may show more rapid physical than mental development, more rapid mental than emotional development, and more rapid emotional than social development. Is there any causative relationship among those events? Perhaps, but present knowledge is so limited that it is possible to establish cause and effect only for the simplest phenomena. For example, poor health will influence all three of the above developmental phases. Figure 2.2 illustrates the complicated, separate, but related design of development.

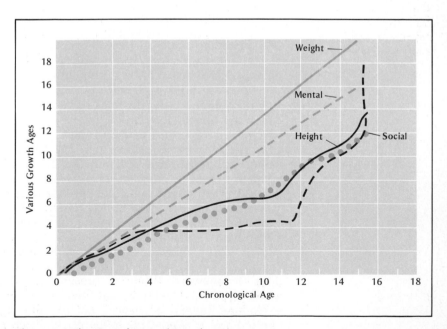

Figure 2.2 The Complexity of Development

Examining Figure 2.2 closely, you can see that the mental age for this youth closely follows the chronological age; thus the IQ is in the normal IQ range, about 100. But note that at age 15, the social age is that of a youngster of 10, the weight age is that of a youth about 18, and the height is that of a boy about 12. Another youngster may show a radically different pattern: normal weight and height, slower mental and social development. The developmental pattern is similar for all but still reflects sharply divergent individual rates.

These facts are significant for educators: chronological age is only a general indication of a child's readiness. Realizing that more than chronological age is involved in pupil assessment, the sensitive teacher is alert to individual differences that necessitate curriculum and instructional variation. Burton (1962, pg. 142) shrewdly observes that many "ages" are important for education: chronological, mental, educational, anatomical, physiological, social, moral, and emotional. He then insists (1962, pg. 151) that, although these different kinds of age reflect real discrepancies, there is a general level of ability that suggests it is a genuinely rare pupil who can do well in everything yet not grasp arithmetic.

THEORIES OF DEVELOPMENT

Tracing children's development, substantial data become available. Longitudinal studies follow the same children for many years, often into adulthood; cross-sectional studies examine many children of different ages simultaneously; experiments are designed to assess behavior under different conditions; careful descriptions of behavior at different ages produce insightful data about developmental changes. The resulting information is so extensive that some means of comprehending it is necessary.

Developmental theories make it possible to order data, interpret and draw conclusions from it, and test the truthfulness of those conclusions. Theories usually reflect a belief in human nature. For example, those who believe that the environment determines behavior look to learning for answers. Those who believe that development proceeds from a struggle between a child's urges and society's restrictions look to psychoanalytic theory for answers. Those who believe development is a series of tasks to master at various developmental levels look to developmental task theory or stage theory (certain developmental characteristics appear at certain ages) for answers. Those who believe that a child, or adult, constructively strives to fulfill potential look to self-realization theories for answers. Table 2.1 presents the outstanding features of several leading developmental theories.

No one theory is "true." Each offers clues to human development and it is possible to learn from each of them. Their impor-

TABLE 2.1
Developmental Theories—Major Figures and Features

	Psychoanalytic Freud	Behaviorist Pavlov, Skinner	Developmental Task Havighurst	Self-Realization Buhler
DEVELOPMENTAL EXPLANATIONS	Passage through psychosexual stages	Respondent conditioning Operant conditioning	Mastery of developmental tasks	The basic life tendencies
ESSENTIAL FEATURES	Id-ego-superego psychosexual stages	Stimuli-responses	Developmental tasks	Need satisfaction
SOURCE OF PROBLEMS	Conflict during development leads to fixation, regression, personality problems	Inadequate connection of stimuli with changing response capacity	Failure to master tasks at one period leads to future difficulty	Negative self-concept leads to frustration
GOAL	Sexually mature individual	Socially acceptable behavior by proper conditioning procedures	Adjustment and happiness through success with developmental tasks	Fulfillment of potential

Source: The Growing Child by John Travers. © 1977 Wiley. Reprinted by permission of John Wiley & Sons, Inc.

tance lies in the perspective they bring to developmental data. Development is regular, organized, and continuous, but to understand it, investigators artificially divide it into periods. The first of these periods is infancy.

Infancy

While there are few direct classroom implications of this period, future development and learning depend upon a normal infancy. It is an age of rapid growth, which combined with adequate nourishment and environmental stimulation enables the child to develop normally. These are the crucial years in which mind and body are shaped. Comparing the helpless newborn organism, who seems capable of little more than expressions of discomfort or pleasure, with the relatively sophisticated 2-year-old, one notes remarkable changes.

Table 2.2 shows that the youngster has grown almost three feet and is using basic sentences. From being unable to differentiate themselves from the surrounding world (in those first days, weeks, and months, children and world seem one), by 2 they know who they are, they comprehend cause and effect relationships, they feel secure and wanted—an amazing transformation. At 2, then, youngsters who have experienced a stimulating environment have acquired a priceless asset: confidence that they can cope with the world. In this section, the characteristics of the period are presented. Chapter 4, which focuses upon the work of Piaget and Bruner, presents theoretical explanations of *how* these changes occur. The importance of early experience, especially for cognitive development, is discussed in Chapter 3.

SOME CHARACTERISTICS OF THE PERIOD

Escalona (1968) summarizes this period by identifying three "landmarks":

1. As babies become aware of things during the first 6 months (bottle, mother, hands, feet), they begin to develop a sense of self. They are distinct from the world; there is something outside themselves.
2. These initial perceptions influence children's judgments about the nature of the world: is it pleasant, does it help me? These feelings may color their reactions to others throughout their lives and here is the significance of the mother-child relationship.
3. Children, toward the end of the period, as they develop new competencies—walking, running, talking—observe that they can control most activities. Such confidence becomes apparent from examining Table 2.2 and noting the physical, motor, and mental abilities that originally helpless children now possess.

Note the steady physical and mental progression. When the typical child integrates these abilities at 2 years, there should be an accompanying feeling of confidence. It is almost as if the youngster shouts: "Look at me. I can run, jump, move things, and talk."

The key ages

Four weeks is the first key age, and although the child cannot creep, walk, or talk, breathing is regular—an important accomplishment. The heart beat steadies and the temperature ceases fluctuating. The child lies on one side more than the other, which

TABLE 2.2
Some Developmental Characteristics of Infancy

Age (months)	Height (in.)	Weight (lb)	Language Development	Motor Development
3	24	13–14	cooing	supports head in prone position
6	26	17–18	babbling—single syllable sounds	sits erect when supported
9	28	20–22	repetition of sounds; signals emotions	stands with support
12	29.5	22–24	single words—*mama, dada*	walks when held by hand
18	32	25–26	3–50 words	grasps objects accurately, walks steadily
24	34	27–29	50–250 words, 2–3 word phrases	runs and walks up and down stairs

may indicate future handedness. There may be definite visual and auditory responses (the child may briefly look at the mother), but it is still too early to make any judgment about normality and abnormality.

The second key age is 16 weeks, when the infant seems quite mature compared to the 4-week-old child. It is a time of rapid cortical organization, demonstrated by eye-hand coordination. The child sees an object and reaches for it, not too successfully because

MERRIM, MONKMEYER

Infant Development

of difficulty in grasping. But here there is a definite developmental sequence emerging: looking, reaching, contacting, grasping, manipulating, and exploring objects. One emerges from the other (Knobloch and Pasamanick, 1974, pg. 48). The child coos and laughs at this age; parents are usually delighted at such sociability.

The third key age is 28 weeks, when maturity is much more evident. Children prefer to sit; they grasp objects rather crudely (more with hand than fingers) and almost everything is put into the mouth. They pick up objects and transfer them from one hand to the other, but the eyes are still more skillful than the hands. Knobloch and Pasamanick describe the child as "socially wise, he knows what is going on around the house."

The fourth key age is 40 weeks, which Knobloch and Pasamanick describe as the transition to an epoch, since so many new and distinct behavioral patterns emerge. Forty-week-olds pluck a small object between thumb and forefinger with "pincer precision"; they begin to creep, and can sit alone almost indefinitely. Now, using the side of the crib, they pull themselves to their feet. An interesting characteristic of the period is their unwillingness to remain supine (lying face up); they either sit up or pull themselves up.

The fifth key age is 1 year and Table 2.2 shows some of the more observable changes: the increase in height and weight, the beginning of meaningful vocalization, and the first steps. The youngster creeps rapidly, much more so than the 40-week-old, and seems both confident and happy. It is a fairly stable period.

At 18 months, the next key age, children are highly mobile; they walk without falling, and may even begin to run. They start to master stairs, which can be a problem since they lack the ability to climb them smoothly. Usually they have a 10- to 30-word vocabulary, but comprehend more than they can say.

End of the Period

The last key age of infancy is 24 months, the climax of the great achievements of the period. Children can run and walk up and down stairs unaided; they communicate fairly well, and are usually toilet-trained. They are leaving infancy and moving into the preschool period and, as they do, their behavior increasingly comes under social control. But their responsiveness to the environment still depends upon their constitutions—especially the organization of the central nervous system.

DEVELOPMENTAL TASKS OF THE PERIOD

Robert Havighurst (1972) has devised a particularly productive means of analyzing the relationship between development and education with his developmental task concept. He defines a developmental task as one which arises at or about a certain period in the life of an individual, successful achievement of which leads to happiness and to success with later tasks, while failure leads to unhappiness in the individual, disapproval by the society, and dif-

ficulty with later tasks. The potential value of Havighurst's reasoning is that, knowing the characteristics of the various ages, adults
can identify those tasks that facilitate development and help
youngsters to master them.

Havighurst states that as children grow they acquire new physical and psychological resources and also face new demands and expectations from society. These inner and outer forces combine to establish a series of developmental tasks that necessitate mastery. There are three sources of these tasks:

1. Physical maturation, such as learning to walk and talk or adjusting to menopause in later life.
2. Cultural pressures, such as learning to read, learning to participate in society.
3. The self, which means the individual's personal goals and values.

As Havighurst notes, when the body is ripe, and society requires, and the self is ready to achieve a certain task, the "teachable moment" has come. For teachers it is an exciting idea: if you can accurately specify the developmental tasks of the school years, your teaching and your students' learning will be easier and more pleasant.

The developmental tasks of infancy are:

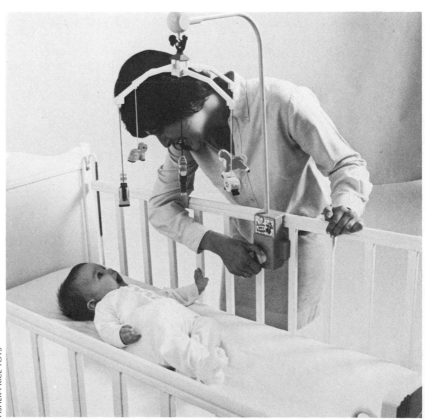

FISHER-PRICE TOYS

Early Institutional Care

Although direct classroom implications of infancy are few, society's changing nature means that more children will experience institutional care such as afforded by day-care centers at earlier ages. Consequently, the type of available care demands cautious and critical scrutiny, as infancy could well be the most important period in a child's life. Burton White, the Harvard child psychologist who directed the massive Harvard Preschool Project, began by studying 3- to 6-year-olds to discover the roots of intellectual competence. As White comments, they were too late—the children already possessed the competencies at 3 years.

White and his associates believe that 10 months is the critical period—it is then that there are few differences among children. But by 18 months, differences in mental abilities among children were evident. Something significant had happened between 10 and 18 months that relates directly to the mother. The children who showed high mental competence had mothers who superbly organized and designed the child's environment, and also provided stimulation when the child's curiosity was piqued. One final note about these children: those more intellectually competent paid far greater attention to environmental objects in the environment. Again, we see the central role of attention, noted earlier in the discussion of the need to study normal children.

What does this have to do with day-care centers? Combining our growing knowledge of infancy with recognition of the need for early environmental stimulation, the answer is clear. Nonstimulating, custodial care is insufficient. Some dangers that day-care centers must avoid are poorly trained staff, overcrowding, impersonal care, and a lack of private periods for children. But a good day-care center may be more stimulating than some children's homes, especially if there is adequate space, outdoor activities, good nutrition, and health care.

More detailed evidence is needed about optimal conditions of day-care centers. Until then day-care centers require careful observation to ensure that they facilitate, and not retard, development.

1. *Learning to walk.* Normally, most children are ready to walk between the ages of 9 and 15 months.

2. *Learning to take solid foods.* Sometime during the second year the child can chew and swallow solid food, thus gradually eliminating the need for nursing and sucking. It is an important task since the manner in which parents treat it (age and abruptness) can affect the child's personality.

3. *Learning to talk.* Havighurst describes the nature of this task as making meaningful sounds and communicating with others through these sounds. As he notes, and can be seen from Table 2.2, the onset of speech readiness is from 9 to 15 months. You shall see later, in the discussion of language development, that a child's social class strongly affects language learning.

4. *Learning to control the elimination of body wastes.* The myriad words written about toilet training have undoubtedly alerted almost everyone to the significance of infancy. Biologically, most children are ready to regulate elimination by the end of this period; culturally, most parents are more than ready to train the child. Although mastery comes gradually, it is a difficult time for both child and parents, and needs careful handling.

CLASSROOM IMPLICATIONS OF THE PERIOD

There are few direct classroom implications of this period. Its importance is the building of a foundation that will facilitate later development and learning. Adequate stimulation, both physical and emotional, furnishes a child with healthy nerves, bones, and muscle growth while simultaneously fostering those feelings of security and confidence so needed in coping with the world.

Early childhood

If infancy has provided a solid basis for future development, a child of 2 to 6 years is ready for more complex stimulation that will further perceptual and abstract abilities. Examining Table 2.3, the physical accomplishments of the period are obvious: growth of about one foot and another 20 pounds. Vocabulary development has increased from slightly more than 50 words to about 2600. There is a marked increase in relatively sophisticated behavior. The child coordinates motor abilities. Copying a square or diamond involves coordination of eyes, arm, hand, and fingers. Intricate language usage appears in which a 5- or 6-year-old's speech shows not only a rapid increase in vocabulary, but a corresponding increase in complexity and abstraction.

SOME CHARACTERISTICS OF THE PERIOD

During these years a definite sense of self emerges as children gain control of their bodies, begin to manipulate the environment with language, and play with other children. They begin to master the environment, but they also must learn to react to authority—parents, first teachers, older brothers and sisters. These are busy years, intellectually and physically, as is apparent from Table 2.3. If a child attends nursery school, there must be ample room for play, sturdy toys and materials, and that indispensable person—a good teacher.

How should parents use television during these years? Cau-

TABLE 2.3
Some Developmental Characteristics of Early Childhood

Age (years)	Height (in.)	Weight (lb)	Language Development	Motor Development
2½	36	30	Identifies object by use (vocabulary of 450 words)	Can walk on tiptoes; can jump with both feet off floor
3	38	32	Answers questions; brief sentences; may recite television commercials; vocabulary of 900 words	Can stand on one foot; jumps from bottom of stairs; rides tricycle
3½	39	34	Begins to build sentences; confined to concrete objects; vocabulary of 1220 words	Continues to improve 36 month skills; begins to play *with* others
4	41	36	Names and counts several objects; uses conjunctions; understands prepositions; vocabulary of 1540 words	Walks downstairs, one foot to step; skips on one foot; throws ball overhand
4½	42	38	Mean length of utterance (morphemes) 4.5 words; vocabulary of 1870 words	Hops on one foot; dramatic play; copies squares
5	43	41	Begins to show language mastery; uses words apart from specific situation; vocabulary of 2100 words	Skips, alternating feet; walks straight line; stands for longer periods on one foot
5½	45	45	Asks meanings of words; begins to use more complex sentences of five or six words; vocabulary of 2300 words	Draws recognizable man; continues to develop throwing skill
6	46	48	Good grasp of sense of sentences; uses more complex sentences; vocabulary of 2600 words	Jumps easily; throws ball overhead very well; stands on each foot alternately

Television

tiously, and even reluctantly, since the 2- to 6-year-old is active, curious, and restless, and using television as a baby-sitter may restrict development. Sitting in front of a television set does little for motor development and less for intellectual development unless it is used wisely. Table 2.3 shows the enormous increase in vocabulary development and sentence complexity, both of which require usage for maximum development. There is the accompanying danger of what television may do to the impressionable child.

Another important, even critical, acquisition of this period is

that of an acceptable sex identity. It is more than recognition of a
boy or a girl by sex organs; it is the realization that I am a boy or
girl. It is a sense of knowing the femaleness of female and the
maleness of male. John Money and his associates (1972) have conducted brilliant work with hermaphrodites at Johns Hopkins and
concluded that a child usually acquires a sex identity at about 3
years. If not, a child may experience some future emotional problems. Money believes that the critical period for the acquisition of
a sex identity may begin as early as 6 months for bright children
and certainly no later than 18 months for all youngsters, and fin-
ishes by about 3 years.

Other key ages are 3, 4, 5, and 6. More coordinated motor ability
allows children to proceed through the day with increasing success. They can feed themselves and help in dressing. Growing language competency makes them enjoyable companions; language
has opened new worlds.

At 4, children dress themselves, brush their teeth, and wash
their hands and face. They begin to tie their shoes. It may be a
difficult time for parent and child since most 4-year-olds test parental limits as well as patience.

By 5 years, children are usually much calmer and more stable.

COURTESY OF THE CHILDREN'S TELEVISION WORKSHOP

Youngsters seem more content, more confident of themselves and more secure in their surroundings. They dress and undress themselves, communicate well with others, and typically play well with other children.

At 6 years, the end of this period, children may again show volatile reactions. They experience new pressures at school. There are expectations that must be fulfilled; there are obligations they must meet. These novel experiences may produce emotional storms that demand care to avoid problems such as school phobia.

DEVELOPMENTAL TASKS OF THE PERIOD

Havighurst focuses upon four main developmental tasks for these years.

1. *Learning sex differences and sexual modesty.* The discussion of this period's characteristics mentioned the importance of acquiring a satisfactory sex identity, which usually appears by 3 years. Interest in the pleasure associated with sex organs, combined with adult interest in sex, emphasizes its critical role. Children must learn to control sexual interest and expression, but in a way that does not make sex evil and cause later sexual problems.

2. *Forming concepts and learning language to describe social and physical reality.* The nervous system gradually matures and permits a child to use environmental stimuli to form categories: boy-girl, animal, round, fruit. As experiences are absorbed and concepts formed, a youngster builds the foundation for later mental development. Linguistic conditions are especially significant during these years as seen in the growth of vocabulary, sentence complexity, and initial reading. Youngsters whose families provide them with meager language experiences put them at a distinct disadvantage upon entering school.

3. *Getting ready to read.* A child gradually learns that signs represent words and that there are many signs (from Table 2.3 you can see that the 6-year-old has an approximate vocabulary of several thousand words). Reading is a good example of the integration of many developmental tasks: society expects the average 5- or 6-year-old to read; psychologically, most 5- and 6-year-olds want to read; physically, the average child can begin to integrate eye, hand, and fingers. Combining this readiness with suitable experiences, most children will be successful and happy—effecting the desirable completion of a developmental task.

4. *Learning to distinguish right and wrong and beginning to develop a conscience.* Children develop ideas of right and wrong chiefly through their parents. How parents use threats, punishment, and praise, coupled with love and affection, powerfully influences a personally and socially acceptable conscience. The roots of moral character are in this period, and the belief today is that moral development parallels cognitive development, that is, a cognitive awareness of what is right and wrong slowly emerges.

FORSYTH, MONKMEYER

Nursery Schools

There are about 1 million children in nursery schools. This number forces any society to examine carefully the care and education offered by these schools. Moore and Kilmer (1973) comment that while all nursery schools claim to provide sound educational experiences, philosophies and curricula differ noticeably. Traditional nursery schools emphasize social skills, the learning potential of play, and the value of creativity, placing little emphasis on formal instruction. Montessori schools offer tightly structured methods and materials, a characteristic that surprises many parents, leading to disappointment and disenchantment with the methods. Many current nursery schools are somewhere between these two examples.

At the Laboratory Nursery School of the Institute of Child Development at the University of Minnesota most of the children are between 3 and 5. Moore and Kilmer portray the program as flexible and informal. The children move around freely, talk with each other, and play alone or in small groups. The children's activities were selected because of their contribution to child development. Science activities, prereading, premath, language experiences, and problem solving all aid intellectual development. Play materials foster social development. Yard equipment encourages climbing, jumping, and balancing, thus contributing to physical development. Art, music, and drama all advance aesthetic development.

Among the characteristics of the 5- to 6-year-old child is limited cognitive activity. Good nursery schools design programs and materials that account for this characteristic, yet facilitate mental development by supplying challenges. For example, the authors note that there must be ample concrete experiences, such as tangible objects, field trips, interesting people, and tasks that demand performance. Nursery schools must have standards of excellence, otherwise they could instill negative personal, social, and intellectual habits that affect the home atmosphere and may transfer to formal schooling.

CLASSROOM IMPLICATIONS OF THE PERIOD

School Entrance

There are two distinct educational possibilities for this period. Almost everyone experiences the first formal introduction into a public or private school system at either kindergarten or first grade. For those of you who will teach the 5- or 6-year-old, growth characteristics almost dictate what you can and should do. Rapid growth suggests a lack of motor coordination that results in awkwardness and difficulty with intricate tasks. Activities and materials should focus upon large muscles. There should be ample time and space for play and physical activity, accompanied by periods of rest.

The 5- and 6-year-old child possesses sharply restricted abstract ability. These children have entered the symbolic world: they think, use language, and mentally retain and transfer material. But they still cannot mentally adjust to change; they cannot reverse their thinking; that is, they may know $2 + 2 = 4$, but stumble when asked what happens if we take 2 from 4. They are still fooled by changes in form; they cannot retain the essence or substance of a problem. If someone pours one of two equal amounts of water into a tall, thin glass, these youngsters (up to about 7) think that there is more water in the taller glass.

It is an exciting time, ripe with educational potential. Table 2.3 illustrates how quickly children grow during these years. Most psychologists would agree that times of rapid growth are critical periods; that is, suitable tasks are learned quickly and easily, but if a suitable task is lacking, for example, learning to read, then mastery of that task becomes difficult at a later age. Havighurst's developmental tasks reflect the critical periods hypothesis. Carefully designed reading programs, both readiness and introductory, that present appropriate materials and instructional techniques are vital. Kindergarten and first-grade teachers must be skillful reading teachers, accomplished in different methods, expert in having the reading program match developmental level, and thoroughly familiar with all reading levels so that previous experiences are utilized and future needs anticipated. There is a saying, almost a cliché, but nevertheless true: every teacher is a reading teacher.

Discussion Questions

1. Return to Figure 2.1 and examine it carefully. Do you think that it encompasses all aspects of behavior? If not, what would you add? How can you justify another category?

2. Do you know any "normal children"? Why do you identify them as such? Most psychologists believe all children manifest abnormality; it is the extent, or degree, of abnormality that affects adjustment. Can you provide several "abnormal characteristics" of your normal children, such as stuttering, temper tantrums, tics?

3. When you consider children in this way, does it affect your judgment of them? How? Why? We mentioned in Chapter 1 that it is dangerous to think of teachers as therapists; but are there any striking causes of abnormalities in your normal children?

4. Would you agree with the interpretation of Figure 2.2? What do you think is its chief significance? Do the data imply that our instruction must be highly differentiated, that is, different programs and activities for the several individual differences of each child?

5. From your knowledge of brothers, sisters, nieces, nephews, or neighborhood children, write a description of infancy. Does it differ from what you just read? Why?

6. What do you consider the outstanding classroom implications of early childhood? If you were a teacher of 3- to 4-year-olds, what would you stress? Why?

Middle childhood

If a child's first six years have been healthy, there now begins one of the most exciting times of life, dominated by school entrance. Suddenly another challenging world emerges, a world in which children must adjust to peers, and a world in which parents are not paramount. There is continuing development of strength and skill and, as the child's world becomes more complex and abstract, expanding mental capacity matches this novel, stimulating environment.

But it is school that is the great adventure. Here a new world opens, where the children contact and are judged by adults other than parents, and by children other than brothers and sisters. Most children both fear and enjoy this experience, and teachers must establish an atmosphere that recognizes the child's physical and psychological reactions to these ambivalent feelings. Teachers and par-

ARLINGTON, MASS. ADVOCATE

ents must accept and encourage those flashes of independence characteristic of early childhood. Children need constructive discipline that helps them towards independence and maturity—a discipline that facilitates maximum self-growth while appreciating the rights and needs of others, both teachers and children.

SOME CHARACTERISTICS OF THE PERIOD

As children enter this new world, they are usually bright, happy, and eager to learn. Their developmental characteristics should be a perfect match for their educational experiences. Table 2.4 presents some of the periods outstanding features.

This is a particularly revealing table. Until this period, boys and girls have almost matched each other, inch for inch, pound for pound. It was possible to present combined data for boys and girls in Tables 2.2 and 2.3. But during middle childhood the differences are so noticeable that separate male-female physical data are neces-

TABLE 2.4
Some Developmental Characteristics of Middle Childhood

Age (years)	Height (in.)		Weight (lb)		Stanford-Binet Test Items	Motor Development
	girl	boy	girl	boy		
7	48	49	52	53	Child can detect in what way two things are similar: apple, peach	Child has good balance; can hop and jump accurately
8	51	51	60	62	Child can read a paragraph of seven or eight sentences and recall five or six major ideas	Boys and girls show equal grip strength; great interest in physical games
9	52	53	70	70	Child can observe card with two designs and after ten seconds draw the designs' main features	Psychomotor skills such as throwing, jumping, running show marked improvement
10	54	55	74	79	Child can repeat as many as 60 digits	Boys become accurate in throwing and catching a small ball; running continues to improve
11	57	57	85	85	Child can find similarities among three things: rose, potato, tree	Boys can throw a ball about 95 feet; girls can run about 17.5 feet per second
12	60	59	95	95	Child can recognize absurdities: we saw icebergs that had been melted by the Gulf Stream	Boys can run about 18.5 feet per second; dodge ball popular with girls

sary. By 12 years, girls are slightly taller, and as heavy or heavier, than boys. Girls mature faster than boys. Girls will also reach the adolescent growth spurt before boys and their greater maturity can cause social and emotional problems for both sexes. Boys may feel awkward and inferior; girls may feel embarrassed by their physical development and by 11 or 12 turn to an older group for social activities.

The figures in Table 2.4 may vary widely, that is, individual children may be taller or shorter, heavier or lighter, but the pattern is clear until about 12: rather slow, steady growth. An example is height: for the more than two-foot gain from birth to 6, there is only about one foot gained from 6 to 12. It is almost as if the body slows for the mind to accelerate. The Stanford-Binet intelligence test is a good illustration. If you examine Table 2.4, the increasing sophistication of mental ability is apparent. Note the difference in the nature of items throughout these years: the testing of a child's capacity to discern relationships and solve more complicated, abstract tasks.

Here, then, is the 6- to 12-year-old. Physically, both boys and girls manifest considerable strength, speed, and skill in physical tasks, especially by 11 and 12. This phenomenon, coupled with the importance of peers, emphasizes the role of sports in the child's life. Traditionally, this applied to boys, but with girls' growing

Some Trends of the Period

ARLINGTON, MASS. ADVOCATE

**Importance of Peer
Approval**

participation in organized athletics, some conclusions hold true for both sexes. Peer approval usually rewards skillful performance and, since most sports of these years are organized, the less coordinated boy or girl may feel frustrated.

Each year, in Little League baseball, Pop Warner football, or youth hockey, some children show greater psychomotor skill, until by 12 some youngsters are highly competent athletes. But at each level, more youngsters drop out of the programs, with an accompanying emotional jolt. It can be a difficult time for youngsters; teachers and schools can supplement these programs to help fill a conspicuous physical, social, and emotional void.

Mentally youngsters can solve more abstract problems. They can conserve, that is, retain the essence of something although its form may change. For example, in our previous example of pouring water into a taller and thinner container, by 7 or 8, children no longer think the smaller container has more water. They *know* the water remains the same. But it is still a restricted mental ability since children must have tangible, concrete objects to manipulate mentally. Verbal, symbolic problems still confuse them. Here is an excellent instance of the school's need to match curriculum and materials with developmental knowledge to encourage intellectual growth.

DEVELOPMENTAL TASKS OF THE PERIOD

Havighurst states that middle childhood has three great outward pushes: out of the home and into the peer group, the physical thrust into the world of games and work, and the mental thrust into the world of adult concepts, logic, and communication. Havighurst (1972, pg. 19) comments that at the beginning of this period children are all possibility, while at the end they have formed their own style and found their own level in these activities. There are nine developmental tasks of the period:

1. *Learning physical skills necessary for ordinary games.* Previously mentioned, this task today applies to more and more girls.

2. *Building wholesome attitudes toward oneself as a growing organism.* This task demands healthy bodily care, plus habits of cleanliness and safety. Since modern society accentuates the body, a child quickly values mastery of this task.

3. *Learning to get along with age-mates.* When children leave the safe influence of the home and go to school with its peer influence, they become social personalities. They must learn the give-and-take of group play, form friendships with strangers, and play fair.

4. *Learning an appropriate masculine or feminine social role.* What does it mean to be a boy or girl in a particular society? While cultural sex differences are diminishing, they still exist, and boys and girls must meet society's expectations, whatever they may be.

5. *Developing fundamental skills in reading, writing, and calculating.* For any youngster to adjust to a complicated, technological society requires considerable expertise in reading, writing, and calculating.

6. *Developing concepts necessary for everyday living.* While the preschool child undoubtedly has several hundred concepts, the 6- to 12-year-old develops several thousand, which enable a youngster to move effectively through his or her environment.

7. *Developing conscience, morality, and a scale of values.* As youngsters grow mentally, they also experience moral development. Initially through parents, and then through the acquisition of rules (games, school, society), they form a sense of right and wrong.

8. *Achieving personal independence.* Personal independence grows, from both parents and teachers. Children slowly gain knowledge and security, and begin to make their own decisions. Both parents and teachers must strive to foster independence, but in a way that permits children to remain close to their parents and to work successfully within definite boundaries.

9. *Developing attitudes toward social groups and institutions.* Children are very impressionable during these years and quickly form attitudes toward politics, ethnic groups, and religion. Once formed, they are not easily changed.

CLASSROOM IMPLICATIONS OF THE PERIOD

The school can meet intellectual needs—a recurrent theme throughout our work—but schools can also aid other developmental phrases. For example, building wholesome attitudes toward oneself in modern society demands sex- and drug-education programs. There is an alarming number of 9- and 10-year-old alcoholics, so many that several large metropolitan hospitals have established children's alcoholic clinics. There is need for accurate information, perhaps in a drug-education program or some separate offering.

The school cannot avoid its role in moral development. Many a school may hesitate about direct intervention in moral development—perhaps rightly so—but its mere existence as an institution that rewards and punishes means that it judges right and wrong, for example, cheating and stealing. Teachers also serve as daily models and their example is potent.

Schools should be both positive and pleasant. Although most children anticipate school and regard it as an important stride toward maturity, the shock of contact with new authority, demands, competition, and isolation may lead to a condition described as school phobia. Unheralded and perhaps unadmitted is the familiar case of crying, vomiting, and feigned illness in order to avoid school. Kahn and Nursten (1964) note that symptoms of the problem are anxiety by both mother and child, recurrent physical troubles, and a child's refusal to believe there is no danger in school. While the emotional climate of the home may be intense and contribute to anxiety about the mother-child separation, the school itself may add to the problem. A first-grade teacher who displays excessive impatience or harshness increases the child's fear of this new reality.

Coolidge et al. (1960) separated children who manifest school phobia into two classes: those who are secure and normal in their relations except for school, and those whose personalities are so disturbed that school phobia is but one expression of their difficulties. Their study indicated that school phobia in young children may predict moderate to severe difficulties later in life. Coolidge, Brodie, and Feenedy (1964), in a ten-year study of children who had evidenced school phobia, again found that frequently it signifies severe problems later in life.

School phobia is still a relatively unstudied problem. Whether it persists or is overcome quickly is probably the best clue to its seriousness. During the first days of kindergarten or first grade most youngsters experience troubled times. It is more characteristic of first grade than kindergarten. Problems with classmates, fear of the teacher, and feelings of isolation and inadequacy magnify a tense situation.

Most youngsters adapt quickly and establish acceptable, usually harmonious, relationships with the teacher, various groups, and individuals. For those children whose troubles persist, the problems seem to reflect a more serious disturbance.

Childhood is usually viewed as a completely carefree, happy time, devoid of any worries or problems. Unfortunately, children frequently suffer stress, anxiety, school problems, and even illness— usually because of home problems. Realizing how some parents treat children, it is a marvel that they are as adjusted as they are. This realization is not a rationale for tolerating disciplinary upsets; it is a plea to search for causes, especially during the years 6 to 12. Anthony (1970) reports that there are two distinct peak periods for clinic admission: for boys at about 9 years and then again at 14; for girls at about 10 years and then again at 15. Even youngsters are susceptible to problems, so be alert to signs of emotional difficulty—the sooner detected, the easier helped.

Adolescence

Experts have written millions of words about adolescents; investigators have studied, tested, and observed them; philosophers have speculated about the nature of adolescence. Yet the words, studies,

ERWITT, MAGNUM

and speculations retain an air of uncertainty, as if adolesence were
a mysterious, magic time that only adolescents can understand.
Why? Is it actually adolescence, or our perception of it that causes
uncertainty?

In a penetrating analysis, Kenneth Keniston (1970) states that

before the twentieth century, adolescence was rarely included as a stage in the life cycle. Today, however, it is considered an integral part of development. Keniston believes that there are major themes that dominate adolescent development:

1. Tension between self and society, as a youth struggles for self-identity, a struggle that may produce conflict with society.
2. Pervasive ambivalence, a desire for independence coupled with a desire to be effective *within* society.
3. Wary probe, an interesting expression coined by Keniston to illustrate the adolescent's testing of the adult world (it is often joined with self-probe)
4. Estrangement and omnipotentiality, in which feelings of isolation alternate with feelings of absolute freedom.
5. Youth-specific identities, which are usually temporary roles that inspire intense commitment: hippie, radical, athlete.
6. Youthful countercultures, a grouping with other youths in a deliberate attempt to remain apart from society.

**Patterns of
Adolescence**

These are some themes suggested by Keniston, and we may better understand their intensity, or lack of intensity, by relating them to what George Goethals (1975) calls "patterns of adolescence." There are three patterns:

1. Adolescence by age grade, in which the adolescent is carefully prepared in specific schools and social rituals until, under watchful adult supervision, the adolescent is accepted into adult society. It is a pattern in which an adolescent has a specific role in a prescribed social hierarchy. There is nothing to achieve since the role is preordained from birth.

2. Rites of passage, in which some moment or ritual signals passage into adulthood. It is an initiation, and if society does not provide it, an adolescent may impose it upon himself, such as stealing a car, buying a car, sexual intercourse. The difficulty is that while the act may have great personal significance, society ignores its significance.

3. A psychological moratorium, which is a period of noncommitment. Goethal remarks that age grading is peculiar to elites, the rites of passage to more primitive societies, and the moratorium to those societies where adolescence and young adulthood determine one's place in the social order.

Whatever the cause, it is a time of unrest, a time to which society must devote more care and attention, if only because of the huge number of youth. Table 2.5 shows the numbers of males and females 14–24 from 1840 to 1990 and the change in each decade.

Note the leap from 1960 to 1970. In that one decade, the increase

TABLE 2.5
Size of Population Aged 14–24, 1890–1990, and Percent Change per Decade

Year	Size (in million)	Percent Change
1890	14.2	
1900	16.5	+16
1910	20.0	+21
1920	20.8	+ 4
1930	24.8	+20
1940	26.3	+ 6
1950	24.2	− 8
1960	26.7	+10
1970	40.5	+52
1980	44.8	+11
1990	41.1	− 8

Source: U.S. Bureau of the Census, Department of Commerce, 1960 Census of Population: General Population Characteristics.

was 13.8 million, more than in the rest of the century. What happened to those youths? The schools absorbed most, helping to explain some of the unrest of the 1960s.

SOME CHARACTERISTICS OF THE PERIOD

Dorothy Eichorn (1974) has analyzed several biological and psychological characteristics of adolescence that have relevance for our social institutions, especially the school. Teachers know the great diversity of adolescent growth: the difference between those who have completed the growth spurt and those who have yet to begin it, although the age may be identical; girls usually begin their adolescent changes about two years before boys. Between 11 and 17 the range of individual differences in physical structure and physi-

Sex and Adolescence

Goethals and Klos (1976) believe that many adolescents have difficulty coping with sex because of conflicts within the American society. The ideal of an idealistic, romantic love combined with a rigid religious ethic can cause considerable confusion. The authors also stress the conflict between the American goal of "rugged individualism" and teenage uniformity. If one adolescent *can* do something, then all should be able to do it, which has no realistic physiological or psychological basis.

Individual adolescent sexual differences are particularly pertinent. Sex means quite different things for boys as compared to adolescent girls. Adolescent girls, with a romantic and affectionate sexual outlook, are often unprepared for the physical expression of sex that many teenage boys desire. Thus adolescents frequently experience intimacy without identity. Kilpatrick, in his penetrating essay, *Identity and Intimacy* (1975), states that identity demands time. The concomitants of identity—trust, commitment, love, friendship —likewise demand time. Have adolescents had sufficient time to acquire that self-identity which permits the fulfillment of intimacy?

Kilpatrick mentions that boys have more difficulty with their sexual identity than do girls, that anxiety about sexual identity continues to plague boys far longer than girls. Boys, sooner or later, must reject their maternal identification, which can be difficult.

Girls, however, do not escape unscathed. While they may be more secure in their sexual identity, they are increasingly unhappy in their sexual roles. Kilpatrick notes that although females feel secure in their femininity they still envy the status and privilege that accompany the masculine role in a male-oriented society.

Is it any wonder that adolescents, buffeted by surging sexual desires, still insecure with their maturing sexual identity, and uncertain about their sexual roles, need understanding and guidance during these "storm and stress" years?

ological functioning at any given age is greater than at any other time. At age 15 boys may vary as much as 8 inches and 30 pounds.

Eichorn uses these data to question age grading and mixed sex grouping. As we mentioned earlier, size and motor skill are rewarded, and slow maturing youths suffer distinct disadvantages. The opposite is also true, and these feelings of frustration and superiority may persist, especially for boys. A well-developed girl in a class of "childlike bodies" has more mature interests than her classmates, which may cause embarrassment and negative reactions. If these disparities are coupled with such adolescent dilemmas as acne, large feet, and awkwardness, the quest for identity is intensified and made more difficult.

Mentally, the adolescent is ready for true abstract thinking—logical and mathematical—without using concrete objects or experiences. This new intellectual capacity extends to emotional and social decisions so that we see the idealistic, romantic adolescent who wants to reform society. Yet adolescents, only now coming

Difficulty with Age Grading

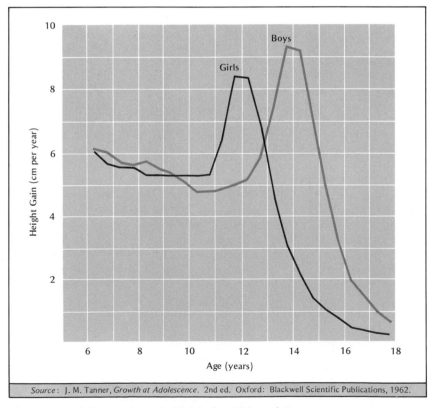

Source: J. M. Tanner, *Growth at Adolescence*. 2nd ed. Oxford: Blackwell Scientific Publications, 1962.

Figure 2.3 Adolescent Spurt in Height for Girls and Boys

ARLINGTON, MASS. ADVOCATE

into their intellectual powers, must begin making educational choices about some future occupation about which they probably know little if anything. With the changing feminine role, these decisions are as significant for girls as boys since occupation determines socioeconomic stations, life style, and children's education.

Vocational choice is one of the adolescent's most serious choices. Surveys indicate that boys and girls themselves believe that a vocational decision is their most critical task, more important than the usual adolescent concerns. Concern about these decisions affects today's 12-year-olds. These concerns have led educators to devise career education programs that begin in the first grade. (We shall return to this important topic in Chapter 16.)

The physical and psychological data suggest a clear pattern of adolescent concerns:

1. Early adolescents show a preoccupation with bodily concerns and sexual interests.
2. As adolescence proceeds, interests shift to include personal truths and values, vocational decisions, and heterosexual role.
3. Toward the period's end, the adolescent has a good sense of self, realistic vocational ambitions, and carefully defined sex pattern.

DEVELOPMENTAL TASKS OF THE PERIOD

Havighurst believes that the years 12 to 18 reflect physical and emotional maturation more than intellectual, which is seen in the following nine developmental tasks.

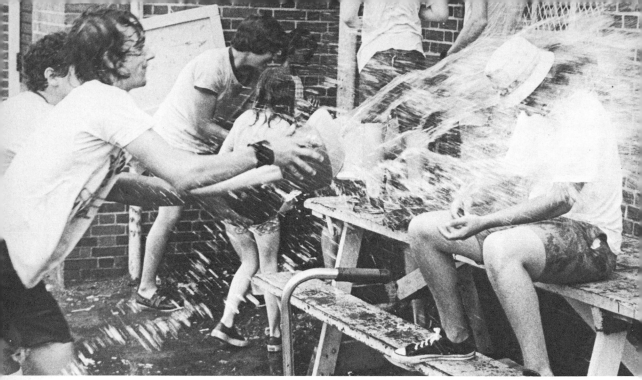

ARLINGTON, MASS. *ADVOCATE*

1. *Achieving new and more mature relations with age mates of both sexes.* During these years boys become men and girls become women. They become members of the adult society working with others and establishing a pattern of sexual behavior. Group approval is probably more important during adolescence than during any other time.

2. *Achieving a masculine or feminine social role.* Adolescents achieve sexual maturity during this period, but culturally defined sex roles are changing and many girls now wish to combine marriage and career. Contraception and abortion have radically altered many girls' lives so that achieving an acceptable feminine sexual role is more complicated.

3. *Accepting one's physique and using the body effectively.* There are extensive physical changes in adolescence, so teenagers need sympathetic advice about early and late maturity to help them accept and understand their physique.

4. *Achieving emotional independence of parents and other adults.* Adolescents begin the task of freeing themselves from childhood parental dependence. Although most authorities focus upon the physical and sexual aspects of adolescence, a satisfactory relationship with parents dominates much of an adolescent's thinking and some adolescents never fully reconcile dependence and independence. Ask any group of college students what their major problems are and invariably parental relations is one of the first few mentioned.

76

5. *Preparing for marriage and family life.* This task relates to that of achieving a satisfactory sex role; times are changing, roles are changing, but most see marriage as a desirable state. The challenge today is to prepare for its varied nature.

6. *Preparing for an economic career.* Given the importance of occupations, considerable care and thought is required to prepare for an enjoyable and productive career.

7. *Acquiring a set of values and an ethical system as a guide to behavior—developing an ideology.*

8. *Desiring and achieving socially responsible behavior.* Both of these tasks indicate the growing maturity of adolescents, their concern with the abstract, and willingness, even eagerness, to discover personally and socially acceptable values that will permit them to function as mature adults in a complex society.

CLASSROOM IMPLICATIONS OF THE PERIOD

Every society must somehow solve the problem of transforming children into adults, for its very survival depends on that solution. In every society there is established some kind of institutional setting, within which the process of transition is to occur, in directions predicted by societal goals and values. In our view, the institutional framework for maturation in the United States is now in need of serious examination. (Coleman, 1974, pg. 1)

The adolescent characteristics, with their attendant developmental tasks, have led many thoughtful observers to ponder the need for change in secondary education. *Youth: Transition to Adulthood* contains the reflections of several social scientists and educators as a Report of the Panel on Youth of the President's Science Advisory Committee. They begin by noting that as child labor has become unnecessary, society has merely lengthened schooltime. But schooling focuses upon cognitive achievement, imposes dependency, and withholds authority and responsibility. Perhaps the time has come to ask not "How much schooling?" but "What are appropriate environments for youth to grow into adults?"

Since schools now provide the general social environment for youth, they share the socialization task with family and peers. Consequently, the time has come to rethink society's treatment of youth, including schools but not limited to them. There should be alternative environments, including cognitive learning but also incorporating other maturational features. These environments would satisfy two general objectives: First they would provide those necessary personal skills that enable youths to expand their personal resources. Second, they would provide opportunities for dealing responsibly with others.

Specifically, Coleman and his colleagues (1974, pp. 3–4) suggest the following objectives within two broad categories:

A.1. To develop cognitive and noncognitive skills necessary for economic independence and occupational opportunities.

2. To develop the capability of effectively managing one's own affairs.

3. To develop capabilities as a consumer, not only of goods, but more significantly, of the cultural riches of civilization.

4. To develop the capabilities for engaging in intense concentrated involvement in an activity.

B.1. To be enlarged by experience with persons differing in social class, subculture, and age.

2. To be enlarged by the experience of having others dependent on one's actions.

3. To be enlarged by interdependent activities directed toward collective goals.

Discussion Questions

1. Examine carefully the IQ test items in Table 2.4. What impresses you most about them? Do they suggest any implications for teaching?

2. Most readers have had some experience, either direct or vicarious, with organized youth sports. Do you approve of them? Explain your answer. How would you improve them? Would you make any suggestions for parents? What is your reaction to the growing participation of girls in these sports?

3. Would you recommend sex education programs in the schools? Drug programs, including alcohol? Give reasons for your answers. How much community preparation is first necessary, if any?

4. Do you think adolescence is actually the time of trouble and turmoil that we make it? Why? Relate your answer to society's expectations.

5. What do you think is the most critical developmental task of adolescence? There should be a variety of answers; try to discover patterns: physical problems, economic difficulties, parents.

6. *Youth: Transition to Adulthood* poses two general objectives: self-development and service to others. These recommendations imply work outside of the school in hospitals, shops, nursing homes. Do you agree with the recommendations? Are they practical?

Some Concluding Thoughts

As an artist must understand the quality and texture of colors and the resulting product when colors are mixed, so a teacher must understand the developmental characteristics of students and the possible results when these characteristics are mixed. For example, most fourth graders are 9 or 10 years old, which are critical years emotionally. Obviously not all 9-year-olds are clinic cases but it seems to be an emotional age, so teachers knowing this, should be alert to those symptoms that signify difficulty.

This is true for all ages and grades, but some ages are more tumultuous than others and require greater teacher sensitivity. Kindergarten, first grade, and adolescence are other emotional ages. But other grades may include these youngsters who are either beginning or ending a turbulent period, thus any teacher undoubtedly encounters a mixture of developmental characteristics. Viewing education developmentally, the significance of "individual differences" is striking, which means adapting both teaching methods and administrative structures to accommodate these differences.

Both educators and psychologists constantly suggest revisions in techniques and structure to fulfill children's needs more effectively. For example, open education became popular, and now the reaction against some of its excesses has begun. In *Youth: Transition to Adulthood*, the authors urge changes in the secondary schools, advocating more work outside the school. Ultimately, all suggested changes at all educational levels acknowledge the primacy of developmental characteristics.

Summary

- While there is considerable individual variation in human development, the sequence is identical for all.

- There are common developmental characteristics that aid us in making judgments about normality and abnormality.

- Infancy is the foundation upon which all else rests, thus accentuating the necessity for a stimulating environment.

- Havighurst's developmental task concept is a useful tool for analyzing developmental characteristics and needs.

- Early childhood shows a remarkable surge in language facility, which should receive environmental encouragement and stimulation.

- The acquisition of an acceptable sex identity is a basic need for all children and illustrates the critical period concept.

- Middle childhood sees school entrance and the opening of a new exciting world that involves adjustment to a new atmosphere and winning peer approval.

- Adolescence, a time of great physical, emotional, and intellectual variety, should find a youth acquiring a sense of identity that results in self-fulfillment.

Suggested Readings

Havighurst, Robert. *Developmental Tasks and Education.* New York: McKay, 1972. Here Havighurst explains his developmental task concept and relates it to developmental periods. A brief but excellent, inexpensive, text that belongs in your library.

Knobloch, Hilda and Benjamin Pasamanick. *Gesell and Amatruda's Developmental Diagnosis.* New York: Harper & Row, 1974. A fine overview and analysis of the first years, with comprehensive chapters on developmental disorders.

Travers, John. *The Growing Child: An Introduction to Child Development.* New York: Wiley, 1977. A thorough analysis of child development from conception to adolescence.

Youth: Transition to Adulthood. University of Chicago Press, 1974. Report of the Panel on Youth of the President's Science Advisory Committee, an engrossing look at what was, what is, and what may be in secondary education.

3

Early Experience and Intellectual Development

(continues)

Introduction

From the developmental overview of Chapter 2 it is possible to trace the growing complexity and abstractness of a child's thought. Since mental ability is a developmental phenomenon, a child's or adult's intellectual achievement results from the interaction of heredity and environment. Heredity, the genetic material that nature provides, delimits potential, but environment determines if children approximate that potential. Recognizing both potential and limitations, psychologists and educators today acknowledge the early years' significance. From birth to about 2 or 3 years represents one of a child's most sensitive periods.

What does it mean to say that early experience affects intellectual development? Does it mean that children at birth need all kinds of gimmicks and gadgets, creating what the famous psychologist William James called "a buzzing, blooming confusion"? Does it mean that tender loving care comes before all? Something must be at work to explain such statements as "Today's children are brighter than ever." Or, "Look at today's knowledge explosion—a monument to human progress."

No, this is not quite correct. The statement needs rephrasing: a monument to the progress of *some* men and women. Why must the statement be restricted to make it more precise? Is it because some men and women are naturally more gifted than others? Yes. Is it because some men and women receive greater opportunities than others? Yes. But it does not mean that *all* those whose opportunities are limited are less gifted than those who are the beneficiaries of more stimulating circumstances.

This is the ancient nature-nurture controversy. Buried for so many years, it angrily burst forth in the late 1960s, with the work of Arthur Jensen and his belief that there are racial differences in intellectual performance. With the resultant heated controversy has come one agreeable consequence. Most (still not all) of the disputants agree that a child's early years are critical for healthy development into a mature, self-sufficient adult.

Some think these years should provide the stimulation that enables a child to grow intellectually, to secure the physiological and psychological foundation that insures cognitive growth. Others disagree with this reference to intelligence and intellectual development; while they feel that heredity tells all, they are still willing to admit that the early years should provide a warm and accepting environment to help a youngster become an emotionally adjusted adult.

This chapter argues that a child's early experiences have a direct bearing on intellectual performance, achievement, and ultimately, healthy adjustment. In this chapter you will not enter the debate over the intelligence test itself—does it measure an individual's intellectual capacity or does it measure achievement (see Chapter 11)? Rather, intellectual performance, or mental test performance, will refer to scores on popular, frequently used tests, such as the Stanford-Binet or the Wechsler.

The argument is as follows: the early years are vital for maximum development; if the experiences of these years are deficient, intellectual performance, partially reflecting this deficiency, will suffer accordingly. The argument includes the word "partially" because there is no escape from genetic endowment. Every human being differs genetically, which obviously results in varied human abilities.

There is no reassurance, however, that children will fulfill their potential. Limited experiences mean limited development, both physical and mental. The well-known American psychologist Jerome Bruner has said that one of the most important features of human development is the extent to which it progresses from the outside in as much as from the inside out. Is there evidence to support the optimistic conclusion that improving a child's environment will also improve intelligence? The encouraging answer is: Yes. Both physiological and psychological studies show a clear pattern. But danger signals also fly concerning the time and duration of childhood deprivation, which must be accounted for in our discussion.

The physiological evidence

Recent neurological advances furnish knowledge that is especially significant for an understanding of nervous system development. Steven Rose, in his fascinating book *The Conscious Brain* (1973) states that one of the features that distinguishes the brain from

ARLINGTON, MASS. ADVOCATE

other bodily organs is that the neurons will not regenerate, either in the child or the adult. Infants are born with nearly all of the neurons that will develop, and the inescapable conclusion is that damage to any of these cells is irreversible.

The brain is the physical basis of mental life. The distinguished Nobel prizewinner John Eccles (1958) has stated that all mental activity, including the supreme activity of creative imagination, arises somehow from brain activity, with its staggering capability: 10 billion neurons in the adult brain, capable of flashing signals instantaneously from one to another across synaptic junctions. Eccles then asks the critical question: What brain activity corresponds to the mind's activity and how does it burst into consciousness? While there is no definitive answer, Eccles speculates that repeated brain activation is necessary to establish vital neuronal patterns. Many and varied experiences are necessary to enable the child to build the physiological foundation which mental life requires.

The Brain Is the Basis of Our Mental Life

Another Nobel prizewinner, Holger Hydn (1967), has discovered that proteins play an important role in learning. Experiments demonstrated that nervous system proteins increased with learning; but after injection with chemicals that inhibited the formation of proteins, learning suffered significantly. His investigations also suggest that protein deficient animals learn more slowly than those on a normal diet.

MALNUTRITION AND ITS EFFECTS

Do we have evidence that children suffer these same consequences when environmental conditions are deficient? If protein plays a key role in learning, and if a child suffers a protein lack, will learning and mental test performance also suffer? Malnutrition studies confirm this assumption and also offer two interesting conclusions. First is that malnutrition does not occur in a vacuum, which means that usually *all* parts of a malnourished child's environment are impoverished. Second is that protein-calorie malnutrition produces results that are strikingly similar to the results produced by early environmental isolation.

Protein-Calorie Malnutrition

Steven Rose (1973) states that one of the most severe environmental alterations, short of actual brain damage, is food deprivation. Cravioto's studies in Mexico (1970) have shown that adults deprived of food maintain their normal level of mental test performance until body weight declines about 30 percent. When malnutrition is eliminated, mental test scores return to normal. Unfortunately, children may not respond similarly. All organisms experience critical or sensitive periods during which proper environmental stimulation produces maximum growth, while a lack of proper stimulation hinders growth. Malnutrition may even pro-

The Critical Periods

Nervous System Experimentation

Human beings have long manifested an intense interest in what makes them what they are. The ancient Egyptians believed that the heart and the head made humans "human," relegating the brain to an insignificant role. Even Aristotle believed that the heart was the thinking organ. While these ancient beliefs are fascinating, more recent research is particularly pertinent, for example:

Year	Person	Finding
1861	Paul Broca	Damage to the brain's left frontal lobe causes language problems.
1904	Ivan Pavlov	The role of the autonomic nervous system in digestion. Later discovered the conditioned reflex in animals.
1934	Wilder Penfield	Discovered brain's control center by electrically stimulating brains of epileptic patients.
1955	James Olds	Accidentally discovered a pleasure center in rat's brain while using electrical stimulation.
1959	James McConnell	Cannibal worms show learning after eating trained worms—multiple experiments involving electrical stimulation of human and animal brains.
1963	John Eccles	Receives Nobel prize for studies of internal activity of nerve cells.
1963	David Hubel Torsten Wiesel	Demonstrated that young animals deprived of seeing at critical developmental stages have abnormal brains and abnormal vision.
1964	David Krech Mark Rosenzweig Edward Bennett Marian Diamond	Demonstrated that an enriched environment produces significant chemical and anatomical changes in rats.
1969	Neal Miller	The conscious mind can control involuntary functions.

The experiments continue unabated. Adam Smith (1975) chronicles a series of controlled tests and speculations that range from mind-changing drugs to the growing popularity of mind control by transcendental meditation. As knowledge of the brain grows, so also will our experimentation.

duce physiological damage. These critical periods seem to be times of rapid neurological growth and organization. Brain growth is an outstanding example of a critical period. From the last trimester of pregnancy to 6 months after birth is a time of great brain growth. It is also a time of great susceptibility to environmental experience. The statistics of this period are particularly pertinent. At birth, the brain is about 20 percent of its adult weight. Estimates are that it weighs about 335 grams at birth, 1064 grams at 2 years, 1190 grams at 4 years, and 1350 grams at 12 years. These figures and times are important since they indicate the time of greatest growth and potential vulnerability. As a result of his studies, Cravioto believes that if protein-calorie malnutrition occurs under 2 years, and if it is sufficiently severe to affect physical growth, there is a real possibility of permanent mental and motor damage.

Examining the physical increase in brain weight, we note that it coincides with the psychological findings of the noted American educator Benjamin Bloom (1964) who has analyzed longitudinal studies of intelligence and concluded that a child acquires 50 percent of his variance in adult intelligence by 4 years. The rapid development of the human brain is seen in Figure 3.1.

These and other speculations refer to the period of the brain's fastest growth. The most sensitive period for brain development probably extends from birth to 18 months. But prolonged malnutrition (18 months to 5 years) may also affect subsequent brain development, though less severely. Sohan Manocha (1972) states that it is only during the period of rapid brain growth that severe physiological damage may ensue. Since the brain achieves about 90 percent of its total growth by 4 years, malnutrition has little effect after this sensitive period. The early peak of brain growth may be a blessing in disguise since most youngsters may achieve maximum brain development before malnutrition can leave its mark. Approximately 60 percent of the world's children between birth and 5 years are malnourished, but the percentage of mentally retarded children is much lower, which may be due to the brain's rapid growth. Youngsters have passed through the brain's sensitive period before malnutrition takes its toll.

Although malnutrition defintely produces the effects previously mentioned, it does not do so on a one-to-one basis. Malnutrition is associated with environmental conditions, such as poverty, poor housing, disease, illiteracy, and a general lack of stimulation. The consequences of any, or all, of these circumstances are similar. For

Accompanying Environmental Conditions

example, Manocha quotes a study of Indians in which malnourished children's body weight was only 60 percent of normal. *But* their home environment was good (warm and affectionate); the children felt secure and wanted; they played with pots and pans and other home objects; there was a good relationship between the parents. The IQs of these children were as high as those of children from upper-class backgrounds. The time and duration of malnutrition and the extent to which recovery occurs after treatment is also significant. If deprivation begins early and lasts some time, the damage may be irreversible. If malnutrition strikes before six months after birth (actually within that sensitive nine-month interval—the

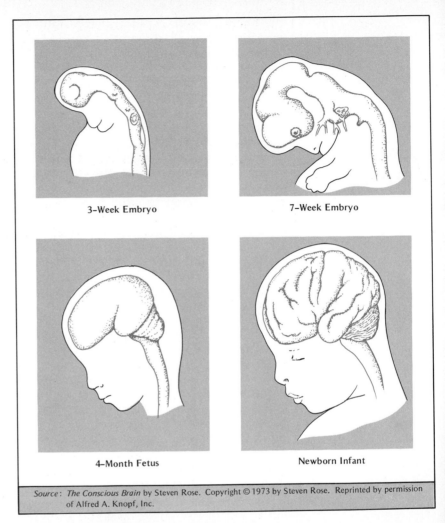

3-Week Embryo

7-Week Embryo

4-Month Fetus

Newborn Infant

Source: *The Conscious Brain* by Steven Rose. Copyright © 1973 by Steven Rose. Reprinted by permission of Alfred A. Knopf, Inc.

Figure 3.1 The Development of the Brain

final trimester of pregnancy and the first six postnatal months) it may influence all subsequent development, both physical and mental. But coming later, the child better tolerates its effects.

Malnutrition and social deprivation seem to produce a similar effect: both frequently appear together; both produce like results so that it is difficult to separate the influence of one from another. Do the malnutrition studies help in understanding the impact of early experience upon a child? The answer is clearly yes. If deprivation, either dietary or social, occurs early in life, and lasts long enough, a child may experience a lifetime of problems—physical, social, and intellectual.

These studies also demonstrate that critical periods are indeed critical. Although it is difficult to specify precisely what critical periods are and when they occur, the evidence seems irrefutable that they exist. John Paul Scott's (1969) experiments with various animals reinforce the critical period concept. He and his wife took a newborn female lamb into their home and reared her on a bottle. She became closely attached to the Scotts, "following them around like Mary's little lamb." After ten days they returned her to the flock. She paid no attention to the sheep, would respond only to the Scotts, and three years later she remained isolated while the rest of the flock gathered together. They had produced a social isolate.

Critical Periods

Scott believes that this is an almost perfect example of a critical period: a brief duration when a small effort produces a major and lasting result. The Scotts then experimented with puppies. Investigators placed a tame pregnant bitch in a field surrounded by a board fence. After the puppies were born they were fed through a hole in the fence. The puppies had no human contact, perhaps a fleeting glimpse of a human through a broken board. Individual puppies were removed at various ages and exposed to humans. Those removed during the first 5 weeks behaved normally and made friendly contact with people. Those removed at 7 weeks manifested considerable shyness, while at 14 weeks the puppies had to be confined after removal because they were so wild. The Scotts thus concluded that dogs have a critical period for social attachments—3 to 12 weeks.

The thalidomide episode of the 1960s is a tragic reminder of human critical periods. Pregnant women who had used this seemingly safe sedative during the first six or seven weeks gave birth to youngsters who either had deformed limbs or missing limbs—a specific example of chemical interference with a critical period, in this case, formation of arms and legs. Women who had taken the drug later in their pregnancy produced normal children. German measles are also dangerous. If contracted during the first two or three months of pregnancy they can cause a newborn to be blind, deaf, or mentally retarded.

Sex Identity

John Money's incredible work with hermaphrodites at Johns Hopkins is another example of human critical periods. A girl, because of faulty hormonal action, is born with internal female sex organs (uterus, ovaries) but an apparent external male organ (penis). She is raised as a male before an accurate sex identity is made. After accurate identification and corrective surgery, she is now reared as a girl. Or consider the boy who has his sex reassigned (becomes female) because an accident caused ablation of the penis. After surgery the child-rearing pattern is female. Will either, or both, of these children adjust to the change?

As Money says, this is the land of the midnight sun of sex. While these cases are fascinating, the major concern is with the timing of the sex reassignment (usually a combination of hormonal and surgical treatment). Money believes that there is little chance of psychological adjustment after 3 or 4 years. He believes that the correct age for developing gender identity, although not quite from birth, begins with bright children at 6 months, and with almost all youngsters from 18 months. So the critical period is from the first months to 3 or 4 years.

> . . . one has a degree of freedom to decide on a change during the first year to eighteen months of life, but this freedom progressively shrinks with each month of subsequent age. The age of establishing conceptual language is also the age of establishing a self-concept. This self-concept is by its very nature gender-differentiated. (Money and Ehrhard, 1972)

A Changing Intelligence

Carl Sagan, in his brilliant essay *The Dragons of Eden* (1977), states that the world is very old and human beings very young. An awesome vista of time has preceded human intelligence, a vista about which little is known because there were no written records and also because limited human intelligence has difficulty in grasping the immensity of the time involved. But over this vista of time human intelligence and human societies have changed.

As Sagan notes, human societies are *not* innovative and change is resisted. But change—significant change—is emerging, and world societies and humans are beginning "to abandon the childhood of their species." Such change is desperately needed, especially today when so many complex problems face the human species. Sagan believes that there must be some way to encourage, in a human context, the intellectual development of youngsters.

Particularly interesting is the author's comment that the real extension of the human brain is now in progress: *stimulating unrepressive learning environments for children is one of the richest and most promising educational tools now available.* Sagan states that the essential human quality is intelligence, and it is in the development of intelligence that any hope for the future exists.

> Unless we destroy ourselves utterly, the future belongs to those societies that, while not ignoring the reptilian and mammalian parts of our being, enable the characteristically human components of our nature to flourish; to those societies that encourage diversity rather than conformity . . . to those societies that treat new ideas as delicate, fragile, and immensely valuable pathways to the future. (Sagan, 1977, pg. 193).

INTERACTION WITH THE ENVIRONMENT

A recurring theme in the malnutrition literature is that a number of problems are associated with a dietary deficit. For example, early malnutrition may cause faulty learning because the child is too apathetic to explore the environment: movement is restricted and stimulation lacking. The malnourished or chronically ill child cannot respond to learning opportunities like the normal child. Lack of movement and its accompanying lack of stimulation may affect the central nervous system.

Richard Held's work (1965) supports this interpretation. Held notes that anyone who has worn glasses initially experienced distortion, which may have been sufficiently severe to influence motor coordination. In a day or two the condition disappeared—the nervous system adjusted so that vision through glasses seemed normal and skillful motor coordination returned. As Held states, information from the environment must produce adaptation. Consequently, the central nervous system must adjust to the growth of the body (changes in distance between the eyes, between the ears), and our motor system must adjust to the bones' and muscles' growth to produce modified, more refined movements. For example, it takes an infant only a few months to develop eye-hand coordination.

The Held Experiment

To test his hypothesis that the central nervous system adjusts to visual distortion, Held devised an experiment in which subjects wore goggles with prisms that made straight lines look curved. He then placed the subjects in a large drum that had an irregular pattern of small spots on the inner surface. The spots looked the same, with or without the prisms; that is, there were no straight lines on the drum which would appear curved through the prisms. Before entering the drum and without the goggles, the subjects all were able to identify straight lines. Upon entering the drum, the subjects (with goggles on) either walked around the drum for 30 minutes or were rolled around in a cart. Leaving the drum the subjects removed the goggles and again examined the straight lines.

Held states that without exception the active subjects perceived curvature while the passive subjects perceived none. The active subjects had adapted to the prisms; the passive had not. These and other experiments mean that the feedback from movement influences perceptual coordination. It also means that youngsters too listless to engage in the ceaseless activity of the normal child will lack vital impressions in the central nervous system. If these links are not made at the appropriate times, it is possible that critical periods have passed and learning may subsequently suffer.

Figure 3.2 illustrates the sequence. Note the passive state of the subject—no interaction with the environment. Those who walked

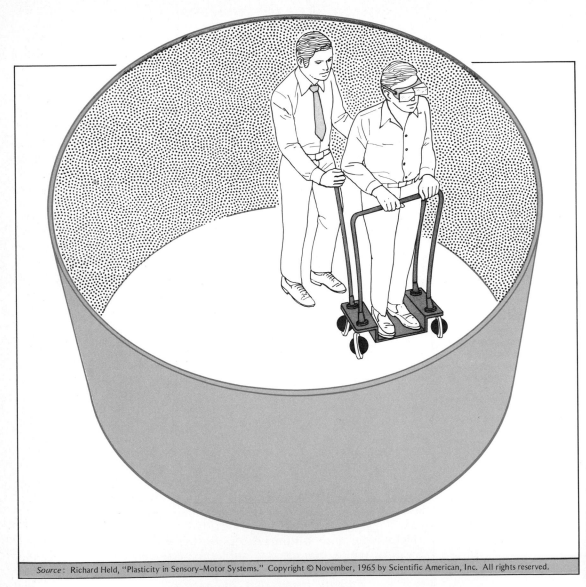

Figure 3.2 Passive Transport of Subject

had interacted with the environment, causing the changes Held described. These are important findings for teachers. Individuals adapt to almost any environmental change provided they use their muscular systems. If learning is to occur, students must interact with their environment; they must be actively involved. If they remain passive recipients, similar to the individual in Figure 3.2, then we may seriously question whether their central nervous systems adjust to produce lasting change.

All of these influences—dietary, chemical, critical periods—stress the significance of the early years. But do psychological influences produce similar results?

Discussion Questions

1. Can you relate Hydn's work to the malnutrition studies? What is the significance of the relationship? Are there educational implications of this evidence? Be specific in your answer.

2. Reexamine the data about developing brain weight. What period shows striking growth? What does this imply for parents? For educators?

3. Do you agree with Scott's definition of a critical period? Why? Do you think that the evidence supports the existence of critical periods? If you agree, what does it mean for the schools? If you disagree, offer evidence that refutes their existence.

4. Richard Held's work is fascinating and replete with educational possibilities. Generally, using no specific subjects or techniques, tell what you think it means for elementary and secondary teachers. Would your suggestions be more difficult for the elementary than the secondary teacher? Why?

The psychological evidence

The results of environmental deprivation, that is, a lack of a stimulating environment, are more difficult to determine. Bloom (1964) defines environment as the conditions, forces, and external stimuli which impinge upon the individual. Extreme environmental influences are greatest in the early and more rapid periods of intellectual growth and least in later years. Bloom then conservatively estimates that an extreme environment affects intelligence by about 20 IQ points, which could mean the difference between a productive life or life in an institution. Health experts also agree that a barren social environment produces effects similar to malnutrition. Is it possible to test the accuracy of this assumption? Animal studies offer some pertinent data, although caution is required in applying conclusions to humans.

THE ANIMAL STUDIES

Since the 1950s, investigators at the University of California, Berkeley, have conducted studies that have startled the scientific and educational community while providing dramatic evidence concerning environmental stimulation and brain development. David Krech, Mark Rosenzweig, Edward Bennett, and Marian Diamond are the people most closely associated with this project. Together, and individually, they have reported consistent findings for over 15 years.

Originally interested in the chemical changes that accompany memory and learning, the investigators wrestled with an old question: Does experience produce discernible brain changes? They reasoned that rats who had a stimulating environment with many opportunities for learning would eventually have a brain that differed from their improverished brethren. Krech humorously states that investigators, assistants, graduate students, and thousands of rats have labored—and some even sacrificed their lives—to discover this evidence (1969).

Experience and Brain Change

The experimental technique was simple: they randomly assigned some animals to an enriched environment, some to deprived conditions. Both groups had an identical diet, but those receiving the enriched condition lived 12 in a cage and had many rat toys—levers to push, tunnels to explore, ladders to climb. The investigators instructed the graduate students to treat these rats with tender, loving care. Their poor, deprived mates were isolated individually in cages and placed in remote parts of the laboratory, devoid of attention. *But* the diet was the same. Figure 3.3 illustrates the different environments.

As the investigators continued their work, they were shocked to find that the brain weights of the two groups had changed. Rosenzweig et al. (1972) report that the rats who had spent from four to ten weeks in the enriched environment had heavier and thicker cerebral cortexes, better blood supplies to the brain, larger brain cells, and more glial cells than the deprived rats. Enriched experience affected the ratio of cortical weight to the rest of the brain. The weight of the cortex increased as a result of environmental stimulation.

The Need for an Active Interaction

Rosenzweig states that other investigators were initially skeptical of their results. But when repeated experiments consistently produced identical results, some scientists swung to the other extreme; that is, they concluded the brain is so plastic that any experience will modify it. Disagreeing, Rosenzweig notes that only the rats who actively interacted with the environment gained in cortical weight. The important conclusion is that an enriched, or stimulating, environment will produce these effects only *if the organism interacts with the objects in the environment.* (This conclusion parallels Richard Held's, that subjects changed only if they interacted with the environment.)

There is little doubt that experience changes many aspects of brain anatomy and brain chemistry. Consequently, the psychological environment seems to be crucial in brain development. If these results apply to humans, there are enormous possibilities for aiding youngsters from impoverished environments.

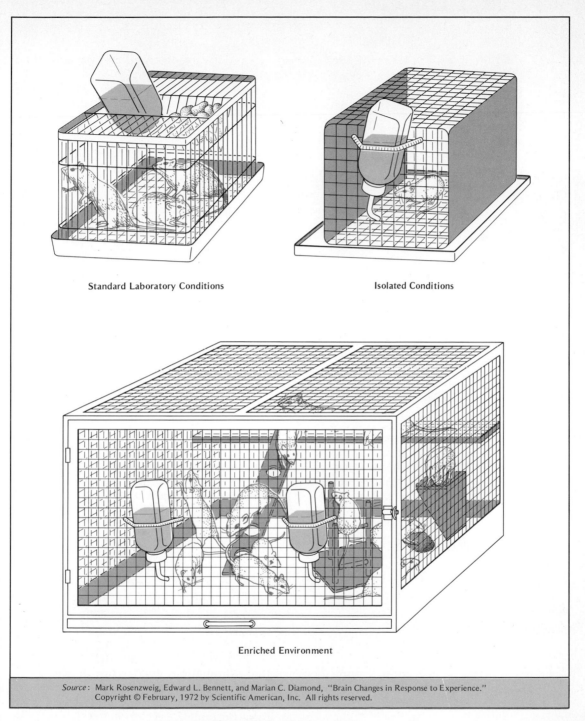

Standard Laboratory Conditions

Isolated Conditions

Enriched Environment

Figure 3.3 Three Distinct Environments

BOSTON, SUMMERTHING

The Role of Stress

Evidence grows that the timing of environmental stimulation is vital for development. Seymour Levine (1960) posed a related and pertinent question: How do the stressful experiences of infancy affect the behavior and physiology of the adult? His basic assumption was that almost all infant experiences involve handling by a parent or some other large figure, and this handling, no matter how tender, may cause stress.

Levine subjected one group of infant rats to mild electric shock; he placed another group in the shock cage but did not shock them; he left a third group undisturbed. He assumed that the third group would be the best adjusted. But it was the third group— *those not handled at all*—that exhibited most problems (such as, acute fear in new surroundings) as adults. The investigators could not discern any difference between the shocked animals and those who were handled but not shocked. Both groups, as adults, seemed more emotionally mature and learned new tasks more readily. Levine believes that stimulation, even painful, accelerates the maturation of the central nervous system. The stimulated animals had brains with higher cholesterol levels, and the animals themselves showed a more rapid rate of development.

Generalizing from these results, Levine states that while heredity undoubtedly determines the basic developmental patterns, organisms will not approximate potential except in interaction with a varied and stimulating environment. With words strikingly familiar, Levine says that stimulation of the infant organism has "universal consequences" upon the adult's behavior and physiology. While caution is necessary in applying these results to humans, the author says that it is hard to believe that these findings are limited to any particular species.

Some aspects of his work obviously troubled him. If painful stimulation produces effects that are indistinguishable from mere handling of the animal, what does this imply for an adult picking up and petting a baby? Perhaps it means that infant stress is necessary for successful adult adjustment to the environment. Are there critical periods for affective stressful stimulation? In Levine's studies only those animals handled immediately after birth responded typically to later stimuli. Finally, he asked: Is it possible

Monkeys, Intelligence, and the Environment

Harry Harlow, studying rhesus monkeys, has vastly broadened our knowledge of various environmental conditions. He and his colleagues (Harlow, Harlow, and Suomi, 1971) report on three laboratory settings. First is the normal laboratory treatment; second is "partial social isolation" (from birth the monkey is kept alone in a bare wire cage); third is "total social isolation" (from birth the monkey is completely isolated).

Monkeys reared in total social isolation for *90 days* were enormously disturbed, and some actually died. Those who survived gradually adjusted to age mates. But if they were totally isolated for *six months* from birth, they were disturbed for life and *never* adjusted to age mates. The only social behaviors that matured were fear and aggression—even against infants. Twelve months total isolation produced a social nonentity.

For many years, Harlow felt that while total social isolation destroyed social and sexual capabilities, learning ability remained unaffected. Normally stimulating environ-

ments were not superior to deprived environments in stimulating intellectual development. Monkeys from different environments performed equally on different learning tasks. But then Harlow says; "My world of happy intellectual isolation was jolted, however, when the socially enriched preadolescents and adolescents, as contrasted with the socially isolated adolescents and controls, proved to be superior at the .001 significance level on our most complex problem-oddity-learning set."

Harlow concludes that an enriched early environment enables monkeys to achieve superior intellectual levels compared to deprived monkeys. While the exact cause of this superiority is unknown, the results of early stimulation are clear. As exciting as this evidence is, caution is essential in any interpretation. These are animal studies, and it is impossible to identify cause-and-effect relationships. They do, however, support the premise that early experiences produce later results.

to erase the effects of a lack of early stimulation (a critical period) by later, remedial stimulation? These are not easy questions; there are no easy answers.

HUMAN STUDIES

It is time now to leave the animals and present the available evidence about humans. Rene Spitz has conducted a classic study of deprived children. In 1945, he reported on an investigation of 164 children during the first year of life. The children came from four sources: professional homes, children from an isolated fishing village (where nutrition, hygiene, and housing were poor), a nursing home, and a foundling home.

At the end of the first year, the children in the foundling home, although at about the same developmental level at birth, had deteriorated. They showed all the characteristics of "hospitalism" (both physical and mental). While hygiene and nutrition were excellent, from the third month the children showed extreme susceptibility to disease. An epidemic of measles struck the community, and while the mortality rate was only 0.5 percent in the community, 13 percent of those up to 18 months, and 40 percent of those from 18 to 30 months of the foundling home children died. Only two of the children 18 to 30 months could walk, talk, or eat alone. Some of these children developed a weepy behavior that soon became **Anaclitic Depression** withdrawal. They would lie on their cots with their faces turned away. They lost weight, suffered from insomnia, and were susceptible to disease. This behavior lasted for about three months, giving way to a dazed look, vacant eyes, frozen faces, and a lack of awareness of what was occurring in the environment. Spitz called this condition "anaclitic depression."

Criticism of Spitz's work mounted as methodological weaknesses were exposed (selection of children, lack of control, obscure details), but Spitz's findings have recurred so consistently throughout the years that today there is general acceptance of his conclusions. One of the conclusions is that while the youngsters' environment was unstimulating, it was mainly the lack of human partners, the lack of social stimulation, that produced the damaging consequences. This is especially true when a mother figure is missing. In Spitz's study, at three months, a child shared a nurse with seven other children. He reasons that there is a time during which restriction of the mother-child relationship causes irreparable harm.

Another famous study is Wayne Dennis's report of children reared in an orphanage in Teheran (1960). Infants were swaddled until 4 months of age; the sides of the cribs were covered so only **Orphanage Conditions** ceilings were visible; there was one attendant for every ten children and toys were minimal. The average child usually sits alone at about 9 months—over 50 percent of the children in the orphanage did not sit alone until from 1 to 2 years. Most children walk by 2 years—only 15 percent of the orphanage children walked between 3 and 4 years. Dennis's work emphasizes the need for early stimulation for healthy development.

DEPRIVATION DWARFISM

Studies continue to show that early experience affects physical and psychological development. Spitz reported his findings in 1945, Dennis in 1960. Lytt Gardner, writing in *Scientific American* July, 1972, reports on cases of what he calls "deprivation dwarfism." Gardner begins with the hypothesis that infants will suffer if their mothers are hostile or even indifferent to them. For example, in a British-occupied German town after World War II, there were two municipal orphanages. Each had about 50 boys and girls from 4 to 14 years old. They had only official rations to eat and were below normal height and weight.

The youngsters in one of the orphanages (Gardner's Orphanage A) for six months received unlimited amounts of bread, extra jam, and concentrated orange juice. The matron in charge of Orphanage A was a cheerful young woman, genuinely fond of the children; the Orphanage B matron was older, stern, and blatantly favored eight of the children in B. The Orphanage A matron left, and the woman in charge of Orphanage B was transferred to A, bringing her eight favorites. Until this time, the children in Orphanage A were taller and heavier than the others. The switch in matrons coincided with the introduction of extra food for the A children.

In spite of the extra food, the youngsters in Orphanage A showed *less* weight gain than those in B who, while not receiving the extra food, no longer had the strict matron. There was an exception: the matron's favorites exceeded *all* youngsters in physical development. Gardner concludes that the youngsters exposed to an unfavorable emotional climate reacted with a reduction in their growth rate.

He then gives a remarkable example of deprivation dwarfism involving twins. A mother gave birth to boy and girl twins. She soon found herself undesirably pregnant again. Her husband lost his job and shortly thereafter left home. Until the time of the new pregnancy, the twins progressed normally, the boy somewhat more rapidly than the girl. But the mother's hostility toward the father was now directed toward the son. The youngsters were about 4 months old when the boy's growth rate slowed considerably. When he was a little over a year, his height was that of a 7-month-old, and his general condition required hospitalization. Figure 3.4 illustrates the developmental differences between the children. In the hospital he immediately began to recover, and be-

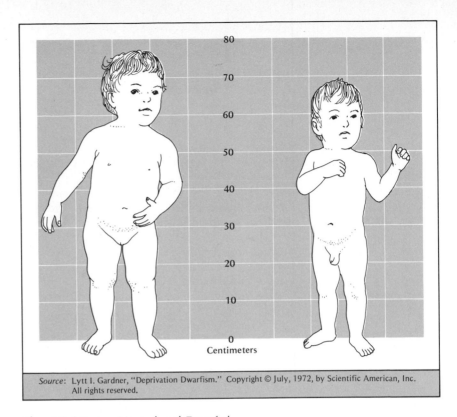

Figure 3.4 Twins, Normal and Dwarfed

fore his release the mother and father reconciled. The boy continued to recover and by 2 years his development matched his sister's.

Gardner speculates that environmental deprivation and emotional turmoil may upset the endocrine system, thus influencing a child's growth. He believes that there are sensitive periods in human development, similar to those in animals, although the timing and type of environmental stimulation needed for normal development remain vague. Gardner concludes that deprivation dwarfism clearly demonstrates the "delicacy, complexity, and crucial importance of infant-parent interaction."

Certain conclusions are now possible: malnutrition affects physical and mental development, perhaps permanently if it is harsh and lengthy; lack of early environmental stimulation affects cortical development in animals; active interaction with the environment affects the central nervous system; early emotional deprivation retards normal development. While the significance of heredity was stressed in the beginning of this discussion, the studies presented make it almost impossible to believe that heredity is everything—

Is Early Damage Reversible?

there can be no normal development without environmental stimulation. But if stimulation is deficient, is the damage permanent? The lack of hard data about the timing and extent of any deficit make simple answers impossible. It is necessary again to accumulate evidence that suggests possible conclusions.

THE SKEELS STUDY

In 1966, Harold Skeels reported the results of a 30-year study. Two children, one 13 months with an IQ of 46, the other 16 months with an IQ of 35, were removed from a state orphanage and placed in an institution for the mentally retarded. They were placed in wards with older, slightly brighter girls and women, 18 to 50 years old, with mental ages ranging from 5 to 9 years. Six months after their transfer, Skeels revisited the institution and was amazed to see these same two little girls running around, laughing, and looking like any normal children of their age. He immediately had them retested and discovered that their IQs had risen spectacularly. They were constantly retested for the next three years and they maintained an increased mental level.

A Different Environment

What had happened? Obviously, the environment caused the change. Although placed with low IQ girls and women, the environment was still more stimulating than the orphanage. They became the darlings of the ward; the older girls and attendants lavished attention on them. Conditions were stimulating, affectionate, and conducive to development.

Skeels next devised the fantastic scheme of transferring other youngsters to an institution for the mentally retarded. Overcoming understandable opposition, Skeels managed the transfer of thirteen youngsters, all under 3 years. He was able to match a control group of similar youngsters, who remained in the orphanage. Every child in the transferred group showed a substantial gain (7 to 58 IQ points), while all but one of the control group showed a substantial loss (9 to 45 IQ points).

More Youngsters Placed

Skeels initially disclosed his findings in 1939, and, as with Spitz, there were justifiable methodological criticisms. In 1966, Skeels reported the results of a follow-up study of these same 25 youngsters. This was about 20 years after the last examination of the children. Amazingly, he located all 13 of the experimental group, and 11 of the 12 who had remained in the orphanage. One of this group had died.

He decided not to administer intelligence tests because of the years that had intervened. Instead he compared their adult educational and occupational level. The two groups invariably followed the expected pattern. The 13 members of the experimental group all were socially competent—none was institutionalized. Of the 11 members of the control group, 4 were institutionalized (1 was mentally ill, 3 were in institutions for the retarded) and the others, with one exception, had been in and out of institutions. The one exception was a successful typesetter for a newspaper in a community of 300,000. Table 3.1 presents Skeels's findings.

TABLE 3.1
Experimental and Contrast Groups: Occupations of Subjects and Spouses

Case No.	Subject's Occupation	Spouse's Occupation	Female Subject's Occupation Previous to Marriage
EXPERIMENTAL GROUP:			
1[a]	Staff sergeant	Dental technician	....
2	Housewife	Laborer	Nurses' aide
3	Housewife	Mechanic	Elementary school teacher
4	Nursing instructor	Unemployed	Registered nurse
5	Housewife	Semi-skilled laborer	No work history
6	Waitress	Mechanic, semi-skilled	Beauty operator
7	Housewife	Flight engineer	Dining room hostess
8	Housewife	Foreman, construction	No work history
9	Domestic service	Unmarried	....
10[a]	Real estate sales	Housewife	....
11[a]	Vocational counselor	Advertising copy writer[b]	....
12	Gift shop sales[c]	Unmarried	....
13	Housewife	Pressman-printer	Office-clerical
CONTRAST GROUP:			
14	Institutional inmate	Unmarried	....
15	Dishwasher	Unmarried	....
16	Deceased	....	....
17[a]	Dishwasher	Unmarried	....
18[a]	Institutional inmate	Unmarried	....
19[a]	Compositor and typesetter	Housewife	....
20[a]	Institutional inmate	Unmarried	....
21[a]	Dishwasher	Unmarried	....
22[a]	Floater	Divorced	....
23	Cafeteria (part time)	Unmarried	....
24[a]	Institutional gardener's assistant	Unmarried	....
25[a]	Institutional inmate	Unmarried	....

Source: H. M. Skeels, "Adult Status of Children with Contrasting Early Life Experiences." *Monographs of the Society for Research in Child Development,* 1966, *31,* no. 3. Reprinted by permission of the publisher.
[a] Male.
[b] B.A. degree.
[c] Previously had worked as a licensed practical nurse.

What conclusions does this study suggest? *Early intervention makes a difference:* change from a barren environment to one more stimulating produces future effects. Skeels naturally draws these conclusions from his work but urges caution until we can identify the best means and techniques of intervention. He warns that children do not automatically absorb the environmental impact but must interact actively with it. Again note the emphasis on a child's interaction with the environment.

Beyond the general conclusions that early experience is important, evidence is still scanty concerning precise cause-and-effect relationships, timing of intervention, and means of intervention. As a result, there are other interpretations that stress heredity, or urge a natural "catch-up" hypothesis.

Other interpretations of the evidence

THE GUATEMALAN STUDIES

Jerome Kagan, the well-known Harvard psychologist, has recently reported on his studies of Guatemalan children (1973). Stating that most developmental psychologists believe that the environment exercises a powerful and lasting influence during the early years, Kagan raises questions about the relationship between cognitive development at 12 to 18 months and cognitive development at 11 years. Visiting remote Indian villages, he witnessed listless, apathetic infants; passive, timid 3-year-olds; but active, intellectually

Age Changes in the Children

competent 11-year-olds. Consequently, Kagan states that the "capacity for perceptual analysis, imitation, language, inference, deduction, symbolism, and memory will eventually appear in sturdy form in a natural environment, for each is an inherent competence in the human person." Here is a statement that would seem to negate much of the importance of early environmental stimulation.

Kagan worked in two Guatemalan locations. One was subsistence villages, moderately isolated, with Spanish-speaking residents. The other was an even more isolated Indian village, whose residents felt psychologically detached and alienated from the nation. Infants in the Indian village spend most of the first 10 to 12 months in a small, dark, windowless hut. Mothers do not work and remain at home. If a mother travels to the market she leaves the

Treatment of the Child

infant with a relative. The child is constantly close to the mother, sitting on her lap or carried on her back. Kagan states that people rarely speak to or play with the child, and the only play toys are clothing, the mother's body, oranges, ears of corn, and pieces of wood and clay. These children manifest extreme motor passivity, fear, silence, and minimal smiling. Kagan claims that a few reminded him of the tiny ghosts of the Spitz study. Children from the other location exhibited similar characteristics.

Jerome Kagan

Results of Tests

Kagan administered a series of tasks to both Guatemalan groups, and they fared more poorly than their American counterparts. But at 15 months, the Guatemalan child becomes mobile, leaves the hut, plays with other children, and encounters a more stimulating environment. As the youngsters continued to age, their scores on cognitive tasks more closely approximated American comparison groups until the 11-year-olds from both cultures were comparable. Kagan notes that the cognitive retardation observed during the first year of life vanished in the preadolescent years and concludes that it seems possible to reverse infant retardation due to lack of stimulation.

If economically impoverished American children do poorly on mental tests, Kagan's work offers hope that the damage may be reversible. If the first environment retards psychological development, children will remain below normal as long as they remain within that environment. But if they encounter a more satisfactory environment, they are able to capitalize on these new opportunities and repair the initial damage. Kagan's results are encouraging, but questions arise.

Some Troublesome Questions

First, was the environment of the village children culturally deprived? They were never out of the mother's sight; she is in constant attendance to fulfill their needs; there is some physical, evidently sufficient, stimulation. Perhaps Kagan's work serves to reinforce several other studies previously mentioned whose chief conclusion was that an emotionally secure environment was the essential element for normal development.

Second, was the deprivation period long enough to cause retardation? One cannot dismiss the duration of deprivation. Remember that the children left the dark huts at 15 months. If, for the sake of argument, we agree that those 15 months represented a deprived environment, the entry into the world at 15 months may have been well within the sensitive period for the development of those cognitive abilities Kagan later tested. For example, Kagan mentions Carmichael's famous study in which tadpole embryos were anesthetized until a control group began to swim. As soon as the swimming pattern appeared, about a week, he placed the anesthetized group in regular tap water and they swam as well as the control group. But when other investigators kept the embryos anesthetized for longer periods of time (about two weeks) the swimming pattern was permanently impaired. While Kagan's results are hopeful, care is needed in interpreting them: if deprivation is not too severe or too lengthy, the child may possibly recover.

Early Experience: A Cross-Cultural Perspective

Kagan believes that his Guatemalan work has educational implications for American youth. Poor test performance by disadvantaged youngsters need not indicate a permanently irreversible intellectual deficit. He states that children differ in the age at which fundamental cognitive processes and early experience influence the time of emergence. Economically deprived American youngsters and rural Guatemalan children seem to be from one to three years behind middle-class youth in cognitive functioning.

Many of these abilities appear by 10 or 11 years of age, which suggests that educators are confusing demonstrated cognitive competence with maturational differences. Kagan stresses that when educators note that poor children consistently lag behind middle-class youngsters, they refer to culturally specific skills such as arithmetic or reading. Children from a lower socioeconomic environment continue their cognitive growth but manifest it in other than academic ways.

If a child's initial environment is barren, both physically and psychologically, the youngster will continue to perform below innate ability while remaining in those circumstances. Moved to a more stimulating environment, a youngster may well overcome any prior damage. Kagan concludes his summary of the data as follows (1973, pg. 961):

> There are few dumb children in the world if one classifies them from the perspective of the community of adaptation, but millions of dumb children if one classifies them from the perspective of another society.

Rapid Growth Periods and the Environment

Kagan's work poses problems that require solutions by those who stress the early years' importance. The questions raised above could help in solving these problems, and Bloom's work (1964) also affords insights. Admitting that we have limited evidence about the effects of early experience, Bloom nevertheless states that development occurs in unequal spurts during our lives. For each stable characteristic there is a time of rapid growth (usually during the early years) followed by slower growth periods. Bloom believes that environmental influences are much greater during rapid growth periods.

Bloom then offers data to support his hypothesis. If ages 18–20 represent the adult growth level, then the following ages represent half of the adult growth level of the selected characteristics.

Characteristic	Age
Height	2½
General intelligence	4
Male aggression	3
Female dependence	4
General school achievement	Grade 3

With the exception of school achievement, the most rapid growth period is during the first four years, and thus the environment's influence, positive or negative, is critical in shaping these characteristics.

Bloom also argues that the developmental sequence testifies to the early year's significance. Each characteristic, at any time, depicts previous development and influences future development. Bloom concludes the evidence confirms the tremendous power of early learning, so much so that the most vital behavioral research must focus upon the effects of early learning and early environments on humans.

THE JENSEN CONTROVERSY

Both the animal and human studies that we have discussed infer that early environmental stimulation is critical for healthy physical and psychological development. But heated controversy abounds about the relative importance of heredity and environment. If heredity is all-important, then environmental circumstances, at any age, make little difference. As Steven Rose (1973) says, we may ask: If one individual is genetically superior to another, does that mean we are powerless to aid intellectual performance?

Beginning in 1969, and continuing today, the writing and research of Arthur Jensen seem to provide an affirmative answer to

Rose's question. Maintaining that his studies show that intelligence is 80 percent inherited, the only logical conclusion is that if any race scores consistently lower than any other race on IQ tests, it must be genetically inferior intellectually. Such labeling of any group creates explosive tensions, especially if accepted as indisputable scientific fact, *or if misinterpreted.*

Some Basic Assumptions

How does Jensen reach his conclusions? He assumes that intelligence exists, that intelligence tests measure it, and that IQ scores, derived from these tests, reflect intellectual capacity. There are practical aspects to this argument. Jensen states that after 5 or 6 years of age there is no better predictor of a child's future scholastic success than his or her IQ score. After 9 or 10 years, the IQ score shows a remarkably high correlation with both prestige and financial level of adult occupation. These findings are particularly important in a technological society, and he believes that to reject IQ tests and scores is to reject civilization as we know it.

Based on studies conducted over the past 50 years, Jensen says that genetic elements are far more important than environmental influences in explaining individual differences in IQ. What are some of these studies? One, constantly used, entailed the selective breeding of rats. By mating fast maze-learning males with fast maze-learning females, and vice versa, the result eventually was two distinct strains of rats (with regard to maze-learning ability), one all fast, the other all slow. Twin studies are another favorite reference, especially identical twins reared apart. Although these twins were separated, their IQs were more alike than fraternal twins reared together. Since identical twins share the same hereditary material, any differences in IQ scores must reflect environmental influence. The identical twins were in different environments, and the closeness in IQ scores demonstrates the great thrust of heredity, minimizing the environment. (Recent controversy about the truthfulness of some of these studies raises serious questions about their usefulness.)

Twin Studies

Jensen states that a reverse pattern also illustrates the greater importance of heredity. Adopted, unrelated children brought up in the same home differ from each other as much as unrelated children reared in different homes. That is, a similar environment has not brought the children to the same IQ level. These unrelated children from the same home differ from each other almost four times as much as identical twins brought up in different homes. The IQs of the adopted children show little relationship to the IQs of their foster parents, but show almost the same relationship to their natural parents as any other child.

In his original controversial article which appeared in the Winter, 1969, issue of the *Harvard Educational Review,* Jensen states that compensatory education has been tried and it apparently has failed. Efforts to raise IQ and improve scholastic performance have not succeeded. Blacks still score lower on IQ tests, and these differences cannot be attributed to the environment, if as Jensen says, intelligence is 80 percent genetically determined. Jensen believes there is no psychological and genetic difference between individual differences and group differences: total the individual differences, and they reappear as group or racial differences. This fuels social and political controversy. Consequently, attempts are made to hide real differences by attacking the IQ test, abolishing grading, and introducing a variety of administrative techniques: special classes for different children, elimination of the self-contained classroom, and reexamination of the total educational system. Jensen believes that these "remedies" simply cover up rather than confront a problem.

Individual Differences–Group Differences

Jensen's work has triggered dispute, demonstration, and demagoguery, since there is no escaping his inevitable conclusion: intelligence is genetically determined; there are racial differences in IQ scores; therefore, there are genetically superior and inferior races. Consequently, if intelligence is mainly (80 percent) due to heredity, society need not, indeed should not, overly concern itself with the question of early experience since it makes little difference.

Jensen's Inescapable Conclusion

There are, however, certain questions that challenge Jensen's hypothesis. Can investigators so blithely disregard the uses and abuses of psychological testing? What does the intelligence test measure? Does it assess capacity or is it actually an achievement test? When you examine the items in any mental test, their cultural dependence seems obvious.

Intelligence—a developmental characteristic

Use of the Stanford-Binet

Jensen's work rests largely upon studies in which the Stanford-Binet intelligence test was used, which is understandable since the Stanford-Binet is one of the most widely used IQ tests, *but* blacks were never included in its standardization. Is it possible, or even fair, to compare blacks with whites on this test? Many other questionable techniques are involved when the two racial groups are compared. For example, black youngsters will score higher when the tester is also black. Rose argues that while IQ scores for American blacks are undoubtedly lower than whites, it is scientifically impossible to conclude that heredity is mainly responsible. Such a conclusion is possible if discussion is limited to the genetics of a single population, containing a common gene pool. Even then speculation would be restricted to differences solely within *that* population. It says nothing about another population. Rose also finds it incredibly naive to assume an identical environment for blacks and whites. A black is black in a white culture. The same

Some Overlooked Facts

applies to a lower-class child in a basically middle-class culture. Common sense dictates that these differences figure in any analysis of differences in IQ scores.

The American psychologist J. McVicker Hunt has said that while we cannot absolutely rule out the possibility of racial differences, the issue remains unimportant while some youngsters, black and white, live in poverty with limited opportunities to learn (1969). Hunt rejects the argument that there are real differences between intelligence and achievement tests. While there are differences, they are differences in degree. Intelligence tests are not as limited as achievement tests to academic curricula, but school experience contributes heavily to the IQ score. Both reflect a current performance level that clearly reflects previous learning. A youngster who is culturally deprived is a youngster who has restricted opportunities to learn, which influences IQ scores.

BENJAMIN BLOOM AND THE EARLY YEARS

Benjamin Bloom (1964) has examined several of the classic longitudinal growth studies to determine how much of the variance in adult intelligence appears during the early years. (The longitudinal growth studies are those that have reexamined the same individuals during many years, some for as many as 30 years.) He found an interesting pattern of relationships: intelligence measured at age 1 has no correlation with intelligence at age 17, at age 2 the correlation is 0.41, at age 4 it is 0.71. By age 11 the correlation with intelligence measured at age 17 is 0.92. Figure 3.5 illustrates the correlations between IQ at these ages.

From these data came the famous, although slightly inaccurate, statement that 50 percent of adult intelligence is present by age 4. As Bloom notes, this amazing statistic suggests the rapid growth of intelligence during the early years and the "possible great influence of the early environment on this development."

Bloom believes that intelligence is a developmental characteristic, and that IQ scores reflect an individual's general learning, which also reflects an individual's opportunities to learn. These opportunities either enhance or restrict verbal learning, interactions with the environment, encouragement of independent thinking, and motivation for intellectual endeavors.

BRITAIN'S NATIONAL CHILD DEVELOPMENT STUDY

The Sample

These conclusions are not restricted to American children. A recent report from Great Britain emphasizes the international flavor of a barren environment. In a massive survey, Britain's *National Child Development Study* measured the growth and development of children born in England, Scotland, and Wales during the week of March 3 to March 9, 1958. A total of 15,000 children were studied at

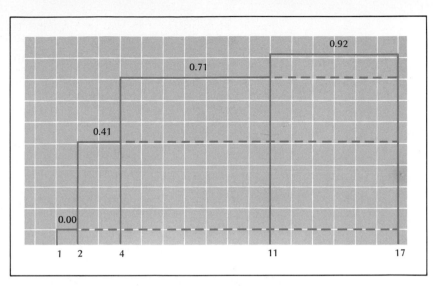

Figure 3.5 Correlations Between IQ at Various Ages

regular intervals for 15 years. Data came from schools, medical clinics, family and social service agencies, supplemented by testing and interviewing of the children.

   The British investigators defined a disadvantaged child as one suffering from the handicaps of a large, low-income family with overcrowded living conditions and one parent missing. These criteria applied to 1 of every 16 children. Any one of these conditions could be catastrophic for a child; the combination of all these usually produces predictable negative results. In the study, a mother's poor physical condition caused health problems for the child: children's general physical development was inferior; school achievement was lower. These youngsters were predominantly white but exhibited the same problems as some American blacks and non-English-speaking children. The conclusion is inescapable: deprived children come from chillingly similar backgrounds.

Disadvantaged
Conditions

   The report's authors do not speculate whether Britain can afford to help its deprived, but whether it can afford *not* to help them since poor developmental conditions are disastrous for child, family, and society. If, as the report suggests, environment is mainly responsible for these developmental difficulties, it makes all attempts at early intervention worthwhile.

EDUCATIONAL IMPLICATIONS

These ideas apply mainly to day-care centers and nursery schools, as we have seen in Chapter 2. If, however, the early years are as vital as accumulating evidence implies, then investigators must more carefully scrutinize parents' roles during this time. (Although intellectual development is the chief concern here, social and emotional development are likewise affected. Anyone who has watched youth hockey or Little League baseball recognizes the support or pressure that a parent exerts on a child.)

What Is Enriching?

Teachers, especially through their knowledge of educational psychology and understanding of children, can help parents to understand how to plan a child's environment more effectively. In talking with parents, teachers should emphasize that a stimulating environment is not necessarily an enriched environment. Surrounding an infant with too many gadgets may actually (although temporarily) retard development and cause emotional irritability. For example, the child with multiple crib gadgets may discover eyes and toes later than the average child, which impedes development of hand-eye coordination.

ARLINGTON, MASS. ADVOCATE

Teachers can also assist youngsters who have gaps in their background. The discussion of the critical period hypothesis implies that *if a deficit is not too severe or prolonged any damage is reversible.* Consequently, teachers who quickly learn about the background of their pupils can become skilled in identifying children with deficits and act accordingly to aid and enrich where possible. Encouragement, group activities, materials, play, remedial work— all will help children to perform more capably.

Discussion Questions

1. What was so startling about Rosenzweig's work with rats? How would you interpret it? What do you think are the major unanswered questions in this study?

2. Were you surprised by Levine's work on stress? What do you see as the main implications of this research? What cautions would you suggest?

3. What is your reaction to the orphanage studies? Do you agree with the conclusion? If so, support your answer. If not, outline and support your objections.

4. Skeels study is fascinating. What do its findings imply for society? Why did he refuse to give IQ tests to the follow-up group? Do you agree with his criteria for adult adjustment? Why?

5. Discussion of Jensen's work provokes intense conflict. Why? Do you agree with his interpretation? If so, link your answer to intelligence testing. If not, use any weakness in his data that you discover.

6. Prepare a brief talk in which you relate the material from brain research and malnutrition to the environmental deprivation studies, including Bloom and Skeels.

Some Concluding Thoughts

After presenting some of the classic and most recent research and opinion, what can you conclude from this discussion? The basic question is not whether the environment influences development, but *how much* it does. If the environment is influential, and all evidence testifies to its potency, then there is the realistic possibility of improving children's achievement and adjustment. Since society is not ready to commence human genetic manipulation, it must focus on environmental conditions. Scientifically, efforts should continue to distinguish the effects of the two. Educationally, socially, politically, and economically, reality must be faced: It is possible to change the environment; vital funds and intensive scholarship should further this attainable goal. Efforts must intensify to specify what environmental experiences, at what age, produce what effects. These questions should direct future research and speculations because conflicting answers have arisen, which only increase present perplexity.

Why do the data of some studies stress the mother-child interaction? Why do other studies emphasize peer interaction? Why do some investigators state that the physical aspects of the environment are all-important? Why do others urge active interaction with the environment?

Another conclusion is that deprived environments need more careful scrutiny. Bruner (1971) has recently stated that it is doubtful if a deficit exists in minority group children; these are superficial differences between different cultural groups. That is, if there is a good diet, warm relationships, and active interaction with the environment, the environment is far from barren. It may be *different* but not *deficient*.

Finally, you should be encouraged from your overview of the early environment literature. The evidence clearly testifies to the possibility of helping children if enrichment reaches them early enough. As efforts continue unabated, the studies and conclusions you have read will improve day-care centers and nursery schools, and will eventually reach into the home, facilitating physical, emotional, and educational development.

Summary

- Brain research is contributing to knowledge of the environment's effect on development during the early years.

- The nine-month period from the last trimester of pregnancy until the sixth postnatal month is a time of rapid brain growth susceptible to environmental extremes.

● Malnutrition is a good example of an environmental deficit that can cause physical and mental impairment.

● There is considerable evidence to support the critical periods hypothesis which compels observers to examine more carefully the nature and timing of environmental intervention.

● Regardless of the kind of environmental stimulation, children must actively use objects, toys, or materials to produce desired changes.

● An extremely deprived environment can create physical and mental deterioration, which may be reversible if detected and alleviated soon enough.

● The nature-nurture, heredity-environment controversy has flared anew because of Arthur Jensen's work.

● Even if the environment determines only one percent of intellectual achievement, it is currently all that can be controlled. Society should concentrate on improving environmental conditions to help children approximate their potential.

Suggested Readings

Bloom, Benjamin. *Stability and Change in Human Characteristics*. New York: Wiley, 1964. A rather technical but informative examination of what the classic longitudinal growth studies mean.

Bruner, Jerome S. *The Relevance of Education*. New York: Norton, 1971. By one of America's (now at Oxford, England) leading psychologists, this collection of essays reflects the author's variety of interests and offers some telling comments on early deprivation.

Havighurst, Robert. *Developmental Tasks and Education*. New York: McKay, 1972. This is a popular paperback that describes Havighurst's interpretation of critical periods and what they imply for education.

Manocha, Sohan. *Malnutrition and Retarded Human Development*. Springfield, Ill.: Thomas, 1972. An excellent overview of the nature, extent, and effects of malnutrition.

Money, John and Anke A. Ehrhardt. *Man and Woman, Boy and Girl*. New York: New American Library, 1974. A compelling summary of what we know about the acquisition of sex-identity.

Rose, Steven. *The Conscious Brain*. New York: Knopf, 1973. A challenging look at man's brain and the consequences of the information. Readable and exciting.

4

The Cognitive Theorists: Piaget and Bruner

(continues)

Introduction

Children are complex. Understanding them requires a knowledge of all their developmental aspects—physical, intellectual, social, emotional—and how these forces interact to produce each student. Investigators have exhaustively examined each developmental aspect until today the data about children are voluminous; the problem now is to organize and interpret it to make it meaningful and practical for classroom teachers. Intellectual development is a good example. The nature of intelligence, its growth pattern, its measurement, and the influences that modify it are legitimate concerns of educational psychology students.

How is the resulting information meaningful? The theoretical explanations offered by Piaget and Bruner seem most satisfactory. These theorists provide a cognitive interpretation of intelligence, that is, the human being is an active participant in intellectual development. The first part of this chapter is devoted to Piaget's ideas: basic concepts, periods of intellectual development, and classroom applications. Bruner's beliefs, similar to Piaget's but with several distinctive features, constitute the chapter's second part.

Piaget the man

Although Jean Piaget has made a renowned effort to understand mental development, his recognition in America came slowly. Partly because of translation (his original writings were in French), partly because of his early disregard of statistical procedures, American psychologists and educators were reluctant to accept his findings. Today with solid documentation of his work and growing personal fame, Piaget is probably the most illustrious developmental psychologist in the world.

Born on August 9, 1896, in Neuchatel, Switzerland, he displayed an early interest in science. He received a doctorate in the natural sciences in 1918 from the University of Neuchatel. During these years he read extensively in philosophy, religion, sociology, and psychology. From reading philosophy he reasoned that biology could aid in solving epistemological problems. Piaget also theorized that external actions, as well as thought processes, have a logical organization. Thought, then, is internal action with an organization analogous to overt action. Consequently, thought and action develop similarly.

Children's Incorrect Answers

After leaving Neuchatel in 1918, Piaget went to the Sorbonne where Simon (who had collaborated with Binet) asked him to standardize reasoning tests using Parisian children. Piaget became intrigued by the processes children employed to formulate their answers, especially incorrect answers. The responses, and thus the processes, differed at different ages.

Early Works

In 1921, he became director of studies at the Rousseau Institute in Geneva. During the years 1921–1925 he published some of his most famous work, including his studies of language, reasoning, and moral judgment. These were initial statements of his system that he later revised. Piaget soon discovered that studying speech was an inadequate technique for analyzing developing thought processes. Also missing from these first statements was a mental basis for logical behavior, the "structures" of Piaget's later work.

From 1925 to 1929, Piaget studied infants' cognitive development and obtained vital information about early mental devel-

Jean Piaget

WIDE WORLD

opment. From 1929 to 1939, he was also associated with the International Bureau of Education, now linked with UNESCO. He resumed his studies of the history of science and investigated children's development of number and quantity concepts, acquiring needed data to support his evolving notion of cognitive structures. Today Piaget directs Geneva's Center for Genetic Epistemology and also teaches, writes, and lectures.

His writings are numerous and difficult. Flavell (1963, pg. 11), an excellent interpreter of Piaget, notes that anyone wishing to study all of Piaget's work must read more than 25 books and over 150 articles. You will find Piaget's ideas challenging and formidable, but you will reap a rich reward for your labors. The insights you will gain from understanding his theory will afford you a unique way of comprehending the intellectual processes underlying children's behavior. There is a belief that the person who truly understands Piaget's theory never again looks at children in the same way.

A Piagetian Glossary

Piagetian theory has its own vocabulary. Here are some terms that you will meet throughout this chapter.

Accommodation. Cognitive structures are modified by "taking in" stimuli from the environment. Action and thought adjust to environmental variations. When you chew and swallow food it changes your biochemical structures; when you incorporate psychological data, it changes your cognitive structures. Accommodation and assimilation, plus organization, together constitute what Piaget calls "the functional invariants."

Adaptation. Ability to adjust to the environment. Intelligence is one form of human biological adaptation. Adaptation consists of assimilation and accommodation.

Assimilation. Taking environmental stimuli into the cognitive structures. It is one of the functional invariants that constitute adaptation. Humans adapt to their environment by assimilation and accommodation.

Centration. Tendency to focus on one aspect of something, while neglecting related aspects. It restricts thinking and is usually seen in younger children.

Concrete Operational Period. The third of Piaget's four stages of cognitive development. It is a time (7–11 years) when children can think logically but only about something concrete. They are still incapable of abstract hypothetical thought.

Conservation. A milestone in children's thinking; they realize that a substance retains certain basic features even when its form is changed (pouring liquid into a taller, thinner glass does not change the volume, only the appearance).

Content. Piaget's term for behavior—talking, acting.

Egocentrism. Children during the early stages of development do not realize that other objects and opinions even exist.

Equilibration. Piaget's term for self-regulation, a tendency to keep assimilation and accommodation in balance.

Formal Operations Period. Piaget's fourth stage of cognitive development, characterized by abstract hypothetical thought (11 years +).

Functional Invariants. The cognitive functions that are always present (hence invariants): organization and adaptation.

Intelligence. For Piaget, one form of human adaptation to the environment.

Operation. To know an object is to act on it. You ← mentally compare it, change it, and then relate it to its original state.

Organization. Refers to cognitive structures; once formed they are not isolated but join with others, thus enabling a person to engage in more complex thinking.

Preoperational Period. Piaget's second period, characterized by the beginning of representation and language (2 to about 7 years).

Primary Circular Reactions. Infants have a tendency to repeat some activity involving their bodies: clenching fists appears in sensorimotor period.

Reversibility. Children acquire the ability to reverse their thinking: $2 + 2 = 4$, $4 - 2 = 2$. Essential for abstract thought.

Secondary Circular Reactions. Infants repeat activities but with objects other than their bodies: tugging a blanket appears in sensorimotor period.

Sensorimotor Period. The first of Piaget's cognitive stages (birth to about 2 years).

Structure. The basic component of mind. Physical structures such as the eyes are used to see, therefore it is logical to assume that cognitive structures are used to think. Children interact with the environment and form cognitive structures.

Tertiary Circular Reactions. Piaget's term to describe an infant's search for novelty: dropping things from different parts of the crib; appears during the latter part of the sensorimotor period.

Key concepts in Piaget's theory

What distinguishes Piaget from other child psychologists is his emphasis on intelligence. His interest in perception is only to contrast it with intelligence; values are cognitive systems with an organization similar to that of intelligence; motivation is significant only as intellectual adaptation. Although Piaget is usually considered a developmental psychologist, he thinks of himself as a "genetic epistemologist." Epistemology is the search for knowledge; genetic epistemology is the attempt to discover how human beings acquire knowledge at different times in their lives. Piaget believes that intellectual development proceeds through four periods and that the knowledge acquired during these different times possesses distinct characteristics. If all children pass through these stages—and growing evidence supports Piaget's theory—then there are important educational implications. Since children think differently than adults, they require appropriate materials and instructional techniques matched to their stage of mental development.

Piaget (1964) states that a child manifests mental development by passage through four successive stages. The first stage which extends from birth to about 18–24 months and which precedes speech is called *the sensorimotor period*. During this time children move from purely reflex activity to primitive mental activity. The second period, which begins with speech (18–24 months) is called *the preoperational period* and extends to about 7 years. Representation, when the child begins to use symbols—words, pictures—occurs in this period. Between 7 and 11 or 12, a third period, called *concrete operations*, appears. Now the child can think logically, but only with concrete objects. It is not until the fourth and final period, *formal operations*, that adolescents and adults consistently evidence logical, abstract thinking.

Note Piaget's constant use of "operations"—preoperational, concrete operations, formal operations. Piaget states (1964) that you

The Cognitive Periods

can understand cognitive development only if you understand the meaning of operation. Knowledge is not a copy of reality. *To know an object is to act on it.* It is not enough to look at it, to picture it. You must modify the object, that is, you do something to it. You compare it with other similar objects, noting similarities and differences; you place it in a particular order; you measure it.

Operations

These mental actions help you to understand not only the subject but also the process of transformation, that is, you gradually understand *how* to think about objects and events. Piaget believes that mental operations are reversible, that is, you can think in opposite directions: you add, but you can also subtract; you join things mentally, but you can also separate them $(2 + 2 = 4 \quad 4 - 2 = 2)$.

Mental operations, which are based originally upon motor activity, are never isolated; they are joined to form mental structures. Cognitive structures are vital to Piaget's theory because they form the basis of intellectual development. For example, as children mature, that is, as they pass through the four stages just described, they act on objects and events—the operations. But with increasing age they act on increasingly complex and abstract material; thus the operations become increasingly abstract until they are capable of formulating local propositions during the formal operations period.

For example, Piaget states (1964, pg. 9) that a number does not exist in isolation. It is a part of a series of numbers, which constitutes a structure. He believes that the operational structures are the basis of knowledge, and changes in the cognitive structures explain cognitive development. Consequently, to understand development is to understand the formation, organization, and function of our cognitive structure.

To illustrate the changes in children's thinking, Richard Gorman (1972) presents a Piagetian problem, children's responses, questions for the reader, and answers that explain Piaget's interpretation.

What makes clouds move?

Age 5: We make them move by walking (magic).
Age 6: God or men make them move (artificial and animalistic).
Age 7: They move by themselves, but the sun and moon also make them move (multiple causes).
Age 8: The wind pushes them (but the cloud produces the wind).
Age 9: Logical explanation.

To the reader: What can you tell from such findings?

A. The child's ideas of physical causality change with age.
B. As they age, children score higher on measures of physical causality.

A. True. Piaget's technique causes the child to diplay different thought processes at different ages.

B. The answers do not represent a higher score; they represent different *kinds* of answers.

Teachers' Interest

This brief discussion of Piaget's work reveals numerous educational implications. For example, if children think differently at different stages then materials and techniques should match these capabilities. His findings about children's acquisition of scientific and mathematical concepts have caused new curricula to be prepared. Piaget also has had a significant influence upon teachers who, once they understand his theory, appreciate the necessity of teaching children at their level of cognitive development. Piaget believes that education's chief aim is to create individuals who can do new things, not just repeat what already exists. Consequently,

Different Structures — Different Results

A good example of how a child's behavior reflects the logic of the underlying structures is seen in the following illustration. If you place six black tokens before a 5-year-old child, give her a pile of orange tokens and ask her to match the black, she can easily do it. When the tokens are in one to one position the child can tell us that both rows have the same number.

But if we now spread the six black tokens and make a longer row, the 5-year-old girl tells us that the row has more tokens!

A 7-year-old child faced with the same problem thinks it is a trick — both rows obviously still have the same number. Piaget even put the tokens on tracks so the child could move and match them.

The 5-year-old (preoperative) child still believed the longer row had more tokens — even after moving them and matching them!

How does Piaget explain this seeming contradiction? Recall what was said about operations — mentally acting upon objects and events, changing them and reversing them. The preoperational child cannot do this; in this example, mentally she cannot reverse the position of the tokens, she simply focuses upon the row's length. The logic of the 5-year-old's structures tells her that there must be more tokens in the longer row. The older child, in the concrete operational period, possesses structures whose logic permits reversibility, thus informing her that the number remains identical.

schools must form minds that can criticize, verify, and select. So pupils must be active, discover by themselves, and *think.*

ROOTS OF THE SYSTEM

Biological and philosophical ideas have influenced Piaget's thinking. For him, problems of philosophy are problems of knowledge, and problems of knowledge are problems of biology. Piaget states (1952, pg. 2) that intelligence is one form of human biological adaptation and its function is to structure the universe.

Philosophical Roots

This guideline—intelligence as adaptation—clarifies the meaning and purpose of genetic epistemology: to discover the psychological structures basic to thinking. Logic is the indispensable element in the search for cognitive structures. If our biological processes possess logic, if our actions possess logic, if our minds possess logic, then logic must also underlie our thinking processes.

The Importance of Structures

If the logic of the structures is the key to understanding the thinking process, then the origin and nature of the structures demand analysis. Piaget turns to biology for help in his studies. He believes that heredity shapes intellectual development, but his interpretation of heredity's role is unique. Heredity acts in *two* ways. The first results in specific biological structures, such as the eye, ear, or nervous system, that determine what humans may perceive. This hereditary function is limited: actions are limited to what is possessed anatomically.

Biological Roots

Heredity's second function is much more general and enables humans to overcome anatomical limitations. Being human means inheriting a method of intellectual functioning. It is a hereditary transmission of function and *not* of a specific structure (Piaget, 1952, pp. 2–3). *It is the second kind of heredity that is critical for intellectual development, because human biological organization then permits the formation of mental structures as the mind contacts reality.* These mental structures change, form groups, and organize into ever more abstract networks that are reflected in ever more abstract thinking during passage through the four stages of mental development. This is essentially Piaget's explanation of cognitive development.

If you understand these basic ideas—the appearance and organization of the structures with their resulting logic—you have a firm grasp of Piaget's system. Perhaps this example will help.

1. We inherit bodily structures.
2. We use the structure of the eye to see.
3. We use the structure of the ear to hear.
4. It is logical, then, to assume that we use the structures of the mind to think.

What are some other key concepts in Piaget's theory?

The Origins of Intelligence

In the *Origins of Intelligence in Children* (1952) Piaget carefully develops his ideas on the origin of mental structures. Structures are central to Piaget's thinking and their evolution from sensorimotor reflex activities to logical propositional thought explains intellectual development. He states that the relationship between mind and biological organization is the beginning of any study of the origins of intelligence (1952, pg. 1).

He then discusses the continuity that exists between intelligence and biological processes. The following sequence explains the route by which children, using their bodily structures, interact with the environment, form cognitive structures, and, as adolescents, finally acquire the logical thought processes that underlie verbal intelligence.

1. Our anatomical structure
            leads to
2. Our reflex system
            which leads to
3. Habits and associations
            which lead to
4. Sensorimotor intelligence
            which leads to
5. Verbal intelligence

If we examine this sequence we can better understand what Piaget means by heredity conditioning our mental development. We are human and thus function mentally as our biological heredity permits: the formation and organization of intellectual structures.

INTELLIGENCE

Intelligence is a consuming interest for Piaget. He is interested in topics such as motivation or learning only as they relate to intelligence. For example, he states (1973) that there are two aspects of a child's development: the psychosocial, which includes all that a child receives from the environment, and the spontaneous, which the child accomplishes alone through discovery. It is the spontaneous aspect that fascinates Piaget. Although related to physical development, Piaget notes (1964) that *total* development depends on the structures of knowledge.

FUNCTIONAL INVARIANTS

Piaget believes that humans inherit a method of intellectual functioning that enables them to adapt to their environment by forming cognitive structures. As they form these structures, they also organize them. Adaptation and organization are intellectual processes constantly used from birth to death. Although different environmental objects are used (for example, toys in childhood, words and propositions in adulthood), the intellectual processes are always identical: adaptation and organization. They never vary, hence the name functional invariants. All else — age, stage, and materials — changes except the functional invariants. Their importance requires further explanations.

A. *Adaptation.* Adaptation consists of two parts: assimilation and accommodation.

    1. *Assimilation.* When we assimilate something we incorporate it, we take it in. Think of eating. We take food into the structure of our mouths and change it to fit the shape of our mouths, throats, and digestive tract. *We take objects into our minds similarly:* We incorporate them into our mental structures, changing them to fit the structures as we changed the food to fit our physical structures. For example, you are now studying Piaget's views on cognitive development. They are unique and require effort on your part to be understood; that is, you are attempting to understand using the cognitive structures you now possess. You are assimilating his ideas; you are mentally taking them in, shaping them to fit your cognitive structures as you physically take food into your mouth.

    2. *Accommodation. But we also change as a result of assimilation.* The food we eat produces biochemical changes; the stimuli we incorporate into our minds produce mental changes. We change what we incorporate; we are changed by what we incorporate. For example, not only are you taking in Piaget's ideas, but they are changing your conventional views on intelligence and cognitive development. Your cognitive structures are changed, and if you understand his concepts you will never look at children in quite the same way again. The change in your cognitive structures has produced corresponding behavioral changes.

        The adaptive process is the heart of Piaget's explanation of mental development. Children take in new objects or events that change their mental structures, thus enabling them to incorporate increasingly different things. For example, while the 1-year-old child cannot incorporate written words (the youngster's structures cannot accept them) the same child of 7 easily incorporates words. The cognitive structures have changed; intellectual growth has occurred. (*Note:* Assimilation and accommodation are two parts of the same process — there is assimilation *to* mental structures, accompanied by accommodation *of* mental structures.)

B. *Organization.* The second functional invariant is inseparable from adaptation. As Piaget states (1952), they are two complementary processes of a single mechanism. *Every intellectual act is related to other similar acts.* Physical structures again are a good example. Reading this text you are balancing it, turning the pages, and moving your eyes. All of these physical structures are organized so that you can read. For you to *under-stand* the material, your appropriate cognitive structures are likewise organized so that they assimilate and accommodate. If some stimulus is radically different, you may be unable to assimilate it because you do not have the necessary cognitive structures; the material remains meaningless.

(*Note:* Be sure that you understand the meaning of functional invariants. If you do, you can more easily grasp how mental development proceeds.)

CONTENT

Flavell (1963, pg. 17) states that content, for Piaget, means raw, uninterpreted behavioral data. It is what the child says or does and is important because a child's behavior is a clue to his or her level of intellectual functioning (one of the four intellectual periods). Cognitive structures are inferred from content and teachers can then attempt to match suitable school materials with the child's cognitive structures.

STRUCTURE

You should now understand the nature, origin, and evolution of structures; they are mentioned here only to show their relationship to function and content. Flavell states (1963, pg. 17) that the search for structures and their developmental changes are Piaget's main quest. They are created by your unique method of intellectual functioning, and they are inferred from behavioral content. The method of intellectual functioning does not change (recall the functional invariants); behavioral content changes, so also do the structures.

SCHEMA

Piaget uses schema to indicate that all actions have a cognitive base. It is a form of classification, and Piaget says (1973) "Indeed, a scheme is what is generalizable in a given action." He constantly uses such expressions as "the sucking schema" or "the grasping schema" to emphasize the mental basis, even during infancy, of action. Perhaps a better example would be that of a child using a stick to bring some object closer, which displays a means-end relationship suggesting that more than random activity is involved.

Study Figure 4.1 and follow the sequence of events beginning with environmental stimuli and culminating in schemata. If you understand this figure, you understand Piaget's system because

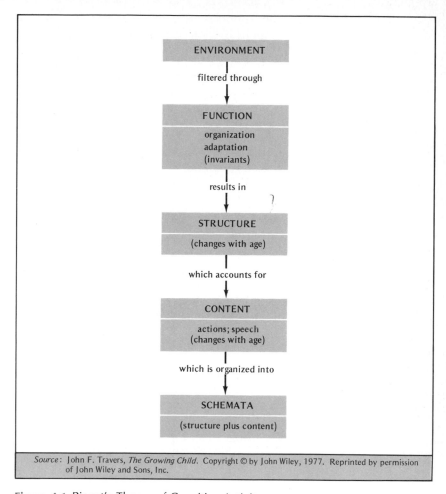

Figure 4.1 Piaget's Theory of Cognitive Activity

you can then use these essential concepts to understand a child's progression through the four cognitive periods.

To illustrate how Figure 4.1 clarifies Piaget's system, recall the child who uses a stick to obtain a distant object. If several questions are posed, a pattern emerges.

1. What are the environmental stimuli? There is a desired object and a means—the stick—of reaching the object.
2. What is the content? The child uses a stick to sweep an object closer to her.
3. Are the functional invariants active? Yes; the child recognizes

(assimilates) the ball that she wants, and the stick that will extend her reach. She accommodates *by changing the use of the stick.* Previously she used a stick to hit something and make a noise; now she changes — she accommodates — and sees the stick as a means to an end.

4. Are cognitive structures involved? Yes; it is the crucial element that explains mental development. The child earlier formed cognitive structures of the ball and its actions, and also of a stick; she has grasped the matter of spatial relations. Suddenly she combines and coordinates the related cognitive structures and uses the stick to reach the ball.

5. How do we apply the schemata? The child recognizes the means-end relationship and combines schemata, which is reflected in a series of related activities.

Both the mechanism and development of intellectual activity is evident. The child not only forms structures but combines and coordinates appropriate structures, which is a more advanced kind of process. Piaget's explanation of mental development and progression through the four cognitive periods are outlined in Table 4.1.

The sensorimotor period

Piaget states (1967) that the period from birth to language acquisition — the sensorimotor period — is marked by extraordinary mental development and determines the entire course of intellectual growth. The child, by perception and movement, conquers the surrounding world. The sensorimotor period has several developmental characteristics that reflect what Piaget calls the "decen-

TABLE 4.1
The Four Periods of Intellectual Development

The Cognitive Periods and Approximate Ages
1. The sensorimotor period (birth to 18–24 months).
2. The preoperational period (2 to 7 years).
3. The concrete operational period (7 to 11 years).
4. The formal operational period (over 11 years).
Note: This is a "stage invariant" theory, which means that the order of the stages does not vary; everyone passes through these stages in this sequence. It is not an "age invariant" theory, which means that a child's age may vary at any one of the periods. For example, although most children reach the concrete operational period at seven years, others may not reach it until eight or nine years.

tering process.'' The sensorimotor child is egocentric, that is, nothing exists that does not center on the body; it is not the egocentrism of adults who know that viewpoints other than their own exist but who simply ignore them. Egocentric infants cannot distinguish between themselves and the external world.

Children, by the decentering process, attain four objectives: they realize that there are permanent objects around them; they acquire a sense of space (that is, that there is a spatial relationship between objects in the environment, and between objects and their bodies); they discover a cause-effect relationship between actions and their consequences; finally, they detect a time sequence in

TABLE 4.2

Outstanding Characteristics of the Sensorimotor Period

	The Six Subdivisions of This Period
STAGE 1.	During the first month the child exercises the native reflexes, for example, the sucking reflex. Here is the origin of mental development, for states of awareness accompany the reflex mechanisms.
STAGE 2.	Piaget refers to Stage 2 (from 1 to 4 months) as the stage of *primary circular reactions*. Infants repeat some act involving the body, for example, finger sucking. (*Primary* means first, *circular reaction* means repeating the act.)
STAGE 3.	From 4 to 8 months *secondary circular reactions* appear; that is, the children repeat acts involving objects outside themselves. For example, infants continue to shake or kick the crib.
STAGE 4.	From 8 to 12 months, the child "coordinates secondary schemata." Recall the meaning of schema—behavior plus mental structure. During Stage 4, infants combine several related schemata to achieve some objective. For example, they will remove an obstacle that blocks some desired object.
STAGE 5.	From 12 to 18 months, *tertiary circular reactions* appear. Now children repeat acts, but not only for repetition's sake; now they search for novelty. For example, children of this age continually drop things. Piaget interprets such behavior as expressing their uncertainty about what will happen to the object when they release it.
STAGE 6.	At about 18 months or 2 years, a primitive type of representation appears. For example, one of Piaget's daughters wished to open a door but had grass in her hands. She put the grass on the floor and then moved it back from the door's movement so that it would not blow away.

their actions (that is, that one comes after another) (Piaget, 1967). The major accomplishments of the period result from the child's using basic hereditary structures, expanding them by the activity of the functional invariants (assimilation and accommodation) and progressing from purely sensory and motor functioning (thus "sensorimotor period") to symbolic activity (language) at the period's conclusion (Travers, 1977).

To illustrate how Piaget's theory differs substantially from other developmental systems, examine the following tables constructed for each period. Observe the difference in how Piaget examines behavior and how he emphasizes a child's action on the environment. Table 4.3 contrasts Piaget's interpretations of the first two years with the more traditional growth characteristics presented in Chapter 2.

Here is an example from Gorman (1972), illustrating Stage 6 (see Table 4.2) of the sensorimotor period.

A 22-month-old youngster picks up a stick and pretends it is a gun.

To the reader: How would you interpret the above behavior?

A. The youngster is using one object to represent another.
B. The child manifests a perceptual alertness not found at previous levels.

A. True. The child displays what Piaget calls the symbolic function—letting one thing represent another. It is the basis for language learning and a great developmental milestone.
B. Perceptual alertness appears earlier and the child displays more abstract behavior here, which is clear evidence of basic representation.

TABLE 4.3
Interpretations of the Sensorimotor Period

Age (months)	Language Development	Motor Development	Piaget's Cognitive Development
3–6	Cooing-babbling	Supports head; sits erect	Primary and secondary circular reactions
6–12	Single syllables; single words	Stands with support; walks with one hand held	Secondary circular reactions; coordination of secondary schemata
12–24	Vocabulary grows from a few to several hundred words	Walks and runs with no difficulty; usually toilet-trained	Tertiary circular reactions to beginnings of representations

The preoperational period

FIVE ACTIVITIES OF THE PERIOD

As children reach two years language is well established and symbolic activity is more frequent. They continue to develop, expand, and integrate their cognitive structures, which explains the steady increase in symbolic activity. Phillips (1975, pg. 64) states that while the sensorimotor child depends upon perceptions of concrete objects, the preoperational child represents a reality that includes past, present, and future.

Piaget and Inhelder (1969) distinguish five activities that characterize the preoperational period.

1. *Deferred imitation*, that is, the child imitates some object or activity when that object or activity is no longer present. The authors use the example of the girl who saw a playmate have a tantrum, scream, and stamp her feet. Sometime after the playmate has left, the girl, laughing, imitated her friend's behavior.

2. *Symbolic play, or pretending*, which was lacking in the sensorimotor period, now appears. Piaget and Inhelder (1969, pg. 53) illustrate symbolic play by the girl who pretended to sleep. She sat down, smiling, but closed her eyes, tilted her head to the side, and put her thumb in her mouth. Another example is the child who was fascinated by bells in a church steeple. Later she stood stiff and straight by her father's desk making loud noises. When asked to stop she replied that she was a church.

3. *Drawing*, which seldom appears before 2 or 2½ years of age, is initially an intermediate stage between play and mental imagery. From drawing the child receives pleasure, similar to that derived from symbolic play, while imitating reality, as with mental images. A good example of a drawing's symbolism is seen in the following sketch of a barber shop by a 5-year-old boy shown on page 132.

4. *Mental images*, which Piaget defines (1973, pg. 84) as internalized imitations, are "static" mental pictures. By static Piaget means that preoperational children reproduce previous objects or events: they do not change them, nor can they anticipate change. For example, recall the 5-year-old who was asked to match red tokens with the blue. She could do it on a one-to-one basis, but when the row of blue tokens was extended, she was frustrated. Thus, she could reproduce, but not anticipate. Piaget and Inhelder comment (1969, pg. 79) that mental images are symbols that provide a fairly accurate picture of the child's level of comprehension.

5. *Language*, which appears with the other symbolic functions, profoundly affects a child's behavior. Thanks to language, a

youngster can talk about past experiences and discuss future actions. Language has become a vehicle for thoughts and ideas and plainly discloses a child's growing symbolic activity.

LIMITATIONS OF PREOPERATIONAL THOUGHT

Although symbolic activity steadily increases during the preoperational period, it is not "good" thought. Recall the name of the period, preoperational, and Piaget's emphasis on operations. The preoperational child's thought possesses several limitations.

1. *Centering, or centration,* which means that a child concentrates upon one part of an activity, neglecting all else. Centering distorts thinking because different parts of an activity remain unrelated. Centering influences all of the preoperational child's thinking. For example, when water from one beaker is poured into a taller, thinner container, preoperational children think the second beaker has more water. They cannot attend to both height and amount of the water.

2. *Egocentrism* means that preoperational children believe no other viewpoint exists except their own. A good example is children's play and speech. Children may appear to be playing together but closer examination reveals that they are in different worlds. Children will talk with themselves and not with others.

TABLE 4.4
Contrasting Views of the Preoperational Period

Age (years)	Language Development	Motor Development	Piaget's Cognitive Development
2–4	Uses sentences; answers questions; vocabulary may approximate 1500 words	Runs, jumps, throws ball overhead; rides tricycle; puts on shoes	Increasing use of symbolism; language, play, drawing
4–5½	Begins to use five- or six-word sentences	Hops, skips, throws ball well; laces shoes	Use of symbolism grows, but is still restricted: I haven't had my nap so it's still afternoon.
5½–7	Uses complex sentences; vocabulary about 3000 words.	Jumps from height; draws recognizable man; dresses and undresses	Approaches logical thinking: Do blue butterflies like the wet? Child: Yes. And the brown ones? Child: They like it dry. Then why are they here with the blue ones?

3. *Irreversibility,* which Flavell believes (1963, pg. 159) is the most important characteristic of preoperational thought, means that children cannot reverse their thinking: $2 + 2 = 4 \quad 4 - 2 = 2$. Flavell notes that preoperational children's thinking often is contradictory because they cannot return to their original premise when they are blocked or confused.

4. *States versus transformations,* which means that preoperational children focus upon some momentary state but cannot join successive states to form a whole. Recall what we said of the preoperational child's ability to construct mental images — it was restricted to reproductive images; it was static.

Ginsburg and Opper (1969, pg. 115) summarize these limitations when they state that a common pattern emerges in the preoperational child's thinking: the inability to deal simultaneously with several aspects of a situation, reflecting an incapacity to shift attention from one aspect to another of a situation. But as the period ends, children slowly decenter their thinking and achieve reversibility, which brings them to the world of operations.

Here is another Piagetian problem posed by Gorman (1972).

Two children — one age 5, the other age 7 — are shown twenty wooden beads, 16 brown and 4 white, and then asked if there are more brown beads or wooden beads.
Child, age 5: There are more brown beads.
Child, age 7: There are more wooden beads than brown beads.

To the reader: How would you interpret these answers?

A. The older child grouped both brown and white beads with the class of wooden beads.
B. The younger child did not understand the question.

___

A. True. The answer required grouping objects, which the younger, preoperational child could not do.
B. Rather than misunderstanding the question, the child could not perform the necessary mental operations. Because of limitations — centering, focusing upon states, and irreversibility — the child could not solve the problem.

Discussion Questions

1. Be sure you understand the meaning of genetic epistemology. Explain the terms and relate them to cognitive development.

2. What does Piaget mean by structure? How did he devise this assumption? Do you agree with him? Explain your answer.

3. Explain the meaning of assimilation and accommodation. Prepare examples of each for the group. Are there times when you cannot assimilate and accommodate? Why? Give examples. Be sure you understand the *mental* as well as physical meaning of the terms. How do they become part of the functional invariants?

4. Explain to the group how Figure 4.1 illustrates Piaget's theory. Now give examples of each step in the figure.

5. What is the great accomplishment of the sensorimotor period? How does it occur? Copy Table 4.2 in your notebook or on the board. Now attempt to add new language and motor behaviors for each period. How do they relate to Piaget's description?

6. Can you devise your own examples of the five activities that characterize the preoperational period? Now explain them using Piaget's interpretation of this period and the basic model (Figure 4.1).

7. Using Gorman's work as a model, can you think of problems that would distinguish the sensorimotor child, the preoperational, and one from the other?

Concrete operations

From 7 to 11 or 12 years, a youngster accomplishes true mental operations. Recall that operations mean mentally acting on an object, changing it, comparing it, relating it to others. Now children can reverse their thinking and group objects into classes. How does

"Doing It in Your Head"

David Elkind (1968) describes concrete operations as the time when children "can do in their heads" what they previously accomplished through their actions. Elkind uses the example of Piaget giving 5-, 6-, and 7-year-old children six sticks and asking them to take a like number from a pile of sticks on a table. The younger children put their six sticks on the table and one by one matched six more from the pile. The older children just took six sticks from the pile; they had mentally counted the required number.

Elkind recounts his own experience of asking a preoperational child if he could be a Protestant and an American simultaneously. The child answered no, reconsidered, and said it might be possible only if you move. His mental structures did not permit him to group Protestant and American into the single class—Protestant American. Concrete operational children have no difficulty with the problem: they can "operate mentally" and combine into classes.

The concrete operational child's greatest achievement is conservation, that is, the notion of permanence. If the surface features of an object are changed (for example, change its shape but retain its substance), youngsters are not fooled. They know that the same amount of material is present, that is, they conserve the essence of the object.

While driving his children outside of Geneva, Piaget was asked by one of them the name of a mountain in sight. The question surprised Piaget because it was a mountain that the child knew well—*from his home*. So Piaget reasoned that a young child has difficulty with change—whether the object changes or a child moves with respect to an object. It is only by conservation that children can cope with a changing world because they are then capable of mental operations.

Piaget explain this remarkable phenomenon? The decentering process, which refers to our physical and social worlds, permits children to perform operations.

These mental operations, however, apply only to concrete operations and not to verbal statements. For example, shown blocks *A, B, C* concrete operational children can tell you that *A* is larger than *B*, which is larger than *C; A,* therefore, is largest of all. But if you tell them that Liz is taller than Ellen who is taller than Jane, they cannot tell you who is tallest of all. Consequently, Piaget designates the period as *concrete operations,* that is, a transition between the first two period's dependence on action and the fourth period's dependence on logical, abstract reasoning.

ACCOMPLISHMENTS OF THE PERIOD

The following are several noticeable accomplishments of the period.

1. *Conservation* is achieved. The classic conservation example uses two identical drinking glasses equally filled. When children are asked if the two glasses hold the same amount, they answer affirmatively. Now, *while a child watches*, one glass is poured into a taller, thinner glass so that the liquid reaches a higher level. Up to about 7 years, a child will say that the taller, thinner glass has more liquid. Or if one glass is poured into a shorter, wider glass, the liquid will be at a lower level. The child, before 7 years, says that the shorter glass has less liquid. Remember: the experiment was done while the child watched. Usually a 7-year-old child immediately states that they are still equal, nothing was gained or lost; this child has conserved the equal amounts of liquid and the transformations were not confusing.

Elkind (1968) states that the older child does not depend on the liquid's appearance. Comparing widths, the wider glass must have more; comparing liquid levels, the taller glass must have more. The problem is insoluble by appearance. The child reasons that since the two glasses had the same amount before pouring, and nothing was lost or added during the pouring, then the amount must be the same. Thus concrete operational children decenter their thinking (that is, they do not focus on only one part of the problem), which enables them to reverse their thinking (they can mentally pour the liquid back into the original glass), and they can understand transformations (their thinking is not static, that is, confined to states).

2. *Seriation*, which is the ability to arrange objects according to increasing or decreasing size, is also achieved. Piaget (1973) states that if you give children different size sticks and ask them to arrange them by size, young children (before 7) form several groups of two or three sticks, putting these in order. They then combine the several groups, with considerable trial and error. Older children compare the sticks, find the smallest which they place on the table, then the next smallest until they are all properly arranged. Piaget notes that each stick is larger than those already on the table but smaller than those remaining.

3. *Classification*, in which children can include subcategories within a larger category, also appears. Recall the example of the 20 wooden beads, 16 brown and 4 white. Preoperational children state that there were more brown beads than wooden beads. They could not combine subcategories into a larger category—the brown beads plus the white beads constitute all the wooden beads. Concrete operational children have no such difficulty.

4. *Number*, which depends upon classification and seriation, also characterizes concrete operational children. Piaget does not mean verbal counting when he refers to number, because a child may be able to count and still not understand the meaning of number. Recall Piaget's experiment with the tokens—youngsters could match them on a one-to-one basis, but when one row of tokens was lengthened, preoperational children thought *that* row had more tokens although the number remained constant. It is not until youngsters realize that one orange is equal to one tree is equal to one person that they understand the meaning of number.

These accomplishments illustrate the difference between preoperational and concrete operational children; they have overcome the limitations of the preoperational period. They decenter, which then enables them to attend to transformations by reversing their thinking. Finally, Piaget states (1967, pg. 41) 7-year-olds begin to liberate themselves from social and intellectual egocentricity. Again, contrast Piaget's views of the 7- to 11-year-old with more conventional interpretations.

To conclude your work on concrete operations, here is another example from Gorman (1972).

What is 12 + 6? How can you get 12 again?
Child, age 5. I don't know.
Child, age 7. $12 + 6 = 18$ $18 - 6 = 12$.

To the reader: What could the older child do that the younger could not?

A. Use addition to solve the problem.
B. Realize that an operation is reversible.
C. Realize that one variable can compensate for another.

A. The older child could add and subtract, but these may be superficial (rote memory) characteristics. Something else is present.

TABLE 4.5
Contrasting Views of the Concrete Operational Period

Age (years)	Motor Development	Stanford-Binet Test Items	Piaget's Cognitive Development
7–8	Good balance; interest in physical games	Detects similarities between two items; can read paragraph of seven or eight sentences	Conservation of substance, length, and liquid
9–10	Skill in throwing and catching; greater running speed; may skate and swim well	Memory shows noticeable improvement on test items	Conservation of weight; classification
11–12	Throws ball accurately for long distance; adept at organized sports	Detects similarities among three items; recognizes abstract absurdities	Conservation; classification; seriation; number

B. True. The older child *understands* that one operation is negated by its opposite operation. The older child's ability summarizes all the essential features of concrete operations.

C. The variables do not cancel each other; it is the operations.

Formal operations

CHARACTERISTICS OF FORMAL OPERATIONAL THINKING

The formal operational period begins at 11 or 12 years for most youngsters and is the culmination of the previous three periods. Ginsburg and Opper (1969) describe formal operations as the time when the adolescent's thought is flexible and effective. That is, adolescents can deal effectively with complex reasoning problems, but they can also imagine many possibilities in a problem. They are not bound by the tangible or concrete, which is the period's major achievement. These authors note that adolescents can compensate mentally for changes (transformations) in their environment.

Piaget and Inhelder state (1969) that decentering is complete and that the adolescent can understand and use hypothetical statements, while reasoning about propositions that are not concrete. They note that adolescents' thinking is so advanced that they can reason correctly about propositions they do not believe and can draw conclusions from statements that reflect only possibilities.

Elkind (1968) describes formal operations as the time in which adolescents can "think about their thoughts," construct ideals, and reason realistically about the future. He offers a good example of formal operational thinking: when younger children are asked to assume that coal is white they reply that coal has to be black, whereas adolescents can accept the unreal assumption and reason from it.

Inhelder and Piaget (1958) illustrate the difference between the concrete and formal operational child by the following example. Present a child with five jars—A, B, C, D, E— that contain colorless liquids. Combining jars A, C, and E produces a yellow color; B is bleach, and D is pure water

$$A \quad B \quad C \quad D \quad E$$
$$A + C + E = \text{yellow}$$
$$B = \text{bleach}$$
$$D = \text{water}$$

The child sees the color, but not how to obtain it. The task is to discover what combination produces yellow, and also the function of B and D. The concrete operational child combines by joining two jars and then tries all five together. The adolescent tests the

Passage Through the Stages

These are the stages, with the operations and structures that characterize each. Piaget raises another basic issue when he questions how an individual passes from one stage to another, that is, what causes the sensorimotor child to become the preoperational child. Four agents encourage passage from one period to another.

1. Maturation, especially of the nervous and endocrine systems, powerfully influences the appearance and functioning of the various structures. Here Piaget recognizes the role of physiological growth and development for normal behavior.
2. Experience, or the actions performed on objects, is necessary for the formation and organization of the psychological structures. Piaget identifies two kinds of experience—physical and logico-mathematical experience. Physical experience is acting upon objects to abstract their properties. Logico-mathematical experience involves the construction of propositions and the combination of these in order to think and solve problems.
3. Social transmission represents the child's capacity to assimilate information from others (parents, teachers, etc.) because of psychological structures. Piaget's interpretation of social transmission should alert educators not to teach concepts that a child's structures cannot assimilate.
4. Equilibration, or self-regulation, is a process that results in states of equilibrium, that is, the child responds to external stimuli (assimilation) by adjusting to them (accommodation).

These four agents explain how a youngster moves from one stage to another. None is alone sufficient but together they help to explain how a child forms structures and uses stimuli to change, organize, and construct new structures, thus preparing for passage to the next cognitive period.

possible combinations of one, two, three, four, and five, thus solving the problem.

Flavell has identified several essential characteristics of formal operational thinking (1963, pp. 204–206).

1. The adolescent's ability to separate the real from the possible distinguishes the concrete operational from the formal operational child. The adolescent tries to discern all possible relations in any situation or problem and then, by mental experimentation and logical analysis, attempts to discover which are true. Flavell notes that there is nothing trivial in the adolescent's accomplishment; it is a basic and essential reorganization of thought processes that permits the adolescent to exist in the world of the possible. Piaget states (1964) that the adolescent employs new operations and forms new structures that are more complicated group structures.

2. Formal thinking is propositional. The adolescent uses not only concrete data but also statements or propositions that contain the concrete data. Flavell says that the adolescent takes the *results* of concrete operations, forms them into propositions, and then makes logical connections between the statements. Summarizing: Formal operations are operations performed upon the results of concrete operations.

3. Imagine adolescents facing a problem. What do they do? First, they isolate all of the variables that they can. Second, they make all the possible combinations of the variables that they can. Piaget calls this procedure "combinatorial analysis."

How do adolescents use formal operations?

First, they organize data by concrete operational techniques (classification, seriation).

Second, they use the results of concrete operational techniques to form statements or propositions.

Third, they combine as many of these propositions as possible (these are hypotheses, and Piaget often refers to this process as hypothetico-deductive thinking).

Fourth, they then test to determine which combinations are true.

CLASSROOM IMPLICATIONS

Flavell suggests that Piaget's work has direct educational relevance:

1. Piaget's techniques may serve to assess the child's level of intellectual development. Assessment results may then guide educators in grade placement and remedial procedures.

2. Curriculum planners can profit from Piaget's developmental findings by attempting to answer two questions. Are there ideal times for the teaching of certain subjects? Is there an ideal sequence for a subject that matches Piaget's description of cognitive development?

3. Piaget's work provides data for the formulation of optimal learning conditions. For example, during the first two periods—sensorimotor and preoperational—youngsters should constantly interact physically with their environment. During the concrete operational period children should have tangible objects to facilitate their acquisition of operations. Finally, the adolescent should encounter verbal problems and attempt to solve them by testing the truth of various propositions.

Piaget, in *Science of Education and the Psychology of the Child* (1971), provides a link between his theory and education that sug-

Knowledge as Action

gests definite guidelines for teaching and curriculum construction. He states that the essential function of intelligence consists of understanding and inventing; that is, children and young adults build cognitive structures by *structuring reality*. The task of educators is to create an environment that enables pupils to assimilate a changing reality into their cognitive structures, modifying them, and forming new structures. Knowledge comes, not from having students copy reality, but from action: from assimilating reality into existing schemata and then accommodating to these new conditions.

A youngster's emerging intelligence, the manner in which it develops, and the material it uses in developing, constitute the basic conditions of education. What are these basic conditions? There are two: Youngsters must interact with their environment and not be passive receptors of "knowledge"; youngsters must interact with materials that match their level of cognitive development. Here the practical considerations of Piaget's work emerge: from analyzing a pupil's *content*, teachers can infer the type of underlying cognitive structure, and then utilize methods and materials that will help their students to *assimilate* and *accommodate*, thus aiding *cognitive development*.

Active Methods

Piaget states (1971, pg. 68) that educators now understand that an active school is not a school of manual labor. The child's early activities require considerable physical manipulation of objects because these actions form elementary logical-mathematical structures. At higher levels (secondary school), authentic cognitive activity may occur through reflections, through advanced abstractions, and through verbal manipulations. These abstract activities suit the cognitive structures of the formal operational adolescent.

Piaget believes that although there is growing theoretical acceptance of activity as the requirement for cognitive development, there has been noticeable reluctance to translate these ideas into practice mainly because active methods cause more difficulty for educators than receptive methods. They demand much more concentrated work from teachers and a sound understanding of child development. Unless these two criteria are met the easier receptive methods will dominate curriculum planning and instruction.

Piaget and the curriculum

Sigel and Cocking (1977) state that Piagetian research has studied cognitive development as it evolves with specific problems— geometry, gravity, time, space, and logic—furnishing specific curriculum guidelines. For example, understanding numbers follows a definite sequence, which has clear implications for curriculum construction. Recalling Piaget's belief that educators need a thorough comprehension of cognitive development, Sigel and Cocking state that classroom teachers should be able to identify a pupil's cognitive level and relate this knowledge to the basic notion of an invariant sequence in cognitive development. Teachers then become agents of social transmission, facilitating a youngster's passage from stage to stage.

To help teachers accomplish this objective, curriculum builders should use the Piagetian framework to develop and order materials. Recognizing that students do not acquire knowledge merely by adding bits of information, but by actively modifying cognitive structures, curriculum experts can employ the stages of cognitive development to shape various curricula. It is insufficient, however, to identify a cognitive stage and then match appropriate material. To cast teachers in such a role eliminates their function as participants in students' development. Sigel and Cocking believe that modern curriculum builders are urging teachers to use naturalistic phenomena rather than repetitive exercises for lessons. For example, young children develop their thinking by seeing the cause-and-effect relationship in wind and cloud movement; they question if an ice cube melts faster in or out of water.

Asking what teachers should stress with elementary school children, Gorman (1972) answers by emphasizing objects, experiences, visual aids, and field trips. His answer reflects a belief that most elementary school youngsters function at the concrete operational level. They can manipulate objects mentally, but the objects must relate to the perceptual, concrete world. Asking the same question about the high school student, Gorman states that activity is as critical for secondary school students as for elementary school pupils. When students compare ideas and beliefs, evaluate evidence, devise conclusions, and relate these events to their cognitive structures, they are suitably active for their level. As Piaget notes (1971), they are personally rediscovering truth.

Gorman provides a rationale for ordering subjects in the curriculum according to Piagetian thought. His scheme is as follows:

Subject	Level	Basis
Foreign language	Primary	Symbolic function
Arithmetic	Grade two	Operational thought
Grammar	Elementary	Concrete operations
Geometry	Elementary	Concrete operations
Specific topics	Mainly elementary	Differing rates of development
Logic	Secondary	Formal operations

Recently, Charleston, West Virginia, school officials, wishing to prevent as many failures as possible, asked Furth and Wachs (1975) to devise a Piagetian program for kindergarten and grades one to three. The authors state that their goal was to aid normal development so that fourth-grade children would master skills but also would be better adjusted, better motivated, and better prepared for future learning.

Interested teachers were trained, and the setting prepared as well as possible. Before choosing specific activities for the children, the authors formulated a rationale that included the following:

1. Thinking is worthwhile in itself. The authors felt that if children could believe this, they could then avoid the negative results of excessive competition, such as the pursuit of higher grades.
2. Structural activities enhance developing intelligence and do not restrict individual freedom. Teachers should prepare varied activities so that children can respond on their own cognitive level. The authors believe that a Piagetian program is midway between open-end and high structured schools.
3. Activities match developmental levels. The activities should challenge a child's thinking but should not be so difficult as to frustrate and cause failure.
4. Children, with their peers, should concentrate upon the activities, and not the teacher, thus permitting the teacher more time to observe and to guide.

The authors believe that the project was successful and rewarding both for children and teachers. They are frank about the limitations and frustrations they encountered but conclude that Piaget's work demonstrates that the ideals of personal freedom and democracy are solidly based in the psychological and biological nature of human knowledge.

Bruner and mental growth

Born in 1915, Jerome Bruner remains a potent figure in developmental psychology, cognitive studies, and education. He received his doctorate from Harvard in 1941, taught there from 1945 to 1973, established Harvard's Center for Cognitive Studies with George Miller, and for the past few years has taught at Oxford. Bruner's interests range over many disciplines and, as Pines (1975) notes, whenever he champions a new idea it is sure to generate excitement and enthusiasm. Yet, as productive and innovative as Bruner is, he has had much less influence than either Piaget or Skinner. His varied interests are perhaps the reason. Pines states that

Jerome S. Bruner

HARVARD UNIVERSITY NEWS OFFICE

Bruner, unlike many of his colleagues, has investigated rat behavior, German propaganda, perception, Freud, cognitive styles, sensory deprivation, learning, child development, innate behavior, and education.

For example, in 1956, he and his colleagues published *A Study of Thinking*, a novel and carefully controlled investigation of how humans form concepts. His most famous work, *The Process of Education*, appeared in 1960. This little book, an analysis of education, instruction, and curriculum construction, has been translated into 22 languages and is still studied by teachers and administrators. Other readable and informative books followed: *On Knowing* (1962), *Toward a Theory of Instruction (1966)*, *Studies in Cognitive Growth* (1966), *The Relevance of Education* (1971), and the controversial social studies curriculum: *Man: A Course of Study*

(MACOS). Bruner's valuable insights deserve our consideration because his view of the child as an information processor, thinker, and creator emphasizes both rationality and dignity (Anglin, 1973).

THE PATTERN OF COGNITIVE GROWTH

One of Bruner's major assumptions is that teaching is an effort to assist growth. He believes that intellectual growth has several discernible characteristics.

Freedom from Environmental Control

1. Increasing independence of a response from an immediate stimulus distinguishes mental growth. We can predict much of young children's behavior from knowing the stimuli around them. But as children grow mentally they are able to maintain a desired response although conditions (stimuli) change. A good example is the proficiency to give the right response in a multiple-choice examination — the youngster maintains the response in spite of assorted stimuli. Children also can change their responses to meet unchanging environmental demands. For example, if an answer is incorrect, and children know it is incorrect, they change their answer (response) to the same question (stimulus).

A Model of the World

2. Intellectual growth depends upon the child's mental construction of a model of the world. (Recall Piaget's insistence on "operations" to form psychological structures.) The child actively constructs a mental picture of the world. Building this mental image of the world permits a child to *use* the information to compare, judge, and predict. It is similar to Piaget's explanation of a child's ability to go from the real to the possible.

Symbolism

3. Growing skill in symbolic activity features intellectual development. Youngsters can say what they have done or will do; they begin to use propositions or statements and thus reflect a logico-mathematical capacity that *did not* previously exist.

Interactions

4. Intellectual development depends on a close interaction between a teacher and learner. There are many tutors in a child's environment — school teachers, fathers, mothers, friends, heroes — and there is still considerable uncertainty about the details of the different relationships. For example, different individuals possess different personalities and thus do things differently. Is the relationship between a permissive teacher and her pupils radically different from the relationship between a firm teacher and her pupils? What is the ideal learning environment for these two examples? Are they identical? More data are needed before confident decisions are possible.

Language

5. Language facilitates teaching and learning, but a child gradually uses it not only for communication but also to bring order to the environment. For example, while the young child uses language to inform others of needs or to identify objects, the older child uses language to represent things or events not present: "To-

morrow I must bring my notebook home to study for the week-end.''

Competence

6. Finally, intellectual development is marked by increasing competence in attending to several possibilities. For example, in Piaget's conservation experiments, when youngsters are no longer distracted by the length or width of the glass but realize that the liquid remains intact, they are attending to several things.

THE PERFECTIBILITY OF INTELLECT

In a perceptive essay, Bruner (1971) states that there are four constraints on intellect; the nature of knowing, an evolving intellect, the growth of intellect, and the nature of knowledge.

1. *The nature of knowing.* Bruner believes that an outstanding intellectual feature is its limited capacity for dealing with information. Confusion can easily overwhelm children's intellect unless

146

Modes of Representation

How can these ideas help us in teaching? Bruner believes that the mental growth characteristics aid a youngster in achieving three levels of representation; that is, a child passes through three distinct cognitive phases.

1. Bruner calls the first level "the enactive mode of representation." The infant knows the world only by acting on it; otherwise the object does not exist. As Bruner notes, there are times in the adult's life when words simply cannot express what is meant (1966, pg. 10). For example, how can you tell someone about "the feel of" the golf or tennis swing?

2. The second level is "the iconic mode of representation," Bruner's expression for perceptual organization. Faced with a series of apparently unrelated tasks, discovering a pattern makes the work easier.

3. The third level is "the symbolic mode of representation." Here the child engages in symbolic activities, such as language and mathematics. Bruner (1966, pg. 14) states that when children translate experience into language they enter the world of possibilities, enabling them to solve problems and engage in creative thinking.

Youngsters learn according to their mode of representation. For example, youngsters at the iconic level need concrete objects and activities so that they can absorb them perceptually. Bruner states (1960) that learning a subject involves three almost simultaneous processes.

1. *Acquisition* of new information, which replaces or expands what the child already knows, is the initial phase. Here the child incorporates environmental stimuli according to the existing mode of representation: by physical action, by forming images, or by abstracting, comparing, and judging.

2. *Transformation* is the second phase. Once youngsters or adults acquire new information then they must manipulate or change it to meet new tasks. Bruner often uses the illustration, "going beyond the information given." For example, your friend passes by the door and says, "Hi, Janie." You do not see her, but immediately think, "There goes Liz." You manipulated verbal stimuli to form the idea of your friend.

3. *Evaluation* is the final phase. Have they successfully manipulated the information? Was it adequate? correct?

Bruner joins mental growth, modes of representation, and learning processes to introduce his idea of the spiral curriculum. He states (1960) that if teachers respect a child's thinking process and translate material into meaningful units (that is, if they match the subject matter to the child's mode of representation) they can introduce great ideas to children at different times and with increasing abstractness. For example, freedom discussed in the first grade differs from a junior high school discussion of slavery, which differs from a high school discussion of the meaning of the Constitution—hence the spiral curriculum.

they learn strategies that reduce the world's complexity. But cognitive organization implies reduction of stimuli, which is a selective process but still must include significant aspects of the environment. Children gradually construct models of the world that not only represent what they encounter but permit them to go beyond specific information. The previous example of picturing and knowing people who speak to you even when they remain out of sight illustrates Bruner's principle.

After youngsters construct these models, they use them to manipulate the environment instead of acting directly on it. For example, the room becomes dark; there is a student sitting by the light switch; I do not cross the room to flick the switch; I ask the student to do it. Bruner says that thought is vicarious action which reduces trial and error.

2. *An evolving intellect.* Bruner firmly believes that human intelligence was substantially altered by using tools. Modern technological societies now have a set of acquired characteristics that passes from generation to generation as part of the cultural pool. He further believes that, as human intelligence evolved, control by the hormonal system decreased and cortical control increased. These two arguments are a constant theme in Bruner's work: with increasing use of symbolism, the role of the central nervous system is enhanced.

These cultural changes have produced educational transformations. Since there is so much skill and knowledge in modern culture, no one can possess it all. Consequently, teachers no longer *show* pupils how things work and let them learn by doing—they now *tell* students because it is more economical. At its worst, this trend can deteriorate into rote, meaningless learning, which is a real danger with highly abstract learning.

3. *The growth of intellect.* Intellectual growth does not proceed smoothly but in spurts followed by periods of consolidation. Bruner believes that these spurts are organized around the emergence of certain capacities; that is, developing abilities dictate that children master one thing before they go to the next.

He states that there is a remarkable amount of "self-reward" from learning during growth. The satisfaction of curiosity, the development of competence, and the achieving and maintaining of desired standards provide a "motor for growth that is stalled only by repeated failure."

4. *The nature of knowledge.* Bruner notes that the past half century has been one of the richest as well as one of the most baffling in the history of knowledge. The amount of new information generated staggers the imagination. Luckily, the possibility of expressing knowledge in various, more or less abstract, modes provides educators with ways of presenting material more meaningfully.

An emerging computer technology, with new ways of storing, relating, and retrieving information, may eventually effect tremendous educational changes. The task now is to rearrange and reorder existing knowledge to reflect theoretical changes. Learning rep-

resents not only knowledge itself but ways of thinking, habits of mind, implicit assumptions, short cuts, and styles of human behavior.

Summarizing these thoughts, Bruner states that the primary task of intellect is constructing explanatory models to order the universe. Converting knowledge into an instrument for this task is a great unresolved goal for the school.

MACOS

Man: A Course of Study (MACOS) is Bruner's attempt to put his ideas into practice. Bruner began working on MACOS in 1960, and by 1975 a completed curriculum was available. Today it is used in about 1700 schools, and some 85 colleges, universities, and educational centers offer teacher education courses for MACOS. Bruner states (1966) that the content of the course is man: his nature as a species and the forces that shape his humanity. The course revolves around three basic questions:

1. What is human about human beings?
2. How did they get that way?
3. How can they be made more so?

To answer these questions, Bruner chose five topics that strikingly illustrate human uniqueness and potential for improvement: tool making, language, social organization, a prolonged childhood, and the urge to explain the world. These topics mirror

The Great MACOS War

The MACOS curriculum has caused one congressional committee to state that its content could be "traumatic for ten- and 11-year-old students." The hard choices that the Netsilik Eskimos faced—abandoning an aged person unable to travel or females who were not as productive as males in securing food—present values inconsistent with American culture. But Dow (1975) states that its purpose was to illustrate that human nature was knowable and that an intelligent understanding of behavior improves chances for survival.

With this goal, the curriculum was designed to portray the human species as unique, possessing language, the capability for social organization, the ability to alter the environment, and a concern for the care of its young. Children, by comparing humans with animals and then examining a specific culture, were expected to grasp more fully the human's capacity for social behavior,

shaped by such cultural innovations as tools and technology. If a human society is to survive, there is a need to know what causes people to love and trust each other, to develop patterns of mutual support, and to share common goals, which is what MACOS attempts to do.

Not so, says George Weber (1975). While he admits that the course's content is technically brilliant, he finds its subject matter unnecessarily controversial, even shocking. Weber believes that 10-year-olds are too young to cope with the course's content, so that indoctrination of the authors' ideas is the principal result. Weber also questions what is *replaced* on the curriculum by MACOS and why the federal government should sponsor this program over others that are available.

MACOS: exciting but controversial. Would you use it?

Bruner's belief that human development is as much from the outside in as from the inside out. Culture is a powerful force in development. The topics also mirror Bruner's belief that matierals should match a child's mode of representation.

The Unit

Youngsters acquire the MACOS concepts by various means: films, filmstrips, short pamphlets, games, exercises—there is no basic text. The first unit contrasts salmon behavior with human behavior; the second unit is based on studies of Lorenz and Tinbergen, concentrating on the behavior patterns of herring gulls, especially parental roles; the third unit focuses on baboons, man's nearest primate relative, and studies group structure and behavior; the final unit analyzes culture by studying the Canadian Netsilik Eskimos. Concluding the course, students should have a deeper understanding of human uniqueness and a more compassionate sensitivity to the common humanity of all cultures.

Growing Criticism

Initially acclaimed—Bruner received awards from the American Educational Publishers Institute and the American Educational Research Association—criticism gradually appeared and became fierce within the last few years. It even reached the floor of the United States Congress (the National Science Foundation originally funded the project) where it was flayed as portraying adultery, bestiality, cannibalism, female infanticide, incest, murder, servitude, wife swapping, and sexual promiscuity. While admitting that the material is scientifically accurate, critics argue that it is inappropriate for 10-year-olds and inculcates values opposed to the American system. Whatever the outcome of the controversy, MACOS is remarkably faithful to Bruner's beliefs about growth and learning.

BRUNER AND PIAGET

Bruner and Piaget share many ideas, and Bruner has often acknowledged his debt to Piaget. Recently, however, Bruner has stated that he differs from Piaget in emphasizing a culture's influence on intellectual development. Anglin (1973) has summarized the similarities and differences between the two. Both believe that mental development involves qualitative rather than quantitative changes in cognitive structures. Both believe that mental development occurs in phases:

Similarities

Piaget	Bruner
Sensorimotor	Enactive
Preoperational	Iconic
Concrete operations	
Formal operations	Symbolic

Their interpretations of the levels are almost identical. Both believe that action in infancy is critical for normal intellectual growth.

Anglin states that there are also important differences. Piaget's work, highly mathematical and logical, is quite formal. Bruner emphasizes more psychological concepts, for example, cognitive conflict hastens mental development. Bruner believes his interpretation of language's role in development differs from Piaget's. Bruner states that *language facilitates mental performance*—it is causally linked to increased mental competence—while Piaget believes that language is *an outcome of growing mental competence.* Finally, Bruner stresses more than Piaget a culture's role. He states that mental development is as much "from the outside in as from the inside out" due to language (as Bruner sees it) and man's use of tools. (Recall that the units of MACOS utilize tool making, language, social organization, prolonged childhood, and curiosity.)

Differences

How real are these differences? Probably minimal since both basically agree about mental development. Bruner questions Piaget's interpretation of maturation and experience, but Piaget believes that two of the four agents that aid cognitive development are cultural: experience and social transmission. Piaget questions Bruner's interpretation of culture, but Bruner believes that material must match the growing child's changing capacities. His famous readiness statement—any subject can be taught effectively in some intellectually honest form to any child at any stage of development—reflects recognition of maturation's importance. He states (Bruner, 1960, pg. 32) that his interpretation of readiness depends on three general ideas: the path of intellectual development (which is essentially Piaget's), the act of learning (which must match the level of intellectual development), and the spiral curriculum (which presents the great ideas and issues in increasingly complex forms). Thus material complements the child's cognitive level—it is an intellectually honest match.

Both Piaget and Bruner have much to offer parents and teachers.

Discussion Questions

1. What does Piaget mean by operations? Explain your answer by applying it to the four cognitive periods.

2. How is the concrete operational child more mentally advanced than the sensorimotor youngster and less than the formal operational adolescent? Give examples.

3. What do the conservation experiments illustrate? Explain by using Piaget's terminology.

4. What does formal operation mean? Give examples. What are the major achievements of the period? Give examples.

5. Give examples of Bruner's growth characteristics, explaining how they distinguish children of different ages. Apply them to Piaget's four cognitive periods and to Bruner's three. Do they help to accentuate the similarities and differences between the two theorists? How?

6. Give specific examples of how Bruner's three learning steps apply to the three modes of representation.

7. Where would you place yourself in the MACOS dispute? Consider both sides of the argument and defend your position.

Some Concluding Thoughts

Although modern schools are devoted to improving the whole child, teachers are primarily interested in mental development. Improving intellectual performance—achievement—is a topic that invariably attracts their attention. The skilled contemporary teacher recognizes that physical, social, and emotional forces influence performance, but any theory that focuses on mental development is especially intriguing.

Piaget and Bruner offer insights into cognitive growth at different ages, and, directly or indirectly, offer accompanying insights into content and techniques. If these essentially similar theorists provide sound data—and research continues to support their ideas—then educational implications derived from their beliefs promise much for the future.

Summary

- Piaget's theory is a stage invariant, but not an age invariant, explanation of cognitive growth.

- Cognitive structures and mental operations are essential Piagetian concepts.

- The functional invariants—organization and adaptation—act to form new structures and expand those already existing.

- Piaget believes that cognitive growth proceeds through four developmental periods: sensorimotor, preoperational, concrete operations, and formal operations.

- Each period has certain characteristics that have important educational implications.

- Jerome Bruner's ideas approximate Piaget's, but he believes that his emphasis upon cultural influences on cognitive development is a major distinction.

- MACOS—an attempt to translate theory into practice—has caused considerable furor.

Suggested Readings

Piaget (Secondary Sources)

NOTE: Piaget's work is difficult to read and understand. The novice reader is urged to begin with secondary sources.

Flavell, John. *The Developmental Psychology of Jean Piaget.* New York: Van Nostrand, 1963.

Ginsburg, Herbert and Sylvia Opper. *Piaget's Theory of Intellectual Development.* Englewood Cliffs, N.J.: Prentice-Hall, 1969.

Phillips, John. *The Origins of Intellect: Piaget's Theory.* San Francisco: Freeman, 1969.

Piaget (Primary Sources)

Piaget, Jean. *The Origins of Intelligence in Children.* New York: International Universities Press, 1952. (This book may well be included as a classic in the psychological literature.)

Piaget, Jean and Barbel Inhelder. *The Psychology of the Child.* New York: Basic Books, 1969.

Bruner

Bruner, Jerome. *The Process of Education.* Cambridge, Mass.: Harvard University Press, 1960.

Bruner, Jerome. *Toward a Theory of Instruction.* Cambridge, Mass.: Harvard University Press, 1966.

Bruner, Jerome. *The Relevance of Education.* New York: Norton, 1971.

5

Personality: Theories, Characteristics, Problems

Introduction

There are three basic components of teaching success: knowledge of content, knowledge of pupils, and instructional skill. This and the preceding chapter stress the importance of knowing pupils— not only knowing them by name, but knowing who and what they

156

are. Chapter 3 opened with the words "Children are complex" and then presented many cognitive complexities. This chapter discusses the importance of the pupil's uniqueness—that is, personality complexities—to teaching and learning. Teachers must comprehend the general principles of the development, organization, and expression of personality while realizing that a pupil's outstanding characteristic is individuality (Allport, 1961, pg. 4).

Knowing pupils aids teaching and learning and alerts teachers to problems that they might otherwise ignore. Current educational policy dictates keeping problem pupils in the regular classroom as long as possible, so understanding personality difficulties is necessary. But teachers should never overestimate their competence—they are not therapists. There is a time for the classroom teacher to work with students; there is also a time to refer troubled students for more expert assistance. A wise teacher never forgets the distinction.

A sympathetic view of personality development and adjustment also helps pupils to mature. Allport suggests that there are several criteria of maturity (1961, pp. 283–296).

1. There is an extension of the sense of self that grows with experience until the welfare of others becomes as important as one's own. Schools should encourage students to accept the responsibility of their actions and to consider how their actions affect others. Talbot (1976) gives the example of youngsters in a Chinese kindergarten: their coats button in the back so that each child has to button another's coat. Responsibility towards others comes early with such experience.
2. The mature personality is capable of intimacy and compassion; that is, the youth or adult possesses a capacity for love and also a respect for the worth and dignity of others.
3. Emotional security characterizes the mature personality. There is a growing ability to tolerate frustration and to express convictions and feelings with consideration for others, that is, without overreacting.
4. Mature personalities are realistic in their judgments of people and situations; as Allport notes, they are in touch with the real world.
5. Mature personalities know themselves—they possess self-insight and their judgment of self is shared by others.
6. Finally, mature personalities have a clear comprehension of life's purpose—they develop a philosophy of life.

Although these criteria characterize the mature personality, they provide objectives for teachers in their work with pupils. But teachers can know pupils and help them toward maturity only if they understand the theories, the data, and the development of personality.

Gordon W. Allport

HARVARD UNIVERSITY NEWS OFFICE

What is meant by personality? Although there are no completely satisfactory definitions, some have received wide acceptance. For example, Allport states that personality is the dynamic organization within the individual of those psychosocial systems that determine characteristic behavior and thought. Allport emphasizes the integration of physical and mental systems (habits, traits) that produce *a particular* individual. A pupil is not a collection of isolated traits.

Guilford similarly defines personality as an individual's unique pattern of traits (1959, pg. 5). By trait Guilford means any distinguishable, relatively enduring way in which one individual differs from others. He then groups traits into the following classes or modalities:

1. *Interest* means a consistent tendency to be attracted to certain activities. Some youngsters are interested in anything musical, others in anything athletic.
2. *Attitude* means a tendency to favor, or not, some social object, event, or activity. Many attitudes are acquired early in life and are difficult to break. For example, racial and religious attitudes usually reflect parental views and are deeply embedded in an individual's personality.
3. *Needs* are consistent efforts to acquire certain conditions or statuses: food, water, sex, success, power. If you can determine what students' needs are, and if you can weave them throughout schoolwork, students will be highly motivated.
4. *Temperament* means a tendency to react in a certain manner, which is often what is meant by personality. *Moody, pleasant, happy, restless* are adjectives often used to describe an individual.
5. *Aptitude* refers to the tendency to perform at a certain level. Some youngsters are "good in" music or sports—they have an aptitude for these activities. A human characteristic is to like what you do well, so aptitudes affect other personality dimensions, such as attitudes, interests, and temperament.
6. *Morphology* refers to body structure. There is a lingering belief that body structures reveal much about personality: fat and jolly, thin and irritable. Everyone is body-conscious and acts accordingly; teenagers are especially aware of every blemish and every extra pound. A positive or negative body image strongly influences all phases of personality. You should be extremely alert to those youngsters who are excessively sensitive about their bodies; they may be difficult to work with because of some real or imagined impediment, and they require perceptive understanding during this period.
7. *Physiology* refers to the basic bodily functions. A malfunction, such as a chemical or hormonal imbalance, has a decided effect on personality.

Guilford, like Allport, stresses the *integration* of traits when he discusses the individual's pattern of traits. His analysis provides helpful insights into pupils' personalities. For example, examining Figure 5.1 carefully, you can see that an adolescent's feelings about an awkward body could cause loss of interest in school, belligerence, or a need for security. Keep Guilford's model in mind as you continue to read. As you study some representative theories and analyze certain personality dimensions, which result in adjustment or problems, refer to Guilford. What are the traits that seem to dominate a particular grade or age? Do they explain the person-

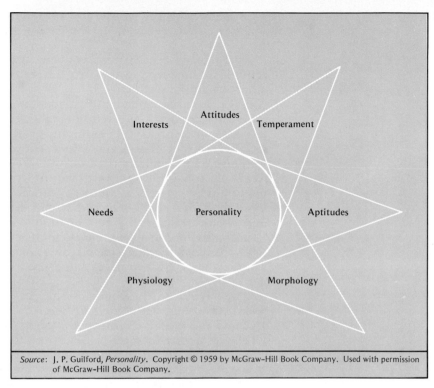

Figure 5.1 Guilford's Modalities of Traits

ality characteristics of the theorists? His work remains a good guide to a complicated topic.

Some representative theories

Personality theories are numerous and represent different interpretations of human nature. For example, psychoanalytic theory accentuates unconscious thoughts, motives, and impulses; learning theory emphasizes stimuli, responses, and reinforcement; humanistic theory underscores the humanity of the personality. Each theory has proponents whose knowledge and perceptions are helpful. Erik Erikson is today one of the leading spokesmen of psychoanalytic theory; Albert Bandura's interpretation of social learning theory has wide current appeal; Abraham Maslow and Carl Rogers are recognized interpreters of the humanistic theory.

After studying these theories, you may believe that one is superior, that it affords you the knowledge about personality that you need. Others may believe that no one theory is adequate for understanding students' classroom behavior and that combining elements from each is most fruitful. Whatever your decision, understand them all. They offer penetrating insights into one or more aspects of personality that will aid you in your work with pupils.

ERIKSON AND THE STAGES OF PSYCHOSOCIAL DEVELOPMENT

Background

The views of Erik Erikson on the search for identity have today become common knowledge. Born in Frankfurt, Germany, in 1902, Erikson soon displayed artistic talent. His settling in Vienna and meeting with Freud led to an interest in psychoanalytic theory and to training with Anna Freud. He also was trained and certified as a Montessori teacher. He came to America in 1933 and was one of the first child analysts in Boston. He has taught at Harvard, Yale and the University of California, Berkeley, and was one of the founders of the Austin Riggs Center in Stockbridge, Massachusetts, a private residential treatment center for disturbed youth.

His field work with American Indian tribes and his treatment of World War II veterans caused Erikson to realize that many emotional problems were due to "identity confusion." He thus expanded Freud's *psychosexual* stages by postulating *psychosocial* stages of development during which the individual has to establish changing concepts of self and reality. Erikson's work is particularly attractive since he emphasizes that each developmental stage has positive as well as negative features (Elkind, 1970).

Rationale for the system

Erikson states that personality emerges from inner and outer conflicts, resulting in a greater sense of inner unity, better judgment, and a more realistic sense of self. These criteria gradually appear as the individual progresses through life's stages and displays a readiness to mature as a result of interacting with a widening circle of persons and experiences. Personality development occurs in eight sequential stages. Each stage contains a crisis (the conflict mentioned above): a period of increased vulnerability and heightened potential and, thus, of possible maladjustment or increased strength.

In his famous *Childhood and Society* (1950), Erikson states that there are two basic assumptions underlying his eight stages:

1. The human personality develops according to the growing person's ability to interact with the environment.
2. Society invites this interaction and attempts to encourage and safeguard the successive appearance of the stages.

Erik H. Erikson

HARVARD UNIVERSITY NEWS OFFICE

Elkind (1970) states that there is a basic theme in Erikson's writings: individuals encounter crises that unify and provide future direction for their activities. Since there are eight stages of life, there are also eight psychosocial crises. These are outlined in Table 5.1.

TABLE 5.1

Erikson's Eight Stages — Crises, Strengths, Influences

Age (years)	Stage	Psychosocial Crisis	Psychosocial Strength	Environmental Influence
1	Infancy	Trust vs. mistrust	Hope	Maternal
2–3	Early childhood	Autonomy vs. shame, doubt	Willpower	Both parents or adult substitutes
4–5	Preschool, nursery	Initiative vs. guilt	Purpose	Parents, family, friends
6–11	Middle childhood	Industry vs. inferiority	Competence	School
12–18	Adolescence	Identity vs. identity confusion	Fidelity	Peers
18–35	Young adulthood	Intimacy vs. isolation	Love	Partners: spouse/lover friends
35–65	Middle age	Generativity vs. stagnation	Care	Family society
over 65	Old age	Ego integrity vs. despair	Wisdom	Mankind

The eight stages

Each of the eight stages represents new abilities, new challenges, and new strengths.

1. *Trust versus mistrust (first year).* Erikson believes that a healthy personality requires a sense of trust, toward one's self and the world, which develops during the first year. Trust requires both physical and psychological comfort. As Erikson notes (1968, pg. 103), an infant's sense of trust arises from the quality of the maternal relationship, not merely from adequate food and physical care. If maternal care is cold and rejecting, mistrust arises and affects all later development. Basic to a sense of trust is hope, which Erikson defines as a belief in the ability to succeed.

2. *Autonomy versus shame, doubt (2–3 years).* During this stage children become mobile and acquire a sense of control of their behavior. They differentiate their world into "I", "you", "mine". If parents accept children's need to attain mastery over the environment, a sense of autonomy develops. If parents are too restrictive, or too critical of inevitable mistakes and accidents, children lose that sense of control and acquire a sense of shame and doubt.

Basic to a sense of autonomy is willpower, which Erikson believes comes from increasing self-control without loss of self-esteem. It is a difficult period for parents: excessive restriction destroys autonomy; excessive freedom can be dangerous. The only solution is to search for a happy balance between the two extremes.

3. *Initiative versus guilt (4–5 years).* Erikson notes that children now realize who they are—they have a lively imagination, they are mobile, they have a good grasp of language. Now their world challenges them to master new tasks, such as dressing, keeping clean, caring for a pet. Parents who encourage children to do things—to play, to help in the home—encourage a sense of initiative; if parents scoff at children's ideas and efforts, a sense of guilt emerges. Purpose is basic to a sense of initiative, since it both motivates children and prepares them for adult tasks.

4. *Industry versus inferiority (6–11 years).* During these school years, children are ready to learn quickly, to plan, and to make things—they possess what Erikson terms a sense of industry. Parents and teachers who discourage children's activities may produce a sense of inferiority in them. Erikson states that if children despair of their skills and their status with their peers, they easily acquire a sense of inadequacy. Development is disrupted if parents have not prepared children for school, or if school fails to sustain the promise of earlier stages (Erikson, 1950, pg. 260). Elkind (1970), however, believes that a child whose sense of industry is frustrated at home may recapture it at school through the efforts of

dedicated and committed teachers. Now the child feels industrious or inferior not only because of parents but also because of other adults. Basic to a sense of industry is competence, that is, achieving a feeling of mastery over the environment.

5. *Identity versus identity confusion (12–18 years).* Adolescents, faced with heightened sexual drives and uncertainties about future adult roles, often become preoccupied with what and how they appear to others as compared to their beliefs about who and what they are. This search for self either culminates in a sense of identity or confusion about who they are. Elkind (1970) believes that adolescents must integrate into a meaningful whole all those roles that they have learned: son, daughter, student, athlete, friend. If

they are successful, adolescents acquire a sense of psychosocial identity; if they are unsuccessful, they remain uncertain as to who they are. Basic to a sense of identity is fidelity, that is, the search for people and ideas to have faith in.

6. *Intimacy versus isolation (18–35 years).* Erikson believes that a sense of intimacy goes beyond the sexual; it is also the capacity to develop a true and mutual psychosocial intimacy with friends, the ability to care for others without fearing a loss of self-identity. If the young adult fails to acquire a sense of intimacy with others, a sense of isolation may appear. Basic to a sense of intimacy is love, by which Erikson means mutual devotion or, as he aptly phrases it, "we are what we love" (1968, pg. 138).

7. *Generativity versus stagnation (35–65 years).* During middle age, individuals think about the future of both society and their own children. Erikson defines it as the concern for establishing and guiding the next generation. If a sense of generativity (similar to productivity and creativity) is lacking, individuals may stagnate, suffering from morbid self-concern. Basic to a sense of generativity

166

is care, which means that individuals assume responsibility for the well-being of the next generation.

8. *Integrity versus despair (over 65 years).* The person who can gaze on his or her life with satisfaction and acceptance of its triumphs and disappointments has achieved a sense of integrity. There is no despair over age, failure, and missed opportunities. Basic to a sense of integrity is wisdom, a detached yet active concern with life and its meaning.

Erikson emphasizes that personality is influenced not only by the individual but also by parents and society. There are strengths and weaknesses in each stage and an individual can overcome the weaknesses of one stage by the strengths of another (Elkind, 1970). The healthy personality masters the environment, has an integrated personality, and is realistic about self and world. Erikson's insights are invaluable for teachers when they determine the psychosocial strength appropriate to the student's age. By encouraging competence and by providing fidelity, teachers can advance the healthy personality, while also facilitating learning.

SOCIAL LEARNING THEORY

Background

Albert Bandura, one of the chief architects of social learning theory, has stressed the potent influence of modeling on personality development. In a famous statement on social learning theory, *Social Learning and Personality Development* (1963), Bandura and Walters note that there is considerable evidence that learning occurs through observing others even when the observer does not reproduce the model's responses during acquisition and therefore receives no reinforcement.

Social learning theory has particular classroom relevance. Bandura and Walters note that children do not do what adults tell them to do but rather what they see adults do. Teacher behavior thus can be a significant cause of behavior. The authors also believe that parents and teachers may become less influential models as television becomes more influential. The importance of models is seen in the authors' interpretation of what happens as a result of observing others.

1. The observer may acquire new responses.
2. Observation of models may strengthen or weaken existing responses.
3. Observation of a model may cause the reappearance of responses that were apparently forgotten.

If pupils witness undesirable behavior, which is either rewarded or goes unpunished, undesirable pupil behavior may result; the reverse is also true. Classroom implications are apparent:

positive, consistent teacher behavior is critical for a healthy classroom atmosphere. To understand the power of modeling, study the pictures shown on page 169 carefully.

Bandura, Ross, and Ross (1963) studied the effects of live models, filmed human aggression, and filmed cartoon aggression on preschool children's aggressive behavior. The filmed human aggression portrayed adult models displaying aggression toward an inflated doll; the filmed cartoon aggression portrayed a cartoon character displaying the same behavior as the humans; the live models displayed the identical aggression as the others. Later all the children exhibited significantly more aggression than youngsters in a control group. Also, filmed models were as effective as

An Explanation of Modeling

Bandura (1972) describes modeling behavior as one person observing another's behavior and acquiring that behavior in representational form without simultaneously performing the responses. There are four processes involved:

1. *Attention.* Mere exposure to a model does not insure acquisition of behavior. An observer must attend to and recognize the distinctive features of the model's response. The modeling conditions also must incorporate the features previously mentioned, such as attractiveness in the model and reinforcement of the model's behavior.
2. *Retention.* To reproduce the desired behavior implies that a person symbolically retains the observed behavior. Bandura believes that "symbolic coding" helps to explain lengthy retention of observed behavior. For example, the observer codes, classifies, and reorganizes the model's responses into personally meaningful units, thus aiding retention.
3. *Motor reproduction processes.* Bandura

believes that symbolic coding produces internal models of the environment that guide the observer's future behavior. The cognitive guidance of behavior is crucial for Bandura because it explains how modeled activities are acquired without performance. But cognitive activity is not autonomous—its nature and occurrence are controlled by stimulus and reinforcement.
4. *Motivational and reinforcement processes.* Although an observer acquires and retains the ability to perform modeled behavior, there will be no overt performance unless conditions are favorable. For example, if reinforcement previously accompanied similar behavior, the individual tends to repeat it. But vicarious reinforcement (observing a model reinforced) and self-reinforcement (satisfaction with one's own behavior) are powerful, human reinforcers.

Without any one of these four processes, it is unlikely that modeling will occur (Bandura, 1972, pg. 50).

Source: Bandura, D. Ross, and S. A. Ross, "Imitation of Film-Mediated Aggressive Models," *Journal of Abnormal Social Psychology,* 1963, 66:8. Copyright (1963) by the American Psychological Association. Reprinted by permission.

The Power of Modeling

live models in transmitting aggression. Research suggests that prestigious, powerful, competent models are more readily imitated than models who lack these qualities (Bandura and Walters, 1963).

Personality

Social learning theorists claim that children acquire response patterns as just described. Thus, children coming from similar social and cultural backgrounds display similar behavior, which remains relatively constant during the early years. Social learning theorists would predict changes in early behavior only if there were an abrupt change in social training (Bandura and Walters, 1963, pg. 25).

Although genetic capacity establishes physical and mental boundaries, environmental influence can significantly alter even the more abstract personality characteristics, such as intelligence. The effect of experiences is highly dependent on the social models and the reinforcement patterns adopted by parents and teachers. For example, a child with below-average intelligence will receive less punishment from lower-class than from professional parents (Bandura and Walters, 1963, pg. 28). The authors believe that all social behavior develops from observing models, reinforcement patterns, and the training methods used to develop and modify social behavior. The classroom implications of social learning theory are enormous. Teachers, as significant adults, are powerful models and influence pupil behavior by the way they treat youngsters and by the kinds of behavior they reward—a sobering thought.

THE HUMANISTS

Rebelling against the Freudian emphasis of abnormality and the behaviorist emphasis on objectivity, a group of psychologists led by Abraham Maslow have insisted upon studying normal men and women. Their work is called humanistic or "third force" psychology. In a popular book, *Motivation and Personality* (1970), Maslow states that he would have preferred calling it *High Ceilings for Human Nature* to stress our "higher nature," that is, our capacity to rise above the abnormal, the mechanical, and the animalistic.

A good example of Maslow's thinking is his analysis of self-actualization, which he describes as the full use and exploitation of talents, capacities, and potentialities—that is, people fulfilling themselves (1970, pg. 150). Personality, then, becomes the growth toward self-actualization. Self-actualization is growth because it does not occur in young people; they have not achieved identity, have not formulated their system of values, have not become sufficiently realistic. They are growing toward this goal as they satisfy their basic needs.

Characteristics of self-actualization

A useful method for analyzing Maslow's meaning of the mature personality is to examine his self-actualization concept which has several important characteristics.

1. An accurate perception of reality is the ability to detect honesty and dishonesty and to judge people fairly. The immature, or disturbed, personality distorts perception so that accurate judgments about people and events are impossible. Doubt, uncertainty, and the unknown do not daunt the healthy personality; rather, they become challenges that stimulate personal growth.
2. Acceptance of self and others produces feelings of personal security and a corresponding lack of shame, guilt, and anxiety. The healthy personality accepts the weaknesses and frailties of human nature, as well as its strengths and motives; the mature personality accepts human nature as it is.
3. Spontaneity and interest in problems outside of the self mark the healthy personality. These characteristics enable such individ-

Abraham Maslow

BRANDEIS UNIVERSITY NEWS OFFICE

uals to further personal growth by their natural interest in things and people around them.

4. A sense of autonomy, which permits relative independence from the environment for personal satisfaction, seems to be a consistent characteristic of the self-actualized person. This independence yields a certain stability, almost stoicism, before life's negative side—ill health, financial reverses, loss of loved ones.

5. Finally, self-actualized people appreciate life; they refuse to become bored. Perhaps this freshness is due to their unerring sense of what is right and their unfailing sense of humor.

These are the characteristics that identify the healthy personality and, as Maslow says (1970, pg. xxii), "Psychological health not only feels good subjectively but it is also correct, true, real."

Carl Rogers

Another leading figure in the humanistic movement is Carl Rogers, who has stated that he shares with Maslow and others the belief that there are three main emphases in American psychology: behaviorism, psychoanalysis, and growth or self-actualization. Rogers argues that our intellect can totally absorb people thereby denigrating their feelings. But in life, in therapy, in relationships with the opposite sex, in marriage, and in parent-child relationships, feelings are as important as intellect (Rogers, 1973, pg. 384).

He further states (1974, pg. 118) that his experiences have underscored the reality and significance of human choice—humans are partly their own architects. But believing in humanism and human choice is not to abdicate responsibility. Rather, responsibility increases because personal and social change are based on human nature, not on conditioning. Belief in humanistic psychology produces a deeply democratic political philosophy, not management by an elite; thus, hard, realistic decisions rest on humanism. Ultimately a new person will emerge—sensitive, self-directing, considerate, and humanistic rather than technological.

Such individuals are always motivated, always seeking. Consequently, the one central source of energy in humans is a function of the whole person and not of some part, such as the intellect. This seeking is a tendency toward self-actualization, toward fulfillment.

> Whether we are speaking of this sea plant or an oak tree, of an earthworm or a great night-flying moth, of an ape or a man, we will do well, I believe, to recognize that life is an active process, not a passive one. (Carl Rogers, 1963, pg. 3)

What is personality?

Rogers has elaborated several propositions that he uses to explain personality (1951, pp. 480–533). For example, individuals exist in a changing world of which they are the center and which they alone truly know. They then react to this world as they perceive it and this personal, perceptual world becomes reality. People react to their world, not as others see it, but as they see it. Humanistic psychologists emphasize this point because to understand others it

is necessary to attempt to see the world as they see it. Also, each individual, striving for self-actualization, reacts as a whole person: intellect, feelings, and body are gradually differentiated into the self as part of the perceptual field. Human development results in part of the private world becoming "me" as a result of my interactions with my environment—objects, events, and people.

Consequently, an individual either organizes experiences into a

Rogers and Learning

Discussing learning, Rogers notes that there are three teacher characteristics that facilitate learning: "realness" in the teacher, accepting and trusting the learner, and a sensitive understanding of the learner (1969). He considers realness, or genuineness, as the most important. When teachers are natural, or real, with students they become more effective, more trusting and accepting of students, and more sensitive to their needs.

These characteristics help teachers to use certain principles that Rogers sees as basic to classroom learning.

1. Pupils have a natural potential for learning; they are curious and anxious to learn about their world. The teacher's task is to provide the conditions that release this desire to learn.

2. Significant learning occurs when subject matter is relevant to students. Learning proceeds more easily if pupils perceive it as nonthreatening and actually aiding their self-concepts.
3. Self-initiated learning by doing is most lasting. Such learning involves the whole student—body, mind, and emotions.
4. Self-criticism and self-evaluation enhance independence, creativity, and self-reliance.

Rogers believes that the most socially useful learning is recognizing that there is a *process* of learning. Pupils who acquire this ability remain open to experiences and comfortably accept the necessity of change.

Behavior and Self

relationship with the self, ignores experiences because they are unrelated to the self, or distorts experiences because they are inconsistent with the self. Finally, each individual adapts behavior that is consistent with the self. Rogers believes that the changes resulting from his personality theory reflect the most important learning of our lives—the learning of self.

Erikson, Bandura, and Maslow/Rogers represent the three major influences in personality theory that Rogers mentioned: neo-psychoanalytic, behavioristic, and humanistic. No one theory holds all the truths, but each contains insights into the human personality that enables you to work more productively with students.

Discussion Questions

1. What criteria would you use to analyze personality? Do your criteria differ from Guilford's, Allport's? How? Defend your answers.

2. Are Erikson's eight stages meaningful for you? Why? Consider your age and stage. Are your crises, strengths, and influences similar to Erikson's? If not, why? Does your answer help you to understand yourself?

3. Has anyone ever influenced you so that you changed your behavior? Who? Under what circumstances? Does it still happen? How do your answers verify, or challenge, social learning theory?

4. What is the core of humanistic psychology? Does it apply to you? How? Can you describe your striving for self-actualization?

5. Rogers's views on learning have definite classroom application. Personal relevance, freedom, and self-evaluation suggest a special classroom atmosphere. Would you be happy in such a classroom? Could you function effectively? (Your answer does not imply a value judgment; however, it demands a recognition of your personality. Some personalities would thrive in a Rogerian classroom; others would find it chaotic. Think about your answer. It may be one of the most important decisions that you make as a teacher.)

Some dimensions of personality

Personality theories attempt to explain how and why people react and adjust as they do. Guilford (1959, pg. 53) states that traits are inferred from behavior, but the traits are properties of a person. Consequently, individuals are characterized by their outstanding traits—gentle, belligerent, nervous, bright, cheerful. Among the more important and widely studied characteristics are aggression, dependency, locus of control, and anxiety.

AGGRESSION

Aggression is any behavior that results in the injury or destruction of an animal, human, or inanimate object (Feshbach, 1970, pg. 161). It may be unintentional (accidental) or intentional (deliberate). Developmental changes in aggression and techniques of controlling it are pertinent topics for teachers because pupils' interactions with peers and authority are frequently the occasion for violence.

Three explanations

Each of the theorists previously discussed offers an explanation of aggression.

1. Freud originally proposed that there were two basic instincts—life and death. The death instinct may be directed either externally or internally. When it is directed externally, the intent is to destroy others. Erikson, while accepting classical Freudian theory, has modified it to include cultural demands as well as instinctual drives.

ARLINGTON MASS. ADVOCATE

2. Applying social learning principles, Bandura (1973) does not believe that people are driven by inner forces or buffeted helplessly by the environment. Behavior is caused by a continuous interaction between the individual and the controlling conditions. Consequently, a culture can produce highly aggressive individuals by rewarding aggression and providing attractive aggressive models.

3. Maslow, basing his views on the principle of striving for self-actualization, believes that humans are capable of hostility and destruction when they feel insecure, thwarted, or threatened. When conditions favor growth, and love and security are furnished, less destruction is found. Maslow, then, interprets aggression as reactive and defensive.

Educational implications

Regardless of cause, aggression, with its painful and injurious results, can create classroom problems that interfere with teaching and learning. Redl (1969) believes that there are three sources of classroom aggression: (1) angers unexpressed at home surfacing at school; (2) internal causes—fantasies, internal turmoil—suddenly erupting; and (3) the classroom itself—teacher, pupils, or frustration with some subject—triggering an explosion.

Redl declares that teachers should know which source generates

Is Aggression Worth the Trouble?

How aggressive are humans? Television, papers, and magazines all stress the growing violence in modern societies. International terrorism is on the rise. But do these widely publicized events mean that the proportions of individuals involved is increasing? Conflicting testimony is found in a study by Thomas Moriarty that suggests we may be a nation of willing victims (1975). Studying daily frustrations, insults, and affronts, Moriarty concludes that most people have adopted a passive attitude for coping with difficulty.

In one study, he asked male college students to take a complicated test of verbal ability. He tested 2 people simultaneously, one of whom was an accomplice who played rock music at top volume. The accomplice was instructed to discontinue the music only at the third request. Of the 20 subjects *16 made no request at all,* but when interviewed, all the subjects were angry at the person playing the music.

In another study, Moriarty had 2 of his accomplices talk loudly in a public library, disturbing 40 people, only one of whom asked them to stop. Under similar conditions in a cinema, 14 of 40 people asked the accomplices to be quiet. In another setting, Moriarty had his accomplice leave a room while a subject came in to take a test. The accomplice then returned and asked the subject if he had found a ring. The subject said no, but the accomplice persisted, finally asking the subject to empty his pockets. *Not one of 10* male subjects refused. Moriarty then conducted the identical experiment at Grand Central Station, using the telephone booths. Of the 20 males, 16 emptied their pockets on request.

Is passivity, rather than aggression, becoming a way of life? Moriarty thinks current social conditions lead people to follow the course of least resistance. The result is a nation of willing victims.

a particular outburst because different causes require different treatments. Usually causes are uncertain, but experience brings diagnostic skill so that teachers can frequently distinguish the home or classroom as the source.

What can teachers do to cope with classroom aggression? Redl suggests several possibilities.

1. *Help youngsters to stop before trouble erupts.* Knowing when to interrupt behavior is a valuable asset—too soon makes a teacher appear fussy, too late may produce an uproar. If a youngster is not going to stop voluntarily, then a teacher should act decisively.

2. *Use "signal interference."* A skillful teacher instantly notices the signs that lead to trouble: fidgeting in one youngster, rigidity in another. New teachers should cultivate this skill, this ability to detect the signals that foretell aggression. Watch youngsters; discover those mannerisms that signal difficulty. Whatever the time, whatever the exertion, the results will make your efforts worthwhile.

3. *Avoid the "tribal dance," which usually involves a dare.* Trouble starts; the teacher acts; the pupil reacts to protect status. The tribal dance has started—the pupil dares the teacher to do something and the teacher must accept the dare or retreat and lose status. Teachers must act quickly to avoid the tribal dance either by ignoring the behavior or by instantly suppressing it, and by knowing those pupils who are susceptible to the ritual. Redl asserts that the truly tough youngster is not usually susceptible—they are not forced to prove their courage. The lesson here is that you should know the danger signals and not put yourself in an impossible situation.

4. *Watch for subsurface effects.* While a pupil may do what you want, there are usually side effects, and the wise teacher will reach a disciplined youngster to prevent feelings of hostility and isolation. Redl states that while we may have to live with aggression, we should not breed it by exposing normal youngsters to classroom experiences that produce frustration.

5. *Finally, recognize your own aggression.* While your hostility may be justified, your maturity and your professional obligation demand that your behavior reduce classroom tension and lessen the opportunities for pupil aggression.

DEPENDENCY

Background

Dependency is behavior that maintains contact between a person (usually a child) and other individuals so that the child receives attention and support from others (Maccoby and Masters, 1970, pg. 75). It is a natural childish reaction, but when it continues into adolescence and adulthood, dependency can become a problem. A child's social behavior arises from its early relationship with the mother. The mother is the initial source of pleasure and pain, and a delicate conflict emerges between clinging and rejecting. Whether a child learns to cope with life's problems may rest on the mother's resolution of the clinging-rejecting conflict.

When does dependency become a problem? To seek help needlessly is a sign of excessively dependent behavior. An example is the child who constantly seeks adult assistance and shows no initiative. Another example is the excessive desire to remain close to an adult. Children constantly seeking attention, approval, and reassurance also show signs of dependency problems. Independence becomes an important goal for most children; almost as soon as they learn to seek help, they begin to learn to manage without it (Herbert, 1974).

Rheingold and Eckerman (1970) describe the striving for independence by noting that infants usually separate themselves from mothers as soon as possible. They creep, later walk away from the

mother, then explore another room, go to the yard, play, go to school; eventually they may leave home for college, or work, marry, and establish their own home. The authors believe that infant separation from the mother is crucial psychologically because even the most attentive and indulgent mother is limited. Children need to explore their environment to instill self-confidence. But the separation should be voluntary. Youngsters enjoy separation from their mothers only when they know they can return anytime.

Dependency and maturity

How do youngsters acquire the independence described by Rheingold and Eckerman? Lois Murphy (1962) believes independence develops by three processes that teachers can encourage:

1. Cognitive growth, which permits the child to encounter and understand new situations.
2. Learning many skills, which helps the child to feel confident in new situations.
3. Learning to reject some novel aspects so as not to be overwhelmed by a new situation.

Dependency has several correlates that help to explain its appearance, consistency, and intensity. A child's sex is closely related to dependency. Most societies reward female dependency, while discouraging it in males. Female independence and aggression cause parental concern, often culminating in strained relations between the girl and her parents. The reverse is true for boys—many fathers reject dependent sons. The tough, assertive male is desired by most parents.

These attitudes reflect cultural biases, which have rigidly defined sex-role characteristics. Parents usually react negatively when a boy plays with dolls, and positively when he plays with cars, balls, or sports equipment. While rigid sex role characteristics are dissolving, the process is agonizingly slow. More girls are playing Little League

Teachers, Parents, and Dependency

Fritz Redl and William Wattenberg, in *Mental Hygiene in Teaching* (1959), state that while younger children are more dependent than older youngsters, some parents and teachers like and encourage dependency. It is a good warning and supports the earlier contention that adults, especially mothers, must resolve the clinging-rejecting conflict.

As youngsters grow, they show increasing signs of independence; by the sixth and seventh grade they become more of a puzzle. The authors believe that these youngsters face two tasks: eliminating childish patterns and their dependence on adult values. They are preparing themselves for adolescent changes and group values. Adults must now develop new relationships with these youths since the pleasant ties of dependency are dissolving.

It could be a hard time for adults. No longer are they children's heroes, and if a parent or teacher is to remain influential he or she must establish a new and different rapport. The authors state that friendship between "almost equals" will form a new bond of mutual respect and responsibility.

Adolescents expect and appreciate advice that is offered with dignity and regard for their near-adult status.

Some youngsters cannot achieve independence, and their schoolwork is designed to win and hold the favor of teachers. The authors consider this to be a bribe and an undesirable personality trait that ultimately leads to avoiding responsibility and a willingness to exchange unthinking obedience for affection. It is a difficult and delicate problem for teachers. Rejection may only increase the insecurity that produced this dependency, but encouragement of the behavior is equally incorrect. The authors suggest that teachers meet reasonable requests while expressing confidence in the student's ability. There will also be occasions when a teacher should tell a dependent student that other pupils also deserve attention.

Teachers walk a fine line with these pupils. They often feel frustrated, but their conscientious efforts are worthwhile since school may be a student's final opportunity to be with a sensitive, concerned adult.

baseball and youth hockey, although with grudging acceptance. Federal regulations are forcing schools and colleges to give greater recognition to female athletic participation. But there is not even grudging acceptance of passive, dependent male behavior.

Persistence of Dependency

Sex role characteristics that conform to society's expectations persist. Maccoby and Masters (1970) note that the relation between childhood and adult dependency reflects cultural expectancies and sex role standards. Prediction is much better for women than for men. For example, passive, dependent girls who lacked independence in middle and late childhood were dependent adults who avoided stress and risks, and chose secure jobs. An interesting finding is that girls independent in childhood and adolescence became dependent upon women friends as adults. The authors believe that passivity and independence are good predictors of adult characteristics. The predictions are poor for men: dependency is more stable between childhood and adolescence than between adolescence and adulthood, a finding consistent with our discussion. Society has constantly discouraged male dependent behavior, and intense adolescent peer pressure could well explain this finding.

LOCUS OF CONTROL

Do you feel that college is a bore? Was that poor mark last semester because the instructor disliked you? Are your good marks this semester due to luck? If you answered "yes" to these questions, you may be an "external," that is, you believe that you have little control over the outcome of your actions—the locus of control is outside you. If you answered "no," you may be an "internal," that is, you believe that you can control what happens to you—the locus of control is within you.

Background

The locus of control concept is usually associated with Julian Rotter (1966, 1971) and E. Jerry Phares (1973). If individuals believe that behavior is rewarded not because of skill but because of luck, they believe in the external control of their actions. If they believe that their behavior deserves success or reward, they believe in the internal control of their actions. Phares states that internal-external (I-E) control of reinforcement is a generalized expectancy that refers to the way that individuals see the connection between their behavior and the occurrence of reward or punishment. People are neither all internal, nor all external, but more or less internal.

Internals seem to have more self-confidence and self-control, work better with others, and have better mental health. Phares notes that internals are more energetic in their efforts to control the environment. For example, internal tuberculosis patients sought more information about their condition, asked more questions, and were more cooperative than externals. Even in prison, internals knew more about the working of the institution and parole. More internals than externals stopped smoking after the surgeon general's report and *did not begin* again.

Source of I-E

Investigation of the roots of I-E have concentrated upon social and family origins. Considerable evidence suggests that lower-class children are external, while children from more affluent, educated background are internal.

Phares (1973) believes that this is only logical since lower-class individuals have little access to power and material goals and have limited social mobility. Rotter (1971) found that middle-class blacks were only slightly more external than middle-class whites, but lower-class blacks were significantly more external than similar whites.

The Family and Locus of Control

The family also strongly influences the I-E continuum. Parental acceptance, encouragement, and support are associated with internals; hostility and rejection produce more externals. Inconsistent parental behavior, that is, uncertainty about appropriate child behavior, also was linked to externals; internal children saw their parents as more consistent in their expectations. Internals and externals seemed to have experienced different child-rearing patterns: internals have parents who encouraged independence; externals have parents who foster dependency, hostility, and aggression.

Locus of control is an important personality variable with significant educational implications. If internal persons are more efficient and better adjusted, then internal is a condition to cultivate. Results from the Coleman Report (1966) showed that among disadvantaged children in the sixth, ninth, and twelfth grades those with high scores on achievement tests were more internal than children with lower scores. Phares states that students learn less when they believe they do not control the occurrence of reinforcement. They do not use past experiences to solve present problems. Consequently, parents and teachers should help youngsters to become more internal; however, specific, effective techniques are still unknown.

FEAR AND ANXIETY

Fear and Its Consequences

Of all personality characteristics none is as potentially crippling as fear. Fear possesses some value—most psychologists agree that fear is essential for self-preservation. Any condition that mobilizes an individual's energies for danger is an asset. But the fear that occurs during an emergency too frequently transfers to other similar conditions where the danger is not as acute and should not be feared. Children easily retreat from any fearful or even challenging

Internal Versus External Control

Rotter's locus of control concept implies that people—adults *and* children—develop an expectancy about the reinforcement of their behavior. Internals believe that their behavior generates reinforcement; externals believe that reinforcement occurs, *not* because of their behavior, but because of luck or fate. An internal locus of control is usually thought to be desirable because of the personality traits associated with internality: lack of anxiety, tolerance, self-confidence, independence, and achievement. Rotter states that internals are more alert to environmental information and more desirous of avoiding failure; externals are supposedly anxious, suspicious, passive, and poor achievers.

From this description internality would seem to be the desired state, and schools should begin to initiate programs to foster internality. While there have been such efforts, cautious criticism suggests externality may not be all bad. It may actually be a realistic way of coping with a hostile environment. Rotter notes that internals sometime overestimate their control, which may produce problems, such as a loss of a sense of psychological security.

Internality, nevertheless, seems to be the more positive condition, especially in schooling. Studies such as Ulrey's (1974) show that improving internality also improves academic work. The author employed a ropes-course technique (teaching youngsters self-sufficiency through camping experiences) that resulted in increased internality that transferred to the classroom.

What should you conclude from the locus of control literature? The evidence seems adequate to warrant your efforts to encourage students to become more internal, while remembering that some externality is not bad. When you reinforce pupils be sure that they know that *their* behavior was responsible for the reinforcement.

predicament, and, unfortunately, a habit of withdrawal, even flight, comes to dominate their reactions. Incompetence marks their behavior; insecurity haunts their inner lives. If these fears are allowed to remain unchecked, the child grows into the adult who is hampered by anxiety, confined by neuroses, and terrified by phobias.

Human beings battle fear all their lives. The early childhood environmental fears become the social insecurity of adolescence, and finally the adult fears about health, job, and death. If adults knew more about childhood fears, how they develop, and how to help children to overcome them, there would be fewer later neuroses.

The classic studies of Jersild and Holmes (1935a, 1935b) found remarkable changes in children's fears at different ages. Under age 7, children fear loud noises, animals, strange persons and objects, and darkness. From 9 to 18, youngsters showed a sharp increase in fear of failure in school and in social relations (Angelino, Dollins, and Mech, 1956).

Many of these fears persist into adult life. Some persevering fears are the fear of animals, bodily harm, darkness, and solitude. These are in addition to the newly acquired fears of sickness, death, financial inadequacy, and many others. Struggling under this burden, some individuals tend to break, and serious problems follow. No one is without fear, but the manner in which children learn to manage their initial hesitations and apprehensions goes far in determining how successfully they shall manage a steadily growing load.

Causes of fear

There are many reasons for the appearance of fear. Children reflect the fears of their parents and those with whom they are closely associated, particularly teachers. Adult fears clearly convey a sense of insecurity about the environment. Fear transfers rapidly by the process of conditioning; that is, nonthreatening aspects of the child's surroundings acquire menacing overtones by association with stimuli that the child has designated as fearful.

Figure 5.2 illustrates the conditioning process. Assuming that some dominant stimulus like a loud noise has aroused a fearul reaction in a child, and that this has happened repeatedly in the presence of one particular doll and during a rainstorm, the youngster develops a fear of both the doll and rain. Admittedly this is an oversimplification but it illustrates the mechanics of conditioning and also affords a clue to the very real possibility of the unknowing transfer of fear.

While the transfer of adult insecurity and failure to recognize fear in children leads to anxieties and uncertainty, there are other sources of fear: school entrance, physical illness, exposure to a constant barrage of sarcasm and ridicule, overprotective parents, and adult example. Always accompanying these potential sources of fear is another: the imagined situation that is not limited by the boundaries of space, time, or objective reality. Children's ability to conjure up terrifying experiences becomes unhealthy if left unchecked because it becomes a way of life, a habit that conceivably can control behavior.

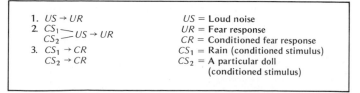

Figure 5.2 The Conditioning Process

Combating fears

To help children avoid unnecessary fear, worry, and anxiety, adults should provide as normal and stable an environment as is both desirable and possible. Children should encounter challenges and learn how to meet anxiety and fear, provided that they have a regular routine and receive sympathy and understanding when and where needed. These conditions are especially pertinent for the classroom.

Jersild and Holmes (1935b) list the following parental methods of meeting children's fears *that are more harmful than helpful.*

1. Ignoring the fear.
2. Ridiculing or punishing the child for the fear.
3. Forcing the child to meet the fear with no attempt to provide reassurance.

Closely related to fear is the phenomenon of anxiety. Exactly where does anxiety become fear? Are there fine lines of distinction between each? To differentiate, the object becomes the distinction between fear and anxiety. Fear has an object; anxiety is fear of a vague object, or of no object at all. Anxiety is a state of apprehension or uneasiness with clear implications for teachers. No one is without anxiety. Yet children are inordinately susceptible to fears and anxiety that well-intentioned but poorly informed adults can intensify. The most effective means an adult can use in combatting fear and anxiety in children is example. If children see that adults are unafraid, they gradually acquire a healthy balance between fear and fearlessness.

If, however, a youngster becomes unnecessarily fearful, parents and teachers should utilize a reconditioning process that would include the following steps:

Combating Fear

1. Identify the nature of the fear.
2. Help the child to realize intellectually that this particular fear or anxiety is groundless. This will not remove the fear but may prevent its passing into the unconscious, ready to reappear when tension or conflict arises.
3. Introduce the fear-provoking stimulus, but joined with other pleasurable stimuli. Children often lose a fear of darkness after having seen slides, or home movies, and enjoyable movies at a theater.
4. Gradually allow the youngster to encounter the fear stimulus alone.

Teachers can play an important dual role in healthy emotional development. First, they should recognize unreasonable fear in children and do all that they can to free youngsters from a needless and harmful burden. Second, they should realize that an educational milieu that is emotionally unhealthy is damaging to the learning process and personality development.

Discussion Questions

1. Do you agree with the definition of aggression? Why? Does it explain all aggressive behavior? Is it too limited? too encompassing? Try to devise your own and show where it differs from, and improves, Feshbach's definition.

2. Are we really becoming a nation of willing victims? What does your personal experience tell you? Do you agree that violence is confined to a small percentage of people? If Moriarty is correct, what does his finding foretell for society?

3. Can you add to Redl's suggestions for coping with the aggressive child in school? Are his ideas practical? useful? effective? The tribal dance is a classroom fact. If you either teach or have done student teaching, can you recount a similar experience?

4. Teachers often do not view the dependent student as a problem. Why? What would be your reaction to the student described? Can you offer alternatives to these techniques suggested?

5. Are you predominantly internal or external? Do you consider it an important dimension of your personality? Were you aware of it before you read this section? How does it affect your behavior? Would an external teacher have difficulty in the classroom? Why?

6. Many students are anxious for many reasons: problems, parental pressure, peer relations. Remembering that teachers are not therapists, can you propose other techniques that teachers can employ to combat pupils' fears and anxieties?

Some personality problems

While most children's personalities develop normally, others tread a rocky path. National Institute of Mental Health figures reveal that 1.5 million youngsters under 18 suffer severe emotional problems. About 10 million more experience moderate difficulty. Since treatment of these youngsters includes as much normal activity as possible, including classroom placement, it is important for today's teacher to know the common developmental problems.

LABELING

An immediate dilemma is labeling. The gifted child, the dyslexic child, the neurotic child are all labels quickly tied to a child. Our discussion of the developmental sequence illustrates the vulnerability of children to physical and emotional strain: physical illness or emotional trauma may produce a temporary crisis, but a label is not so temporary. Any label may cause psychological problems because of the tensions and pressures it creates; for example, the label "gifted" may provide academic pressure and strained relations with peers; temporary parental illness may cause a child to appear neurotic. Experts may label a child "brain damaged" or "learning disabled" but only with solid, supporting evidence. Amateur labeling—neurotic, "mental," abnormal, disturbed—is dangerous and may well induce in a child what is actually nonexistent.

But problems exist; teachers should recognize them, and should know when to treat and to refer. You should remember that all children experience problems. It is the rare child who does not display "emotional problems," "psychological difficulties," or "behavior disorders" at some developmental stage. If you recall Havighurst's analysis of developmental stages, there are many opportunities for a child to stumble.

Herbert (1974) states that family and school are the child's most important social representatives during the formative years. They must change a totally dependent, primitive, hedonistic infant into a self-sufficient, sophisticated, and responsible community member—the socialization process. Parents and teachers have expectations of a child's progress and behavior; children become a problem when they do not meet these standards—they are considered to have "problems," "disorders," or to be "maladjusted."

To help distinguish the problem child and avoid labeling, Herbert poses several questions about the child's behavior.

1. Is the behavior suitable for the age, intelligence, and social situation?
2. Is the environment (home, school) making reasonable demands of the child?
3. Is the environment meeting the child's crucial needs?
4. Does the behavior prevent the child from leading a happy life in which to grow, enjoy social relationships, and work and play effectively?

A PROBLEM'S INTENSITY

Answering these questions emphasizes that *intensity*, that is, exaggerated or extreme behavior, is the problem. For example, the aggressive child who causes destruction or the withdrawn child who lacks emotional responses is the one with difficulties. Shepherd and his colleagues (1971) studied 6000 English children from 5 to 15 and reported extreme behavior by age. Tables 5.2 and 5.3 report the results. Note the persistence of certain problems that could have classroom implications: irritability, restlessness, disobedience,

TABLE 5.2
Extreme Behavior in Boys—Ages 5 to 15

YEARS:	5	6	7	8	9	10	11	12	13	14	15
Very destructive	3	2	2	—	2	1	1	1	2	1	2
Fear of animals	3	3	2	1	1	2	2	1	1	1	—
Fear of strangers	2	1	1	1	—	*	*	1	2	*	4
Fear of the dark	9	6	8	8	10	7	6	5	2	2	2
Lying	5	3	5	2	3	3	3	5	4	2	2
Dislike of school	4	5	5	3	5	5	5	6	7	10	4
Stealing	—	1	1	1	1	*	1	1	2	1	—
Irritability	10	7	13	11	12	14	11	14	11	9	16
Food fads	19	20	22	22	22	18	23	19	17	17	16
Fear of other children	1	*	—	—	*	1	1	1	1	*	—
Always hungry	11	10	10	14	16	13	16	19	15	23	39
Small appetite	11	13	17	14	11	10	13	9	7	5	—
Worrying	4	5	5	7	6	5	3	3	5	4	5
Complaining	7	6	8	5	4	3	4	4	3	2	2
Restlessness	23	19	25	21	22	19	20	18	15	17	20
Underactivity	1	2	1	1	1	2	2	4	3	6	2
Jealousy	6	2	4	4	4	5	3	4	2	3	2
Wandering	3	1	2	3	3	3	3	4	4	8	2
Withdrawn	2	2	4	3	3	3	2	3	3	2	7
⌠ Disobedient	17	11	14	12	12	13	13	14	11	12	9
⌡ Always obeys	8	7	7	8	7	6	7	7	9	9	16
Truanting—at all	1	—	1	—	*	2	—	2	1	4	16
Tics	*	1	1	2	1	2	1	2	2	1	2
Mood changes	4	3	3	2	5	3	4	4	2	2	2
Reading difficulty	7	18	21	27	25	17	21	22	13	13	9

Source: M. Shepherd, B. Oppenheim, and S. Mitchell, *Childhood Behavior and Mental Health.* New York: Grune & Stratton, 1971. By permission of Grune & Stratton, Inc.
Note: * = less than 0.5 percent.

reading difficulty. The ages also are informative: restlessness peaks at 7 years, irritability and disobedience during the teen years, while reading difficulties increase during middle childhood and are more prevalent for boys than girls.

What are the major problems for each developmental stage?

INFANCY

When children experience problems it is a common practice to point an accusing finger at the early environment, especially the mother. Early experience may be the culprit, but nurses and mothers know that children, even those from the same family, differ markedly from birth in their reactions. We usually regard personality as learned, but Thomas, Chess, and Birch (1970) have chal-

TABLE 5.3
Extreme Behavior in Girls—Ages 5 to 15

YEARS:	5	6	7	8	9	10	11	12	13	14	15
Very destructive	2	—	1	—	*	*	—	*	—	1	—
Fear of animals	5	5	3	3	3	1	2	2	1	1	7
Fear of strangers	1	*	2	2	*	2	1	1	1	2	—
Fear of the dark	11	5	8	7	8	8	6	5	4	5	4
Lying	2	2	1	1	3	1	3	1	1	3	2
Dislike of school	1	3	2	4	3	2	3	3	5	7	4
Stealing	1	—	—	—	*	—	—	*	—	1	—
Irritability	10	9	9	10	12	10	12	10	11	16	11
Food fads	20	19	20	22	21	23	17	17	15	17	9
Fear of other children	—	*	1	1	*	1	*	1	*	1	—
Always hungry	5	6	6	10	9	10	10	13	15	11	16
Small appetite	21	17	21	18	13	12	12	8	7	8	5
Worrying	5	7	4	4	6	4	7	5	1	4	5
Whining	7	5	5	3	6	2	5	4	3	5	—
Restlessness	20	16	20	16	13	13	13	11	11	10	4
Underactivity	—	2	1	1	2	3	3	4	7	7	5
Jealousy	8	4	5	5	6	3	4	3	3	6	4
Wandering	*	*	—	1	1	*	1	2	1	2	4
Withdrawn	2	1	2	2	3	2	2	3	2	3	7
{ Disobedient	10	10	8	8	11	7	10	10	12	14	14
{ Always obeys	8	7	7	9	9	8	14	11	12	10	12
Truanting—at all	*	1	1	*	1	*	*	1	1	3	4
Tics	1	—	1	1	1	*	—	*	—	1	—
Mood changes	5	2	4	3	5	3	5	5	7	7	14
Reading difficulty	5	7	14	14	10	13	10	11	5	7	4

Source: M. Shepherd, B. Oppenheim, and S. Mitchell, *Childhood Behavior and Mental Health.* New York: Grune & Stratton, 1971. By permission of Grune & Stratton, Inc.
Note * = less than 0.5 percent

lenged this hypothesis. Studying 141 children from birth for 14 years, the authors state that distinct temperamental differences *persisted throughout the 14 years.*

Are Some Personality Characteristics Innate?

The authors identified three temperamental types. The "positive" child has regular bodily functions, moderately intense reactions, and a positive approach to new conditions. The "difficult" child has irregular bodily functions, intense reactions, slow adaptation to environmental change, and is generally negative. The "slow-to-warm-up" child has low activity, initially withdraws from new stimuli, adapts slowly, and has low intense reactions.

Forty percent of the children were positive, 10 percent negative, and slow-to-warm-up children comprised 15 percent of the sample. Thus, the authors could classify 65 percent of the children; the rest (35 percent) were a mixture of all characteristics. They believe that knowing a child's temperamental characteristics can aid parents in helping children to avoid behavior problems and teachers in helping youngsters to learn. For example, knowing that a child's restlessness is not necessarily related to the school, teachers would be more sympathetic and allow him or her to run errands or do the boards. Slow-to-warm-up children require patience, kindness, and considerable repetition. Difficult children need patience but also firmness; frequently, if these children experience some success, teacher-pupil relations are eased.

Herbert (1974) states that infants' grasping, smiling, and crying shape parents' behavior. Temperament, age, sex, and responsiveness all influence the mother, who reacts according to the infant's individuality. The infant also responds uniquely to the mother's treatment. The child is dramatically transformed during infancy, from total dependency to considerable self-sufficiency. Parents, using an infant's absolute dependency, have the power either to enhance or to disrupt development. Recalling the emphasis upon intensity of reaction, some common infant problems are autism (unnatural withdrawal), feeding and sleeping problems, fearfulness, and night tensions.

EARLY CHILDHOOD

During early childhood, youngsters grow physically, mentally, linguistically, morally, and socially, and their circle of friends expands noticeably, especially at the period's conclusion. Herbert (1974) identifies several characteristic problems of early childhood:

1. Dependency, which is problem behavior when a child constantly and needlessly seeks help.
2. The anxiety and conflict associated with toilet training.
3. Problems of self-restraint — irrational, sexual, aggressive, and inquisitive.
4. Problems of oversocialization and undersocialization. Development should enable children to control impulsive outbursts and to avoid forming an excessively rigid conscience that burdens them with guilt and discomfort.
5. Problems flowing from an inability to express oneself meaningfully or to comprehend others.

Common early childhood problems include phobias, nightmares, speech problems, masturbation, and enuresis. Thoughtful adults can help children minimize these problems and form constructive attitudes toward themselves and others. Herbert believes that early childhood is a watershed because youngsters change the relationship with their parents and form new friendships. Most teachers work with older children but should realize that personality characteristics change slowly. If teachers believe that early patterns re-

quire modification, patience and care are needed to help youngsters master tasks that they should have achieved earlier (Redl and
Wattenberg, 1959).

MIDDLE CHILDHOOD

Mental, physical, motor, and social skills expand rapidly as children begin formal schooling. Herbert notes that children extend
their social universe by school attendance; and teachers, school
mates, and friends become powerful influences. As they achieve
success in school and feel competent and accepted, their self-concept improves.

School Phobia

As challenging, exciting, and productive as school can be for the
6- or 7-year-old, it still is the first prolonged separation from
home. A familiar, playful existence is lost as the child plunges into
more exacting disciplines and the rough and tumble of school life
(Herbert, 1974, pg. 230). Some children find it overwhelming and
"school phobia" appears. School phobia means that a child has an
unreasonable fear of school, or some part of school life. On school
mornings, these children cry, plead illness, keep going to the toilet, perhaps vomit.

Parents become angry, usually to no avail. When asked when
the problem began, most parents reply that it appeared dramatically and suddenly. But, as Herbert notes, most cases have a history—previous isolated cases of school refusal, increasing irritability, restlessness, disturbed sleep, abdominal pain. It occasionally
follows a legitimate absence when the child expresses anxiety
about missed work.

Many of the families of school-phobic children had a high in-
cidence of neurosis (more boys than girls have this problem), but
the children have normal intelligence. School phobia has no one
outstanding cause but seems to result from multiple causes. Treatment should include physical and psychological examinations, remedial work when and where needed, and perhaps a change of
class or school. Cooperation between teachers and parents is essential, and if intervention is swift, the prognosis is good.

Other problems appearing in this period are truancy, stress,
anxiety, psychosomatic problems such as asthma, and underachievement. You will face these problems daily, and, while you
are not a psychotherapist, you should be prepared to meet them.
The best therapy that you can provide is a secure nonthreatening
classroom. Children know when they are accepted and wanted;
they appreciate a teacher who treats them with dignity and respect. Such an atmosphere encourages children to accept others,
which is an important step in emotional development and mental
health.

Hyperkinesis

A particular problem of middle childhood is hyperkinesis (hyperactivity, minimal brain dysfunction). Coleman (1976) describes the characteristics of the hyperactive child: short attention span, distractibility, impulsiveness, poor motor coordination, low frustration tolerance, mood inconstancy, hypersensitivity, and lack of inhibition. They talk and move incessantly, appear quite immature, and do poorly in school. There is no specific cause of hyperactivity, but family problems, difficulty during the birth process, and early injury or illness seem closely linked with it. A conservative estimate of the number of these children ranges from 1.5 to 2 million.

Drugs, tranquilizers, or stimulants especially are commonly prescribed for hyperkinesis; a treatment that is increasingly criticized. Since hyperkinesis is a label for a cluster of symptoms that appear for multiple reasons, many physicians, psychiatrists, and educators are reluctant to mask the actual causes of the problem by using drugs. It is still the predominant treatment, however, and teachers should know what drug is used, how often it is to be taken, and any possible side effects. Physicians and parents should consult teachers about the drug's effect on behavior in and out of the classroom.

Hager (1973) has some warnings for teachers: Be alert to the symptoms; realize that it is a medical problem requiring medical diagnosis; do not make direct referrals to parents or physicians; finally, exercise caution before referring to the school psychologist.

ADOLESCENCE

It is not easy to be an adolescent in modern society. There are enormous pressures—to achieve, to adjust, to avoid drugs, to learn moderation with alcohol, to control sexual impulses, to be independent without rupturing parental relations. Most adolescents succeed admirably; some do not. Redl and Wattenberg (1959) believe that adolescents' main task is becoming adults. They must discard childish ways and adopt adult patterns, which can cause problems if conditions, especially at home and school, are unfavorable. If adults treat a teenager like a child, adult status seems unattainable.

Recall the adolescent characteristics discussed in Chapter 2: the cognitive ability to think abstractly, the adolescent growth spurt, the emotional uncertainty. These characteristics, coupled with such developmental tasks as achieving independence, achieving satisfactory sex and social roles, and adjusting to changing societal expectations can be the occasion for adolescent problems. To illustrate the possibilities for difficulty, Coleman (1976) offers the following as adolescent problems.

Alcoholism
Delinquency
Depression
Drug usage
Family relations
Psychosomatic disorders
Schizophrenia
Sexual delinquency and deviations
Suicide

It is an impressive list, but most adolescents avoid these problems. Those working with adolescents should know the possibilities for problems but also realize that most teenagers will escape them given adult understanding and guidance. If adults establish that new relationship previously mentioned (friendship between al-

Adolescent Suicide

Twenty-five thousand Americans commit suicide each year. Twenty times this number attempt self-destruction. Of these, almost 7 percent are adolescents, and suicide is now the second leading cause of adolescent death, following only accidents. Three times as many males as females commit suicide. Depression, isolation, and excessive alcohol and drug usage are symptoms that should alert parents and teachers to youngsters in turmoil.

Smith et al. (1976) states that statistics show that when boys decide to kill themselves they really want to die, unlike females whose tendency to use an overdose of drugs (which takes time) often indicates a basic desire to be rescued. Smith notes that "subintentional" self-destruction needs more study. For example, some adolescents under severe physical, psychological, and sociological stress take fantastic risks: driving cars, walking railings on balconies, swimming almost out of sight.

The author states that studies of adoles-

cents hospitalized for attempted suicide show that school adjustment is a related problem. Poor grades and discipline problems frequently caused school dropout, which corresponded with the hospitalization. A significant number of suicides occur in the spring when school tension peaks. But school failure usually reflects a deeper problem: depression due to a parent's death, divorce, family conflict.

Smith believes that teachers should know the distress signals, both direct—"You'll be sorry when I'm dead"—and indirect—"That won't matter where I'm going." Note any abrupt change in the quality of schoolwork, any sudden signs of excessive alcohol and drug usage, extreme behavior that might signal the onset of mental illness, and truancy. Try to get the adolescent specialized treatment, without acting yourself as a therapist. Know the warning signs; know the referral agencies. As the author concludes, adolescent suicidal gestures are unconscious cries for help.

most-equals) they can offer support and advice to youth when they most require it.

This section is not intended to provide comprehensive coverage of personality problems; it is intended to alert you to the kinds of problems you could meet at various ages. Most youngsters experience few growth problems, but some develop problems sufficiently serious to warrant special consideration and perhaps treatment.

It is possible to conclude with a positive statement. Herbert states that normal problems have a good chance of disappearing as the child ages. School phobia, tics, shyness, nervousness, tantrums, reading problems, hypersentitivity, and speech problems are short-lived. Most problem children will attain an adequate adult adjustment (Herbert, 1974).

Discussion Questions

1. Do you agree that most children with personality problems, excluding the severely disturbed who require special care, should be in a regular classroom? Defend your answer by listing the advantages for the problem child and the disadvantages for the class. Are there also disadvantages for the problem child?

2. Is labeling something that should concern teachers, or is it an exaggerated problem? Do labels actually "stick to" children? If you think it is a problem, is it intensified or helped by placing problem children in a regular classroom?

3. What was your reaction to the work of Thomas, Chess, and Birch? Are the results helpful for parents? teachers? Can you suggest any practical, classroom implications of this study?

4. How could the classroom atmosphere contribute to school phobia? What do you see as the teacher's role with the school-phobic child? Are there class activities that could help this youngster?

5. The hyperkinetic child is a serious classroom problem. Given the warning about hasty referral, what do you think teachers should do when they suspect a problem? How do you react to the mounting criticism of drug treatment? Is it necessary if the child is to remain in the classroom? Defend your answer.

Some Concluding Thoughts

Combs and Snygg (1959, pg. 239) describe the adequate personality as one who has achieved a high degree of need satisfaction. These individuals have positive self-concepts and feel that they can meet environmental demands. Any negative perceptions of the self are accommodated with a total positive view and cause no disturbance of personality. Such an individual is able to accept any perception and integrate it within the self-structure; thus, acceptance enhances adequacy.

Adequate personalities are people who: (1) perceive themselves in a positive manner; (2) are able to accept themselves and others; and (3) identify with others. Adequate personalities behave more efficiently than those who are less adequate: they are more flexible in their adjustment to the environment; they are more able to engage in constructive, creative work that increases their value to themselves and to society.

Reversing the above criteria, the inadequate personality has a negative view of self and environment. These distorted perceptions cause a sense of threat with a resultant feeling of anxiety. As perceptions are vague and uncertain, behavior gradually assumes the same characteristics.

Finally, examining the specific forces behind adequate personalities, certain conditions constantly appear: they are physically healthy; they possess a willingness to accept themselves as they are while they strive for self-improvement; they seek varied experiences that widen the opportunity for perceptions; they seek goals and values that encourage change in the perceptual field; and they develop the ability to react rationally to threat. Teachers, by their own example and the classroom atmospheres they create, can help youngsters to become adequate personalities.

Summary

- Personality, while difficult to define, refers to a person's individuality—that special integration of habits or characteristics that define uniqueness.

- Erikson, emphasizing psychosocial influences, theorizes that humans pass through eight developmental stages.

- Social learning theory, especially Bandura's work, stresses the reinforcement of behavior and a model's influence on a child's behavior.

- The humanists, represented by Maslow and Rogers, argue that personality development is an unfolding of human potential as both children and adults strive for self-actualization.

- Certain personality dimensions such as aggression, dependency, and locus of control seem to be outstanding features of a child's behavior.

- These personality characteristics have direct classroom implications because the teacher's treatment of the anxious child will differ from that of the aggressive child, and the internal will differ from the external in reactions to the teacher, peers, classroom, and subject matter.

- While most children develop normally, problems occasionally arise that affect classroom performance and relations with the teacher.

- Personality problems usually vary with age, and teachers should be alert to the type of problem they could encounter at different grades.

- Most children outgrow the more common problems and become adjusted adults.

Suggested Readings

Allport, Gordon. *Pattern and Growth in Personality*. New York: Holt, Rinehart and Winston, 1961. An interesting, informative analysis of personality growth.

Bandura, Albert and Richard Walters. *Social Learning and Personality Development*. New York: Holt, Rinehart and Winston, 1963. A thorough, readable account of social learning theory and its practical applications.

Erikson, Erik. *Identity: Youth and Crisis*. New York: Norton, 1969. An enjoyable presentation of a famous psychoanalyst's description of the life cycle.

Guilford, J. P. *Personality*. New York: McGraw-Hill, 1959. An excellent work that presents basic ideas and data about personality and its development.

Herbert, Martin. *Emotional Problems of Development in Children*. New York: Academic Press, 1974. A superior overview of development and possible problems.

6

Language Development and Reading: Emergence into the Verbal World

Introduction

Children speak, read, and write. Most normal youngsters have mastered the basics of their language—vocabulary, grammar, and meaning—by 4 years. This relatively effortless acquisition raises some questions. If youngsters acquire language so easily (compare language learning to mathematical or scientific learning) what happens between 4 years and adolescence? Scores on the college entrance examinations have declined steadily. Recent results show a 20 percent decline in the number of students scoring at superior levels on the verbal test. Colleges report increasing numbers of high school graduates who cannot spell, read fluently, or write their native language—even in schools of journalism. University professors constantly complain about doctoral students who cannot write grammatical sentences.

Many reasons are given for declining scores and abilities. Some blame the tests, but college board officials reply that today's tests are easier than before. Others blame television. Youngsters have little occasion to read or write when free time is spent watching television. Still others claim that as higher education becomes more accessible, greater numbers of disadvantaged students are taking college boards. Less prepared, they score lower, but this still does not fully explain the decrease in high scores. Finally, some blame the schools. Students decide that it is foolish to take a rigorous English course when they can elect an ESP course, sit in a circle for a semester, and mentally try to bend spoons.

Whatever the reason, students' verbal ability has become a problem that teachers cannot avoid. Youngsters who have language difficulties are seriously disadvantaged. They will experience verbal problems in all school work; they will meet greater resistance in acceptance to higher education; they are severely handicapped in job competition. Language permeates our lives; there is no escape. Bereiter and Englemann (1966), noted for working with the disadvantaged, state that a list of possible language uses would be as long as a list of possible human activities. These authors believe that a minimum teaching language is necessary for learning to occur. It must satisfy certain criteria:

1. It must represent reality, preferably by using symbols.
2. It must clearly indicate truth and falsity so that pupils know whether they are right or wrong.
3. Both teacher and child must share the minimum teaching language.

If these criteria are not met, all learning suffers.

Before analyzing this critical aspect of our lives, some distinctions are necessary. *Communication* refers to any process that transmits information. It includes language, speech, telephone, telegraph, computer—it is all-inclusive. *Language* is more restricted and usually refers to verbal or nonverbal communication between organisms. Students speak to each other; they write letters to relatives; they may use body language to convey ideas. Bees and dolphins use an involved language to communicate; chimpanzees have demonstrated mastery of language.

Speech is even more restricted; it is used only by humans and distinguishes more than anything else what is human. To say that language distinguishes the human is technically incorrect; yet the term, as applied to humans, is so widely accepted that it is diffi-

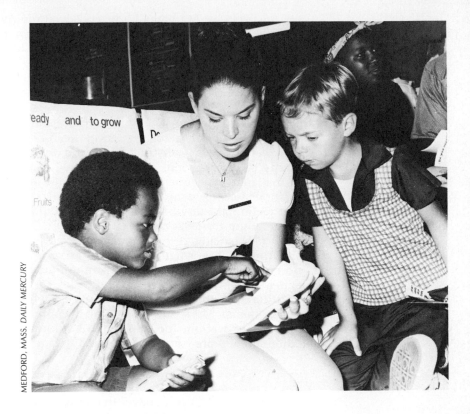

MEDFORD, MASS. DAILY MERCURY

cult, if not confusing, to separate the two. When human language development is discussed, speech is the issue, but "language arts" is technically correct because it implies both oral and written conversation. Wherever distinctions are made between animal and human communication, speech will be used exclusively.

To understand language and its educational application certain topics are particularly pertinent. This chapter will: (1) introduce some fundamental language concepts stressing our need for linguistic competence; (2) review several theories of language acquisition; (3) discuss language development—what is to be expected at different ages, and what programs have been devised to capitalize on development; and (4) conclude with an analysis of reading as a special instance of language.

Language: an overview

A word of caution is necessary before beginning any analysis. There are many and conflicting theories of language acquisition; there are also many and conflicting theories of language and reading instruction. Margaret Early (1976), studying the last decade's research on reading and writing, advises teachers to temper enthusiasm with common sense. Ten years ago teachers were told to concentrate on language structure: phonology (sound), morphology (meaning), and syntax (grammar). A few years later they were told to focus on children's feelings and why they used the language they did.

Attempting to combine both emphases, teachers realize that language develops in a set sequence: steadily increasing vocabulary, simple to complex constructions, short to long sentences, growing ability to comprehend. Teaching should capitalize on a knowledge of the language sequence, but when knowledge is scanty, teaching methods become confused. Early concludes that phonics, meaning, and feeling are all vital, and teachers should strive for skill mastery and reading for personal pleasure.

Such balancing of the language curriculum stresses the language situation; that is, language changes according to the student's purpose and the circumstances surrounding language usage. Encouraging students to read, write, and speak for different purposes and in different settings expands language facility, both in and out of school. James Moffett (1968) states that other than art, music, and physical education, the only school subject is language, since all other subjects are learned through language.

THE IMPORTANCE OF COMMUNICATION

John Pierce (1972) has stated that our very existence depends on communication in countless ways. Genetic messages determine who and what we are. Our internal communication network—nerve impulses and chemical messages—enables us to live and function as we do. For example, a breakdown in cellular communication enables cancer cells to grow. When the word communication is used, it usually means external communication, the processes by which humans communicate with each other. As Pierce notes, without external communication, we might exist but we would be lonely, ignorant individuals.

Lack of external communication would produce:

Life's Vital Property

1. A lack of accumulated skill and knowledge.
2. A failure in society that would force us to struggle for those vital necessities we take for granted.
3. A lack of the satisfaction derived from contact with others.

The Visual Image

Television can be a distraction from reading, writing, and even speaking. As Gombrich (1972) notes, this is a visual age in which both children and adults are bombarded with pictures from morning until night. The day may begin with television cartoons or news, television programming in school or office, and finally re-

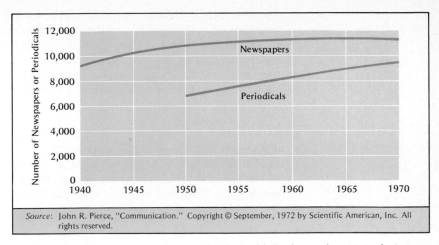

Figure 6.1 Newspapers and Periodicals Published in the United States, 1940–1970

laxation with television in the evening. During the day these visual images are supplemented by newspaper and magazine pictures, billboards, sketches, maps, graphs, picture books, movies, or slides. Figure 6.1 illustrates the stability or slight increase in the number of newspapers and magazines through 1970; whereas Figure 6.2 illustrates the dramatic increase in radio and television sets until by 1970 almost every home possesses one of each. These two figures clearly demonstrate the competition that language faces from visual images and partially explain the decline in verbal abil-

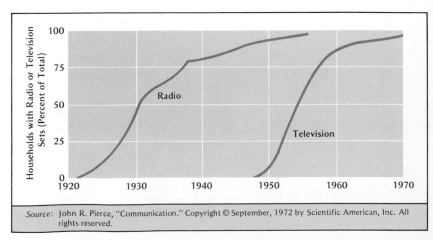

Figure 6.2 Dramatic Increase in Mass Communication, 1920–1970

ity previously mentioned. Still, such increased usage and acceptance of imagery should not be an excuse but a challenge to educators to discover techniques for using imagery to motivate students to improve language ability, for, as Gombrich states, the visual image is supreme in its capacity for arousal, but alone it cannot match the range and function of language.

COMMUNICATION AS LANGUAGE

Although the impact of imagery is increasingly important, language ultimately determines human success and adjustment. The more teachers understand language, the more effectively they can work with students. John Savage (1973) has described several linguistic characteristics.

1. Language is human, and only humans can employ oral and written language symbols to represent their thought.
2. Language is speech, which is uniquely human. By school age, most youngsters have mastered their language: they can efficiently use the sounds of their language (phonology); they know the meanings of various sounds (morphology); and they have learned how to arrange language units (syntax).
3. Language is symbolic and arbitrary. Language symbols represent reality so that you can discuss ideas and convey meanings not immediately apparent. For example, teachers ask youngsters what they did last summer and, using symbols, youngsters explain experiences not presently observable. But the symbols are arbitrary; there is no natural connection between letters and reality, only commonly shared agreement about usage.
4. Language is systematic, dynamic, and complete. While language changes (new words and new standards are accepted), it is systematic (for example, the formation of plurals and the arrangement of elements) and complete (we can communicate all our ideas and experiences through language).
5. Language is a cultural phenomenon. Any language reflects the culture of the people who speak it and thus serves their needs, values, and customs.

How do these linguistic characteristics help you to understand how people talk together? William Moulton (1965) states that to answer this question you must know what happens inside the speaker, how the communication reaches the receiver, and what happens inside the listener. Three major accomplishments are necessary. First is encoding, in which speaker *A* wishes to convey some meaning to receiver *B* and must fit the message to the language. The message must also fit the grammar of the language before it becomes part of a sound system.

Encoding

The second accomplishment is transmission of the message,

Transmission which commences when the brain activates the speech organs. The speech organs now produce a speech sound that generates sound waves. These reach listener *B*, cause ear vibrations, and eventually stimulate *B*'s brain.

Decoding The final accomplishment is decoding, in which the listener uses the sound and grammar of the message to interpret it. Moulton uses an excellent example. Assume that phonologically you decode a message as "I hope this'll suture plans," which is semantically illogical. We return to phonological decoding: the sounds are the same. But grammatically two arrangements are possible:

1. I hope this'll suture plans.
2. I hope this will suit your plans.

Now all aspects of decoding—phonological, grammatical, and semantic—are complete and you accept the message.

LANGUAGE AND EDUCATIONAL PSYCHOLOGY

There are three basic requirements for good teaching: knowledge of subject, knowledge of pupils, and effective communication. This section will link knowledge of subject with knowledge of pupils. As Kean and Personke note (1976), every subject has its own vocabulary and methodology, and teachers will be better instructors of language and reading if they understand the meaning of language.

Phonemes

Linguistics is the scientific study of language, and when linguists examine a language they isolate three major components: sounds (phonology), meaning (morphology), and grammar or construction (syntax). Any language possesses certain fundamental distinctive sounds. These are the phonemes of that language—the smallest language unit. Kean illustrates the distinctiveness of phonemes by using two similar sounding words: *thin, shin.* The initial sounds differ sufficiently so that they are distinctive and thus qualify as phonemes.

Morphemes

While phonemes affect meaning (for example, adding an *s* can change a singular to a plural), they possess no meaning themselves. The morpheme may be a word (free morphemes) or part of a word (bound morphemes). For example, *cat* and *be* are free morphemes; *s* and *ed* are bound morphemes. Peter Farb states (1973) that morphemes allow a speaker to signal relationships: *Jack is older than Jill.* Morphemes also permit the speaker to indicate number, an important consideration in English; for example: cats, pails, roses.

Farb believes that morphemes carry a considerable burden in the English language. *Cat,* for example, tells us that there are three phonemes, so arranged that they convey the meaning of an animal. Consider also the string of morphemes: *Jack fetch pail water.* It is not grammatical because it lacks those morphemes necessary to signal relationship: *ed, a, of. Jack fetched a pail of water* is a grammatical sentence.

Grammar

Morphemes are meaningfully arranged in the grammar or construction of a language. The acceptable constructions of a language are the syntax of that language. Moulton states (1970) that the function of syntax is arranging morphemes in meaningful sentences. Recent grammatical studies have shown that any speaker can say and any listener can understand an infinite number of sentences. Thanks to grammar no two sentences you speak, hear, or read are identical (excluding trivia, such as "How are you?").

Teachers, then, know their subject; they understand the basics of language and reading. The second major requirement for successful teaching is knowing the pupils. Your reading thus far has focused on children's developmental sequence so that you can match materials and instruction to their capabilities. Understanding Piaget, for example, literally dictates when abstract work can commence. Figure 6.3 illustrates the dynamic interaction between learning and maturation.

Note the place of language in this sequence. One-year-olds say 1 or 2 words; 2-year-olds, about 40 or 50 words; 3-year-olds, about 1000 words; 4-year-olds manifest language mastery. Reading and writing, as meaningful processes, involve considerable abstraction and during the early school years require many and varied concrete examples. Here is the great value of educational psychology:

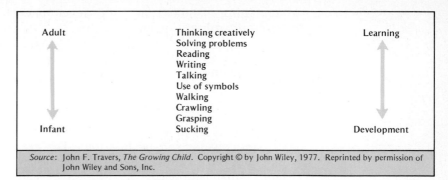

Adult	Thinking creatively	Learning
	Solving problems	
	Reading	
	Writing	
	Talking	
	Use of symbols	
	Walking	
	Crawling	
	Grasping	
Infant	Sucking	Development

Source: John F. Travers, *The Growing Child*. Copyright © by John Wiley, 1977. Reprinted by permission of John Wiley and Sons, Inc.

Figure 6.3 Learning and Development: The Dynamic Interaction

Are Humans Unique?

Do humans alone possess language? If language refers to communication, the answer is no. If it refers to speech, the answer is yes. There seems little doubt that animals develop complex communication systems and can be taught to learn other, complicated methods. For example, Allen and Beatrice Gardner, at the University of Nevada, taught the chimp, Washoe, the American Sign Language. By 4 years, Washoe could use 85 signs; by 6 years, she had mastered about 140 signs. Washoe did not merely respond to the Gardners but frequently initiated communication.

David and Ann Premack, at the University of California, Santa Barbara, have attempted to teach the chimp, Sarah, to read and write using plastic pieces to represent words. At 6 years, Sarah had a vocabulary of about 130 terms that she used with 75–80 percent reliability. The Premacks built Sarah's vocabularly by initially feeding her banana-slices. Then the slices were moved beyond her reach and a pink plastic disc was placed near her. She had to put this piece on a nearby language board to reach the fruit. After she had mastered this task, Sarah had to put a piece of blue plastic on the board to obtain an apple slice. Gradually she learned to combine words into sentences to acquire food.

Do the chimps' accomplishments erase human uniqueness? Joyce Fleming believes so (1974): chimps develop vocabularies and combine symbols to produce different combinations; therefore, language is not unique to humans. Roger Brown (1973) thinks not and believes they are disbarred from full linguistic participation by the first requirement: vocal production and aural reception. Peter Farb also thinks not. Noting Washoe's lack of grammatical understanding and Sarah's restricted ability in generating sentences, he states that the chimps, even if we omit their lack of vocal ability, possess a distressingly limited vocabulary. He quotes Bertrand Russell's saying that no matter how eloquently a dog may bark, he cannot tell you his parents were poor but honest.

combining insights from child development (for example, Piaget's work), learning, (for example, the principles of cognition and behaviorism), and basic language knowledge, teachers become more perceptive in their use of materials and techniques, which facilitates learning and adjustment.

LANGUAGE CAN BE FUN

Language is far more than syntax, phonology, and morphology. Its use and misuse can be hilarious. For example, Peter Farb (1973) mentions slips of the tongue. *Spoonerism* was coined after the syllabic transpositions of the Reverend William Spooner of Oxford University. Addressing a stranger using his pew in the college chapel, he said: "Excuse me, but I think you are occupewing my pie." Or, speaking to a group of farmers: "I have never before addressed so many tons of soil."

Silence in the Classroom

Nancy Naumann (1975), in an interesting reversal of communication, describes what happened on the day the teacher kept her mouth shut. Accidentally stumbling on the idea of becoming a silent class member, she decided to test the wisdom of encouraging self-directed children. Occasionally writing on the board or using body language (she raises an interesting question: Have you ever tried to teach division without using words), she found that she had the children's rapt attention. Naumann claims the experience was worth the risk of a slipped disc and vividly demonstrated the importance of discovering other than traditional classroom communication techniques. She believes that it also vividly demonstrated the importance of peer teaching.

Discussion Questions

1. Be sure that you understand the distinctions among communication, language, and speech. Discuss human's uniqueness according to the distinctions that you have just made. Analyze speech as a communication system.

2. Using the criteria of Bereiter and Englemann, explain how a minimum teaching language is critical for teaching success. Elaborate on the relationship between symbols and reality.

3. Place speech in Shannon's universal communication system. Does it meet the criteria? What does it tell you about the minimum teaching language? List some classroom variables (including speakers and listeners) that would classify as noise sources.

4. Distinguish among phonology, morphology, and syntax. Give specific examples of each, showing how each affects message transmission.

5. Language can be fun. Imagine that you are trying to encourage pupils to write compositions. Think of some techniques that make an enjoyable search for meaning and grammatical accuracy. For example, a school librarian had youngsters write their own books (admittedly brief), laminate the covers, catalog them, and present them to the school library during a coffee hour for parents, teachers, and administrators. An unruly class of sixth graders participated enthusiastically for about five weeks. What are *your* ideas?

Language acquisition: the theories

Joseph Kess (1976) states that language has perhaps been the most important influence in human development. The quality of human language that distinguishes it from animal communication is its abstractness. Humans can use language for planning and reminiscing as well as conversing. Consequently, investigators have long believed that if they could understand the nature of language they would be able to understand the nature of humans. Scholars have proposed many, often conflicting, theories or models to explain how humans acquire language.

Reber (1973) has developed a model to encompass conflicting theories. It has three parts:

1. The associationist orientation, represented most prominently by Skinner, which emphasizes learning principles, especially conditioning.
2. The process orientation, a cognitive interpretation, espoused by Piaget and Bruner.
3. The content orientation, which stresses an innate language capacity, whose leading exponent is Noam Chomsky's.

These theorists—Piaget, Bruner, Chomsky, Skinner—have devoted considerable attention to language, and understanding their beliefs inevitably clarifies and improves your use of language.

PIAGET: THE LANGUAGE AND THOUGHT OF THE CHILD

Language and Cognition

To understand Piaget's interpretation of language development it is necessary to recall his work on cognitive structures. Children's behavior provides evidence about their stage of intellectual development and the underlying cognitive structures. Flavell (1963, pg. 271) states that the major theme of Piaget's work on language is that *language is a symptom of existing cognitive structures*. If you recall Reber's three categories, the cognitivists believe that cognitive mechanisms explain a child's acquisition of language. Consequently, human cognitive ability is not linked solely to language; it also explains the logic and regularity of other activities.

Piaget theorizes that there are four major cognitive stages: sensorimotor, preoperational, concrete operations, and formal operations. The behavior, including language, of each stage says much about children's cognitive structures. If children lack conservation, they have a limited ability to communicate. But when they master their language, they greatly expand the range and rapidity of their thought, thus signifying an underlying abstract and complex network of cognitive structures.

Piaget and Inhelder (1969, pg. 86) state that there are three differences between sensorimotor and verbal behavior.

1. Sensorimotor behavior is linked to actions; verbal behavior can rapidly represent long chains of actions.
2. Sensorimotor behavior is restricted to immediate space and time; verbal behavior can range over vast expanses of space and time, liberating thought from its immediate confines.
3. Sensorimotor behavior proceeds by a step-by-step process; thought and verbal behavior can represent many things simultaneously.

Piaget begins his analysis of language development by asking the question: "What are the needs which children tend to satisfy when they talk?" To answer this question, Piaget recorded the speech of two 6-year-old boys for a month and classified their speech into two major categories.

A. *Egocentric speech,* in which children do not care to whom they are speaking or if anyone is listening. There are three subdivisions of egocentric speech.
   1. Repetition, which is not communication and is used for pleasurable purposes; it has no social character.
   2. Monologue, in which the child does not address anyone but talks to himself or herself; again, this is not communication.
   3. Collective monologue, in which no one listens to the child, although other youngsters are present; the child's egocentric speech precludes others from participating.
B. *Socialized speech,* in which the child exchanges thoughts with others, criticizes someone, questions another, and definitely attempts to interact with others. Even though the 6-year-old is capable of socialized speech, it is still limited, that is, there is no effort to explain or to search for causes; most of socialized speech consists of commands and criticisms. Piaget estimates almost 50 percent of the 6-year-old's speech is egocentric.

Verbal Understanding

It is not until youngsters are about 7 or 8 that there is any genuine verbal understanding between them. Before 7 egocentrism predominates and youngsters cannot give a faithful account of anything. Younger children are not lying or romanticizing; they are

TABLE 6.1
Piaget — Language and Thought

Period (age in years)	Outstanding Characteristics	Language Equivalent
Sensorimotor (0–2)	1. Egocentrism 2. Organizes reality by sensory and motor abilities	1. Language absent until final months of period
Preoperational (2–7)	1. Increasing symbolic ability 2. Beginnings of representation	1. Egocentric speech 2. Socialized speech
Concrete operations (7–11)	1. Reversibility 2. Conservation 3. Seriation 4. Classification	1. Beginnings of verbal understanding 2. Understanding related to concrete objects
Formal operations (over 11)	1. Development of logico-mathematical structures 2. Hypothetico-deductive reasoning	1. Language freed from the concrete 2. Verbal ability to express the possible

still egocentric and have no desire to communicate with others or to understand them. They simply invent as the spirit moves them.

As the child passes from the sensorimotor to the preoperational period, language usage increases strikingly, as a result of symbolic capacity. But, as Piaget constantly warns, language does not create the symbolic function but merely helps to develop it. Table 6.1 illustrates how verbal behavior reflects developing cognitive structures.

BRUNER AND THE SYMBOLIC MODE OF REPRESENTATION

Language and Thought

Bruner believes that cognitive growth is characterized by increasing symbolic skill until the child reaches the "symbolic mode of representation" and uses language and mathematical skills fluently. Language is crucial for mental development and is not merely a symptom of underlying cognitive structures. Bruner believes that language has a strong influence on thought for youngsters between 4 and 12. It releases the student from dependency on immediate experience and permits thinking about absent people, objects, and events.

Bruner asks the question "How does language affect the cognitive processes?" He believes that language is central to any consideration of the nature of intellectual development. The child acquires not only a way of saying something but also a powerful instrument for combining experiences, an instrument that the pupil can use for organizing thoughts about things (1966, pg. 105).

Bruner examines external language functions and then attempts to link these functions to thought to show that considerable thought is internalized dialogue. Thus, these language functions should appear in thinking. He believes that there are six discernible language functions:

1. The referential, or what the message signals: "There goes the dog."
2. The emotive, which expresses the feelings of the speaker: "Damn! I cut my finger."
3. The conative, which indicates the intent of the message: "Will you get my hat, please?"
4. The phatic, or the way something is expressed to maintain contact with the listener: "Yeah, yeah, yeah," during a telephone conversation.
5. The poltic, which emphasizes word combinations and not rules: "He's real cool, man."
6. The metalingual, or concern with verbal precision: "Is stick or twig the better word?"

Bruner concludes that language serves many functions, pursues many aims, and employs many voices. It commands as it refers, describes as it makes poetry, adjudicates as it expresses, creates beauty as it clarifies, and serves multiple needs as it maintains contact. So the style of our minds is partially due to internalizing the language function.

Language instruction was an integral part of MACOS. Bruner believes that certain precautions are necessary if language is to be an attractive subject. For example, teachers should avoid initially teaching children what language should be and having them memorize parts of speech. MACOS introduces language as communication—how animals and humans send and receive messages. Discussion usually leads to an analysis of communication systems and the difficulty of referring to things not present—what signs are preferable?

Pictures, diagrams, code construction, and charades are all used to illustrate the productivity and arbitrariness of language. To help pupils grasp the type and sequence of words, Bruner uses the following example.

1.	2.	3.	4.	5.
The	man	ate	his	lunch
A	lady	wore	my	hat
My	son	drove	our	car

The children are asked to mix words but to use the same sequence. They quickly learn that if they choose words in the proper sequence, they obtain something sensible, even if it is silly or, untrue; for example, "My lady ate our car." Instructors can use these examples as an introduction to more complicated grammatical concepts.

The course then provides opportunities for discussion of language acquisition and returns finally to language's role in shaping human thought. Bruner's ideas are challenging and useful for, as he states, he wishes to stimulate "a livelier sense of the distinctively human nature of human language."

PSYCHOLINGUISTICS AND NOAM CHOMSKY

Cognitive theorists believe that language appears as cognitive structures develop; psycholinguists believe that every speaker has an intuitive grasp of his or her native grammar and also intuitively understands the correct way to use the language. Farb (1973) states that psycholinguistics explains one of language's mysteries: A child hears relatively few utterances (most of which are grammatically incorrect) but, using the "scanty and flawed information," during the preschool years discovers the grammatical complexities of native speech—with no special instruction!

The only explanation (according to psycholinguists) is that children possess an innate competence for language acquisition just as they possess an innate capacity for walking. No one has to tell children *how* to walk—they talk and walk without consciously knowing how they did either. Not only do children quickly manifest this competence, they also display an ability to produce and understand at an amazing rate sentences they have not heard previously.

Joseph Kess states (1976) that language is a characteristic human behavior and that psycholinguistics is an outgrowth of psychology and linguistics. Linguists study language structure and devise rules to illustrate how a language functions. Psychologists study
Psychology plus Linguistics
human behavior. Kess notes that the psycholinguist must explain not only the language data but also the processes by which language is acquired and maintained. Most modern psycholinguists reflect Noam Chomsky's views of language structure and the theory of language.

Chomsky's distinction between competence (the speaker's innate ability and knowledge of language) and performance (the speaker's use of language) is critical in psycholinguistics. Kess states (1976, pg. 77) that natural language is *infinite*; speakers constantly create new sentences. (How many sentences in this book are repeated?) The speaker's ability to generate new sentences, grammatically correct, is called generative transformational grammar.

Noam Chomsky

MASSACHUSETTS INSTITUTE OF TECHNOLOGY

**Generative
Transformational
Grammar**

Psycholinguists use grammar to signify what is characteristic of a language, that is, its components and its rules, or its structures. So grammar provides data about the language and about the speaker's ability to form and interpret meaningful utterances. Understanding the rules and using the language, the speaker can generate an infinite number of sentences. Chomsky (1965) believes these sentences can have both a surface and deep structure. For example, a sentence may have a single deep structure:

The infant ate the candy quickly and this bothered her mother.

But there may be many different surface structures:

The mother was bothered by the infant eating the candy quickly.

That the infant ate the candy quickly bothered the mother.

The infant, eating the candy quickly, bothered the mother.

Each sentence has the same meaning (deep structure), but its phrasing varies (surface structure). A *transformation* has occurred.

LAD

Chomsky believes that all humans have an innate capacity to acquire language, a result of our uniquely human biological inheritance. He calls it our *Language Acquisition Device* (LAD). Chomsky also states that no one acquires a language by learning all the possible sentences of that language. Instead of learning billions of sentences, a child unconsciously acquires a grammar that can generate an infinite number of sentences in his or her native language. Peter Farb states that not every human being can play the violin, do calculus, jump high hurdles, or sail boats; no matter how excellent his teachers. But every person constantly creates utterances never before spoken on earth. Farb then gives the example of presenting a cartoon to 25 English speakers and asking them to describe in one sentence what they see. The different sentences that each speaker will generate will provide the raw material for 20 billion grammatical sentences that will require 40 human life spans to be spoken!

Psycholinguistics is fascinating, especially when you remember that bright children and stupid children, trained children and untrained children, all learn about the same linguistic system (Farb, 1973, pg. 246).

SKINNER AND VERBAL BEHAVIOR

"Men act upon the world, and change it, and are changed in turn by the consequences of their actions." With these words, B. F. Skinner began his analysis of language in his famous *Verbal Behavior* (1957). Skinner's work is essentially a learning theory called *operant conditioning*. In a series of significant writings (1938, 1948, 1953, 1957, 1971) he has unfailingly alienated or enchanted his readers.

Social Control

Kess states (1976, pg. 35) that Skinner believes society functions on behavioristic principles; that is, our lives are determined by controlling agencies: religion, parents, school, and government. Children acquire their values, beliefs, and even their personalities by cultural control. How does society exercise this control? Skinner's answer is that any culture, or portion of that culture, provides reinforcement for desirable (socially approved) responses.

There are two major behavioristic explanations. One is Pavlov's classical conditioning, in which a neutral stimulus accompanies a natural stimulus and gradually acquires the ability to elicit the desired response (See Chapter 1).

Operant Conditioning

Skinner seriously questions the widespread application of Pavlov's model to human behavior. He advocates operant conditioning, which does not depend on identification of a stimulus as a cause of behavior. If the individual emits a desirable response, the environment reinforces it; if the response is undesirable, then the environment either ignores or punishes it: it attempts to eliminate the undesirable response. (Operant and classical conditioning are described in considerable detail in Chapter 7.)

Kess believes (1976, pg. 37) that language seems to be a response emitted without identifying stimuli, and operant conditioning is crucial for Skinner's explanation of language. Skinner (1957, pg. 2) defines verbal behavior as behavior reinforced through the mediation of other persons. Vocal verbal behavior is especially important as a form of human language and is an excellent example of operant conditioning. Parents establish a response repertoire in the child by *reinforcing a response.* Skinner states that the response must appear at least once to be reinforced. Its initial appearance need not be perfect, that is, parents reinforce any approximation of the correct word. Progressive *approximation* ultimately produces sophisticated verbal behavior.

Progressive Approximation

Children acquire verbal behavior when their relatively unpatterned vocalizations are selectively reinforced and slowly attain an acceptable standard. Acquiring verbal behavior requires no identification of the stimuli occurring before the verbal behavior appears. It is difficult, almost impossible, to determine the stimuli that produce specific vocal responses. But prior stimuli become important in *controlling* verbal behavior. For example, when a response is repeatedly reinforced in the presence of a certain stimulus, the individual tends to emit the reinforced response in the presence of the prior stimulus. As a child you were repeatedly told to greet someone you met. When you did, your parents expressed approval reinforcement. Now when anyone enters your office or classroom, you automatically say, "Hi, may I help you?"

Skinner has devised several terms to describe different types of verbal behavior (1957, pp. 35–90). These are described in Table 6.2.

Kess concludes his analysis of Skinner's work on language by stating that many critics have rejected it because of Skinner's avoidance of the problem of meaning. But, as he notes, all other explanations of language also possess their deficiencies.

Discussion Questions

1. How does Piaget relate language acquisition to his belief in cognitive structures? What is the source of language? Using your previous work on Piaget (Chapter 5) explain to the class how both egocentric and socialized speech match Piaget's cognitive theory.

2. Examine Table 6.1 carefully. How do the cognitive characteristics of each period explain the language characteristics of that same period? Is Piaget's interpretation of language consistent with his cognitive explanation? Use specific examples to illustrate your answer.

TABLE 6.2
Terms from Skinner's *Verbal Behavior*

Term	Meaning	Example
Mand (derived from command, demand)	A specific response followed by specific consequences. Characteristic of children, no prior stimulus control, usually reflects some need.	"Wait!" is usually followed by someone waiting; "Quiet!" is usually followed by silence.
Echoic (verbal behavior controlled by verbal stimuli)	Children produce a sound similar to one heard and are usually reinforced for producing it.	Mother says, "Daddy"; child days, "Da da"; mother approves.
Textual (verbal behavior controlled by a stimulus such as a text)	An individual controlled by a text is a reader. A vocal verbal response is controlled by a nonauditory verbal stimulus.	*You* are the best example: you read this text.
Intraverbal (verbal behavior that has no exact stimulus—response relationship as echoic or textual behavior)	Children and adults exhibit verbal responses that have no one-to-one correspondence to the stimulus.	How much is two plus two? Four.
Tact (verbal behavior evoked by some object or event)	Correct response to the object or event is reinforced. Refers to the physical environment.	Children are taught to respond to the physical environment. Upon seeing a glass of milk, they say "milk" and are reinforced.

3. Bruner's work closely parallels Piaget's, but there are differences. How do they differ in their interpretation of language acquisition? Illustrate how Bruner matches his theory of language with his cognitive theory. Is he consistent? Defend your answer.

4. How does Chomsky's work differ from Piaget's? Does the LAD help to explain these differences? Explain the term *generative transformational* grammar. If your language had only two kinds of words, nouns and verbs, and the nouns are both subjects and objects, you would have three word places: subject-verb-object. How many sentences could you generate? Does the result of your arithmetic help you to understand Chomsky's theme?

5. What is operant conditioning? Give an example. Explain how progressive approximation shapes a child's language development. Distinguish tact from intraverbal behavior.

The Rationale for Verbal Behavior

In a fascinating interview with Mary Harrington Hall (1967) Skinner challenged other theorists to show what their theorizing had produced. Had they produced token economies, teaching machines, mechanized baby cribs, or behavior modification techniques? Skinner, of course, believes that their theories led to more theories, while his work changed child-rearing practices, therapeutic techniques, schools, prisons, businesses, and could change international politics if given the opportunity.

To understand and control behavior, Skinner stated that it is fundamentally important to know what a person is doing when he or she is reinforced. There are three parts to this relationship:

1. The stimulus, or the situation.
2. The behavior, or the response.
3. The consequences, or the reinforcement.

The more known about each of these, the better adults (parents and teachers) can control behavior, because it is then possible to establish schedules of reinforcement.

He believes that linguists have misunderstood his work on verbal behavior and have contributed little to our understanding of language because of their dependence upon mentalistic concepts. By insisting that analysts "look inside the person" for explanations of verbal behavior, they have overlooked the situation in which the person is speaking.

> I have found it necessary from time to time to attack traditional concepts which assign spontaneous control to the special inner self called the speaker. Only in this way could I make room for the alternative explanation of action which it is the business of a science of verbal behavior to construct (Skinner, 1958, pg. 460).

Language development

How does a knowledge of language structure and language theories help teachers? If youngsters master the essentials of their language as 4-year-olds, and if these same youngsters experience reading and writing difficulties as adolescents, then something intervened during these years to cause problems. There are many possible explanations—home, friends, media—*but* the school is also a major influence during these years and should correct any potential difficulties. Understanding language enables educators to construct a more meaningful language curriculum and improve language instruction. If teachers can match a child's language capabilities with appropriate materials and instruction, reading and writing improvement should be the logical result.

THE DEVELOPMENTAL SEQUENCE

Youngsters develop their language in the following manner:

1. At about 3 months, children imitate the sounds they hear, enjoy making sounds, and laugh aloud.
2. As 1-year-olds they can usually say 2 or 3 words, and know their own names.
3. At 3 years, their vocabulary has increased to about 1000 spoken words and several thousand comprehended words; they can talk in sentences.
4. As 4-year-olds most youngsters have mastered their language's complexity.

Figure 6.4 illustrates the increase in a child's vocabulary. Note the sudden acceleration at 3 years. This language explosion occurs at about the same age in every healthy child throughout the world.

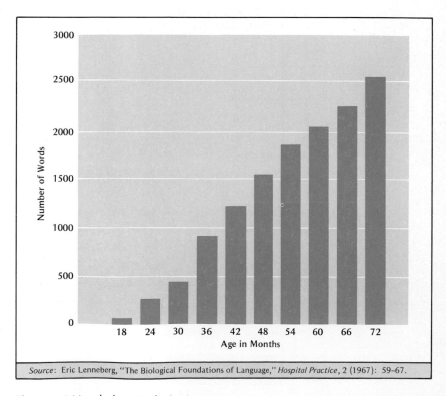

Source: Eric Lenneberg, "The Biological Foundations of Language," *Hospital Practice*, 2 (1967): 59–67.

Figure 6.4 Vocabulary Explosion

Lenneberg believes (1967) that it is a human characteristic inexplicable by reinforcement principles.

Figure 6.5 represents language's developmental sequence. Note the kinds of changes—not only quantitative, but also qualitative. A child develops increasing facility with language, including nouns, verbs, adjectives, conjunctions, and prepositions. Knobloch and Pasamanick (1974, pg. 5) state that language behavior furnishes clues to the organization of the child's central nervous system. Articulate speech depends on the social environment but also requires sensorimotor and cortical readiness. For example, preverbal stages prepare for verbal phrases, inarticulate vocalizations precede words, and language refinement comes by social reinforcement.

Figure 6.5 and the developmental milestones discussed in Chapter 2 illustrate normal language development during the early years. What can teachers expect by school age? Has the average child mastered discernible language skills other than those that seem innate? Table 6.3 presents some typical language accomplishments for the 6- to 10-year-old child.

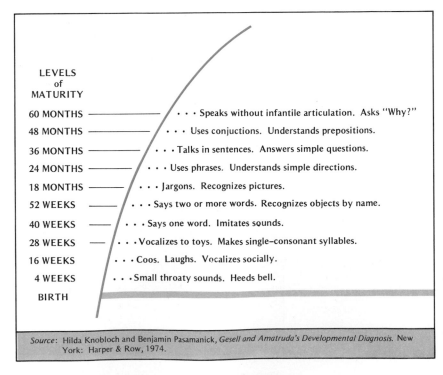

LEVELS
of
MATURITY

60 MONTHS ——————————— · · · Speaks without infantile articulation. Asks "Why?"

48 MONTHS ——————————— · · · Uses conjuctions. Understands prepositions.

36 MONTHS —————————— · · · Talks in sentences. Answers simple questions.

24 MONTHS ———————— · · · Uses phrases. Understands simple directions.

18 MONTHS ———————— · · · Jargons. Recognizes pictures.

52 WEEKS ——————— · · · Says two or more words. Recognizes objects by name.

40 WEEKS ————— · · · Says one word. Imitates sounds.

28 WEEKS ———— · · · Vocalizes to toys. Makes single–consonant syllables.

16 WEEKS ——— · · · Coos. Laughs. Vocalizes socially.

4 WEEKS —— · · · Small throaty sounds. Heeds bell.

BIRTH

Source: Hilda Knobloch and Benjamin Pasamanick, *Gesell and Amatruda's Developmental Diagnosis*. New York: Harper & Row, 1974.

Figure 6.5 The Developmental Sequence of Language

TABLE 6.3
Some Typical Language Accomplishments

Age (years)	Language Accomplishment
6	1. Vocabulary of about 2600 words 2. Understands use and meaning of complex sentences 3. Uses language as a tool 4. Possesses some reading ability
7	1. Motor control improves; able to use pencil 2. Can usually print several sentences 3. Begins to tell time 4. Losing tendency to reverse letters *(b,d)*
8	1. Motor control improving; movements more graceful 2. Able to write as well as print 3. Understands that words may have more than one meaning *(ball)* 4. Uses total sentence to determine meaning
9	1. Can describe objects in detail 2. Little difficulty in telling time 3. Writes well 4. Uses sentence content to determine word meaning
10	1. Describes situations by cause and effect 2. Can write fairly lengthy essays 3. Likes mystery and science stories 4. Masters dictionary skills 5. Good sense of grammar

An examination of Table 6.3 reveals that most school age youngsters have a fairly sophisticated language knowledge. Their vocabulary, both speaking and comprehending, is enormous, they display considerable skill in reading and writing, and they begin to use their language for many varied purposes (needs, demands, humor, formal and informal communication).

THE LANGUAGE ARTS

Five years is a critical age for children: they begin formal schooling and their mastery of their native language encounters specific instruction. Five-year-olds understand language structure and can form and understand an infinite number of sentences, have a considerable vocabulary, and their speech is clearly recognizable. As Kean and Personke (1976) note, a classroom full of first year children is a miraculuous collection of quite accomplished speakers of

Skilled Speakers

English. Consequently, these authors believe that teaching language arts is not "teaching English," which the children know, but assisting youngsters to refine their reading and writing skills.

Teachers should encourage children's speech and writing, expand their language productions, and respond to children's language in correct forms. Since language acquisition is a constantly developing process, the language arts program must consider the entire developmental sequence. Knowledge of the language capabilities of each age and grade affects instruction, materials, and organization of the language arts curriculum.

The language arts curriculum

Kean and Personke (1976) specify eight language arts topics that deserve special consideration.

Black English

While language may be a problem for any youngster, it often represents a serious obstacle for black children, especially those who use "Black English." Farb (1973) believes that there are three basic interpretations of Black English.

1. It is a completely different language, despite its similarity to Standard English.
2. It is a radically different dialect.
3. It differs no more from Standard English than any other dialect.

Farb believes that the second interpretation is correct and results from five major influences: African languages, West African pidgin, a Plantation Creole, Standard English, and urbanization in the northern ghettoes. Black English does not sound like Standard English because it frequently uses different sounds and a different grammar. For example, Standard English uses *is: He is working.* Black English emphasizes the auxiliary verb *be: He be working,* which means

that the person has been working steadily, while *He workin'* means that the person is working now.

Farb concludes that Black English is neither a mispronunciation of Standard English nor an accumulation of errors in Standard English. Both Black and Standard English share sufficient similarities so that kindergarten and first-grade teachers are often unaware that a black youngster may speak another dialect that is not Standard English. For example, the black child who says "they toys" and "he work" for the printed "their toys" and "he is working" has quickly translated Standard English into his dialect—Black English.

Many linguists now believe that ghetto children should learn Standard English as a second language. Such youngsters actually become bilingual. Whatever the school's decision, teachers, realizing some youngsters' difficulties, must patiently attempt to adapt much of the Standard English work.

1. *Oral language.* Every classroom is an environment that helps or hinders a student's oral language. Talking is an important part of learning, and teachers should encourage class discussion (including all class members), individual reports, reading, plays (including puppertry), and oral interpretation of literature. These activities can greatly facilitate speech development.

2. *Listening.* Listening is an important language skill for everyone, but especially for youngsters in a traditional classroom. To help children become good listeners, teachers should have an oral presentation and then ask students about important details: a story's sequence, its meanings, its validity, and its main idea.

3. *Semantics.* Words mean different things and children acquire a "semantic sense" rather slowly. Encouraging children to read widely and use a dictionary should be an integral part of the language arts program. Charades and word puzzles are popular classroom techniques.

4. *Composition.* Children must learn to write their language in a clear, concise manner or they will suffer a lifetime language handicap. Composition—the organization and written presentation of an idea—has long been a key element in the language arts program. Motivating children to write by using an exciting topic, helping them to organize their ideas, having them put these ideas on paper, constructively criticizing them, and eventually encouraging them to permit others to read their work are all essential to good writing instruction.

5. *Handwriting and spelling.* Spelling, a cognitive skill, and handwriting, a motor skill, are the tools of written communication and represent the encoding process—changing ideas into symbolic language. Both manuscript and cursive writing should be in the program, and while there is today a tendency to scoff at handwriting instruction, many children's illegibility is a growing concern. Legible letters and words, meaningfully communicated, should be a standard expectation in all classrooms. Students also should develop a "spelling conscience," a desire to spell words properly, which a teacher can combine with both handwriting and composition to make instruction and learning more pertinent.

6. *Usage, grammar, and mechanics.* Forming and combining words, punctuating them, and using them accurately are the bases of effective written communication. As the language program develops, correct usage (which is highly debatable, as the problems of dictionary editors evince), growing syntactical ability, and accurate punctuation should be a daily goal.

7. *Literature.* Children should learn a love of reading at an early age. Relevant, interesting, and exciting materials are avaiable for readers of all levels and are well worth a teacher's effort to obtain them. (The next section of this chapter is devoted to a more detailed discussion of reading.)

8. *Media.* When we consider the time that children spend, and will spend, with television, film, magazines, newspapers, and radio, media requires serious study so that children learn to become intelligent consumers. The authors offer the following guidelines: Know the media capability of your school, know what children are watching on commercial television, and present viewing suggestions. With their sex and violence themes, television and movies are powerful magnets; so teachers and parents must join to discover what kinds of shows children are watching and to exercise some control over viewing habits. Parents and teachers should also make their feelings known to local stations and national networks, either as individuals or organizations, if television is to be a positive force in education and development. (We shall consider children as producers of media in Chapter 15.)

Reading: a special case of language

A youngster who cannot read cannot succeed. Although there may be exceptions to this blanket assertion, they are rare. Reading disability retards educational progress, restricts educational level, limits occupational and financial success, and impedes social mobility. The reading phase of language development is probably the most important subject in the curriculum and, unfortunately, one of the most controversial. Experts simply cannot agree on content, materials, and instruction.

Problems of Definition

There is a cliché—true, as are most clichés—that states that every teacher, kindergarten through senior high school, is a reading teacher. Consequently, every teacher should have some knowledge of the reading process. First, what is reading? Here few authorities produce identical definitions. Miles Zintz (1975, pp. 6–7) believes that reading encompasses three definitions.

1. Reading is decoding written words to produce them orally.
2. Reading is understanding the author's language in a printed passage.
3. Reading is the ability to grasp the meaning of words so that a paragraph's or story's ideas are clear.

Differences in reading programs are mainly differences in emphasis in these three interpretations.

THE TRIED, THE TRUE, AND THE NEW

Jeanne Chall, in her *Learning to Read: The Great Debate* (1967), states that American children learn to read in almost any kind of building you can imagine: wooden compounds on stilts, ancient

multistory brick buildings, and modern, glass-walled structures. Some youngsters are in crowded classrooms with screwed-down desks, while a few minutes away you will find 20 or 25 children in a roomy, airy space equipped with a bewildering variety of materials. So children learn to read under amazingly different conditions.

To explain this phenomenon, Chall believes that from about 1930 to 1960 there was a fairly discernible consensus about beginning reading methods that included these principles.

The Tried and the True?

1. Reading should include word recognition, comprehension, interpretation, appreciation, and application.
2. Children should begin with meaningful reading (whole words, sentences, and appropriate stories).
3. When children have a sight vocabulary of about 50 words, they should commence phonetic structural analysis.
4. These skills should be taught from grades one to six.
5. Teachers should avoid isolated analytical drills.

223

6. There should be a reasonable readiness period, small group instruction, and considerable word repetition.

From about 1960, these principles were subjected to mounting attack. Beginning with Rudolf Flesch's *Why Johnny Can't Read* (1955), growing criticism led to such new reading programs as those emphasizing phonetic analysis, alphabetic principles, the Initial Teaching Alphabet (ITA) that modified the alphabet to correspond to actual sounds, the language experience method, the Montessori technique, and programmed instruction. Summarizing these, Chall believes that they represent three major innovations.

The New

Dyslexia

Some youngsters, otherwise intelligent and normal, have abnormal reading difficulties. Dyslexia, that mysterious problem involving words and symbols, strikes one child in seven. Estimates are that 75 percent of all juvenile delinquents suffer from dyslexia, but it respects no barriers—Thomas Edison, General George Patton, Woodrow Wilson, and Albert Einstein all were dyslexic (Young, 1975). Dyslexia seems to result from some blocking in the brain's organizational ability so that letters are transposed and reversed—*b* becomes *d*, *not* becomes *ton*, *oil* becomes *710*.

Nelson Rockefeller, a Phi Beta Kappa from Dartmouth and a famous dyslexic, states that he often sees letters and numbers backwards. Excerpts from his diary (when he was 11) show "engen repar schop" for engine repair shop. He is still a miserable speller, but he overcame his handicap by learning to cope. He learned that he needed extra concentration while reading so that even today he rehearses his speeches carefully and has aides check his spelling.

Woodrow Wilson could not master the alphabet until 9; at 12 George Patton still could not read. But these famous figures succeeded in spite of their handicap. Others are not so fortunate. Ridiculed by classmates, labeled as lazy or stupid by teachers, troubled by routine schoolwork, they not only fail but also feel overwhelmed.

What can parents and teachers do to help these children? First, know the symptoms: persistent spelling errors, reversals, upside-down letters, illegible handwriting, confusion about left and right, and up and down, a history of delayed spoken language, and personal disorganization. Not all children who manifest some of these symptoms are dyslexic, but if a pattern appears, have the child tested.

Second, if suspicious, have the child examined physically, expecially in vision, speech, and hearing. Ensure that the home life—eating, sleeping, and play—is regularly scheduled. Minimize abstractions.

Then, if dyslexia is confirmed, refer the child to a program that provides systematic tutoring, especially in phonics.

The results are encouraging. If properly treated, the dyslexic can avoid failure associated with language problems.

1. There is a noticeable attempt to facilitate earlier acquisition of the alphabetic principles.
2. There is a perceptible effort to increase individualized instruction.
3. There is an endeavor to make content more realistic, meaningful, and vital.

Although these may be the major themes in all of the newer programs, there are, nevertheless, differences among them. As Savage and Jones note (1973–1974, pg. 26), these differences are important since they lead to different materials and techniques.

THE READING PROCESS

Regardless of controversy over methods, curriculum programs, and materials, what happens when a child reads? William Gray states (1948) that adults are so accustomed to reading that they seldom think of it as a complicated process. They rapidly discern the author's ideas without stopping at each word. Their eyes sweep along the printed lines and, from their experience they instantly assign the meaning to words that the author intended. For example, Gray uses two sentences that illustrate an author's intent to convey different meanings to the same word.

1. Each boy had played in the band.
2. Each boy had a band around his arm.

Although reading seems to be a single smooth operation, Gray believes that reading consists of four steps.

Reading: A Four-Step Process

1. Word perception initiates the process by enabling us to identify the printed symbol and assign the proper meaning to it. For example, in the above sentence we read *band*, not *bank*, and realize that the author means a musical group.

2. Comprehension, the next phase, leads to meaning: accepting some ideas and rejecting others. You form a chain of ideas, which are usually those that the author intended.

3. Reaction to the author's ideas prompts readers to assess their value, accuracy, or worth. Knowledge of the subject determines your reaction; little knowledge or experience causes you often to accept the author's ideas, while substantial knowledge causes you to be more critical. (Gray's third step is a good example of problems associated with a complex, technological society. Uninformed about many magazine and newspaper topics most readers tend to accept the printed word as unfailing truth.)

4. Integration of ideas allows you to assess the total meaning of the author's message. You balance the various ideas of the passage and either accept or reject them. Either decision broadens your experiences so that you continue to bring a deeper perspective to future work.

Gray states that each step is dependent upon its predecessor. Children determine meaning only if they accurately perceive abstract symbols, which implies the need for certain prerequisite skills. Discussing learning to read and reading to learn as two concurrent processes, Zintz (1975, pp. 17–18) describes a necessary sequence of reading skills.

A. *Developmental: How-to-read skills*
   1. Word recognition skills
   2. Comprehension skills
   3. Study skills
B. *Functional reading*
   1. Location activities
   2. Specific skills for study/comprehension
   3. Selection and organization
   4. Summarizing
   5. Providing for remembering
C. *Recreational reading*
   1. Reading as a "free time" activity
   2. Locating books of interest in the library
   3. Developing tastes for a variety of reading material
   4. Giving pleasure to others through oral reading
   5. Fixing permanent habits of reading every day

BILINGUAL EDUCATION

There is currently national interest in bilingual and bicultural education. Growing ethnic pride and a legally supported concern with minority children have caused schools with minority populations to introduce bilingual programs. Although you may not teach in the native language program (unless you are expert in the language), you probably will have youngsters in your class for whom English is *not* the native language.

The Legal Mandate

Teitelbaum and Hiller (1977) trace the legal mandate for bilingual education to the Bilingual Education Act of 1968, which provided federal funds for bilingual programs and its updating in the Bilingual Education Act of 1974. The landmark court case was *Lau v. Nichols* (414U.S. 563 -1974), in which Chinese public school students brought suit against the San Francisco Unified School District in 1970.

The issue was not the lack of services to meet their linguistic needs; it was whether non-English-speaking students receive an equal educational opportunity when they are taught in a language they do not understand. When lower courts rejected their claims, they appealed to the United States Supreme Court. The Supreme Court found in their favor, stating that schools must take affirmative steps to remedy English language deficiencies, steps that exceed merely providing the same books and teachers to all pupils. While the court's decision did not precisely demand bilingual education, it provided grounds and status for programs servicing those youngsters who did not speak English.

Basic Problems

Christian (1976, pg. 17) states that the ideal bilingual educational pattern would consist of learning to read and write the home language during the school years, continuing to learn in and through it together with the school language during the entire period of formal education, and developing maximum skills in both languages throughout the lifetime, with the nature and complexity of skills varying with the professional and personal needs of the individual. The author notes that where the home language differs from the school's, literacy in the home language is typically used to aid in acquiring the school language. Once this occurs, *the school loses interest in the home language.*

That this is one of the basic problems in bilingual education is seen in John-Steiner and Souberman's (1977) explanation of why bilingual programs are so demanding and complex. It is necessary:

1. To identify those children who would benefit from such programs.
2. To decide which model of learning and teaching would be most effective with these children.
3. To devise a different curriculum.
4. To recruit and train personnel.
5. To encourage a joint effort by both community and school.

The authors believe that too often there is indecision about either maintaining the native language while developing new language skills or dropping it after the first few years. Most existing bilingual programs consist of structured lessons in English and

Hope for the Future

some rehearsal and practice in the native language. The intent is to produce individuals who can converse, write, and read with ease in two languages.

Wright (1973) is both gloomy and hopeful, stating that the most conspicuous failure group in today's American educational system is composed of those children whose home language is *not* English. A lack of programs, a scarcity of qualified teachers, little agreement on which languages for bilingual education, all contribute to present problems. But the author is optimistic. In Boston, for example, while there is a Puerto Rican population of 10,000, only 63 Puerto Rican students graduated from high school. You may think this is shameful, but only 4 students graduated between 1965 and 1969. Bilingual education, slowly but surely, is progressing.

READING AND EDUCATIONAL PSYCHOLOGY

The primary purpose of educational psychology is to improve teaching and learning. Since learning to read is so vital, and teaching methods so controversial, perhaps the application of learning principles to reading will help you to make psychologically and methodologically sound decisions. There are several characteristics of learning that can help you to examine the reading process more critically. Figure 6.6 illustrates these characteristics.

1. *A motivated individual.* Learning is impossible without motivation. The teacher's problem is to discover *how* to make young-

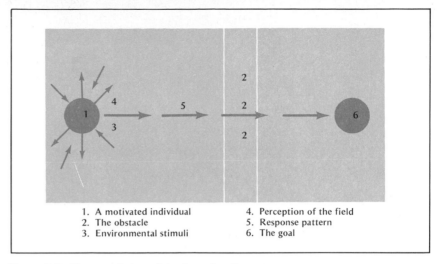

Figure 6.6 Characteristics of the Learning Process

sters want to read. They can use obvious methods (grades, rewards, punishment), which is external motivation, but teachers strive for *internal motivation,* that is, that the students themselves desire to read. Today, especially, the obstacles facing teachers are formidable. As you saw in the opening pages of this chapter, visual imagery is stimulating, appealing, and requires little effort to comprehend. To combat this challenge, educators must design and use materials that have exciting content, reflect children's current interests, and have a vocabulary suited to their reading level. If children, early in their school lives, use interesting materials and encounter teachers who make a story's content real and touching and who themselves display a love of learning, then youngsters may acquire an early love of reading. It is not an easy task, but it is rewarding.

2. *The obstacle.* Symbols, words, sentences, and stories become the reading obstacle. Teachers must choose material wisely so that students are neither completely frustrated, which would block learning, nor unchallenged, which would also block learning because there is nothing to learn.

3. *Environmental stimuli.* What stimuli will a teacher use? Depending upon grade, age, and reading level, symbolic stimuli are a teacher's tools. Beginning with concrete examples (an orange, then a picture of an orange) the teacher gradually leads the child to recognize the abstract symbols that mean orange. There are several established psychological principles that can guide a teacher's use of stimuli: going from the concrete to the abstract, from the simple to the complex; using as much reward as possible; constantly applying and transferring reading (that is, it is not an isolated subject that uses isolated symbols), and formulating meaningful learning sessions (both in content and time).

4. *Perception of stimuli.* A youngster perceives the learning situation according to his or her experiences and immediate stimuli. Stimuli—letters, words—must be clear to avoid confusion and prevent problems. For example, teachers must help pupils attend to pertinent stimuli—*b*, *d*, *pet*, *pat*, *pit*. Many youngsters will avoid future reading problems if they learn to perceive symbols accurately. But it is more than the perception of unrelated symbols; almost immediately youngsters should begin to focus on relationships, which means that teachers should introduce youngsters to words as soon as possible. They thus develop a habit of searching for relationships that will extend to words, sentences, and paragraphs, enabling them to determine and compare ideas, enriching their interpretation of what they read. The search for relationships is continuous.

5. *The response pattern.* Youngsters respond *as a whole* to their

reading materials—cognitively, motorically, and emotionally. The teacher's responsibility is clear here: diagnosis and sound judgment. Is the child sufficiently mature physically to hold a book and turn pages? Is the child sufficiently advanced cognitively to interpret symbols? Is the material designed to instill a fondness for reading? No one can answer these questions better than the classroom teacher.

6. *The goal.* Does the child want to read? If so, then the task is easier and amounts to carefully directing activities. If not, then obstacles require identification and removal, and the task becomes more difficult, requiring greater and continuous emphasis on motivation.

The learning characteristics themselves are related. Learners want something—to learn to read. They are blocked and must use the environment (teacher and materials) to reach their goal. As they use the classroom stimuli, with like, dislike, or indifference,

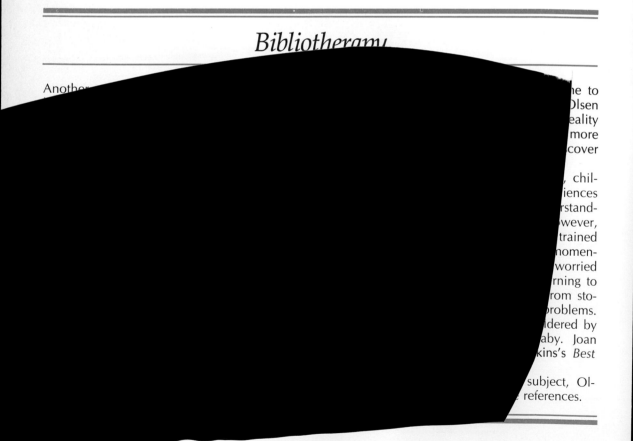

Bibliotherapy

Another

they combine letters into words, words into sentences, sentences into paragraphs until they can read and understand a whole story. Reading and educational psychology have mutual benefits: understanding sound psychological principles helps teachers with their instruction, while the reading process is an excellent example of educational psychology in action.

THE PROGRAMS — ELEMENTARY AND SECONDARY

Reading programs today are offered from preschool through college. When children begin formal education they usually enter one of several reading programs. Zintz (1975) states that there are five major options: a language experience technique, a basal reading series, individualized reading, a modified writing system, and programs stressing phonics.

1. *Language — experience.* Teachers encourage youngsters to tell stories about their experiences or ask them to draw a picture and then tell a story about it. The teacher then writes one or two of the child's sentences on a board or notebook, gradually accumulating many of the child's stories. The objective is to make children sensitive to their language, develop their vocabulary, and then advance them to books with controlled vocabularies.

2. *Basal readers.* These are a carefully graded series of texts and supplementary materials designed to provide a sequence and integration of basic reading skills: vocabulary development, word

BOSTON COLLEGE PUBLIC RELATIONS

analysis skills, and evaluative skills. The first books contain a limited number of sight words so that children immediately experience meaning in words, rather than isolated drill with letters or syllables. Although basal readers are criticized because of their sterile content, their scope is a great help to many teachers: readiness workbooks, preprimers, a primer, a first reader, and then usually two books for each grade. Films, filmstrips, tapes, and vowel cards may accompany the program.

3. *Individual reading.* The belief that reading is an active, cognitive, individual process produced the individualized reading concept. Children proceed at their own rate by selecting their own materials. Estimates are that each classroom requires at least 100 books, changed each month, with a wide range of difficulty. Most of these are trade books. Each child has a weekly meeting with the teacher, comparing records and encouraging class reporting.

4. *Modified writing systems.* An example of a modified writing system is the Initial Teaching Alphabet (ITA), which uses 44 symbols instead of the conventional 26. No capitals are used and emphasis is on sound, not spelling; for example, "girls and bois lern to reed."

5. *Phonics-based system.* Skill in attacking printed words by analyzing them into sounds is an example of a phonics system. Today phonics is usually considered a *part* of the total reading program; for example, it would be essential in Gray's first stage — word preception.

Since children can learn to read in many ways, schools should use varied techniques to suit unique learning styles. There is no escaping an obvious conclusion: teachers must master the basics of several different programs.

Reading at the secondary level

Burmeister (1974) states that teachers soon find little distinction between teaching reading and reading content, that is, helping students master content usually means teaching reading. The author furnishes a good example of the reading range that secondary teachers can expect. Assuming you will teach tenth-grade social studies, how low will the poorest reader be, and how high the best? Circle the grade levels:

1 2 3 4 5 6 7 8 <u>9 10 11</u> 12 13 14 15 16 17 18

(The answer is on page 236.)

Burmeister (1974) suggests several techniques to help secondary teachers when they give reading assignments. The first is use of the Directed Reading Activity (DRA), which entails five steps. *Step*

DRA

1 is preparing students for their reading by discussing familiar but related topics, introducing new and difficult words they may encounter, reviewing outlining skills, and perhaps presenting some pertinent visual material. *Step 2* includes previewing the assignment, ensuring that students understand what they are to do and why they are to do it. In *Step 3*, the students read silently. In *Step 4*, they discuss it, write about it, or illustrate it. In *Step 5*, the teacher attempts to extend their activity by having them do related work in magazines, newspapers, drama, or experimenting.

Another technique is the SQ3R, which permits more student independence than DRA. There are also five steps to the SQ3R plan.

SQ3R

1. *S — Survey.*   Read the title, author, table of contents, preface, chapter introductions, glossary, and appendices. Try to obtain a general idea of the book's intent.
2. *Q — Question.*   Examine the main headings and ask questions of yourself: What does it mean? Have I ever seen this before? What can I relate to it?
3. $R_1 — Read.$ Now read to answer your questions.
   $R_2 — Recite.$ Recite the answers to yourself, and evaluate their validity. (Continue using Q, R_1, R_2 until you finish the chapter.)
   $R_3 — Review.$ Review the total chapter by surveying it, then attempt to form your own outline.

These are only two techniques that teachers of all subjects can use. Burmeister argues strongly that if secondary school reading is to improve, a school-wide commitment is necessary. Individual teachers cannot accomplish this feat, nor can all skills and interest develop in one year. The author suggests the formation of a school-coordinating committee, consisting of the principal, a reading consultant, a guidance counselor, a librarian, a representative from each academic department, and possibly a school board member. The coordinating committee would try to formulate a secondary school reading program that reflects both the school's and community's aspirations. The task is difficult but possible, and if you recall the opening words of this chapter, it is well worth the effort.

Discussion Questions

1. Give meaning to the statement that every teacher is a reading teacher. How can this be so at the secondary level? Use specific examples in your answer.

2. Using Gray's four steps of the reading process, demonstrate how learning to read could be explained by a behaviorist such as Skinner and a cognitivist such as Bruner. Apply their theoretical concepts to each step.

3. Which of the elementary reading programs appeals to you? Why? What would cause you to use more than one program? What could limit your selection?

4. Apply the SQ3R technique to this chapter. Did it help you? Why? Will you continue to use it? Will you have your students use it (if appropriate)? Explain your answers.

Some Concluding Thoughts

Language and reading are lifelong activities, and if children develop language problems, they face a lifetime of restricted opportunity. Whether some cultural disadvantage or some early unnoticed problem is the cause, there is no escaping the effect. If teachers possess knowledge of their language and its development, and if they recognize the significance of good reading instruction, they may both inspire the good reader and aid the poor reader.

Educational psychology's role is especially pertinent to the language program. Challenging materials and provocative methods have a distinct relationship to the learning process, and teachers can use these materials and methods more effectively if they have a sound knowledge of educational psychology. But language instruction need not be grim. As Savage notes (1973), almost everyone takes language for granted; so, to focus students' attention on its importance, have them attempt to communicate with classmates *without using language.* The results should highlight language but also lead to an interesting discussion of body language. Try it with other means such as code or signs; students will soon realize language's advantage as a communication medium.

Summary

- Understanding language, its structure and development, aids all phases of teaching and learning.

- Reading and writing face intense competition from television for students' attention.

- Phonology, morphology, and grammar are the chief components of language.

- Language (speech) is uniquely human; so understanding language furthers our knowledge of students. Theorists such as Piaget, Bruner, Chomsky, and Skinner have proposed explanations of language acquisition.

Answer: 6 and 15 for a good class, 5 and 13 for a poor class, 5 and 15 for a typical class.

- Language development has an observable pattern, which helps educators to match materials and instruction with appropriate language levels.

- Reading skill largely determines success or failure at *all* educational levels.

- Reading seems to follow a four-step process: perception, comprehension, reaction, and integration.

- There are many and varied reading programs at the elementary level with which teachers should be familiar.

- Reading instruction does not end at grade six; secondary teachers should be familiar with the many successful techniques available to aid both reading and achievement.

Suggested Readings

Burmeister, Lou. *Reading Strategies for Secondary School Teachers*. Reading, Mass.: Addison-Wesley, 1974. An excellent reference for programs, problems, and techniques in secondary reading.

Chall, Jeanne. *Learning to Read: The Great Debate*. New York: McGraw-Hill, 1967. A fine overview of reading programs—materials, methods, and controversies.

"Communication." *Scientific American* 227 (September, 1972). The entire issue is devoted to communication and is a superb source.

Farb, Peter. *Word Play*. New York: Knopf, 1973. Witty and informative; if you are interested in language, try this.

Kean, John and Carl Personke. *The Language Arts: Teaching and Learning in the Elementary School*. New York: St. Martin's Press, 1976. A thorough review of language and its place in the elementary school. Good presentation of basic ideas and suggested classroom activities.

Savage, John. *Linguistics for Teachers*. Chicago: Science Research Associates, 1973. A superior collection of articles about linguistics, "the magic word" in language.

Zintz, Miles. *The Reading Process: The Teacher and the Learner*. 2nd ed. Dubuque, Iowa: Brown, 1975. A comprehensive analysis of contemporary reading instruction.

Part Three
The Learner and Learning

7

The Nature of Learning

Introduction

Students learn. They learn in school, often with difficulty, and out of school, usually with ease. For example, Liz is a college freshman who does fairly well in school but detests reading assignments. Yet she holds a part-time sales position in the jewelry department of a large store, which entails hours of home reading about emeralds, jade, and diamonds. She studies cheerfully, steadily, and successfully.

Or consider Ellen, a 15-year-old high school sophomore who dislikes mathematics. She works at the cash register a day and an evening a week in a local store. She has no difficulty with the constant computations including discounts, which involves fractions. John is a typical 14-year-old boy: lazy, experiencing a growth spurt, and sensitive to any suggestion of work. This tired, listless male, however, is capable of performing a graceful ballet around first base for hours under a broiling sun.

Those of you who have knowledge of school bands will agree that youngsters participate eagerly under trying conditions. The hours of practice, the miles of drill, the interminable parades, and endless competitions are a grueling ordeal. But these same children, who protest studying, homework, and tests, never miss a practice even though they miss lunch or dinner, become ill on lengthy bus trips, or faint in the heat.

These are difficult learning situations, but youngsters will move any obstacle to achieve a desired goal. They are motivated, and since motivation is such an important topic, we shall devote an entire chapter to it. The purpose of this chapter is to analyze the nature of learning—what it is, what forms it may take, and how teachers can help students retain and transfer their learning.

MEDFORD, MASS. *DAILY MERCURY*

It is impossible to exaggerate the importance of learning in our lives. It is the most important method of adjusting to our environment, and our analysis of the learning process is no abstract exercise. If you recall the statistics of Chapter 1, there are about 60 million students partaking of formal learning. Phillip Jackson, in his fascinating book *Life in Classrooms* (1968), states that on a typical weekday morning between September and June millions of American youngsters bid their families goodbye, pick up their lunch boxes and books, and spend the day in enclosures called elementary school classrooms. Here is where tests are passed and failed, where amusing things happen, where insights occur, and where skills are acquired. Each of these classrooms, the materials used, and the instructional techniques employed reflect a commitment to a psychology of learning.

Students' learning capacities are enormous but different. For example, consider yourself. You undoubtedly learn some things more quickly than others. Why? One explanation is that certain kinds of materials appeal to you. Some may learn readily from textbook reading; others effortlessly solve mathematical problems; still others need to form a picture of what is to be learned. By studying the learning process and understanding different theories you will both help your students' learning and improve your own teaching.

Different interpretations of learning

ASSOCIATIONISM VERSUS COGNITIVE THEORY

Learning theorists differ radically in their explanations of how people learn. The chief distinction is between the associationists and the cognitive theorists. The differences are important. Associationism offers a relatively mechanical model of human learning and emphasizes careful control of stimuli and responses. Cognitive theorists believe that inner processes substantially affect learning and help to explain individual differences. These underlying beliefs dictate different classroom materials and techniques. Neither theory answers all of our questions about how pupils learn. Table 7.1 illustrates some outstanding figures in the history of learning, plus their primary concerns.

Before scrutinizing the important theorists of Table 7.1, you should consider some critical questions that Hilgard and Bower raise (1966, pg. 68). They state that a comprehensive learning theory should answer those questions that an intelligent nonpsychologist would ask about everyday learning.

1. *What are the limits of learning?* Individuals differ in learning capacity and their ability to learn different things. The authors wonder if practice overcomes innate differences in capacity.

TABLE 7.1
Great Names in Learning Theory

ASSOCIATIONISM (ALSO CALLED BEHAVIORISM, S-R THEORY, CONDITIONING)		COGNITIVE THEORY (ALSO CALLED FIELD THEORY, GESTALT THEORY, PERCEPTUAL THEORY, PHENOMENOLOGY)	
Name	*Concern*	*Name*	*Concern*
Greek philosophers (Aristotle)	Principles of association (similarity, contrast, contiguity)	Classical Gestalt school (Wertheimer, Koffka, Köhler)	Insight
English philosophers (Locke, Berkely, Hume)	Association of ideas	Kurt Lewin	Life space
Alexander Bain	Turned to *S-R*	Jerome Bruner	Perception, concept formation, education
Edward Thorndike	Connectionism	Arthur Combs, Donald Syngg	Phenomenology
John Watson	Behaviorism		
Ivan Pavlov	Classical conditioning		
Edwin Guthrie	Contiguous conditioning		
B. F. Skinner	Instrumental conditioning		

Source: John F. Travers, *The Growing Child.* New York: John Wiley, 1977.

2. *What is the role of practice in learning?* Practice helps, but what precisely is known about it? Is it the amount of practice that is significant or is it the condition of practice? Is practice even harmful?

3. *How important are drives and incentives, rewards and punishments?* Theorists agree that reward and punishment can control learning and that it is easier to learn something exciting than dull. But questions remain. Are the results of reward and punishment equal and opposite? How do intrinsic and extrinsic motivation affect learning?

4. *What is the place of understanding and insight?* If people realize why they do certain things they may do them better. But they can also do some things very well with little understanding! You are probably unaware of your eye movements across the page; yet, obviously, you can read. Are these different kinds of learning?

5. *Does learning one thing help you to learn something else?* How do

students transfer learning? How can teachers help them? How much can they transfer?

6. *How does the process of remembering and forgetting work?* Memory is tricky; people often remember what they would like to forget, and forget what they would like to remember. What is involved in memory? How can teachers help pupils retain their learning?

These questions deserve answers. For example, if you are a math teacher, you want to know if there are ideal practice conditions that aid students both to retain and transfer their math learning to chemistry and economic classes. Classroom control always worries new teachers and is a major contribution to teaching success or failure. If there are tested, proven psychological principles about reward and punishment, teachers should understand them. Sarcasm or ridicule may control young children, but at what price? Sarcasm with older pupils may lead to further and more serious disciplinary problems. Remember these questions and decide if any one theory answers them all satisfactorily.

Associationism

Table 7.1 indicates some other names for associationism: *behaviorism*, *S-R* theory, *conditioning theory*. While some minor differences divide the associationists, they agree that students react to stimuli, and, consequently, those who manipulate the stimuli (parents, teachers) should be able to predict and control behavior.

THORNDIKE'S CONNECTIONISM

Edward Lee Thorndike (1874–1949), following an early interest in animal behavior, believed that all learning is explained by connections (or bonds) that are formed between stimuli and responses. These connections occur mainly through trial and error, which Thorndike later designated as learning by selecting and connecting. Thorndike formulated laws of learning, which were not inflexible laws but rules that learning seemed to obey. The three major laws as formulated in his *Animal Intelligence* (1911) and *The Psychology of Learning* (1913) have had direct application to education.

The Law of Readiness

The Laws of Learning   When organisms, both human and animal, are ready to form connections, to do so is satisfying and not to do so is annoying. As Hilgard and Bower note (1966), Thorndike believed that readiness is an important condition of learning because satisfaction or frustration depended on an individual's state of readiness. He states (1913, pg. 133) that readiness is like an army sending scouts ahead or a train whose arrival at one station sends signals ahead to open or close switches.

The Law of Exercise

Any connection is strengthened in proportion to the number of times it occurs and in proportion to the average vigor and duration of the connection. Conversely, when a connection is not made between a stimulus and response for some time, the connection's strength is decreased. Continued experimentation and criticism forced Thorndike after 1930 to revise the original law of exercise. He realized that practice alone was insufficient for improvement. There must also be a strengthening of the bond by reinforcement, that is, the law of effect must also operate.

The Law of Effect

Probably the most important of Thorndike's laws, it states that responses accompanied by satisfaction are more firmly connected with the situation; responses accompanied by discomfort have their connections weakened. The greater the satisfaction or discomfort, the greater is the strengthening or weakening of the bond. In 1932, Thorndike revised the law to stress that reward has a much greater strengthening effect than punishment has a weakening effect.

For many years, Thorndike had a powerful influence on educational practice, because of his insistence on a scientific basis for education. Hergenhahn (1976) states that Thorndike believed good teaching begins with knowing what you want to teach—the stimuli. You must also identify the responses you want to connect to the stimuli and the timing of appropriate satisfiers. As Thorndike would say:

1. Consider the pupil's environment.
2. Consider the response you want to connect with it.
3. Form the connection.

Thorndike's remarkable energy and drive led to an astounding number of publications and provided education with the scientific cloak it so desired. Still the theory's mechanical nature left the question of meaning and understanding unanswered.

WATSON'S BEHAVIORISM

John Watson (1878–1958) believed that Ivan Pavlov's work—classical conditioning—proved that there was no need for a "mind" or "consciousness" to explain human behavior.

He soon was convinced that learning was mainly conditioning—the substitution of one stimulus for another. In his experiments, Pavlov, a physiologist and winner of a Nobel prize in 1904, noticed that digestive juices flowed when the experimental animals merely anticipated food. Saliva flowed at the sight of a dish or an attendant, perhaps even at some sound the attendant made. These are *not* natural stimuli. Food in the animal's mouth is a natural stimulus; it, not these other stimuli, is expected to cause saliva.

A natural (unconditioned) stimulus causes a natural (unconditioned) response. Some neutral stimulus, associated with the original unconditioned stimulus at the time of the response, gradually acquires the ability to elicit the response. This is the conditioned stimulus. Learning is conditioning, and conditioning explains all "higher mental activity." The process is as follows:

a. $US \rightarrow UR$

b. $CS \rightarrow US \rightarrow UR$

c. $CS \rightarrow CR$

(US = food; UR = saliva; CS = sight of the attendant or conditioned stimulus; CR = saliva or conditioned response)

Thus the ability to elicit the response CR has shifted from US to CS. This is the famed conditioned reflex; the dog has "learned."

Watson was fascinated by Pavlov's work and believed that his search for an observable substitute for mind was over. Watson (1930) recognized three kinds of learning: emotional, manual, and laryngeal. These types of learning, based on conditioning, explained all human behavior.

Emotional Learning

Humans have three inborn emotions: fear, rage, and love. These are bodily responses that slowly develop into our complex emotions by conditioning. Many of a student's interests, attitudes, appreciations, and values are a direct result of the conditioning process. Also significant is the increasing interest in conditioning therapy, especially in the removal of fears and phobias. For example, in Watson's famous experiments with Albert, the child was given a rabbit with which to play. Each time Albert touched the rabbit, he was startled by a loud noise. The child gradually learned to fear not only rabbits, but *all furry objects*. (See Figure 7.1.)

Manual Learning

"Manual habits" was Watson's phrase for organization of the trunk, arms, legs, and feet. The human body undergoes ceaseless stimulation, from within and without, and responds with ceaseless movement. During this stimulation, activity constantly occurs. The more sophisticated and integrated manual responses evolve from simple responses by conditioning.

Language Learning—Thinking

"Laryngeal habits" was Watson's term for thinking. Language is a manipulative habit whereby the larynx is controlled by its at-

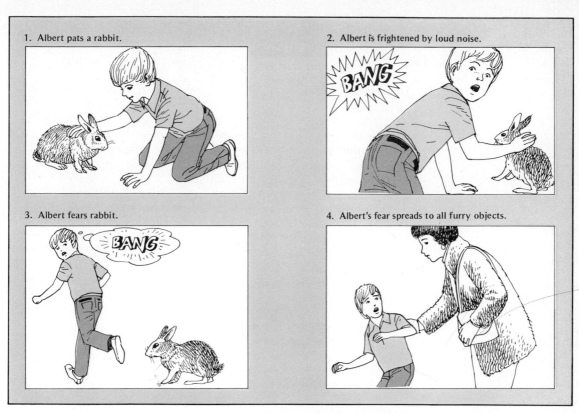

1. Albert pats a rabbit.

2. Albert is frightened by loud noise.

BANG

3. Albert fears rabbit.

BANG

4. Albert's fear spreads to all furry objects.

Figure 7.1 Albert Acquires a New Fear by Classical Conditioning

tached muscles as air is expelled. The result is a conditioned vocal response that grows from original unlearned responses. The unconditioned stimulus is some change in the muscular or glandular tissue of the throat. The unconditioned response is some unintelligible, uncontrolled vocal reaction. Word conditioning depends upon these stimuli and responses as the individual associates sounds with objects, events, and persons, and slowly achieves a more skillful manipulation of laryngeal habits. Thought, obviously, is not restricted to the larynx, since thought and expression are possible even when the larynx is removed. Any bodily response may then become a word substitute: a shake of the head, or shrug of the shoulders.

All three habit systems actually function in any reactions, but usually one predominates and, as humans are rational beings, the laryngeal habits dominate life. It is the integration of the three systems that shapes an individual's personality. Watson's place in psychology is secure because of the complete break he made with psychology's philosophical tradition.

SKINNER AND OPERANT CONDITIONING

It may be well to pause here to clarify the rather subtle distinctions among the various interpretations of conditioning.

1. *Classical conditioning.* This is Pavlov's interpretation of conditioning. A neutral stimulus, present when an unconditioned stimulus elicits a response, will, on repetition, gradually acquire the ability to produce a similar response. It now is termed a *conditioned stimulus*, and the process frequently is referred to as "conditioning," or "classical conditioning," and is characterized by something being done to the organism.

2. *Instrumental conditioning.* Unhappy with existing explanations of behavior, B. F. Skinner (b. 1904) focused upon an organism's responses to explain its behavior. In several major publications, *The Behavior of Organisms* (1938), *Science and Human Behavior* (1953), *Verbal Behavior* (1957), *The Technology of Teaching* (1968), *Beyond Freedom and Dignity* (1971), *About Behaviorism* (1974), and in a steady flow of articles, Skinner has reported his experiments and developed and clarified his theory. He has never avoided the challenge to apply his findings to practical affairs, as have many other theorists. Education, religion, psychotherapy, and other subjects have all felt the repercussion of Skinner's thought. There is little doubt that his work, still continuing at a vigorous pace, will be a source of influence and controversy for many years.

The following are the chief differences between the two views.

Classical Conditioning	Instrumental Conditioning
1. Known stimulus	1. Unknown stimulus
2. Elicited response	2. Emitted response
3. Type *S* conditioning	3. Type *R* conditioning

Type *S* refers to conditioning of stimuli. Type *R* refers to conditioning of responses.

Operant and respondent behavior

For Skinner, behavior is a causal chain of three links: (1) an operation performed upon the organism from without; (2) some inner condition; and (3) a kind of behavior. Lacking information about inner conditions, investigators must manipulate the environment and, consequently, must always go beyond the second link in the causal chain. For example, a pupil is listless and disinterested during class. Skinner scoffs at those who say the child is unmotivated. What does this mean? How can you explain it behaviorally? The problem is that the teacher or counselor searching for causes has stopped at the second link: some inner condition. The answer lies in the first link: something done to the child, such as lack of breakfast, physical difficulty, or trouble with parents.

B. F. Skinner

HARVARD UNIVERSITY NEWS OFFICE

Respondent Behavior

Behavior is a process, changing and fluid, yet some organizing principle must explain behavioral data. Skinner believes it is possible to classify behavior as either respondent or operant, which distinguishes his system from conventional stimulus-response psychology. Advocates of the customary stimulus-response basis of behavior were concerned with stimulus substitution, that is, a neutral stimulus acquires the power to elicit a response that was initially elicited by another stimulus.

Operant Behavior

With operant conditioning the concern is not with stimuli. The response appears without identifying any stimulus or without manipulating the environment (Skinner, 1953). Skinner is concerned with not a single but a class of responses. Reinforcement is dependent upon the response and it is important to remember that reinforcement does *not* strengthen the response. (It has already occurred.) What has changed is the probability of future responses in the same class (Skinner, 1953).

Elicited Responses

When an identified stimulus causes a response, the resultant behavior is called respondent. Responses are elicited by the stimuli. But there is a much more prevalent kind of response that appears and that resists identification with any stimulus. A response thus occurs apparently unrelated to anything in the immediate environment. These responses are called *emitted responses*, and Skinner refuses to speculate about the stimuli that cause them. He believes

Emitted Response

that knowledge of the stimuli acting at the time of an emitted response is irrelevant. Emitted responses, which lack any recognizable stimuli, constitute Skinner's classification of operant behavior.

Skinner holds that most human behavior is operant—that is, response patterns appear that cannot be linked with any stimuli. For example, we see a youngster walking to the library. The actions (responses) are clearly evident; but why is the child walking down the street, going into the library, selecting certain books, and finally returning home? What stimulus, or stimuli, set these responses in motion? Here you clearly see the dilemma facing the observer who feels compelled to attribute responses to pronounced stimuli.

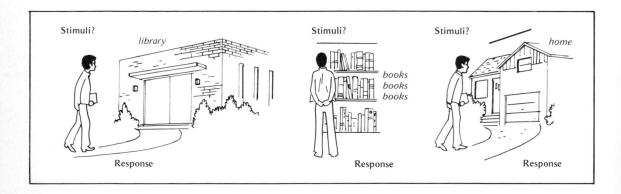

Conditioning

If there are two types of responses there must be two types of conditioning; in Skinner's theory these are called type S and type R conditioning. Type S conditioning is Pavlovian and describes the conditioning of respondent behavior. For Skinner, type S conditioning is relatively unimportant because most human behavior is operant; he also has serious reservations that many other agents are involved in classical conditioning.

Type S Conditioning

Type R Conditioning

Type R conditioning, which is the conditioning of operant behavior, is far more significant in Skinner's scheme. (As an aid in distinguishing the two types of conditioning, it may be helpful for the reader to note that S in type S conditioning emphasizes the stimulus, while the R in type R conditioning emphasizes the response.) The response is reinforced. The experimental evidence for type R conditioning resulted from bar pressing by rats in the famous Skinner box.

The Skinner Box

A hungry rat explores the box (which is as free from distracting stimuli as possible) and after a number of trials learns to push the bar to receive food. The animal must *push* the bar; it is the only way by which it can obtain food. It actually *does* something to alter the environmental conditions; it is *instrumental* in securing reinforcement (hence the term "instrumental conditioning"). It *operates* on the environment to secure reinforcement (hence the term "operant conditioning"). Neither Skinner nor anyone else knows why the rat initially pushes the lever.

Reinforcement

The unusual quality and distinctive feature of Skinner's system is his insistence that reinforcement neither precedes nor accompanies but *follows* the response. If Skinner's theory has a basic law, it must be that of reinforcement: When any response is reinforced, that behavior will probably reappear under similar circumstances. But, as you so well understand, our daily endeavors lack continuous reinforcement. The worker at the plant usually receives a yearly increase in salary; the author receives royalties long after the book is written; the student receives periodic grades. If reinforcement is so vital, several serious questions are raised by the conditions of practical, daily living. Ultimately, all questions become one: What kind of intermittent reinforcement is most effective?

Intermittent Reinforcement

Skinner believes that there are two kinds of intermittent reinforcement: *interval* and *ratio*. *Interval reinforcement* refers to a schedule whereby the animal is reinforced at definite established time intervals; for example, it may receive a food pellet every 30 or 60 seconds after the previous reinforcement. The animal reduces its responses immediately after reinforcement and then slowly increases its responses as the time for another reinforcement approaches.

A *ratio schedule* means that the animal is reinforced after a certain number of responses. The animal may receive a food pellet on every fifth, tenth, or twentieth response. If the ratio is slowly altered, an amazing number of responses may result from a very low number of reinforcements. Skinner also has developed *variable* schedules for both interval and ratio reinforcement, whereby the animal could be reinforced at any time or after any response (Skinner and Ferster, 1957).

Finally, Skinner accepts the principle of *secondary reinforcement*. For example, an animal presses a bar and a light appears, followed by food. After conditioning is established, bar pressing is sharply reduced in the dark by no reinforcement. If the conditions are again changed and pressing the bar produces light, then the number of bar-pressing responses increases significantly, and the light itself is now a reinforcer. Skinner designates the light as a *generalized reinforcer*. He uses money as an obvious example of a generalized reinforcer because money is associated with a great many primary reinforcers.

Shaping behavior

One of Skinner's great appeals is his willingness to apply his theories. If he is correct, behavior is controlled by the behavior-reinforcement association. Responses are regulated by the reinforcements that accompany them. If the organism makes a response that the individual in charge of reinforcements thinks is correct or desirable, then that response leads to a goal—food for the animal, good grades or praise for the human. Skillful manipulation of reinforcements will refine or shape the responses until they reach a suitable level.

In one of Skinner's famous experiments, he teaches a pigeon to make a complete circle to the left to secure food. Whenever the hungry pigeon makes the slightest movement to the left the behavior is rewarded. But each movement must be slightly more to the left than its predecessor. Skinner gradually shapes the pigeon's behavior until it makes a complete circle to the left. Using this technique, he can cause animals to perform remarkable feats, for example, pigeons to play Ping-Pong.

Here, as elsewhere, note the key role of reinforcement in controlling behavior for Skinner. While you may think of reinforcers as rewards, they also may act as punishment. Skinner identifies a *positive reinforcer* as a stimulus whose *presentation* strengthens behavior. A *negative reinforcer* is a stimulus *whose withdrawal* strengthens behavior. What happens when a teacher or parent withdraws a positive reinforcer (a child cannot go to the movies) or introduces a negative reinforcer (slapping, scolding)? Skinner believes that these two conditions describe punishment. Punishment has certain discernible effects.

1. *It is confined to the immediate situation and may have no effect in the future.* A good example is gum chewing. Look at your classmates during your next class. Some will almost surely be chewing gum. Ask if any one of them had ever been punished for chewing gum in school. Invariably some will recall that during elementary school they either had to stay after class, do extra work, or wear the gum on their nose. Yet here they are chewing noisily.

2. *There may be a future effect if the punished behavior later produces conditioned stimuli that evoke unpleasant emotional responses.* For example, when a youngster begins to chew gum in school, the memory of previous punishment arouses feelings of guilt and anxiety that will inhibit gum chewing. One immediate difficulty is that previously punished behavior may become acceptable under different circumstances. For example, a boy or girl from a devoutly religious family may have had premarital sex followed by feelings of remorse, guilt, and acute anxiety—all forms of self-punishment. It is possible that these feelings become so intense that they affect sexual life after marriage.

3. *Any stimulus accompanying the aversive stimulus may be conditioned to that behavior.* A pupil who has a nagging, sarcastic teacher in the first or second grade may react with fear to any classroom setting.

Should teachers resort to punishment? The practical answer is yes. Problems arise in a classroom where a teacher must act quickly and decisively or lose control of an entire class. But teachers should use punishment sparingly, carefully, and as a last resort. One reason is that we simply do not understand punishment's effects. If you must use it, here are some suggestions.

1. *If you must punish be sure that you later have the student do something that you can reinforce positively.* Do not have your use of punishment produce a hostile, defiant pupil who sees teachers as nothing more than punishing agents.
2. *Punish individuals, not classes.* Nothing is so ludicrous as having an entire class remain late, or do some exercise, because one or two individuals caused trouble.
3. *Avoid using school subjects as punishment.* There is no better

Skinner and Teaching Failure

In a perceptive analysis, Skinner ponders the reasons for teaching failure (1968). There is still excessive reliance upon aversive control (punishment). While corporal punishment is either frowned upon or prohibited, ridicule, sarcasm, criticism, banishment, and extra work have all filled the void. While they may be less objectionable than corporal punishment, students still spend considerable time doing things they dislike.

You can force students to read books, listen to talks, and take tests, but these activities are usually accompanied by unwanted by-products. Students soon devise ways to escape aversive stimuli. They come late, they are truant, they feign illness, they develop school phobia, or they simply "turn off" the teacher. They may even become disruptive. Vandalism increases.

It is not enough to provide attractive settings, to use multisensory materials to hold students' attention, or to make material insultingly simple. Students do not learn what they are shown or told unless positive reinforcement follows. Students remember certain things they have seen or heard during the day *because of the consequences that followed.* A young girl may be reinforced by her mother's attention when she tells her whom she saw in the store on the way home. These consequences are lacking when the same girl's teacher merely shows her, as one of many, a film or slides. Teaching will become more pleasant, and teachers more successful, when they abandon aversive techniques in favor of designing personally satisfying schedules of reinforcement for students. Skinner believes that programmed instruction is one alternative to aversive control.

way to teach students to dislike math or spelling than having them solve hundreds of extra problems or copy endless lists of words.

4. *Avoid sending youngsters to others for punishment.* You only inform students that *you* cannot control them. Also, the student will develop antagonistic or fearful feelings toward the principal or whoever dispenses punishment.

5. *If at all possible, ignore aggravating behavior.* Skinner calls this extinction. Some youngsters like to be punished. It is a way of getting attention and is reinforcing. By not supplying the attention or reinforcement, the behavior disappears. If a pupil's behavior is so disruptive that it affects an entire class, then naturally it cannot be ignored. You must act.

No one can tell you the best way for you to control a class. You yourself must discover what works best for you. You will encounter problems; everyone does. Refuse to panic and try various techniques until you discover your most effective method. Always remember that positive reinforcement is much more pleasant for you and the student than punishment. Problems are minimal in a pleasant, exciting atmosphere that encourages activity and cooperation.

Educational implications of Skinner's operant behavior theory

Skinner has been a critical observer of current educational practices (1968). He uses the teaching of arithmetic as an example. Youngsters must learn special verbal responses: words, figures, signs that refer to arithmetic functioning. Teachers must help pupils to bring this behavior under stimulus control.

Teaching Arithmetic

For example, children must learn to count, add, subtract, multiply, and divide before they can solve intricate mathematical problems. How are these procedures taught? Skinner believes that regardless of progressive or open education, youngsters still learn to avoid aversive stimulation, that is, punishment. While teachers seldom strike youngsters today, they still criticize and give them low marks, send them to the principal, or warn their parents.

Skinner questions the school's use of reinforcement. Reinforcement should be immediate and when considerable time elapses between response and reinforcement little, if any, learning results. Also, reinforcement is too infrequent. Pupils depend on a teacher, usually only one teacher, and Skinner estimates that during the first four school years teachers can arrange only a few thousand behavior-reinforcement contingencies. But efficient mathematical behavior during these years requires from 25 to 50 thousand contingencies of reinforcement. Consequently, mathematical instruction is inefficient and children not only are poor mathematicians but they also come to detest anything numerical.

Are You Good at Arithmetic?

One may agree or disagree with Skinner's views, but his identification of the reluctant mathematician is perceptive. Why is it that so many of us freeze at the sight of numbers? If you are comfortable with figures, you can easily solve the following problems. If you are one of the "frozen" your lack of arithmetic sense will show instantly.

1. Examine the following columns of figures for about 30 seconds. You will not be able to add each; that is not the purpose. After scanning each column, select the four that have the highest totals.

A	B	C	D	E	F	G	H	I
3	9	5	7	1	8	3	2	3
8	0	3	7	2	5	9	8	4
3	8	8	5	3	2	1	4	3
6	2	2	2	4	3	6	5	1
8	7	5	4	5	6	5	7	9
5	1	2	6	6	1	5	6	3
2	1	2	6	6	1	5	7	9
7	4	9	3	8	8	7	9	6

2. Fill in the blanks to make this a correct multiplication example:

$$
\begin{array}{r}
-7 \\
\times 8- \\
\hline
--- \\
--- \\
\hline
2--8 \\
\end{array}
$$

3. Place addition signs between the eights so that they total 1000:

8   8   8   8   8   8   8   8

These are relatively simple arithmetic puzzles. Some of you will do them instantly, some will experience difficulty. Can you explain why this is so, relating your answer to Skinner's work? Incidentally, youngsters in the fourth, fifth, and sixth grades will achieve similar results. Try it with them.

Answers: 1. H = 48, A = 42, G = 41, D = 40
2. 27 × 84
3. 888 + 88 + 8 + 8 + 8

As Skinner notes (1968, pg. 19), there would be little value in criticism if improvement were impossible. He suggests two major revisions.

1. The schools should search for reinforcements that they now possess and are not using. For example, children are fascinated by anything mechanical—paints, paper, scissors, and puzzles—which furnish feedback and are *not* punishing. It is not the amount of reinforcement that is significant. It is the *kind* of reinforcement—a small amount of positive reinforcement can be extremely effective.

2. Having discovered some useful reinforcements, how can the school make them contingent upon the desired behavior? The only way is to divide the material into small units and make reinforce-

ment contingent upon the successful completion of each step. Teachers thus almost insure positive reinforcement and eliminate dependence upon aversive stimuli. The best means of obtaining these results is by using teaching machines.

These are general proposals but Skinner's work has specific implications for the classroom teacher.

1. *Reinforcement is a powerful tool in controlling behavior, and teachers should be aware of its consequences.*

2. *The smile, the nod, even the grunt can all positively reinforce pupils.* Pupils also reinforce teachers in much the same way. There is a story (fictional?) of the college class who, after having learned about shaping behavior, only nodded their heads in agreement and understanding when the instructor moved to his right during the lecture. By the end of the semester he gave all of his classes standing by the windows—as far right as he could move!

3. *The famous "Premack principle" is of great value.* David Premack has stated (1965) that all organisms engage in some activities more than others. After noting a pupil's preferred activities, you can then use them to reinforce less frequent activities. To utilize the Premack principle effectively, you must know and understand your pupils to identify their preferred activites. For example, boys who lack the math sense mentioned earlier may love to play ball. A shrewd teacher, knowing these likes and dislikes, could promise them a ball game after they complete their math work.

4. *Aversive stimulation (punishment) may well cause more problems that it solves.* You should use it sparingly and carefully, although there are occasions when nothing else will suffice. If possible, have the offending pupil do something—and do it fairly quickly—that you can positively reinforce.

5. *Be aware of the timing of your reinforcement.* Obviously it is impossible to reinforce all desirable behavior, but if you decide that certain behavior is critical, then reinforce it immediately. Do not wait three, five, or seven days before reinforcing.

6. *Decide precisely what you want your students to learn and then arrange the material so that they make as little error as possible.*

This is called *sequencing.* Sequencing will encourage you to know both your students and subject even better than you do now. You must know the abilities of your students to arrange a subject in appropriate steps, and you must also know the range of your subject to make logical divisions and to determine what and when to reinforce.

Behavior modification

One of the most popular applications of operant conditioning is called *behavior modification,* which is based on the principle that people are influenced by the consequences of their behavior. As Kanfer (1973) notes, however, there is more to it than merely attaching reward or punishment to a behavior. It requires skill, patience, and theoretical expertise to define the problem and select appropriate reinforcers. When a teacher complains about a pupil's misconduct, lack of attention, underachievement, or nervousness, a practitioner of proficient behavioral modification will:

1. Carefully observe the child's behavior.
2. Carefully observe the teacher's behavior.
3. Carefully observe the classroom setting.
4. Carefully observe the home environment (if the problem is sufficiently severe).

5. Identify the conditions that cause problems.
6. Initiate behavioral intervention.

Becker (1973) argues strongly that Skinner's work has been a potent influence on classroom practices because it has effectively demonstrated the relevance of learning principles to teaching and learning. He believes that a teacher's verbal behavior, if carefully used as a reinforcer, can successfully alter 80 to 90 percent of all classroom behavior problems. Teachers have various other reinforcers that are also effective. Social reinforcers, such as a smile or nod, or even the teacher's physical presence, can strengthen desired behavior. Activity reinforcers—those things that children like

---

An Example of Behavior Modification

David Phillips (1974) has described a public school behavior modification project with which he was associated. It involved 75 children in a total school population of 750. These children were identified as socially maladjusted, emotionally disturbed, or retarded. Little attention was paid to standardized tests; instead, when a child manifested a learning or social problem, the problem was immediately and directly treated. Another assumption was that when students do not learn, they have not been taught.

Phillips states that it was difficult to identify satisfactory reinforcers. Food was used for a few children, but social reinforcers (praise, group play) were the chief means. The children immediately received points (marks on a piece of paper) when they exhibited desirable behavior. These were then turned in at the period's conclusion and actual reinforcers given. Phillips reports that most of the pupils are now functioning successfully in a regular classroom. He believes that certain principles emerge from this project.

1. Define the problem objectively and behaviorally. Avoid saying, "The child has a

bad attitude"; state the problem precisely, "The child is constantly out of his seat."
2. Measure the strength of the undesirable behavior. For example, how many times does the child leave his seat? Does he do it more in some classes than others?
3. Attach some consequences to the behavior; if you want to change the behavior, you must change the consequences. Be certain that the reinforcers you select are meaningful for the *pupil,* not for *you.*
4. Arrange the contingencies of reinforcement carefully. Reinforce small improvements in the desired behavior. You can do this by immediately approving a child's behavior, *if you are a positive source of reinforcement.* For example, your praise may reinforce one child but not another. Or you may arrange a token system whereby pupils receive some symbol that they may later redeem for the actual reinforcer.
5. Assess the efficiency of your contingencies of reinforcement. If they are not successful, perhaps they are inappropriate or there is an excessive delay between behavior and reinforcement.

to do—become powerful reinforcers. These techniques, however, demand more than a "warm and positive" classroom environment.

While warmth and acceptance are highly desirable, to meet the requirements of behavior modification the teacher's behavior must follow specific pupil responses. As Becker notes, it matters *when* the teacher praises *whom* and for *what* behavior. Knowing when to do what, for which behavior, and with what resources, and knowing how to monitor and test treatment effectiveness continuously, is the challenging aspect of behavior modification (Kanfer, 1973, pg. 4).

Skinner's influence has been enormous and is felt in social planning, education, programs for the emotionally disturbed and mentally retarded, even business. One final thought, however, requires reinforcement: reinforcement is a powerful influence on behavior. Even if you do not believe in elaborate Skinnerian programs, be aware of the potency of your approval (or its lack) and attempt to use it with discrimination to encourage desirable behavior.

Discussion Questions

1. Each of us favors one of the two major learning theories because it reflects our belief in human nature. Answer the questions posed by Hilgard and Bower according to what you now believe about learning. Which class of learning theories do you favor?

2. Be sure that you can distinguish between classical and operant conditioning. Which is Pavlov's? Skinner's? What is the main distinction between the two?

3. What is the meaning of: operant, instrumental, respondent, elicited, emitted? Give examples of each. Illustrate how these terms appear in classroom behavior.

4. How do you react to the notion of shaping behavior? Do you think it actually is possible? Would it work in the classroom? Defend your answer.

5. Do you believe in using punishment? If you answer no, suggest other means of classroom control. If you answer yes, how would you avoid unforseen consequences? Can you add any other practical suggestions for using punishment to those proposed?

6. Do you think that the Premack principle is feasible? How would you use it? Realistically, does a teacher have the time to discover what reinforces all of his or her pupils? Explain your answer.

7. Do you agree that behavior modification principles should be used in the classroom? Can teachers do it? How would you react to a rigidly planned learning atmosphere where token economies dominate a pupil's behavior? Do you see any ethical problems?

Cognitive theory

Cognitive theory includes classical Gestalt psychology and its modern versions, such as topological, perceptual and phenomenological psychology. For the cognitive theorists, *reaction to a stimulus is relatively unimportant*. What assumes significance is the individual's perception of the relationship in the environment. Experience consists of, not isolated and separate S-R bonds, but the organized pattern of an individual's field.

THE GESTALTISTS

Concern with the "Whole"

Field theories had their origin in classical Gestalt thought. Max Wertheimer (1880–1943), studying the perception of movement (for example, watching movies), became convinced that conventional explanations, such as movement as a composition of visual S-R bonds, were completely inadequate. These accounts failed to explain the "wholeness" of the problem. Two famous psychologists, Wolfgang Köhler (1887–1962) and Kurt Koffka (1886–1941), served as subjects in Wertheimer's studies and later were responsible for the popularity of Gestalt theory, especially in the United States.

The Gestaltists claimed that experience is not the sum of parts because there is a form or wholeness that is destroyed by analysis. The word "gestalt" means a configuration, shape, or form. Since all events in nature occur within some field, it is the totality of the field, its properties and structure, that explains all events happening *within* the field.

Köhler (1969) offers an excellent example. He arranged two lamps behind a screen, with a straight rod between them and nearer the screen. A double switch permitted rapidly turning on and off of both lamps. Both lamps cast shadows at different locations (see Figure 7.2). When one lamp is turned on, then off, and then the other lamp turned on, a shadow appears and disappears in both places. There is no actual movement from place to place. When the shadows are made to appear and disappear rapidly, an observer sees one shadow moving back and forth across the screen.

How can we interpret the results? Köhler states that when stimulations occur in different places under certain conditions the visual processes are not independent S-R bonds—the processes must interact. Thus, individuals react to the perception of events. To understand why students behave as they do, teachers must know as much about them as possible and try to see the classroom and learning through their eyes. So often things are not as they really are but only as they seem to be to students.

Within each field (for example, the classroom), the figure-ground relationship is critical. The process of attention enables a

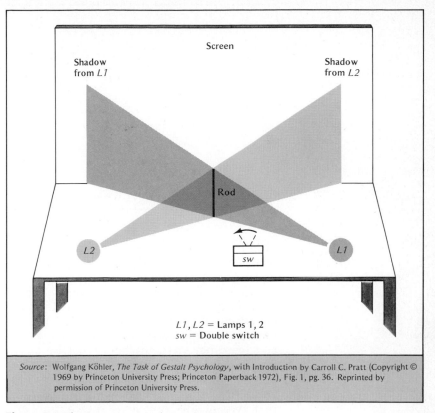

Figure 7.2 The Appearance of Movement

Source: Wolfgang Köhler, *The Task of Gestalt Psychology*, with Introduction by Carroll C. Pratt (Copyright © 1969 by Princeton University Press; Princeton Paperback 1972), Fig. 1, pg. 36. Reprinted by permission of Princeton University Press.

pupil to be aware of a thing, or teacher, or event as distinct from the background. Yet it is the background that enriches a student's perception of something, and the better you understand the various relationships of background to a thing or person, the richer will be your perception. Insight is unquestionably the most basic concept in Gestalt thought. It is by insight that an individual learns, solves problems, and thinks creatively. Insight is a consciousness of vital relationships, and it supplies structure or organization to a previously disorganized field. Insight is a form of perception, a kind of neural organization, and the more intelligent, mature person achieves insight more readily than a less gifted individual. There is little doubt that prior experience also facilitates insight.

To illustrate how the relationship of parts within a field affects your perception of reality, examine the following carefully and report what you see:

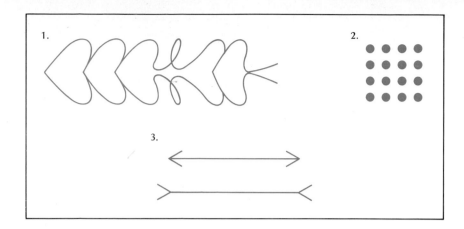

In the first figure you probably did not recognize the common word "men" because of the altered nature of the lines. In the second figure you probably identified a square—although it consists of circles! You ignored the circles at the corners because of the relationship among all the circles. In the third figure, both lines are exactly the same length.

These simple examples are extremely informative about teaching and learning. First, teachers must be alert to the way that pupils see their work. Second, teachers must arrange materials so that pupils see meaningful relationships and are not bewildered by obstructions in the field. Reading is a good example. If you recall the first two of the four steps (perception and comprehension), it is easy to understand how pupils experience difficulty. If their perception is distorted (they do not recognize a word because they cannot perceive the relationship among letters), they cannot comprehend the author's meaning. Learning consequently suffers.

Hilgard and Bower (1966, pp. 257–258) list several features that distinguish field theory.

1. *Since learning depends upon the differentiation and restructuring of fields, any higher type of learning depends upon a natural capacity for responding in such a manner.* Difficulty in differentiating and structuring a field is often attributed to poor instruction rather than an individual's innate capacity.
2. *Field theorists believe in the value of practice, but insist that changes occur within repetition, not as a result of repetition.* Repetitions enable an individual to discover new relationships in his or her field.
3. *Humans have an inherent tendency toward completeness that the Gestaltists designate as the principle of closure.* Attainment of a goal modifies behavior because of the results of closure; that is,

activities leading to a goal are transformed because of their success or failure.

4. *Perception of relationships is constantly stressed in Gestalt thought and implies that problems are solved sensibly and structurally rather than mechanically or randomly.* Teachers should constantly encourage pupils to search for relationships.

5. *Transfer of learning occurs because of transposition.* The perception of relationships that is discovered in one circumstance becomes applicable to another. Although there will be similarity between the two situations, there need not be identical elements. Rather a similarity of patterns or relationships is perceived. For example, pupils recognize "Song Sung Blue" regardless of the key in which it is played.

Lewin's Topological Psychology

Gestalt psychology has had many illustrious advocates. Aside from the original Berlin group of Wertheimer, Koffka, and Köhler, Kurt Lewin (1890–1947) developed his own theory as a result of work with classical Gestalt thought (Lewin, 1935, 1936, 1942). Lewin came to the United States in 1932, where he taught at Stanford, Cornell, Iowa, and the Massachusetts Institute of Technology. His theory is more precisely known as "topological" psychology because of its emphasis upon the individual's perception of environmental forces acting upon him—that is, the "mapping" of the person's life space.

Wertheimer (1959) summarizes the principles of problem-solving behavior and simultaneously provides a concise statement of the Gestalt interpretation of learning. We can begin by recounting the famous story of Gauss, the great mathematician. When he was 6-years-old and attending a local grammar school, the teacher presented the class with the following problem:

"Who will be first to get the sum of
$$1 + 2 + 3 + 4 + 5 + 6 + 7 + 8 + 9 + 10?"$$

While the rest of the class was still working, Gauss raised his hand with the answer.

When the teacher asked how he attained it so quickly, this 6-year-old boy replied that if he had added $1 + 2 = 3$, then $3 + 3 = 6$, and $6 + 4 = 10$ to completion, it would have been time consuming and error prone. Instead he saw that $1 + 10 = 11$, $2 + 9 = 11$, $3 + 8 = 11$, $4 + 7 = 11$, $5 + 6 = 11$. There are five pairs: $5 \times 11 = 55$. Gauss, with his uncanny mathematical sense, had unconsciously discovered and used an important theorem: $Sn = [(n+1)(n/2)]$. (Recall what was discussed earlier: Why do some students and adults develop a "feeling" for mathematics while others never capture it? Can you link teaching to this phenomenon?)

Wertheimer uses the Gauss story and asks why so many find

the task difficult. He believes that students must learn problem-solving behavior and he offers the following guidelines.

DO NOT

Be bound and blinded by habits.
Repeat slavishly what you have been taught.
Proceed mechanically with a piecemeal attitude, piecemeal attention, and piecemeal operations.

DO

Look at the problem openly and as a whole.
Try to discover how the problem and the total situation are related.
Try to discover regularity by perceiving the relationship in the problem.

The early Gestaltists have made us conscious of the need to examine wholes, to perceive relationships, and to discover patterns. Their influence continues and is seen in Jerome Bruner.

BRUNER AND THE PROCESS OF EDUCATION

We have previously studied Bruner's thoughts on intellectual development, language acquisition, and MACOS. In 1960 he wrote a remarkable little book called the *Process of Education*, in which he presented his ideas on teaching, learning, and curriculum design. Bruner is a cognitive theorist who has refined many of the early Gestaltist ideas to meet contemporary challenges.

He states that there is one inescapable component of human learning—the opportunity for exploration. This basic belief is far removed from the Skinnerian warning that learning should proceed by minute steps. Students are encouraged to explore, to discover, to make mistakes and use them to further their "learning how to learn."

Bruner and learning

Bruner develops four major themes in analyzing learning: structure, readiness, intuition, motivation.

1. *Understanding a subject's structure is central to Bruner's thinking.* He states (1960, pg. 17):

The first object of any act of learning, over and beyond the pleasure it may give, is that it should serve us in the future. Learning should not only take us somewhere: it should allow us later to go further more easily.

As he notes, grasping a subject's structure is understanding it so that many other things can be related to it meaningfully—to learn structure is to learn how things are related. Pupils can only grasp a subject's structure if they understand its basic ideas. The more basic the idea that students learn, the more they can apply it to other topics. Ensuring that pupils understand a subject's fundamental structure makes the subject itself more comprehensible, aids memory, facilitates transfer, and helps to build a "spiral curriculum."

The spiral curriculum is an excellent example of an attempt to develop structure. For example, World War II has become a major topic in contemporary history. Using the principles of the spiral curriculum, it is successively taught at higher grade levels in an increasingly abstract manner. Figure 7.3 illustrates the process. Note the increasing abstraction and complexity of the presentation. Completing their study, pupils should have a good grasp of the subject.

2. *The spiral curriculum is closely linked to Bruner's second theme—readiness.* His famous statement that any subject can be taught effectively in some intellectually honest form to any child at any stage of development implies that the basic ideas of science, mathematics, and literature are as simple as they are powerful. If teachers begin teaching the foundations of these subjects in an appropriate manner consistent with pupils' intellectual level, as described by Piaget, pupils can learn important basics at any stage of mental development. Then, by applying the principles of the spiral curriculum, they can steadily proceed to more complex forms of the subject.

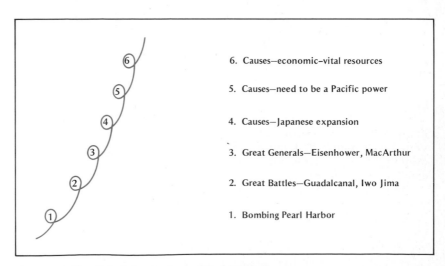

6. Causes—economic—vital resources

5. Causes—need to be a Pacific power

4. Causes—Japanese expansion

3. Great Generals—Eisenhower, MacArthur

2. Great Battles—Guadalcanal, Iwo Jima

1. Bombing Pearl Harbor

Figure 7.3 The Spiral Curriculum—World War II

3. *Once students obtain a detailed knowledge of a subject, they can begin to expand their hypothetical abilities; that is, they can make an informed guess.* Knowing a topic deeply and widely enables them to proceed by implicit perception; they can grasp something without detailed analysis. They can make their informed guess and then subject it to critical analysis, thus fostering both problem-solving and creative behavior.

4. *Motivation is Bruner's final indispensable learning ingredient.* He questions the value of excessive emphasis upon examinations, grades, and promotions with respect to a desirable lifetime commitment to learning. Children always have mixed motives for learning: pleasing parents and teachers, competing with peers, and acquiring a sense of self-mastery. It is difficult to inspire intrinsic motivation in a child; so Bruner realistically states that, if you teach well and what you teach is worth learning, there are forces in our society that will provide the external prod to have children become more involved in their learning processes.

Bruner and Teaching Success

Bruner describes a junior high school course he taught that illustrates these principles (1966, pg. 109). One unit related Caesar's decision to cross the Rubicon and drive for Rome. The class had Caesar's commentaries, nothing about his opponent Pompey, and some letters from Cicero. The class immediately divided into Caesarians and Pompeyans and tried to obtain more information about strategy. Would Caesar move his army through a narrow valley unless he had previous reassurance that the inhabitants were friendly? Bruner states that the pupils reasoned like politicians.

One group of troublesome students provided an excellent analysis of the corrupt Roman political system and sympathized totally with Caesar. Pompey "had no guts." When these students compared Roman to current politicians and equated Roman governmental problems with current difficulties, the course came alive.

Here you see an excellent example of theory translated into practice. Bruner believes that any act of learning involves three processes:

1. The acquisition of new information. What was the political situation in the valley?
2. Transformation, or manipulation, of knowledge to make it fit new tasks. Was the Roman political situation similar to contemporary American politics?
3. Evaluation, or determining if the manipulated knowledge is adequate. Does understanding and applying current information help to comprehend the Roman issues?

A learning episode occurred, which reflected what had gone before it, and which permitted generalization beyond it.

Anyone at any age is ready to learn; allow children to explore and make educated guesses; allow them to make mistakes; teach them the structure of a subject, not minute and isolated facts: Bruner's ideas are far removed from Skinner's and imply a radically different interpretation of how children learn. You may want to try both techniques in your classroom, but be sure you also understand *why* these theories differ. They reflect opposing views of human nature. You probably are more comfortable with one than the other; so be sure you understand your own beliefs. You will be much more effective with those theories and practices that are compatible with your beliefs.

As there are specific classroom implications for Skinner's work, so Bruner also has some specific recommendations. He notes that there are many mechanical aids for teachers (films, tv, programmed instruction) but the chief facilitator of learning still remains the teacher. If you believe in cognitive learning principles, Bruner suggests (1960, pp. 88–92) that you consider the following:

1. *If you desire to teach effectively, you must master the material to be taught.* (There probably is no better way of learning a subject than teaching it.)
2. *Remember that you are a model.* Unimaginative, uninspiring, and insecure teachers are hardly likely to spark a love of learning, especially since students quickly sense a lack of commitment.
3. *Remember that, as a model, students will identify with you and often compare themselves with you.* It is a sobering thought, but it can motivate you to search constantly for ways to better your teaching and furnish a stimulating classroom atmosphere.

The learning process

Travers (1972) analyzes the difficulty in defining learning and the search for a sufficiently broad expression that permits wide usage. He begins by quoting Allport's statement (1961) that theories of learning, like everything else in psychology, depend upon the investigator's conception of human nature. Thus, there is no commonly accepted definition of learning because there is no commonly accepted view of human nature.

He also stresses the split between those who value definitions of learning as a process and those who emphasize learning products. Although the "within" of man is uncharted territory, focus upon learning products forces attention upon outer manifestations and ignores the reality of the inner operation that caused these

Learning as a Process

outer characteristics. While learning is a process, studying what is learned deserves attention because it is possible to infer the inner activity from the outer and observable phenomena. These behavioral changes indicate learning, and if they are lacking you may well question whether learning has occurred. Travers (1972, pg. 9) then summarizes the inner and outer working of learning and defines it as a process that results in the modification of behavior. He also insists that such behavioral changes must be attributed to learning and not to maturation, fatigue, or drugs.

Chapter 6 mentioned the characteristics of learning: a motivated individual, an obstacle, environmental stimuli, perception of the field, response pattern, and the goal. These characteristics function in all learning. For example, Travers (1972, pp. 21–23) describes the learning sequence as follows: A child sees family members enjoying reading and she wants to learn to read (motivation). But there is an obstacle: she is unfamiliar with letters, combinations, and meanings. So a goal is established: learning to read. Now environmental stimuli are important; in our example they would be colorful, relevant, and appropriate reading materials. Once in school, the process continues and the child builds a sight vocabulary (she perceives the field). Simultaneously the youngster refines and expands her response pattern: she combines letters into words, words into sentences, sentences into paragraphs, and paragraphs into stories. She has learned to read—the goal is attained. Figure 7.4 illustrates the learning sequence.

THE FORM OF LEARNING

The learning process results in different types of learning, which can be classified into four categories:

1. *Motor learning.* If you reflect upon the sequence of activities that is required for the execution of a "simple" motor skill, you soon realize how complicated it is. Separate phases of the skill are mastered; this is called *differentiation*—the discrimination and identification of the elements of the task. Once the separate parts are performed satisfactorily, you must recombine them. This is called *integration*. There is also some mental commitment. Learners ma-

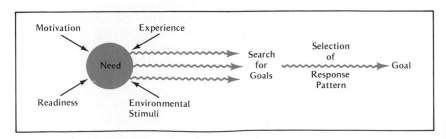

Figure 7.4 The Learning Sequence

BOSTON, SUMMERTHING

nipulate muscles; they also must understand the relationship of parts to whole and the goal. Playing golf is a good example. You must learn to grip the club and position your feet correctly, to move your body and club in a smooth swing, and then to swing the club in an inside out direction to hit the ball. After learning these individual tasks, you combine them into a smooth, effortless swing.

2. *Rote learning.* How do human beings memorize anything? First they must have an objective. Next, they must begin to make the necessary associations: word to word, line to line, and stanza to stanza. The rate and retention of learning improve if there is some comprehension of the material. Finally, there must be repetition until the verbal associations are firmly implanted.

3. *Comprehension.* This is a more intricate kind of learning. Pu-

MEDFORD, MASS. DAILY MERCURY

pils seek relationships, hunting for a cause-and-effect connection. But before discovering relationships they must form concepts, which are generalizations gained from experience with specifics.

4. *Problem solving.* Can pupils use their knowledge in adjusting to novel changes in the environment? First, they must know that a problem exists, otherwise there will be no drive toward solution. Next, they search the environment for possible clues to the solution and decide which of these is most promising. They now test tentative solutions. The logical and psychological soundness of their hypotheses reveals much about mental ability. Since students must use preceding levels of learning in problem solving, the abil-

ity to reach systematic, and perhaps even ingenious, solutions discloses an innate capacity to perform on the abstract level.

WHAT INFLUENCES LEARNING?

Regardless of the learning type (verbal, motor) there are certain conditions that decisively affect learning. These conditions, or variables, may be individual, task, or method variables. Garry and Kingsley (1970) offer the classification scheme outlined in Table 7.2.

The three classes of variables coupled with the organizational intricacies of any school system vividly illustrate the complexity of the learning process. The following study is a good example.

A recent survey of the Philadelphia school system offers some hard data about influences on learning. The variables studied were class size, school size, teacher experience, and rating of teachers colleges.

1. *Class size.* Elementary school classes up to 33 have no negative effect on achievement. Classes of 34 or more have a negative effect on all elementary pupils. Elementary students who are below grade level gain in classes below 28. For junior high school students, classes of 32 or more negatively affect achievement. Senior high school English classes that did not exceed 26 had the highest learning rates. If you examine Figure 7.5 you can judge the range of class size for the sixth, eighth, and twelfth grades and relate them to achievement data.

TABLE 7.2
Variables Affecting Learning

Individual Variables	Task Variables	Method Variables
Maturation	Length of material	Practice
Age	Difficulty of material	Degree of learning
Sex	Meaningfulness	Recitation
Previous experience	Retroactive inhibition and interference	Knowledge of results
Capacity: mental age, intelligence, aptitude		Whole versus part
		Sensory modality used
Physical handicaps		Set
Motivation		Guidance
		Incentives

Adapted from Garry and Kingsley, 1970.

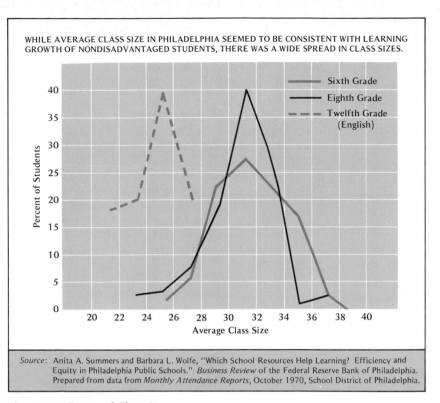

Figure 7.5 Range of Class Size

2. *School size.* Smaller schools seem to produce increased learning at the elementary and senior high levels. School size seems to be nonsignificant at the junior high level. One interesting finding concerning junior high school is that an eighth grade that is part of an elementary school increases pupil achievement growth by 4.3 months. Figure 7.6 shows the great variety in the size of Philadelphia schools.

3. *Teacher experience.* An interesting finding in the Philadelphia elementary schools was that high achievers do better with experienced teachers while low achievers do better with new, relatively inexperienced teachers. The older, more experienced teachers may be more impatient with slow learners. In the junior high schools, English teachers with ten years teaching experience seem to benefit all students, while math teachers with the same experience actually reduce the learning rate. One possible explanation is that these math teachers were teaching the new math without prior training in it. Figure 7.7 shows years of teaching experience.

4. *Rating of teachers colleges.* The data are not conclusive, al-

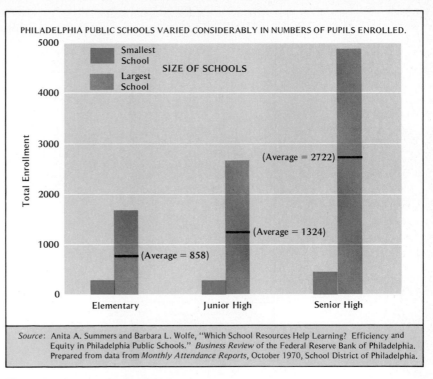

PHILADELPHIA PUBLIC SCHOOLS VARIED CONSIDERABLY IN NUMBERS OF PUPILS ENROLLED.

Source: Anita A. Summers and Barbara L. Wolfe, "Which School Resources Help Learning? Efficiency and Equity in Philadelphia Public Schools." *Business Review* of the Federal Reserve Bank of Philadelphia. Prepared from data from *Monthly Attendance Reports*, October 1970, School District of Philadelphia.

Figure 7.6 Range of School Size

though elementary school pupils achieved better if they had teachers from highly rated colleges.

If all of these variables affect learning—and they do—is there any hope of matching a student with an ideal learning environment? Is there a suitable learning environment for students' learning styles? You may well ask whether there is anything that does not affect learning. The answer is no and is the reason that teaching is challenging and frustrating, exciting and fulfilling.

LEARNING STYLES AND LEARNING ENVIRONMENTS

Smith and Bentley (1975) have devised an ingenious technique for analyzing learning styles and attempting to match them with appropriate teaching styles. Students learn through many channels: hearing, sight, touch (especially important during the early years), and even taste and smell. Some students require substantial teacher help; others achieve more independently. Some pupils learn more as passive group members, others as active members.

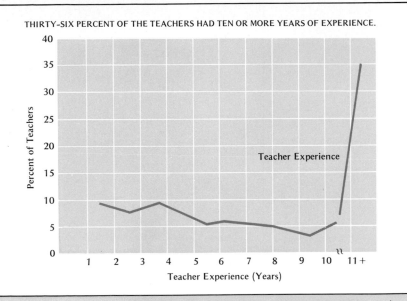

Figure 7.7 Years of Teaching Experience

The size and composition of the group also affect learning. Some learn slowly; others grasp ideas quickly. These and many other conditions suggest the need for specific learning environments. To design an effective learning environment three questions must be answered.

1. *How do the individual students learn best?* Again, knowing your students will permit you to construct groups and conditions that will promote the learning of individual pupils.
2. *Does all learning occur within the school?* What sources are available outside the classroom that will motivate pupils and advance learning? These sources must be pertinent so that learning occurs; recreation is something else. Teachers are facilitators of knowledge, not tour directors.
3. *Has there been adequate planning?* Adequate implies that you, the classroom teacher, are a key figure because you know if your students rely primarily upon reading or listening, or if they function better in small groups.

Smith and Bentley illustrate three different kinds of teaching and learning styles that reflect both teachers' and learners' personalities.

I. INTELLECTUALLY DIRECTED TEACHING AND LEARNING STYLES

Teacher	Learner
Always displays composure	Works alone frequently
Appears aloof	Uses library frequently
Demonstrates academic excellence	Self-directed
Reads widely	Reads well
Little team work	Few extracurricular activities
Quiet	Quiet
Quotes authorities	Displays persistence

II. EMOTIONALLY DIRECTED TEACHING AND LEARNING STYLES

Teacher	Learner
Many plants and animals in classroom	Likes art work
Environmentally conscious	Enjoys caring for plants and animals
Sense of humor	Good in group
Uses play and drama	Enjoys informal learning situations
May be good in motivating, but weak in basic skills	Takes drama, art, or music lessons

III. METHODICAL, STRUCTURED TEACHING AND LEARNING STYLES

Teacher	Learner
Manages time well	Disturbed by schedule change
Stays on schedule	Wants specific instructions and directions
Aided by lesson plan	Wants to know what will be in test
Divides work into attainable goals	"How many pages should I write?"
Achieves goals	Sets attainable goals
Innovates cautiously	Hesitates to experiment

Some Interesting Questions

These are only a few of the many teaching and learning styles that the authors suggest. Analyses of teaching and learning styles raise some interesting questions. Is it realistic to expect teachers to individualize their instruction and to form ideal groups? The answer is yes, because all conscientious teachers are attempting it

Studies of Learning Environments

Psychologists, teachers, and administrators are increasingly alert to the significance of the learning environment. Using the *Student Opinion Survey in Chemistry,* a scale measuring student attitudes toward chemistry, Heikkinen (1973) discovered that the learning environment is more important than the type of course in determining student attitude. Comparing students in Interdisciplinary Approaches to Chemistry (IAC) courses, which are both innovative and humanistic, with students in traditional high school chemistry courses, Heikkinen found that the type of course had little affect on students' attitudes toward chemistry.

Many studies associated with Harvard Project Physics have also focused upon the learning environment. For example, Walberg and Anderson (1968) studied physics achievement as related to the students' perceptions of the classroom climate. Students who showed the greatest achievement gain perceived their classes as socially homogeneous, a cohesive group working toward a desirable goal. Students who grew in scientific understanding, not just specific facts, saw their classes as well organized with little friction among class members.

Laurenz (1974) studied the relationship between the classroom learning environment and students' attitudes toward science. She used the Learning Environment Inventory which measures such dimensions as cohesiveness (friendship among class members), formality (following rules), speed (keeping up with work), favoritism (good students are given special projects), and competitiveness (cooperation among students). There are a total of 9 scales and 105 items. She found that the favoritism scale in biology, and competitiveness in chemistry, best predicted class attitude.

Interest and research in studying learning environments will continue, and will provide increasingly more sophisticated data about classroom conditions.

now, and the more accurate information they obtain, the better they will become at it. Another question is whether teachers *should* create these ideal conditions? An objection is frequently raised that youngsters will meet different kinds of people and situations in life so they should encounter varied situations in school that will help them to cope in the future. No learning environment is so rigidly structured that variety is lacking. By attempting to make learning conditions as compatible as possible, teachers aid growth, development, and learning and thus help their students acquire that necessary maturity to encounter all situations.

Discussion Questions

1. How would you define learning? In what category would you put it (behaviorist or cognitivist)? *Specify* how you think your definition meets the objections to any definition.

2. Think of something you have learned—something obvious. Now use Figure 7.4 to illustrate how these characteristics functioned in your learning. Could this analysis improve your teaching?

3. Attempt to relate learning variables to the Philadelphia study. Can you identify those individual, task, or method variables that change because of organizational conditions?

4. Can you think of any other variables that affect learning? Prove that they are not included in the Garry and Kingsley scheme.

5. List those features that you consider important in teaching (knowledge, humor, compassion). What does it tell you about your teaching style? What type of learning environment would you create?

Some Concluding Thoughts

This chapter began by describing some examples of youngsters who want to learn. To attempt to explain what happens during the learning process is to travel a tortuous path. The conflicting explanations may often seem a theoretical exercise, but closer examination reveals that the theories have far-reaching and practical consequences. Thinking as a behaviorist you will do things differently in the classroom than as a cognitivist, and you may use different materials.

While most people are eclectic in their beliefs, they tend to prefer one explanation over the other, and this influences all they do. For example, a strict Skinnerian will help students avoid error. Pupils often remember their mistakes, especially when test results are delayed days or weeks. Consequently students receive small bits of information that almost eliminate the possibility of error. A cognitive belief encourages discovery and insight, and risk taking. The possibility of error is constant, but error is used to facilitate further learning; that is, it becomes a part of learning how to learn.

The learning environments resulting from these two theories are radically different. One is tightly controlled, the other is open; one urges self-activity, the other is more restrictive to avoid mistakes. You should make *no* value judgments about either theory. Each can be highly effective with a sympathetic teacher. It is a matter of personal belief and style. Know as much as you can about both and then shape the learning environment to suit you and your students.

Summary

- There are two basic and conflicting theories of learning: behavioristic and cognitive.

- While there have been many interpretors of behaviorism, the most well-known contemporary figure is B. F. Skinner. His work is called operant, or instrumental, conditioning to distinguish it from Pavlov's classical conditioning.

● The nature and scheduling of reinforcement is critical for Skinner and has produced a method of behavioral control called behavior modification.

● The Gestalt psychologists—Wertheimer, Koffka, Köhler—rejected an *S-R* explanation of behavior and believed that individuals reacted to wholes by perceiving relationships.

● Jerome Bruner is one of the most popular modern cognitivists, and his work has produced notable educational change.

● Any definition of learning reflects the author's interpretation of human nature; thus, definition frequently becomes philosophical rather than psychological.

● Learning takes many forms, but there are sufficient common elements to designate them as the characteristics of learning.

● Many variables affect learning, and we may conveniently group them into individual, task, and method variables.

● There is growing interest and research into the issue of learning styles and learning environments.

Suggested Readings

Bruner, Jerome. *The Process of Education.* Cambridge, Mass.: Harvard University Press, 1960. A remarkable little book that had an enormous impact upon curriculum and instruction. It is available in paperback and you would both enjoy and profit from it.

——. *The Relevance of Education.* New York: Norton, 1972. A collection of essays in which Bruner addresses contemporary issues.

Garry, Ralph and Howard Kingsley. *The Nature and Conditions of Learning.* Englewood Cliffs, N.J.: Prentice-Hall, 1970. A good, basic learning text that investigates learning, learning theory, and the variables that influence it.

Skinner, B. F. *Science and Human Behavior.* New York: Macmillan, 1953. If you want to understand Skinner, read this text. It still remains the best summary of his work.

——. *The Technology of Teaching.* Englewood Cliffs, N.J.: Prentice-Hall, 1968. A collection of Skinner's essays in which he details his ideas about education, schools, and teaching.

Travers, John. *Learning: Analysis and Application.* 2nd ed. New York: McKay, 1972. A thorough presentation of the learning process, types of learning, learning theories, and motivation.

8

Motivation and Learning

281

(continues)

Introduction

Chapter 7 opened with examples of a teenage girl studying gemology for long hours and of preteens practicing with the band in blistering heat. These children are motivated; they want to exert themselves—even punish themselves—to achieve a goal. Why do students, teachers, administrators, and parents act as they do? Motivation is the answer. Every experienced classroom teacher would agree that when pupils want to learn something the process is remarkably smooth.

The current interest in gymnastics is a good example. Children must first master the basic tumbling skills—forward and backward somersaults, cartwheels—before they can use balance beams and parallel bars. The initial learning can be painful; yet youngsters have produced a gymnastics boom.

STRICKLER, MONKMEYER

Why? Much of the impetus came from the 1972 and 1976 Olympics, when Olga Korbut, the tiny 83-pound Russian girl, and Nadia Comenici, the 14-year-old Rumanian, astounded television audiences with their electrifying performances. Suddenly millions of children saw a new world unfold, a world in which they envisioned themselves sending a disciplined body through graceful maneuvers. For many, no obstacle was too great to overcome.

The television cameras at the 1976 Olympics provided a prod, called extrinsic motivation, for many youngsters. Teachers use this in the classroom when they give grades, comments, and promotion. But what of the youngster who continues gruelling practice, who punishes herself daily with no external prod? This is called intrinsic motivation, and it is what teachers hope to inspire in students—in this case, a love of physical fitness, in the classroom, a love of learning.

What is it that produces intrinsic motivation? Ryder, Carr, and Herget (1976) have analyzed footracing, studying the records of Olympic champions, and have concluded that today's running records are still below human physiological limits and that the restraints on performance are psychological.

These authors believe that a highly competitive situation produces a level of performance in the finest athletes that they cannot match under less challenging circumstances. They state what is needed is not better runners but bigger challenges. It is the competition that heightens performance, which introduces an issue with which you should be familiar. What is the role of com-

MEDFORD, MASS. *DAILY MERCURY*

petition, both in school and society? This question deserves study since it is so important, but remember the beliefs of these authors and also ponder the question of why two-thirds of the people who establish a world record never set another.

In Chapter 6 the application of the characteristics of learning to reading was discussed. The first characteristic was a motivated student. Without desire, there will be little interaction with the environment and little learning. (You may want to reread Chapter 3 to review the need for children to interact with their environment.) Desire causes restlessness, which then furnishes the energy for initiating the learning process: selection of an appropriate goal, response to stimuli, and refinement of activity.

Partially motivated students lack these characteristics. Their drive is weak; thus, they select inappropriate goals and carelessly determine the means of attaining them. Their responses are random and usually lead to failure. Poorly motivated students are often a continuing cause of disciplinary problems.

Why are you reading this text? Obviously, you desire to pass a certain course—but is that the only reason? For some, the answer is yes. Others, however, may have strong interest in psychology and read this text not only to pass but because they want to learn more about motivation—they are interested in it. Still others see little relevance of the book to the course and less to their future goals. They will have difficulty learning from the text.

So motivation looms large in any study of learning and also in classroom management. To help clarify this critical and expansive topic this chapter first explores its meaning and then studies various explanations of motivation and attempts to discover how and why leading theorists view it as they do. A special and sensitive issue today is women's motivation, especially their need to achieve. Do women actually prefer to lose in certain situations? Are they *afraid* to achieve? What does all of this mean for the classroom teacher? From studying the motivational literature is it possible to derive practical suggestions that help both new and experienced teachers in classroom management? For example, youngsters should be comfortable with figures and enjoy working with them. Try these with your pupils. (Answers are below.)

1. Divide 20 by ½ and add 3. What is the answer?
2. A farmer had 17 sheep. All but 9 died. How many survived?
3. How much is twice one half of 987654321?
4. How much is $1 \times 2 \times 3 \times 4 \times 5 \times 6 \times 7 \times 8 \times 9 \times 0$?

Finally, it may be interesting for you to stop and consider what is *your* motivation for teaching.

The meaning of motivation

Your students have tremendous abilities. They possess boundless energy; they can respond quickly and accurately to varied stimuli; they perceive relationships and organize their behavior; they are

Answers: 1. 43; 2. 9; 3. 987654321; 4. 0

increasingly capable of more abstract work; they are striving, effective, complex organisms. Do they manifest this behavior in your room? Yes—even if it is directed toward undesirable goals. Murray (1964, pg. 1) states that students use their capabilities according to their motivation: desires, wishes, wants, needs, yearnings, hungers, loves, hates, and fears.

Try to analyze the motives of your students. Do they want to come to class? Do they love to learn? Or do they hate learning and dread coming to school? Why do they feel as they do? If they enjoy their work, try to discover what they like and how you can improve the classroom atmosphere. If they are reluctant scholars, try to discover what has gone wrong. Is there anything you can do in the classroom to channel their interest into academic pursuits? (Later in the chapter you will find some practical suggestions for improving students' motivation.)

WHAT IS MOTIVATION?

Motivation is a term, admittedly vague, that describes an inner restlessness that urges an organism into activity. These inner tensions are often called drives, needs, desires, or wishes. Motives are usually divided into physiological (hunger, thirst, sex) and secondary (acceptance, achievement, success). There are several theories that attempt to explain motivation but unfortunately they are as conflicting and contradictory as theories of learning or personality. Still, it is doubtful if any topic other than motivation is more important to teachers. Teachers could avoid more classroom problems if they knew more about the issue of motivation—knew more about it *and acted upon their knowledge*. Motivation acts to arouse, sustain, and direct behavior. Applying these motivational functions to the classroom (especially to students' behavior), the practical value of motivational knowledge becomes more apparent.

Will students learn even if they are not motivated? Obviously they will learn something, but will they learn what we want them to learn, even in an atmosphere in which both students and instructors have established objectives? A student may learn to despise the subject that is being taught; another may learn to think of the class as a recreation period among the more serious moments of the day.

Class members may well be motivated, but not toward desirable goals, and learning may occur, but not the learning that was originally intended. Everything we know about learning clearly indicates that it suffers if motivation is faulty. Arousal is limited, perhaps minimal; behavior is extinguished before objectives are attained; attention is directed elsewhere and energy dissipated; the learning process has failed.

Dramatic? Oversimplified? Hardly, since motivation supplies the fuel for learning. But, again, what is motivation? The basic, honest answer is that no one can say with any degree of certitude.

Cooking in the Classroom

It is much easier to describe motivation than to explain precisely what it is. Motivation, like learning, has many interpretations, but it is relatively easy to describe motivated students. For example, Barbara Wilms (1976) recounts how preschoolers acquired general academic skills while learning to cook. Simple math and science, vocabulary, and physical skills are all involved in cooking. One teacher drew picture cards to illustrate recipes, thus permitting children to progress by themselves. If a cup of milk was needed, the picture showed a measuring cup of milk with the word "milk" printed on top. The children soon were able to use teaspoons,

eggs, and bowls, and began reading the printed words to the teacher.

While one-half- and one-quarter-cup measures were used they were not called fractions, but the children learned the words and their meaning—cut something in two for halves, into four for quarters. Foods popular with various nationalities were used to encourage ethnic cooperation. The author concludes that the children not only acquired skills and learned cooperation, they also presented adults with a unique view into preschoolers' minds and how the world looks to them.

The best investigators can do is describe those conditions of behavior that seem to result from motivation. That is, something acts to produce a certain kind of behavior, maintained at a definite energy level, and directed toward a specific objective. Most students of the topic would agree that motivation arouses, sustains, directs, and integrates a person's behavior; otherwise there is little agreement. As with theories of learning and personality, certain theories of motivation will appeal to you more than others. You will have a feeling of greater ease and confidence working within the guidelines of a particular system.

Motivation affects all aspects of behavior

Edward Murray (1964, pp. 11–20) has illustrated how motivation influences all aspects of behavior.

1. *Perception and attention.* Your perception of your world depends mainly upon physical stimuli. Why do people attend to some stimuli and not others? Past experience and maturation largely determine attention. If you show hungry children and adults ambiguous pictures—with difficult-to-identify elements—they usually claim they see some food. There is overwhelming experimental evidence to suggest that motivation influences perception.

2. *Remembering and forgetting.* Feelings and emotions influence how well people recall past events: they usually tend to remember

pleasant events more easily than unpleasant, unless the unpleasant are so vivid that they force themselves into their consciousness. Murray reports a study involving failure that has strong implications for the classroom. College students memorized a list of nonsense syllables, such as *MOU, BIV*. They quickly learned the list perfectly, and then they had to learn a simple motor task—tapping a pattern with cubes. No matter how well they did, they were told they had failed and that their performance was an indication of poor college performance. They were then asked to recall the nonsense syllables. Their memory was adversely affected (they made many more mistakes) although failure was associated with the motor skills and not the verbal material. Control subjects who were not told they had failed with the cubes had no difficulty. When the experimental group was told they could take the cube-tapping test again, the investigators told them that they were now succeeding. They then retook the examination on the nonsense syllables and now *did as well as they had at the beginning, before the first cube-tapping test*. Think about this experiment and what it means for the pupil who has had a lifetime of failure.

3. *Thinking and fantasy.* Motivation also influences how people use information. Both problem solving and creativity reflect motives—the desire to achieve a specific goal, and the wishes and dreams of fantasy.

4. *Learning and performance.* Motivation's effect on learning is striking and has long intrigued psychologists and educators. There are two basic issues here:

a. Does motivation facilitate learning? The answer—derived from experiments with animals, children, and adults—is indisputably affirmative.

b. Does increasing the intensity of the motive and drive always aid learning? Here the evidence is clear but less precise. Increasing the motive's intensity facilitates learning and performance to a point. Beyond that point, which varies from person to person and task to task, learning and performance may deteriorate.

How Much Motivation

Intense motivation seems to facilitate learning simple tasks; moderate motivation aids learning complex tasks. This is called the Yerkes-Dodson law, which states that ideal motivation for learning decreases with increasing task difficulty. Broadhurst (1957) trained rats to swim through an underwater y-shaped maze. At the fork, the rats had to choose between a bright door leading out of the water and a dark, locked door. When the door was brightly lighted, the rats learned quickly; when less brightly lighted, they found the task more difficult.

Broadhurst now varied the conditions of the experiment. There were three levels of illumination: easy, moderate, and difficult, which represented the task difficulty. Motivation was the need for air, which can be intense. He varied the time—0,2,4,8 seconds—that the rats were submerged before permitting them to swim the maze. With the easy task (selecting the bright door), the ideal motivation (air deprivation) was 4 seconds. With the difficult task (dark door) ideal motivation was 2 seconds.

Similar results appear in the classroom. Moderate tension may help in a test, but increasing anxiety may adversely affect learning and performance. Also, the anxious student performs well on easy tasks, but has difficulties with harder work—in spite of ability. Motivating students is obviously desirable, but the intensity of motivation must allow for the nature of the task and the pupil's anxiety.

Murray sensibly warns that motives seldom act in a simple and direct way. Several motives, whose satisfaction would involve conflicting behavior, may be acting on any one person. Since needs are hierarchical—arranged by intensity of need—both adults and youngsters tend to satisfy those that are most demanding.

Charles Cofer and Mortimer Appley (1964, pg. 5) state that when people ask about motivation, they want to know:

The "Flow Experience"

The exhilaration that comes from intrinsic motivation is described by William Furlong as the "flow experience" (1976). Flow is the fun in fun and occurs when people are totally immersed in what they are doing. They lose their awareness of self and time, concentration increases, and feedback is enhanced. Flow is possible in both physical and mental activities.

The use of "flow" began with the work of Dr. Mihaty Csikszentminalyi at the University of Chicago. While teaching at a small liberal arts college he became fascinated by the sheer enjoyment that soccer players derived, while the hockey players—the school's status athletes and only representatives in big-time sports—exhibited little of the same enthusiasm.

Was it some difference in intrinsic rewards that the sports offered? He pursued the question into other nonstatus activities: handball, mountain climbing, long-distance swimming. The common denominator he found was flow—described in many ways, but always with the same meaning: Individuals intensely aware of what they are doing, but unaware that they are aware.

Recalling our discussion of moderate motivation, here is a "formula" for flow.

1. *Fit the difficulty to the skill.* Here is one of the prerequisites of learning: the nature of the challenge. If it is too easy, boredom results; if it is too difficult, anxiety arises. Teachers can increase a pupil's motivation by insuring that the match is correct, thus providing some success that will produce positive feedback.
2. *Focus attention.* Furlong states that any activity can cause flow if a person focuses well enough. What can you do to help pupils focus their attention on something they dislike or, at best, are neutral about? Can you relate the subject to something they find interesting? Provide for success. Involve them with their peers. Not all activities will cause flow, but the mere increase in attention may well improve discipline and learning.
3. *Forget time.* The ability to concentrate upon *this* moment, not the past or future, enables teachers and students to receive immediate feedback.
4. *Relax and wake up.* Relax but stay alert; notice what you are doing and how you are doing it. The combination of a relaxed body and alert mind is the ideal—the perfect balance between anxiety and boredom. A skilled teacher attempts to achieve the happy combination of optimal tension and cheerful relaxation in the classroom atmosphere. Think for a moment about yourself and how pupils see you. Do you project an image of competence and acceptance that encourages pupils, or do they sense anxiety and insecurity, which then affects *their* performance?
5. *Training for flow.* Concentrating on the here and now, using any techniques that prevent tension and distraction, aids the appearance of flow.

Furlong describes an ideal state, but one that you can attempt to create in your pupils. Actually, teachers have always attempted this in their efforts to instill intrinsic motivation in students. The effort is well rewarded; even work becomes play.

1. If something in the environment caused the behavior.
2. If some internal urge, wish, or desire caused the behavior.
3. If some goal or objective caused the behavior.
4. If some combination of the preceding caused the behavior.

Answering these questions suggests that either inner or outer forces, or both, may cause behavior. Biological needs, such as hunger, pain, and discomfort, motivate an infant's behavior, while psychological needs, such as security, belongingness, and achievement, motivate the growing child and adult. By combining these needs certain conclusions are possible.

Motivation results in self-activity, physical changes, emotional changes, perceptual changes, and cognitive changes. Melton (1950) states that motivation has three functions in learning.

Functions of Motivation

1. It energizes the organism, thus sustaining activity when a goal is not immediately available. Evidence indicates that the energizing function acts as a mediating process. It is affected by the activity it originates, and this facilitates or inhibits continuing activity.
2. It directs the organism's activity. Not all goals satisfy all needs; particular goals are selected because of the nature of the guiding motive.
3. It exercises a selective role by determining if the consequences are satisfactory, which influences later performance.

MEDFORD, MASS. *DAILY MERCURY*

But the analysis is not as simple as it might appear. When youngsters begin school, they already possess complicated motivational systems. They have definite interests, attitudes, opinions, fears, desires, habits, and skills. When the school attempts to impose a new set of goals, many of which are highly unreal for children, trouble frequently arises. If they seem compatible with their interpretation of the environment, they succeed. But if the barrier between them and a goal remains intact, motivation falters and frustration results.

Unless students are able to reorganize their behavior and again attempt to reach the goal, their behavior becomes nonadaptive. It is exactly here that most learning theorists, in a presentation of learning characteristics, pause and exhibit concern about the reaction of failure, frustration, or thwarting. Students may become aggressive and display hostility toward classmates, teachers, or anyone in authority. They may refuse to alter their behavior and continue to fail; the consequences—emotionally, socially, and academically—have already been mentioned.

What then does motivation mean for the teacher? A simple answer is: Everything. Motivation is the difference between a pleasant, happy class in a harmonious learning atmosphere and exactly the opposite. The more that teachers know about motivation and the more effectively they manipulate motives, the more successful is the teaching-learning process.

Great stress is placed upon goals, objectives, or purpose in the behavioral sciences. This is as it should be, for anyone in pursuit of a goal is an active, dedicated individual who is willing to tolerate almost any hardship in order to reach that goal. But, in this description of individuals striving for goals, there are several ideas that deserve additional comment.

Intrinsic and extrinsic motivation

Unless a goal has meaning for a student, progress toward it undoubtedly lacks force and direction. Teachers can make goals real and vital to students only as they know the abilities, interests, and needs of their pupils. This is a time-consuming, formidable task, but one that is richly rewarding. Human beings are anxious to acquire any technique that promises to make their lives easier and more comfortable. For teachers, the advice to know their students should be at the top of any list of "teacher aids."

Know Your Students   But knowledge of students implies more than recollection of names, marks, and routes home. It means answering such questions as: How many brothers and sisters? What is the socioeconomic status of the family? How is education regarded in the home? What is the emotional climate of the home environment? What interests the student outside of school? It takes time and ef-

BOSTON COLLEGE PUBLIC RELATIONS

fort to answer these and similar questions, but teachers who take the time and make the effort have gone a long way toward preventing disciplinary problems and preparing for significant learning in a smoothly functioning class. The more teachers know about individuals, and the more they know about motivation, the more skillful teaching will become and the more productive learning will be. The educational milieu, with its establishment of goals that are sometimes too distant to seem real to students, has need of insights into the nature and application of motives.

There is a dual approach to motivation—extrinsic and intrinsic. Intrinsic motivation should be the goal of teachers, since it results in students themselves wishing to learn in order to achieve objectives. By relating their knowledge of student ability, need, and interest to educational goals, teachers can provide the basis for intrinsic motivation. As this is not always possible, extrinsic motivation, such as marks, prizes, and degrees, is employed. When teachers rely on these methods they should attempt to have students transfer this external, temporary drive to an internal, lasting motive.

Why do nonmotivated students become discipline problems? One of the most widely reported articles in the psychological liter-

**The McGill
Experiments**

ature, "The Pathology of Boredom," by Woodburn Heron (1957) offers some clues. Beginning with the assumption that monotony is an important and enduring human problem, investigators at McGill University studied the effects of a prolonged monotonous environment. How do humans react when nothing is happening?

Experimental subjects were male college students who were paid $20 a day to participate. They lay on a comfortable bed 24 hours a day for as long as they wished to stay, taking time out for eating meals while sitting on the bed. They wore plastic visors that prevented pattern vision; cotton gloves prevented touch perception; the hum of an air conditioner and the use of rubber pillows stifled auditory perception.

Before the experiment the subjects stated that they were going to plan their studies (exams, term papers), but all reported that they were unable to think clearly about anything for any length of time and that their thought processes became distorted. Concentration was impossible, and they began to drift mentally; some said that their minds became full of sound and color. After prolonged isolation they saw images—hallucinations over which they had little control.

Heron states that a prolonged monotonous environment produces childish emotional responses, disturbed visual perception, hallucinations, and a changing brain wave pattern. Pilots, truck drivers, and long distance swimmers all report the same results. He concludes that a changing sensory environment is essential for humans. While few, if any, classrooms approximate sensory deprivation, everyone has experienced monotonous classroom atmospheres. If these experiments are accurate, and continuing evidence supports their results, then a monotonous classroom will cause restless pupils, discipline problems, and frustrated teachers.

Discussion Questions

1. From your knowledge of the characteristics of learning, explain how motivation is the key to the learning process. Give a specific example, using a subject with which you are familiar.

2. Relate a lack of motivation to classroom problems by recalling your own experiences. Can you remember a class in which you were definitely nonmotivated? Why? Was it because of your personal condition, or was it something in the environment? What happened?

3. Using your answer to the previous question as a basis, explain how your lack of motivation affected all aspects of your behavior, as outlined by Murray.

4. How did you react to the Broadhurst experiment? Has intense motivation ever affected your performance? In school? on tests? How do you respond whenever it happens now?

Young Audiences

A rapidly expanding, national, nonprofit organization called Young Audiences is an example of motivation in action. Its objective is to introduce children to some of our greatest living artists and thus bring youngsters into contact with varied aspects of our culture. Young Audiences has enabled 1500 artists to give 11,000 programs, and if you multiply the number of programs by the number of student viewers you can understand its widespread enrichment and its encouragement of pupils to pursue interests they might never have envisioned.

Young Audiences began in 1949 when some amateur musicians in Baltimore played for neighborhood children. They became so popular that they visited schools and fascinated children. Growing recognition led to the incorporation of a national headquarters in 1952 and today there are about 40 chapters across the country. Among the participating artists are Leonard Bernstein, Marian Anderson, Isaac Stern, Artur Rubinstein, and Beverly Sills.

Observers describe Young Audiences as a teacher's dream. Schools supply the space and pupils, Young Audiences supplies the performer and group that best suits the children's needs, informs the teacher about the program so that the children are prepared, and prepares the artist for the children's level. A single performer charges about $200 and Young Audiences pays half. It is able to be so generous because of the amazing response to its fund-raising appeals.

As interesting as this idea is, consider its motivational aspects: attention, desire, feedback, encouragement, goals. As Beverly Sills asked, Who likes art, music or ballet? Is it just some elite group? No, those who appreciate the arts encountered them early in life and obtained expert instruction, thus acquiring intrinsic motivation.

Check your telephone directory to see if there is a chapter in your community. If not, write to national headquarters:

Young Audiences
115 E. 92nd St.
New York, New York 10028

It will be worth the effort and money; perhaps your local PTA will help financially. Try it.

---

5. The McGill experiments are deservedly famous. Did you ever experience a similar condition because of sensory deprivation? Describe it. If not, do you recall your reactions when you were bored in class? What did you do? What *do* you do?

Explanations of motivation: the theories

A good teacher motivates students by recognizing their needs and by arranging the classroom environment to meet these needs. But the recognition of needs implies an interpretation of human nature, the same kind of interpretation that we saw in our analysis of learning. That is, those who think that human beings are striving, active individuals interpret learning as a cognitive process. Those who believe that humans react to stimuli and schedules of reinforcement appeal to a behavioristic interpretation. The same holds true for most motivation theorists. To illustrate motivational theories, the work of Skinner, Bruner, Maslow, and McClelland will be reviewed.

SKINNER AND MOTIVATION

In *Science and Human Behavior* (1953), Skinner says that human nature is the same the world over only in the sense that behavior always varies with environmental change. The independent variables controlling behavior are not the same the world over. Genetic endowments differ widely and most environments are more different than alike, which causes great individuality. Skinner uses culture as an example of how motivation affects environmental differences. An individual's hunger depends not only on the availability of food but also upon the culture that controls what is eaten and when it is eaten. Sex depends not only on the availability of a partner but upon one's ethics and religion. So motivation depends upon both social and nonsocial conditions.

Skinner believes that "deprivation" and "satiation" explain motivation. Deprivation refers to the individual who is deprived of physical exercise and feels rewarded by activity, as well as the individual who is deprived of food or water. Satiation produces feelings of satisfaction, a sense that behavior has been rewarded. Considering motivation as a relationship between deprivation and satiation, Skinner can abandon those troublesome "inner causes of behavior," such as needs, drives, and wants.

These inner causes, or mental explanations, curtail the search for truth. As Skinner (1971) notes, if you ask people why they went to the theater and they reply that they felt like going, you are usually satisfied. It would be more profitable if you knew what had happened when they previously went to the theater, what they had read about the play, and what else induced them to go. Behavior is shaped and maintained by its consequences (Skinner, 1971, pg. 18), thus producing the "industrious" person and the "lazy" person, the motivated student, and the nonmotivated student. These are not traits; they are behaviors that result from schedules of reinforcement. If pupils obtain reinforcement for certain behavior, they tend to repeat it with vigor. Exactly the opposite is also true.

Motivation and the student

In the *Technology of Teaching* (1968), Skinner states that the word "student" means one who studies, who is eager and diligent. Unfortunately, not all students fit the category and Skinner believes that teachers must critically examine motivated behavior to iden-

Skinner and a Modern Emile

Responding to charges that his ideas eliminate an individual's freedom and dignity, Skinner has replied with a barrage of countercharges that vividly and practically illustrate his views on motivation. The philosopher Jean Jacques Rousseau (1712–1776) published in 1762 *Emile,* in which he described ideal education as that in which children would be reared apart from human society because it is so evil and vicious. Emile is to discover all things himself; there is to be no authority in his life. Using Rousseau's *Emile* as an example, Skinner in a 1973 article, "The Free and Happy Student," demolishes the concept of the free school. Emile never believed in working very hard; he never thought very clearly; he preferred feelings to the life of the intellect.

Today's Emile is also a muddled thinker who seems quite unhappy. He dislikes school—either dropping out, playing truant, or actively destroying it—and seems to thrive in a world of unprecedented violence. Perhaps today's Emile, motivated by his new freedom, has become more creative than his peers of past, repressed generations? No; one only has to look at the highly regimented youth groups who ape each other's clothes, style, and speech to doubt their creativity. Any products they manage to create are severely restricted because of their lack of knowledge.

Perhaps today's Emile is a more effective citizen? Reluctantly, Skinner concludes that, alas, this is also doubtful. Dropping out of school seems to be a forerunner of dropping out of life. Too many youths refuse to accept responsibility for even their own lives and are content to live off the contributions of their more industrious brothers.

As Skinner says, these are exaggerations, but they clearly indicate a direction. Still, students should not study merely to avoid the consequences of *not* studying—punishment. Students then engage in truancy, vandalism, or apathy (either nonmotivated or motivated for the wrong reasons and the wrong goal). But they will not study when given "freedom"; they simply come under the control of other conditions. Consequently, the teacher must improve control over education, not abandon it.

How? It is a difficult assignment that necessitates the arrangement of positive reinforcers so that the teacher can compete with conditions that cause disruptive behavior. Tokens, credit point systems, and programmed instructions all have proven to be successful techniques. Students are encouraged when they are praised for correct behavior and not merely punished for incorrect behavior. They come to feel free and happy both in the classroom and when their formal education ends because they have established behavioral patterns that produce success, pleasant relations with others, enjoyment in their work, and a deserved sense of accomplishment. This is Skinner's explanation of intrinsic motivation.

Skinner is a good and witty writer. You would especially enjoy this article.

tify those conditions under which all students will study effectively. One technique is to discover the consequences of studying, that is, what reinforces students when they study. Knowledge, prestige, and money are some of the ultimate advantages of study-

ing but, as Skinner notes, they are the ultimate and not the immediate reinforcers valuable to the teacher.

Skinner states (1968, pg. 148) that "on-the-spot reinforcers" such
as the rod, sarcasm, ridicule, and failing grades often produce unwanted consequences; for example, youngsters quickly learn to
hate school. A better alternative is personal reinforcement. Attention, approval, and affection may characterize a teacher's behavior.
These may also cause difficulty because students frequently engage
in disruptive behavior to obtain a teacher's attention.

Skinner believes that the teacher should use any available reinforcer *provided* there are no harmful by-products and that the student's resulting behavior eventually comes under the control of
frequently encountered reinforcers. That is, motivation should shift
from the extrinsic (teacher-controlled) to the intrinsic (student-con-
trolled). It is not the reinforcers themselves that are important; it is
their relationship to the preceding behavior. Unless there is intermittent reinforcement for behavior, intrinsic motivation seldom
develops.

Desirable behavior depends upon the requirements for reinforcement; that is, students should produce an optimum amount of
behavior before they are reinforced. The teacher can then continue
to reinforce desirable behavior until studying becomes "good" in
itself. Skinner is remarkably faithful to his basic belief that proper
contingencies of reinforcement ideally control behavior and make
students eager and diligent and ready to enjoy what is taught
them for the rest of their lives.

BRUNER AND MOTIVATION

In *The Process of Education* (1960) Bruner states that any attempt to
improve education inevitably begins with the motives for learning.
What results from emphasis upon examinations, grades, and promotion? Does it intensify motivation? How intense should motivation be? Bruner believes that there is some ideal level of arousal
between apathy and wild excitement, since passivity causes boredom while intense activity leaves little time for reflection and
generalization.

But there is an even deeper problem. Immediate arousal may
not produce future interest in learning. Reliance upon audiovisual
aids may produce passive people who merely wait for someone or
something to excite them. There is no immediate solution; perhaps
the best that teachers can anticipate is that pupils will develop intrinsic motivation from the use of external motivation. The problem of producing intrinsic motivation is growing, especially in
technological societies where the media is ever present and success
depends upon entertainment value.

One possible solution is Bruner's notion of "discovery learning," which captured many educators' imagination with its in-

Discovery Learning   sights into classroom motivation. Arguing that discovery is rearranging or transforming evidence so that one goes beyond the evidence to form new insights, Bruner states that discovery proceeds from the well-prepared mind. Encouraging discovery causes students not only to organize material to determine regularities and relationships but to avoid the passivity that blinds them to the uses of the information learned. The result is that students learn to manipulate their environment more actively and achieve considerable gratification from personally coping with problems.

Bruner emphasizes that the goal of discovery learning is to

Removing Perceptual Blocks

Students frequently lack motivation because they simply are unaware of how to attack a lesson, do a paper, study, or do any independent work. Increasing competence means increasing motivation. People like to do what they do well. Adams' ideas on conceptual blockbusting offer excellent suggestions that could help students *start* (1974). He believes that there are several perceptual blocks.

1. *Difficulty in isolating the problem.* Students just cannot identify the problem, which may be answering a question or completing a written exercise. They use inadequate clues to leap to a solution (usually incorrect), or they use misinformation. One of a teacher's first tasks should be to help students isolate the problem — what precisely the student is to do. Students will learn that their initial effort saves time and poses solutions.
2. *Tendency to limit the problem too closely.* Everyone, especially children, tends to be bound by his or her experience. If pupils solved a particular problem by addition, they are reluctant to try multiplication on the next problem. They impose imaginary boundaries and refuse to cross them. Teach your students once

they have identified a problem to try different methods, not just what was previously successful.
3. *Seeing what you expect to see.* This is closely related to the second obstacle and can be disastrous for motivation. Recall the discussion of the development of a "mathematical sense," which many lack. Why? The answer probably is that you could not isolate the problem (new symbols, new vocabulary). When you succeeded you tended to repeat the solution, right or wrong, and as you failed, you *came to expect failure.*
4. *Failure to utilize all sensory inputs.* Students need help and often rely excessively upon a single channel of communication. Concentrating upon words, they may neglect illustrations that help to clarify; they may not use tapes or discussion with others as sources of information. Teachers should help their pupils to use as many, and different, inputs as possible.

One conclusion is clearly apparent from Adams's work — helping students to acquire a technique or to recognize, isolate, and solve problems is also a powerful motivational technique.

have pupils use their information in solving problems in many different circumstances. Kolesnik (1976) believes that a basic assumption underlying discovery learning is that individuals behave according to their perceptions of their environment. That is, students see meaning in knowledge, skills, and attitudes when they themselves discover it. The teacher's task in encouraging discovery learning is to arrange classroom materials and activities so that students learn with a maximum of personal involvement and a minimum of teacher intervention.

There is no one successful formula that you can follow to inspire discovery learning. As Kolesnik states, it is more a matter of your attitude. Can you tolerate the frustrations and mistakes that will inevitably occur? It is far removed from a set plan with rigidly prescribed objectives. Kolesnik summarizes it nicely when he notes that discovery methods imply providing facilities, encouragement, challenges, and opportunities for individuals to find out and think for themselves (1976, pp. 132–133).

A Warning

Piaget (1961) warns, however, that not *all* pupil activity satisfies his interpretation of interacting with the environment. Genuinely concerned with what he calls "intuitive methods," he believes that they have retarded the acceptance of cognitive activity techniques. For example, some theorists believe that "active" means only physical activity, which is true at elementary levels but which ignores the personal rediscovery of truth through interior and abstract reflection. Appropriate logico-mathematical experience is true cognitive activity and meets the requirements of discovery learning.

Finally, Bruner believes that children will always have mixed motives for learning. They must please parents, impress peers, and acquire mastery. Within the educational environment how can teachers help children to appreciate the world of ideas? One recommendation is to increase a subject's inherent interest by insuring that teachers present ideas at their pupils' level so that youngsters achieve a sense of discovery. If teachers succeed, they can not only teach a subject but also instill attitudes and values about intellectual activity.

It is worth quoting Bruner here.

> If teaching is done well and what we teach is worth learning, there are forces at work in our contemporary society that will provide the external prod that will get children more involved in the process of learning than they have been in the past (1960, pg. 73).

Bruner believes that these external prods come from a growing educated class who believe in the value of education and share a desire for their children to secure the best schooling possible.

Finally, Bruner notes that knowledge of results (feedback, reinforcement) is valuable if it comes when learners compare their results with what they attempt to achieve. Even then, learners use feedback according to their internal state. Information is least useful when learners are highly anxious or concerned with evaluating only one possibility (similar to limiting the problem too closely). Bruner, like Adams, believes that information is most helpful when it is at the learner's level and encourages self-activity and intrinsic motivation.

MASLOW AND MOTIVATION

Abraham Maslow has explained motivation in a way that many teachers and students have found realistic and appealing. In *Motivation and Personality* (1970), Maslow argues that investigators should study normality and resist generalizing from abnormality. As he notes (1970, pp. xii–xiii), growth, self-actualization, health, the search for identify and autonomy, and the yearning for excellence all represent a widespread, perhaps universal, human tendency.

The hierarchy of needs

Maslow believes that there are five basic needs: the physiological needs, the safety needs, the love and belongingness needs, the esteem needs, and the need for self-actualization. These needs are related, that is, a lower need must be partially satisfied before a higher need becomes potent.

   1. *Physiological Needs.* These are the basis of motivation and unless they are satisfied, everything else recedes. As Maslow says, they are the most prepotent of all the needs. A starving person is unlikely to be overly concerned about esteem or belonging needs; all energies are aimed at securing food. Although most Western societies have virtually eliminated starvation, some interesting questions remain. What happens to the student who suffers from poor nutrition? Many adolescents have notoriously poor diets, which affect both their energy level and classroom performance. They can become passive, sluggish, and sullen and manifest all the characteristics of the nonmotivated student. If a student's behavior changes throughout the day—and it is not due to trouble or dislike of the subject—check his or her eating habits as the first diagnostic step.
   2. *Safety needs.* Once the physiological needs are met, Maslow believes that higher needs emerge. He calls these the safety needs: security, stability, protection, freedom from fear and anxiety, need for structure and limits. These needs appear more frequently in children, whose reactions are less inhibited. Children want a predictable, lawful, orderly world, and when it is threatened, the safety needs predominate. Maslow states that child psychologists,

teachers, and psychotherapists have discovered that children need, almost demand, freedom with limits rather than unrestricted permissiveness. There are also clear and unmistakable implications for the classroom. Sarcasm, ridicule, or open hostility in the classroom cause students to construct their own safety measures—often at the expense of learning. Students refuse to participate; they fear the consequences and thus refuse to explore and discover. There is no motivation for learning, only a desire for self-preservation. Think about Maslow's safety needs in relation to your classroom atmosphere.

3. *Love and belongingness needs.* If the first two need categories are satisfied, the desire for friendship, family, and children arises. There is a strong wish to avoid feelings of strangeness and loneliness. Today's modern society—mobile, lacking traditional ties, often rootless—contributes greatly to the frustration of these needs. Encounter groups, weight-watching groups, group therapy—the noticeable trend toward groups in all aspects of our lives—testifies to the potency of these needs. It is not a need for sex. Maslow emphasizes that sex is only one component of the love and belonging needs, which reflects an individual's search for a warm and accepting place with others. The educational ramifications are legion. Youngsters whose families move frequently are often confused and lonesome. How can you help? Youngsters who encounter hostility and rejection at home bring their defensiveness to school. What can you do? The youngster whose color, race, or religion causes difficulty with peers feels no sense of belongingness with the group. Can you incorporate this need into your curriculum? The answers to these questions should guide you in identifying your students' needs.

4. *Esteem needs.* All people need a good opinion of themselves and also need the respect of others. Thus there is a need for competence and mastery and a need for recognition. But the feeling of competency and the respect of others should be based on solid achievement; that is, it should be deserved. Teachers should provide opportunities for students to satisfy this need; that is, they must enable them to achieve and to secure reinforcement. As providers of the reinforcement teachers must insist on satisfactory performance (depending on the student's ability), otherwise our efforts become mockery. Students quickly discern that anything is rewarded, and the process becomes meaningless. If you know your students, you can set tasks they can master and that you can honestly praise and reward. Every student should experience some success.

5. *Need for self-actualization.* With all these needs satisfied, Maslow states that people still may feel discontented and restless *unless* they do what they feel capable of doing. As he states, what people *can* be, they *must* be. The satisfaction of this need seems to come later in life; with youth teachers can only guide, encourage, and

reward so that youngsters begin to recognize their potential. Maslow's ideas are particularly pertinent for teachers since they provide a rationale for understanding motivation and a basis for understanding a pupil's behavior. As teachers and students satisfy their physical needs, a new and different set of psychological needs emerges and is satisfied, which gradually leads to a feeling of self-fulfillment. Finally, most people are partially satisfied and partially dissatisfied in all their basic needs. It is only when a lower

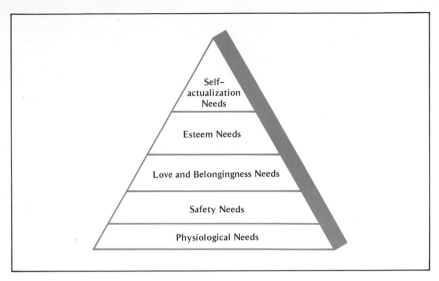

Figure 8.1 Maslow's Hierarchy of Needs

need is not satisfied, or barely satisfied, that higher needs do not appear. Maslow's theory is a remarkably perceptive picture of human nature. Figure 8.1 illustrates the hierarchy of needs.

McCLELLAND AND NEED ACHIEVEMENT (*nAch*)

David McClelland has long been fascinated by the achievement motive. What is the need to achieve? Why does it vary from individual to individual? Does it differ from society to society? It is this latter question that provoked interesting and significant research since McClelland stated (1961, pg. 36) that achievement motivation is partially responsible for economic growth. But how is it possible to assess *nAch* in countries as massive as America and Russia?

First, it was necessary to devise a technique of measuring *nAch*. McClelland describes the basic methods of measuring *nAch* as follows: Subjects are given tasks that arouse the achievement needs. For example, male college students were told that the tests they were taking directly indicate their intelligence and reliably discriminate people of high ability. The subjects believe they are to be evaluated by some standard of excellence and thus will desire to do well.

When the tests were completed, the subjects' fantasies were studied by having them respond (write a five-minute story) to pictures about work flashed on a screen. The themes of these stories were then compared to those of similar subjects who had not been

Use of Children's Readers

aroused by the test and its instructions. The stories written under the aroused conditions contained more references to standards of excellence, to doing well, or wanting to do well.

The next phase was to measure *nAch* nationally. McClelland and his associates decided to measure the imaginative productions of modern nations by examining stories written for children (1961, pg. 70). The author believes these stories are ideal because they provide interesting material for the child and also because their themes and plots reflect the motives and values of their societies. (McClelland quotes Margaret Mead as saying that any culture has to get its values across to its children so simply that even a behavioral scientist can understand them!)

nAch and Economic Growth

Twenty-one stories written in 1925 and 21 more written around 1950 were collected from each country. As many countries as possible were used: 23 countries for the 1925 period, 40 countries for the 1950 period. Thirteen hundred stories were tabulated for three motives: *n* Achievement, *n* Affiliation, and *n* Power. McClelland next attempted to use this technique to predict economic growth. Using national income figures and amount of electricity produced, he found that the children's stories of 1925 were excellent predictors of economic growth.

Are there educational implications in McClelland's work? Perhaps his work in India suggests some answers. Working with Indian businessmen, he had them rewrite their answers on projective tests until they reflected high *nAch.* He then had them play business games in which they set attainable goals and used problem-solving techniques to reach the goals. He found that the businessmen who took the course started more businesses, invested more capital, and created more jobs than the control group (McClelland and Winter, 1969). If increasing a pupil's *nAch* is desirable then teachers should provide opportunities for students to tell stories that are high in *nAch* and have them play educational games in which they learn to set realistic goals and achieve them by logical steps.

TABLE 8.1
Motivational Theorists and Their Basic Ideas

Name	Theory	Concern	Explanation of Motivation
Skinner	Operant conditioning	Reinforcement	Schedules of reinforcement
Bruner	Cognitive	Intrinsic processes	Mixed motives
Maslow	Humanistic	Hierarchy of needs	Satisfaction of needs
McClelland	Achievement	Need to achieve (*nAch*)	Changes in need to achieve

Discussion Questions

1. Explain how Skinner uses satiation and deprivation in his explanation of motivation. What is the role of reinforcement?

2. Skinner obviously used Emile as an extreme to support his views, but do you think there is truth in what he says? How else would you explain the antischool attitude of many students?

3. Do you think that Bruner is realistic or idealistic in his interpretation of motivation? Are the "external prods" in contemporary society that enthusiastic about education?

4. Be sure that you understand Maslow's hierarchy. Although there is yet little empirical evidence to support it, his hierarchy provides a remarkably rational explanation of motivation. Can you suggest other classroom implications of each of his needs?

5. Does McClelland's work with *nAch* appeal to you? Why? How would you assess your own *nAch*? Be realistic. Would it be possible to use his training techniques in the classroom to raise students' *nAch*. Should you?

Women and motivation

INTRODUCTION

The need achievement studies have led to some fascinating conclusions about women's motivation. Matina Horner (1969) touched a sensitive nerve when she showed that women frequently have a fear of success. They believe that they can do well academically as long as they do not surpass men. Asking subjects to write stories about successful members of their sex, she found that most college women wrote unpleasant things about successful women, while only a few college men did likewise for successful men.

The Cues

She gives the example of Phil, a college sophomore, who does well academically and wants to be a doctor. When asked to write a story to the cue "After first-term finals, John finds himself at the top of his medical school class," Phil writes that John is conscientious, hard working, and eventually will graduate at the top of his class. When Monica, another honors student, replies to the cue "After first-term finals, Anne finds herself at the top of her medical school class," she replies that her medical school colleagues are so disgusted with Anne that they beat her.

When Phil and Monica take achievement tests, Monica scores higher than Phil. But when they compete against each other on similar tests, Monica becomes nervous while Phil performs superbly. How can we explain this glaring discrepancy? Horner states that women consistently obtain higher test anxiety scores than men and that the intellectually motivated woman pays an especially high price because she is refusing the standard role of what "women ought to be."

Girls equate intellectual achievement with loss of femininity. Horner believes that the bright woman is caught in a "double bind"—she worries about not only failure but success. Failing, she knows she has not lived up to her ability; succeeding, she knows she is flaunting society's expectations for her. What results is a motive to avoid success.

The Double Bind ✦

Horner administered the John and Anne cues to 90 girls and 88 boys, all undergraduates at the University of Michigan. Negative replies were of three types: anxiety about becoming unpopular, unmarriageable, and lonely (Anne will be a proud and successful but very lonely doctor); doubts about femininity (Anne feels guilty, has a nervous breakdown, quits medical school, and marries a successful young doctor); denial that girls could be so successful (Anne talks to her counselor who tells her she will make a fine nurse).

Male Versus Female

Sixty-five percent of the girls' stories fell into one of these categories, compared to fewer than 10 percent of the boys' stories. None of the boys' stories reflect the bitterness and hostility of the girls'. When she had the girls compete against the boys on achievement tests, they did more poorly than when they had taken similar tests *alone*. Horner believes her findings indicate that women will try to succeed intellectually only when they are not competing with men. In 1974, Monahan et al. had adolescent boys and girls write stories about successful boys and girls. Both sexes were more negative about the successful girls, while both were positive about male success.

THE CHANGING STATUS OF WOMEN

Horner's work reflects women's role in society, home, and school. Blake (1974) states that during the 1960s most developed countries witnessed protests about women's status. More young women have married between the ages of 25 and 34 in 1970 than in 1950, but more married women returned to work in 1970 than in 1950. Their work experience differs qualitatively from men. For example, while women are well represented in the professions it is usually at the lower status level. In 1970, teaching and nursing accounted for 63 percent of the professional women in the United States, while only 7 percent of the physicians and 1 percent of the dentists were women.

While economic reasons are mainly responsible for the increase of working women, there is also a relationship between education and work. As Blake notes (1974, pg. 143), in almost all the developed countries the proportion of women receiving a baccalaureate degree has increased and better-educated women are more concerned with vocations. But this causes problems unless the well-educated women leave the traditional feminine jobs. The female labor supply is rapidly becoming overeducated for these positions.

Substantiating Horner's findings, Blake states that most women accept their position. In 1972, a national poll asked American women whether they preferred "a loving husband who takes care of me" to making it on their own. Half, including those women under 30, said they frequently felt that having a loving husband was more important, and another fifth said they occasionally had this feeling—altogether 70 percent. The percentage was even higher for older women. Similar survey data in all the developed countries show no great discontent among women; they seem as satisfied with their lives as men.

Blake draws some interesting conclusions from these data.

Myths and Sex Differences

Eleanor Maccoby and Carol Jacklin (1974a) examine male and female differences and conclude that many myths have arisen. As they state, physical differences are obvious and universal, but psychological differences are not. They then analyze several of these myths.

1. *Girls are more social than boys.* No evidence supports this belief; both sexes are equally as interested in social stimuli. In childhood, girls are no more dependent than boys, nor are they less willing to remain alone.
2. *Girls are more suggestible than boys.* Boys are as likely as girls to imitate others and to react to social pressure.
3. *Girls have lower self-esteem than boys.* Throughout childhood and adolescence both boys and girls have similar self-confidence and self-satisfaction. Where differences appear, girls feel more social competence, while boys feel more dominant and powerful. It is during the college years that boys feel more confident about their performance, but these authors doubt

that this means girls have lower self-esteem.
4. *Girls lack motivation to achieve.* Maccoby and Jacklin believe that when competition is eliminated, girls' *nAch* is equal to or superior to that of boys. It is only with competition that girls' *nAch* suffers.
5. *Boys are more analytic than girls.* There is no sex difference on tests of analyzing ability; that is, both sexes show equal ability at restructuring a problem to reach a solution.

These findings came from an exhaustive survey of over 2000 books and articles that reported on sex differences in motivation, social behavior, and intellectual ability. One basic finding was that when sex differences appeared (mathematical, spatial, visual) it was not until about 11. The authors believe that these myths survive because parents and teachers focus upon sex characteristics that they expect to observe in boys and girls and then reinforce the expected and desired traits.

1. The socialization of women exerts powerful pressures to develop those personality characteristics and behavioral traits that are congruent with the role of wife and mother.
2. American women are socialized for defeat in those tasks in which men are socialized for success.
3. It seems unlikely that many women will swim upstream in these societies as they are currently structured.

CHANGING STATUS — CHANGING *nAch?*

Alper (1974) reviewed the literature on women's *nAch* and raised several pertinent questions. Would time and women's changing status change the results? Did the original tests (such as Horner's) adhere too rigidly to a male model of *nAch?* Finally, is it really true

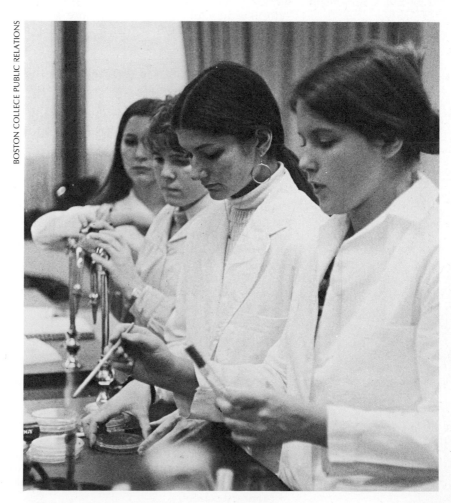

BOSTON COLLEGE PUBLIC RELATIONS

WROS

that American women do *not* want to be achievers? Avoiding the sex-stereotyped cue (Anne in medical school immediately prejudices the results), she attempted to link achievement to role. The Wellesley Role Orientation Scale *(WROS)* was one result. It measures three beliefs:

1. What traits college girls designate as feminine or masculine.
2. What roles they see as appropriate for themselves.
3. What careers they see as more appropriate for men.

High WROS scores indicate a preference for the traditional feminine role, and vice versa.

Role and Achievement

When asked to respond to pictures of two women in a chemistry laboratory and two men in a machine shop, with one person working and one watching in both pictures, women with low WROS scores told significantly more success stories than did those who had high WROS scores. That is, high achievement is clearly linked to role:

1. Those who do not see themselves in the traditional role place a career ahead of being a wife and mother, or believe that it is possible to combine career and marriage, or think it is impossible to combine both and it is better to avoid marriage.
2. Those who see themselves in the traditional role believe that motherhood comes before a career and that they could not, and should not, attempt to combine both.

Alper then poses the critical question: Are low WROS scores actually better achievers than high? She believes that the evidence suggests they are. The studies are fascinating; the evidence is mixed. As Alper states, methodological differences cause confusing results, and life for the achievement motivation researchers is never easy.

Motivation in the classroom

INTRODUCTION

After the discussion and the theories, the question still remains: what does motivation mean for the classroom? How can it help both teachers and students? Frymier (1974) reports on a study related to academic achievement involving about 20,000 students. Certain clear motivation patterns emerged.

1. There are definite sex differences in motivation. By junior high school, girls have more positive motivation than boys. Frymier believes it is due to a predominant female influence during elementary school.

Nursery Schools and Sex Differences

As interesting as these studies are, what do they imply for the classroom? Probably the oustanding conclusion is the need to be aware of and avoid sexual stereotyping. This is easy to say, but difficult to practice. It is much easier to visualize girls playing with dolls rather than computers. Also remember that social learning begins early. Serbin and O'Leary (1975) believe that as early as nursery school, children learn that boys are aggressive and can solve problems, while girls are submissive and passive. They observed 15 preschool classrooms and discovered that teachers react differently to boys and girls. They reinforced, usually by their attention, typical male-female patterns, such as a boy's aggression and a girl's dependency.

These investigators also found that teachers actually teach boys more than they teach girls. Difference in mathematics, verbal ability, and problem solving appear and are reinforced in these early preschool days. Boys receive more directions and are allowed to explore, fail, and discover for themselves, while there is a noticeable tendency for teachers to do something for the girls (stapl-

ing papers, for example) rather than let them do it for themselves. The authors conclude that such differentiated treatment of children limits the intellectual and psychological development of both sexes.

But stereotypes resist change. Tavris (1975) reports on an ambitious study, involving over 1000 children in kindergarten, fifth grade, and ninth grade, that attempted to teach sexual equality. The children read stories, saw movies, and conducted plays all designed to show that women and men are more alike than different. To their surprise, while the girls showed acceptance of a more liberated role, *fifth and ninth grade boys* became even more traditional in their views. Peer pressure and constant examples of male power do not make them sexist—just realistic.

While these programs may help, they also create other problems. The boys held to their traditional ideas; the girls began to reject them, thus increasing the possibility of misunderstanding and resentment unless considerable caution is exerted.

2. Motivation is linked to social class. Disadvantaged youngsters have less motivation for academic learning than those more affluent.

3. Motivation to learn is enduring. While it is not fixed, motivation changes slowly, which has both positive and negative aspects. The eager youngster is not easily discouraged, but the reluctant scholar does not change overnight.

4. There is optimal motivation for individuals. That is, everyone has a personal, ideal motivational level; beyond this, learning deteriorates, which reflects the Yerkes-Dodson law. Frymier simply says that too much motivation is bad; too little is undesirable.

From these patterns, Frymeier believes it is possible to distinguish the motivated student. For example, enthusiastic students

have positive self-concepts and value the abstract and the aesthetic. They also seem to differ in their perception of time, that is, while aware of the past, they also anticipate the future. Nonmotivated pupils seem to cling to the past and fear the future. The motivated youngster also seems to tolerate ambiguity and welcome new experiences.

E. Paul Torrance, well known for his creativity studies, states that external pressures seldom, if ever, force a student to learn, study, or behave properly. Creative learning produces an inner stimulation that makes rewards and punishment unnecessary. Torrance (1970) also believes that teachers can foster internal motivation by changing goals and suggests several techniques.

1. *Have students encounter incompleteness in many ways, such as in pictures and stories.* Ask them to name something that the story does not mention. Use mysteries, puzzles, projects, and constant surprise.
2. *Have students produce something and then use it.* For example, Torrance describes a class in which the pupils were shown a picture of a pond and told to imagine they could be anything in the pond they wanted: frogs, fish, mosquitoes. The children then drew some experiences they might encounter in the pond and wrote stories and songs about them. The teachers used these experiences for arithmetic: If there are three frogs on shore and three on a log and they all jump in, how many will be in the pond? Producing and using something seems to be a powerful motivational tool.

Classroom in the Sky

Lee Conway (1976) described an unusual motivational device called "Classroom in the Sky." While few teachers could employ it, the project illustrates innovative planning that motivated seemingly unmotivated students: the disadvantaged, the poor readers, the failures, those with behavioral problems and poor self-concepts. But, as Conway states, a light, 150 HP single-engine airplane produced basic and positive behavioral changes in these youths.

A foundation grant provided the money for flying time. The program consisted of four units: in-school aerospace instruction; field trips to airports, control centers, and a naval air station; small-group tutoring in mathematics and navigation; actual flight instruction.

During the preceding year, 60 percent of these boys had been suspended at least once. Problems continued when the project began (they thought they were in the "dummy class") but by year's end they were coming to class even when sick. In that first year, significant gains resulted: attendance increased dramatically, no project student was suspended, behavior improved enormously, reading and math scores both increased significantly.

The project began in 1968. In 1975 Conway began a follow-up study; the youths were now about 21 years old. Stunning changes had occurred.

1. Fifty-six percent of the youths were either in college or armed forces training schools and maintaining a B average. Three had won scholarships. Others of the original group were working so they could go to college, and two others had obtained private pilot licenses.
2. Parents, who were involved in the project from the beginning, had continued to support the boys in college, at considerable personal sacrifice.
3. Employment was remarkably high for these boys; only two of the original group were unemployed.
4. Self-esteem had soared. When questioned about feelings of self-pride, only two still retained doubt and insecurity.
5. There was a growing sense that they had control over their destinies. (Recall Rotter's locus of control discussed in Chapter 5; these boys could now be classified as "internals.")

While not all schools can have a "classroom in the sky," the implications are legion. All have one main theme: knowledgeable teachers, searching for interesting and exciting activities, stimulate intrinsic motivation.

3. *Have pupils ask questions.* Students want to ask questions but teachers frequently discourage them for many reasons: insecurity, lack of knowledge, lack of time. Teachers should both encourage children to ask relevant questions and then take time either to answer them or guide youngsters to those sources where they can find the answers by themselves.

COMPETITION: YES OR NO?

In his great book *Economics* (1975), Paul Samuelson, speaking of markets and prices, states that a competitive system is not a system of chaos and anarchy but possesses order and logic. It works. We opened this chapter with a discussion of the motivation of Olympic athletes and noted that Ryder et al. believe the world does not need finer runners but keener competition. It is the competition that makes the person.

No

Why then is competition an issue that so troubles educators? For example, Joseph Wax (1975) states that competition is an educational incongruity increasingly difficult to justify. Competition seeks advantage at a cost to another and brings pain to someone when schooling should be a joy. Aggression and hostility are the products of encouraging some children to triumph over others. No great psychologist or educator—Socrates, Freud, Skinner, Dewey—advocated competition.

But Michael Grenis (1975), rebutting Wax, states that there is nothing basically wrong in creating a competitive group climate.

Yes

To do otherwise is to mislead students and fail to prepare them for the competition they will inevitably encounter. Honesty demands that schools recognize excellence. Children themselves know that some are smarter than others. What schools must provide is the opportunity to compete fairly. Every child must experience success, but there should be no institutional guarantee of a reward for every effort, no matter how trivial. Otherwise, true achievement becomes meaningless. Grenis believes that setting reasonable goals and attaining them is an important learning activity—both for school and life.

The arguments, pro and con, are endless, and Wax and Grenis are typical. What can you conclude from them?

1. *Competition is a fact of life—in the home, in school, in work.* Wax states that races should be run and scores should be kept.
2. *Intense competition can be psychologically, even physically, damaging.* The Yerkes-Dodson law and Broadhurst's experiments showed the negative result of excessive motivation and apply equally well to competition, which is a sharp stimulant to motivation. Recall the athlete who, under enormous pressure from some unthinking coach, hides a potentially crippling injury "to help the team to win."

ARLINGTON, MASS. ADVOCATE

3. *Excessive emphasis upon grades and honors turns a student's focus away from the intrinsic value of learning to the transient value of material objects.*

4. *Intense competition with others turns youngsters against each other and, if prolonged, leads to undesirable concentration upon self—I must win—regardless.* Under these conditions, too often the end justifies the means and unhealthy behavioral patterns become routine.

5. *In spite of these negative features, competition can be healthy and probably belongs in the classroom.* But teachers must work, and work diligently, to instill competition with self. This is what Ryder et al. meant in their study of racing. There is a world record: Am I good enough to beat it? Am I doing the best I can? Competition with self is closely related to many other motivational topics: the setting of reasonable goals, a moderate level of self-competition, a realistic level of need achievement. Teachers who strive for intrinsically motivated students by encouraging realistic self-competition not only foster learning, they also provide a means for coping with life.

TEACHING, MOTIVATION, AND YOU

In their excellent text *Mental Hygiene in Teaching* (1959), Redl and Wattenberg state that people are usually highly motivated when they choose an occupation. Whether it is for satisfaction, status, or some personality attribute, motivation will decisively affect performance, just as it affects students' learning. The authors suggest several motives for teaching and, ordinarily, a combination of them explains any one person's choice.

1. *Status.* While not the most highly paid profession, teaching still commands respect from most people. A secure, accepted social position is thus assured, which can be extremely important for many individuals.

2. *Family pressure.* Having someone in the family a teacher can easily be a family ambition. To obtain and maintain parental affection, a person could select teaching.

3. *Love for a particular subject.* Some subject may be very appealing, and the only way to continue to study it *and* earn a living may be to teach.

4. *Identification with a teacher.* The power of identification is strong and if some teacher was especially admirable and had a warm relationship with students, he or she becomes a model to follow.

5. *Love of young people.* Some simply like young people. They find them stimulating and enjoy their company. One way to acquire youthful companionship, and be paid for it, is to teach.

The authors also include several other motives: the need for power, need for security, desire for affection.

Stop for a moment and try to identify your motives for teaching. It will help you to become a better teacher. As Combs et al. (1974) state, people do what they need to do, but to tell teachers what they need to know to be effective teachers has limited value. The authors consider that time spent in examining and evaluating beliefs leads to the identification of those needs that bear directly on self and are powerful motives. For example, the problems that beginning teachers see usually are not those of experienced teachers: a need to maintain discipline in a classroom versus a need for a larger raise. Thus the basic motive usually remains—love of children, fondness for a subject—but secondary motives may change.

John Gardner, in his thoughtful essay on excellence (1961), states that we must understand that high motivation is as precious a commodity as talent and that if we do not have a system that searches for motivation as well as talent we must resign ourselves to poor leadership. Combs et al. agree that we must more seriously consider teacher motivation. They state that a teacher is not only a professional, he or she is a unique flesh-and-blood human being with wants, desires, goals, hopes, and fears. These motives carry into the classroom and influence teacher performance and classroom atmosphere.

Discussion Questions

1. Have times changed sufficiently since Horner's work so that women's fear of success is diminishing? Your experience with your friends is probably the best practical indication. Whether you answer yes or no, do you think your answer applies *nationally*?

2. Do you think that Alper's attempt to link achievement with role perception is more revealing than Horner's work? Why? Again, from your experience, how do you rate your friends in the relationship between achievement and traditional or career roles?

3. Study Maccoby and Jacklin's myths about the sexes. Do you agree with those presented? Why? How do you explain equality in self-esteem and equality in *nAch* when *competition* is eliminated?

4. In your experience do schools really teach girls "to shut up"? Many would argue that just the opposite is true: Schools reinforce traditional feminine behavior patterns. Which do you believe is more accurate? Why?

5. It might be interesting for you to identify your motives for teaching. List those motives that have drawn you to teaching. Which are most powerful? Have you always had them? Which do you think are most likely to change?

Some Concluding Thoughts

Motivated students plus motivated teachers produce the ideal classroom. Or do they? There is little dispute about motivation's key role in learning, so why question the opening statement? It is vital to determine what motives are acting, and at what intensity. If youngsters want to learn and teachers enjoy youth and teaching, the combination is ideal. But if youngsters are determined to win at any cost or a teacher is satisfying a need for power, a different kind of motivation is surely needed.

What needs, both teachers' and students', are functioning? Where do they belong in Maslow's hierarchy? Why have they appeared? The answers to these and other motivational questions guide our classroom action and determine both what and how we teach. As teachers, the motivational literature offers help in daily work as well as some cautions. Do you treat boys and girls alike? Do you use classroom competition wisely? Do you attempt to instill in your students competition with self? Do you search for innovation in your classroom techniques?

Assessing yourselves and your students, you can decide what incentives to use, how much or little to prod one youngster or another. You come to know yourself better and thus better understand your students. But in your desire to motivate, remember you are a teacher, not an entertainer. There comes a time when students must meet standards and follow a reasonable code of conduct. If you overlook everything and reward everything, motivation is lost and achievement becomes meaningless.

Summary

- Motivation is basic to learning and without it little or no learning results.

- A precise definition of motivation is difficult, but it arouses students and directs them toward a goal.

- Motivation is not selective; it affects all aspects of behavior, from perception through performance.

- While motivated students are obviously desirable, the degree or intensity of motivation needs careful scrutiny.

- Teachers reasonably attempt to motivate most students by incentives (extrinsic motivation) but hope for a sincere love of learning (intrinsic motivation).

- Many theorists, such as Skinner, Bruner, Maslow, and McClelland, have offered explanations of motivation.

- Women's *nAch* has raised interesting, and educationally pertinent, questions about female motivation in current societies.

- Innovation and competition both are motivational techniques that require skillful use.

Suggested Readings

Bruner, Jerome. *The Process of Education*. Cambridge, Mass.: Harvard University Press, 1960. Bruner's fascinating little book that explores teaching. His chapter on motives for learning is especially good.

Cofer, C. N. and M. H. Appley. *Motivation: Theory and Research*. New York: Wiley, 1964. This is the "bible" of motivation; thorough, comprehensive, well documented.

Maccoby, Eleanor and Carol Jacklin. *The Psychology of Sex Differences*. Stanford University Press, 1974. A massive compilation of the latest research on sex differences, examining the relationship between sex and such characteristics as intelligence and achievement. Probably the best reference to date.

Maslow, Abraham. *Motivation and Personality*. New York: Harper & Row, 1970. Maslow's finest interpretation of his beliefs about the human personality and the needs that motivate it.

McClelland, David. *The Achieving Society*. New York: Van Nostrand, 1961. A fascinating account of the development of the achievement motive studies and their practical application.

Murray, Edward. *Motivation and Emotion*. Englewood Cliffs, N.J.: Prentice-Hall, 1964. A good, brief summary of motivational research and theory.

Skinner, B. F. *The Technology of Teaching*. Englewood Cliffs, N.J.: Prentice-Hall, 1968. As usual, Skinner puts his ideas to practical test. This book, well written and still timely, has interesting sections on motivating students by reinforcement.

9

Types of Learning I: Cognitive

(continues)

Introduction

Verbal learning still reigns supreme in the classroom. Unfortunately, most discussions of verbal learning have little value for teachers. Unending and complicated flow charts, or highly theoretical analyses of principles, offer little help to hard-pressed instructors. These presentations lack meaning and furnish no structure for teachers to employ in their daily work. For example, if you consider how children acquire concepts—those categories in which things are grouped because of certain similarities—you suddenly realize that youngsters form these categories quite naturally.

David Ausubel (1968) has wrestled with the complexity of verbal learning and concluded that children from birth through the early elementary years form concepts intuitively. That is, they acquire the concept of chair by abstracting a chair's common features from repeated use of different chairs. Later children mature cognitively and can understand verbally presented concepts.

Since most learning proceeds verbally, pupils must be able to relate new learning to their previous learning—they must have some *structure* to which they can relate this new material. Teachers must know that what they are teaching is *potentially* meaningful to their pupils, that is, that students can relate it to their present structure of knowledge. Since this process is the heart of most classroom learning, it is the focus of this chapter.

It is impossible to overemphasize the significance of meaningful learning since continued abstract learning, problem solving, creativity, memory, and transfer all depend on the meaning a youngster gives a subject. To illustrate how meaning affects all verbal learning, try this experiment yourself. Read the following famous story, "The War of the Ghosts" (Bartlett, 1950), and when you complete this unit ask your instructor to have you write what you remember of it. Read it just this once; at the end of the chapter obvious patterns that appear in your story will be identified.

The formation and use of ideas determines the success or failure of education. Training for a skill that may soon be obsolete in a technological society is an inadequate goal. Students must understand what they are doing, which is only possible by forming clear concepts of the task or subject. Only then can they adjust to change.

You do not form isolated concepts. You compare, combine, and form patterns of ideas in your constant struggle to adapt to the environment. Such mental activity is thinking. Educators often say that they want their students to think, which is a desirable objective, but one frequently ill defined. One task of this chapter is to examine the process of concept formation and attempt to demonstrate clearly underlying psychological principles and classroom application.

Solving problems is also a form of mental activity that teachers should encourage. It is arduous work to pose meaningful problems for students and then to guide, not direct, them to solution. Problem-solving techniques remain with a student throughout life and affect success or failure in personal happiness and occupational

"The War of the Ghosts"

One night two young men from Egulac went down to the river to hunt seals, and while they were there it became foggy and calm. Then they heard war cries, and they thought: "Maybe this is a war party." They escaped to the shore, and hid behind a log. Now canoes came up, and they heard the noise of paddles, and saw one canoe coming up to them. There were five men in the canoe, and they said:

"What do you think? We wish to take you along. We are going up the river to make war on the people."

One of the young men said: "I have no arrows."

"Arrows are in the canoe," they said.

"I will not go along. I might be killed. My relatives do not know where I have gone. But you," he said, turning to the other, "may go with them."

So one of the young men went, but the other returned home.

And the warriors went on up the river to a town on the other side of Kalama. The people came down to the water, and they began to fight, and many were killed. But presently the young man heard one of the warriors say: "Quick, let us go home: that Indian has been hit." Now he thought: "Oh, they are ghosts." He did not feel sick, but they said he had been shot.

So the canoes went back to Egulac, and the young man went ashore to his house, and made a fire. And he told everybody and said: "Behold I accompanied the ghosts, and we went to fight. Many of our fellows were killed, and many of those who attacked us were killed. They said I was hit, and I did not feel sick."

He told it all, and then he became quiet. When the sun rose he fell down. Something black came out of his mouth. His face became contorted. The people jumped up and cried.

He was dead.

Source: T. C. Bartlett, *Remembering: A Study in Experimental and Social Psychology.* London: Cambridge University Press, 1932.

---

success. Life is not a lecture, and our schools should not penalize students by neglecting to furnish them with the tools to cope with environmental pressures.

Adjustment to environmental forces increasingly demands new responses. These often must be unprecedented, not only for the individual but for society. Creative thinking is recognized today as a desirable, even necessary, type of mental activity. History supplies many stories about the suspicion with which the creative individual was once viewed. Today both enlightened educators and society have reversed this attitude: schools actively search for signs of creativity and are demanding better ways of identifying the creative student. The problem surrounding the search for and development of creativity deserves your attention.

Verbal learning is critical for academic success and thus, in most societies, it is also critical for occupational success. To help students benefit from instruction, teachers must structure material so that pupils both see meaning and acquire new insights. Although verbal learning is divided topically, this chapter repeatedly returns to the theme of structuring material for concept acquisition, problem solving, and creative thinking.

Concept learning

As you adjust to your environment, you react in a manner that defies an explanation dependent upon the presence of observable stimuli. You respond to pressures from within as well as without. When asked a question or faced with a problem, you usually pause, reflect, and then respond. During the pause you search for clues, combine past experiences, and recall past similar situations.

For example, suppose that you were asked this question: What is a cloud? Presumably, you are reading this book in a study, library, or some enclosed area. Nevertheless, you can "picture" a cloud. Somewhere, sometime you formed a concept of a cloud and now upon demand you can recall this idea. You do not have a concept of a particular cloud, but of *any* cloud. By your ability to abstract, you have taken all that you know about clouds, removed the individual features of any particular cloud, and now constructed a mental category of *clouds*. By abstraction, a concept has resulted. The symbol *cloud* now represents not a unique, individual object but a class of objects that possess common properties.

Once the concept is formed, you can respond to the environment more efficiently and far more economically. There is no need to go to a dictionary and look up the meaning of cloud, no need to go to a geology book to discover the properties of clouds, no need to seek photographs of clouds. Using the verbal stimulus of the question, you can respond with a description of a cloud, or with a list of characteristics, or with whatever is desired. Your response is based not upon immediate activity but upon a previously acquired concept of a cloud.

MEANING AND STRUCTURE

Students acquire concepts when material is somewhat familiar or can be organized into structures. Try this experiment yourself. It is similar to what your students encounter. Memorize the lists of words on the top of page 325.

As you attempt to recall them, certain patterns emerge. You probably had difficulty with the words in Column A—they were meaningless. Column B was easier—not only did the words possess meaning, they clustered around two key words: *book* and *steel*.

The Role of Meaning Column C was probably the easiest—the words were logically or-

A	B	C
nok	book	read
mak	steel	the
yik	paper	following
zeb	smoke	pages
xih	store	very
weh	cover	carefully
quh	words	to
niv	mill	learn
vih	grass	about
zah	page	concepts

ganized into a meaningful structure. Teachers have a dual task: they must either relate new material to what students already know, or they must make new material as meaningful as possible.

The teacher's task is similar to that faced by the Gestalt psychologists (see Chapter 7). For example, Köhler (1969) states that when individual objects become part of a larger structure, they acquire different and more significant meaning. While Köhler is concerned with perceptual psychology, he nevertheless provides direction for teachers, especially in verbal learning. Frequently the individual object acquires new meaning when absorbed into a larger unit. Recall one of the classic Gestalt techniques: What do you see in the following diagram.

Most readers say that it is a square, but it is a square of circles; individual identity is absorbed by the larger unit. Four of these "circles" now become "corners."

Teachers can capitalize on their pupils' tendency to group; that is, students want to organize and structure, and you can help them by recalling certain principles.

1. What do you see in the following figure?

You saw two groups of circles, not ten isolated circles. In beginning algebra, students often have trouble with this type of problem.

$$2a + 4a - (-9 + 3a) = 36 - 3 - (+3a - 48)$$

Where to begin the solution often baffles them. Why not insist that they begin with those things that are close. For example:

$$6a - (-9 + 3a) = 36 - 3 - (+3a - 48)$$
$$6a + 9 - 3a = 36 - 3 - 3a + 48$$
$$3a + 9 = 33 - 3a + 48$$
$$3a + 9 = 81 - 3a$$
$$6a + 9 = 81$$
$$6a = 72$$
$$a = 12$$

These detailed steps are only a beginning, but the smartest students frequently encounter difficulty in their initial contacts with these equations. No matter how you do it, teach them to group those items that are close.

2. Objects that are similar form natural groups. What do you see in the following figure?

+ + + + + + +
+ + + + + + +
+ + + O O + +
+ + + + + + +

You saw a group of crosses *and* a group of circles because we group similar things. To return to our algebraic problem:

$$6a - (-9 + 3a) = 36 - 3 - (+3a - 48)$$

Why not next stress similarity? For example, the first step was to teach youngsters to group those things that are close: Combine whole numbers and similar unknowns on each side of the equation. Now insist that they concentrate on similar things. They should combine all the a's, and then all the whole numbers, finally solving for a. Instructors do this now, but making it a conscious effort will help both teachers and pupils.

3. There is a natural tendency toward closure. What do you see in A, B, C, D, E?

O   ⊝   ⊝   ⊝   ⊝
A   B   C   D   E

Some readers conclude "face" as early as *B*. We have a desire to complete things, which is the famous Zeigarnik effect (named after Bluma Zeigarnik, a student of Kurt Lewin). The Zeigarnik effect, or drive toward closure, can be a practical aid for teachers. Using the same algebraic equation, let beginning students occasionally work backwards; for example, $6a = 72$, $6a + 9 = 81$, $3a + 9 = 81 - 3a$. Thus you and they can capitalize upon their tendency toward completion. While teachers will not use this frequently, it can be helpful, especially with the novice who is bewildered by grouping unknowns, changing signs, and transforming numbers.

Closure

Closure also aids recall. English teachers and history teachers can employ this psychological principle by teaching their students never to stop reading or writing at a logical conclusion. For example, when I complete my writing for today I will try to leave it in the middle of a sentence. Tomorrow, returning to my work, I can begin immediately because the thought was unfinished and the incomplete sentence acts as a stimulus. If I stop at the end of a paragraph or section, it is often difficult to begin again. Try this with your students; you may be surprised by the results.

These basic perceptual principles aid meaning because students can then organize material. So teachers should attempt:

1. To use the familiar to introduce the novel.
2. To relate new material to some structure that the students already possess.
3. To stress any meaningful relations within the material.

Before beginning a detailed analysis of concept formation, the importance of meaning and structure for teachers needs further emphasis. Köhler has stated (1971) that we often experience difficulty in thinking and problem solving because "facts" are buried by their surroundings—they are "camouflaged." Can you find the digit 4 in the following figure?

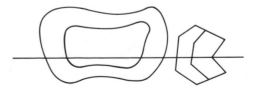

It is buried within unfamiliar shapes and you probably had trouble finding it. Students have exactly the same trouble discovering concepts and finding meaning within unfamiliar subjects. Student's past experiences should be used to introduce organization into their work. From organization and structure flows meaning.

THE NATURE OF THE CONCEPT

What is a concept? Are all concepts similar? Are they formed in the same manner? Before discussing the instructional implications of concept formation some experimental evidence and descriptive data will provide historical perspective and will help you understand the significance of concepts for both teaching and learning.

A Determining Tendency

Ach (1921) warns that dependence upon associations for the development of concepts is inadequate. His experiments illustrated that concept formation is an active, creative process and not merely a passive reception of obvious associations. The memorization of words and their connection to objects will not result in concepts. Concepts are acquired as the solution of problems. For Ach, the critical element in concept formation is a "determining tendency," which is the individual's image of the goal.

Emergence of Common Elements

Moore (1910) flashed a series of five geometrical figures to his subjects until they were able to isolate the one figure common to each series. He stated that the common element was acquired at the expense of the surrounding elements. Two distinct phases in the isolation of the common element were apparent. First, the common element was recognized but not clearly enough to be definitely isolated. There was only a vague awareness that something was common to all. Secondly, as repetition continued, the common element emerged more clearly. It was now definitely isolated. Both Moore's and Ach's studies reflected the *active* search by the individual.

The Hull Study

The well-known study by Hull (1920) is especially interesting. Dissatisfied with existing methods of studying concept formation, he endeavored to discover if one method of learning concepts was more effective than others. He presented his subjects a series of 144 Chinese characters selected from a standard Chinese dictionary. Each group or pack of characters had common elements. The subject was expected to learn the name of the character by its common element.

Simple to Complex

Some of his conclusions are particularly pertinent for teachers. First, concepts are learned more efficiently by proceeding from simple to complex. But the simple to complex sequence, in itself, is not the explanation. Rather, concepts are learned more rapidly and thoroughly when substantial time is devoted to presenting the character under simple conditions. Students should not be rushed into complex experiences with the concept until they have been exposed to more simple experiences.

Abstract plus Concrete

Second, a combination of abstract and concrete examples results in greater functional efficiency than the use of either alone. Telling a class the common element in any concept, with no alternate method, is unsatisfactory. Students must recognize common elements both in and out of their natural location. This is a sharp reminder to educators that their students must experience the concrete aspects of subjects as well as the abstract.

Use of Error

Finally, the awareness of individual concepts evolves gradually. Errors are either discarded or corrected by continuous development, and it is here that the trial-and-error technique is most consequential. Students must actively engage in the search for the correct common elements that constitute the concept.

In a fascinating study, originally published in Russia in 1934 and translated into English in 1962, Vygotsky comments upon the traditional method of studying concept formation. First, there is the technique that he calls method of definition. The concepts that a child has are investigated by the verbal definition of the contents. This technique is inadequate because it neglects the dynamic process by which the concept developed. The investigator is not as concerned with the child's thinking as with the verbal reproduction of knowledge. Nor is the investigator concerned with the perceptions and mental refinements of sensations that are indispensable to concept formation.

Second, there is the technique that focuses upon psychic processes to the complete exclusion of the role played by some symbol (words). The subject is expected to discover some common trait in a series of discrete impressions, abstracting it from all other nonessential traits (Vygotsky, 1962, pg. 53).

Thought and Language

What is needed is some procedure that combines both of these methods. Vygotsky felt that this could best be accomplished by introducing nonsense words for which there are no familiar concepts. The nonsense word could be attached to a combination of object attributes for which no concept or word now exists. For example, *saltin* could mean bright and cheerful. The process does not depend upon previous knowledge but requires active intellectual research. Vygotsky (1962, pg. 53) believed that such techniques focus upon the functional conditions of concept formation.

From his studies of more than 300 children, adolescents, and adults, Vygotsky concluded that concept formation occurs in the following three basis steps:

1. *A syncretic form of thinking.* The first step in concept formation occurs when children group, without any basis, a number of disparate objects. They thus unite diverse elements into one articulated image because of some chance impressions (Vygotsky, 1962, pg. 60).

2. *A complex form of thinking.* Individual objects are combined in the child's mind, not only by personal chance selection, but because of bonds actually existing between these objects. Thinking in complexes is a kind of objective thinking, but it is not conceptual since the bonds between objects are concrete and factual, rather than abstract and logical. (Note: Syncretic thinking depends upon purely subjective bonds; complex thinking depends upon actual similarities or perceptual bonds between objects.)

3. *The formation of potential and true concepts.* In potential concepts, single traits are abstracted; the true concept appears when abstracted traits are synthesized, and these abstracted syntheses become the chief instrument of thought.

Vygotsky summarizes his study by stating that the processes that result in concept formation begin in earliest childhood, but that the intellectual functions necessary for concept formation develop and ripen only at puberty. Before that, certain intellectual functions have the same relationship to true concepts as the embryo to the fully formed organism.

Recent research reported by the Wisconsin Research and Development Center for Cognitive Learning illustrates the growing complexity of concept learning experimentation (Levin, 1976; Klausmeier et al., 1974). Both laboratory experiments and classroom studies of children from 4 to 15 years contributed to the formulation of a model of conceptual learning and development (CLD). Klausmeier and his associates recognized that the ability of children to acquire concepts depends on both external (appropriate instruction) and internal conditions (maturation and learning). The CLD model traces concept attainment through four successively higher levels: concrete, identity, classificatory, and formal.

1. Levin (1976) notes that concept attainment at the *concrete level* means that individuals recognize an object previously encountered. For example, recognizing a red ball implies the cognitive operations of attending to the ball, discriminating it from other environmental objects, representing it internally (usually by forming an image of it), and then remembering the representation.

2. Concept attainment at the *identity level* means that individuals recognize an object when viewed from a different perspective or sensed in a different modality (hearing something you originally saw, such as church bells). While attending, discriminating, and remembering are again instrumental, generalizing appears as a new cognitive operation.

3. Concept attainment at the *classificatory level* means that individuals can generalize that two or more things are somehow alike. For example, when youngsters treat a toy dog and an actual dog as dogs then they have attained the concept of dog at a basic classificatory level. While they can provide examples of nonexamples of a concept, youngsters at this level cannot define the word that represents the concept nor can they explain the basis of their classification.

4. Concept attainment at the *formal level* means that individuals can define *both* the name and the attributes of the concept. Klausmeier states that children possess the concept of tree at the formal level if, when presented with examples of trees, shrubs, and herbs, they identify the trees, call them by name, define a tree's attributes, give an accepted definition of tree, and explain how trees, shrubs, and herbs differ. Acquiring the names of concepts and their attributes enables individuals to think symbolically and to acquire additional concepts by language.

The four levels of concept attainment emerge in an invariant sequence; that is, children exhibit a distinct developmental trend in concept acquisition. Klausmeier and his colleagues observed other interesting phenomena: the attainment of a particular concept varies among children of the same age (17 percent of the third-grade children attained equilateral triangle at the formal level, but 83 percent did not); the same children acquire different concepts at different rates (30 percent of the ninth graders attained "noun" at the formal level, while 90 percent attained "cutting tool" at the formal level).

Educational
Implications There are major educational implications in this work. It is an interactionist interpretation, which means that environmental conditions influence concept attainment. Klausmeier states that instructional conditions can facilitate conceptual development. He uses the example of the ninth-graders who did not attain "noun" at the formal level. These students probably will never do so *without further* instruction; that is, instruction must match conceptual level.

You should identify those concepts that students are to learn in a specific subject and decide at what level each of your students should attain them. For example, some students may be able to attain certain specific concepts at the formal level, while others may be restricted to the identity level. Then you should state each concept's defining attributes, furnish examples and nonexamples, and devise test items.

It is a demanding but richly rewarding task. By employing these techniques you can respond to the plea that educators formulate means for relating levels of concept attainment, internal conditions of concept learning, and instructional conditions (Klausmeier et al., 1974).

THE CONSTRUCTION OF CATEGORIES

Your economical movement through myriad environmental stimuli reflects your ability to place objects in categories and then invent a name for the category. *Book, pupil, teacher, car, doll,* and *water* are examples of your tendency to categorize. With this talent, you avoid the necessity of responding separately to each and every object in your environment. When you hear the word *book* you need not seek an actual book to ascertain its characteristics. If you have a concept of book, you have placed it in a category with other similar objects that are made of bound sheets and have pages with words and illustrations. Upon hearing *book* you recall the concept that possesses the common properties of that category.

A Study of Thinking   Bruner, Goodnow, and Austin (1956) have analyzed categorizing and believe it explains why humans are not overwhelmed by environmental complexity. These authors state bluntly that categorizing is an inventive act and the category formed becomes a tool for further use (1956, pg. 2). Once the object is placed in a category (the concept is formed), you utilize it when you encounter a similar stimuli pattern in the future. You need not repeat the process of categorizing.

There are two main types of categories—the identity category, by which stimuli are classed as forms of the same thing, and the equivalance category, by which you respond to different things as though they were the same thing. Categories, then, are composed of things that either are the same, or are considered to be equivalent.

These authors (1956, pp. 232–233) stress that categorizing entails two distinct activities. First, there is concept formation, or the construction of a category by the generalization of response to a specific stimulus, by the uniting of several individual concepts (female presidents of the United States) or by pure invention. Next, there is concept attainment, which is the location of attributes that distinguish a certain category. This is the search for exemplars and nonexemplars of any category.

Bruner, Goodnow, and Austin summarize the importance of categorizing as follows:

1. *Categorizing reduces the complexity of the environment.* Abstraction enables us to group objects and respond to *classes* of objects rather than to each and every thing we encounter.
2. *Categorizing permits us to identify the objects of the world.* We identify objects by placing them in a class, and when similar objects are met, we can say, "Ah, there is another one of those little redheaded Venusians."
3. *Categorizing allows humans to reduce their need of constant learning.* Each time we experience an object, we are not forced to form a new category; we merely categorize with no additional learning. This object has attributes *X, Y, Z*; therefore, it belongs to the category entitled *car.*
4. *Categorizing provides direction for instrumental activity.* When we see a road sign that reads "Danger Ahead" we alter our driving to the anticipated conditions. We become more alert, proceed more cautiously, and drive more slowly.

Conceptual Blockbusting

Analyzing verbal learning uncovers many learning blocks. Fear, anxiety, habit, and inexperience, either singularly or combined, all produce conceptual blocks. James Adams (1974) has presented some ideas about "conceptual blockbusting" that you will examine throughout this chapter. He identifies several major perceptual blocks—those obstacles that prevent us from clearly perceiving some issue, or the information needed to solve a problem.

1. *Difficulty in isolating the problem.* Problems, including those characteristics necessary to construct categories, are frequently hidden by inadequate clues or misleading information. For example, is the problem with some course you dislike really the instructor's fault, or is it because you have not allotted enough time to it, and thus are doing poorly? Clearly perceiving the problem is the first step to thinking clearly. Take the time to define the problem precisely or you will waste time needlessly. There is usually considerable information given that will help you, if you look for it. What exactly is required? What data are available to help me? How can I utilize the data to find the solution?

2. *Delimiting the problem too closely.* There often is a natural tendency to restrict thinking to the traditional, or to those techniques that have "worked in the past." Most readers will not exceed imaginary boundaries; they are trapped by their past. The constraint is within them, not the problem. *The boundaries are in the problem, and the more widely you teach students to search within the problem's boundaries, the more their verbal learning will improve.*

3. *Failure to utilize all sensory inputs.* Senses such as sight and sound, taste and smell, are closely linked and supplement each other. As Adams notes, problem solvers need all the help they can get, but from the first day of school they are assaulted verbally and usually become less competent visually. Einstein, for example, said that words played little part in his thinking, while images appeared to be critical.

Everyone encounters these blocks, but their quantity and intensity varies from person to person. Pupils are usually unaware of them, and one of a teacher's tasks should be to help pupils examine issues more carefully, using these guidelines.

---

5. *Categorizing encourages the ordering and relating of classes.* Since we react to systems and patterns, once we place an object in a category we vastly increase the possibilities of establishing relationships for that particular object.

TYPES OF CONCEPTS

Certain conclusions are now possible:

1. Both children and adults exhibit the power of abstraction.

2. There is general agreement about the nature of a concept (an abstracted property or properties).
3. There is wide disagreement about the precise manner in which concepts are formed.

Categorizing because of an element or a relationship differentiates *kinds* of concepts. Bruner, Goodnow, and Austin (1956, pg. 41) state that there are three category types, depending upon the method of combining properties. These are conjunctive, disjunctive, and relational concepts, which have the following meaning.

1. *Conjunctive concepts* rely upon the joint presence of several attributes. These attributes are abstracted from many individual experiences with the object, thing, or event. So there are categories, such as *boy, car, book,* and *orange.*

2. *Disjunctive concepts* are composed of concepts any one of whose attributes may be employed in classification. The authors (1956, pg. 156) remark that members of a disjunctive class exhibit defining attributes so that one or another of the attributes enable an object to be placed in a particular category. A good example of the disjunctive category is the strike in baseball. A strike may be either a ball thrown by the pitcher that is over the plate and between a batter's shoulders and knees, or a ball at which the batter swings and misses, or a ball that the batter hits foul (outside of the playing limits of the diamond). Anyone of these attributes enables the observer to classify it as a strike.

3. *Relational concepts* are formed by the relationship that exists among defining attributes. The authors illustrate this category by using income brackets. There are many income levels or classes, all of which exist because of the relationship among income, eligible expenses, and number of dependents. The combination of these properties determines an individual's income class. These are relational categories.

The authors conclude that categorizing implies more than merely recognizing instances. Rules are learned and then applied to new situations. The various categories (conjunctive, disjunctive, relational) are really rules for grouping attributes to define the positive instances of any concept.

HOW CONCEPTS ARE FORMED

The meaning of concepts should now be clear: the concept of anything implies knowing what that thing is. Concepts extend over a wide range of complexity. Some may be simple, such as *boy, girl, dog, water.* Others are much more subtle and demand a combina-

tion of terms and interpretations to capture their essences: *loyalty,*
suborbital, deoxyribonucleic acid. Students must master the significant concepts of their environment, for concepts are the heart of all
learning.

**Concept Formation
Begins**

When environmental stimuli contact the individual they initiate
the process of concept formation. Sensation is the first step in this
process. Sense organs react to some of these stimuli that are bom-
barding them and produce a nerve impulse that ultimately is interpreted by the central nervous system. The senses of sight, sound,
smell, touch, and the like, all contribute to this first phase.

What happens with faulty sensation? If sensations are vague,
distorted, or inaccurate, the concepts formed will likewise be
vague, distorted, and inaccurate. So the warnings that teachers
constantly receive about the physical deficiencies of their pupils
are real. The youngster who is slightly deaf or the adolescent who
shuns eyeglasses will experience faulty sensations.

Note that we react to some, not all, stimuli. Given our many
sense organs and the infinite variety of stimuli impinging upon
them, it is impossible to react to everything. Why do we react to
some and not others? There are three possible answers. First, some
stimuli demand our attention. They so overwhelm everything else
in our environment that we must respond to them. Second,
frequently we want to react to certain stimuli. Call it motivation,
readiness, set, or emotion, we associate pleasure with this or that
combination of stimuli and are drawn to it. Third, our past experiences influence our reaction. We are inclined to the familiar and
normally will recognize and respond to it more rapidly than to the
unknown.

The role of perception

We do not respond to our environment on a one-to-one basis. For
example, examine the following figure.

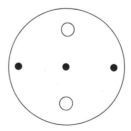

What do you see? Undoubtedly your reply would be something
like, "I see a circle with dots and smaller circles inside it." You
would not say, "I see one dot, and another dot, and another dot,
and a small circle, and another small circle, and a line around all

of them." You grouped the stimuli and expressed your answer in some related manner. You utilized your past experience by combining it with this present experience. When someone asks you what time it is, do you carefully observe all of the minute markings on your watch? No, your past experience enables you to ignore the irrelevant and concentrate on the section where the hands are.

The Figure-Ground Relationship

You organized the relevant stimuli, ignored the irrelevant, and moved them into the background. This is the famous figure-ground relationship. The more prominent qualities of the stimulus pattern emerge more clearly (figure), while the less prominent qualities recede (ground). In the example of telling time, the hands resting on the minute markings of five o'clock are the figure, while the remainder of the face of the watch represents the ground.

Perception is giving meaning to the discrete, meaningless stimuli that initially aroused awareness. The meaning that you give any stimulus depends upon the manner in which you pattern it. For example, a young boy hears a sound. From his past experiences he realizes that it is a whistle. As he continues to relate this stimulus to his experience, perceptual meaning becomes richer. He notes the time element; the whistle always blows at seven o'clock morning and evening. Passing through town one evening at seven o'clock, he hears the whistle coming from the fire station. He has located its source. Now when he hears it, he identifies it as the seven o'clock whistle coming from the firehouse.

How you structure stimuli determines the quality of the percept and, ultimately, the concept. Teachers should use materials that form a meaningful pattern for youngsters. The strong reaction against history as the memorization of dates, and against geography as the memorization of places, is a negative example of perceptual meaning. Presented as a mass of sheer facts, students are unable to form patterns and establish meaningful relations among such stimuli, or to link them with their own past experiences. The result—a distorted concept of all aspects of history and geography and a distressing tendency to avoid these subjects later in life. Teachers must ensure that their courses are both logically and psychologically sound; administrators, that the curriculum is logically and psychologically sound. The range of experiences furnished students should provide them with percepts that are an asset to the construction of clear and concise concepts.

Students need help in achieving this objective. They are not always favorably disposed to certain subjects, nor is their background always sufficiently satisfactory to rely upon similarity or familiarity as a tool. Teachers must often link their materials to some interests extrinsic to both student and school. Only then can they guide the pupil to see relations and to acquire meaning. This in itself is no easy chore; it requires a thorough knowledge of individual pupils. But the effort is richly rewarded when pupils acquire awareness and begin to discern meaning in their classroom material.

The concept develops

Stimuli, then, produce sensations and perceptions, but the process is still incomplete. You can form mental representations of objects, things, people, and events even when they are not present. When a particular novel you are reading contains a description of a "pale blue sky laced with fleecy white clouds," abstraction occurs. You have a concept of what each term means. You need not find a dictionary and hunt for the meaning of *pale.* Nor must you hurry outside and examine a blue sky. The same is true for the remainder of the description.

If a pupil is sufficiently mature and has acquired the meaning of each of these terms, the verbal symbol alone will arouse the concept. Again note the economical way in which you adapt to the environment once concepts are developed. The sheer physical necessity of search is removed once you attain concepts. The development of most concepts requires considerable search, physical effort, and time. Concept attainment often demands years of hard work for richness of meaning to evolve.

For example, infants' first experiences with an orange are relatively meaningless. (See Figure 9.1.) They probably push it, watch it roll, and play with it. They cannot discriminate between the orange and a ball. Next, as children, they may begin to associate the orange with the kitchen, or with meals, or with food. They see other family members peel it, cut it, slice it, and eat it. Undoubtedly they are given pieces to eat. Now the association of this round, orange object with food is more firmly established. As they grow and as the process continues, they hear the word *orange* mentioned each time the identical object appears. While they are feeling it, pushing it, and eating it, they are also attaching a verbal symbol to the object.

The process continues. Some oranges are small, others are large; some are bright orange, some are rather pale; some are seedless,

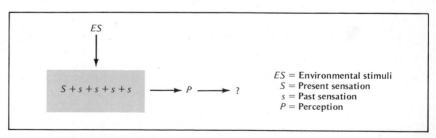

Figure 9.1 The Developing Concept

Figure 9.2 The Concept Is Formed

some are not; some are juicy, some are not. *But they gradually real-ize that they are all oranges.* The property common to all oranges is formed. Now when they hear or see the word *orange* the concept is not of an apple or banana but of this object they have learned to call orange. Figure 9.2 illustrates the complete process.

TEACHING CONCEPTS

Youngsters throughout their school career are literally surrounded by a world of words. As they develop meaning for these symbols and actually wield them in practical application, students can fully utilize their environment. Consequently, teachers should structure classroom experiences to provide as many rich and meaningful im-pressions as possible. The following principles should help.

1. *Remember that concepts are only as valuable as the meaning they convey.* Be careful that you do not accept the symbol alone as evi-dence that students have attained a concept. You should contin-ually probe to guarantee that meaning is associated with the sym-bol. For example, you probably can define *concept* but can you describe it, give examples, and explain the various types?

2. *Provide varied experiences for the learner.* Students should en-counter the concept under different conditions. Where possible they should see and feel and talk about it, contacting the object with as many senses as possible. Learners should occasionally en-counter examples of what a concept is not. That is, some negative examples are effective if mixed with many positive, clear instances.

3. *Utilize assorted methods of presenting the concept; different tech-niques of presentation are most efficient.* Teachers cannot be satisfied with one method, whether it is telling, discovery, or reading. A combination of methods is distinctly indicated.

4. *Encourage self-activity in the search for common elements.* This principle is almost a subdivision of item 3 above. Many methods are urged, but teachers should not rely exclusively upon a telling technique. All learning increases with a student's activity, which is also true for concept formation. Students should spend substantial time in searching for the necessary properties of the concept. The time spent should be proportionate to the other methods employed by the teacher for the acquisition of any concept. That is, a teacher must decide, at least initially, how much time should be given to search, and how much to telling. The concept's abstractness will unquestionably influence the teacher. For example, teaching a child the concept of *ball* entails considerable self-activity. Learning about deoxyribonucleic acid demands substantial teacher direction, especially in the initial phases of concept acquisition.

5. *Permit the learner to apply the concept.* Once students have partially attained the concept, they should begin to use it. They should read it and explain it; they should furnish it as a missing word; they should use it to solve problems. Above all, if they are to use it outside the classroom, teachers should supply experiences that are not routinely educational. Pupils must realize that they can use it at home, work, or play, which is exactly what is meant by concepts aiding in the economical adjustment to the environment.

Once concepts are acquired, they are vital components in our thinking, reasoning, and ability to perceive relationships. The quality of a child's concepts is the best measure of probable success in learning because meaning is basic to learning. Also, concepts determine what adults know, believe, and do. Concepts, then, are vital in all phases of life. They order the environment, add depth to perceptual relationships, clarify thinking, and, particularly, facilitate the entire learning process.

Discussion Questions

1. What did you learn from memorizing the word tests? Was there a steady increase in recall as meaning appeared, especially when you could discern an organized structure? Can you think of a similar example, using subject matter?

2. Gestalt experiments are a good illustration of our tendency to organize our environment. Provide examples showing how proximity, similarity, and closure can be used with subject matter.

3. Think of some instances that you can present to the class enabling them to form concepts. Begin with simple geometric figures from which it is fairly easy to isolate the defining characteristic(s). Now proceed to more abstract, verbal material, and keep teaching until the group has mastered the concept. What does this experience tell you about:

    a. Using concrete or abstract material?
    b. Using some proportion of both?
    c. Using positive or negative instances?
    d. Using some combination of both?
    e. Using teaching directed methods or encouraging
       discovery through self-activity?

4. From your participation in the last questions, can you describe *your* attempt to derive the concept? Does it agree with the process presented in this chapter? As a result, can you suggest additional techniques you would use in your teaching?

Students, schools, and problem-solving behavior

INTRODUCTION

How would you answer this question: *If a human being has an inoperable stomach tumor, how can the tumor be removed by rays that destroy organic tissue at sufficient intensity without destroying the healthy tissue surrounding it?* This problem by Karl Duncker has become a classic in the literature. Think about it briefly; when problem-solving behavior is analyzed, see how your answer matches several possible alternatives.

Problem-solving behavior should become a way of life for students. Unfortunately classroom conditions frequently prevent this technique from widespread usage. The number of students, nonteaching duties, or insufficient time restrict the preparation necessary for introducing problems. But once students form concepts, once they have mastered the facts, teachers should encourage their pupils to use them, both for true learning and for application later to daily living.

Learning as Problem Solving

Solving problems entails obtaining a goal that students desire, an obstacle, unsatisfactory responses, and finally, reorganized behavior. These words should sound familiar; they describe the characteristics of learning previously mentioned. All learning, then, is problem solving; there may be different forms—psychomotor, verbal, or affective—but these are differences in form; the core remains identical. So the more you know about problem-solving behavior, the more you discover about teaching and learning.

Solutions to problems are required whenever you cannot achieve a desired goal by customary responses. Now you commence a search: Exactly what is the problem? Are there any clues available that I could use? What information that I now possess can I employ here? What new information is needed? How can I relate it to my present knowledge so that the barrier to the goal is removed?

The initial phase of problem solving requires recognizing that a problem exists and probing for necessary data. Additional activity is needed. Can you apply present knowledge to this problem? Does it work? If not, why not? As you examine the process of problem solving, another question emerges: What produced a successful solution? This question has caused many investigators to view problem solving as an orderly sequence of steps; others see it as a kind of insight: suddenly, for no apparent reason, the solution appeared.

OBSTACLES TO SOLUTION

One fact is certain. When the stimulating situation is unusual, your response must be unusual. It is the novelty of response that causes difficulty. Human nature is such that it resists change; it tends to rely upon the familiar, and familiar responses often interfere with needed novel solutions.

Human behavior possesses a rigidity that defies change. You cannot find solutions, not because of any deficiency in motivation or intelligence, but because you customarily respond in definite ways. This phenomenon is called *set* and implies inflexible thinking; you cannot change either the direction or function of your thinking. That is, in a given problem, you continually see 4 as $2 + 2$ and never as 1   1   1   1, and seldom search for different alternatives. Unless you teach students to use problem-solving techniques, this rigidity can persist throughout a lifetime. Luchins's water jar problem is a good example (Table 9.1). Try it yourself.

Problem 1 illustrates the procedure: Fill the smaller jar three times from the larger. Now do the rest of the problems. You probably devised the formula $B - A - 2C$ to solve the problems. But examine Problems 7–11. Each of these requires only one simple arithmetic computation (Problem 7: $23 - 3 = 20$) but almost everyone continues to use the formula. You have developed a set. Have your students attempt them; it is a valuable experience.

TABLE 9.1
Luchins's Water Jar Problem

Problem	Given the Following Empty Jars as Measures			Obtain the Required Amount of Water
1.	29	3		20
2.	21	127	3	100
3.	14	163	25	99
4.	18	43	10	5
5.	9	42	6	21
6.	20	59	4	31
7.	23	49	3	20
8.	15	39	3	18
9.	28	76	3	25
10.	18	48	4	22
11.	14	36	8	6

Source: Adapted with permission of University of Oregon Books. Copyright 1959 by Abraham S. Luchins.

ANALYSIS OF PROBLEM-SOLVING BEHAVIOR

Admitting that the conditions of the problem may either facilitate or inhibit solution, investigators have formulated some interesting explanations of how problems are solved. While theorists may disagree about explanations, they agree that solving problems is the essence of learning. Students' lives outside of school are a series of problems; within school they should be preparing to adapt. This is the true meaning of transfer of learning.

Students must acquire the ability to manipulate their environment mentally. Again note the emphasis upon economy. Pupils should not respond immediately; rather they should test the situation mentally. People who engage in meaningful problem-solving behavior devise several possible responses. They then test them mentally. This process will unquestionably result in the elimination of several of the possible solutions. They will disregard some as manifestly impossible. Of those that survive this initial exclusion, one or two will appear more suitable than the remainder. They then actually test this most promising procedure. Figure 9.3 illustrates the manner in which the correct response is attained.

Students who mentally test responses are spared the frustration of many incorrect responses. They are not either right or wrong on one response because they do not wildly follow each and every possible clue. But this process of mentally testing solutions is difficult to teach to students. The next task is to evaluate some analyses of problem-solving behavior.

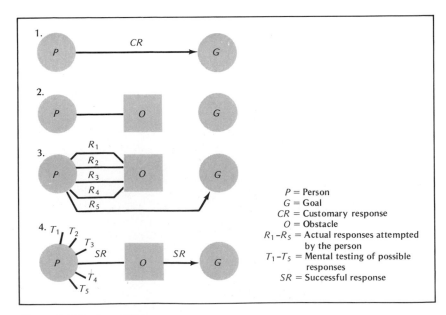

Figure 9.3 Testing of Responses

Dewey's descriptive theory

One of the most enduring explanations of problem-solving behavior is John Dewey's classic, *How We Think* (1933). Originally published in 1910, it has served as a model for scientific investigation and a logical method for studying thought. Dewey (1933, pg. 12) remarks that reflective thinking begins when there is doubt or perplexity that leads to a search for material that will resolve the doubt and dispose of the perplexity. The first phase is the prereflective, which establishes the nature of the problem to be solved. The last phase is postreflective, which results in a feeling of mastery and satisfaction.

Between these limits of reflection are states of thinking. These include (Dewey, 1933, pp. 106–108):

1. *Suggestions, in which the mind anticipates possible solutions.* This mental activity inhibits direct action and encourages thinking.
2. *Recognition of the nature of the problem.* Assess the conditions that caused the perplexity, and locate and define the problem.
3. *The use of hypotheses to initiate and guide the search for relevant material.* From the definition of the problem, possible solutions arise. As you relate these tentative solutions to the facts that you have gathered, you modify them until you derive a hypothesis.
4. *Mental testing of the hypothesis.* The mind elaborates upon the supposition or hypothesis, slowly refines it, and shapes it as a possible solution for this problem.
5. *Actual testing of the hypothesis.* Here you attempt to verify the solution by overt action.

Dewey (1933, pg. 115) emphasizes that these five phases of thought need not follow one another in a set order. The solution may come at any intermediate time, or the solution may not be final; it may lead to new suggestions. Some of the phases may be passed over quickly and the burden of solution may fall upon a single phase. Also, any one phase may be so complex that it includes subphases. But failure to solve a problem lies in some inadequacy in one or all of the five stages.

Although Dewey's theory is provocative and affords penetrating insights into the problem-solving process, it does not answer all questions about such behavior. First, one of the chief criticisms of this analysis is that it occurs after the person has solved a problem. It is easy to review some troublesome problem and, upon reflection, believe that it was solved in a clear and logical manner. Possibly—but the difficulty remains that it is an accomplished fact, which appears much more simple after than before the solution.

Second, the testimony of outstanding thinkers tends to refute this neatly organized process. Ghiselin (1955) relates several examples in which the solution "came in a flash"—an insight suddenly yielded the solution. After wrestling with the obstacle with little success an individual would leave it and begin to work on something else. Suddenly, and for no apparent reason, the solution appeared. It did not seem to follow the logical testing of tentative solutions. Possibly the individual, subconsciously, continued to ponder and evaluate the data, and Dewey is correct. Present knowledge, however, suggests mediating processes that are not as logically arranged as descriptive theories propose.

Guilford's problem-solving model

Guilford (1966) has constructed a model for problem solving that is based upon his concept of the structure of the intellect. Assuming that much can be learned about mental processes from the study of computers he offers the diagram reproduced in Figure 9.4.

Most behavior involves problem solving, and, with the knowledge accumulated since 1901, it now appears more complex than Dewey's steps. Guilford states that problem-solving behavior begins with input, either environmental or somatic. The input must pass through a filter, which determines if it will have any influence on behavior. The memory storage affects all steps, beginning with the filter. (Guilford uses filtering as a functional synonym for attention.) Evaluation occurs throughout the process as the individual constantly checks and corrects. Note that it is not the final step in problem solving.

Once the problem is structured (a cognitive operation that depends upon memory and evaluation), the search for answers starts. If there is a solution, behavior ceases at Exit III. Exit I represents avoidance of the problem; Exit II, leaving the problem for some reason. If the solution is inadequate the process begins again at the second cognition block. The input blocks depict the use of new information. This process or cycle may occur repeatedly as a person copes with the environment.

Concepts and problem solving

Klausmeier and his colleagues (1974) stress that problem solving depends on concept attainment. When an individual needs a response but lacks the necessary means, such as concepts or methods, a problem arises. These authors believe that problem solving is the most complex form of human intellectual activity since it enables children and adults both to adapt to the physical and social environment and to change it.

With maturity, students encounter increasingly abstract materials that force them to relate several concepts to form the principles that are necessary to solve complex problems. Klausmeier believes that the conceptual learning and development model suggests that pupils who have attained concepts at the classificatory and formal

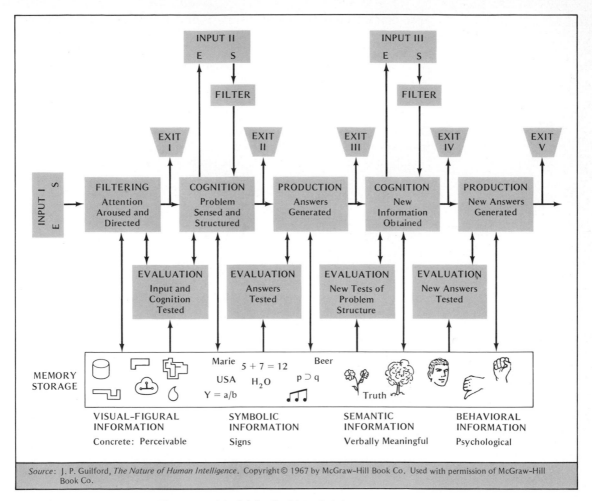

Figure 9.4 Model for Problem Solving

levels will have greater success solving complex problems. He also speculates that not only do concepts aid in solving problems but, by so using concepts, greater knowledge of the concept itself develops.

Klausmeier's CLD model is a good example of a growing experimental trend in studying problem-solving behavior. Investigators are more frequently using the classroom to analyze the cognitive processes involved in problem solving. As Wittrock and Lumsdaine note (1977) researchers are more willing to state and to test alternative models of the cognitive processes employed in school learning, especially those used in solving problems.

Problem-solving experiments

The Tumor Problem

Numerous studies provide penetrating insight into the problem-solving process. Some have become classics. Did you solve Duncker's problem? Some suggested that the rays should be sent through the esophagus; others that the intensity of the rays be weakened; finally, there emerged the suggestion to send scattered rays through a lens and concentrate them at the tumor's location. Duncker, studying the various answers, concluded that incorrect responses were not random trial-and-error replies, but a method of specifying the problem. As the subject more accurately comprehends the problem, solutions become more perceptive.

Another classic is the Bloom and Broder study (1950). Students were instructed to think aloud as they attempted to solve problems. Tape recordings were made of the efforts of six successful and six unsuccessful college students. They summarized their findings in four categories:

1. *Comprehension of the nature of the problem.* Successful problem solvers seized upon some clue and immediately began to construct a solution. Those who were unsuccessful missed clues and often misinterpreted the problem.
2. *Comprehension of the ideas contained in the problem.* A major difference between the two classes of students was in the ability to utilize knowledge already possessed to solve a problem. Frequently, the unsuccessful students possessed the necessary information but could not group the ideas contained in the problem.
3. *The style of problem-solving behavior.* Successful students were more active in their thinking aloud. They also simplified the problem whenever possible, and would analyze it into parts if they could not solve the whole problem. The unsuccessful students guessed at solutions and did not attempt analysis.
4. *Attitudes toward problem solving.* The successful students felt they could solve the problem, while the unsuccessful felt powerless when confronted by a problem. They were discouraged easily and were positive that thinking would be of little help.

Problem solving and teaching

Just at this time I left Caen, where I was then living, to go on a geologic excursion under the auspices of the school of mines. The change of travel made me forget my mathematical work. Having reached Coutances, we entered an omnibus to go some place or other. At the moment when I put my foot on the step the idea came to me, without anything in my former thoughts seeming to have paved the way for it, that the transformations I had used to define the Fuchsian functions were identical with those of non-Euclidean geometry. I did not verify the idea; I should not have had time, as upon taking my seat on the omnibus, I went on with a conversation already commenced, but I felt a perfect certainty. On my return to Caen, for conscience's sake, I verified the result at my leisure (Poincaré, in Ghiselin, 1955, pg. 37).

Did Poincaré solve his problem by reorganizing the field, as the Gestaltists claim? Or did he follow a logical sequence, as Dewey suggested? Did he feed input through a filter into a cognitive mechanism, as Guilford theorizes? Or did he continually propose mental solutions until the correct answer appeared, as Duncker believes? Whatever the correct explanation—and there is no one correct interpretation—pupils can improve their problem-solving methods. There are several procedures you can use to help them.

1. *Teach them to organize the problem.* What, precisely, does the problem require? What, precisely, am I asked to do? What, precisely, am I given? What, precisely, shall I do? Algebra is an excellent tool to illustrate the necessity of organizing the problem, especially when word problems are used. For example:

The perimeter of a rectangle is 25 feet greater than the sum of its length and width. If the length is 15 feet longer than the width, what are its dimensions?

a. What is required?	The rectangle's dimensions.
b. What am I asked to do?	Solve for length and width.
c. What am I given?	The perimeter and the length.
d. What shall I do?	Use the given data.

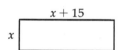

The perimeter $(P = x + (x + 15) + x + (x + 15))$ is 25 feet greater than the sum of l and w.

    e. Solve:

$$x \times (x + 15) + x + (x + 15) = x + (x + 15) + 25$$
$$4x + 30 = 2x + 15 + 25$$
$$4x + 30 = 2x + 40$$
$$2x = 10$$
$$x = 5$$

If you can teach your students to examine what the problem gives and then to organize the problem's elements, they will begin to proceed more logically than previously.

2. *Analyze the difficulties in individual students' problem-solving behavior.* These difficulties usually result from any or all of five causes:

a. *Intelligence.* Even if some pupils have relatively low ability, you can still improve their problem-solving technique, but keep the problem manageable for them; that is, the problem cannot be too abstract. For those of greater ability, problems should become progressively more abstract.

b. *Motivation.* Often pupils are so discouraged by previous attempts to solve problems that they either stop immediately or guess. No one has taken the time to help them. If you provide tangible help and manageable problems, they will show immediate improvement.

c. *Information.* Either the problem does not provide sufficient data, or pupils cannot relate information they possess to the problem. You must know your students so that you can satisfactorily match problem with pupil.

d. *Experience.* If students have had little instruction or practice in solving problems, they are usually bewildered. You must actively demonstrate techniques and then let them practice with simple problems.

e. *Set.* Teach students to look initially for several possible solutions and to test them mentally to determine which is most feasible. Emphasize that they should *not* necessarily use the first solution they devise. If the class is mature enough you could have them try both the nine-dot and the water jar problems.

3. *Correct students' difficulties.* If you return to Bloom and Broder's experimental work, you will find a guide for remedial work. Teach pupils to search diligently for clues that organize the problem and to use their existing knowledge, plus the problem's data, to solve it. By urging students to separate the problem into meaningful parts, you not only aid analysis by helping them to simplify it, but you also encourage a more positive attitude about their ability to solve problems.

4. *Teach—directly teach—problem-solving techniques. Do not assume that presenting a problem to students will automatically trigger some problem-solving mechanism.* Teach the ideas discussed here and stress the use of errors. Note—the *use* of errors. Recall Duncker's belief that each error represented a tentative solution. Students must learn to expect errors, but not to cease searching for a solution. Why was it an error? At what stage? Do I need more information? Can I use here what I learned elsewhere? These are the questions that can help pupils to use error intelligently.

5. *Give your students the opportunity to solve problems.* Success in life is determined by the ability to see, to analyze, and to solve problems. Admittedly it is a time-consuming process, and it would be much easier to tell students the answer. But that offers little support when they meet other, different obstacles. It is the *technique* that will transfer and assist your students in all situations.

Nowhere in your teaching can you better serve your students than by helping them to remove those "intellectual blocks that result in an inefficient choice of mental tactics or a shortage of intellectual ammunition" (Adams, 1974, pg. 63).

Encouraging creativity

I turned my chair to the fire and dozed. Again the atoms were gamboling before my eyes. This time the smaller groups kept modestly in the background. My mental eye, rendered more acute by repeated visions of this kind, could now distinguish larger structures, of manifold conformation; long rows, sometimes more closely fitted together; all twining and twisting in snakelike motion. But look! What was that? One of the snakes had seized hold of its own tail, and the form whirled mockingly before my eyes. As if by a flash of lightning, I awoke.

(Koestler, 1964)

Has anything similar ever happened to you? Have you ever done something totally novel, at least for you? Is some solution completely new to you—such as designing a unique study, fitting some extra part into a toaster or iron so that it works, or discovering a solution to a math problem that is *not* in the back of the book—were you creative? Or must some technique be new to society to be designated "creative"?

THE CREATIVE PROCESS

Creative thinking applies to a thought process that constructs original answers, solutions, or ideas. Usually creativity is associated with responses that are novel to society as well as to the individual. Problem solving entails the correct answer. For creativity there is no correct response; it is new, or original, and unique, which makes creativity so difficult to discover and encourage in a person. Society is chiefly concerned with the conforming, or correct response. Consequently, when an individual proposes anything radically new, the first inclination is to distrust and reject it. Accurate measures to discover the truly creative are one of the major needs in education today.

Creativity Described

Creativity has had a brief history in American education. In 1950 Guilford, in his presidential address to the American Psychological Association, noted this neglect by psychologists and urged more extensive research. A possible reason for neglect is the lack of agreement about definition or methodological approach. For example, Ghiselin (1955) states that creativity begins with a vague, confused excitement—almost a hunch. It never proceeds by purely conscious calculation; only outside consciousness can creativity

find the necessary freedom to encounter the unknown. Still, the goal of creativity is not mere novelty but use. Initially, practical application may be remote or unknown, but the inventor usually seeks some end that seems valuable.

Ghiselin believes that creativity is not completely spontaneous; there are important and conscious elements in the process. He notes that even the most original mind must have attained more then ordinary mastery of a subject. He states, "The artist must labor to the limit of human development and then take a step beyond." This mastery, this courage characterizes all creativity. Understanding, discipline, hard work, and patience are the marks of creativity.

How to Explain It

Studies of creativity focus upon either products, persons, or processes. Wallach notes (1970) that studies of products have examined mature adults, concentrating on occupation, salary, publication, listing in such sources as *Who's Who in America*, and inventions. Studies of both children and adults have chiefly scrutinized personality characteristics. For example, successful architects (a group thought to be highly creative) possess the skills of juggler, lawyer, business expert, artist, and engineer. Studies of processes have tried to identify specific and distinct psychological processes in the creative. These range from initial attempts to discover stages in the process to modern endeavors to separate creativity from intelligence. Some of these descriptive techniques follow.

STAGES IN CREATIVE THINKING

As with problem solving, there have been descriptive attempts to explain creativity. Wallas (1926) suggested four distinct stages:

1. *Preparation.* The problem is isolated and data gathered in this stage. Even when the needed idea suddenly appears, there has been substantial effort to identify the nature of the problem and the kind of basic material needed to solve the mystery.
2. *Incubation.* Once the initial, preparatory stage is complete, there seems to be a lull, or rest period. The necessary facts are gathered, and they are applied to the heart of the problem. If the problem is such that a creative response is needed, it undoubtedly will not appear immediately. A period of frustration, in which the thinker may turn to other tasks, attends each discovery. Somehow the mind continues its search; it seeks to uncover new relationships among familiar facts.
3. *Illumination.* Suddenly the idea, solution, or new relationship materializes. All the facts "fall into place." Is it insight? Is it the natural product of a logical succession of steps? Is it some cortical phenomenon? The truthful answer is that no one knows. For some reason, vital new methods, data, or relationships become clear to the thinker.
4. *Verification.* The idea is new and appealing. It has exciting possibilities. But does it work? Does it relate the parts into a meaningful whole? Here the idea must be tested against the cold reality of fact.

These stages are not the final answer to the quest for the explanation of the creative process. Stein and Heinze (1960) suggest that there may be additional or overlapping stages, and they argue convincingly that conscious effort alone is insufficient to produce creativity. But, as Wallach notes (1970), these techniques are so similar to problem-solving behavior that it becomes impossible to differentiate creativity from problem solving. Merely using the term "creative" avails us nothing.

THE CREATIVE INDIVIDUAL

Who are the creative people? Do they possess any special characteristics that aid in their identification? In an interesting essay, Taylor (1961) offers a tentative description of the creative individual. He first insists that *creative* is not identical with *gifted* because the latter is closely associated with intelligence test scores. Gifted is too restricted an interpretation of creative since intelligence test items tend to have a low correlation with the characteristics of the creative individual. As Taylor (1961, pp. 73–77) examines the creative person, he lists several categories of characteristics:

1. *Intellectual.*   Certain customary cognitive elements are essential for creative thinkers. These include memory and evaluation. Divergent elements, such as originality, flexibility, and sensitivity, are indispensable. Another outstanding intellectual characteristic of the creative thinker is the ability to sense problems, a realization that some ambiguity prevails.
2. *Motivational-interest.*   Creative people are curious; they like to manipulate ideas. They have a high achievement need that is linked with an intellectual persistence. They seek challenges, prefer the complex, and can tolerate uncertainty. An inevitable conclusion is that the creative have an intense commitment to their work.
3. *Personality.*   The creative person would tend to be independent, inclined to take risks, resourceful and adventurous, extroverted, and complex. Although listing specific characteristics is an unsatisfactory tactic, other authorities, in their generalizations, agree with Taylor. Rogers (1959) discerns three inner conditions of the creative: (1) an openness to experience that prohibits rigidity; (2) the ability to evaluate according to one's needs; and (3) the ability to experiment and to accept the unstable. Barron and Roe (1958) propose that the attributes of creativity are found in the interaction of the individual's intelligence, personality, motivation, and personal history.

Taylor (1961) concludes that the psychological processes involved when people use existing knowledge and systems differ from those used to produce new knowledge and systems.

Torrance (1970) discusses the use of tests and other behaviors to identify creative individuals. Creativity tests require individuals to supply multiple responses to a problem, for example, the different

Blocks to Creativity

James Adams discusses new ideas and asks his readers to try a game. Divide the class and have them be various animals as follows:

Last Names Begin With	They Are
A–E	Sheep
F–K	Pigs
L–R	Cows
S–Z	Turkeys

Now have each person take a partner and look him or her in the eye. The instructor will count to three and everyone is to make the sound of his or her animal as loudly as possible. Adams believes that everyone will experience one of the greatest blocks to creativity—that of feeling like an ass. Expressing a new idea and convincing others of its value produces exactly the same feeling. He believes that there are several other blocks.

1. *Fear of taking a risk.* You have constantly been rewarded for the right answer; suddenly to propose something new risks the disapproval, sarcasm, and ridicule of others. If you ever have a novel idea that seems risky, Adams suggests that you write a "catastrophe" report—what would happen if everything went wrong. Is it worth it or not?
2. *No appetite for chaos.* Insecurity often produces an inability to tolerate ambiguity. Some people must have everything, physical *and* mental, in a proper place; they cannot endure vague and ill-fitting ideas.
3. *Judging rather than generating ideas.* This is the safe way, but if you judge too early in the process, many fragile ideas that could possibly lead to other ideas are lost.
4. *Reality and fantasy.* Lack of imagination soon stifles creativity since the creative individual needs controlled access to it. The imagination cannot restrict itself to one sense, although people are primarily verbal, but must employ sight, taste, smell, and touch as well. What does blue smell like in this situation? How does it feel? *Creativity requires the manipulation and recombination of experience.*

---

uses of a wire coat hanger. Responses are scored for fluency, flexibility, and originality (Thorndike and Hagen, 1977). Children who achieve high scores on creativity tests produce more ideas that are original and give more explanations of unfamiliar toys than their less creative classmates. Torrance matched youngsters by intelligence, sex, race, and teachers and found that the most creative pupils were known for their "wild and fantastic" ideas, their original drawings. Their work also displayed a lack of rigidity and traces of humor.

Torrance urges parents not to depend solely on tests as indicators of creative potential. Children spontaneously exhibit creative activities that teachers can encourage. Classroom activities can also foster creativity. Torrance urges that pupils encounter incompleteness, which can be incorporated into pictures, stories, and written work. Another technique is to have pupils produce something—a drawing, a story, a biography—and then do something with it. For example, elementary school pupils could act out their stories, while secondary school pupils could write a play based on the biography.

The manner in which pupils react to these techniques reveals much about their creativity. Those who generate multiple responses, who are not limited by the dimensions of a problem, and who ask novel questions show signs of creativity. By the use of methods similar to those suggested by Torrance, teachers can help those who appear to lack this ability.

MacKinnon (1962) presents another fascinating account of the search for creativity. He states that there are three conditions to creativity: responses that are novel, responses that solve a problem, and fullest development of the creative response. Thus creativity is characterized by originality, adaptiveness, and realization.

MacKinnon's research involved 40 architects who were selected by experts because of their observed creativity. They were studied by problem-solving experiments, self-report techniques, affective inventories, and responses to stressful situations. He found that the highly creative have a good opinion of themselves, express self-criticism, and are inventive, independent, industrious, and enthusiastic. He also discovered a low positive correlation between intelligence and level of creativity, and a clear preference for the complex, for intuitive perception as opposed to sense perception, and for introversion as opposed to extroversion. The creative person is relatively uninterested in small details, and is more concerned with meanings and communications, exhibits cognitive flexibility, intellectual curiosity, and verbal skill.

FOSTERING CREATIVITY

The response to creative children in the classroom is the same as to creative adults in society: caution, suspicion, and a feeling that they are different. But these are the minds that society needs, and teachers can begin early to help youngsters think rationally, solve problems, and search for the novel. These guidelines may help.

1. *Be certain that the material you use to encourage creativity in the classroom matches the developmental level of the children.* If you recall Piaget's stages of cognitive development, you know that younger children cannot comprehend and use abstract subjects, so, at these early stages, while you can still encourage them to be innovative, you must use content suitable to their mental ability.

2. *Give children experience in deriving as many and different re-*

sponses to a problem as possible. Select a word, for example, *book,* and ask them to think of as many uses as possible for it. List them on the board and then ask the children for more uses. You are then fostering divergent thinking, and not just requiring one "correct answer." What can one do with a book? Obviously, read it. But one could also use it as a doorstop, a weight, or rule in an emergency.

For older students the technique is basically similar. If you teach secondary school pupils, ask them to imagine, to go beyond the data. For example, assume that the class is studying the opening of the American West. They could write essays that employ the basic facts but reach far beyond. A popular book takes the life of General Custer, presents the facts, and then asks the readers to assume that Custer, critically wounded, survived Big Horn and had to stand trial for his role in the massacre. *The Trial of George Armstrong Custer* is a lesson in creativity. Try something like it.

3. *Encourage your pupils to search for relationships.* Creativity tests often ask you to name one word that links three apparently unrelated items. *Stool, powder, ball:* Can you think of something that "fits" each of these? Stretch your imagination, refuse to be bound by purely logical definitions. Do you have it? Of course— *foot.* Devise other lists that require similar thinking, or check *Mednicks Remote Association Test* from which this example was taken.

4. *As Dacey (1976) notes, the most important aspect of creativity is the ability to tolerate ambuiguity.* Fear of failure, fear of the unknown—the drive toward closure mentioned earlier—makes people (especially children) almost desperately desire some answer, suitable or not. Directly teach pupils that it is better to pause, to muse, to think of alternatives, to search for "the better way."

5. *The techniques are clear and amusing, but always remind students that true creativity rests squarely upon knowledge of subject, hard work, and patience.*

6. *Try the* Journal of Creative Behavior *for more suggestions to foster creativity.* First published in 1967, it contained in that initial year several lists of suggestions for stimulating creativity.

Discussion Questions

1. Why is Duncker's tumor question a good example of problem solving? Give specific examples of good and bad techniques of solving the problem.

2. Is your thinking ever "rigid"? What does this mean? Were you trapped by the water jar problem? Give an example of a situation in which you displayed rigid thinking.

3. Try the Bloom and Broder technique with your classmates. Be sure your problem is clear yet manageable. Could you classify their an-

swers? Were they similar to the four categories suggested by the authors?

4. Algebraic word problems are an excellent source of problems. Find a basic algebra text that contains the answers and try to solve the problem by organizing the data that the problem gives. Remember—students face this same dilemma and any help you can provide will greatly benefit them. Can you add to the procedures that were mentioned in this chapter?

5. Are you creative? Why? How do you define creativity? Does your behavior "match" your definition? What do you use for criteria in judging creativity?

6. If your instructor permits, try Adams's suggestion about the animal noises. How did you feel? Did you ever try to convince others to accept something "different" that you devised? Were you afraid of their reaction?

Helping students retain their learning

Assuming that students are ready and motivated to learn, and that they learn, what else should concern us? Pupils should *remember* what they have learned. There is little value in leaving learning in the classroom. Students should use their knowledge in the constant and changing process of adapting to life, which is impossible unless they retain their learning. Consequently, retention is a topic that demands our interest, both to acquire as much data as possible and to suggest practical implications of this data.

How important is memory? The moment that the question is raised, memory's role in human behavior becomes striking. Without memory, you become a proverbial lost soul, wandering in a world that constantly poses new problems without offering any clues to their solution. As it is almost impossible to imagine such a situation, case studies, stories, films, and plays about amnesia assume an unreal dimension. Why are some things easy to remember, while others are difficult? Why do some memories vanish within a short period of time, while others persist for a remarkably lengthy period? The questions are thus posed: Is there a difference between short-term (*STM*) and long-term (*LTM*) memory? Where and how is the memory stored? What is eidetic memory (the ability to scrutinize a page of material for a moment and then reproduce it exactly)? Why is there a difference between rote memory and memory with understanding?

Adams (1974) suggests a simple exercise that entails memory and also provides a clue to how you may help students with their retention. Examine the following list and picture the entries, putting a *c* for clear, *v* for vague, or *n* for nothing after each depending on the image's clarity.

1. The face of a friend
2. Your kitchen
3. A jet passenger plane
4. A running cow
5. The earth from orbit
6. A rhododendron
7. Jimmy Carter

The clarity of your images depends upon how sharp your original perception was, your motivation on originally encountering the object, the visual character of the object (it was probably easy to recall Jimmy Carter because he has been in the news so much), and, finally, the image reproduction mechanism of your brain. Students, with your help, can improve retention by practicing, by attending more carefully to objects, and by linking the subject or problem to some organized structure that they already possess. Try to offer varied experiences that your students can later use as cues to aid their long-term memory.

SHORT-TERM VERSUS LONG-TERM MEMORY

Is there a difference between *STM* and *LTM* in method of storage and cause of loss? For example, you look up a strange number in the telephone directory; within minutes, the number can be lost. On the other hand, you may remember a poem, a story, a play, a face, a situation (room, hall) for years. Are there two distinct mechanisms for *STM* and *LTM* storage, or are they two sides of the same coin? Unless students make a conscious effort to learn incoming information, that is, to transfer it from *STM* to *LTM,* they forget it rapidly. Hilgard, Atkinson, and Atkinson (1975) view *STM* as a rapidly decaying system and *LTM* as permanent storage.

Stimuli enter *STM,* and if recalled and relearned to the point of overlearning, students will retain the information. This practice, called rehearsal, limits the information that *STM* can retain. After students feel secure about their knowledge, it may transfer to *LTM.* If decay occurs in *STM* before data are transferred to *LTM,* the data are lost—forgotten. But once transfer occurs, *it is permanent,* although memory may fail if the cues are not pertinent. The authors' interpretation of the *STM-LTM* process is seen in Figure 9.5.

Why some items are permanently stored and subject to recall is, presently, an unanswered question. Guilford (1967, pg. 302) speculates that for permanent storage to occur some perseverative activity, or automatic rehearsal, is necessary. A selective mechanism operates that determines which items are to be permanently stored and which are not. Most experiences need not be stored and a selective mechanism may also act to prevent overloading. What does this imply for intentional learning as opposed to incidental learning? Probably the distinction between intentional and incidental learning offers more promise than the distinction between storage and nonstorage.

FACTS ABOUT RETENTION

If youngsters rapidly learn a large amount of nonmeaningful material, they will forget it just as quickly. The rate of loss slows when most of the material is forgotten. But occasionally a surprising phenomenon seems to occur. After a rest period, there may be an actual gain in retention.

For example, after 30 minutes of studying 20 spelling words, pupils may be able to spell 15 of them correctly. Yet the next morning they may spell 17 correctly. This *reminiscence* is troublesome to ex-

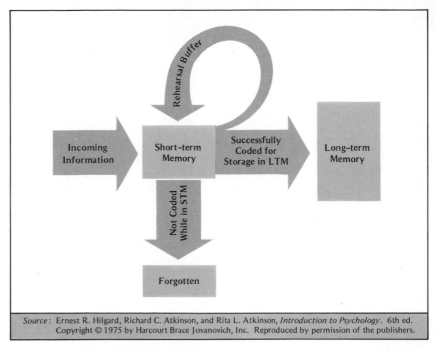

Source: Ernest R. Hilgard, Richard C. Atkinson, and Rita L. Atkinson, *Introduction to Psychology*. 6th ed.
Copyright © 1975 by Harcourt Brace Jovanovich, Inc. Reproduced by permission of the publishers.

Figure 9.5 A Two-Process Theory of Memory

plain. Is it true learning, or is it the product of faulty experimentation? There are two possible causes of reminiscence.

1. Fatigue developed during the original learning and affected retention, which then improved after rest.
2. The experiment was faulty because the initial test of retention was actually another learning experience that aided performance in the next test of retention.

Position of Material

Another important item for teachers to notice is the position of items to be memorized. The beginning and end of any memory task is learned much more easily than the middle elements. Undoubtedly this is a function of *interference*; isolated items are learned more readily and retained longer. What can you do to help students with that difficult middle section? One technique is to furnish some organization or structure to which they can relate it. For example, ask them to select two or three words in the section that have particular meaning for them and have them use these words as clues. Or have them imagine a picture related to the section, or use some words to form pictures.

This helps to reduce interference, which may produce the following phenomenon.

Tasks		Retention
A. Task 1		Test Task 1
B. Task 1 Task 2		Test Task 1
C. Task 1 Task 2		Test Task 2

Procedure A is the control; there is no interference. Procedure B is *retroactive inhibition;* that is, new material (Task 2) interferes with previously learned material (Task 1). Procedure C is *proactive inhibition;* that is, previously learned material interferes with the recall of new material.

Teachers should strive to eliminate inhibition by ensuring that the material to be learned is meaningful and organized. Learning meaningful material to mastery lessens students' susceptibility to interference. If students comprehend the meaning inherent in any material they learn it more rapidly and retain it longer. What is meant by meaning as an aid to memory is seen in two fundamental facts. The meaningfulness in material depends upon either some pattern that the learner recognizes (1, 7, 13, 19, 25, 31) or the familiarity of the material (previously learned details).

Memory as a Library   Broadbent (1966, pp. 281–295) suggests that human beings are systems that store information and that nervous systems encounter the same problems as a library. Like the library, they may store information in different places and organize it in a different manner. Since information is received through the senses, you may "tag" the information before you store it; information from the right ear is tagged accordingly and stored, as is information from the left ear, right eye, and the like. Selection operates during perception as well as recall, and thus provides two separate divisions from which you can retrieve. As information arrives in the nervous system, it is stored in an active manner that entails analysis and transformation (neural information may be stored in acoustic fashion). Storage may be under different headings; retrieval without the one correct label under which an item was stored is possible by use of different characteristics. Broadbent (1966, pp. 294–295) raises the interesting question, What is education? Certainly it is not storing information (how much algebra or history do you recall?); perhaps we are not "loading the shelves, but could we be writing the index?"

FORGETTING

Forgetting, unfortunately, is a normal process and here does not refer to an abnormal loss of memory occasioned by aging, shock, or brain injury. Under normal daily conditions, what causes students to forget previously acquired material? Theorists have proposed several explanations.

1. *Forgetting as disuse or fading.* Once an item is learned, unless it is used it is forgotten. Deterioration develops and learning slowly fades. This is probably the most popular belief, but today psychologists question it. For example, if subjects memorize a list of words to errorless recall, and then wait for various times before testing, the loss is similar to that illustrated in Figure 9.6. The exact details of the curve may vary depending upon the nature of the material, the degree of overlearning, and other material studied between the time of learning and the time of recall. But note two items with important implications for teaching: the rapid decline after initial learning and the stability of retained materials with increasing time.

Hilgard, Atkinson, and Atkinson (1975) note that there are other possible interpretations of the "forgetting" curve. Certain skills, such as riding a bicycle, swimming, or ice skating, show remarkable endurance. Even some verbal material is not quickly forgotten. You probably recall some lines from an elementary school play or show, while forgetting something you learned last semester that decay over time does not explain; other variables, such as motivation, also must influence retention. Still, time exacts its toll and you should consider this in your teaching by conducting periodic, *meaningful* reviews.

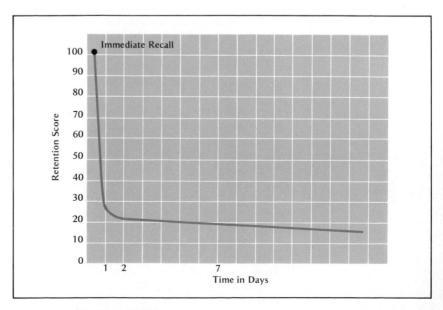

Figure 9.6 The Curve of Retention

2. *Motivated forgetting, or repressed forgetting.* Unquestionably there are experiences that you try to forget because of the unpleasantness, fear, or anxiety associated with them. If sufficiently severe, amnesia—either partial or total loss of memory—results. The extent of repression as a cause of normal forgetting remains unestablished because of the lack of experimental control that can be introduced.

3. *Forgetting because of interference.* Psychologists agree that most forgetting happens because new learning interferes with past learning. The proactive-retroactive process illustrates this theory. Perhaps Guilford (1967) best summarizes the problem when he notes that there is positive evidence for the effects of both decay and interference. You should consider both in your teaching.

4. *Forgetting because of extinction and reorganization.* Because of disuse and a lack of reinforcement, students forget a response. When forced to recall it, they apply newly acquired experiences and undoubtedly reshape the original response so that it may or may not suit the original stimulus. This explanation, essentially behavioristic, incorporates portions of the other theories.

IMPLICATIONS FOR EDUCATION

Given the present understanding of the forgetting and retention phenomenon, some prominent principles to remember would include:

1. *Constantly urge students to remember.* By that is not meant obvious exhortation by the teacher. It refers to student self-activity, whereby material acquires both meaning and personal significance; that is, it is organized and stored. For example, overlearning is significant for memory. Overlearning more sharply distinguishes the item to be stored and facilitates coding, which lowers the possibility of negative transfer, and increases the possibility of positive transfer. The chief danger for teachers to recall (!) with overlearning is the chance that the material may be too isolated and restricted to one function (Guilford, 1967, pg. 304).

2. *Comprehension, not mere mastery of facts, should be the aim of instruction.* This depends upon the kind of material and how it is presented. As words are remembered better than nonsense syllables, so solutions of problems are better remembered than isolated facts. Teachers should guide students to perceive and use relationships within the material and between the topic and the learner's background. Throughout this work on verbal learning, three essentials have been stressed: meaning, organization, and structure.

3. *Provide distributed rather than mass practice and insure that overlearning occurs.* It is much better to teach 10 foreign language

Current Memory Research

Estimates are that your *STM* can retain between five and ten pieces of information—but unless you constantly repeat that information you forget it in less than a minute. *LTM,* however, has enormous retentive power lasting, perhaps, throughout your lifetime. Discussing these and other phenomena, Ruth Winter (1977) reports on some of the world's most advanced work on memory currently underway at the Bell Research Laboratories in New Jersey.

Investigators now believe that *STM* is stored and retrieved in acoustical form through words that you repeat to yourself. Think of how you try to remember a telephone number: You constantly say the number over and over again, and if someone speaks to you during the process, you forget the number. But if you glance at something *written,* interference is less likely.

Testing *STM,* volunteers were asked to memorize a brief list of numbers (8, 2, 6, 5, 1). They were then required to decide quickly if some number—say 8—were in the list. Some subjects were at a loss how they knew; others said they silently repeated the list. Investigators discovered that none of the subjects used either technique. What they found was startling. Subjects can search 25–30 memorized digits per second. Try to count to 30; you will be unable to approximate that rate. Also when the subjects searched their lists, they did not stop as soon as they reached the required digit; they continued through the entire list. When the researchers demanded that they stop at a specific digit, the *search was slower.*

Testing *LTM,* they are attempting to discover how words are organized in memory and how they are retrieved. The findings suggest that words are arranged systematically, with words of similar meaning kept together. Subjects were asked if a row of letters, such as *teacher* or *pable,* were proper English words. Decisions were made in less than a second. Incredibly, words in *LTM* storage, stored close together in the brain, permit a more rapid search than those in *STM.* The search rate for *STM*—25–30 words per second—would be just too slow to search the thousands of words stored in *LTM.*

A husband and wife team at Ohio Wesleyan University, Harry and Phyllis Bahrick, devised an ingenious method for testing. They obtained high school yearbooks from more than 1000 persons associated with the university. The yearbooks ranged from a few months out of high school to the 1920s. The subjects in the experiment were from 17 to 70, and they were asked to identify pictures and names from their yearbooks. Recent graduates could identify nine out of ten of their classmates' pictures—but so could people who had graduated 30 years earlier. The same pattern held true for the ability to recognize names. Here is startling evidence for the capacity of *LTM* to store, almost permanently, pertinent facts and information.

Will you remember this for your next quiz?

words a day for five days than to force memorization of all 50 words in a single period. Periodic review of lecture notes is superior to cramming. Once recall is complete, practice should continue.

4. *Conduct periodic reveiw.* Teachers should review soon after learning and at short intervals, gradually widening the time between reviews. Review need not be dogmatic, formal sessions. Quizzes, assignments, and use of material are effective review techniques. Periodic reviews are especially significant when you recall the retention curve, which dramatically illustrated the initial loss of learning. Meaningful reviews are an excellent tool to overcome this loss.

5. *Reduce interference.* Recalling the proactive-retroactive inhibition paradigm, teachers, and especially administrators, should try to schedule subjects that reinforce and do not interfere with each other.

For teachers, the customary method of recall is to ask students to retrieve information in its original form. If you present cues (questions) different from the form in which the information was originally stored, students experience much greater difficulty. Consequently, teachers should use questions carefully, so that they may aid a pupil to acquire a method of problem solving or to think creatively. To demand recall in the original form is to promote convergent thinking (certainly but not always a needed and desired technique) at the expense of divergent thinking. Here is a great unstudied problem that demands much more attention and research.

Helping students transfer their learning

INTRODUCTION

Once learning and retention have occurred, the obvious question becomes: What do students do with this material? The goals of education demand more than classroom mastery of topics. If students can learn and retain that learning (which they can), then they must take their new knowledge with them when they leave school (which they do). Implicit in all educational objectives is the use of learning. Whether for personal accomplishment, professional skill, or social adjustment, students should use what they have learned, which introduces the transfer of learning; that is, learning one topic influences later learning. Transfer may be either positive (when learning one topic helps the learning of another) or negative (when learning one topic hinders the learning of another).

THEORIES OF TRANSFER

Two questions concerning transfer arise: How does it function? How can teachers facilitate the process? To answer the first ques-

"The Saber-Tooth Curriculum"

School curricula have always caused controversy. One of the chief causes has been transfer; that is, should subjects remain in the curriculum because of their intrinsic and lasting value to us as human beings, or should subjects be selected on a more transitory basis—what is practical for the here and now. Simply put, should students study Latin because of its inherent value or automotive mechanics because there is a temporary shortage of skilled mechanics?

In an amusing essay, *The Saber-Tooth Curriculum,"* Harold Benjamin deftly presents the problem. A member of an ancient tribe decided to prepare children better for adulthood. What needed to be done? One of the major survival activities was catching fish with bare hands, so why not teach them fish grabbing at an early age so they could become skilled adults. After this instruction, these children had a decided advantage as adults over those who had not received instruction. Gradually everyone in the community received this teaching.

But conditions changed and the waters grew so muddy that it was almost impossible to catch fish with bare hands. After generations of dodging fish grabbers, the fish grew more intelligent, and the fisher could not see them. The community found itself in a difficult situation, and the thinker who had originally devised fish-grabbing techniques had died.

But one of the younger men, in desperation, tied a few branches together and formed a net. Soon he was catching as much fish as the entire rest of the tribe. Others asked if these new techniques could be taught to children. But the wise old man of the tribe said no, it would not be true education; it would only be training. Besides, there was no room in the curriculum for such frivolous subjects; they must maintain standards which would be lowered if fish grabbing with bare hands was dropped.

Amusing? Yes. Pertinent? Yes. Apply these ideas to your curriculum, and decide which you would accept. Should subjects be more relevant? Or does relevance imply impermanence, which destroys any society? It is not an easy question to answer. Think about it.

tion, many theories attempt to explain transfer. One of the oldest is the formal discipline theory that assumes that the mind has distinct faculties, such as memory, reason, and judgment. As muscles are strengthened by exercise, so these faculties are strengthened by encountering difficult subjects. Studying Latin, Greek, and mathematics should improve all of the mind's faculties.

Identical Elements

First challenged by William James at the end of the nineteenth century, formal discipline was thoroughly refuted by Thorndike in the first part of the twentieth. Criticism showed that practicing memorization did not improve its rate or quality, nor did difficult subjects of themselves improve reasoning or judgment. Good students selected difficult objects, so the formal discipline theory was immediately biased. Thorndike claimed that transfer appears only when the learner sees the identical elements in both situations.

Thus Thorndike's theory of identical elements was born (1906, 1911, 1913).

The theory of identical elements is not limited to the transfer of facts. Skills, methods, and even attitudes transfer. Criticism of Thorndike's work was directed at its rigid and inflexible nature. The curriculum soon was aimed at the mastery of specifics, and little thought was given to principles, relationships, and generalizations. Methods degenerated into mere drill. In fairness to Thorndike, these deviations were due mainly to the excessive and misguided zeal of his disciples. Thorndike himself, through his lengthy career, displayed a consistent ability to see the good in new evidence and to adapt his own work accordingly.

Generalization Theory

As a reaction to the specificity of identical elements, Charles Judd (1908) proposed a theory of transfer based upon generalizations. Testing two groups of boys on their ability to hit a target under water, Judd discovered that the boys who were taught the principles of light refraction had greater success when the depth of the target was changed. When individuals understand the principles of the problem, they transfer this knowledge more effectively. The theory of generalization is really a continuation of Thorndike's work, without its limitations. There must be something identical in both situations, and there must be some similarity between situations, but it need not be confined to specific elements.

Transposition Theory

A further refinement of the generalization theory is that of transposition. As an outgrowth of Gestalt theory, transfer is accounted for by the student's understanding of the structure or pattern of the problem. When the individual perceives, not only the facts and principles in any problem, but also the relationship of facts to principles and principles to goals, then transfer occurs.

Here is an amusing but effective method of testing your pupils' ability to transfer language. You can use this technique with a variety of subjects: history, geography, even arithmetic.

Can you change the incorrect letter in each of these four words so that each reads correctly: QUIST, PUAH, EFIT, EET PLINT? (Answers appear below.)

WHAT INFLUENCES TRANSFER?

Task Similarity

There are certain conditions that exercise a decided impact upon what and how much will be transferred. Ellis (1965) provides an excellent example of a major influence on transfer: task similarity. Imagine a change in the rules governing traffic flow; instead of stopping at a red light, drivers now must stop at the orange.

Answers: QUIET, EXIT, PUSH, WET PAINT.

Positive Transfer

Would this bother them? Probably not too much, because orange is similar to red and it would be easy to transfer the stopping habit. As Ellis states, learning to make the same response to new but similar stimuli results in positive transfer. That is, we can do it fairly easily.

Negative Transfer

Let us change the conditions more radically. Now, instead of stopping at red, drivers must stop at green, and go on red. The pattern is completely reversed. What will happen? Undoubtedly there will be a sharp increase in the number of accidents. Drivers are now making new, and opposite, responses to the same stimuli, which leads to interference or *negative transfer*. Understanding the similarity among tasks to predict the possibility of transfer is an important task for teachers.

An experiment by Ellis offers a striking illustration of similarity's effect on transfer. Subjects were presented with pairs of words; the first of the pair was the stimulus, the second was the response. They had to associate them so that on seeing the stimulus word they could provide the correct response. There was no logical connection between the stimulus and response words. The subjects first learned the associations. Two days later they learned a second list of stimulus-response words where the stimulus words were similar but not identical to the original words. There were several degrees of similarity in the stimulus words in the second list. For example: *agile-nimble-lively*. *Agile* and *nimble* are highly similar; *lively* is less so. Subjects learned the original list and *either* a list of high or moderate similarity. The word combinations appear in Table 9.2.

The results showed that Group I far surpassed Group II on a

TABLE 9.2
Similarity and Transfer

GROUP	ORIGINAL LIST		TRANSFER LIST	
I	*Stimuli*	*Responses*	*Stimuli*	*Responses*
(High stimulus similarity)	Agile Empty Liquid	Modest Unclear Weary	Nimble Vacant Fluid	Modest Unclear Weary
II	*Stimuli*	*Responses*	*Stimuli*	*Responses*
(Moderate stimulus similarity)	Agile Empty Liquid	Modest Unclear Weary	Lively Hollow Flowing	Modest Unclear Weary

Source: Henry C. Ellis. *The Transfer of Learning.* New York: Macmillan, 1965.

later test; Ellis concluded that the greater the degree of stimulus similarity, the greater the amount of positive transfer.

Ellis mentions several other influences on transfer.

1. *Learning to learn is seen when students become progressively better at tasks the more that they do them.* This is an example of task similarity involving not similarity of specific stimuli but a similarity of learning techniques, that is, a general method of attack.
2. *The degree of original learning is an important element in transfer.* More practice on the original material results in greater positive transfer.
3. *Personal variables, such as intelligence, motivation, and past experience, are important, but extremely difficult to control, influences on transfer.* Your personal knowledge of your students is probably your best weapon to ensure transfer since you know something about the structure and organization of this past learning. Consequently, you can usually relate some aspect of their experience to new material to facilitate transfer.

IMPLICATIONS FOR EDUCATION

Today psychologists recognize the strengths and weaknesses of these theories and believe that transfer occurs because of a combination of events. For example, all of the theories agree that transfer is a fact, that learners must perceive something similar in both situations, and that, the more efficient the original learning, the more substantial will be the transfer. If courses in driver education are offered, the students should obtain licenses and have good safety records. If algebra is taught to help in physics and chemistry, then students should manifest this ability in science classes. From the discussion of theories, experiments, and practice, it is possible to suggest certain guidelines that would increase your students' positive transfer.

1. *Teach to overlearning.* Repeated studies clearly indicate that the more experience students have with the task to be transferred, the more successfully they transfer it. Since most academic material is verbal, you should probably give verbal examples of transfer and then provide a variety of circumstances that actually encourage your students to use the material. Actively foster transfer in class discussion, assignments, and quizzes.

2. *Be certain that the material you teach is well organized.* More meaningful material is more easily transferred. Meaning, organization, and structure have been stressed throughout this chapter. It is deceptively easy to teach mechanically, to accept rote answers, and to test automatically when working with verbal content. If you can urge students to transfer principles and generalizations, they will transfer not only specific content but study methods as well.

3. *Use advance organizers if possible.* When you are about to teach abstract material it may be useful to furnish your students with what David Ausubel calls "advance organizers." These are some general principles that you furnish your students so that the abstract material they are encountering will possess more structure than if they had met it unprepared. You must know both your students and subject to formulate effective advance organizers because your introductory work reflects what you think is important and it must match your students' ability level.

4. *Emphasize the similarity between classroom work and the transfer situation.* If you are concerned with transfer, you must attempt to make the classroom condition similar to the transfer situation. For example, most algebra tests involve word problems, so as soon as possible have your students work with word problems, perhaps incorporating terms from chemistry and physics. If you teach reading, be sure that the letters and words you teach have the same form that the youngsters will see in their readers. As Ellis stresses, sometime during your teaching, students should receive practice under conditions similar to the working or transfer environment.

5. *Specify what is important in the task.* Identifying the important features of a task helps youngsters to transfer these elements or to guard against potential difficulties. For example, children frequently confuse b with d, so teachers should stress the distinction and give them considerable experience with words containing these letters. Again in algebra, students consistently forget to change signs $(+ -)$ when moving terms from one side of the equation to the other. Constantly calling students' attention to the re-

"The War of the Ghosts"

The moment of truth has now arrived. Write the story of "The War of the Ghosts" as you remember it. Now compare it to the original. What did you omit? What did you change? How does your story compare to these samples?

After an interval of 20 hours one subject produced the following first reproduction:

"The War of the Ghosts"

Two men from Edulac went fishing. While thus occupied by the river they heard a noise in the distance.

"It sounds like a cry," said one, and presently there appeared some men in canoes who invited them to join the party on their adventure. One of the young men refused to go, on the ground of family ties, but the other offered to go.

"But there are no arrows," he said.

"The arrows are in the boat," was the reply.

He thereupon took his place, while his friend returned home. The party paddled up the river to Kaloma, and began to land on the banks of the river. The enemy came rushing upon them, and some sharp fighting ensued. Presently, someone was injured, and the cry was raised that the enemy were ghosts.

The party returned down the stream, and the young man arrived home feeling none the worse for his experience. The next morning at dawn he endeavored to recount his adventures. While he was talking something black issued from his mouth. Suddenly he uttered a cry and fell down. His friends gathered around him.

But he was dead.

Eight days later this subject remembered the story as follows:

"The War of the Ghosts"

Two young men from Edulac went fishing. While thus engaged they heard a noise in the distance. "That sounds like a war cry," said one, "there is going to be some fighting." Presently, there appeared some warriors who invited them to join an expedition up the river.

One of the young men excused himself on the ground of family ties. "I cannot come," he said, "as I might get killed." So he returned home. The other man, however, joined the party, and they proceeded on canoes up the river. While landing on the banks, the enemy appeared and were running down to meet them. Soon someone was wounded, and the party discovered that they were fighting against ghosts. The young man and his companion returned to the boats, and went back to their homes.

The next morning at dawn he was describing his adventures to his friends, who had gathered round him. Suddenly, something black issued from his mouth, and he fell down uttering a cry. His friends closed around him, but found that he was dead. (From F. C. Bartlett, *Remembering: A Study in Experimental and Social Psychology.* London: Cambridge University Press, 1932.)

Is yours similar? Since these ideas in the story are unrelated to your experiences, you tend to omit considerable detail and, simultaneously, to make the ideas more logical and the story more concise. *You have altered it to fit your mental organization; you have imposed structure upon it.* The process is similar to Piaget's assimilation-accommodation model. Students do exactly the same: They either shut out unrelated, meaningless material, or they change it radically. This example should reinforce what has been discussed in this chapter: the importance of meaning and structure, and of those variables that affect memory, forgetting, and transfer.

quired change of sign, instructors should provide numerous instances that require transposition.

6. *Try to understand how the learner perceives the possibility of transfer.* Instructors teach what they know and have organized. How do students view the process? Is it meaningful to them? Do they see how they can use the material in different circumstances? If you attempt to see your teaching and the subject from your pupils' viewpoint, you may present it quite differently, capitalize more on their background, and offer more practical possibilities of transfer. This is more easily said than done, but once you try it you will be more conscious of the need for meaning, organization, and structure.

Discussion Questions

1. What did you learn from Adams's image formation exercise? What image did you form clearly? Why? Does this suggest certain techniques for helping students form clear images of what you are teaching?

2. There are little hard data about the memory process. From the description, which elements do you think are decisive? What can you do to incorporate these elements into your teaching? Be specific.

3. Try memorizing a list of nonsense syllables. Memorize until you are able to make two errorless repetitions. Test yourself 24 hours later. How much did you recall? The usual loss is about 20 percent. What does this tell you about your students' retention? Having done this, what can you suggest that would improve retention?

4. What was your reaction to "The Saber-Tooth Curriculum"? Some abstract topics improve methods of study and transfer, but it is also easy to argue for the popular, or practical subject. Where do you stand? Be objective and be ready to defend your answer.

Some Concluding Thoughts

Verbal learning, that critical yet frustrating aspect of learning, is one of the most important tasks that teachers face. From the basic concepts of elementary school arithmetic, geography, or science to the highly abstract concepts of university chemistry or psychology, verbal learning permeates students' lives. Youngsters who miss basic concepts in the lower grades and never acquire appropriate learning styles will encounter considerable difficulty in school and, perhaps, never realize their full potential.

What is especially critical about verbal learning is its effect both in and out of school. It is not learning that is confined to one situation; it affects behavior at school, home, work, and play. Pupils with a rich conceptual background, skillful problem-solving techniques, and the courage to tolerate ambiguity and face failure in searching for different and more beneficial solutions have an enormous advantage over others who lack these skills. They respond more effectively in all situations because they have learned and have retained and transferred that learning to every circumstance they meet. Teachers can play a substantial role in helping students obtain these goals.

Summary

- Meaning, structure, and organization form the basis of verbal learning since, without them, learning becomes rote and mechanical.

- There are basic psychological processes, such as the tendency toward closure, that teachers can use to help students bring meaning and structure to their work.

- Helping students to categorize enables them to cope more effectively with their environment and improves learning by organizing and bringing structure to otherwise unrelated material.

- One of the most persistent obstacles to solving problems is rigidity of behavior; that is, a mental set interferes with the consideration, or even search, for other possible solutions.

- While there is no clear explanation of problem solving, you can help students improve their technique by insisting that they organize the problem and use all available data.

- Some students may be more creative than others, but certain methods, such as requiring many different responses, help foster creativity and structure the classroom environment so that students gradually acquire the ability to tolerate ambiguity.

- Since all evidence suggests that interference is the greatest threat to memory, you should be cautious about both subject method and the sequence of presentation, and recall the facts about proactive and retroactive inhibition.

- If transfer is the ultimate goal of education, your teaching should be well organized, with the pertinent material labeled and taught to overlearning and with adequate opportunity to use it in a variety of situations.

Suggested Readings

Bruner, Jerome, Florence Goodnow, and George Austin. *A Study of Thinking*. New York: Wiley, 1956. One of the best analyses of concept formation that is available.

Dewey, John. *How We Think*. Boston: Heath, 1933. If at all possible, read this classic and learn how little we have progressed beyond Dewey.

Ellis, Henry. *The Transfer of Learning.* New York: Macmillan, 1965. Probably still the best single source of our knowledge of transfer.

Ghiselin, Brewster, ed. *The Creative Process.* New York: New American Library, 1955. Fascinating personal accounts of how famous individuals produced unique discoveries.

Wallach, Michael. "Creativity." In *Carmichael's Manual of Child Psychology,* edited by Paul Mussen. New York: Wiley, 1970. Excellent presentation of background, theories, research, and problems relating to creativity.

10

Types of Learning II: Psychomotor and Affective

Introduction

While learning characteristics may remain identical and motivation may be an ideal, learning may take many forms, depending upon the content. For example, a highly complex psychomotor skill is involved in the seemingly simple act of kicking a football. Look closely at the illustrated sequence and attempt to describe the boy's activities.

You undoubtedly noticed him dropping the ball, striding, and kicking. Simple? Hardly. First, the boy had to position himself correctly; that is, he stood a certain distance from the ball, held his hands in a comfortable position to receive the ball, and assumed a balanced stance. Each of these acts not only involved the body, but also required a decision—cognitive activity was necessary. Once the ball was in his hands, he had to hold it properly at a certain height from the ground. Next, he had to stride correctly, both to obtain maximum power and maintain balance. Finally, he had to snap his foot into the ball at precisely the right angle. These are some of the components of kicking a football: physical, cognitive, and emotional. Imagine the tension that the boy feels, especially under game conditions with hundreds, perhaps thousands, of spectators.

The other forms of learning discussed in this chapter—attitudinal, moral, value, and interpersonal skills—exhibit identical learning characteristics, but differ radically in their appearance. Teachers often ignore these topics, usually because they are treated briefly, if at all, in both texts and courses. One of the purposes of this chapter is to emphasize their importance and to suggest methods and materials that will enrich all learning. But to utilize these various forms of learning throughout the curriculum requires precision.

Educators generalize easily: Teaching machines are superb; audiovisual accessories are essential; teachers should follow the principles of learning; conditioning is vital to the learning process. What precisely is meant by these statements? What kind of machines? What kind of learning? What type of conditioning? What does "affective" mean? It is only by analyzing and discriminating that these sweeping statements become practically useful.

Generalizations about the learning process can cause trouble if they are too broad or inapplicable to specific learning situations. If, however, exact meanings are clearly comprehended, they may furnish useful insights. For example, consider the statement, "conditioning is vital to the learning process." If you realize that conditioning includes both classical and instrumental conditioning and that certain material is better learned by these techniques than others, the statement has a practical purpose.

For example, students like or dislike certain subjects, and their feelings are subtly influenced by conditioning. Now you can better understand the problem: how to have students achieve successfully and also develop pleasant feelings about the subject. Precise knowledge of terms has produced a more desirable objective and a more unified method of achieving that objective.

Students must master many types of learning and utilize different learning styles. Human variability precludes acceptance of any one learning theory or theory of behavior that is applicable to all learning. Consequently, there is no one teaching method, or teaching aid, that is equally appropriate to all types of learning. Robert Gagné's work provides a useful format for classifying the various types of learning.

Gagné and the outcomes of learning

There are inherent dangers in any attempt to categorize learning. Gagné notes that while students may learn history, algebra, biology, or football, such categories fail to encompass learning that is not confined to school subjects. Furthermore, the same form of learning occurs in different subjects, and different forms of learning occur within the same subject. For example, learning to short-circuit an ignition to steal a car is not encouraged in school; nevertheless, it meets all the criteria of learning. Students constantly master verbal information in all subjects, but may acquire a motor skill, verbal information, and attitudes in one subject. Gagné insists that various types of learning require different kinds of instruction.

THE OUTCOMES OF LEARNING

Gagné (1974) believes that there are five major categories of learning outcomes: verbal information, intellectual skills, cognitive strategies, attitudes, and motor skills. Each category possesses sufficient identity to justify its existence as an independent class distinguished from other kinds of learning.

1. *Verbal information.* Students learn a tremendous amount of verbal information in school—names, facts, generalizations. Verbal information is a primary means for transmitting knowledge from generation to generation. Gagné believes that information is verbal when students can state it, but they need not store it that way. Recall the discussion concerning learning styles—many pupils will prefer to store knowledge as visual images. The most critical aspect of acquiring verbal information is its inclusion within a larger meaningful unit. Once organized, verbal information facilitates further learning. For example, before a student can teach according to Piagetian principles, he or she must know assimilation, accommodation, structure, schema, and the characteristics of the cognitive stages. The teaching strategy for verbal information is clear: The instructor must provide a meaningful context when presenting new material.

2. *Intellectual skills.* Gagné states that intellectual skills comprise "knowing how" rather than the "knowing what" of verbal information. Since students—and all humans—cannot assimilate and integrate limitless items of information, they learn how to connect isolated symbols into words and sentences, or how to add, subtract, multiply, or divide mathematical symbols and derive meaningful totals. Gagné believes that intellectual skills proceed from the simple to the complex and are interrelated because complex skills depend upon simple skills. The sequence is from discriminations to concepts to rules to higher-order rules.

Discriminations refer to the student's ability to distinguish among environmental stimuli, for example, cars from trucks, Pontiacs from Chevrolets, hardtops from sedans, convertibles from hardtops. Finer discriminations are learned in school, *b* from *d*, *a* from *o*, *m* from *n*, red from orange, 6 from 9. Without these it is impossible to form concepts, which are classes of similar discriminations: a car has wheels, a chair has legs. Once concepts are acquired and relations established among them, it is possible to formulate rules, which include both the ability to verbalize them and illustrate them in action. Frequently, simple rules are combined into complex combinations and these higher-order rules enable students to solve problems.

Teaching intellectual skills demands several steps (Gagné, 1976, pg. 33):

a. Prerequisite skills are needed as a basis for abstract learning.
b. Pertinent cues are needed to help students retrieve previously learned material.
c. Additional, more subtle, cues are needed to encourage students to combine the simpler skills in their problem-solving activities.

3. *Cognitive strategies.* Gagné defines cognitive strategies as internally organized skills that govern the individual's attention, learning, remembering, and thinking (Gagné, 1976, pg. 34). Students use cognitive strategies in thinking about what they learn and in solving problems. Teachers can help students develop their cognitive strategies by providing instances for their practice. For example, there should be classroom opportunity to recall and transfer material: questions in an English class that would require retention and transfer of Civil War battles, generals, and politics from history classes. They should encounter *novel* problems that force them to think about what they have learned and to use it in a different way. The classic nine-dot problem is a good example. Try it yourself. Connect these nine dots with four straight lines without taking your pencil from the paper.

·   ·   ·

·   ·   ·

·   ·   ·

You are forced to think differently about number and lines and to break from the conventional to solve the problem. (The answer appears at the bottom of the next page.) Although this is simple, students usually see the purpose: to think differently about things. Try it with your class and then begin to substitute subject matter for the dots and force them to use facts in new and challenging ways.

4. *Attitudes.* Gagné defines attitudes as learned dispositions that influence the choice of personal action toward classes of things, persons, or events (1976, pg. 35). Schools want pupils to acquire favorable attitudes toward country, school, subjects, and people of different religion or race. Attitudes are further analyzed in this chapter, but Gagné's comments about instruction are interesting. Verbal instruction is ineffective in establishing or changing attitudes. It is far more effective to use models to demonstrate the desired attitude, to have students engage in activities that change their attitude, and ensure that these responses are reinforced. For example, if a teenager dislikes others because of race or religion, have him or her work with younger children of that race or religion (tutoring, coaching) and encourage communication efforts.

5. *Motor skills.* Motor skills cross curricular lines. Reading, writing, physical education, and vocational education are good examples. Motor skills are this chapter's first major topic, so Gagné's thoughts concerning instruction are pertinent. Reinforced practice is vital to acquiring these skills. Students also need to understand the sequence of movements. Motor skills offer an excellent example of the integrated nature of learning: physical, cognitive, emotional.

Psychomotor learning

INTRODUCTION

Psychomotor learning (motor learning, motor skills, skill performance are synonymous) is a neglected type of learning; this could cause unnecessary hardship for students. Psychomotor learning underlies every aspect of pupils' and adults' lives and is not confined to sports, as important as they are to boys and girls. Youngsters talk, walk, run, play children's games, write, read, ride bicycles, throw, kick, type, use machines, drive cars—the list is endless.

Some of these activities have more educational significance than others; some appear to have little psychomotor involvement, such as reading. But closer examination of reading reveals greater psychomotor activity than suspected. Holding a book requires eye-hand coordination to keep it at a suitable angle, level, and distance for reading. Unless the eye muscles are sufficiently developed the eye will not move smoothly across the page and return to the beginning of the next line.

**Reading: A
Psychomotor Skill**

Try this experiment. Ask one of your classmates to stand in front of the class and read a paragraph. Those in the first rows should see rather startling eye movements, similar to those outlined in Figure 10.1.

If you actually watched your classmate read you probably were startled by the eyes' movements. They did not flow smoothly across the page as you might have suspected; they moved in a series of jerks, which are the fixation pauses during which words are read. Youngsters whose eye muscles cannot control eye movements do not return accurately to the next line; their eyes skip lines and may even wander down the page. Subtle psychomotor activity thus appears in a highly verbal situation.

Education, play, work, and sports all encompass psychomotor activities; thus, they are basic to everything that people do. But psychomotor skills are more than the compilation of separate, simple parts. Skills imply proficient performance, and the individual who masters the varied movements becomes the successful performer—on the job, in school, on the fields, in the bowling alleys. But successful performance occurs only when the learner discriminates the separate movements, masters them, and then integrates them into a smooth, polished skill. Mastery occurs only when there is comprehension of individual parts and their relationship to the whole (cognitive activity), and commitment plus moderate intensity (emotional activity).

Before analyzing these skills more carefully, one intriguing phenomenon demands discussion. In examining motivation (see Chapter 8) Ryder et al. (1976) were quoted as saying that what is needed is not better runners but bigger challenges. Their study of footracing reveals some amazing data. If you are unfamiliar with track records, you still probably know that the four-minute mile was considered a miracle in 1954. Consider today's record: 3:49.4. Ten seconds for 100 yards has always been the mark of the great sprinter. Today's record: nine seconds, a 10 percent reduction. Why? Diet, training methods, and scientific analysis have all contributed to record-shattering performances. The authors believe that there must be a physiological limit to human running speed, but it has not yet been identified. They conclude that the barriers to outstanding performance are psychological. Hence their belief that the world does not need better runners but bigger challenges.

Answer:

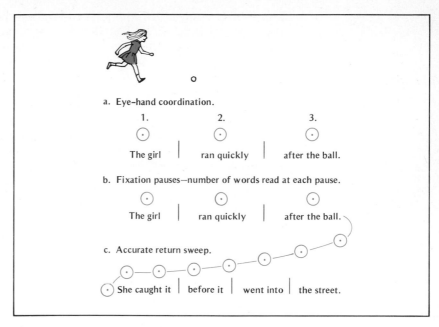

Figure 10.1 Psychomotor Activity in Reading

The Bigger Challenge

What do these results mean for education, especially the acquisition of psychomotor skills? An interesting comparison can be made. If performances in some related fields—physical education, sports—are constantly improving, why are performances in other related, admittedly more subtle and complex, activities, such as reading, writing, and speech, declining. Time, money, and effort have been lavished on the schools, but an objective observer would readily concede that the results have been disappointing.

Is the barrier to outstanding educational performance also psychological? Before answering, there must be clarification of "bigger challenge" and "outstanding performance." Recall Chapter 8's conclusion: foster competition with self. If teachers are to remove psychological barriers, they must thoroughly understand children's capabilities. Thus they can determine *appropriate* bigger challenges, successful completion of which is outstanding performance. Moderate competition with self and others may remove self-imposed psychological barriers.

A TAXONOMY OF HUMAN PERFORMANCE

Psychomotor activities permeate human lives but, as Fleishman notes (1975), some system for classifying these skills remains elusive. If such a system were available, generalization and predictions would improve both our knowledge about performance and our ability to transfer the results of training from one task to another. Gross classifications, such as "psychomotor" and "cognitive," are of little value. Detailed task analysis is good but too restrictive since it so often applies only to one particular task.

Merrill (1972) has proposed that the following five categories are pertinent to schools.

1. Physical education and recreation skills (including sports, dance, exercise)
2. Communication skills (including typing, handwriting, shorthand)
3. Language skills (including speech and gestures)
4. Vocational skills (including crafts, tool usage, machine usage)
5. Fine arts skills (including painting, singing, using musical instruments)

Fleishman, however, believes that these broad categories overlook the great performance diversity *within* each of these categories. What is needed is a system that precisely identifies the required learning skills, criterion performance levels (what is acceptable), the range of individual differences, and the possibility of transferring educational learning to job requirements.

THE NATURE OF PSYCHOMOTOR LEARNING

The learning characteristics previously discussed apply equally well to psychomotor learning. Try to teach writing, typing, or drawing to unmotivated students who ignore environmental stimuli, miss vital perceptual relations, and produce erratic responses with little, if any, notion of the activity's purpose. The frustrations and problems are as great here as in any subject. You should recall the learning characteristics also before beginning instruction—forcing yourself to consider objectives, uncomplicated stimuli, and accurate responses.

Perceptual-Motor Abilities	*Physical Proficiency Abilities*
1. Control precision	1. Extent flexibility
2. Multilimb coordination	2. Dynamic flexibility
3. Response orientation	3. Static strength
4. Reaction time	4. Dynamic strength
5. Speed of arm movement	5. Explosive strength
6. Rate control (timing)	6. Trunk strength
7. Manual dexterity	7. Gross body coordination
8. Finger dexterity	8. Equilibrium
9. Arm-hand steadiness	9. Stamina
10. Wrist-finger speed	
11. Aiming	

The role of individual differences

Individual differences are also highly significant in skill learning. Some activities require considerable strength, for example, football. Other skills demand precision; the clumsy boy or girl will struggle with activities demanding finger and hand coordination, such as repairing a vacuum cleaner or rebuilding a carburetor. Development and experience loom large in acquiring these skills. Fleishman (1975), studying hundreds of tasks, believes that certain abilities account for skilled performance. He and his colleagues have identified 11 perceptual-motor and 9 physical proficiency abilities that constantly affect performance, shown opposite.

These abilities are almost a catalog of individual differences.

The elementary school youngster learning to write lacks finger dexterity, arm-hand steadiness, and wrist-finger speed among the perceptual-motor abilities, and flexibility among the physical proficiency abilities. Different tasks require different combinations of abilities. For example, football demands considerable trunk strength, while long-distance running places a premium on stamina; typing requires dexterity and speed; mechanical drawing needs precision, steadiness, aiming, and dexterity. Identifying the critical abilities greatly aids instruction: What are the needed abilities? Does each student possess the maturation to begin? If not, what is needed to help them? Thus you can utilize books, films, demonstrations, and practice to produce a sequential program, ranging from readiness to skilled performance.

Cratty (1970) studied popular motor activities, such as play and sports, and derived various social correlates for each age. The role of individual differences is evident: intellectually slow youngsters of 7 or 8 begin to have difficulty comprehending complex rules; some youngsters thrive on competition; others begin to avoid it. Cratty designates the 9- to 10-year-old stage as a time of observable individual differences; if excessive anxiety is associated with the skill, performance then suffers. (Recall the discussion of the Yerkes-Dodson law in Chapter 7.)

Cratty comments that social development is linked to psychomotor learning and that different patterns emerge at different levels (1970, pg. 239). For example, during middle childhood the environment exerts considerable influence upon psychomotor learning because of economic conditions. Do parents enjoy an economic standard that can afford a child athletic equipment and facilities, such as tennis racquets and weights, and educational tools, such as calculators and slide projectors? Sex differences, although dissolving at this age, still appear, with boys enjoying more vigorous activity. Adolescence continues this sex differentiation with boys achieving substantial recognition because of physical prowess, although girls' sports now bring increasing status. So individual differences in psychomotor learning affect, and are affected by, cognitive and emotional achievement.

The various abilities, such as strength and speed, and ages at which they appear, with their social, emotional, and intellectual counterparts, relate to "students," not to specific boys and girls. Any youngster's attainment of a skill's standard of excellence varies because of his or her developmental level. Imposing a single standard for all ensures failure for some and frustration for most, if not all. Individual differences impose individual standards within a range of acceptable performances. The high school football coach who views himself as a potential Vince Lombardi (the late, hard-driving coach of the Green Bay Packers professional football team), and drives growing boys by standards obviously impossible for their age, may produce permanent physical damage. All instructors should avoid setting arbitrary standards and then insisting that *all* attain them.

CHANGES DURING PSYCHOMOTOR LEARNING

A motor skill is a finely organized series of movements intended to achieve a definite goal. Acquiring the fine organization that produces skilled performance demands comprehension of the skill, practice until overlearning occurs, and motivation—the characteristics of learning. Changes occur during this process that help to clarify the nature of psychomotor learning.

1. *Discrimination of parts.* Learning a skill necessitates analyzing in into its parts, which can temporarily cause poorer performance. For example, a youngster may hit a golf ball fairly well, or build a wooden cabinet or closet using a regular saw. But individuals will never become proficient unless they begin again; the golfer learn-

ARLINGTON, MASS. ADVOCATE

ing the many individual parts of the swing; the novice carpenter learning the movements required of more sophisticated tools. Although a necessary part of instruction, instructors should always teach the part as it relates to the whole, otherwise any integrated smooth performance is lost.

2. *Integration of parts.* After learners have identified and mastered the individual parts, they must combine them into a unit. Learning a skill involves both the elimination of unnecessary parts and the addition of new, more sophisticated responses. Once the learner has mastered individual parts, these responses may undergo modification through integration into the total act. For example, while practicing a forehand shot in tennis, the learner is told to stride evenly and with the forward foot. During a game that forehand shot will be lengthened and abbreviated due to body position at time of contact, while the stride may be shorter or longer depending on direction of body movement. The integrated act determines the particular form of the part. It is not simple repetition of the isolated part; just as H is hydrogen and O is oxygen, H_2O is water. Each part modified every other part in the total act.

3. *Perception of the task.* If the final act is more than the sum of its parts, perception must account for the change. The learner perceives the goal to be attained by mastering the task, and then perceives the parts of the skill and their relationship to each other that will lead to mastery. Increasing mastery produces decreasing perception; responses become more habitual. Typing is a good example: the beginner concentrates furiously; the skilled typist works almost automatically *unless* something changes the conditions, such as an employer or principal stressing the importance of a particular document.

4. *Precision of movement.* Awkward movements are refined; unnecessary movements are dropped; new movements are integrated. Miller et al. (1960) describe the process as the initial appearance of slow, awkward movements entailing considerable conscious effort, practice, and the final attainment of rapid, precise, more involuntary movements.

Fleishman and Hempel discuss changes in various abilities as proficiency increases. Figure 10.2 illustrates these changes. If you examine it carefully, you will see the changes that occur during skill learning. In this task, learning to use different switches as a response to different light patterns, spatial relations explain about 30 percent of the score on the first trial, but only about 8 percent on the fifteenth trial.

Figure 10.2 is an excellent portrayal of the changes that occur during skill learning, and Fleishman (1975) believes that his studies (similar to those in the figure) illustrate:

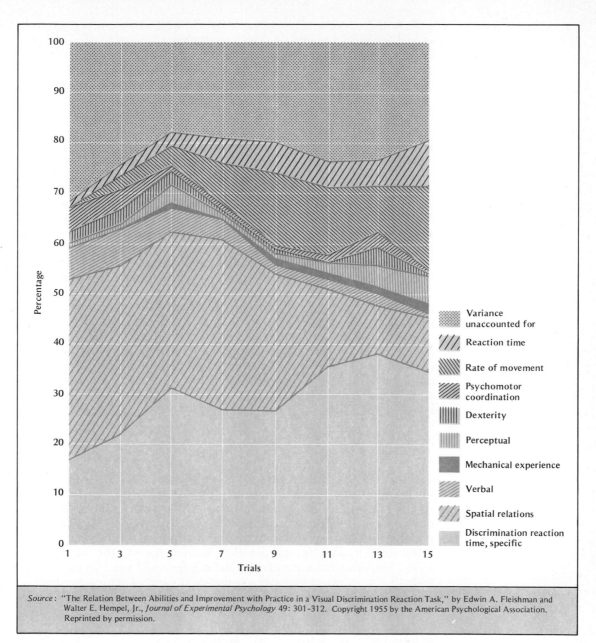

Source: "The Relation Between Abilities and Improvement with Practice in a Visual Discrimination Reaction Task," by Edwin A. Fleishman and Walter E. Hempel, Jr., *Journal of Experimental Psychology* 49: 301–312. Copyright 1955 by the American Psychological Association. Reprinted by permission.

Figure 10.2 Changes in Abilities as Proficiency Increases

1. That the specific combination of abilities contributing to task performance changes as practice continues.
2. That these changes are progressive and systematic, and are finally stabilized.
3. That the contribution of verbal and mental abilities to psychomotor skills is initially large but decreases with practice and improvement (the declining perceptual involvement previously mentioned).
4. That an increase in specific abilities is needed for mastery of a particular task.

A good example of the changes that occur during skill learning is driving an automobile. Do you remember those first times behind the wheel—your fear, almost overwhelming fear, that you would hit something, or worse, somebody? Do you recall the tight feeling in your stomach, hands clutching the wheel so tightly that they ached? There was a forced, almost painful consciousness of things to do: position yourself comfortably; adjust seat belts; start car (don't race the motor!), hands in the classic ten minutes of two position; move the gear selector to the correct setting (again, you pushed it past DRIVE; move it back); the jerky steering movements. Now you start the car immediately, perhaps ignoring seat belts; you move the gear selector without bothering to glance at it (you have the "feel" for it); the car is started and turned almost simultaneously with little conscious thought. You have eliminated all unnecessary movements and are now master of a smoothly integrated skill.

TEACHING PSYCHOMOTOR SKILLS

Everyone is a teacher of motor skills. Whether it is a parent showing a child how to build a kite or drive a car, a teacher instructing sewing, music, or shop class, or an office worker demonstrating how to refuel a copier, teaching motor skills is inevitable. In teaching these skills, one immediate requirement surpasses all others: instructors must possess detailed knowledge of the skills they teach. They must comprehend what the finished product looks and feels like; they must know the individual parts of which the task is composed; they must understand how the parts are best integrated and be able to inform students how they can evaluate their own performance. Simply put—instructors must know their subject. To emphasize this requirement, examine Figure 10.3. The subject must draw a star that she sees reflected in the mirror. The actual star is shielded from sight. While the subject realizes that small, straight lines are necessary, the right-left relationship is reversed and causes difficulty and the usual habits will not work. The subject must correct movements, make mistakes, gradually eliminate

Figure 10.3 Mirror Drawing Experiment

them, and finally produce a smooth reproduction. It is an excellent technique to illustrate the problems youngsters have in learning new skills and helps instructors improve their techniques. Try it yourself. You'll enjoy it.

Verbal Instruction

Skill teaching usually begins with verbal instruction so that learners may understand the objective, the sequence of events, and the relationship of parts. This verbal initial phase emphasizes the cognitive aspects of motor learning, without which students will always lack the finesse that marks skilled performance. Proceed cautiously; you want to explain and clarify, not confuse and frustrate because of excessive details.

Demonstration

Demonstration should follow verbal instruction. The instructor may demonstrate or show movies, pictures, slides, or models to illustrate the task, while simultaneously commenting on the skill's final form. Demonstration not only provides examples of expert performance, it also aids comprehension. The student, as an observer, can almost feel the skilled act.

Finally, the learner must attempt the act. Instructors walk a thin line here. They must not allow learners to make repeated mistakes, which could then become part of the skill and be extremely difficult to eliminate. But they should not comment too quickly because then the skill remains the instructor's, not the student's. Learners will err, but if they themselves cannot eliminate the errors, then the instructor should furnish guidance—verbal demon-

Practice

stration. Practice should be organized, relevant, and meaningful. If not, motivation is lost, errors are learned, and boredom quickly appears. Spaced practice (intervals, perhaps a day, between sessions) is better than massed practice (several sessions per day,

some following each other). Under spaced conditions, the learner has time to think, to integrate mentally the parts, and to avoid fatigue. Practice should also reflect the actual connections of the skill; that is, if speed is vital, then practice must emphasize speed and accuracy. If accuracy is the basic requirement, then emphasis should be upon accuracy, followed by speed.

Learning a skill with instruction usually follows the classic learning curve seen in Figure 10.4. The curve represents several instructional phases. The fairly rapid initial rise indicates that the

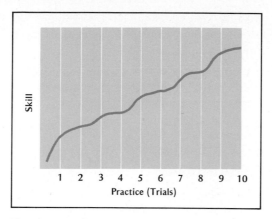

Figure 10.4 The Learning Curve

student begins in ignorance and is highly motivated. Several "plateaus" will appear: times when improvement seems to disappear, due to carelessness, loss of motivation, or new demands of the skill (moving from letters to words in learning to type). Finally the ultimate level is determined by the ability and desire of the student.

Nixon and Locke (1973), using instruction in physical education as an example, summarize some key points in teaching psychomotor skills. They state that children are not taught how to move because they are "prewired" for movement at birth. The environment directs these movements to specific goals, and the culture, with its reward system, causes children to place great importance on physical skills.

Psychomotor learning permeates everyone's life. As vocational education, physical education, games, and sports combine with the new thrust of career education, more time, attention, money, and research will focus on the teaching and learning of motor skills.

Discussion Questions

1. Recall Gagné's insistence that different kinds of learning require different types of teaching. From your study of his five categories, do you believe it is possible to differentiate different kinds of teaching? Why? Give examples based upon his categorization.

2. Can you think of techniques that you would use to facilitate your students' mastery of cognitive strategies? If you do not have access to a classroom (student teaching, observation), try it in your educational psychology class. Present your classmates with a novel problem and ask them "to think about their thinking" as they work. Discuss the results and apply them to elementary and secondary school students.

3. Have you ever mastered a psychomotor skill? (Sewing, typing, mechanics, hockey?) How did you achieve mastery? How would you *teach* it to others?

4. Return to Figure 10.2. Explain the initial and final percentage of time spent on each ability required by the task.

Affective learning

INTRODUCTION

Learning psychomotor skills can be frustrating, as can any learning. If frustration prevails during initial learning or any plateau period, negative attitudes appear that may discourage future learning. How you "feel" about anything often determines your success or failure with a particular task—including teaching.

What is true for you is true for your students: how they feel about school will influence their learning. In a time of uncertainty, anger, and violence, attitudes are formed and hardened early and

Responsibility in Children

Nathan Talbot, reporting on the Harvard Interfaculty Seminar on Children (1976), discusses fostering in children an attitude of responsibility toward others. Since children in primitive societies are expected to act responsibly toward others by 3 years—and do—Talbot muses about ways that American children can develop likewise and believes that the most effective technique for encouraging humaneness in children is to be certain that they are taught, expected, and encouraged to be decent toward others.

For example, even in the regimented Chinese society, children are taught to love and help each other during the early days of nursery school. If a child falls, the teacher will tell the other youngsters that they must help each other and ask them to help the fallen child. Also, Chinese youngsters wear winter jackets that button up the back so, since they

cannot button their own coats, they must help each other. As Talbot notes, helping others becomes a habit.

Brighter children help slower classmates. Five-year-olds assume classroom tasks, such as clearing tables and sweeping floors. They are encouraged to be productive at an early age. For example, they plant seeds for vegetables; a manufacturer pays them to pack crayons for export. The money is then used to buy something for the classroom.

Many American nursery schools provide similar experiences, but Talbot notes that encouraging these attitudes is not universal, and he believes that America must rank it high on any national agenda of child-rearing priorities.

You would enjoy Talbot's practical and reassuring book.

brought intact into the classroom where they affect everything a student does. For example, the busing issue has touched the lives of millions of Americans and produced heated and conflicting attitudes that have turned some schools into armed camps. Why has there been such a wide attitudinal difference? Some communities prepared for years and softened, if not changed, negative attitudes. Other communities fanned the fears of violence into rigid attitudes that will take years to modify. What can you do to foster a positive attitude toward learning? Initially, you should learn as much as possible about the nature and formation of attitudes.

THE AFFECTIVE DOMAIN

Learning and Feelings

Educators agree that students' feelings influence their learning. Their feelings about school, the teacher, the subject, and many other persons, objects, or events are all a teacher's concern. Attitudes, opinions, beliefs, values, interests are formed not only in school but also at home, from friends, and from past experiences. Nowhere do humans differ more, and often more violently, than in their affective behavior. Before any attempt is made to analyze these expressions of feelings, two basic issues need examination. How do people acquire those feelings, and how easily are they changed? Both of these topics are significant for the daily life of the classroom.

Development and change of affective behavior

A Pattern of Development

Home and family shape many attitudes, opinions, values, and interests during the early years; thus, these affective responses reflect social class differences. As Bloom notes (1964, pg. 133), affective responses also incorporate cognitive elements. Longitudinal data on the development and stability of affective responses—interests, attitudes, values—are still scanty, but suggest surprising stability for personality characteristics. For example, Bloom believes that by an average age of 2, one-third of the adolescent variance in aggression and dependency is predictable; by age 5, the amount has increased to one-half. Figure 10.5 illustrates the development of several characteristics, including ego development.

Note the ego development curve, especially its slower growth during the first 5 years and the earlier attainment of the plateau. Bloom believes that basic values show stability, but their expansion in particular attitudes varies during the years.

What causes changes in attitudes and values is important because teachers have an opportunity to modify their pupils' attitudes before that plateau around 18 years. Berelson and Steiner (1964) examined the relationship between affective response and social strata and reasoned that, in the United States, differences exist because of the following:

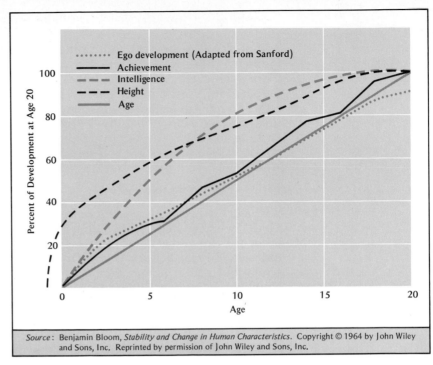

Figure 10.5 Curves of Development for Selected Characteristics

1. *Residence.* There are wide differences among geographical regions (particularly between the North and South in political and religious matters), and between rural and urban populations.
2. *Ethnic status.* Nationality, race, and religion all influence values, attitudes, opinions, and interests.
3. *Class.* Whether defined by income, occupation, education, or heredity, class will produce significant differences in affective responses. Suprisingly, an important and often overlooked fact is that the lower-class members are much more authoritarian than those of the upper class. This has major educational implication in determining methods and materials for schools. For example, before students from deprived areas are given the freedom necessary for problem solving and creative activity, there should be a period of careful preparation to avoid discipline problems.
4. *Age.* Youth today seems to follow social class leadership more than religious leadership.
5. *Sex.* Although sexual stereotypes are cracking, there is still considerable expectation that boys will value such activities as politics and sports; girls, sewing, and reading.

Once affective responses are formed they are fairly stable if they are steadily reinforced by family, group, or social class. When people are emotionally involved—that is, when the decision is other than rational—they are less likely to alter their views. Teachers should be especially conscious of the reluctance of students to change their beliefs. A surface concession to achieve a grade or degree may hide a remarkably stable underlying value or attitude. Behavior changes more rapidly, perhaps more superficially, than affective beliefs.

Difficulty of analysis

If individuals change their behavior to meet the demands of a situation, yet retain values or attitudes opposite to observed behavior, the problem of analysis is more apparent. For example, how often are people friendly to an individual that they actually dislike? If this example is characteristic of affective behavior, how can an investigator derive reliable data? The hidden nature of affective responses is the first, and perhaps major, obstacle to analysis.

Masking Our Feelings

Another problem is measurement. There are limitations in today's techniques that objectively assess an individual's attitudes, opinions, values, and interests. The many reasons for this are all related to an ability to mask feelings. Thorndike and Hagen (1977) state that respondents may not be open and forthright. To sample a student's learning in algebra or chemistry, the subject itself is a basis for questioning. The student is either right or wrong on the selected items. The discipline itself is the criterion.

What Is Measured?

Measuring a student's attitude toward religious freedom and expression demands that a person state an attitude toward the contribution of Jews, Protestants, and Catholics toward democracy. Two thorny problems arise. First, what criteria will satisfactorily evaluate the answer? There is no positive and unwavering certainty to any answer. Is the investigator truly impartial in the choice of criteria used to judge the answer? Is the student totally right or wrong considering previous experiences with this issue? Answers to questions in the affective realm lack the objective certainty of the answers to questions in algebra or chemistry.

Second, there is a cognitive element in any affective response. Although the essential component is feeling, another is intellectual involvement. Students make decisions about attitudes as information increases with maturity. Assuming, then, that blind, irrational, emotional responses are normally few, pupils will reflect upon a question about religious expression and weigh the consequences of their answer.

With the present unsophisticated methods of measurement, it is easy for subjects to disguise their feelings. It is relatively simple to follow the pattern of questions and to realize what answers will make one appear inflexible and prejudiced. It is possible to camouflage feelings.

There is no external, objective criterion against which the subject's responses can be evaluated. The criterion is the veracity of the subject, which, as described, may be highly questionable. Investigators are placed in the unenviable position of matching the person's responses against overt behavior. They are entirely at the mercy of the subject.

Changing Affective Responses

Other delicate questions remain. Should teachers attempt to change attitudes and opinions? This behavior develops within the family and peer groups; altered attitudes may alienate both. Knowing this, should a teacher still aim to transform faulty attitudes? While no one answer is possible, the degree of potential tension will govern the teacher's effort. If a student might encounter considerable unhappiness, a teacher may have to be content with moderating objectionable attitudes and hope that increasing maturity and independence will produce the desired result.

Objectives for Affective Learning

This is far from satisfactory for teachers, but judgment often dictates a temporary compromise. Since the student probably lacks the ability to judge that a change in opinions or belief is good, another question arises. Who is to decide what are good attitudes, opinions, values, interests, and appreciations? Is it the school board, the superintendent, the principal, or the teacher? Again, the answer is complex, but the collective judgment of the members of a school system should formulate objectives that are consistent with the school's philosophy of education. These objectives should include statements of purpose that indicate specifically what affective behavior is preferred. A school system that follows this policy attracts teachers who agree with its philosophy; this circumvents unrest and furnishes teachers with practical direction in their daily work.

THE AFFECTIVE DOMAIN: A TAXONOMY

Categories of Objectives

Any discussion of, or attempt to formulate, meaningful objectives for the affective characteristics is hampered by vagueness. What is meant by interests, attitudes, values, or appreciations? The little agreement about meaning has been a major reason for educators to avoid affective objectives. In a concerted effort to eliminate much of the confusion, Krathwohl et al. (1964) classified objectives into three categories: cognitive, affective, and psychomotor. Affective objectives are those that emphasize feelings: love, an emotion, or some degree of acceptance or rejection. These objectives are usually designated as interests, attitudes, appreciations, values, and biases. They range from simple attention to the complex attributes of character and conscience (Krathwohl et al., 1964, pg. 7).

Since affective responses are characterized by intense feelings

Internalization

that distinguish one from another, the authors had to find a continuum that would relate them, which led to ordering the components of the affective domain. The continuum encompasses being aware of, attending to, responding to, and organizing phenomena. "Internalization" best summarizes this continuum and refers to the incorporation within oneself of something that becomes one's own. Internalization implies that external control of behavior yields to inner control. It also implies that the continuum proceeds from simple to complex and from concrete to abstract.

Krathwohl et al. (1964, pg. 33) state that internalization commences when students attend to something. As they give their attention to the subject, they differentiate it from the remainder of the perceptual field. Next, they deliberately seek it as it acquires emotional significance and value. As internalization proceeds, it includes other similar and valuable objects. They continue to respond to it so that their reactions to it and others like it become almost automatic. Finally, the values placed upon this phenomenon and others similar to it are interrelated to form a new set that will aid in a constant search for success and adjustment.

The categories and subcategories of the continuum are as follows:

1.0 Receiving (attending)
    1.1 *Awareness.* Learners are conscious of something; they need not attend to it, but are merely aware that it is there.
    1.2 *Willingness to receive.* People attend to something and do not attempt to avoid it.
    1.3 *Controlled or selected attention.* People differentiate a stimulus from the perceptual field; the student looks for a particular stimulus.
2.0 Responding
    2.1 *Acquiesence in responding.* People comply with the expectations or requests of others.
    2.2 *Willingness to respond.* People display a capacity for voluntary activity. They act because they wish to do so.
    2.3 *Satisfaction in response.* They feel pleasure at their response. Now the activity has emotional significance.
3.0 Valuing
    3.1 *Acceptance of a value.* Learners ascribe worth to a phenomenon, behavior, or object; for example, reading.
    3.2 *Preference for a value.* Learners not only accept a value, but they seek it out, they want it; for example, looking for good books.
    3.3 *Commitment.* Learners act to further the thing valued, to extend their involvement with it. Loyalty and conviction are characteristic of this category; for example, students believe that books and reading are the path to knowledge.

4.0 Organization
    4.1 *Conceptualization of a value.* Abstraction enables learners to perceive how this value relates to those that they now hold, or those that they are developing; for example, the criteria for a good book.
    4.2 *Organization of a value system.* Learners can accommodate a complex of values, even disparate values, and form them into an ordered relationship. This relationship ideally should be harmonious and internally consistent; for example, students learn to value a book whose views differ from their own.
5.0 Characterization by a value or value complex
    5.1 *Generalized set.* There is an internal consistency to the learner's system of attitudes and values. It may be a predisposition to act in a certain way, or an unconscious set, or orientation, that guides action without conscious forethought. The generalized set permits learners to reduce a complicated environment to manageable parts; for example, they may change their opinion as a result of reading a different but logical interpretation of some issue.
    5.2 *Characterization.* Learners develop a consistent philosophy of life.

Source: Krathwohl, David R., Benjamin S. Bloom, and Bertram B. Masia. *Taxonomy of Educational Objectives, Handbook II: Affective Domain.* New York; McKay, 1964.

Krathwohl et al. (1964, pg. 36) found that the usual terms for affective characteristics (interests, attitudes, values, appreciations, and adjustments) were not confined to any one particular category but extended over several sections of the continuum. For example, interest ranged from awareness to preference for a value. Appreciation extended from controlled attention to preference for a value. Attitude and value ranged from a willingness to respond to a conceptualization of a value. Figure 10.6 illustrates the comparison of the usual affective terms with the taxonomy continuum.

Clarifying affective terminology can help teachers since the affective domain permeates all aspects of school life. Throughout the school years, maturing students are acquiring preferences, attitudes, and values that influence the extent, pleasure, and efficiency of learning. Moral development and values clarification are good examples of affective learning's impact.

MORAL DEVELOPMENT

The School as a Moral Force

Moral education is in the air. As Purpel and Ryan state (1975), the moral education of children is one of the school's oldest missions and one of our newest fads. Educators, from the ancient Greeks to contemporary Americans, have envisioned the school as a key

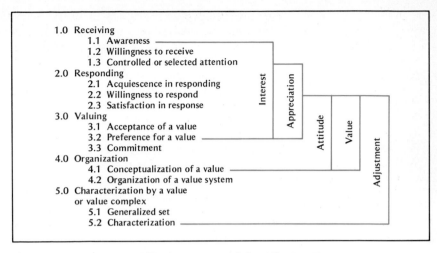

Figure 10.6 Customary Affective Terms and the Affective Taxonomy

force in the moral development of children. These authors define moral education as direct and indirect intervention of the school that affects both moral behavior and the capacity to think about "right or wrong."

While educators almost unanimously agree that moral education *should* be a critical objective for the schools, they have been equally as reluctant to assume the overt role of moral educator. Dacey (1976) notes that from a close alliance with the church during colonial days, the school's role in character development steadily diminished until the "last vestige of religiosity" was removed by the Supreme Court's decision against school prayer.

Church, State, and School

But a changing society has turned the tide. Shaken by political assassinations, Vietnam, Watergate, youthful rebellion against traditional values, crime, a shattered family structure, and stunned by the blinding speed of change, people, especially parents, are searching for "something" and often turn to the schools for help. Purpel and Ryan offer an excellent example of staggering change: over a few years the American people have turned from valuing frugality to valuing conspicuous consumption back to valuing ecological frugality.

What is the school's role in this search for a national conscience? The authors address several troublesome issues, chief of which is the school's pluralistic character. The conjunction in schools of races and religions with different values causes many to believe that moral education belongs in the home and church. Others believe that another task should not be added to schools already failing to offer intellectual education.

The authors rebut these objectives by noting that moral education already occurs *every day in every classroom.* Revolution in history, abortion in biology, honesty in heroes all introduce moral issues. Some schools offer moral education courses based on Lawrence Kohlberg's work or values clarification using Sidney Simon's ideas. More subtle, but perhaps more pervasive, is the teacher's behavior. Purpel and Ryan conclude that teachers are moral educators and the question is not "Should we?" but "How should we?"

Several recent surveys support their conclusion. In 1973, the Phi Delta Kappa membership was asked to rank 18 educational goals. Moral development was placed third, surpassed only by the development of reading and writing skills, and the development of feelings of self-worth and pride in work. In 1975, 1000 members of the same organization were sent a moral education questionnaire; 561 members replied.

Most of the respondents defined morality as concern for the rights of others, followed by decisions about right and wrong. While 75 percent worried about rising crime and 72 percent were bothered by political corruption and the breakdown in family life, only 26 percent were greatly concerned by changing sexual habits and decline in religious affiliation. Surprisingly, 27 percent felt that mass media could be an effective moral educator.

What does this survey suggest? First, there is a powerful plea that schools and teachers accept their role as moral educator. Second, the school's impact on moral development commences early—almost at initial school entrance. Third, schools can best fulfill their role as moral educator by active programs of moral education.

Kohlberg and moral education

Kohlberg and Piaget

One of the most popular moral education programs is Lawrence Kohlberg's. Applying Piaget's cognitive development theory to moral development, Kohlberg believes that moral stages emerge from the child's active thought about moral issues and decisions (Kohlberg, 1975, pg. 670). Kohlberg's stages of moral development are summarized in the box on page 402. Before you analyze them you might want to review Piaget's reasoning about the formation and development of cognitive structures, as presented in Chapter 4.

A Famous Moral Dilemma

Kohlberg emphasizes that the moral stages are structures of moral judgment, which may differ from the content of moral judgment, that is, moral judgment may differ from moral action. For example, one of his most famous moral dilemmas involved stealing an expensive drug to save a dying woman. The woman's husband cannot raise the money—what should he do? When the dilemma was posed to a national American sample, 75 percent said that it was wrong to steal the drug (but most said that they would),

Lawrence Kohlberg

which is essentially Stage 4 reasoning (law and order), but with indications that some reasoning has progressed to the post-conventional level.

Moral education

Given current concern with moral development, schools today must offer some kind of moral education program that also respects American pluralism. Those that have begun have usually taken Kohlberg's work—the use of moral dilemmas to aid moral development—and adapted it to particular community needs.

Kohlberg suggests that if schools wish to encourage morality and justice in children, the classroom itself must be just since mo-

Kohlberg's Stages of Moral Development

Level I. Preconventional (about 4 to 10 years).

During these years children respond mainly to cultural control to avoid punishment and attain satisfaction. There are two stages:

Stage 1. Punishment and obedience. Children obey rules and orders to avoid punishment; there is no concern about moral rectitude.

Stage 2. Naive instrumental behaviorism. Children obey rules but only for pure self-interest; they are vaguely aware of fairness to others but only for their own satisfaction. Kohlberg introduces the notion of reciprocity here: "You scratch my back, I'll scratch yours."

Level II. Conventional (about 10 to 13 years).

During these years children desire approval, both from individuals and society. They not only conform, but actively support society's standards. There are two stages:

Stage 3. Children seek the approval of others, the "good boy-good girl" men-

tality. They begin to judge behavior by intention: "She meant to do well."

Stage 4. Law-and-order mentality. Children are concerned with authority and maintaining the social order. Correct behavior is "doing one's duty."

Level III. Postconventional (13 years and over).

If true morality (an internal moral code) is to develop, it appears during these years. The individual does not appeal to other people for moral decisions; they are made by an "enlightened conscience." There are two stages:

Stage 5. An individual makes moral decisions legalistically or contractually; that is, the best values are those supported by law because they have been accepted by the whole society. If there is conflict between human need and the law, individuals should work to change the law.

Stage 6. An informed conscience defines what is right. People act, not from fear, approval, or law, but from their own internalized standards of right or wrong.

The Teachers' Role

rality comes not from books but from a moral atmosphere—the hidden curriculum. Teachers need not relinquish authority in providing a moral atmosphere; instead of depending upon rewards and punishments, the teacher's authority should come from a mediator's role. The teacher should ascertain that the children understand the nature of the conflict or dilemma because, as Kohlberg's studies have shown, youngsters rarely understand moral decisions more than one stage above their own. But they understand, and occasionally use, all stages below their own.

Any moral education program consists of several elements:

Basis of a Moral Development Program

1. Establishing a youngster's present level of moral development through the use of moral dilemmas.

2. Exposing the student to the next higher stage of moral reasoning.
3. Fostering discontent with the present level of moral functioning by presenting problem situations.
4. Encouraging open discussion about the previous three conditions.

For example, Blatt (1975) discussed moral dilemmas with four classes of junior and senior high school students for one semester. As students were at Stages 2, 3, and 4, their discussion of the dilemmas was at different levels. The teacher supported the stage above the lowest level, that is Stage 3 rather than Stage 2. When the students understood Stage 3 reasoning, the teacher then challenged that level using arguments from Stage 4. At semester's end, all students were retested; about 50 percent had progressed to the next stage, while control groups showed no change. Thus, it seems possible for schools to further moral development.

TEACHING FOR MORAL DEVELOPMENT

Two practical suggestions for classroom instruction entail the use of moral dilemmas and actual experience.

Using moral dilemmas

Paolitto and Hersh (1976) state that moral dilemmas are thought-provoking dialogues that probe the moral basis of people's thinking. It is a real or imaginary conflict situation involving competing claims, for which there is no clear, morally correct solution. Since most students have had little experience in resolving moral dilemmas (their parents make the decision or their age dictates automatic response to authority), these authors urge that teachers initially be active during the discussion and only later introduce more complex issues, that is, the next stage above the student's present moral level. They suggest certain kinds of questions for teachers:

1. Asking "why" to help students identify the dilemma and discover their level of moral reasoning; for example, Why is yours a good solution?
2. Complicating the circumstances to add a new dimension to the problem. For example, in resolving the dilemma of whom to throw from an overcrowded lifeboat, students frequently avoid answering by stating that it would be possible to save the extra people by tying them to the boat by ropes. But the teacher says that there are no ropes in the boat; so, who should go into the water: a mother or her teenage son?

3. Presenting personal examples, such as some item from television that describes survival after a plane crash, to emphasize moral dilemmas in the student's daily life. Who should receive the food: the injured or the healthy? Or a more personal dilemma: should an entire class be punished for the actions of a few?
4. Alternating real and hypothetical dilemmas, so that students are not embarrassed by premature self-disclosure.

Paolitto and Hersh state that teachers, as moral educators, must assume the social perspective of the students' moral levels and then create conflict by presenting different and higher moral reasoning.

Using actual experiences

Richard Graham (1975) has devised a scheme called action learning which he defines as learning from experience and associated study that is, or could be, accredited by an educational institution. Graham believes that adolescent and youth literature strongly supports his idea but that few programs have yet evolved. (See Chapter 2 for the theoretical rationale of this concept with adolescents and Chapter 16 for innovative programs of career education.) The author has attempted to match his practical proposal with Kohlberg's theory. The results appear in Table 10.1.

Graham believes that present knowledge of cognitive development and experiential learning indicates that the school cannot offer all experiences needed for maximum development. While most Americans complete the adolescent transition, few reach the level of principled judgment (Kohlberg believes that only 10 percent of adults attain this level). Consequently the match between

TABLE 10.1
Matching Moral Level with Action Learning Assignment

Kohlberg's Stages of Moral Development	Graham's Action Learning Assignment
Stage 1. Fear of punishment behavior	Following directions precisely, as in the military
Stage 2. Self-interest behavior, both in obeying rules and in relations with others	Accepting piece-rate jobs; some sales jobs
Stage 3. "Good boy-good girl" mentality	Group work, as in a fast-food outlet, secretaries in a pool, or shared production work
Stage 4. Law-and-order mentality	Supervisory assignment, correctional work—wherever rules clearly prescribe behavior
Stage 5. Moral decisions based on a legalistic interpretation	Personnel work, counseling; any position of decision making, resolving conflict according to fundamental principles of fairness

an individual and experience should reflect moral, cognitive, and social development to maintain continued personal development.

The author concludes that action learning assignments should match the individual's cognitive-social-moral level or permit the student to realize that the assignment is characteristic of the next higher stage. Graham gives the example of an assignment involving the care of retarded children and states that a student at Kohlberg's Stage 2 could see the task as Stage 3, liking and being accepted by others at the institution. For the Stage 3 person, the assignment could represent the Stage 4 characteristic of following institutional rules exactly. It is not only a field assignment that is important; the nature of the assignment determines future growth and development.

Note the preconditions, the development of prerequisite abilities that will aid in the resolution of moral dilemmas, and the step-by-step analysis that proceeds from clarifying the issue, to obtaining data, to means of obtaining a solution, to applying the solution to similar situations.

VALUES CLARIFICATION

A second major effort to implement moral education, devised by Sidney Simon, is called "values clarification." While value is used in the traditional sense—something possessing worth—Simon places little emphasis upon the content of values; his objective is to clarify the valuing process, that is, how people form their values. As Simon and de Sherbinin (1975) note, there is no place to hide from your values because everything you do reflects them. Even to deny values is a "value indicator."

Values clarification consists of knowing what one prizes, choosing those things that one prizes, and incorporating them into daily living. The late Louis Raths first devised the term during the fifties, reflecting his interpretation of John Dewey's ideas. Knowing, choosing, and living with one's values implies the following seven subprocesses (Simon, Howe, Kirschenbaum, 1972, pg. 19):

Prizing
1. Prizing and cherishing
2. Publicly affirming, when appropriate

Choosing
3. Choosing from alternatives
4. Choosing after consideration of consequences
5. Choosing freely

Acting
6. Acting on your values when necessary

7. Acting on your values with a pattern, consistency, and repetition

The authors believe that values clarification does not indoctrinate particular values but helps students use these seven processes to bring more meaning to their lives.

Simon and de Sherbinin (1975) list several specific objectives of values clarification:

1. *It brings purpose to people's lives.*   The authors believe that when children know what they want, they use time more efficiently and work more purposefully. Children who participate in values clarification sessions feel more positive about themselves and learning.

2. *It increases a person's productivity.*   The authors state that this is not a commercial or mechanistic result; they argue that productivity produces gratification. As students can no longer master an entire body of knowledge, they require some process to identify

MEDFORD, MASS. *DAILY MERCURY*

what will be of value to them. Values clarification thus causes productivity, pleasure, and gratification.

3. *It aids critical thinking.*   Students can better penetrate to the substance of an argument and rationally evaluate it.

4. *It furthers human relations.*   When people know what they want, and act on that commitment, they become better human beings.

Values clarification work takes many forms: as a specific part of a course (usually English, history, or social studies), as a special elective course, or as part of career and drug education programs. Whatever the vehicle, values clarification proceeds by practical *strategies.* For example, here is a summary of the first strategy:

Purpose

To aid students in deciding if they are obtaining what they want from life. The individual who settles for anything rather than pursuing goals is not guided in life by personal values. Life for this person never is meaningful.

Procedure

The teacher asks the students to list from 1 to 20 on a piece of paper and than asks them to list 20 things they enjoy doing. The teacher encourages the students by saying that the list can include both important or trivial things. When the students finish, the teacher tells them to code this list as follows:

1. Place a dollar sign next to any item costing more than $3.
2. Place the letter *A* beside those things that you like to do alone, and *P* next to those things with people, or *A-P* for both.
3. Place *PL* next to those things that require planning.
4. Place *N5* next to those that would not have been listed five years ago.
5. Use the numbers 1-5 to rank the five most prized items.

Teachers can then help students to evaluate them against their present status in order to bring more meaning to their lives.

The criticism

Both Kohlberg and Simon have their critics. Richard Peters (1975) believes that Kohlberg grossly neglects the "good-boy-good girl" level of morality since few individuals ever emerge from Stage 3 and 4. If principled learning eludes most, the goal should be to ensure that most citizens are comfortable with, and understand, the conventional level of morality. Also, since most people learn morality, they need reinforcement for their moral behavior. Peters argues that Kohlberg has ignored the importance of reinforcement and modeling in moral development.

John Stewart (1975) analyzing values clarification, argues that it is a superficial system lacking a conceptual basis. Where Kohlberg attempts to trace moral development through unfolding cognitive structures that emerge from the individual-environment interaction, Stewart believes that Simon focuses on the content of values. Stewart also argues that values clarification, through its strategies (especially that of public affirmation), exposes an individual to enormous peer pressure.

Whatever your opinion about these issues, they testify to a growing concern with moral development that affects more and more classrooms.

Discussion Questions

1. You have experienced various learning activities throughout your academic career. You succeeded at some, did fairly well with others, and failed with yet others. Recall one incident that you remember clearly and decide if some affective element influenced the outcome. What was it? Would you clarify it as an attitude, opinion, or value? Has this happened more than once?

2. What are some things that you value? Can you trace one of them, using the affective taxonomy from its roots to the final form? Try it. If you falter along the way, decide why it happens.

3. Be sure you understand Kohlberg's stages. Devise some moral dilemmas and present them in class. Analyze them. What does it tell you about identifying moral values?

4. Try Simon's strategy of listing 20 valuable things (or any of his other strategies) and decide if it reflects what you value and what satisfies you. If there is conflict, what do you suggest?

Some Concluding Thoughts

Learning takes many different forms that require unique instructional techniques. Before teachers can devise effective strategies they should understand the complexities of the various forms of the emotional and cognitive components. Psychomotor skills are frequently camouflaged, which results in inefficient learning, while verbal skills often have an unexpectedly large motor element. Consequently, instructors must incorporate psychomotor knowledge into all their teaching and constantly recall that their instructional demands must accommodate their students' maturational level. Whether subject matter stresses task components or student abilities, instructors must make a concerted effort "to match the mix," that is, match their instruction and expectations to their students' capabilities.

Affective learning, which can be as subtle as the psychomotor nature of all skills, demands equal consideration. Students' opinions, attitudes, interests, and values influence everything they do—including their learning. Recognizing the affective aspect of learning is insufficient in itself; teachers frequently must change an attitude or opinion, try to raise moral levels, or help students clarify their values. It is a sensitive task, one receiving careful scrutiny today. Regardless of formal programs, teachers can immeasurably help their students by awareness of their own behavior. Be a suitable model.

Summary

- Robert Gagné's study of the conditions of learning is one of the most popular attempts to categorize learning outcomes.

- Psychomotor skills are an integral component of *all* learning, and the skilled performer enjoys considerable status in most societies.

- Analysis of psychomotor skills usually focuses upon the task's characteristics or the abilities required to master the skill.

- Knowing the changes that occur during skill learning helps teachers to evaluate their effectiveness during instruction.

- Although many difficulties arise during the analysis, teaching, and evaluation of affective learning, the affective taxonomy aids clarity.

- Kohlberg's theory of moral development offers some hope for introducing formal instructional programs into the schools. One of its strongest features is its evolution from Piaget's cognitive theory, linking stages of moral development to emerging cognitive structures.

- Values clarification is an additional attempt to help schools formulate programs involving sensitive moral issues.

Suggested Readings

Cratty, Bryant. *Perceptual and Motor Development in Infants and Children.* New York: Macmillan, 1970. An excellent overview of motor development during the first 12 years.

Fleishman, Edwin A. "Toward a Taxonomy of Human Performance." *American Psychologist* 30 (December 1975): 1127–1149. A thorough review of present attempts to analyze psychomotor learning.

Gagné, Robert M. *Essentials of Learning for Instruction.* New York: Dryden

Press, 1974. A good summary of Gagné's present views on categorizing learning.

Kohlberg, Lawrence. "The Cognitive-Developmental Approach to Moral Education." *Phi Delta Kappan* LVI (June 1975): 670–677. A clear summary of Kohlberg's ideas, with his views on moral education. The entire issue is worth your close scrutiny.

Krathwohl, David R., Benjamin Bloom, and Bertram Masia. *Taxonomy of Educational Objectives. Handbook II: Affective Domain.* New York: McKay, 1964.

Second Handbook of Research on Teaching. Chicago: Rand McNally, 1973. There are valuable insights into teaching psychomotor skills in Parts 3 and 4.

Simon, Sidney, Leland Howe, and Howard Kirschenbaum. *Values Clarification: A Handbook of Practical Strategies for Teachers and Students.* New York: Hart Publishing, 1972. Here Simon and his colleagues offer 79 strategies to aid students in discovering and clarifying their values.

11

Measuring and Evaluating Ability and Achievement

Introduction

Teachers use tests. They use them to assess their pupils' abilities, achievement, aptitudes, personalities, interests, and weaknesses. Then, using the test results, teachers and administrators make scientific judgments about curriculum, pupil placement, materials, and methods. Or do they? Teachers speak glibly about precise measurement. But how often do they refuse to accept some test's

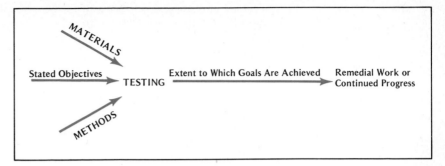

Figure 11.1 The Integration of Educational Activities

negative results because they like a particular pupil? This is called the "halo effect." Or how often do they question positive test results about a pupil who creates classroom problems?

Reliable measurement or personal judgment—which will influence you? You should repeatedly recall this question during your reading because if you refuse to accept the outcome of good testing, how valuable is any test? Should schools continue to invest substantial sums in testing programs? It is impossible to eliminate personalities, which always color judgments, but if you acquire confidence in the tests you use, your judgment will be based upon more than personal discretion. Consequently, your pupils will benefit and your teaching will become more effective.

Only some means of measurement can determine the attainment of objectives, the degree of learning, the success of teaching, and the desirability of curriculum material. Changes in pupil behavior are the best criteria to assess learning and are the data that you must accept and use to improve both teaching and learning.

Educators can defend the success of teaching, the value of curriculum, or the amount of learning only by some demonstrable proof. Proof requires evidence; in education such evidence is obtained by testing. The preceding work was concerned with discovering objectives and the methods of attaining these goals. Here is your third major task: testing. Figure 11.1 illustrates the integrated nature of these three enterprises.

Figure 11.1 graphically illustrates the key position of testing in the teaching-learning process. Desirable objectives have been formulated, methods and materials have been selected to attain these objectives, and the results of testing indicate whether learning has occurred. If it has, students advance to more difficult materials; if it has not, then review and repetition are needed.

The above procedure, which is the most common use of the classroom test, focuses upon student achievement. What have students learned as manifested on this test? Have they achieved enough objectives to move on to the next level? The vital role of objectives is clearly seen: they must be sharply defined and stated in language that permits measurement; that is, they must specify behavioral change. The results plot the future path of both teacher and learner.

Unfortunately, most interpretations of test usage are restricted to this relatively narrow view. But testing also has a guidance function. Depending upon the nature of the test scores, the results will portray the specific type of remedial work required, or the exact kind of advanced material that would be most suitable. Careful interpretation of test scores greatly furthers the diagnosis of learning difficulties, both for an individual and a class.

Can teachers remove themselves from testing? The answer is as plain as it may be painful. If an individual, or class, has failed to attain objectives, teachers search for the cause. There are three immediate possibilities: the student (physically ill at the time of testing, bothered by a personal problem), the difficulty of the material, and the teachers' methods. If the class is typical, if the material has been proven to be successful with other similar groups, then teachers can consider several possibilities: lack of background information, too rapid or limited student activity when the material demanded more personal involvement. The lesson is clear: professional teachers will also use test results as a form of self-evaluation.

Testing can also help teachers and administrators in their search for appropriate subject matter. If students consistently fail, or experience difficulty, or score unusually high, you may question the nature of the subject matter. Objectives, methods, materials, and diagnosis all reinforce the belief that testing is at the vital core of education. Testing must also provide information about the conditions of learning. What do you know about the motivation of the class? Do they realize they are faced with a problem? Are you providing the opportunity for them to practice the desired behavior? Have they been given sufficient time? Are they deriving satisfaction from their work? How much direction is necessary? Are they obtaining feedback? Both learning and teaching become more efficient as additional knowledge about the conditions of learning is acquired.

Surprisingly, theorists concerned with education as it should be often are more aware of the importance of testing than many practitioners who are inherently suspicious of testing. Teachers frequently feel that testing is an added burden that interferes with real teaching and learning. But the use of carefully constructed tests is time well spent. Try to assess the quality of materials, the effectiveness of teaching, and the worthiness of objectives without testing. If testing is avoided, or merely tolerated, it is impossible to judge these issues without resorting to guessing. When one realizes that tests, both teacher-made and standardized, may alter a student's future, it is apparent that poorly made and questionably interpreted tests can cause lasting damage. Grades, promotion, college acceptance, and employment opportunities all reflect the results of testing. Why then are teachers notoriously careless in the construction of tests and the interpretation of test results?

One reason is that teachers are also notoriously confident about their judgment of pupils. They know what their pupils can do; in many instances they view testing as superfluous. Another reason is that a good test is extremely difficult and time consuming to construct. What are the objectives I wish to sample? How are they related to this particular context? Will these items adequately measure the objectives? Still another reason is the dependability of the score. The student may feel ill; she may have had trouble at home; there may have been a discipline problem in class just before the test; the test itself may have left much to be desired. Admittedly, each and all of these events will bias the test score. But the purpose of this chapter is to alert you to these obstacles and to suggest techniques for limiting any negative effect they could have.

To accomplish this purpose, you shall examine both the teacher-made and standardized test. What exactly is the meaning of measurement? Are there problems innate in the nature of measurement? What is the relationship of measurement to educational objectives? The assessment of objectives implies a good instrument. What are the characteristics of a good test and how can you build these into your tests? What types of tests should you know? What are some items that represent the various tests? Finally, how should you use test data in marking, grading, and reporting to parents?

Why test?

If personal judgment is so important in decisions about pupils, why test? If the halo effect—good pupils are smart—acts constantly to affect all our assessments, why test? It is precisely because of personal involvement that you need some more objective measure of pupils. Philip Jackson (1968), in his fascinating *Life in the Classroom*, discusses the importance of evaluation in a pupil's life.

WHO EVALUATES?

Sources of Evaluation

Jackson notes that the dynamics of classroom evaluation are complex and difficult to describe because evaluation comes from more than one source, the conditions of communications vary, and the quality may range from intensely positive to intensely negative. The chief source of evaluation is the teacher, who makes continuous judgments about students' work and behavior and then communicates that judgment to the students and others (administrators, parents). It is a constant process that keeps students steadily informed of their progress.

But others also pass judgment. Classmates frequently join in the evaluation of a peer. "Who can help Janey?" Judgment frequently occurs spontaneously when students may laugh at someone, grin at an answer, or even applaud something outstanding. Students constantly evaluate themselves. The youngster who is asked to read a selection and cannot, the youth who is asked to solve an algebra problem at the board and fails—these pupils themselves pass judgment on their behavior.

Others also pass nonacademic judgments. Peers are among the most critical judges of personal characteristics—he's a dummy; she's a teacher's pet; he's a sissy; she cheats. Students know and accept this kind of evaluation because they themselves join in it. Friendship and popularity are largely based on these kinds of evaluations. Thus, there are three sources of evaluation:

1. The teacher
2. Peers
3. Self

They evaluate three kinds of behavior that relate to:

1. Academic achievement
2. Institutional adjustment
3. Personal characteristics

Frequently all sources are judging all kinds of behavior. For example, the girl who is a constant do-gooder may see herself as doing the "right thing," while peers, and even the teacher, are repelled by her behavior; each of the sources simultaneously makes judgments about the behavior itself—smart, teacher's pet, "pain-in-the-neck."

What influences evaluation?

Brophy and Good (1974) have studied student differences that affect teachers and reached some interesting conclusions. If one-third of the youngsters who begin first grade do not graduate from high school, there must be some obvious reasons for this high, and unacceptable, dropout rate. Who are these students? As the authors note, there is considerable knowledge about them. They are more likely to be boys, to come from lower-class or broken homes, and to be low achievers. These are the dropouts, and you must face a difficult question: how much do teachers' personal opinions affect academic decisions?

The Dropouts

Attractive or Unattractive: Does It Matter?

Other than tests, what do teachers use for evaluating papers? The halo effect is an encompassing, humorous term that is probably true but not very helpful. More specifically, what causes teachers to place a halo over some pupils and not others? Among the more powerful judgmental influences are the teacher's expectations of a pupil's behavior and also the physical attractiveness of children. There is a persistent cliché that attractive children are more intelligent and more socially desirable.

Clifford and Walster (1973) sent completed, above average report cards, together with photographs, to fifth-grade teachers and asked them to assess each child's IQ and personality. The photographs were of attractive and unattractive children. Regardless of the pupil's or teacher's sex, the attractive children received more favorable evaluations than the unattractive. Dion (1972), hypothesizing that observers perceive attractive children as more socially desirable than unattractive, studied the effects of presenting observers with information about severe misbehaviors of both attractive and unattractive children. The stereotype held. Observers classified the unattractive children as chronically antisocial, while attractive children committed only "temporary pranks."

Rich (1975) believed that these and other studies, while informative, had methodological weaknesses that affected their results. He determined to restudy the question of whether teachers treat attractive children differently from unattractive children and then to discover if academic and personal information about children will change teachers' opinions. The subjects were 144 female elementary school teachers. They read about some severe misbehavior that an attractive or unattractive child, whose photograph was attached to the record, had committed. They were then asked to assign blame for the behavior (for example, pushing another boy or girl downstairs), to evaluate the child's personality characteristics, and to recommend punishment. The study's next phase entailed the teachers' receiving a report card—good, average, or bad—of the child. They were then asked to reevaluate the child for blame, personality, and punishment.

In the pre-report-card phase there was a significant difference between the treatment of unattractive boys and girls: unattractive girls were least blamed for misbehavior while unattractive boys were blamed most often. Unattractive boys were also most recommended for stronger punishment. A definite attractiveness-sex interaction emerged during the pre-report-card phase, with the unattractive boy the consistent target of teachers.

The post-report-card results were comparable to the introductory conclusions. Teachers more readily blamed attractive children for misbehavior, but unattractive boys again were teachers' primary targets.

Rich concludes that it is impossible to postulate a general physical attractiveness stereotype; what consistently emerges is the attractiveness-sex interaction. While physical attractiveness obviously influences, it seems no longer acceptable to suggest that teachers are victims of the "what is beautiful is good" syndrome especially if the evaluating adult is a female teacher. More sophisticated arguments are necessary.

Brophy and Good believe that within any class there are group and individual differences that strongly influence teachers' judgments.

A. *Influential group differences*
   1. *Social class differences.* There has been a persistent pattern of findings regarding teachers' attitudes toward children from different social classes. A student's socioeconomic status (*SES*) was the strongest variable determining teachers's attitudes toward their pupils. Teachers believe that the *SES* of first-grade children is a better predictor of academic success than IQ, and they still believe it at the sixth-grade level. More teacher reinforcement is given to middle-class than lower-class children. Lower-class children are not expected to meet the goals of middle-class children. The authors conclude that the data clearly show that *SES* predicts both teachers' perceptions and treatment of their children.
   2. *Race.* There is little clear evidence about racial impact on teacher-student interactions. Research seems to show that while teachers give less attention to black students and have lower expectations for them, Indian and Eskimo children in Alaska who attend village elementary schools and then go to urban high schools experience similar problems. While most studies are confounded by the race, sex, and *SES* interaction, the authors conclude that teachers are likely to have negative attitudes toward minority group children.
   3. *Sex.* While evidence clearly suggests that school is more meaningful for girls and that they do better, there may be an excellent reason for this difference. Female teachers predominate in elementary schools and they simply may favor girls. Nevertheless, boys get into more trouble and do more poorly than girls. Thus girls have more favorable attitudes toward school.
B. *Influential individual differences*
   1. *Student achievement.* Students who achieve well have more favorable interactions with their teachers, while low-achieving students experience more conflict with their teachers. Brophy and Good believe that these differences are magnified when a school uses a tracking system. Students in the high track usually come from high *SES* homes, instructors enjoy teaching them, and because of their rich and varied backgrounds, these students learn from each other.
   2. *Student personality.* Since both students and teachers have their individual personalities, it is difficult, if not impossible, to make sweeping statements about a cause-and-effect personality relationship. But teachers react differently to different students and certain cautious generalizations are pos-

sible. Teachers prefer conforming, orderly students the most, followed by those who are dependent and acquiescent. Least liked are independent, active, and assertive students. So these individual personality characteristics affect teachers' reactions, which then may bias teachers' assessments.

3. *Other influences.* These include physical attractiveness, speech characteristics, and writing neatness.

Does Ability Level Make a Difference?

The authors conclude that student characteristics affect teachers' perceptions, which then affect how teachers treat students. Another example of how individual differences affect teachers' behavior is reported by Heller and White (1975). Their initial premise is that a teacher's verbal approval or disapproval powerfully influences pupil behavior, which becomes effective in increasing appropriate classroom behavior. The investigators then sought to determine if teachers' approval and disapproval varies with ability levels. They observed five social studies and five mathematics instructors teaching both high and low ability classes in a New York City junior high school.

The authors discovered that teachers emitted more disapproving statements in low-ability classes than in the high and these disapprovals were mainly managerial, that is, they attempted to control social behavior. The rates of approval did not change from one ability grouping to another. But there were significant differences in the rate of disapproval from one group to another for social studies teachers. These teachers showed much more disapproval with their low-ability classes. While these results may be isolated, what is there about low-ability students that produced notable differences in teachers' reactions? Here is a glaring example of how student achievement affects teachers' behavior.

THE NEED FOR TESTS

If teachers' personal evaluations are so significant, and if they are strongly influenced by the previously mentioned forces, then you may ask whether tests serve any practical function. That is, realistically, are tests used for any other reason than impressing parents and soothing accreditation agencies? There can be but one answer: tests must be used to balance, and perhaps even overcome, teachers' prejudices.

Testing and Teaching

Brown (1970) states that teachers consciously strive to eliminate, or minimize, anxiety, unfairness, dishonesty, and humiliation, but examining and evaluating is essential for effective education. While some tests (both standardized and teacher-made) are better than others, most thoughtful teachers accept the fallibility of their personal judgments when based upon irregular, uncontrolled observations. Tests provide a more extensive and objective basis for judging. Ebel (1965) summarizes the role of testing when he notes that testing does not eliminate teacher observation; it extends, refines, summarizes, and records these observations.

Chauncey and Dobbin (1963) state that carefully constructed tests serve several functions:

1. *They assess the learner's development.* The authors believe this can be the most important use of achievement tests. Having some estimate of a student's ability to learn, periodic assessment can inform instructors if pupils are progressing satisfactorily.
2. *They aid in student guidance.* Students constantly face choices: activities, courses, careers. The best predictor of future success is past progress in similar activities. How else can teachers effectively assess achievement and predict performance in any field without testing?
3. *They aid in curriculum planning.* Times change; needs change; curricula must change. Since the goal of education is to prepare youngsters, both personally and professionally, teachers must continually question methods, materials, and the curriculum. You cannot answer the question, "Are youngsters prepared?" without testing both ability and achievement.
4. *They aid in promotion and admission decisions.* Performance dictates promotion and admission to higher levels of education or a profession. It is as simple as that. Tests, again both standardized and teacher-made, are needed to access satisfactory performance at these critical points.
5. *They aid in school assessment.* Testing is *one* way of determining if the school itself is performing satisfactorily. That is, does it prepare students in the basic skills of reading, writing, and calculating, while simultaneously meeting community demands and comparing favorably with national norms?

You should now have some idea of the difficulties and advantages of testing. That testing is needed seems apparent. That testing has weaknesses is also apparent. But granted these limitations, tests in the hands of a skilled teacher are an excellent educational tool. You can best argue for the need of tests by stating: to teach without testing is unthinkable.

Meaning in measurement

TERMINOLOGY

Many terms are used, often confusingly, in testing. For example, "test" usually means some device that provides a sample of behavior; occasionally some authors will use test in the sense of eval-

Can Tests Eliminate Schooling?

Can, or should, testing eliminate schooling? Marlowe (1976) describes a new examination that is certain to fuel the flames of the testing controversy as nothing has done for the last decade. The test, called the California High School Proficiency Examination, is a four-hour assessment of skills designed to determine if a 16- or 17-year-old needs to spend further time in high school. If students pass the test, they have earned their diploma.

It is essentially a reading test that enables students to demonstrate that they can read directories, understand written directions, and do basic mathematical calculations. Marlowe describes it as a very practical and useful test, requiring little, if any, literary, historical, or artistic knowledge. Little writing is required, and the student's writing is examined only if the final score is close to the cutoff point.

While California has strict rules concerning physical education, no knowledge or demonstration of citizenship is required. There are no questions regarding the American system of government. Marlowe states that *maybe* this test is valuable in making schools prove that their students can meet minimal standards, but it seems doubtful. There are serious implications to this latest procedure, one of which is that the state can grant diplomas, regardless of the needs and wishes of the local community, and colleges must accept students that the state says are ready, regardless of the high school's evaluation.

Can, or should, tests eliminate schooling?

---

uation, that is, a collection of all evidence needed to make decisions about students. To avoid ambiguity, the terms used in this chapter, and the text, have the following meaning.

Test

A test is a sample of behavior. It tells us something, not all, about that behavior. An arithmetic test, for example, samples addition or division. It tells us nothing about a student's knowledge of fractions. Mehrens and Lehmann (1975, pg. 3) state that a test is the presentation of a standard set of questions to be answered. When students answer these questions, you obtain a numerical measure of the characteristic you have tested.

Measurement

This is a more inclusive term that implies abstracting information about students by employing several techniques: observation, rating scales, and other instruments. Educators then derive a numerical score from using these instruments to assess certain behavior: reading, science, mechanical aptitude. Measurement scores reflect students' achievements.

Evaluation

This is the most inclusive term and implies the use of tests, measurements, behavioral records, inventories, and other instruments so that teachers or counselors can make decisions about students. Where tests and measurement provide quantitative measures, evaluation guides you toward *qualitative* judgments. You are concerned not only with a numerical score, but with how much students have progressed during the year: have they achieved their original objectives? An interesting, and popular, analysis proposes two types of evaluation: formative and summative. Bloom, Hastings, and Madaus (1971, pg. 207) describe formative evaluation as a continuous process that quickly assesses weaknesses and suggests remedial techniques so that instruction can remain effective. Summative evaluation occurs at the end of a unit or course and its primary objective is marks, teacher assessment, and curriculum evaluation. While vital, a teacher who relies solely on summative evaluation leaves no time for remedial work.

Standardized tests

Mehrens and Lehmann define a standardized test as one that is commercially prepared and samples behavior under uniform procedures. Uniform procedures means that the same fixed set of questions is administered with the same set of directions, the same time, and with the scoring procedure carefully detailed. The testing experts usually administer the test to a norm group (usually a large, national sample) so that any one student's performance can be compared to others throughout the country. Standardized tests are usually classified according to what they measure. There are three general categories:

1. Aptitude tests, which are intended to assess students' general or specific abilities; for example, intelligence tests supposedly assess a student's total ability. (The current raging controversy concerning what intelligence tests measure will be discussed later.) There are other, more specific aptitude tests that measure mechanical, musical, artistic, and many other aptitudes.
2. Achievement tests, which measure accomplishment in such subjects as reading, arithmetic, language, and science.
3. Interest, personality, and attitude inventories, which assess noncognitive behavior.

Teacher-made tests

While teachers use many techniques in evaluation, probably the most popular is the written paper-and-pencil type that they themselves construct. These may be either subjective or objective. Since teachers chiefly rely on their own tests to assess learning and to evaluate pupil progress, these tests will receive considerable attention in this chapter.

Norm-referenced tests

A norm-referenced test yields a score that enables you to compare it with the scores of others who took the same test. For example, when you grade an essay test you compare each student's answers to those of other students and decide that the answers, compared to the others, warrant a *B*. A score on a standardized achievement test provides a score that tells how a student compares to some national group that took the test.

Criterion-referenced tests

A criterion-referenced test provides a score that informs us of the extent to which a student has achieved predetermined objectives. There is *no* comparison with others. Criterion-referenced tests are increasingly popular because of renewed emphasis on individualized instruction, behavior objectives, and mastery learning. As Thorndike and Hagen state (1977, pg. 5), there is no question as to whether one student is better or worse than another; the focus is on reaching a particular standard of performance.

Validity

Thorndike and Hagen (1977) define validity as the extent to which a test measures what it is supposed to measure. Of all the essential characteristics of a good test, none surpasses validity. If a test is not valid, it has no value. For example, if a test designed to measure academic achievement in a particular subject uses questions that are phrased in difficult language, it does not test geography or history as much as reading. Its validity is questioned, since it is not measuring what it claims. Validity is specific. A test may be valid for one purpose, and no other. To administer a spelling test for the purpose of determining a student's achievement in grammar is invalid.

There are three kinds of validity.

1. *Criterion-related validity* is present if the results of a particular test parallel some other, external criteria. Thus test results are sim-

Mastery Learning

The issue of norm- and criterion-referenced tests is today so significant that it deserves additional comment. Individualized instruction, with its insistence on specific objectives, has stressed the need to discover how well students achieve or master objectives. Consequently, there is a close link between mastery learning and criterion-referenced testing. Block and Anderson (1975) state that mastery learning is a philosophy about teaching—a belief that all students can and will learn well most of what they are taught under appropriate instructional conditions.

Bloom (1974), whose ideas have strongly influenced the development of mastery learning, states that John Carroll's model for school learning initially caused him to consider the relationship among student aptitude, instruction, and learning time. He notes that the basic problem is time. The top 20 percent of students, under nonmastery conditions, will attain material that it

Summary Position Statements on the Mastery-Discrimination Controversy

Advocates of discrimination testing believe that—

1. Mastery can be only arbitrarily defined and that there are important decisions to be reached from knowledge of degrees of achievement.
2. Most subject matter is not so structured that understanding one concept requires "complete mastery" of a previous concept.
3. Varying time rather than amount learned is not the most beneficial or efficient instructional strategy.
4. All students need not, and probably should not, learn many (if any) things to the same degree of proficiency.
5. Even if item 4 were a reasonable goal, what we know about individual differences suggests that even by making time a variable, student proficiencies are not likely to be very homogeneous.
6. If differential learning exists, it is wasteful not to measure it, since it is a potential aid in decision making.

Advocates of mastery testing believe that—

1. Mastery is definable in a meaningful, useful way, and degrees of mastery for many subjects either do not exist or are unimportant.
2. Most subject matter is hierarchically structured.
3. For hierarchically structured subjects it is an unwise pedagogical decision to attempt to teach higher concepts if the basics have not been mastered.
4. Therefore, it is better to allow variations in the time spent in learning than in the amount learned (that is, it is better for a student to learn fewer things more thoroughly).
5. All pupils enrolled in a course should learn the same things from that course.

Source: From *Standardized Tests in Education,* Second Edition by William A. Mehrens and Irwin J. Lehmann. Copyright © 1969 by Holt, Rinehart and Winston. Copyright © 1975 by Holt, Rinehart and Winston. Reprinted by permission of Holt, Rinehart and Winston.

takes the remaining 80 percent of students another two years to attain—four-fifths of students need two extra years to attain the mastery reached by the other one-fifth. Under mastery conditions—that is, determining what all children should learn, stating predetermined objectives—criterion-referenced testing flourishes. Differences between the two tests are summarized in the table on page 424.

Mehrens and Lehmann conclude that both criterion- and norm-referenced tests are needed. Current school organization, with learning time identical for all pupils, requires norm-referenced tests. As individualized instruction increases, mastery learning and criterion-referenced testing will spread.

---

ilar or not similar to another example of behavior that is manifested simultaneously or in the future by the pupil. If students do well on some standardized reading test that measures all aspects of reading, they should likewise do well in completing and understanding geography and history reading assignments. You can comprehend how this kind of validity is valuable for the teacher, particularly in assessing the validity of teacher-made achievement tests. As Thorndike and Hagen state (1977), some other measure is taken as the criterion of success.

2. *Content validity* testifies to the test's success in sampling behavior that has been the goal of some activity, such as instruction. Does the test adequately represent the material that was presented? For example, an instructor teaching the geography of Europe spends considerable time on Western Europe and briefly mentions Eastern Europe. If he then attempts to remedy this imbalance by testing extensively the pupil's knowledge of Eastern Europe, he violates content validity.

3. *Construct, or congruent, validity* exists when the particular subject that the test is measuring can be compared with some other manifestations of the subject. If, for example, a teacher claims that the test measures understanding and not facts, there should be some other criterion that measures understanding with which the results of the test can be contrasted. If the test measures anxiety, then its results should be similar to judgments made about individuals designated as anxious. Thorndike and Hagen (1977) state that construct validity tells us if the test scores correspond to some meaningful trait or construct.

Reliability

Thorndike and Hagen (1977) define reliability simply: a measure is reliable to the extent that an individual remains nearly the same in repeated measurements. A test is reliable if it is consistent. Do two forms of a test yield similar results? If the test is repeated after a certain interval, how consistent are the results? There is always some error present in any test since fluctuations in human behavior are uncontrollable and the test itself may contain possibilities of error. Its language may be so ambiguous as to be misleading. Correcting essay examinations also introduces the chance of error.

You should note carefully the distinction between reliability (consistency) and validity (accuracy). A valid test must be reliable, but a reliable test need not be valid. For example, a test may have an inherent error in it. A teacher may ask for the names of the nations that constitute SEATO but inadvertently may have written NATO in the test. A scoring key was devised that indicates the names of the SEATO countries. Naturally, pupils will give the wrong countries *consistently*. The test is consistent, but it is not valid.

These are some of the major concepts used in measurement. If you want more information about specific tests, such as reliability and validity data, you might examine Oscar Buros's *Eighth Mental Measurement Yearbook,* which lists, describes, and criticizes each new standardized test. Also, the *Standards for Educational and Psychological Tests* (1974), published by the American Psychological Association, is an excellent guide to both desirable test standards and proper test usage. Table 11.1 summarizes the terms and their meanings.

PROBLEMS IN MEASUREMENT

Test Limitations

Tests, measurements, and evaluations are vital for successful education, but that should not blind you to some of the difficulties inherent in the measurement process. All measurement is subject to error; in the behavioral sciences, the testing conditions, the person giving the test, the person taking the test, and the test itself are potential sources of error. These reservations about measuring instruments should not discourage you; educational and psychological measurement continues to show remarkable refinement. Instruments have become more precise, statistical techniques have become more sophisticated and yield more information from test scores, and techniques of test administration have greatly improved.

Yet problems remain. For example, when you consider the limitations of the test itself, the lack of true zero is apparent. If a student scores zero on a geography test, does this imply no geographical knowledge? Obviously not. It means that knowledge is zero on the geographical material that the particular test was measuring, but it tells us nothing more about the student's geographic information.

The Teacher's Role

Again, how much does the teacher influence the results of any examination? The disciplinary attitude toward measurement, the

TABLE 11.1
Testing Terms: Meanings and Examples

Term	Meaning	Example
Test	Sample of behavior	Arithmetic test
Measurement	Multiple techniques of assessment: tests, observation, ratings	1. Arithmetic test 2. Stanford-Binet IQ test 3. Behavior Rating Scale
Evaluation	Use of tests and measurements to make qualitative judgments	Because of these data, many students should not take advanced algebra
Standardized test	Test commercially prepared under uniform conditions	Scholastic Aptitude Test
Teacher-made test	Paper-and-pencil test constructed by teacher	What are the characteristics of a good test?
Norm-referenced test	Test that compares one student with all others taking it	Scholastic Aptitude Test
Criterion-referenced test	Test that provides information about mastery of objectives	Although mainly teacher constructed, commercial publishers are now entering the field
Reliability	Is the test consistent in its results?	Student achieves similar scores on alternate forms of test, or on taking the same test after some time interval
Validity	Does the test measure what it says it measures?	Teach the Jefferson presidency; test the Jefferson presidency

"life or death" view, or the indifferent approach, influence results. The testing milieu has not yet been subjected to the complete control that measurement experts desire. As continued efforts add to knowledge of the classroom's psychological atmosphere, testing itself will undoubtedly improve.

But the individual remains the chief variable in our analysis of measurement problems. A student's knowledge is not the primary concern. The most worrisome element is the opportunity to demonstrate knowledge. In teacher-made tests, the student's outlook on testing is important. If, as Cronbach (1970) says, the test is elevated into *the* measure of achievement, the learning process is distorted. He believes that tests that tell what needs to be reviewed, or where the student can next progress, are constructive and serve a valuable motivational purpose. But tests that are given because the class is through with a certain topic are appropriate only for Judgment Day.

Problems in test construction

Issues about testing are not the only measurement problems. Any test constructor faces two major problems: determining what to measure and deciding how to measure it. Both of these obstacles are carefully considered in the good test.

What to Test

The question of what to test implies that the test must measure what was taught. To the degree that test constructors are successful in endeavors to relate test items to what was taught, to that same degree will their test be reliable and valid. For teacher-made tests, you may question whether there is any difficulty in testing what was taught. After all, students were exposed to the same teacher, methods, and materials. The answer is not that simple.

Temporarily ignoring the conditions of testing—classroom atmosphere, student health, and related factors—the test itself may fail to assess a student's learning. Did you know why you were teaching—that is, were the objectives stated in behavioral terms that permitted measurement? Did the test adequately sample the material that was taught—did it stress the content that you emphasized as important? Some teachers have a distressing habit of accentuating certain aspects of a subject and then testing other sections. This supposedly insures broader coverage. Yet it is obviously unfair to the pupil. Did you construct items that concentrated only upon a small amount of the material that was taught? Are the items comprehensible to the student?

What Kind of Test?

Focusing upon test items, other problems become apparent. The essay test, for example, allows students to express their own ideas in a creative fashion and permits them to demonstrate such elements as organization and grasp of a subject and its application to a particular problem. It is also deceptively easy to construct. But it samples only a limited amount of material, favors the articulate student, and is difficult to mark.

Conversely, the objective test samples much more subject matter than the essay examination, has greater objectivity of scoring, and reduces the verbal element in a student's response. But it is unwieldly in the measurement of problem solving and creative behavior, emphasizes factual information, frequently promotes guessing, and is time consuming to prepare.

Determining what to measure and deciding how to measure it thus remain real obstacles for the teacher. Ebel (1965, pg. 14) urges teachers to avoid absolute standards. If most students receive an A on a test, or almost all fail another test, you can assume that the test is at fault. Often teachers postpone constructing a test until the last moment, with the result that the test is hastily written and inadequate to sample a student's attainment of objectives. Ebel (1965, pg. 15) also warns instructors to beware of the trivial and ambiguous.

What can you conclude from recognition of measurement error?

Accept Limitations

You should accept the possibility of error, but not let it paralyze you. Achieve as much as possible using existing tools—both standardized and objective. With this attitude you will use an instrument as skillfully as possible. Consciously try to eliminate, or at least minimize, those conditions that cause error; both you (your teaching) and your students (their learning) will benefit.

Discussion Questions

1. Do you believe that the halo effect exists? Have you ever been the recipient of this attitude? Did it affect your achievement or your relations with peers? Since it is a common weakness, what would you do to avoid it?

2. Brophy and Good's analysis of the influences on evaluation is alarming. Do you agree with them? Why? Be specific and furnish examples.

3. Controversy rages about tests; some critics even urge that schools and teachers should abolish tests. Considering both weaknesses (Brophy and Good's inherent measurement problems) and strengths (Chauncey and Dobbin), what is your attitude? How would you defend it against an opponent?

4. Distinguish among these terms: test, measurement, evaluation. Give examples of each. How are they related? What is the role of each in a school-wide evaluation program?

5. Be sure you understand the distinction between norm-referenced and criterion-referenced tests. Which do you believe is more beneficial to *students?* Why? Explain the strengths and weaknesses of each.

6. What is your reaction to mastery learning? If you favor it, indicate what it means for *bright* students. If you oppose it, indicate what it means for slow students. Consider your answer carefully—there are serious and far-reaching consequence to these decisions.

Measuring ability

There is frequently considerable confusion about the term "ability" or "aptitude." Does it refer to some general ability, a global capacity of the individual that is designated as intelligence? Or does it refer to a range of special abilities: musical, artistic, mechanical, verbal? Here, when you see ability or aptitude, it is used to signify a student's general ability or intelligence.

THE NATURE OF INTELLIGENCE: AN OVERVIEW

Intelligence testing became popular with Alfred Binet's work. At the turn of the century Parisian school officials were determined to identify those pupils who either could not or would not learn. Realizing that teachers' judgments were fallible, the schools turned to Alfred Binet for some reliable method to distinguish between the two categories. Binet then was the director of the Laboratory of Physiological Psychology at the Sorbonne and had long been interested in both child and abnormal psychology. In 1905 he published, with Theophile Simon, his former student, a set of tests designed to measure general intelligence. Binet himself revised it in 1908 and 1911, and Terman adapted it for American use in 1916 as the now famous Stanford-Binet test. More than 60 years after its initial publication (with significant modification) it still remains the standard by which all other tests are measured.

Cronbach (1970) declares that Binet solved four problems that every test designer faces: what to measure, items to measure it, a measuring unit, and validity. For Binet, what to measure meant, "What is intelligence?" He was unimpressed with the prevailing theory of intelligence. The nineteenth century was dominated by faculty psychology, which assumed the mind was composed of distinct faculties, such as perception, memory, imagination, attention, and reasoning. Faculty psychology became so influential that the question was not whether mental faculties existed but how many there were.

Binet abandoned the notion of these separate functions in favor of the concept of general intelligence. He discovered that youngsters who did well on tests of judgment also did well on memory, vocabulary, and so forth. Thus there seems to be some unifying thread connecting them—the idea of *general intelligence*. Binet wished to tap the higher mental abilities because he felt that intellect consists of judgment, common sense, initiative, and the ability to adapt oneself.

Although his test measured judgment, memory, and vocabulary, he did not conceive of a segmented intellect whose parts could be measured separately. More accurate assessment would measure the combined effects of reasoning, judgment, imagination, and attention on complex tasks. One of Binet's great legacies was his assumption that in the selection of tests it makes little difference what kind of tasks are employed provided that in some way they are a measure of the child's general intelligence.

David Wechsler

Dissatisfied with the Binet scale because of its limitations with adults, David Wechsler, a clinical psychologist at New York's Bellevue Hospital, felt the need of an instrument that could more precisely identify the subnormal adult. Like Binet, he also had to make certain assumptions about intelligence. From clinical data Wechsler concluded that adult intelligence differs from intelligence at age 15 or 16. The intelligence level appears to drop after the early twenties, which caused Wechsler to formulate his theory of mental deterioration.

Wechsler agreed with Binet about general ability but believed that individuals vary in different abilities. Wechsler stated that intelligence is global because it explains the person's behavior as a whole, and it is also an aggregate because it consists of abilities that are dependent but qualitatively different.

Yet intelligence is not the mere sum of these abilities. Wechsler gives three reasons for this.

IQ as a Global Concept

1. Intelligent behavior is more than a function of the number and qualities of abilities; it also depends upon the way in which these abilities are combined.
2. More than intellectual ability is involved—for example, drive and incentive.
3. An excess of any intellectual ability seems to add little to the efficiency of behavior as a whole.

Wechsler believed that intellectual ability is decisive only as a necessary minimum. Beyond a certain point any ability does not aid in personal adjustment. But theorists can only evaluate intelligence by measuring the various abilities. Wechsler compares this with existing knowledge of electricity: electricity is not identified with the methods of measuring it. Like electricity, general intelligence is a kind of energy: its ultimate nature may be unknown, but its presence is inferred by the things people do. Wechsler concludes that intelligence is no simple quantity that may be expressed by a single factor such as general ability, or *g*. Intelligence is this and more. It is the ability to use this energy in meaningful responses to life's situations.

INTELLIGENCE TESTS

Binet and Wechsler also devised highly original ways of testing intelligence. Controversy about these and other intelligence tests has raged fiercely for several years and today shows no sign of relenting. The chief criticism is that they penalized certain parts of the population, such as those with language problems and the culturally deprived. A school system that places great emphasis upon IQ test scores, and little else, could assign potentially bright students to a slow group and assume that this is their proper level throughout school. The damage done to such pupils may last a lifetime. Although these cases are becoming less frequent because of greater sophistication about the tests, the issue remains. The basic question is: What do IQ tests measure?

Our concern here is more with the test itself. If one student has

Race and IQ: The Jensen Controversy

One of the fiercest controversies swirling around intelligence tests is the racial interpretation of test scores. Until 1969, there was general agreement that while both heredity and environment contributed to intelligence scores, when socially disadvantaged youths scored poorly, environment probably was the chief cause. This was especially true of black youngsters. But then Arthur Jensen stated in the *Harvard Educational Review* that blacks consistently scored 15 points lower than whites on IQ tests. What infuriated many observers was his further assumption that 80 percent of our intelligence is determined by heredity. Thus, racial differences in intelligence test scores are genetic differences. The issue suddenly became one of racial superiority or inferiority.

Jensen skillfully used examples of how genetic defects depressed IQ scores, and also used studies of monozygotic (identical) twins to build a strong, statistical case. But the twin studies have long aroused skepticism, today more so than ever, because of the possible fraudulent basis of some of the seminal studies.

He also ignored the great environmental studies, particularly the Skeels (1966) work, that clearly demonstrated how an enriched environment can positively influence IQ. Bloom (1964), analyzing the major longitudinal studies, concluded that an extremely depressed environment can depress IQ scores by about 20 points.

And so the battle rages unchecked—heredity or environment—which is more decisive? But if we can momentarily narrow the focus of the controversy for our purposes in this chapter, we can raise an interesting and critical question. If environment *can* change IQ scores, what does the intelligence test measure: ability or achievement?

a reading difficulty, does this mean that he is less intelligent than another student who is a better reader? Obviously the answer is no, and much of the present criticism of intelligence tests is directed at this inconsistency.

Critics claim that intelligence tests measure learning, not capacity. This is especially true of the verbal intelligence test, and it is the main reason that testers are devoting more time to construction of nonverbal intelligence tests in which they hope to eliminate the interference of language in assessing capacity. Another criticism of the tests involves the influence of cultural differences. Admittedly, students from different cultures may have a language problem, but there are even more obstacles in the accurate measurement of their intelligence. Their backgrounds often differ from those of most middle- and upper-class students. But if the intelligence test refers to anything cultural, culturally different persons are penalized, not because of any intellectual deficiency but because of experiential shortcomings.

Qualities of intelligence tests

These examples help to explain the current unhappiness with intelligence tests. Some school systems have gone so far as to eliminate intelligence test scores from pupils' records. Whether this is wise remains to be seen. Rather than ban intelligence tests, a more reasonable solution would be to accept both the worth and limitations of these tests and to interpret scores correctly.

Criticism of Intelligence Testing

Some indication of a pupil's capacity to learn is necessary and involves two main issues. First, what is intelligence? Although theorists disagree about the nature of intelligence, there is agreement that intelligence exists because of the things that people can do. They learn to tie shoes, speak a language, and master an occupational skill. Second, what is the best method of measuring this capacity to learn? Although evidence suggests that intelligence is more than a mere collection of parts, the way to measure it is to assess various examples of behavior.

Perhaps now the problem of language difficulties and cultural deprivation is more apparent. Good intelligence tests correlate highly with the ability to comprehend and the ability to learn, both of which are highly dependent upon experience. Nonverbal tests attempted to eliminate cultural biases but they have received a mixed reaction. Mehrens and Lehmann (1975) believe that they are less useful measures than those that are environmentally influenced. Wechsler (1966) claims that the results of these tests have restricted application because they correlate poorly with verbal aptitudes and are also poor predictors of learning ability and school achievement. Unfortunately these tests have not proven to be free of cultural influences. Pictures and symbols all acquire meaning, and performance items tend to become measures of special abilities rather than measures of general intelligence.

Although criticisms of intelligence tests are often accurate and justified as a warning against overemphasis, these tests still provide an indication of an individual's capacity to learn, adjust, adapt, think abstractly, or solve problems.

Individual intelligence tests

The development of the first Binet-Simon scale was previously traced. The 1905 scale, consisting of 30 items, was revised in 1908 and 1911. There were several American versions of the test; one of the first of these was Goddard's translation in 1911. The most lasting revision, prepared by Lewis Terman in 1916 at Stanford University, is commonly called the Stanford-Binet. Anastasi (1976, pg. 191) remarks that Terman and his associates revised the tests so thoroughly that they virtually constructed a new test. The original version of the Stanford-Binet was revised in 1937 and 1960.

The Stanford-Binet Test

Although Terman died in 1956, the 1960 manual retains his

name as one of the authors, with Maud Merrill. In discussing the 1916 revision, these authors (1960, pg. 5) state that the original revision incorporated the essential features of the Binet scales: the use of age standards, various types of mental functions, and the fundamental belief in a general intelligence that is measurable. The 1916 edition presented tests that were arranged according to difficulty by age levels and provided standards of intellectual performance from age 3 to 16. An individual's achievement on this test was expressed as mental age scores, which then could be converted into an IQ.

To illustrate the kind of content employed in the 1960 edition, two age levels are presented here.

For the 5-year-old:

1. *Picture completion: Man.* The subject is presented an incomplete drawing of a man and asked to fill in the missing parts.
2. *Paper folding: Triangle.* The tester takes a 6-inch square of paper, folds it into a triangle, and then folds it into a smaller triangle. The subject is then asked to duplicate the tester's actions.
3. *Definitions.* The subject is asked the meaning of *ball, hat,* and *stove.*
4. *Copying a square.* The child is given three trials to reproduce a square that he or she is shown.
5. *Pictorial similarities and differences II.* The subject is presented with 12 picture cards and asked to discover whether the objects on each card are similar or different.
6. *Patience: Rectangles.* The subject is given two rectangular cards, one of which is divided diagonally into two triangles and then asked to join the two cut pieces and form a triangle.

For the average adult:

1. *Vocabulary.* The subject is asked the meaning of a list of 40 possible words. The subject is asked to define each until 6 consecutive words are failed. The words range in difficulty from *orange* to *sudorific* and *parterre.*
2. *Ingenuity.* The subject is presented with oral problems and asked to reason to their solution.
3. *Differences between abstract words.* What is the difference between *laziness* and *idleness, poverty* and *misery, character* and *reputation?*
4. *Arithmetic reasoning.* The subject is asked to solve three arithmetic problems without paper and pencil. The difficulty of the problems is as follows: at 15 cents a yard how much will 7 feet of cloth cost?
5. *Proverbs I.* The subject is expected to tell the meaning of certain proverbs. For example: "Don't judge a book by its cover."
6. *Orientation: Direction II.* The subject is expected to reason di-

The IQ

For Binet, the notion of mental age was vital. Normal children should be able to do the same things that others of their age normally do. For this theoretically normal person, the IQ would be 100, which is determined by dividing mental age by chronological age. If the test yields a mental age of 10 years, 6 months, and a youngster's chronological age is 10 years, 6 months, the IQ is 100.

A. $IQ = \dfrac{MA}{CA} \times 100$

B. $IQ = \dfrac{10 \text{ years, 6 months}}{10 \text{ years, 6 months}} \times 100$

C. $IQ = \dfrac{126 \text{ months}}{126 \text{ months}} \times 100 = 100$

If the mental age is greater than the chronological age, the student is above normal; if the mental age is less than the chronological age, the pupil is below normal. For example, if a student's mental age is 12 years, 10 months, with a chronological age of 11 years, the IQ is as follows:

A. $IQ = \dfrac{MA}{CA} \times 100$

B. $IQ = \dfrac{12 \text{ years, 10 months}}{11 \text{ years}}$

C. $IQ = \dfrac{154}{132} \times 100 = 116$

Or the pupil whose mental age is 8 years, 6 months, and whose chronological age is 10 years:

A. $IQ = \dfrac{MA}{CA} \times 100$

B. $IQ = \dfrac{8 \text{ years, 6 months}}{10 \text{ years}}$

C. $IQ = \dfrac{102}{120} = 85$

The 1916 version was immensely popular since it tried to measure a functional intelligence, had been standardized on a fairly large sample, and offered detailed instructions for its administration. But as the test was widely used, several deficiencies appeared. It was not adequate below the age of 4, and at adult levels, the standardization population was too restricted geographically, and too few subjects were tested. These defects combined to stimulate the 1937 revision.

This was a comprehensive revision by Terman and Merrill of Terman's 1916 work, while still retaining the essential features of Binet's original scale. It assumed the existence of a general intelligence and used age standards as its criteria. The same kinds of test items were employed: analogies, opposites, comprehension, vocabulary, similarities and differences, verbal and pictorial completions, absurdities, drawing designs, and memory items. Two scales were furnished, Form L and Form M, which differed in content but were mutually equivalent (Terman and Merrill, 1937, pg. 3).

In the 1960 revision the authors combined Forms L and M of the 1937 edition. They (1960, pg. 20) state that there was less need for an alternate form in 1960 because other individual intelligence tests were available. The 1960 revision again contained the chief characteristics of the Binet Scale (an age scale designed to measure individual intelligence).

rection from an oral description. For example: Suppose you are going east, then turn to your right; in what direction are you going now?

7. *Essential differences.* The subject is expected to distinguish between such concepts as ability and achievement.

8. *Abstract words III.* The subject is asked the meaning of such words as *generosity, independent, envy, authority,* and *justice.*

Through the years the Standford-Binet has been one of the outstanding predictors of an individual's ability to learn. Properly administered and interpreted, it can be an invaluable instrument.

The other significant individual intelligence test was devised by David Wechsler. There are three forms of Wechsler's tests:

The Wechsler Tests

1. The Wechsler Adult Intelligence Scale (WAIS)
2. The Wechsler Intelligence Scale for Children (WISC)
3. The Wechsler Preschool and Primary Scale of Intelligence (WPPSI)

With these scales, Wechsler believes that intelligence can be measured throughout anyone's lifetime from 4 years to old age. The Wechsler is not an age scale. It consists of subtests, each of which yields a point score. The subtest scores are converted into standard scores, which can then be expressed as an IQ.

The 1955 WAIS consists of 11 subtests; 6 of these subtests comprise the verbal scale, and 5 the performance scale. Three IQ scores are thus derived: a verbal IQ, a performance IQ, and a total IQ. The separation into verbal and performance scale is especially valuable for diagnostic purposes.

Originally Wechsler was unhappy with existing methods of measuring adult intelligence, and in 1939 his first adult intelligence scale was published under the name of the Wechsler-Bellevue Intelligence Scale. One of the major difficulties of the initial scale was its standardization sample. There were 1081 subjects chosen from the city and state of New York, ranging in age from 7 to 70, and this immediately raised questions about the use of New Yorkers as a standard for the rest of the country. Some of the female subjects were parents of children brought to the Bellevue Mental Hygiene Clinic; others were volunteers solicited from Coney Island beach. This population was sufficiently questionable to make anyone familiar with tests decidedly uneasy.

An attempt was made to remedy these defects in the 1955 scale by using a representative national sample for its standardization. The test was lengthened, which also increased its reliability. A brief description of the subtests follows (1–6 verbal, 7–11 performance).

1. *Information.* There are 29 questions designed to sample knowledge that the normal adult in our society is expected to possess.

2. *Comprehension.* There are 14 of these items that require subjects to state what they would do under circumstances that could be anticipated in daily living.

3. *Arithmetic reasoning.* There are 14 problems involving basic arithmetic. It is a good sign of mental alertness, and subjects who do poorly in arithmetic reasoning frequently experience other difficulties.

4. *Similarities.* There are 13 items that require an identification of likeness. It is simple to administer, interesting to adults, seems to assess general intelligence, and offers reliable clues to an individual's thought processes.

5. *Memory span for digits.* Digits are presented orally, which the subject reproduces, first in regular sequence and then backward.

6. *Vocabulary.* Forty words are presented and the subject is asked the meaning of each. A person's vocabulary indicates not only schooling, but also general intelligence, because the words anyone knows reflect learning ability, verbal information, and the extent of ideas.

7. *Digit symbol test.* This is essentially a substitution test, long popular with psychologists. Subjects must associate certain symbols with other symbols, and their speed and accuracy provide a good measure of intelligence. Symbols must be associated with digits.

8. *Picture completion.* There are 21 pictures, each with some part missing. The subject must discover and name the missing part.

9. *Block design.* Subjects must duplicate designs of increasing difficulty, using red and white cubes. This test correlates well with total score and individual items, and was the best performance item since it seems to combine both analytical and synthetic skill.

10. *Picture arrangement.* The subject must arrange a series of pictures to tell a story. The pictures are quite similar to the comics in the newspapers. It is a suitable sign of an individual's ability to respond to the totality of any problem, and Wechsler also stated that it signifies social intelligence.

11. *Object assembly.* The subject is required to unite the parts of a hand or profile. This test has a particular qualitative appeal because it reveals much of the subject's thinking and working habits.

The Wechsler scales are highly regarded. Because of the distinction between verbal and performance scale, they also enable the tester to diagnose mental problems that are hindering performance.

Group intelligence tests

While individual intelligence tests are the best measuring and diagnostic instruments now available, they are both costly and time consuming. Consequently group intelligence tests are used more frequently in the schools. Their popularity has grown since the Army Alpha (verbal) and the Army Beta (nonverbal) were used in World War I for screening and placement. Since more than one million recruits had to be classified quickly, some reliable device was needed to facilitate this process.

The American Psychological Association appointed a committee under the guidance of Robert Yerkes to determine how the psychological profession could help in the war effort. From this interest, with its accompanying military need, the first group intelligence test emerged. After the war these tests were cleared for civilian use just as the value of testing was recognized in America. The Alpha and Beta was revised frequently and became the model for other group intelligence tests.

1. *Pintner General Ability Tests—Verbal Series.* This battery contains group intelligence tests from the kindergarten level through the freshman year of college. Thorndike and Hagen (1977) report that the test has good reliability, an excellent manual, and five methods of interpreting scores, but its administration is more demanding than for other group tests.

2. *Otis-Lennon Mental Ability Tests.* This is one of the most popular series of tests used in the public schools. There are tests available that extend from first grade through college. Reliability is good, the tests predict academic achievement, they yield a single IQ, and are easy to administer and score.

3. *The Lorge-Thorndike Intelligence Tests.* Tests are furnished that range from grades 1 to 12. The tests through third grade are nonverbal; the other tests give both verbal and nonverbal scores. It is thought to be among the best of the group intelligence tests because standardization techniques and norms are superior. Anastasi (1976) states that the intent of the authors was to measure abstract intelligence, which they define as the ability to work with ideas and the relationship among ideas.

4. *Terman-McNermar Tests of Mental Ability.* This is a widely used and carefully constructed test that was prepared specifically for the high school level. It is entirely a verbal test consisting of seven subtests: information, synonyms, logical selection, classification, analogies, opposites, and best answer. Thorndike and Hagen (1977) observe that it is a well-standardized and well-constructed measure of verbal ability.

Group tests are undoubtedly less interesting and decidedly restrict a subject's answers, both of which will affect performance. Although group intelligence tests are both convenient and time saving, they yield less accurate scores for individuals than do the individual tests. You should use and interpret them with considerable caution.

Using ability tests

Oliver Wendell Holmes once said that there were no more than 500 "civilized" people in the world. Houts (1976) uses this quote to question the meaning of intelligence, as others could question Holmes's use of civilized. He argues that intelligence tests are indistinguishable from achievement tests, and they may damage a child if accepted as a final judgment. A major problem as mentioned in the Jensen discussion is that while IQ scores are supposedly *individual* scores, we frequently employ them to make *group* judgments.

Houts believes that no one should interpret current criticism of standardized tests as an attempt to abandon assessment. Rather, it is an attempt to develop new assessment techniques that will meet new societal objectives: education's purpose is not to sort people, but to educate them; not to eliminate people, but to educate as many as possible; not to isolate groups, but to enrich society *because* of racial diversity.

What, then, are desirable purposes of standardized testing? Mehrens and Lehmann (1975) believe that there are four types of educational decisions—instructional, guidance, administrative, and research—and that standardized tests should help formulate these decisions.

Measuring achievement

Achievement tests are devised to permit students to demonstrate what they can do with the information, skills, and ideas they are supposed to have learned in school. The ability tests discussed are intended to measure intellectual skills that have been acquired over years from many sources; the achievement test measures skills acquired over short periods of time in *school*.

How can the characteristics of the good test be applied to those instruments that teachers construct? Validity, reliability, and practicality are, more often than not, lacking when a teacher decides it is time for a test and sits down to write a series of questions in 10 or 15 minutes. Tests possess desirable characteristics only after careful consideration.

TEST CONSTRUCTION

The "good" test is the product of a series of steps that usually follow this pattern:

1. *Planning the test.* The first step in planning the test is to recall the objectives of the unit or subject. (You might want to review the objectives section of Chapter 1.) Will this instrument give evidence of the degree to which the students have achieved these goals? What exactly is the purpose of this test? Is it a pretest to discover weaknesses and strengths, or will the results be used as a basis for evaluating a pupil's academic achievement? How many and what kind of questions should be used? Does the test reflect the emphasis of instruction? These are some of the questions that you should answer in this planning stage.

2. *Preparing the test.* One of the best methods to use in preparing a test is to prepare questions as you teach a lesson. Certain items will be of more interest or need additional work, or be of more importance, and no one but you can determine what material is of greatest importance to your class. A variety of items designed to hold student interest is a desirable goal in test construction. More items than are necessary should be prepared so that you can eliminate those that are least suitable in the final draft. You should also remember to group the various items such as true-false or multiple choice.

Finally, you should be certain that the correct answers come by chance, not by arrangement. For example, in the true-false section, true and false answers should not alternate regularly. Students sense any pattern, and the test then does not adequately sample behavior.

3. *Administering the test.* You should administer the test in a simple and relaxed manner. Directions should be such that pupils understand exactly what is required, and the length of time permitted. The test conditions should be as ideal as possible.

4. *Evaluating the test.* Stanley (1964, pg. 200) states that test evaluation should have two purposes: to determine the quality of the test itself and to determine the quality of the pupil's responses. Did the test serve its purpose? Does it indicate to what extent students have attained objectives? Did each item show roughly the desired 50 percent level of difficulty? Did it discriminate between high and low pupils, and did the results match external criteria that the teacher has? The answers to these questions will help you to discover just how effective is the instrument that you have devised.

THE ESSAY TEST

In planning your test you will decide what type of item best demonstrates to what degree your students have attained the desired objectives, and also what items will discriminate them. Teachers have long claimed advantages for the essay examination that are not subject to either proof or disproof. Whether they evaluate higher thought processes more effectively than the objective test is an unsolved question. That there are advantages as well as disadvantages is apparent; and, since teachers place so much value upon it, the essay test remains the most widely used classroom test and deserves careful study and thought.

Because they are so widely used, Thorndike and Hagen (1977, pg. 266) state that the value of the essay question for assessing pupils' ability to use information, to organize materials, or to use language effectively depends not only on writing appropriate questions but also on structuring the situation so that other elements do not obstruct the desired appraisal. For example, insufficient time may restrict a student's response. To help you avoid these pitfalls, the authors suggest that you:

1. *Determine the cognitive operations you want the pupils to use and understand the kind of response that represents these abilities.* For example, if a political science teacher wants students to think critically about election processes, then an essay question should force students to weigh rhetoric against fact, to question emotional appeals to an electorate, and to examine conflicting interpretations of issues. Responses should reflect these criteria.

2. *Phrase your questions so that they demand some novelty in students' responses.* A common student complaint is that essay questions have them reproduce material; novelty in the question can prevent charges of a lack of originality. As the authors state, if you begin questions with "compare," "contrast," "predict," "illustrate," students are compelled to select, organize, and use their knowledge (Thorndike and Hagen, 1977, pg. 265).

3. *Write essay questions that clearly and unambiguously define the students' task.* For example, "Discuss the organizations that contribute to the health of the community," is poorly phrased. What does "discuss" mean? Does it mean list, criticize, or evaluate? What kind of organizations? What type of contributions? Thorndike and Hagen state that this, and similar items, force students to guess.

4. *Consider carefully your students' maturity when you devise questions and be certain that your question specifies the behavior you want.* If you phrase your questions accurately you will help your pupils to display what they really know, and you will make your scoring of the answers easier and more exact.

There is general agreement that the validity and reliability of the instrument is improved if the test is lengthened. Carefully controlled questions, which limit the time and also the length of a pupil's responses, are helpful as they allow a greater number of items to be incorporated into the test. The obvious danger is that you may construct an instrument similar to an objective test after you originally decided that an essay test was more suitable.

The pertinence and phrasing of the question is critical in an essay test, which is one of the reasons that the construction of such a

442   THE LEARNER AND LEARNING

The Essay Test: Pros and Cons

The advantages of the essay test are:

1. It is fairly easy to construct.
2. It may be administered simply; questions may be written on the blackboard.
3. It emphasizes wholes rather than parts.
4. It better illustrates a pupil's ability to recall, organize, reorganize, and apply knowledge. Also, a pupil's expression of ideas may well reflect learning that is impossible to measure objectively.

The disadvantages of the essay examination are:

1. Its validity is questionable because of the small amount of material it samples.
2. Teachers often are tempted to grade other factors than content, for example, spelling or grammar. Also, if a student is more articulate than his or her classmates, it is often troublesome to distinguish between fact and form.
3. The difficulty of scoring the answers to essay questions is tremendous. Study after study has shown the wide difference among teachers in grading essay tests. It is a true saying that students often pass or fail essay tests depending on who marks the paper and who takes the test.

Essay tests will continue to be used widely so you should be aware of several precautionary steps that you can take to insure effective essay questions. Probably most important is to realize under what conditions the essay test may be better used than the objective examination. Before you can make a sound judgment about the suitability of conditions you should know the various kinds of essay questions and the purposes they serve. A classic source is Weidmann (1933, 1941) who classifies essay questions as follows:

1. Who, what, when, which, where
2. List
3. Outline
4. Describe
5. Contrast
6. Compare
7. Explain
8. Discuss
9. Develop
10. Summarize
11. Evaluate

test is deceptively simple. It is probably more difficult to construct high-quality essay tests than objective tests because it is more difficult to insure that the characteristics of the good test are present.

In improving essay tests, however, most of the specialists' time and thought have been given to improving scoring procedures. Authorities agree that the following principles facilitate the scoring of an essay test:

1. Be sure that you do not know whose paper you are scoring.
2. Score one item at a time on all tests.

3. If any other behavior is to be scored, it should be done separately from the content of the test.
4. If the results of a test are crucial for any reason, have another person score the test, or do it a second time yourself.

Other suggestions would be to know exactly what is needed in the answer—that is, attempt to have several specific points that the student must mention to achieve the maximum score. To insure that all students take the same examination, avoid the use of optional questions. If you recall these warnings in the construction and scoring of essay tests, your tests will be more precise tools in the measurement of learning.

THE OBJECTIVE TEST

There are purposes for which objective tests are better suited than the essay examination. Their range of coverage in a relatively brief period and the objectivity of scoring make them an attractive tool, although the time and care that must go into the construction of the items are also recognized. One of the major criticisms constantly directed at the objective test is its apparent emphasis on fragmented, factual knowledge. Recognizing the justice of this criticism, psychologists and educators have labored to devise test items that sample a depth of knowledge far more extensively than tests which formerly measured only factual information. Nevertheless, you cannot ignore the purpose for which the test is designed. A teacher may need to ascertain the amount of factual material students possess before attempting instruction in a more advanced unit. Or comprehension or analysis may be the purpose. The type of test must suit the purpose of the teacher. Convenience should not be the decisive element.

Most teachers will use a variety of items to serve their purpose. Objective items may be classified into two general categories.

1. The supply type (free response, simple recall, completion).
2. The selection type (alternative response, multiple choice, matching).

The supply type usually asks a question, or leaves a sentence incomplete, and the student must furnish his or her own answer. The selection type of item restricts the student's possibilities of answers to those that are presented in the item.

Supply items

The simple recall items and the completion item are fundamentally the same. In both instances, the subject responds with either one or a few words. The simple recall type usually takes the form of a direct question, while the completion item normally is presented in a sentence with one or several key words missing. For example:

1. Who is the present president of the United States?
2. The next election for president of the United States will be held in the year —————— .

Great care is needed to have directions sufficiently clear so that pupils know exactly what is expected without "leading" them. Remember to avoid textbook language, word questions to offer only one possible correct answer, and avoid excessive blanks in completion items.

Selection items

The more common alternative response item is the *true-false, right-wrong, yes-no* variety. A declarative sentence is the usual form of a true-false item, and the subject indicates whether the statement is *T* (true) or *F* (false).

Directions: Mark each of the following statements true or false. If the statement is true, circle the *T;* if it is false, circle the *F.*
T F Jimmy Carter became president of the United States in 1977.

Since these items are factual, students will often guess. So, when you use true and false items:

1. Again, avoid textbook language.
2. Avoid clue words, such as "always," "never."
3. Balance the number of true and false statements.

The *multiple-choice* item presents students with a question or incomplete statement and several possible responses, one of which is correct (unless more than one response to each item is permitted, which is the *multiple-response* type). The typical multiple-choice item reads as follows:

Directions: For each of the following questions, there are several possible answers. Select the response that you think is correct for each question, and write the number of that answer in the blank space to the right of the question.
1. Who is considered to be the "father" of classical behaviorism?
   a. Lewin
   b. Watson
   c. Skinner
   d. Thorndike

The multiple-choice item is thought to be the best of the objective items. When it is used the direct question is the preferred form; at least four possible responses are needed (all of which should be plausible); all answers require consistency and equal length.

The *matching test* usually utilizes two columns, each item in the first column to be matched with an item in the second column. A typical matching item is the following:

Directions: Below are two lists, one containing the names of individual psychologists, the other the names of schools of psychology. Match the individual with a school of psychology by writing the number of the school before the name of the appropriate individual in the space provided.

_____ Watson	1. Gestalt
_____ Skinner	2. Functionalism
_____ Thorndike	3. Dynamic psychology
_____ Koffka	4. Behaviorism
_____ Woodworth	5. Topological
	6. Connectionism
	7. Programming
	8. Structualism
	9. Contiguity

In writing the matching item, the instructions should be simple, clear, and precise; otherwise they can confuse students. Also include more than the required number of responses, keep homogeneous material in both columns, and keep the list of responses fairly short. The matching item is best suited for a test of factual material.

Objective items should be selected for a particular purpose, carefully written to suit the appropriate reading level of a class, and free from ambiguity. You must rely on your own judgment, based on your knowledge of a class, to allot sufficient time for the objective test. There is no other reliable guide, although a rule of thumb is 100 true-false items or 75 multiple-choice items are appropriate for a 50-minute period. Ross and Stanley (1954) quote Ruch (1929) as suggesting that for factual material three recall or four recognition items per minute are reasonable; for more comprehensive items the rate should be one or two recall and two or three recognition items per minute.

As an illustration of the searching and analytical nature of many of today's objective tests, the following selection from Bloom et al. (1956, pg. 156) is offered. These are sample test items from the *Taxonomy of Educational Objectives.*

Items 12 to 14 are based on the following paragraph:

(1) Hamlet is given a command by the ghost of his murdered father to take vengeance upon the murderer, Claudius. (2) He is not able to do so immediately because he does not have sufficient proof that Claudius has murdered his father. (3) In the process of finding this proof, Hamlet unwittingly allows the king to discover his suspicions. (4) As the action proceeds, Hamlet cannot take vengeance because he never has a real opportunity to do so. (5) As the action ends, Hamlet becomes involved in a duel arranged by Claudius which has as its consequence the death of the hero and his adversary, as well as the more important of the subordinate characters.

12. A discussion and evaluation of the statement given above would revolve most around the points made in
    a. Sentence 1.
    b. Sentences 2 and 3.
    c. Sentences 2 and 4.
    d. Sentence 5.

13. Assume, temporarily, complete agreement with the statement. In discussing various parts of the play, which among the following would you tend to minimize?
    a. Hamlet's interview with the ghost in Act I.
    b. The lapse of time between Acts I and II.
    c. The play within the play.
    d. Hamlet's departure for England.
    e. The short lapse of time between the play within the play and Hamlet's departure for England.

14. Which of the following statements about Hamlet is least inconsistent with the general position taken in the statement?
    a. Hamlet is a man of action.
    b. Hamlet is by nature a meditative person, not accustomed to meet problems by direct action.
    c. Hamlet is an intellectual, over whom someone more shrewd even if less learned has the advantage in the world of practical affairs.
    d. Hamlet is normally a sensitive, good-natured person, who, however, during the period covered by the first four acts of the play, is in a state of melancholy—a condition induced by his father's death and accompanied by a great lethargy.

Finally, Bowman (1960) offers several concise steps to aid teachers in the construction of their tests:

1. Determine the real purposes of a unit of work; actually write them out to aid teaching and testing.
2. Decide what specific kinds of behavior manifest attainment of these objectives and are subject to measurement.
3. Familiarize yourself with the different types of test items and with the principles of test construction.

4. Practice writing the various kinds of items. Sample them in class.
5. Keep a record of how pupils respond to each item. The pupils who do well on the entire test should do better on each item than those whose score is lower.
6. Begin a collection of good, discriminatory items.
7. Keep an open mind about the first form of the test. There is no way of telling how easy or difficult a test is until it has been used.

Constructing a good test is not an easy task; it is time consuming, difficult, and even frustrating. But you cannot obtain an accurate appraisal of your students without accurate measurement.

Discussion Questions

1. What do you mean by ability? Does your definition agree with Binet's and Wechsler's? What criteria would you use in defining it?

2. Review the questions that Binet had to answer when he devised his intelligence test. Do you think that these provide adequate guidelines? From reading this section, from your personal test-taking experience, how would you answer these questions — generally or specifically? Give examples.

3. Be sure you understand the Jensen controversy. Again, from your personal knowledge, do you think Jensen underestimated the environment's impact? Why?

4. Now, do you prefer essay or objective tests? Why? If you were the classroom teacher, which would you use? Why? In your answer, state the pros and cons of both.

5. Write several essay questions for this chapter. Have various class members correct them and then compare scores. What do the results tell you about essay tests?

6. Write an objective test for this chapter. Administer and score it. What does preparation, administration, and scoring tell you about objective tests?

Using test data

Some of the purposes of both standardized and teacher-made tests have been mentioned: assessing ability, measuring achievement, determining the degree to which objectives have been attained, and guiding educational divisions. But now it is time to be specific in suggesting how test data are used. Three uses should immediately concern you: marking, grading, and reporting. *Marking* refers to your assessment of a test or an oral or written report; *grading* refers to your evaluation of tests, reports, essays—whatever you assigned for a definite period of time; *reporting* refers to the manner in which you communicate these results to children and parents.

MARKING

Thorndike and Hagen (1977) define a mark—no matter what the educational level—as a judgment of one person by another. You should be concerned with how you mark one test, one book review, one oral discussion. Sometimes your judgment may be informal, as when you discuss an oral report with a student, or mark and comment on an essay examination. Occasionally your mark may be quite mechanical as when you simply total the number of correct items in an objective test and assign marks on the basis of number right. A certain percentage of your class receives an *A, B, C, D,* or *F.*

Marks are usually relative; that is, the marks you assign to the members of one class may differ from the marks you assign to the members of another brighter class. (Here we see one of the reasons that criterion-referenced tests are becoming popular.) The way *you* feel influences your marks. Unfortunately there is considerable evidence to support this conclusion. Imagine yourself with a migraine, or having just received an A in a graduate course—would your marking be identical in both situations? Repeated studies had teachers grade the same essay answers; the results ranged from *A* to failure.

What can you do to improve your marking technique?

1. *Be sure to mark (or somehow indicate) any work you assign.* Nothing frustrates pupils more than spending substantial time on a project and not having teachers react to it. Your assignments are quickly labeled "busy work," and, if done at all, contribute little to learning. The best rule of thumb is: If you assign written work, mark it; if you assign readings, discuss them, so all students feel involved and realize that you always respond to assignments.

2. *Return work immediately or as soon as possible.* Unless students receive reinforcement, they quickly forget, or worse, remember error. Giving a test one day and not returning it for a week or two is poor teaching. If you believe that tests aid teaching and learning then they become an integral part of your work, not something added at the end of a unit or course. If you delay furnishing test results, students find it difficult to use your corrections; too much has happened since the tests. If serious weaknesses are uncovered, but the test was some two weeks ago, students probably should

The Effects of Teachers' Comments

Ellis Page (1958) conducted a famous study of marks and the effects of teacher comments. He wished to determine if teachers' comments improve student performance and which comments were effective. Previous studies had inherent difficulties: outsiders conducted the experiment, tests were contrived to mask the treatment, and praise or reproof was often random (classroom comments are definite and specific). Page's study eliminated these problems by leaving classroom procedures untouched, except for written comments upon the tests.

Seventy-four teachers randomly selected one of their classes to be an experimental group. The total student group consisted of 2139 secondary school students. The teachers initially administered whatever test came next in the course. They then scored the tests as usual—A, B, C, D, or F—and then randomly assigned each paper to one of three groups. The *No Comment* group received a mark and nothing else. The *Free Comment* group received whatever comment the teacher deemed appropriate. The *Specified Comment* group received uniform comments previously designated for each mark.

A. Excellent! Keep it up.
B. Good work. Keep at it.

C. Perhaps try to do still better?
D. Let's bring this up.
F. Let's raise this grade.

The teachers returned the test with no unusual attention.

The effects of these comments were judged by the scores the same pupils achieved on the next usual test. The results were:

1. The *Free Comment* students achieved higher scores than the *Specified Comment* group, which did better than the *No Comment* pupils.
2. The results were consistent for all schools in the sample.
3. Although teachers had expected the better students to profit more from their comments, no evidence supported their expectations.

Page concludes that when secondary school teachers write truthful but encouraging remarks on student papers, they have a measurable and potent effect on students so that learning improves. You would find this study fascinating to read, and it would be well worth your time.

not have commenced new work; if they did well, they could possibly have bypassed the introductory work of the next topic. Think carefully about the timing and return tests.

3. *If possible, personally comment on the test.* If it is an objective test, pupils will appreciate some remark even if only "You did quite well in this test." Essay tests provide more freedom to comment.

4. *Be specific in your comments; telling students they are wrong has* *little effect.* Your comments should indicate precisely where the error is and, if necessary, how to correct it. Tell students exactly where their answers are superior so that they can capitalize on their strengths.

5. *Mark the student's work, not the student.* This chapter has constantly cautioned against the halo effect, which is especially dangerous for objective marking.

6. *Avoid sarcasm, and belittling or ridiculing remarks.* You have the experience, the authority, and power in the classroom. Use it wisely, and not to enhance self-importance. A successful teacher works with students, so be careful of your remarks; they can hurt and discourage sensitive, developing personalities.

7. *You must make a personal decision, which is often based on available time, whether to have pupils repeat their work and correct errors.* Merely mentioning mistakes does not remedy them. If possible, have pupils actually rework their errors after they have determined where they blundered.

GRADING

Most schools insist that teachers periodically grade their pupils, which means that you must judge a student's work for two or three months and decide upon *A* or *B,* 90 or 72. What contributes to the grade? Is it the mere average of all test scores, or should it also include students' attitude, improvement, or participation? Thorndike and Hagen (1977) believe that you can only answer this question by determining the purpose of grading.

The Purpose of Grading

If a grade is intended to indicate competence in algebra, then it should probably consist essentially of marks assigned to subject matter: tests, reports, final examination. Specialized schools or programs can then strictly interpret a grade and judge a student's readiness for a course or program. Such grades are probably characteristic of most secondary schools, while elementary school grades often represent some combination of competence, effort, and general attitude. A combination is difficult to interpret and even at the elementary level it is better to assign a competence grade and to report on attitude, interest, or comprehension in some other way.

Grades as Discipline

One danger in assigning grades, both at the elementary and secondary levels, is the opposite of the halo effect—using grades to discipline or punish the unruly pupil. It can be more subtly done in grading than in marking. If you mark harshly on a test, it is obvious that you are not marking *content.* Something else is influencing the mark. But unless a grade represents competence—and pupils, parents, teachers, and administrators have agreed on this—many other forces will affect the final grade.

In a perceptive essay, Orville Palmer (1962) discusses seven classic ways of grading dishonestly.

1. *Abdicating.* The first, and most indefensible, way of grading dishonestly is by abdication. Some teachers may scorn testing; they refuse to believe it has a purpose in teaching and learning. Consequently they either use hastily devised tests or none at all. It is hard to decide which is more harmful to pupils. With no testing, everyone understands that a course grade represents a teacher's personal opinion; no one is sure of what a disorganized collection of test scores represents.

2. *The "carrots and clubs" system.* This is another dishonest method, wherein grades represent many different things for different teachers: tests, entire course work, spelling mistakes in history tests, and halo effects. Enough has been said of the purpose of grading to alert you to the dangers of marking something other than merit.

3. *Defaulting.* Grading by default was briefly popular in the 1960s when many instructors and schools were reluctant to grade pupils. Many college professors refused to give tests and assigned everyone an *A.* Secondary and elementary teachers gave as few tests as possible. Academic dishonesty soon became apparent because no one could determine how students were prepared for new, more difficult, work. Many pupils, at all levels, found themselves progressing into programs or schools for which they had neither the interest, competence, or ability. Today there is intense national interest in improving all aspects of education: tests, marks, and grades.

4. *Being a zealot.* Test, test, test! These teachers turn their classes into a nightmarish endurance contest. The danger here is so obvious it needs little comment, but consider the possible outcome: student dislike of the course, teacher, and school.

5. *Changing rules in midstream.* The "tough" teacher eases standards; easy markers panic when the principal mentions how well their students are doing. The pattern is reversed; students are bewildered; the learning atmosphere becomes tense and mistrustful.

6. *Psychic testing.* This is an alarming extension of abdication, default, and the halo effect. "They do not require tests; they know who will receive *A*'s or *F*'s." Most students are frightened by this type of teacher, and, in college especially, they will shun the course.

7. *Being a perfectionist.* Some teachers, striving for impossible perfection, inform their class that no one receives an *A* and only geniuses need expect *B.* Failure is rampant.

Unfortunately you have probably experienced one, or several, of the above. To avoid these pitfalls remember: decide specifically what the grade is to represent—have it firmly in mind when you assign grades (this should be a decision accepted by teachers and administrators and communicated to parents); all teachers in a school should participate in determining both what contributes to a grade and what various grades represent: *A* is clearly superior work, *B* is good, *C* is average. If you are a beginning teacher, or if you have transferred to a new system, discover what the testing procedures are and determine what grading system is used and what it means. You will help both your students and yourself and avoid unnecessary unpleasantness.

REPORTING

Report for Whom?

Parents wish to be informed of their children's educational progress, which is probably the rationale for report cards. Children usually know how they are progressing; teachers know; it is only the parents who need this extra communication. You should remember parents' needs in both formulating the report and in any succeeding parent-teacher conference. With this as a guideline, you can use reports to strengthen the link between home and school. Here is the main benefit of any reporting system. Schools and teachers should know how much support they will receive from parents, what advantages or disadvantages the child has, what is the parents' attitude toward education. Parents should know what are the objectives of teachers and schools, how their child meets these objectives, and what they should reasonably expect their child to attain.

Other than informing parents of their children's progress, a reporting system should bring together parents and teachers so that both home and school can combine to encourage and help children. Unfortunately most new teachers dread these conferences. They feel insecure and defensive, especially if the child has earned poor grades. To evade or to be vague can be disastrous. Honest, and *hopeful*, evaluation is the only rule. To portray a child as superior to both ability and performance disserves everyone: parents' expectations are unduly heightened; children quickly sense adult dishonesty; teachers avoid a crucial task. If home and school are to work together, there must be honesty, tempered by mature judgment.

The Parent-Teacher Conference

What to report

No reporting system is completely satisfactory. Either the report of academic progress is slighted (*John is doing very nicely*), or there is excessive emphasis upon a grade (John - C). For example, the traditional report card supplies letter or numerical grades with little interpretation—*A, B, C,* 95, 85, 75. There may be a column where teachers check attitudes as satisfactory or unsatisfactory. Such cards are more typical of elementary than secondary schools.

A-B-C

A less rigid system may use two categories: *satisfactory* or *unsatisfactory*, which provides a less rigid classification. Doubts persist

U-S

Progress or Not?

about such reports. Satisfactory, or unsatisfactory, compared to what? How much realistic information is conveyed to parents in this system?

A third, equally unsatisfactory, technique is to use even broader categories: *John is progressing. John has shown improvement since the last report. It is necessary to discuss John's progress so please arrange a conference.*

Given these conditions, what can you do?

Testing and Society

While evaluation techniques concern you personally, tests, grades, and reporting also have had great social impact and weigh heavily in significant policy decisions. Concluding your work on measurement and evaluation, you should look beyond the classroom and view testing's wider role. Three examples will illustrate the relationship between testing and society.

The National Assessment of Educational Progress (NAEP), which began in 1964, is intended to provide information about the knowledge, skills, concepts, understandings, and attitudes of young Americans, and to measure the achievement changes that occur. Learning skills were tested in reading, writing, mathematics, science, social studies, citizenship, music, art, literature, and career development. Learning is assessed by a wide variety of test items. Some of the early findings are: students from the northeastern section of the country achieve higher than all other geographic areas, while those from the southeastern section are lowest; girls continue to achieve higher than boys except for mathematics and science; the parents' educational level is highly correlated with students' achievement (Ahmann, 1976).

During the 1960s, educators associated with the International Association for the Evaluation of Educational Achievement (IEA) have tested more than a quarter of a million students in 22 countries throughout the world. The results suggest that social class powerfully influences achievement; nevertheless, schooling significantly affects math, science, literature, and second-language learning.

David Cohen and Michael Ganet (1975) analyzing the use of research to reform educational policy conclude that current premises are faulty. They note that since social policy has become big business, its problems have multiplied. While tremendous amounts of money are spent on policy research, little is spent on assessing the consequences of research. Evaluations of Head Start and similar programs raise serious questions about existing early-intervention policy, yet there has been little change in policy. The authors offer the penetrating insight that norm-referenced tests were used to assess these programs. When unexpected results appeared, investigators questioned the tests themselves, which caused the boom in criterion-referenced tests.

While each of these examples is in itself fascinating, what should capture our attention is the major social role played by testing.

1. *It makes no difference what system you prefer; you must use the school's system.* The best advice is to study it thoroughly so that you can report objectively and thoroughly.

2. *Know exactly what constitutes your evaluation of a pupil.* If you assign a C, or 75, or satisfactory, or progressing normally, be sure that you realize exactly what contributes to the grade: tests, home assignments, class participation, library research, and reports.

3. *Beware of personal opinion in any objective reporting.* When you judge a pupil's work unsatisfactory, or nonprogressing, or even C, avoid the halo effect. Separate the subjective from the objective even if the report is just a comment. For example, state precisely what the child has accomplished, and then relate it to ability or aptitude. Answer the question: Can you objectively defend your grade as free from bias?

4. *Use any subjective evaluation cautiously but honestly.* Whether it is a written comment, or an attitude checklist, make your judgment as fair as possible but tell parents exactly what you think. For example, if the youngster is obviously not working up to ability, tell them; if a youngster's classroom behavior is damaging achievement, tell them.

5. *Use a parent-teacher conference wisely.* Here you have a unique opportunity to improve the home-school cooperation. If you are prepared, if you can justify your grades and comments, then the conference no longer becomes something to dread, but a tool to help pupils. But you must be able to produce test scores, marks, or essays and reports, and a record of completed assignments to support objective grades. You must be prepared to furnish detailed reasons for your personal evaluation. There is no greater persuasive argument than facts.

Discussion Questions

1. What marks did you assign to the essay questions that other class members wrote for you? How did you arrive at them? Did you comment on the answer? Did your friends learn anything from your comments?

2. In marking essay tests, how would you avoid the halo effect's influence? Did the Page study convince you of the need to comment on students' work? Explain your answer.

3. After studying this chapter, what do you think *should* contribute to a grade? Can you defend your answer against the argument that either subjective or objective elements are all that are necessary?

4. If you had your preference what kind of reporting system would you employ? If you were in a school whose reporting system opposed your belief, what would you do to ensure both accuracy and accord with other teachers?

5. The relationship of testing to public policy is both fascinating and controversial. Can you devise arguments that either support or oppose the role of testing in evaluating such policies as busing, early intervention programs, or federally sponsored programs? You need not have detailed information about these issues; concentrate on what you know about testing and decide if it has a place in formulating public policy.

Some Concluding Thoughts

Teachers frequently evade examination periods, because they either misunderstand the intimate tie between instruction and evaluation or doubt their ability to construct a valid and reliable instrument. Yet successful teaching is difficult, if not impossible, without means of ascertaining a student's strengths and weaknesses. Ideally, perceptive teaching demands accurate assessment of learning at school's opening to determine the level of instruction, during the year to measure progress, and at year's end to weigh the ultimate achievement of each pupil.

The results of measurement help teachers to determine if students have achieved objectives and what steps are necessary to insure continued progress or to provide remedial help. The results of measurement can also help to determine what students know and what they can acquire through independent effort. But no teacher can guess that students know material; there must be more concrete proof of such knowledge. Measurement supplies such evidence.

The issue frequently is not student knowledge; often it entails a *lack* of knowledge. Specifically, the teacher needs to know what are a student's weaknesses, what caused them, and what kind of remedial work is necessary. Measurement again supplies evidence that illustrates the nature of the problem and what kind of remedial work is required.

Measurement also supports instruction. If standardized test results show that students should do average or higher work, but classroom achievement test scores are consistently low, it is usually a classroom problem. If the test is valid and reliable, if the students are reasonably motivated, and if materials are properly designed for the particular level, and students still fail to achieve as well as anticipated, teachers should logically question teaching techniques.

Properly employed, measurement is an essential feature of *both* teaching and learning. As Figure 11.1 illustrated, measurement concerns both teacher and learner. Unless learning is measured, and the results expressed in intelligible terms, there are no reliable means of defining improvement and no direction for future progress. You have an obligation to yourself and to your students to comprehend thoroughly the nature and use of standardized tests and also to ensure that your own tests are as good as possible.

Summary

- Evaluation is a complex, ceaseless process that involves children, teachers, parents, and administrators.

- Teachers' evaluations are subject to many powerful influences.

- Properly used, tests can serve specific, positive purposes.

- Testing has its own terminology, which must be mastered to distinguish the various aspects of evaluation.

- Ability, or aptitude, tests, which are the source of heated controversy, are still widely used.

- There are certain indispensable criteria for good test construction that every teacher should know and apply.

- Teachers should carefully weigh the advantages and disadvantages of essay and objective tests and construct those that best meet pupils' needs.

- It is easy to use test data carelessly, but marks, grades, and reporting methods are so important for pupils that they require time, thought, and care.

Suggested Readings

Bloom, Benjamin, J. Thomas Hastings, and George Madaus. *Handbook on Formative and Summative Evaluation of Student Learning.* New York: McGraw-Hill, 1971. An encyclopedic analysis of evaluation that is to be used as a handbook for all phases of evaluation.

Brophy, Jere, and Thomas Good. *Teacher-Student Relationships: Causes and Consequences.* New York: Holt, Rinehart and Winston, 1974. A perceptive view of the effect of individual student differences upon teachers.

Chauncey, Henry and John Dobbin. *Testing: Its Place in Education Today.* New York: Harper & Row, 1963. An excellent, brief presentation of the dos and don'ts of good testing.

Ebel, Robert. *Measuring Educational Achievement.* Englewood Cliffs, N.J.: Prentice-Hall, 1965. A fine text that focuses on classroom testing.

Mehrens, William and Irvin Lehmann. *Standardized Tests in Education.* New York: Holt, Rinehart and Winston, 1975. One of the most precise, pertinent overviews of standardized testing.

Thorndike, Robert and Elizabeth Hagen. *Measurement and Evaluation in Psychology and Education.* New York: Wiley, 1977. An excellent, basic source.

Part Four

The Learner and Individual Differences

12

Slow and Gifted Learners

(continues)

Introduction

Learning takes many forms; it also reflects many abilities. As a teacher in a "normal" classroom you will, nevertheless, encounter many youngsters of unusual ability—both those who are gifted and those who are slow, sometimes extremely slow, learners. You may well wonder why, in an era of multiple special classes, you need knowledge about these pupils. There are two reasons:

1. The more you know about the characteristics of special children, the more accurate are your recommendations for placement.
2. You frequently have these children in your class for a considerable time.

Most of these youngsters, unless they are obviously and severely handicapped, elude diagnosis for several years, sometimes into secondary school, which means that classroom teachers are responsible for their learning. Are there special methods, curricula, and programs suitable for these youngsters *in the classroom?* Working with them, understanding them, and learning about them will aid in your suggestions for their future, especially today when teachers' opinions are critical in the evaluation of these pupils.

Kirk (1972, pg. 4) defines an exceptional child as one who deviates from the average or normal child in:

1. Mental characteristics
2. Sensory abilities
3. Physical or neuromuscular characteristics
4. Social or emotional behavior
5. Communication abilities
6. Multiple handicaps

This chapter will concentrate on the intellectually gifted and the mentally retarded, the upper and lower extremes of the intelligence scale. These children especially elude detection. Lack of motivation, for example, could well mask high intelligence; while an appealing hard-working child may mask slow learning. Figure 12.1 illustrates the percentile distribution of IQ. If you examine Figure 12.1, you will note that those below 70 IQ represent 2.63 percent of the population; Termans labels these mentally retarded. Those above 140 IQ represent 1.33 percent of the population; Terman calls these the gifted. Using intelligence tests and IQ scores causes problems, but Figure 12.1 presents a graphic portrayal of the extremes that could be your concern.

The slow learner

One of the most dramatic reassessments of exceptional children has been due to the relatively recent surge of interest in mental retardation. After decades of neglect, the public has come to support federal, state, and local programs designed to educate, rehabilitate, and care for exceptional children, a large number of whom are mentally retarded.

BACKGROUND

Marie Crissey (1975) has traced the shifting attitudes to mental retardation from past to present and speculates about the future. She believes that although there was growing concern for the handicapped that accompanied the great revolution of the eighteenth century, it was not until Itard's work with "Wild Boy of Aveyron" that special treatment of exceptional children was attempted.

Itard and Sequin

Itard's student, Edward Sequin, believed that the mentally retarded deserved some education, and he incorporated existing educational and psychological knowledge into his programs, which

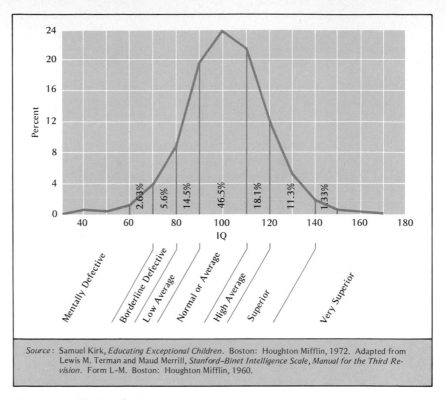

Source: Samuel Kirk, *Educating Exceptional Children*. Boston: Houghton Mifflin, 1972. Adapted from Lewis M. Terman and Maud Merrill, *Stanford–Binet Intelligence Scale, Manual for the Third Revision*. Form L-M. Boston: Houghton Mifflin, 1960.

Figure 12.1 IQ Distribution

were soon applied to large numbers of youngsters. Sequin believed in accurate *diagnosis,* followed by appropriate means, which, as Crissey notes, implies that he was more interested in behavior than pathology.

Sequin left France in 1848 and eventually settled in America, where he became instrumental in establishing programs for the mentally retarded in the Northeast. In 1876, there were sufficient institutions to form the organization that later became the American Association on Mental Deficiency. In spite of Sequin's clear views on ideal institutions for the mentally retarded, Crissey believes that a growing emphasis on heredity and the rise of intelligence testing doomed his ideas. If heredity explained mental retardation, and if these youngsters were criminally inclined, then society must segregate them—get them out of sight. Intelligence testing and the "fixed IQ" seemed to confirm the existing hereditary bias. Individuals were committed for life; numbers increased; conditions deteriorated; Sequin's ideals were abandoned.

A Depressing Trend

Crissey believes that at about the time of World War II frustrated parents began to organize in large numbers and to have

The Wild Boy of Aveyron

No discussion of mental retardation is complete without mentioning the "Wild Boy of Aveyron." Harlan Lane's recent account is particularly appealing and presents many of the problems still facing the handicapped: accurate diagnosis and adequate treatment.

One day in 1797, some peasants in the southern central region of France (Lacaune) observed a naked boy running through the fields. Repeatedly observed during the next 15 months, he was finally captured, escaped, and recaptured on July 25, 1799. He again escaped and for the next 6 months was seen near the surrounding villages, where people occasionally fed him. Finally, on January 8, 1800, perhaps driven by hunger, he approached a local farmhouse and thus began a new era in education.

He was placed in an orphanage, but confinement frustrated him and he twice escaped. During the ensuing pursuit and capture he was seen running on all fours. Word of his capture soon reached Paris and the youth became the center of speculation. Fortunately, there were those with some knowledge of handicapped children, and after observation at a local school, the boy was transferred to a Parisian school for deaf-mutes.

The case fascinated the people of France, and many saw it as an opportunity to answer those troublesome questions that have always plagued men: Was the boy left in the woods because he was an idiot, or was he an idiot because he was left in the woods? What is nature and what is nurture? What happens when animal impulses are unchecked by society? The Wild Boy of Aveyron might possibly be the key that unlocked the door into human nature.

Federal Support

greater impact. With the support of President Kennedy, who had a mentally retarded sister, federal support became available, and efforts to improve the conditions of mental retardates became almost a crusade. Today questions about intelligence testing, evidence refuting the "fixed IQ," and a recognition that environmental elements can cause mental retardation have reversed the depressing decline in conditions surrounding the mentally retarded. But questions remain. Is the community ready to accept greater responsibility for the care of the mentally retarded? As knowledge about retardation grows, will there be accompanying application? While the figure may pose problems, it is much more hopeful than in 1880.

Dramatic, controversial, fascinating, the Aveyron story is all of these. But you will not meet any wild boys in your class; you will more likely try to help youngsters like Eddie.

Today Eddie is 19 years old, physically strong, and works in a local gas station. Usually pleasant, Eddie is perfectly capable of pumping gas, cleaning windshields, and getting coffee and donuts. It is only when you await change from a $20 bill that you notice Eddie's difficulty. If you are a new customer, one of the other attendants immediately helps; if you are known and trusted, you tell Eddie what change to give you. Eddie is a good example of an educable mentally retarded boy who is adjusting satisfactorily. Experiencing immediate difficulty in school, he was placed in a special class when he was 11. Learning rudimentary skills, he acquired sufficient knowledge to enable him to service cars—gas, water, battery, washing. The station owner feels strongly about the boy and has given him an opportunity that many other similar youths never receive. There is one problem—Eddie is usually pleasant, but several mechanics mock him and send him on foolish errands, which infuriates him when he realizes what they have done. Human nature being human, these conditions are perhaps inevitable. Still, given this one drawback, Eddie enjoys a unique situation where he has proven himself a valuable asset and shown the wisdom of attempts to bring these youths as close as possible to normal lives.

DEFINITIONS

Who are the mentally retarded? Robinson and Robinson (1970) state that, because of the continuing controversy about intelligence, it is not surprising that discussion about the definition of mental retardation still continues. People who are mentally retarded are limited in their ability to learn and are generally socially immature; some are further handicapped by emotional and physical disabilities. A more precise definition is:

> Mental retardation refers to significantly subaverage general intellectual functioning existing concurrently with deficits in adaptive behavior and manifested during the developmental periods.
>
> (*Manual on Terminology and Classification in Mental Retardation.* Washington, D.C.: American Association on Mental Deficiency, 1973.)

The Robinsons (1970) believe that this definition, which originally appeared in similar form in 1959, reflects a changing view of mental retardation. It indicates a concern with present behavior without speculating about future performance; it suggests the use of intelligence tests *plus* numerous other sources of information; it avoids treating mental retardation as incurable because recent data shows that cultural deprivation and emotional problems may severely limit intellectual performance. Mental retardation is viewed as a behavioral symptom, not necessarily stable, accompanied by any number of other symptoms.

Number of Retarded   Estimates reveal that about 6 million Americans—about 3 percent of the population—are mentally retarded. Causes of mental retardation include genetic and chemical abnormalities, early childhood deprivation, damage to the central nervous system, toxic agents such as lead, and viruses. Premature infants and those born to women over 35 years seem especially vulnerable. Mental retardation causes more childhood disability than any other physical, emotional, or mental problem.

Classification

You have probably seen several different categories of mental retardation, which can be confusing. To help you distinguish categories, terms, and meaning, examine carefully the following three systems.

The first classification scheme reflects Table 12.1.

1. The *profound mentally retarded,* representing about 1.5 percent of the retarded population, require total care. Infant mortality is high in this group.

2. The *severe mentally retarded* encompass about 3.5 percent of this population. They are usually institutionalized, requiring constant supervision; they may acquire language and self-care skills only after extensive training. Genetic problems and neurological damage usually cause severe mental retardation.

3. The *moderate mentally retarded* constitute about 6 percent of the retarded. Although many reside in institutions, some adults may live with their families and can do household chores. Brain damage and Down's syndrome (mongolism) are the chief causes of

TABLE 12.1

Estimated Distribution of Retarded Persons in the United States by Age and Degree of Retardation

Degree of Retardation	ALL AGES		AGE BY YEARS	
	Number	*Percent*	*Under 20*	*20 and Over*
Total	6,000,000	100.0	2,455,000	3,545,000
Mild (IQ 52–69)	5,340,000	89.0	2,136,000	3,204,000
Moderate (IQ 36–51)	360,000	6.0	154,000	206,000
Severe (IQ 20–35)	210,000	3.5	105,000	105,000
Profound (IQ 0–20)	90,000	1.5	52,900	37,100

Source: The Problem of Mental Retardation. U.S. Department of Health, Education and Welfare, Office for Handicapped Individuals. Washington, D.C.: U.S. Government Printing Office, 1975.

moderate mental retardation, which is usually diagnosed in infancy and early childhood.

4. The *mild mentally retarded* represent about 89 percent of the retarded and they can customarily adjust satisfactorily with help in more complicated, abstract matters, such as finances. Eddie is a typical example of a mild mental retardate. Only about 1 percent are institutionalized, usually during adolescence and for behavior problems, not low intelligence. As youngsters they are eligible for special classes, but only *one in three* is actually placed (Robinson and Robinson, 1970), a startling statistic that should convince you to learn about these children since you eventually will have them in your class. Causes of mild mental retardation typically are early environmental deprivation, emotional problems, or some central nervous system difficulty. Table 12.2 summarizes the behavior associated with each of these four categories.

5. A final category, frequently used but not appearing in Table 12.1, is borderline mental retardation (IQ 68–83). The Robinsons state that these individuals blend with the normal population and, with proper training, can achieve social and vocational adequacy. This group and those mild mental retardates who remain undetected form a class often called "slow learners."

The second major, and also popular, scheme is offered by Kirk's educational classification (1972).

1. *The educable mentally retarded child.* This child cannot profit from regular elementary school work but may develop minimum

TABLE 12.2
Adaptive Behavior Classification for the Retarded

Mild	Development slow. Children capable of being educated ("educable") within limits. Adults, with training, can work in competitive employment. Able to live independent lives.
Moderate	Slow in their development, but able to learn to care for themselves. Children capable of being trained ("trainable"). Adults need to work and live in sheltered environment.
Severe	Motor development, speech, and language are retarded. Not completely dependent. Often, but not always, physically handicapped.
Profound	Need constant care or supervision for survival. Gross impairment in physical coordination and sensory development. Often physically handicapped.

Source: The Problem of Mental Retardation. U.S. Department of Health, Education, and Welfare, Office for Handicapped Individuals. Washington, D.C.: U.S. Government Printing Office, 1975.

academic skills (rudimentary reading, writing, and calculating), sufficient social adjustment to achieve independence, and minimal occupational adequacy for self-support. The educable retarded child often escapes detection until classroom work becomes steadily more abstract, particularly in the fourth grade, when special-class placement is recommended. As you will see in Chapter 13, this child may now remain in the regular classroom under the spreading policy of "mainstreaming," that is, keeping as many handicapped children as possible with normal youngsters.

2. *The trainable mentally retarded child.* Kirk believes that this child is not academically educable or capable of independent social adjustment and occupational success. The trainable retarded child can acquire self-care skills, achieve family adjustment, and offer some economic aid in the home or institution.

3. *The custodial mentally retarded child.* This child is severely, or profoundly, mentally retarded, lacks self-care ability, and requires constant help and supervision throughout his or her lifetime.

The third classification system is by Koch and Koch (1976), who estimate that more than 60,000 mentally retarded babies will be born in the United States this year. Of these, one-fourth will be moderately or severely handicapped. These authors grapple with the classification problem, reasoning that when doctors tell parents their child is mentally retarded they mean that the child will probably have an IQ score of less than 70. The extent of the handicap and its behavioral consequences determine the severity of the retardation. They use the following scheme as the basis of their discussion.

1. *Mild retardation (IQ 50–70).* These individuals, remain undetected for years. They are educable and can learn simple academic skills. Properly educated, they can mingle with the normal population, marry, and keep simple jobs.

2. *Moderate retardation (IQ 30–49).* They can learn simple speech and are trainable. They require lifelong supervision, but can acquire self-care skills, such as toilet training, dressing, feeding, and cleaning themselves.

3. *Severe retardation (IQ 0–29).* They are incapable of toilet training; some may never walk or talk. They are institutionalized early in life and require lifelong care.

What can you conclude from these schemes? Those who have an IQ of 50 or above can be educated for a relatively independent life. Those whose IQ place them in the severely or profoundly retarded range require treatment in protected environments. All but a small percentage can achieve some independence; the number who actually do depend on the quality of care and understanding they receive.

The Wild Boy: II

The Wild Boy of Aveyron was in a Parisian school for deaf-mutes. The next phase entailed a detailed description of the boy. Among the highlights were the following:

1. External appearance. The child appears no different from any other. About 12 to 13 years of age, he is 4½ feet tall with normal features. His body is covered with scars, which seem to have been caused by burns. When walking he rocks from side to side; he cannot swim. His body is well proportioned. He seems to experience occasional convulsive fits.
2. Sensory processes. His senses seem good. He is not deaf, but obviously, because of his isolation, has a defective speech mechanism. The sense of smell and taste are much more developed than those of the ordinary youngster. He has excellent vision.
3. Speech deprivation. He has absolutely no speech and communicates by cries and inarticulate sounds. He normally used these sounds to express emotion.
4. Instinct. The child uses purely animal functions and his desires do not exceed his physical needs. His chief concerns

seem to be nourishment, rest, and independence. He expresses no affection.
5. Nourishment. He dislikes bread, meat, soup, and eats only potatoes, nuts and acorns. He is acquiring a taste for meat—either raw or cooked. He is obsessed with eating; it is the one thing that completely absorbs him. If he has extra food, he buries or hides it.
6. Suspicion of imbecility. He exhibits survival intelligence; but when not concerned with food, there is only animal functioning. He reflects on nothing; he has no imagination or memory.
7. Character. When flattered, he is sweet and complacement. He is unaware of right and wrong. When frustrated, he becomes agitated, shows rage, strikes his head, bites, rips, scratches, weeps, and cries out. He detects children of his own age.

This account, retaining the terminology of the original report, provides only some of the fascinating clues to a primitive existence that produced behavioral symptoms that were quickly labeled retarded.

The classification suggested by the American Association on Mental Deficiency is probably the most widely used today; you can also translate it easily into Kirk's educational categories. But the most important idea that you should take from studying the classification schemes is that all the authors agree that detection of mild mental retardation is slow, often taking years; consequently, you may bear the educational responsibility for these children.

CHARACTERISTICS OF THE SLOW LEARNER

Youngsters you will meet are not likely to exhibit the extreme behavior of the Wild Boy but they will manifest less intense symptoms—not a lack of speech and communication, but difficulty in communicating; not a survival intelligence, but difficulty with the complex and abstract. These characteristics appear early, often at birth or during early childhood, and remain undetected because adults overlook the qualitative nature of a child's difficulty. The retarded have problems adjusting to society's demands because of limited intellectual capacity; yet, frequently years pass before teachers or parents recognize the qualitative difference in behavior, which is why you so often see special treatment or placement recommended when the child is 10 or 11 years old.

Qualitative Differences in Behavior

Knobloch and Pasamanick (1974, pg. 149) state that in all deviant development the task is to determine if the subsequent retardation and behavioral difficulties are deep-seated or transient, generalized or delimited, ameliorable or ineducable. These authors believe that many cases escape recognition in infancy because observers fail to make critical distinctions among different degrees of immaturity, that is, qualitative distinctions. Since other disabilities resemble retardation, it is important to discover normal potential that is masked by misleading visible defects. Table 12.3 presents some developmental characteristics of the mentally retarded that should help you to understand why detection remains elusive.

If you examine Table 12.3, moving from mild to profound, note how realistic the descriptions are: "often not distinguished from normal until later age"; "can learn academic skills up to approximately sixth grade level by late teens." The child's qualitative distinctions remain obscured until difficulty with abstract material becomes so obvious that it is apparent the youngster is not experiencing a simple, temporary learning difficulty. Even the description of the moderate category poses identification problems: "can talk or learn to communicate"; "fair motor development." It is only with the last two categories that difficulties are evident.

Difficulty of Retention

It is the child with mild mental retardation whom you will typically have in your classroom; either because of lack of detection, or because school officials feel that these youngsters can be mainstreamed into classrooms supervised by regular teachers. Your first task is to recognize and understand these children. The Kochs (1976) believe that society's first obligation to the retarded is an enlightened understanding attitude. The retarded have the same rights and feelings as all people; they deserve society's best efforts to correct or alleviate their handicaps, including an education designed to facilitate whatever ability they possess, so that they can approach as normal a life as their potential permits. Probably most important, the retarded deserve respect so that they can live with dignity and self-respect (Koch and Koch, 1976, pg. 88).

Knobloch and Pasamanick offer other criteria to distinguish normal from mentally retarded children at 28 weeks and 3 years.

The comparisons in Table 12.4 are particularly interesting because they are more specific than most. For example, at 28 weeks,

TABLE 12.3

Developmental Characteristics of Mentally Retarded Persons

Degrees of Mental Retardation	PRESCHOOL AGE (0–5) Maturation and Development	SCHOOL AGE (6–20) Training and Education	ADULT (21 AND OVER) Social and Vocational Adequacy
Mild	Can develop social and communication skills; minimal retardation in sensorimotor areas; often not distinguished from normal until later age.	Can learn academic skills up to approximately sixth-grade level by late teens. Can be guided toward social conformity. "Educable."	Can usually achieve social and vocational skills adequate to minimum self-support but may need guidance and assistance when under unusual social or economic stress.
Moderate	Can talk or learn to communicate; poor social awareness; fair motor development; profits from training in self-help; can be managed with moderate supervision.	Can profit from training in social and occupational skills; unlikely to progress beyond second-grade level in academic subjects; may learn to travel alone in familiar places.	May achieve self-maintenance in unskilled or semiskilled work under sheltered conditions; needs supervision and guidance when under mild social or economic stress.
Severe	Poor motor development; speech is minimal; generally unable to profit from training in self-help; little or no communication skills.	Can talk or learn to communicate; can be trained in elemental health habits; profits from systematic habit training.	May contribute partially to self-maintenance under complete supervision; can develop self-protection skills to a minimal useful level in controlled environment.
Profound	Gross retardation; minimal capacity for functioning in sensorimotor areas; needs nursing care.	Some motor development present; may respond to minimal or limited training in self-help.	Some motor and speech development; may achieve very limited self-care; needs nursing care.

Source: The Problem of Mental Retardation. U.S. Department of Health, Education, and Welfare, Office for Handicapped Individuals. Washington, D.C.: U.S. Government Printing Office, 1975.

the youngster experiencing mild difficulty examines something in either hand, behavior that the normal child exhibits at 16 weeks. At 3 years the normal child uses complex language, while the child with a mild mental difficulty exhibits language behavior that a normal 1½-year-old child uses. Knobloch and Pasamanick believe that it is the degree of behavioral impairment that enables observers to interpret the extent of mental deficiency. Even with careful observation it is impossible to distinguish among the various categories; one merges with another, for example, the milder forms of mental deficiency shade into dull normal. These authors stress that lowered intelligence alone does not constitute mental deficiency; it is the symptom together with integrated and organizational capacities that permit a sharp distinction between normality and mental deficiency.

TABLE 12.4

Comparative Development at 28 Weeks and 3 Years of Age: Normal, Mild, Moderate to Severe, and Profound Mental Deficiency

28 WEEKS	Maturity Level	3 YEARS	Maturity Level
ADAPTIVE BEHAVIOR		**ADAPTIVE BEHAVIOR**	
Normal: reaches, grasps, transfers	28 wk	*Normal:* builds 3-cube bridge	3 years
Mild: regards object in hand	16 wk	*Mild:* builds tower of 3–5 cubes	18–21 mo
Moderate to Severe: disregards or only glances at object in hand.......	8–12 wk	*Moderate to Severe:* dangles ring by string	52–65 wk
Profound: stares vacantly; may hold object reflexly without regard	0–4 wk	*Profound:* grasps object near hand or on contact; or stares vacantly; or drops object in hand..............	4–16 wk
GROSS MOTOR BEHAVIOR		**GROSS MOTOR BEHAVIOR**	
Normal: sits leaning on hands for support, head erect	28 wk	*Normal:* climbs stairs with alternating steps	3 years
Mild: sits supported, head steady but set forward..........................	16 wk	*Mild:* walks well........................	18–20 mo
Moderate to Severe: sits supported, head unsteady...........................	8–12 wk	*Moderate to Severe:* stands or toddles...................................	52–65 wk
Profound: head drops....................	0–4 wk	*Profound:* sits supported, head steady or wobbly; or lifts head in prone...................................	4–16 wk
LANGUAGE BEHAVIOR		**LANGUAGE BEHAVIOR**	
Normal: vocalizes m-m-m	28 wk	*Normal:* speaks in sentences, using plurals....................................	3 years
Mild: laughs aloud........................	16 wk	*Mild:* names 1–2 pictures..............	18–21 mo
Moderate to Severe: smiles; coos	8–12 wk	*Moderate to Severe:* says 2–6 words....................................	52–65 wk
Profound: vague throaty sounds	0–4 wk	*Profound:* laughs; or crying and vague ejaculation	4–16 wk
PERSONAL-SOCIAL BEHAVIOR		**PERSONAL-SOCIAL BEHAVIOR**	
Normal: takes feet to mouth.............	28 wk	*Normal:* feeds self, little spilling......	3 years
Mild: anticipates feeding.................	16 wk	*Mild:* carries and hugs doll............	18–21 mo
Moderate to Severe: watches moving person	8 wk	*Moderate to Severe:* gives toy on request.................................	52–65 wk
Profound: stares blankly at persons ...	0–4 wk	*Profound:* anticipates feeding; smiles on social approach; or stares blankly at persons.............	4–16 wk

Source: Hilda Knobloch and Benjamin Pasamanick, *Gesell and Amatruda's Developmental Diagnosis.* New York: Harper & Row, 1974.

Identification of slow learners

Difficulty in Diagnosis

Clarizio and McCoy (1976, pg. 223) state that correctly identifying a disorder is basic since this simultaneously suggests the treatment. Reliance upon IQ scores is unsatisfactory because persons having identical IQ scores vary enormously, and also because there are no specific behaviors associated with an IQ score. The authors believe that one must accept the complexity of mental retardation and attempt to identify it by employing a team of professional specialists.

Some Suggestions for Identification

The President's Committee on Mental Retardation, in discussing tests to determine this condition, state that they range from chromosomal analysis to intelligence and social adaptability tests of school children. Several states require screening tests for infants soon after birth to discover chemical and neurological abnormalities that can produce retardation. Tests of sensory and motor development are used in infancy to assess developmental progress. Intelligence tests are given as soon as possible and related to observation of the child's adaptive behavior, that is, the behavior that the youngster employs to meet environmental demands.

Clarizio and McCoy (1976, pp. 224–230) recommend the following steps in identification and diagnosis of retardation.

1. *Familial and developmental history.* Has the child suffered any injuries or major illnesses? Is any relative retarded? Was there any developmental lag in sitting, feeding, dressing, and talking?

The Wild Boy: III

Jean-Marc-Gaspard Itard was 26 years old when he first met the Wild Boy of Aveyron at the Parisian Institute for Deaf-Mutes. Itard believed that the "savage" was not inherently defective, but lacked a language that would enable him to perform the higher mental processes. A patient and careful observer of his charge, Itard attempted to identify the major causes of the boy's difficulties, sensory, motivational, and verbal. He then attempted to correct them, beginning with sensory activity and progressing to language and, finally, to abstract thought.

The remedial conditions must suit the child's needs, and Itard believed his first task was to create a healthy and positive environment. By providing "positive reinforcement," Itard gradually introduced specific objects, pictures, and sounds to teach particular skills. As Lane notes, Itard shifted the instructional focus from the materials to the learner.

Itard had five major instructional objectives:

1. To interest the Wild Boy in his surrounding social life by making it pleasant for him.
2. To capture his attention by energetic stimulation, even by intense emotion.
3. To extend the range of his ideas by giving him new needs and increasing his social contacts.
4. To aid speech development by subjecting him to the necessity of imitation.
5. To make him exercise the simplest mental operations for satisfying his physical needs.

2. *Measures of intellectual ability.* IQ scores are still the most widely used standard for measuring retardation. Given the limitations of intelligence testing, they should be only one method of determining retardation.

3. *Social competence.* Failure to meet social demands—dropping out of school, job failure, criminal activity—has long characterized the mentally retarded. Observers must carefully evaluate this criterion since many nonretarded individuals manifest the identical behavior; its significance is as *one* of a cluster of causative agents.

4. *Learning.* Difficulty with learning has also been a standard sign of retardation. The more severe the retardation, the poorer the learning; the more abstract the learning, the greater the difficulty.

5. *Other symptoms.* Language difficulties, emotional problems, cultural disadvantages may either result from retardation or be isolated difficulties that affect performance. These, like social competence, can only be interpreted as part of a total evaluation, never alone.

After examining the two troublesome topics of characteristics and identification, what can you conclude? One inevitable conclusion is that it is frequently difficult, if not impossible, to determine where one kind of behavior ends (for example, dull normal) and another begins (for example, mild retardation). A second deduction is that isolated behavior—poor reading scores, moodiness, withdrawal, lethargy—cannot be used to identify the retarded. A complete evaluation, such as those suggested by Clarizio and McCoy, is mandatory.

Dangers of Labeling

Finally, labeling is a dangerous practice widely employed when discussing the handicapped. Once a child receives a label, it can stick for life. Kirk notes (1974) that being mislabeled is unfortunate and frightening because the term "special" once applied leads to unending special classes. Reevaluation rarely occurs; only one child in ten who is labeled retarded ever returns from a special class.

Abandoning identification is no solution since it produces a dreamworld where everyone is assumed to be alike. The task, as Kirk sees it, is to feel less bound by categories and to derive better programs for particular difficulties.

Still, exceptional children in regular classrooms pose real dilemmas for teachers. If they are to be successful they must possess the training to provide for an enormous range of student ability, from the retarded to the gifted. Funds must be available to provide specialists who can work with both teachers and students in diagnosing and alleviating particular problems.

CAUSES OF MENTAL RETARDATION

Mental retardation has many causes: genetic, prenatal, perinatal, postnatal, and cultural (Kirk, 1972, pg. 172). An example of a ge-

BOSTON COLLEGE PUBLIC RELATIONS

PKU

netic cause of retardation is phenylketonuria (PKU), which occurs in about one of 10,000 births. A genetic abnormality produces a lack of the necessary enzyme to transform phenylalanine, which then increases in the body, and finally affects the central nervous system. If detected immediately, by a simple urine test, it is easily remedied by a proper diet; if not, the result is mental retardation. Another genetic cause is some chromosomal abnormality, such as Down's syndrome or trisomy. A normal person has 46 chromosomes; a victim of trisomy has 47, resulting in mental retardation.

Rubella

Two prenatal causes that can cause mental retardation are rubella (German measles) and the Rh factor. If, during the first three months of pregnancy, a woman contracts German measles, her child may be mentally retarded. Before the age of vaccines, rubella produced over 2000 handicapped children each year. The Kochs note that there has been a growing laxity in immunization programs and they recommend a premarital blood test for German measles.

Rh Factor

Eighty-six percent of all humans have the Rh factor in their blood. The difficulty arises when an Rh negative woman marries an Rh positive man. Usually the firstborn escapes the problem since the blood of mother and baby are separate. But at delivery the mother's blood may absorb some Rh positive blood; during her next pregnancy, her blood system, which has now formed antibodies, begins to attack the blood of the fetus, destroying red cells. The brain is deprived of oxygen and mental retardation results. Today there is a vaccine, that, if given to the Rh negative women just after birth, will prevent her system from forming the destructive antibodies.

Perinatal Causes

Among the perinatal causes (those occurring immediately preceding or during birth) are brain injuries, asphyxia, and prematurity. Prolonged and difficult labor, forceps damage, or some other mechanical element may cause brain injury resulting in retardation. Asphyxia, or lack of oxygen, may also cause brain cell damage. The Kochs (1976) estimate that 300,000 premature babies are born in the United States each year. Ninety percent weighing less than 1 pound will be retarded, as well as 40 percent of the 3-pound babies and 10 percent of the 4-pound infants.

Cultural Causes

Although prematurity obviously relates to time of delivery, it is also related to the environment. It is the poor who have the highest prematurity rate, almost five times as great as for middle-class women. The negative effect of a deprived environment was thoroughly examined in Chapter 3, where the potential nervous system damage that could result from sterile surroundings was noted. At a time of great growth and organization of the nervous system, the environment exercises as even more potent effect.

Knobloch and Pasamanick (1974) make a sharp distinction between mental deficiency, caused by brain damage, and mental retardation, which they believe comes from poor environmental conditions. But they recognize that evidence suggests both categories may represent the lower end of the normal curve because of heredity. Nevertheless, they argue strongly that environmental deprivation produces not mental but behavioral deficiencies sufficiently severe to require therapeutic intervention. For example, they state that data show an increasing subnormality that reflects socioeconomic status. Table 12.5 outlines the evidence, taken from a study of 1000 infants, they use to support their view.

Examining Table 12.5, you see the use of a developmental quotient (DQ), which is an expression of maturity level based on observation of performance. Less than 0.2 percent of whites in the upper half of the socioeconomic table had DQs of less than 75, while the evidence for blacks and those in a lower socioeconomic status ranged from 1.5 to 2.5 percent. What is especially startling in this table is the figure for 3-year-old blacks. The percentage of those DQs less than 75 jumped from 2.0 at 40 weeks to 8.1 percent at 3 years. Interpreting the causes and future affects of mental retardation caused by cultural elements is uncertain.

Any discussion of causes suggests preventive measures. The President's Task Force on the Mentally Handicapped states that prevention is preferred to treatment and rehabilitation, and the opportunities for prevention cover the lifespan. For example, some retardation due to maternal infection, malnutrition during preg-

TABLE 12.5

Percent of Population with Adaptive Developmental Quotients Below 75, by Age and Socioeconomic Status (Adjusted for Proportion of Premature Infants in Each Group)

	AGE	
Socioeconomic Status	40 Wk	3 Yr
White upper half	0.2	0.3
Black upper half	1.5	0.6
White lower half	2.5	2.3
Black lower half	2.0	8.1

Source: Hilda Knobloch, and Benjamin Pasamanick, *Gesell and Amatruda's Developmental Program*. New York: Harper & Row, 1974. From data in Study of Prematures, Baltimore, Maryland, Knobloch, H. Pasamanick, B: "Predicting intellectual potential in infancy." *Am I Dis Child 106;* 43–51, 1963. Copyright 1963, American Medical Association.

nancy, and birth injury is preventable if proper prenatal and obstetric care are available. Prematurity seems to have a close relationship to low socioeconomic status, which implies service to women who meet these criteria. Genetic counseling may help to prevent metabolic error. It is now possible to prevent damage from rubella and Rh factor incompatibility. As Skeels's study (discussed in Chapter 3) shows, unfavorable environmental conditions can cause mild, but common, retardation.

Specifically, the task force recommended:

Specific Recommendations

1 Prenatal and perinatal services for all who need them.
2. National day-care programs, from infancy to school age, that involve children's families and collaborate with health, educational, mental health, and social services.
3. The expansion of existing programs to detect problems of social adjustment and intellectual competence in preschool and primary school children.
4. More and better programs that educate for parenthood and provide information to young parents about clinics, social agencies, and adult education courses.
5. Development of programs designed for youth organizations in poverty areas.
6. Stimulation of intensified research into the causes of retardation.
7. Avoidance of all drugs during pregnancy except those prescribed by a physician.

EDUCATING THE SLOW LEARNER

Educational Characteristics

Kirk (1972), devoting considerable thought to slow learners, has formulated several plans for their education. For example, he be-

The Wild Boy: IV

The previous discussion left Itard preparing a course intended to achieve specific objectives for the Wild Boy, whom he named Victor. Itard attempted to sharpen the boy's senses by proper diet, clothing, and rest. While taste and smell improved, sight and hearing did not. Itard tried to socialize Victor by initially providing food (primary reinforcers) for certain behaviors and then linking those to social contacts, which gradually produced a minimum form of socialization.

Teaching him how to speak was Itard's most difficult task. Painfully, by imitation, Victor acquired a few words and Itard felt he could distinguish five vowels and four consonants, but the major obstacle was Victor's successful communication by gestures. Slowly he acquired a primitive language and the use of some signs.

Itard continued his work with Victor for another four and one-half years. He attempted to refine Victor's hearing until he could make fine discriminations; by carefully graded exercises, he taught Victor to match words, and then to associate the words with appropriate objects. Victor gradually increased his vocabulary and began to construct sentences. Itard summarizes his failures thus far: hearing and speech are almost totally inadequate; intellectual reasoning is slow and painful, and emotions confused. He also lists his accomplishments: improvement in sight and touch, the basis of symbolic thought, the ability to name objects, a partial degree of socialization.

Victor's education now ceased; he remained institutionalized until he died, approximately in his forties. Lane credits Itard for treating Victor as a developing child and not a miniature adult, for providing a suitable milieu, for his patience in manipulating stimuli and responses, and for leading Victor into a social life. He faults Itard for ignoring Victor's initial skills and especially for faulty language instruction. Nevertheless, Lane concludes that Victor made enormous progress under Itard's tutelage. Perhaps Itard's work was doomed because of Victor's prolonged isolation, which may have caused him to miss too many critical periods.

lieves that the educable mentally retarded child can acquire rudimentary education in basic academic skills, sufficient social adjustment to live independently, and minimal occupational adequacy. Most of these youngsters are not diagnosed as extremely slow learners until they attend school and begin to fail. Where other youngsters are ready for reading, spelling, and arithmetic at about 5 or 6 years, the low ability child displays readiness at about 8 to 10 years. Kirk estimates that these youngsters' school progress match their mental development, which is about one-half to three-quarters the rate of the normal child; that is, they cannot do a year's work in a year's time. When they complete formal education, their school achievement will range from the second- to sixth-grade level.

These youngsters receive education in different regular class-

The Early Years

room programs, in special classes, and in residential schools. While the most common procedure is to place them in special classes, mainstreaming (providing special services to the child in a regular classroom) is a growing phenomenon. Few preschool programs offer special classes, usually because of a lack of early identification Frequently, if a principal, teacher, and psychologist believe that some children will fail the first grade, they are retained in kindergarten. Kirk believes that a better procedure is to identify children who are having difficulty in kindergarten and provide them with special help in language, perception, and adaptation skills. If resource teachers are available, this technique may compensate the environmental deprivation and prepare for later school tasks.

Elementary Program

For these children, learning failures commence almost immediately in the first grade, and Kirk believes that they could benefit from one of three plans: (1) Keep them in the regular grade but provide extra instruction by a resource specialist; (2) enroll them in a special class, but allow them some time in the regular classroom; or (3) place them in a special class for the entire day. The degree of retardation and the available service will usually determine the decision. By 9 or 10 years of age, the failing child is typically placed in a special class, and the school's efforts are designed to teach the basic subjects of reading, writing, and arithmetic and to improve the child's basic adjustment to the environment.

The Secondary Program

Today some systems have special classes for those in junior and senior high school. One teacher of the basic subjects usually remains with them for the greater part of the day, with some additional classes in music, art, or industrial training. The secondary program is designed to further their knowledge of the basic subjects, to improve "home" skills such as home economics and household mechanics, and to ensure an understanding of physical and mental health.

Teaching Suggestions

Understanding more about the needs and abilities of slow learners, what can you do to help if you identify some in your classes? Watson (1973) and Kirk (1972) offer some practical suggestions.

1. *Provide carefully guided instruction.* This will help avoid failure, and their performance will enable you to emphasize positive features. These youngsters work best with a carefully designed, step-by-step technique, similar to previous suggestions for mastery learning. Considerable repetition is usually necessary, and you should adapt material appropriately for the slow learner. Use as much positive reinforcement as possible.
2. *Avoid any kind of competition or comparison between normal or gifted students and slow learners.* Constant failure has a damaging impact on anyone's self-concept.

3. *Discover any specific skills slow learners may possess.* If possible, let them demonstrate them for other students.
4. *Be careful of environmental stimuli.* Too many stimuli, especially if they are similar, confuse these children. For example, *ough* in *through, thought, trough.* Here similar letters demand different responses.
5. *Be careful of both the number of things taught and the abstractness of the material.* Sheer numbers can overwhelm anyone, especially these youngsters. The more abstract the material, the greater the difficulty the low ability youngster will have with it.

Conclusions

An issue underlying this discussion of the slow learner is the question of special-class placement or retention in a regular classroom. One of the early, significant attacks on special classes for the mildly retarded was made by Lloyd Dunn in 1968. Arguing that the results of this policy have been tragic and that the practice is

MEDFORD, MASS. DAILY MERCURY

now obsolete, Dunn believes that the time has come to do something better for slow learners. It is known that these youngsters learn much from normal students in a regular class and that they make as much—or more—progress in regular classes as in special classes. Furthermore, the problem raised by labeling—once labeled, forever labeled—can be avoided. He states that improvements in regular-class programs such as team teaching and flexible grouping now enable teachers to work more effectively with slow learners.

But Macmillan (1971) urges caution in abandoning special classes unless regular classrooms are altered. Macmillan believes that one reason for special education's apparent lack of success is its emphasis on cognitive variables as opposed to motivational variables. For example, most retarded children expect failure, manifest "negative reaction tendencies" (adults have reacted unfavorably toward them), and are outer directed (they distrust their own ideas and solutions and become dependent on others). Consequently, Macmillan argues that disputes about the value of special classes are useless; the question to answer is: Which placement is most advantageous for which child? The slow learners—whether in a special class or regular class—will still have a high expectancy for failure, excessive negative reaction tendencies, and outer directedness. These emotional-motivation characteristics need treatment to help the slow learner in either a special or a regular class.

Whether you believe in special-class placement or not, this section concludes as it began: You will inevitably teach some of these youngsters. Know as much about them as possible and recall the teaching techniques presented here.

Discussion Questions

1. Examine Figure 12.1 again. From our discussion of intelligence and intelligence testing, do you think this breakdown should be the basis for categorizing children? If you disagree, what would you suggest?

2. Do you know a boy or girl like Eddie? If so, describe him or her to the class, including home conditions, and schooling. Knowing this individual, and recalling your own academic experience, what is your opinion of the growing tendency to keep the mildly retarded in a regular classroom?

3. There is considerable confusion about defining and classifying retardation. Of the three systems described in this chapter, which do you prefer? Why? Specify both theoretical and practical issues in your answer.

4. Comment on the characteristics of the retarded, using *one* of the classification schemes presented and stressing the type of youngster you may find in your class. Which category will most likely remain in school for several years? Why? List the instructional principles you would want to use with them.

5. Discussing programs for the retarded, a heated argument usually ensues about the pros and cons of special classes. Do you think the mildly retarded belong there? What are the alternatives? Be practical in your answer; that is, consider the demands on the classroom teacher, the reaction of the class, and the need for special resources in a time of shrinking budgets.

The gifted learner

The gifted child is again a source of concern, since, after decades of neglect, there is the realization that we may be squandering an enormous potential for good. A recent international conference on the gifted reported such instances as these:

Tim's parents realized they had a problem when he wrote his second love letter to a pop singer and when he began to recite the alphabet backwards. Tim was 3.

Barbara's mother was stunned when the family physician told her to get this girl into school immediately. Barbara was 18 months old.

About 2 percent of the school population is gifted, that is, have IQs of 140 plus. Henry Collis, director of Britain's National Association for Gifted Children, believes giftedness is a mixed blessing since, if not properly managed, it can bring enormous problems. How do parents and teachers treat young children who can outwit computers, solve complicated mathematical problems in their heads, delve into, and understand, the mysteries of science, or easily acquire foreign languages? Parents often are bewildered and teachers frustrated and intimidated by these youngsters until, finally the child feels different.

A concomitant problem is identification. Due to a lack of motivation or an unchallenging education, they may escape identification. One of the conference's reports stated the issue simply: gifted children can be tomorrow's dropouts and delinquents, or tomorrow's leaders, inventors, scientists, and artists if we can help them to fulfill their potential. Our discussion of gifted children will be remarkably similar to that of the mildly retarded: problems of identification, education, and prevention of emotional disturbances. The letter shown in the box on page 482 written by a 16-year-old college freshman is both instructive and moving.

Don't Make Me Walk When I Want to Fly

My name is John. I'm 16, and I have two younger brothers, Mark and Todd. On our school records, a green clip identifies all of us as *Ex Chs,* which for years mystified me, but which you know stands for Exceptional Child—the smarty pants variety.

My parents were told that my IQ is in the 160s and that my brothers weren't far behind. School was easy, and I was in the top five percent on SAT scores. Maybe I'm innately bright, but I have another theory as to why I became an *Ex Ch.*

Here's how I explain myself. I was born right after my grandfather's death, and my grandmother became a great influence in my life. At first it was almost full time. She spent her waking hours reading, showing, telling, taking me places—the latter starting when I was less than one year old.

Influence number two was almost as potent. My aunt is a reviewer of children's books. From the day I was born, boxes of books arrived at my grandmother's house. I can honestly say that I can't remember when I couldn't read. My grandmother thinks I recognized words at two, and it's probably true, for both my brothers did. Anyway, I spent hours on my grandmother's lap following along as she read, and I guess I learned automatically.

The other major contributors to my early life were my mother and father. My dad is a carpenter, and early he taught me how to use tools, how to measure exactly, how to be thirfty and neat in what I made. Under him, I developed precise skills. He's also an outdoor man and spent many hours with my brothers and me gardening, hiking, and camping. I learned innumerable lessons from my father, who is a truly great guy in a thousand ways.

My mother gave me order and oughtness in a low-key sort of way. I can never remember not folding my clothing neatly at night. Changing my clothes after school was automatic, and they got hung up, too. My brothers and I shared a room and each guy made his own bed—a hard, fast rule. Even on weekends when we got up ahead of our parents to watch cartoons, no one dared look at TV if his bed wasn't made. From my mother I also learned the rules of politeness—how to meet grown-ups, how to accept gifts. Don't knock it. This training gave me a lot of confidence.

It wasn't until I went to kindergarten that I realized I knew more or thought more complexly than other kids. Sunday school had been sort of vague. I would sit and read the Sunday school papers, but I honestly didn't know that the other kids couldn't read them.

In kindy I was a marked kid. I handed out papers for the teacher, read stories to the other kids, and once I even marked papers for the first-grade teacher. I didn't learn much except an important lesson that I've been learning ever since: One's peers are suspicious and resentful of you when you do things more quickly or better than they do. I soon found ways to hide or play down what I know, and I find myself still doing it today.

Since this is a letter for teachers, I want to tell you mostly what happened in school. Unlike many schools, it *did* try to take care of the *Ex Chs* in a variety of ways.

Skipping

I'm sorry to report that I got skipped twice. After my kindergarten performance, the first-grade teacher didn't want me. (Maybe it was those papers that I marked.) Anyway, the principal convinced my parents I should start the next year in second grade.

At first I found myself behind the others in both motor and formal skills. I didn't write as small and neatly as they did, and had to do a lot of practicing at home for the first couple of months. Also, the kids who had been in first grade knew how to do their workbook exercises and they had less trouble sitting at their desks for long periods of time. Yet, I soon noticed that my classmates, who I was in awe of because they were older, made some pretty simple judgments and decisions which the teacher accepted. I learned to keep quiet.

My second skipping came after I was in fourth grade for two months. I felt the teacher wanted to get rid of her *Ex Ch* so she pushed me off on the fifth-grade teacher. It was the best break of my elementary years. I'll tell you why later—but I paid for it in high school.

Absolutely, I don't recommend skipping for *Ex Chs*. It may be an immediate solution, but it's a long-range detriment. It's no fun being 13, 14, and 15 in tenth, eleventh, and twelfth grades.

Enrichment

If schools don't skip *Ex Chs,* then they have to provide more of the stuff that's called enrichment. Schools aren't set up for innovative enrichment—they could learn a lesson from my grandmother—but I'll describe what happened. A student interested in science or math was accommodated fairly easily. There were kits for them to build, experiments to do, advanced workbooks in math, and so on. Unfortunately, I was interested in books, social situations, aesthetics, and languages; so I was more of a problem. The school didn't have kits for me.

For example, in the summer between second and third grades, I met a Spanish boy. That fall I asked the principal if I could learn Spanish, but he turned me down because there was no teacher to help me, and he wouldn't let me do it on my own. I think the prospect of a seven-year-old third grader learning Spanish independently may have been too much for him to accept.

Language and communication

My fifth-grade teacher was an elderly lady near retirement. She was a jewel, and I cried at her funeral last year. She may have had no training in what to do with an *Ex Ch,* but she was a natural. First, she talked to me about anything and everything. She introduced me to old-fashioned diagraming which I found to be great fun. We played games, with her trying to concoct a sentence that I couldn't diagram. She brought me Latin books and I would stay after school and talk Latin to her. Latin was the only other language she had ever learned, but from that experience I learned that I have a knack for languages. Today, I speak fairly fluent Spanish, French, and German, having learned the first two in high school and teaching myself the latter with the use of tapes, records, and self-study books.

She gave me Lamb's *Tales from Shakespeare,* then took me to see Hamlet and I became a disciple of the Bard . . . and was she ever sneaky! She insisted I train my memory and gave me passages of Shakespeare to memorize. I fell for it, seeing myself as the next John Gielgud. Today I'm grateful. Memorizing is not only a wonderful tool, it gives comfort and support in lonely moments.

She built my vocabulary by introducing me to complex words, and in our private conversations we used them freely—you never heard such talk! You may have sensed that she and I were almost clandestine in our special relationship. In front of others she treated me like them and I understood. Fifth grade was my happiest year, and I never had a better teacher.

Special efforts

While I was in fifth grade, a new young principal who cared about *Ex Chs* came to our school. He set out to identify us and give us special things to do. Some of his projects were what I called, *so-whats,* but my brothers loved them. I didn't, but I respected him so much that I did them anyway. For example, he taught us how to estimate the height of a flagpole by measuring its shadow. He showed us how to estimate the number of bricks used to build our school. Today I amuse myself in boring situations by doing *so-whats.* In high school courses that were dull, I'd figure how many bricks would be needed to box in the room. Doodling is another good *so-what.* I find I can keep myself out of a lot of trouble by doodling.

The principal organized chess games and encouraged games such as Monopoly and 3-D checkers. He liked games and I think we all learned from playing them.

Special projects

By the time I was in sixth grade, the principal had convinced someone in authority that there should be a resource teacher to set up special projects for *Ex Chs.* He meant well, but we were better off when he was taking care of us.

Don't think me a snob, but the person who thinks up *Ex Ch* projects better be a former *Ex Ch.* Our resource teacher wasn't and didn't have much of a sense of humor. In October I was assigned a research project on Columbus. (Original idea, wasn't it?) The whole thing was pretty boring, but I did it and got into a lot of trouble. As part of the assignment, I was to do a piece of original writing. I wrote a funny (to me) soap-opera skit. My plot was that Isabella and Christopher were having an affair. Ferdinand discovered it and sent Chris off on the high seas. Further, Ferdy got his revenge by using Isabella's money to finance the project. The

teacher went into shock and called my parents.

Responsibility

My brothers and I were encouraged to earn our own money. I started with a paper route and soon had both brothers involved. We had it down pat, both distribution and collection. We paid our father a dollar to drive us to deliver Sunday papers.

Once we mastered paper delivery, we began looking for a way to earn greater profits. Since we had our own tools, which our father had taught us how to care for and use, we opened a gardening service. Throughout junior and senior high school we had all the lawns we could care for. Of course there were some family donations but most of the $3,100 I had in my savings account when I graduated from high school I had earned.

Aesthetics

Starting in sixth grade (my parents had reservations, and I told none of my friends) I enrolled in ballet class. Today I don't want to be a ballet dancer and I'm through my John Gielgud period, but the ballet class was a great experience. I enjoyed the expressive movement, the music, the costumes, and even learned how to do some choreography.

I experimented on my grandmother's piano and took enough lessons to give me a limited facility. My tastes in music differ from my brothers; so my father helped me fix my own equipment in the headboard of my bed, and I listen with earphones.

The future

As maybe you can guess, I hope to be a writer and am studying toward that end in college. I think I would also like to teach literature or languages in college.

In conclusion, I'd have to say that I came

out of elementary school relatively un-scathed. No teacher was ever really mean to me, and my fifth-grade teacher and the principal were great—I group them with my parents and grandmother in a special closed set.

But elementary school could have been a lot better. I spent a lot of time standing still, doodling, and pretending. Undoubtedly, the teachers had a lot of other children who needed their attention more than I did.

I want to finish with an idea and a question. The idea is, if you have an *Ex Ch* in your room, remember he has problems of his own. Be supportive, even protective, and never put him down in front of his peers. Help him fly when the world around him is walking.

The question—would you have wanted me in *your* room?

Source: Instructor, January 1977, pp. 68–72.

In or Out?

BACKGROUND

Robert Trezise, in an article entitled, "Are the Gifted Coming Back?" (1973), stated that no other group of students has been so in and out of favor during the last 60 years as the gifted. Although some gifted were identified early and easily because of their great talent, it was not until the advent of the intelligence test that a systematized and standardized technique became available to categorize intelligence. It was then, Trezise states, that the gifted first came "in." But a problem quickly arose: what could the schools do with these youngsters? The author questions whether these youngsters were truly accepted; in spite of Terman's study of genius, which clearly demonstrated that the gifted were not misfits, the feeling persisted that the gifted were not really normal.

Trezise traces these ambivalent feelings about the gifted to two prevailing views of democracy: Jeffersonian, which encouraged the identification and education of an intellectual elite, and Jacksonian, which stressed an equalitarian approach to all men. For example, Sputnik changed the concept of giftedness momentarily; panic produced a belief that the gifted were a national resource, and accelerated programs sprang up everywhere. As Trezise states, it was almost smart to be gifted. The moment of glory was brief. Controversy about intelligence tests challenged the value of IQ scores, and public opinion shifted to a concern with the culturally disadvantaged.

Today interest in the gifted has increased dramatically and currently there is a director of education for the gifted and talented in the Department of Health, Education, and Welfare. Regardless of shifting emphases that reflect social concerns, there has always been a need for programs for the gifted. Trezise states that no one denies that thousands of brilliant, talented youngsters are languishing in schools. Such talent remains underdeveloped, and many of these youngsters find school boring and useless. The gifted may well be the most educationally deprived youths in school.

WHO ARE THE GIFTED?

Recent United States government reports reflect this interest in the gifted, stating that the gifted are a minority who need special attention. They are a minority, characterized by their exceptional ability, who come from all levels of society, all races, and all national origins, and who represent both sexes equally They are unusually endowed; not merely competent, they are extraordinary: the Newtons, Einsteins, Edisons, and Lands.

Some Famous Examples

If these children are so talented, why do they require special attention? For every Einstein who is identified and flourishes, there are probably dozens of others whose gifts are obscured. Thomas Edison's mother withdrew him from first grade because he was having so much trouble; Gregor Mendel, the founder of scientific genetics, failed his teacher's test four times; Isaac Newton was considered a poor student in grammar school; Winston Churchill had a terrible academic record; Charles Darwin left medical school.

Schools frequently fail to challenge the gifted, and their talents are lost to themselves, professions, and society. You may well wonder why extraordinary children fail with ordinary educational programs. Most schools are designed for the average; as the slow learner has difficulty keeping up with average classmates, so the gifted has difficulty staying behind with average classmates. The gifted lose their motivation and either reconcile themselves to mediocrity or become discipline problems.

But the curriculum is not the only issue facing the gifted. There are several others.

1. *Failure to be identified.* In a recent survey, the U.S. Office of Education reports that 60 percent of schools reported *no* gifted students. Teachers and administrators simply fail to recognize them.
2. *Hostility of school personnel.* Hostility has traditionally been a problem for the gifted. Resentment that they are smarter than teachers, dislike for an "intellectual elite," and antagonism toward their often obvious boredom or even disruptive behavior, have all produced a hostile atmosphere for the gifted.
3. *Lack of attention.* The "in and out of favor" phenomenon that we described causes this condition. Estimates are that only 3 or 4 percent of the nation's gifted have access to special programs.
4. *Lack of trained teachers.* There are remarkably few university programs to train teachers for these children.

In 1969, Congress passed P.L. 91-230, which amended the Elementary and Secondary Education Act of 1965 and directed the

Commisioner of Education to investigate existing programs for the gifted and to make suggestions for improvements. The first step was to define giftedness, and the Office of Education questioned over 200 experts and derived the following definition:

> Gifted and talented children are those, identified by professionally qualified persons, who by virtue of outstanding abilities are capable of high performance. These are children who require differentiated educational programs and/or services beyond those normally provided by the regular school program in order to realize their contribution to self and society.
>
> "High performance" might be manifested in any or a combination of these areas:
>
> 1. General intellectual ability
> 2. Specific academic aptitude
> 3. Creative or productive thinking
> 4. Leadership ability
> 5. Visual and performing arts
> 6. Psychomotor ability

This definition is widely accepted today and, applying it to the current school population, experts conservatively estimate that a "minimum of 3 to 5 percent of the school population" are "gifted and talented" for federal program purposes. The 1970–1971 school population (elementary and secondary) was about 51.6 million; using the 3 to 5 percent figures, there are 1.5 to 2.5 million gifted children.

IDENTIFYING THE GIFTED

Since the most generous estimate claims that only 80,000 of the nation's 2 million or more gifted children are receiving appropriate education, the problem of identification becomes more meaningful. Identification may be by an individual intelligence test (if the youngster is fortunate enough to take one), a group intelligence test (which may, for many reasons, miss identifying the gifted), achievement tests (which may not identify a gifted underachiever), and parental or teacher observation.

Getzels and Dillon (1973) believe that existing knowledge suggests other procedures in addition to the above techniques.

1. *Manifest talented accomplishments.* Certain types of superior performance simply demand attention. Artistic and musical talent are outstanding examples, but more subtle achievement may be unrecognized; for example, the youngster who consistently exhibits leadership.

2. *Observations of potential talent.* Experienced and informed ob-

servers, especially teachers, may be sufficiently astute to recognize great potential. The authors give the example of The School of the Art Institute of Chicago, where teachers give grades on work performed, but also rate artistic potential. Significant signs would include constant drawing and the use of art to express personal feelings, time spent on special projects, such as making telescopes, extra reading of scientific literature, or a tendency to prove conclusions experimentally.

3 *Tests of potential talent.* These are aptitude tests designed to predict specialized talents, in art and music, architecture, mechanics, and such. The authors make the interesting comment that present studies and tests omit humanistic talents—for love and compassion, for empathy and altruism, and for living gracefully—and they wonder if these talents lie beyond psychological and educational purview.

"Genetic Studies of Genius"

In 1921, Lewis Terman began one of the most ambitious studies of the gifted ever undertaken, known as the *Genetic Studies of Genius.* Terman wished to identify over 1000 children in the California schools whose IQ was so high that it placed them within the highest 1 percent of the nation's child population. Teachers were asked to name the brightest children in their school who were then given a group intelligence test. Those who scored highest were then administered an individual Stanford-Binet test. The original criterion for inclusion in the study was an IQ of 140. One interesting finding appeared: of the youngsters nominated for the study, more of the youngest in the class qualified for the final study than of those nominated by teachers as the brightest.

This phase of the study yielded 661 subjects (354 boys and 307 girls). An additional 365 subjects came from volunteer testers in schools outside of the main survey. Both of these groups consisted of subjects from eighth grade or lower. Another 444 subjects, all junior and senior high school students, were selected by their scores on group intelligence tests. These 1470 subjects were selected from a school population of one-quarter million. Fifty-eight more subjects were added during the first follow-up in 1927–1928, providing a grand total of 1528 subjects.

Terman and his associates collected additional information about the subjects: developmental histories, school information, medical data, anthropometrical measurements, achievement test data, character test data, interests, books read over a two-month period, data on the nature of their play, word association tests, and, finally, home ratings. These data were eventually used to supply information about the characteristics of the gifted compared with their average peers.

What is especially interesting about Terman's work is his method of identifying the gifted—by almost sole reliance upon intelligence tests.

The study of mathematically and scientifically precocious youth

One of the most fascinating studies of the gifted is occurring at Johns Hopkins University. Julian Stanley has given one of the early reports on its progress that is an outstanding practical example of identifying and educating the gifted (1973). Stanley begins by stating he is pursuing a theme that has been sadly neglected: the value of tests for the quick, tentative identification of intellectually promising youths. He believes that high test scores are probably the best single clue to high potential, but cautions against an either-or view; that is, to use no tests or only to use tests. A logical conclusion is that the more we test an initially high-scoring youth, the greater can be our dependence on test data. A combination of achievement, aptitude, personality, and interest measures lets us reliably predict which pupils will succeed the most.

Use of Test Scores

Stanley states that in their study of precocious youth they have leaned heavily on test scores with excellent results. He gives the example of a 13-year-old eighth grader who took a computer course at Johns Hopkins one summer. His scores on all tests were so high that Stanley had him admitted to Hopkins in the fall of 1969, when he was still 13, and had him take honors calculus, sophomore physics, and an introduction to computer science. Of a possible 4.00 (A) grade point average, this boy received 3.69. He received his A.B. in 1973, and began doctoral work that fall when he was not quite 18. Stanley notes that without that initial testing, he would not have been identified as gifted.

These experiences encouraged Stanley to solicit foundation support for the study of mathematically and scientifically precocious youth (SMSPY). It is interesting to compare Stanley's and Terman's techniques of identifying gifted youth. Both relied on tests, but Stanley used a battery of tests: intelligence, achievement, aptitude, interest, and personality. Gallagher states that while the tendency today is to urge a variety of techniques to identify the gifted, standardized tests of mental ability are the most widely used method. If the tests do not measure all that is essential in giftedness, then some youngsters are lost because of testing inadequacy.

CHARACTERISTICS OF THE GIFTED

Almost all recent studies of the gifted have confirmed what Terman found and reported in his *Genetic Studies of Genius,* a fascinating series of five volumes extending from 1925 to 1959 (Kirk, 1972). It is both engrossing and informative to review some of Terman's discoveries based on the subjects previously described (Terman and Oden, 1947).

1. *General health and physique.* The gifted group was equal to or superior to the general population in general health, height, weight, and freedom from serious defects. They were identified as physically superior in childhood and retained this advantage. The death rate among the gifted is definitely below that of the general population.

2. *Mental health and general adjustment.* The gifted were judged by three criteria: satisfactory adjustment, some maladjustment, and serious maladjustment. Eighty percent were satisfactorily adjusted, 15 percent showed some maladjustment, while 5 percent manifested serious maladjustment. Alcoholism was a problem for 1.5 percent of the men and 1 percent of the women; five men and two women sought hospitalization as a cure. Four males served time in reformatories. Eleven men and six women (about 1 percent of the group) reported homosexuality.

3. *Intellectual status as adults.* Initial testing of the subjects (1921) yielded an average IQ of 152. Terman states that in 1940, the subjects had an average IQ of 134. Bright children become bright adults.

4. *Educational history.* About 90 percent of the gifted men and 86 percent of the gifted women entered college; 70 percent of the men and 67 percent of the women graduated. Terman concludes that these figures are about eight times as great as for the total California population. Of the graduates, 68 percent of the men and 60 percent of the women continued graduate studies. Fifty-one percent of the men and 29 percent of the women received graduate degrees, including 54 doctors of medicine, and 73 doctors of philosophy.

5. *Occupational status.* Compared to the general California population, eight times as many of the gifted entered the professions. Terman concludes that the gifted were filling positions of responsibility and exercising leadership to a reliably greater extent than average college graduates. The earned income of the gifted group was higher than that of the average college graduate, which was considerably higher than that of the general population.

6. *Marital status.* The marriage rate for the gifted was about the same as for the general population: by 1945 about 84 percent of both men and women were or had been married. Terman also attempted to assess marital adjustment and happiness of his group, and, by comparing the gifted, and those who had married the gifted, with a less-gifted group, he estimated that the gifted seemed to be slightly happier and as well adjusted as the general population.

What did Terman conclude from these data?

1. The group included about 25 scientists who have either achieved, or will achieve, a national reputation. Any randomly selected group of 1500 individuals would typically produce 2 or 3.

Lewis Terman

2. The number of published, talented writers is several times the normal expectation.
3. About a dozen of the doctors seemed destined for eminence, again, far beyond the normal expectations.
4. There is no way of evaluating those who have no desire for recognition, but who desire only personal contentment. Are they more content than their counterparts in the general populations?

Terman's monumental studies have left a legacy of dedicated research and a path which other researchers have followed, mainly to confirm his original findings. Thanks to his work, the myth of the gifted child—neurotic, sickly, isolated, unable to adjust—has largely been dissipated.

EDUCATING THE GIFTED

The burgeoning interest in the gifted comes when communities are tightening school budgets; when there is increased, intense competition for federal funds, school officials must be as prudent as they are enthusiastic. Much can be accomplished with existing resources. For example, nongraded schools, flexible grouping, and team teaching—all time-tested "innovations"—can be used to chal-

TABLE 12.6
What Is Special About Special Education?

XX—Major change X—Minor change	PROGRAM MODIFICATION		
	Content (what is taught)	Pedagogy (how it is taught)	Learning Environment (where it is taught)
SEVERE-CHRONIC (needed for all of school career)			
Moderate and severe mental retardation	XX	XX	XX
Deafness and severe hearing loss	XX	XX	XX
Blindness and severe visual impairment	X	XX	X
Autism and schizophrenia	XX	XX	XX
Orthopedically handicapped	—	X	XX
Severe communication problems (cleft palate, cerebral palsy)	—	XX	X
TRANSITIONAL (needs may be met by limited, intensive treatment)			
Educable retarded	XX	XX	XX
Hard of hearing	X	XX	X
Partially sighted	—	X	X
Emotionally disturbed	X	X	X
Articulation problems	—	X	X
Specific learning disabilities	XX	XX	X
Gifted	X	X	X

Source: James J. Gallagher, "Phenomenal Growth and New Problems Characterize Special Education," *Phi Delta Kappan* LV (April 1974): 517.

Using Existing Resources

lenge gifted students. Gifted students should have time to pursue topics more deeply than their classmates; clusters of schools should combine their gifted children regularly for special enrichment programs that would be beyond the resources of any one system; schools should employ community expertise in such fields as art, photography, journalism, drama, and creative writing, for their talented youngsters.

Harold Lyons, former Director of Education for the Gifted and Talented, believes that the key to educating the gifted is to formulate individual programs for them so that they encounter daily challenges. But he warns that talented youngsters lucky enough to have their gifts recognized are often forced into *cognitive* enrichment programs, which flaunts today's multifaceted definition of gifted. Lyons argues for the affective as well as the intellectual dimension, so that the gifted can develop their capacity for love, empathy, awareness, and ability to communicate as human beings.

Cognitive and Affective

It is a timely warning that could do much to thwart the persistent feeling that the gifted are "different." Such education requires teachers who have received special training that enables them to work with gifted students at their level and foster both the freedom and discipline vital for the fullest development of talent.

Before discussing specific techniques for educating the gifted, examine Table 12.6 carefully. Since this chapter and the next concern exceptional children, it is interesting to observe the degree of change in various programs.

Gallagher has attempted to identify the kinds of changes that have already occurred in special-education programs. Using his key, you can quickly note that programs for the gifted have undergone only slight change. Programs for most of the other exceptional children have received major alterations. Why? The answer lies in Trezise's account of the "in and out of favor" status of the gifted. Gallagher's survey reflects the time when only *ten* states had a full-time individual responsible for gifted and talented education. *Seventy-five* percent of all gifted children who received any special education were located in these ten states.

Only 12 American colleges offered graduate training for teachers of the gifted. With concern growing, what can be done for the gifted? There have traditionally been three major techniques for offering the gifted "something extra": *acceleration, enrichment,* and *special grouping.* Given current financial restrictions, changes will undoubtedly occur within these categories, supplemented possibly by federally formed options.

Acceleration

Acceleration means some modification in the regular school program that permits a gifted student to complete the program in less time or at an earlier age than usual (Getzels and Dillon, 1973). There are several variations: school admission based on mental rather than chronological age, skipping grades, combining two years work into one, eliminating more basic courses, and early admission to high school and college.

Getzels and Dillon believe that research findings on acceleration are definitely positive; Kirk, noting that most studies have focused on acceleration of one or two years and not several, urges that you be cautious in interpreting the results. Returning to the *Genetic Studies of Genius,* Terman concluded that the controversy focused on the relative importance of intellectual and social values in education. If intellectual performance is the sole criterion, then acceleration should relate directly to mental age. For example, the 6½-year-old youngster with a mental age of 10 years can achieve at fourth-grade level by the end of the *first* school year.

If such children must remain in a regular classroom, Terman be-

Pros and Cons

lieves that they still achieve far more than their classmates. In spite of such remarkable achievement, Terman states that these young-sters often acquired bad work habits. To him the basic question is how much we can risk social maladjustment to ensure a pro-gram sufficiently vigorous to command the attention and respect of the gifted. Terman flatly states that the risk of maladjustment is much less than is commonly believed. Also, the problem of social immaturity among the accelerated would lessen if more of the gif-ted were accelerated since larger numbers would remove the feel-ing of conspicuousness.

Terman believes that no generalizations are possible; decisions must depend on the individual child's characteristics. As a guide-line he suggests that programs should enable the child with an IQ of 135 and higher to enter college between the ages of 16 and 17 years. Getzels and Dillon are more dubious, however. They state that the cultural values favoring a standard period of dependency

An Example of Acceleration

Julian Stanley, whose work was mentioned earlier, believes that any learning for the gifted is doomed to frustration if it omits acceleration (1976). Concluding that most of the gifted-child research was buried with Lewis Terman in 1956, Stanley states that acceleration is vastly preferable to various enrichments that frequently degenerate into busywork, unrelated to the student's *specific* talent, or merely present advanced material earlier, guaranteeing future boredom.

Stanley believes that grade acceleration and subject matter acceleration should proceed simultaneously. Using an example from the Johns Hopkins program, he describes a verbally and mathematically brilliant boy who took one course each semester and summer from age 12 to 15. He also skipped the second, eleventh, and twelfth grades which, combined with subject matter acceleration, enabled him to enter Johns Hopkins at 15 years, 2 months (recall Terman's suggested age for college entrance) with 39 college credits.

Stanley states that most gifted boys and girls want to accelerate, which they do with ease and pleasure. Of their 44 early college entrants, only one experienced initial difficulty, which he quickly conquered. Such procedures are relatively inexpensive and may actually save a school system time and money. For example, identification of the gifted, grade skipping, some special courses, early high school graduation, and arrangement for early college placement require little extra funding.

Addressing himself to the social and emotional needs of accelerating students, Stanley concludes that those gifted students who *desired* to accelerate had few problems. While there is considerable individual variation, Stanley reasons that most of the gifted are also more socially and emotionally mature and not to challenge them by acceleration is to refuse "to extend the reach and the grasp of our brilliant youths."

---

and formal education are stronger than the social or individual needs for achievement and independence: when research findings clash with cultural values, the values will most likely prevail (1973, pg. 717).

Enrichment

Enrichment is a term designating different learning experiences in the regular classroom. Kirk (1972) states that enrichment techniques usually follow one or more of these procedures.

1. Have teachers attempt to challenge gifted pupils by assigning extra readings and assignments and permit them to participate in related extracurricular activities. For example, if parents can arrange the time, they could take a scientifically advanced stu-

dent to special classes at an institution like the New England Aquarium.

2. Grouping the school's gifted so they are together occasionally, enabling interested teachers to challenge their abilities by group discussions and independent research.

3. Provide special offerings, such as extra language or advanced science.

4. Employ for each school system a special teacher who could move from school to school, identify the gifted, aid regular teachers, and actually work with the gifted in seminars or group discussions.

Enrichment has its advantages and disadvantages. The major disadvantage is the tendency to provide the gifted with busy-work and call it enrichment. More of the same is *not* enrichment. Another disadvantage is that extra work, discussions, or classes may

Can We Be Equal and Excellent Too?

In his widely heralded book, *Excellence,* John Gardner asks the question: Can we be equal and excellent too? He states clearly his concern with the fate of excellence in modern society. Individuals are unequal in their native gifts and motivations; they will be unequal in their achievement. All must have equality of opportunity, which society has not achieved.

Gardner believes that only high ability and social education equip an individual for constructive and innovative behavior, and schools must conduct the vital talent hunt. The search for talent involves the use of tests, whatever feelings of trepidation they introduce. But, as Gardner states, tests are designed to do an unpopular job, and, in spite of their weaknesses, they have removed the talent hunt from the status of hereditary privilege. The major mistake in test usage is to apply the results beyond the academic or intellectual performance they were designed to assess.

The search and recognition of talent, which is intended to bring the best qualified to positions of leadership, necessitates rigorous selection processes. Here Gardner notes that the selection process is not simply to eliminate the less able but also to eliminate the poorly motivated. The survivors will be individuals not only of superior ability but also of superior character. Consequently, society must enlarge our view of education because the goal is nothing less than the construction of a greater and more creative civilization. The fostering of individual development within a framework of national and world values is a national task. Individual fulfillment must become an authentic national preoccupation. Excellence implies more than competence—it implies a striving for the highest standards in all our endeavors. Can we be equal and excellent too?

not match the talent and interests of the gifted child. The chief advantages are that it should provide challenging, meaningful work for gifted youngsters, while *they remain with their peers.* If teachers can satisfactorily adjust their instruction, enrichment can deter gifted youngsters from social and emotional maladjustment that *could* accompany acceleration.

Special grouping

Special grouping implies self-contained special classes, or even special schools, and not to the temporary groupings mentioned under enrichment. Considerable controversy swirls around self-contained units for the gifted, some of which relate to the Jeffersonian versus Jacksonian concepts mentioned earlier. Should a democracy encourage and establish an intellectual elite? Aside from the philosophical issue, there is no evidence indicating a clear superiority of special grouping over other techniques. Getzels and Dillon (1973, pg. 716) conclude that the research is inconclusive and experts remain uncertain as to the social desirability of grouping or its effect on achievement.

Teaching the gifted

All teachers inevitably become teachers of the gifted for two reasons: (1) Some gifted defy identification and remain with regular instructors for many years; and (2) most schools that have recognized the need for special provisions for the gifted have adopted enrichment techniques that keep gifted children in the regular classroom. Thus, since you will find the gifted in your classroom, you should recall Terman's description of their characteristics.

Most learn to read before starting school (20 percent of this group read before they were 5). They demonstrated quick understanding, insatiable curiosity, extensive information, excellent memories, and encyclopedic interests. Remember his warning: more than one-half of the children with IQ of 135 or above were already two full grades beyond the one in which they were enrolled. Terman's gifted preferred abstract school subjects, but showed about the same interest in games and sports as regular pupils. *Gifted girls share the same school interests as gifted boys,* which means that gifted girls differed sharply from average girls in scholastic preference.

Using these characteristics as a guide, you may find these suggestions helpful for teaching the gifted.

1. *Learn to recognize the signs of giftedness.* Terman's discouraging conclusions about the failure of parents and teachers to recognize unusual talent should be a warning to everyone. As the gifted return to educational prominence, you will probably be more sensitive to these youngsters and become more capable of discovering hidden talent. If you suspect unique talent, arrange for individual testing, both intelligence and aptitude. Avoid guesses; confirm your intuition.

2. *Help the gifted; do not reject them.* Once you have identified gifted students, plan to help them. This is easier said than done because teachers busy with 20 or 30 students can consider extra work with a gifted student an imposition. Try to shun such feelings and recall that they are exceptional students with deep, often unmet, needs. They may be personally difficult because school bores them, or you may feel intimidated by their quickness. Be honest with yourself; recognize the reasons for your feelings; try to challenge them. If you succeed and follow their progress, you can take pride in a job well done.

3. *Avoid hostility toward the gifted.* Discipline problems and feelings of inadequacy can often produce open hostility toward these students. There is no solution except for you to realize why you feel this way, and to determine to recognize these pupils for what they are: youths with real needs who require help.

4. *Remember that they are similar to other students.* You should help to bring together the talented with the other students to remove feelings of isolation, or of "being different." Terman's findings that the gifted have the same interest in games and sports should be a definite help to you. Also, remember that the intellectually gifted student is not necessarily physically gifted, or that the artistically talented may not be mathematically superior. These facts should help you guide the gifted's social and emotional development.

5. *Recognize where your talents lie.* As someone who has survived many years of academic trial, you possess certain talents. Recognize them and use them in your work. For example, if you like to excell in literature, you can be of enormous help in arranging reading programs for gifted students; your knowledge of books will permit you to make pertinent suggestions for those with other talents—the artistic, the scientific. *Use your talents.*

6. *Watch for signs of boredom.* Recall Terman's guidelines: the gifted are usually at least two years beyond grade placement, sometimes three or four. Gifted youngsters will quickly become restless if immersed in a regular curriculum. What can you do?

7. *Remember these specific suggestions.* First, *the gifted are excellent readers.* Outline a reading program that challenges them, keeps them interested, and encourages them in any special talent they possess. Do not use reading materials that they will meet in the next grade; you only ensure future, more serious, problems, and do later teachers a deep disservice. Second, *the gifted enjoy working with abstract materials and complex relationships.* Provide situations where they work with other gifted or some complex problem or project you have devised. Encourage discussions and seminars where they can express and support their beliefs and yet be challenged by equally inquiring minds. You may want to search the Educational Resources Information Center (ERIC) for possible programs and techniques.

Third, *the gifted are insatiably curious.* Use this curiosity to fill their free time when they complete assignments before their classmates. For example, Terman discovered that the gifted enjoy collecting. Determine the interests of your gifted and have them build collections—books, rocks, fish, whatever they enjoy that is educationally profitable. Permit them to go on field trips with parents, other classes, or by special arrangement. Combine this with both written and oral reports. Be careful, however. You must treat judiciously their use of free time, otherwise classmates may become envious and the gifted pupil soon feels different and isolated.

Although they have similar interests in games and sports, their interest is more mature. For example, when most youngsters quickly acquire an interest in baseball, it centers on the physical aspects of the game. It is the gifted child who wants to know rules, who interprets disputes, or who quotes batting averages. Use this interest to motivate them to read, calculate, or even invent a board game.

8. *Know what your state department of education is doing.* Determine if your state department of education has anyone coordinating efforts for the gifted. Those states that have such coordinators will offer excellent suggestions for programs, teaching techniques, and related literature.

Discussion Questions

1. You need to answer one question concerning the gifted that will guide your thinking and decisions. Do you believe that the gifted should be treated according to Jeffersonian or Jacksonian principles? Use this question to guide class discussion.

2. Why do the gifted so often remain unidentified? What are the implications for parents and teachers? From reading this section, what would you recommend as a basic means of identification?

3. Do you know any gifted? How were they educated? Are they "different"? How would you rate them according to Terman's characteristics of the gifted?

4. Which of the traditional methods of treating the gifted do you favor? Why? Suggest specific techniques you would adopt for each of the procedures. Can you determine advantages and disadvantages to these procedures other than those mentioned?

5. Devise your own specific suggestions for teaching the gifted. Do they differ radically from those proposed? Are they realistic with regard to money, time, and resources?

Some Concluding Thoughts

In this chapter we have discussed the extremes of the normal curve of intelligence—the slow learners and the gifted learners. Because there are frequently problems in identifying these exceptional children, you will have them in your class, often for an entire year. They require understanding, and the better you understand their abilities, needs, and problems, the more effectively you will work with them and contribute to an encouraging classroom atmosphere.

It is important to understand the characteristics of these children so that your expectations are realistic. What can you anticipate from a mildly retarded child? How much academic work can they accomplish? Why are the gifted sometimes classroom problems? How much should you challenge them? The gifted need extra stimulation but you must also consider their relationship to peers when classmates notice this special attention.

Teaching these pupils is a special task, but there are techniques that you can employ that will enable you to meet their needs more effectively. With today's tendency to mainstream exceptional children, you can be certain that you will have these pupils.

Summary

- Today's concern with exceptional children and the growing desire to maintain them in regular classrooms ensure that you will have them in your classes.

- While there are several classifications for the mentally retarded, it is the mildly retarded whom you will find in your class, especially during the early years.

- You should be aware of the characteristics of slow learners so that you can alert administrators, arrange testing, and devise suitable programs, especially for those who may appear retarded because of cultural deprivation.

- Know and utilize the recommended techniques for teaching the mildly retarded in regular classrooms.

- It is relatively easy to miss identifying gifted children if their talents are masked by boredom, restlessness, and behavior problems.

- Today's definition of gifted includes a wide variety of talents, and specialists urge that a battery of intelligence and aptitude tests be used in attempts to identify gifted pupils.

- Terman's classic studies have provided invaluable information about the gifted, especially about their characteristics, which enable educators to devise suitable strategies for teaching gifted students.

Suggested Readings

Clarizio, Harvey and George McCoy. *Behavior Disorders in Children*. New York: Crowell, 1976. Excellent overview of exceptional children and their needs.

Kirk, Samuel. *Educating Exceptional Children*. Boston: Houghton Mifflin, 1972. Probably the best single source, analyzing all kinds of exceptional children. Particularly valuable for suggestions about curriculum and teaching techniques.

Knoblock, Hilda and Benjamin Pasamanick. *Gesell and Amatruda's Developmental Diagnosis*. New York: Harper & Row, 1974. Fine source of comparative developmental rates, with specific behavioral differences that help to distinguish the normal from the retarded.

Lane, Harlan. *The Wild Boy of Aveyron*. Cambridge, Mass.: Harvard University Press, 1976. Fine historical account of a classic study. Valuable for its insights into the development of methods of treating the retarded.

Skeels, Harold. "Adult Status of Children with Contrasting Early Life Experiences," *Monographs of the Society for Research in Child Development* 31, no. 3, 1966. One of the great environmental studies with which you should be familiar.

Terman, Lewis and Melita Oden. *The Gifted Child Grows Up*. Stanford University Press, 1947. Every student should know and use Terman's enduring series, *Genetic Studies of Genius*, of which this comprehensive report is Volume IV.

13

Mainstreaming Exceptional Children

Introduction

The previous chapter discussed slow and gifted learners as special examples of exceptional children—special because they may remain undetected as such for years. Meanwhile, they receive instruction intended for the "average" student, which may cause difficulty. Today, however, a remarkable phenomenon is sweeping across American education, a phenomenon that guarantees a steady flow of exceptional youngsters into your classroom. Called mainstreaming, it has been praised by its admirers as the greatest educational change since school integration, and damned by its critics as a headlong plunge into chaos. Typically, reality lies somewhere between these two extremes.

It is a novel movement about which little hard evidence exists. Consequently, the task here is to trace briefly the roots of special education and attempt to determine how it produced legislation leading to mainstreaming. What, precisely, is mainstreaming and what does it imply for individual states and school systems? To answer this questions one of the most advanced programs in the nation will be examined: Chapter 766 of the Acts of the Commonwealth of Massachusetts. Finally, what does mainstreaming mean for you? No teacher will escape its effects, beginning with changes in teacher education programs and extending into the classroom.

Initially, a brief overview of mainstreaming may help you to understand better some of the specific aspects of the movement we shall analyze.

WHAT IS MAINSTREAMING?

Mainstreaming means integrating physically and mentally handicapped children into regular classes. Most exceptional children,

with the exception of slow and gifted learners, have readily discernible characteristics that quickly mark them as special-class students. In the past, they were educated apart from their peers. But in 1975, Congress passed the Education for All Handicapped Children Act of 1975, which ensures every child some form of public education and urges integration into regular classes as soon as possible for all but the most severely handicapped. Beginning with funding of $200 million in the first year and increasing to over $3 billion in 1982, the bill all but dictates including most exceptional children in regular classes.

The United States Office of Education states that there are approximately 8 million handicapped children of school age, which represents 12 percent of the 6 to 19 age group. Officials estimate that only one-half of these receive appropriate education. But why should they enter regular classes? Proponents of mainstreaming believe that a special class isolates the exceptional child academically and socially, furthermore, normal youngsters benefit from association with the handicapped.

While special-class placement may not result in superior academic performance, mainstreaming may be a mixed blessing for some exceptional children: insensitive classmates can make life miserable for the handicapped. Teachers' organizations generally favor mainstreaming, with reservations, but individual teachers feel uneasy. Administrators realize that proper planning may require funds to install ramps, elevators, and other special equipment; otherwise, school life could become excessively difficult for a handicapped youngster.

This attitude to mainstreaming, favorable but cautious, reflects an awareness of the dangers of pendulum swings in education; for example, from enthusiasm for special classes to a rush away from them. Some believe that the current zeal for mainstreaming, resulting from excessive expectations for special classes, may, in turn, lead to excessive expectations for mainstreaming. There is a need for both quality special education and appropriate integration of exceptional children into regular classes. Ardent advocacy of one extreme or the other can only damage the hopes of exceptional children.

Background

WHO ARE THE EXCEPTIONAL CHILDREN?

Different Emphases

Exceptional children are those who deviate from the normal because of certain characteristics. Cruickshank (1975a), whose analysis of the special-education movement is followed here, states that the term "exceptional child" represents many different medical, psychological, and educational groupings of children. Table 13.1 presents the different emphases of medicine, psychology, and education and helps to illustrate why definition is difficult. Each discipline emphasizes different functions and uses different techniques, which is reflected in definition. For example, while medicine focuses on physiological aspects, education concentrates on behavior; while medicine is concerned with prevention and medical treatment, psychology focuses on measurement and psychological therapy.

Any classification of exceptional children would include the following:

1. Intellectually exceptional
2. Crippled
3. Learning disabled
4. Emotionally disturbed
5. Deaf
6. Hard of hearing
7. Speech impaired
8. Visually impaired
9. Multiple handicapped

TABLE 13.1
Emphases of Medicine, Psychology, and Education

Discipline	Levels of assessment	Relevant factors	Definitional emphasis
Medicine	Physiological	Etiology Prevention Medical treatment Changes in function and structure	Biological events Genetic events Neurophysiological events Structure and function
Psychology	Psycho-educational correlates to learning	Measurement Cognitive development Remedial treatment	Cognitive development Psychological events
Education	Behavior	Prevalence Classification Management Behavior modification Developmental methods Corrective treatment	Educational consequences Social-emotional behavior Motivation Observable behavior

These categories are frequently used, mainly because they represent those handicaps eligible for federal support. Each class may be further subdivided. Intellectually exceptional comprises both gifted and retarded. Crippled embraces a wide variety of physical handicaps: cerebral palsy, clubfoot, epilepsy, polio. Learning disabled applies to those children diagnosed as minimally brain damaged, suffering from minimal brain dysfunction or central process dysfunction, or perceptually handicapped. Emotionally disturbed refers to those children who fail to mature socially and emotionally. Deaf and hard of hearing are distinct handicaps requiring different educational treatment. Speech impaired includes those youngsters who manifest speech disabilities because of many different reasons. Visually impaired refers to both the partially sighted and the blind. Finally, there are those youngsters who experience multiple handicaps; for example, a crippled child may simultaneously suffer emotional upset.

Labeling

As Cruickshank concludes, exceptional child is an umbrella term that encompasses many different groups of children with different degrees of disability. These differences illustrate the dangers of labeling. For example, cerebral palsied children so differ from each other in the degree of disability, intelligence, and perceptual abilities that it is impossible to make generalizations about their learning capabilities. The same is true for other handicapped students: homogeneous groups are actually nonexistent. While groupings may be an administrative necessity, teachers must meet the specific learning deficits of the *individuals* within any group.

THE ROOTS OF SPECIAL EDUCATION

Residential schools for the blind, deaf, and mentally retarded were among the first and most obvious concessions to special education that appeared in the early nineteenth century. A less publicized, but profound, influence on people's attitudes toward the handicapped was America's wars, especially the two world wars. Compulsive military service in World War II required massive screening that produced a staggering number of rejects. Their communities had accepted these men and, after rejection, they returned to their regular lives. Tens of thousands of others were maimed during the war, returned to their homes, and were again accepted, thus causing a gradual erosion in prejudice against the physically disabled.

Other influences combined to lessen ignorance and bias. From timid beginnings, parents organized to form local, state, and national associations, which demanded, and received, professional attention and federal support. They have been remarkably successful as you can judge from Table 13.2. Even before P.L. 94-142 (the mainstreaming act), large amounts of federal money were appropriated for the handicapped.

But, as Cruickshank notes, special education's progress depended on discoveries in medicine, physics, biology, chemistry, and psychology. For example, electronics has evolved a new technology for educating the deaf and hard of hearing; it has also produced highly sophisticated sensors in canes for the blind that

TABLE 13.2

Funds Expended, by Type of Handicapped Children and Number of Children Served; Under Part B, EHA; P.L. 89–313; Title III, ESEA; and the Vocational Education Act Fiscal Year 1971

Type of Handicap	Funds Expended	Number of Children Served
Trainable mentally retarded	$ 27,050,007	122,760
Educable mentally retarded	44,435,853	324,777
Learning disabled	10,210,496	58,442
Emotionally disturbed	14,467,346	84,439
Other health impaired	5,704,420	23,004
Crippled	3,237,589	23,409
Visually impaired	5,204,166	30,302
Deaf	10,379,537	38,577
Hard of hearing	6,167,349	46,227
Speech impaired	5,615,557	167,501
Total	$132,472,320	919,438

greatly enhance mobility. Research has created drugs that permit epileptics and hyperactive children to remain in the classroom.

Current Changes

As communities recognized the needs of exceptional children, and as research made more of these pupils ready for *some* education, a sharp demand for special-education teachers arose. All of these forces—wars, parental action, federal support, community acceptance, and more professionals—have brought special education to an unprecedented peak of favor. Today continuing change occurs: there is a growing tendency to eliminate the large institutions for smaller regional or community centers. Mainstreaming, or integrating the exceptional child into regular classes, is the contemporary controversy. Accompanying each change is the demand for quality care of the exceptional child.

But does quality imply either special education or mainstreaming? A potential danger of mainstreaming is that there may be overemphasis upon normal development, which can be misleading when educating exceptional children. The exceptional child is a child with differences; it is these differences that special education has attempted to help. If there were no differences, there would be no need of special education (Cruickshank, 1975*a,* pg. 22). Exceptional children may require separate transportation, ramps, wheelchairs, speech therapy, or special reading materials. Special education's task has been both to provide for the normal and special needs of the exceptional child and to avoid duplicating general education.

Why Special Education?

Here is the potential value of mainstreaming. If a child's needs are not too demanding, they may best be met by a combination of regular-class work and specialized help. It is only after determining the degree of a child's differences that a decision is possible about education: does the child require special placement, or is the difference mild enough so that a modification of a regular-class program will suffice? When parents, teachers, and children are satisfied with a thorough diagnosis, a thoughtful curriculum designed to meet unique needs, and realistic goals, then a rewarding balance between mainstreaming and special education will emerge.

THE ROLE OF THE SCHOOLS

The public schools must educate all children but most states traditionally excluded exceptional children from such legislation. Two recent court decisions—one in Pennsylvania, the other in Washington, D.C.—have provided a legal basis for educating all children. In the Pennsylvania case a suit was filed on behalf of all the mentally retarded who were excluded from public education. The court subsequently ruled that no mentally retarded child should be deprived of full public education and training. Pennsylvania schools were ordered to *discover* all mentally retarded individuals

Landmark Legal Decisions

between the ages of 6 and 21 and to furnish them free education appropriate to their needs.

The Washington, D.C., case, going beyond this ruling, filed suit on behalf of *all* handicapped children. The court ruled that the Constitution of the United States guaranteed a free public education to all children, including the handicapped. The court also ruled that lack of funds was not a valid reason for excluding the handicapped. These two decisions altered the nature of special education and gave great impetus to the mainstreaming movement and the federal legislation that ensures the educational rights of all children.

Educational planning for exceptional children

To comprehend fully the implications of mainstreaming, you should first understand existing plans to educate exceptional children. Such knowledge will not only help you to appreciate the many needs that youngsters may possess, but also help you to devise strategies best suited to meet those needs. Cruickshank and De Young (1975) group these plans into six categories.

1. *The residential school.* The residential, or boarding school for blind children appeared as early as 1930. Other institutions designed for the mentally retarded and the deaf quickly materialized. These institutions have been severely criticised for several reasons: they remove children from their normal contacts (family, peers), social stigma accompany placement ("He's in the deaf school"), the services provided often are inferior, and financial support is frequently scanty. The authors believe that residential schools have been, and should continue to be, an integral part of the total educational program; they state (1975, pg. 65), the challenge of the residential school is not its cessation, but its increase in quality and stature.

2. *The community special school.* Immediately preceding World War I many communities developed local programs for exceptional children, chiefly because parents wanted their children near home and city growth permitted such extensions. Two kinds of school emerged: one designed to serve a single type of exceptional child (for example, mentally retarded), the other to provide for different handicaps. Transportation can be a problem and youngsters are still separated from their peers. But the children are at home; they still contact their neighborhood peers; and multiple services are available.

3. *The special class.* Special classes are located in regular school buildings for groups of exceptional children: mentally retarded, blind, deaf, physically handicapped, gifted. Special-class children are close to peers but have those distinctive services that their differences demand. Good special classes serve children well, but the major disadvantage is segregation, which both parents and courts have protested and which has produced mainstreaming. But for children who need highly specialized treatment, a special class of homogeneously grouped children designed to meet specific developmental needs is usually accepted by children, parents, teachers, and administrators (Cruickshank and De Young, 1975, pg. 73).

4. *The resource room.* To blunt criticism of the special class's segregation, some school systems have hired special-education teachers who remain in one room. Children come to the resource teacher for help for their special needs. The resource room has been mainly used for the partially sighted, the hard of hearing, the physically handicapped, and the learning disabled. The child remains with the regular class, with all its advantages, but still has convenient specialized help.

5. *The itinerant teacher program.* Kirk states (1972, pg. 20) that speech correctionists, social workers, school psychologists, reme-

dial reading teachers, learning disability specialists, and other special-education personnel may deal with children on an itinerant
basis. They may serve several schools and travel great distances to
meet with exceptional children. Kirk gives the example of a speech
therapist who may meet with a youngster several times weekly,
while an itinerant teacher of the visually impaired may come only
once a month. It again has the advantage of keeping children in
their regular classes while offering specialized help. It is essentially
a tutorial service, which is also quite effective with hospitalized or
homebound children.

6. *Mainstreaming.* In the 1970s, integration of exceptional children into regular classes became a groundswell movement that
eventually produced federal legislation—P.L. 94-142—that ensures
each handicapped child a free appropriate public education.
Cruickshank and DeYoung (1975) state that, if mainstreaming, or
integration, is to succeed, school personnel must observe certain
guidelines: *all* exceptional children do not belong in regular
classes; regular teachers and administrators must understand the
nature and needs of exceptional children; there must be adequate
financial support; there must be a total program for exceptional
children; that is, these youngsters must go on field trips or excur-
sions as well as participate in reading or mathematics classes. The
authors recommend cautious planning since the needs of a generation of children are at stake.

Finally, the authors plead for *selective placement,* which involves
the careful and complete assessment of the abilities and limitations
of child, home, and community by professionally qualified persons
representing numerous disciplines, and the ultimate joint recommendation of an evaluation team regarding the optimum educational placement with regard to the realistic opportunities that present themselves (Cruickshank and DeYoung, 1975).

Program requirements

Regardless of the educational plan, a good program requires certain basic features. The necessity for early discovery and selective
placement of exceptional children has been mentioned. Addition-
ally, state and local programs should undertake an initial survey,
followed by a continuous census, to determine their actual needs.
School personnel probably should initiate the survey and refer
suspect children for further screening.

The Survey

Ulrey (1976), stressing the need for early testing, states that
some knowledge of a child's developmental history and a brief test
can often identify a child who is *at risk;* that is, a child who has a
high probability of developing some handicap. While the technology is available to identify such children, most problems remain unrecognized until they become obvious. Testing specialists

MASSACHUSETTS EASTER SEAL SOCIETY

urge a systematic screening of preschoolers that involves four stages.

Stage I. Paraprofessionals administer brief tests and interviews for gross sorting.

Stage II. A psychologist examines at risk children to determine if more comprehensive testing is necessary.

Stage III. A team of specialists evaluates the child and recommends treatment.

State IV. A definite treatment and follow-up program is arranged.

Such screening implies the need for psychological services, another ingredient of a good program. The success or failure of the survey, screening, and continuous census requires skilled personnel using and interpreting appropriate tests. Not only must such psychological services provide information about children but also teachers need to be sufficiently competent to comprehend and apply testing results. Teacher education programs must ensure that students understand the purpose of a particular test so that they can grasp why mentally retarded or epileptic, brain-damaged, or emotionally disturbed children function as they do.

Another essential for a good program, especially with the ad-

Staff Training

vent of mainstreaming, is the continuing accessibility of in-service training. Some type of staff training will be essential for teachers who have little, if any, knowledge of the needs of exceptional children. Teachers, like others, often react to stereotypes, and it is only through positive staff orientation that exceptional children can succeed in the new environment.

Elementary school teachers have been chiefly concerned with exceptional children because of the emphasis on early discovery and the elementary school's acceptance of developmental principles and individualized instruction. But with current changes more secondary school teachers will contact exceptional children.

The Secondary School

For example, traditionally, secondary schools have resisted accepting educable mentally retarded students and only grudgingly admitted them to vocational or mechanical programs. Cruickshank's statement about the educable mentally retarded student (1975*b*, pg. 123) applies to all secondary school exceptional students: high school personnel today are challenged to provide programs that will continue the efforts of the elementary school to develop healthy community attitudes, to foster minimum skills, and to encourage the maximum employment potential of exceptional students.

Conclusion

Integrating the exceptional child into the regular classroom is now a legislative mandate. To appreciate fully the task that lies ahead, you must realize just who are the exceptional children and how society has historically provided for them. You must know the specialized programs and plans that have been proposed, some of which, such as resource rooms and itinerant teachers, will coexist with mainstreaming.

Discussion Questions

1. Any discussion of exceptional children raises the issue of labeling. Other than those discussed in these two chapters can you think of advantages and disadvantages of categorizing children?

2. The role of the wars in forcing acceptance of the handicapped is fascinating. Do you know any handicapped veterans? Have they been accepted? What are people's reactions? Has the veteran adjusted satisfactorily by both his own and society's standards? Was he able to continue his education?

3. After reading the brief descriptions of the various educational plans to provide for the exceptional (residential schools, special classes), what is your initial reaction to mainstreaming? List what you see as its major advantages and disadvantages.

4. The Washington, D.C., and Pennsylvania court cases are far-reaching decisions. The Pennsylvania decision ordered the schools to discover all mentally retarded individuals between 6 and 21 years old, which would entail some screening technique such as Ulrey suggested. Do you think this is feasible? What is your reaction to Stage I?

5. What types of exceptional children could succeed in secondary schools? Refer to the categories at the beginning of the chapter. List the problems that you think secondary school teachers face in teaching exceptional children. What types of preparation do you think they should have?

The mainstreaming movement

Mainstreaming, or integration of exceptional children into regular classrooms, means that the mildly handicapped—of all categories—will require additional classroom support. Special-education teachers will function as resource personnel, helping the regular teacher with the exceptional child's schooling. It is important for you to realize that help will be constantly available as you work with these youngsters. Otherwise, the regular classroom will become a "dumping ground" with unfortunate consequences for children, parents, teachers, and schools.

The rationale for mainstreaming, which underlies all of the court cases, is as follows.

1. Carefully planned educational programs will facilitate better learning for all handicapped youth.
2. Education extends beyond the academic: children learn to cope with their environment, to accept, and to be accepted by, their peers, to adjust emotionally to their personal capacity, and to acquire a sense of competency and independence.
3. The sooner that children begin education, both normal and special, the greater will be their learning (Weintraub and Abeson, 1974).

WHY MAINSTREAMING?

Doubts about special education's effectiveness and isolated court cases are not themselves powerful enough to produce a national groundswell of support and federal legislation. Other forces must have been at work. Birch (1974) believes that mainstreaming derives from multiple complex motives.

1. *The capacity to deliver special education anywhere has improved.* Special education's technology is now so mobile that there is little difficulty in bringing considerable specialized materials to children, which is especially true of self-instruction devices.

2. *Parental intervention is more direct, both through the courts and in the schools themselves.* Parents, never desiring special-class placement of their children, have demanded that special support be offered to appropriate children in regular classes. Where parents believed that such support was lagging, they petitioned the courts for help, winning landmark decisions in Pennsylvania and Washington, D.C.

3. *A repugnance for labeling, coupled with serious doubts about the accuracy of psychological testing, raised grave doubts about the wisdom of special-class placement.* Calling a child "retarded" or "disturbed" may produce a self-fulfilling prophecy: children begin to act delinquent, slow, or disturbed simply because they are treated as such. Since the initial label may have come from test results, a youngster may be unfairly penalized. A disadvantaged student with poor verbal ability frequently does poorly on verbal tests. As Birch states, since children are often placed in special schools and special classes because of low test scores, a growing challenge to the tests themselves has arisen. Many urban administrators, discovering that many more of their pupils were classified as mentally retarded than national estimates, adapted the regular curriculum to compensate for pupils' weaknesses. As a form of compensatory education, Birch believes it was a straw in the wind blowing toward mainstreaming.

4. *Economic conditions favor mainstreaming.* Not only does mainstreaming match the national mood, it may also prove economically sound. As costs for real estate, building materials, and labor spiral, the possibility of extended use of school buildings becomes attractive.

5. *Economics, doubts about special education, and idealism have combined to produce mainstreaming.* While money is always an issue, a spirit of sympathy and compassion for the handicapped has unquestionably been a major motive. When realism and idealism combined with serious doubts about special education's efficacy, change was inevitable.

As Birch notes, no single element caused current changes, but a combination of all produced a steady evolution from the early residential schools. Today many parents and educators believe that both handicapped and nonhandicapped youth suffer when the exceptional are isolated. Youngsters who never contact the handicapped miss an opportunity to develop compassion and understanding. Early interaction removes, for the nonhandicapped, awkwardness, unease, and feelings of repulsion and scorn. For the

handicapped, security, confidence, and feelings of acceptance result naturally when accurate, selective placement has been made.

FEDERAL LEGISLATION—P.L. 94-142

In 1975, Congress, reacting to the pressures described earlier, passed P.L. 94-142, the Education for All Handicapped Children Act of 1975. The intent of the act is clear—to help the more than 8 million handicapped children in the United States become all that they are capable of becoming. The act defines special education as specially designed instruction that may include placement in a special class, a special program in a regular classroom, home in-

Mainstreaming and EMR Children

While evidence favoring mainstreaming is scanty, as is evidence condemning it, studies are appearing that provide tentative support. For example, Gottlieb, Gampel, and Budoff (1975) attempted to assess the impact of mainstreaming on educable mentally retarded (*EMR*) children. The authors observed 22 youngsters who had been randomly assigned to segregated and integrated placements. Originally, all the students were attending classes in schools destined for demolition. In the new school, 11 pupils were assigned to regular classes, while the remaining 11 were placed in a special class.

The youngsters were observed in May, while they were still in special classes in their original school, in November after reassignment to the new school, and again in May. Those in regular classes spent the day there, except for 40 minutes in a remedial learning center. Those in special class remained there for the day, taught by special-education teachers.

The authors observed several behaviors: attention, distraction, out of seat, restlessness, self-stimulation, uncoordinated motor response, aggressiveness toward peer, positive verbal response from peer, and negative verbal response from peer. After one year of integration, the ex-special class pupils exhibited more prosocial behavior than did those who remained in *EMR* special classes. They also manifested more prosocial behavior than did those in a regular-class sample.

The authors interpret the results to show the beneficial effect of regular-class teachers and students. Special-class youngsters had only their classmates as models, who still engaged in inappropriate behavior because there were so few inducements to change. The authors also rationalized that the integrated child may fear return to the special class if he or she misbehaves.

There was one disturbing finding: regular-class children do not choose integrated *EMR* children as friends. The authors believe that given the positive results of integration, further study is needed to determine the causes of this lack of acceptance.

struction, hospital instruction, institutional placement, or special training in physical education. The essential element in any specially designed instruction is that it must be based on individualized educational programs to meet each child's needs.

The Individualized Educational Program

The individualized education program is a written statement that specifies instructional objectives and indicates what special education and related services (such as transportation and help like special therapy, physical therapy, psychotherapy, recreation, and medical services) the child will receive. The plan must specify the child's present level of functioning and include *annual goals.* Educators, parents, and, if possible, the child should participate in its formulation.

Congress found that more than half of the handicapped children

The Timetable

receive no appropriate educational services; 1 million of these are totally excluded from the public school system. If any school system is to receive federal support under this act, it must have provided free appropriate public education to all handicapped between the ages of 3 and 18 by September 1, 1978. By September 1, 1980, the same opportunity must be available to those between 3 and 21. Appropriate education means that handicapped children are educated with the nonhandicapped whenever possible. Special classes or schools should be used only when the handicap is so severe that regular-class education, with support, is unsatisfactory.

Testing

The legislation addresses an especially sensitive issue in special education: testing. Parents and critics of special education have accused the schools of crudely assigning disadvantaged youngsters to special classes based on faulty testing procedures. This has been particularly true for the mentally retarded special class, since youngsters who score poorly are assumed to be abnormally slow. Too frequently, normal youngsters with an English-language difficulty have been identified as retarded. The new law requires safeguards in using tests for placement so that racial and cultural discrimination is eliminated. No test is the sole criterion for placement. Parents or guardians also have the right to examine all pertinent records used for their child's identification, evaluation, and educational placement. If parents question the assessment, they may obtain an independent evaluation of their child.

The Right of Appeal

Parents are to receive a written notice in their native language about any change in identification, evaluation, or placement of their child. The legislation defines native language as the language normally used by a person with limited English-speaking ability. If parents remain dissatisfied with placement and education, they may initiate a due process hearing, which is to be conducted by someone not presently responsible for the child's education. All participants will receive a verbatim record of the hearing. If still dissatisfied, parents or guardians may carry their grievance to the appropriate state agency and, ultimately, to the courts. While a decision is pending, children remain where they were before the appeal.

The legislation is breathtaking in its scope and illustrates why some observers believe that it will produce the most sweeping changes in education since the desegregation impetus began in 1954 with *Brown* vs. *Board of Education of Topeka*. What is important here is your role in the process because there is no escaping involvement. Somewhere in the identification, evaluation, and placement procedure, you will be asked to comment on the child's classroom performance. Some states have the teacher play a key role in presenting current and past educational information. Since the legislation also requires each state to develop and implement a comprehensive system of personnel development, you will inescapably have changes in preservice education, or if you are now teaching, you will have some form of in-service training. Sooner or later you will encounter the ramifications of P.L. 94-142. Mainstreaming is here to stay.

MAINSTREAMING: AN INTERPRETATION

Birch (1974) states that the idea and its accompanying terminology are so new that confusion can result. Unless there is agreement on what is meant, the ideals of mainstreaming will not see fulfillment. Birch believes that most state directors of special education agree with several basic principles.

Regular Classes

Mainstreaming involves placing handicapped students in regular classes, whenever possible, and offering specialized help there. Regular-class teachers must adapt content and techniques to en-

A Study of Teachers' Attitudes

Mainstreaming is proceeding at an unprecedented rate, its impetus derived from the mistaken belief that it is a magical solution rather than an experiment supplying special education services for mildly handicapped youngsters. Gickling and Theobald (1975) state that mainstreaming enthusiasm has outraced its research support. But, as these authors suggest, if mainstreaming is to have any chance of success, it is important to understand teachers' and administrators' perceptions of this new movement.

They sampled regular and special-education personnel, both elementary and secondary, in rural and urban populations. They also assessed what teachers believed *their* needs to be under these novel circumstances. Altogether, 326 Tennessee teachers and administrators from both regular- and special-education classes responded to a 46-item questionnaire; the ratio of regular educators to special educators was three to one. The results were provocative.

These results are shown in the table on pages 520–521. Items one to six illustrate teachers' attitudes toward special classes. Items one, four, and five clearly show that about two-

thirds of the special-education personnel believe that special classes are restrictive. Only 50 percent of regular-education personnel agreed with item one. Note the high agreement on item six: from 60 to 70 percent believe that special-class placement reflects socioeconomic and racial bias. Thus we can conclude from items one through six that large numbers of both regular and special educators think that special classes restrict and discriminate against exceptional children.

But a warning emerges from the data in items seven through fifteen. Discrepancies abound. For example, items one through six indicate a general dissatisfaction with special classes. Items seven through fifteen show that while a large majority of both special and regular personnel believe special classes were not providing adequate academic services for the handicapped (item nine), nevertheless 60 percent of both groups thought that special classes were more effective than regular classes for the mildly handicapped. Note especially item eight — less than 15 percent of both elementary and secondary regular teachers believed that they possess sufficient skills to aid exceptional children.

It is a disturbing study. Perhaps regular educators are merely insecure with the unknown, but there is no strong teacher support for mainstreaming. The authors conclude that for mainstreaming to succeed, teachers' attitudes cannot be ignored. A mandate for mainstreaming has been given, but before systems initiate programs, there should be assessment of teachers' needs and planning for specific in-service programs. Otherwise, mildly handicapped children can only suffer further reversals.

Questionnaire Item	PERCENTAGE OF "YES" RESPONSES PER QUESTIONNAIRE ITEM						
	Regular Educ. $N = 230$	Special Educ. $N = 96$	Sec. Regular Teachers $N = 67$	Sec. Special Teachers $N = 25$	Elem. Regular Teachers $N = 122$	Elem. Special Teachers $N = 49$	Elem. Sup./ Admin. $N = 29$
TEACHER ATTITUDE TOWARD EQUAL EDUCATIONAL OPPORTUNITY FOR EXCEPTIONAL CHILDREN							
1. Being placed in a special-education self-contained classroom restricts the chance for a student to fully participate in activities, such as service organizations, clubs, sports, normally available to regular-classroom students.	48.2	66.3	50.7	68.0	47.1	75.5	48.3
2. If given a chance, special-education students would participate in most school activities.	68.5	78.5	60.3	84.0	70.7	83.7	86.2
3. Public schools' philosophies and objectives are limited to the range of normal children.	68.8	58.5	62.7	56.5	69.7	64.6	67.9
4. Children placed in self-contained special-education classes are more likely to be seen as different than if permitted to stay in regular classes.	61.3	73.0	56.5	66.7	62.7	81.3	69.0
5. A child is socially isolated from his peers when placed in a self-contained special-education class.	56.4	71.4	49.3	72.0	61.5	72.9	67.9
6. Special-education placement practices have been free of socioeconomic and racial discrimination.	29.4	41.9	36.4	26.1	23.9	41.3	34.5
TEACHER COMMITMENT TOWARD INTEGRATING EXCEPTIONAL CHILDREN INTO REGULAR CLASSROOMS							
7. Under normal conditions the regular-classroom teacher feels imposed upon to help special-education students.	48.9	31.0	47.1	30.4	48.7	31.1	46.4

Questionnaire Item	PERCENTAGE OF "YES" RESPONSES PER QUESTIONNAIRE ITEM						
	Regular Educ. N = 230	Special Educ. N = 96	Sec. Regular Teachers N = 67	Sec. Special Teachers N = 25	Elem. Regular Teachers N = 122	Elem. Special Teachers N = 49	Elem. Sup./ Admin. N = 29
8. The regular-classroom teacher feels he/she has the skills to help special-education students.	15.2	10.5	14.7	13.6	12.8	10.9	18.5
9. Special self-contained classes seem to be adequately providing academic services for the mildly handicapped and do not need to be changed.	39.2	32.2	35.9	34.8	42.1	26.1	29.6
10. Special self-contained classes for the mildly handicapped have proved to be more effective than regular classes have been for these students.	62.1	59.3	72.1	62.5	58.2	53.1	44.8
11. If there was a movement away from self-contained special classes for the mildly handicapped, would regular-classroom teachers be willing to accept special-education students into their classes?	59.3	47.5	57.8	54.5	64.5	54.5	70.4
12. The regular-classroom teacher would feel more comfortable if special education would assist in providing services in the regular classroom.	80.6	80.0	88.2	77.3	83.5	76.1	57.1
13. If time were available to work with special-education personnel, regular-classroom teachers would take advantage of this opportunity.	95.3	91.6	97.7	91.3	94.6	90.7	93.1
14. In the future, I strongly recommend the use of resource rooms for mildly handicapped children.	85.8	82.0	90.2	88.0	82.7	77.1	82.1
15. In the future, I strongly recommend the use of self-contained classes for the mildly handicapped.	45.9	41.6	55.6	33.3	41.4	35.4	37.9

Source: Edward Gickling and John Theobald, "Mainstreaming: Affect or Effect." *The Journal of Special Education* (Fall 1975): 317–328.

compass all children in normal activities with attainable goals for each child. These procedures apply from preschool programs through secondary education, and, at each level, the handicapped child reports to the regular-classroom teacher. Exceptional children will spend at least half of each day in the regular classroom.

If suitable help is to be available for mildly handicapped pupils, then the burden cannot fall alone on regular-classroom teachers. Resource rooms and special education teachers must be accessible so that exceptional children can receive either small-group or individual instruction and assignments, in which both special and regular teachers ideally should cooperate. Although grades and reports are the regular teachers' responsibility, both regular and special teachers should mutually agree on them. These special resources should also be open to regular pupils who may temporarily need them.

Birch (1974) succinctly summarizes the mainstreaming process: exceptional children will enter a regular kindergarten or first grade, where they will simultaneously receive special support. Special-class placement follows only when the need is obvious and agreeable to child, parents, and school officials (now demanded by

Mainstreaming Terminology

Jack Birch has presented some concise and practical suggestions for understanding mainstreaming. One treats the new language arising from the movement. Some of the more common terms and their meaning follow.

Adaptive education. Synonym for special education

ARD committee. Admission, Review, and Discharge committee that monitors programs of exceptional children

All-out pupils. Exceptional children placed in regular class with special help

Alternative programming. Synonym for mainstreaming

Clinical center. Resource room

Consultation room. Resource room

Floating room. Resource room

Helping teacher. Special-education teacher

Inclusion. Mainstreaming

Integration. Mainstreaming

Learning center. Resource room

Modified plan. Mainstreaming

Progressive inclusion. Scheduling exceptional children into regular class as children improve and/or teachers develop more expertise with the handicapped

Resource room. Special teachers' space for providing specialized help for those exceptional children placed in regular classes. May entail individualized or small-group instruction

Self-contained program. Total instruction by special-education teachers

Self-contained special education class. Exceptional students spend the entire day in a special class

Stair stepping. Gradually moving special-class pupils into regular classes

P.L. 94-142). The intent of special-class placement is to prepare these pupils for return to regular classes. Youngsters are selected for mainstreaming because of their needs, and the mainstreaming program's ability to satisfy these needs, rather than because of the severity of the handicap.

A NEED FOR THOUGHTFUL MAINSTREAMING

Martin (1976) states that most educators have incorrectly and rigidly categorized children into normal and handicapped, believing that the two groups differ radically in nature and in the learning challenges they present. He believes that this belief is based on two false assumptions:

1. The numbers of exceptional are so small that they are of no vital concern to the school.
2. The exceptional have learning problems that are unique and irrelevant to regular education.

Teacher Training

Recently, however, educators realize that almost 50 percent of school children experience problems, some of which require special help. Martin suggests that initially educators must rethink basic teacher training so that all teachers are qualified to work successfully with a wide variety of individual differences. Given the Gickling and Theobold data, Martin's suggestion is particularly pertinent. Unless teachers possess competence *and* understanding, mainstreaming has little chance of success.

It is a difficult task, probably far more difficult than educators now realize. Changing adults' attitudes presents unique obstacles; their beliefs and their stereotypes resist change. Some experienced teachers will find change formidable, and in-service programs must be ready to cope with silent opposition. But teachers' willingness to work with exceptional children is the key to mainstreaming success.

Martin is also concerned with the "naive, mad dash to mainstream children, based on hopes of better things for them." He views the major barriers as:

1. The lack of adequate training for experienced classroom teachers. Efforts are falling behind the pace of mainstreaming. Skills and competencies alone are insufficient; there must be attitudinal change that can only come from practical involvement.
2. Several logistical problems. Scheduling, materials, and finances pose real obstacles.
3. Failure to evaluate precisely the child's attainment of specific educational objectives. School officials then must rely on subjective judgments about classroom success or failure, and whether the exceptional child should remain in a regular class.

Changing Classrooms

What happens when exceptional children appear in regular classrooms? Molloy (1975) states that mainstreaming implies a classroom environment that will not encumber exceptional children and should enhance their learning. He believes that ordinary schools can absorb most exceptional children by changing nothing but administrative policy. Accommodating some exceptional children, however, will necessitate physical changes. For example, about 18 percent of exceptional children are physically handicapped and present the most obvious physical needs: ramps for wheelchairs, wide doors, appropriate toilet facilities, and attainable drinking fountains.

Some Outstanding Examples

For example, one California school was designed for integrating physically handicapped with regular youngsters. There are nine separate areas for special-education teachers to work with children: regular classrooms, a separate platform area with curtains, a small area separated by portable partition, several physical therapy cubicles, an occupational shop, imitation home living room, a physical therapy weight room, a hydrotherapy room, and special outdoor playgrounds. There is also a common teacher room and other shared space to encourage communication among the various therapists, special-education teachers, and the regular staff—all of whom normally travel independent routes.

Other school systems now are making similar provisions. For example, educators have long felt that hearing-impaired children could not cope with open space mainly because of acoustical interruptions. A Massachusetts school for the deaf adapted barn spaces into "defined areas." These were activity centers for reading, science, art, math, and more sophisticated space for photography and the development of listening skills. Two spaces were labeled "high gear"—where children could discharge excessive energy—and "monster"—for audiovisual activities. Molloy notes that the activity centers produced some interesting side effects. When children repeatedly used the high gear area it was a signal some other activity failed to interest them—the environment signaled the staff when a change was necessary.

There are many other examples: sensory stimulation centers for the blind to heighten sensitivity to sounds, textures, and proximity; open, stimulating, but well-organized areas for emotionally disturbed children; the learning center concept for the mildly mentally retarded where several areas (centers) are formed adjacent to but separated from the regular classroom. (The centers are actually graded groups where the child is prepared to return to the regular class.)

Summarizing these classroom adaptations, Molloy argues that teachers have discovered that they enrich the learning of all students. Consequently, mainstreaming offers opportunities to improve facilities and curricula for all students. But he likewise presents two warnings.

1. Never make classroom changes that will not benefit all students.
2. Always make the educational environment as realistic as possible; avoid the abstract and imaginary. Exceptional children will inevitably encounter the harsh realities of life beyond the classroom; they deserve practical preparation.

Discussion Questions

1. Based on the discussion thus far, do you agree with the mainstreaming concept? Be specific in your answers; use the rationale for mainstreaming as a basis for your answers.

2. Analyzing Birch's motives for mainstreaming, do you believe that the timing is appropriate? Why? Why not? Defend your answer by using the five motives presented.

3. Do you think that the federal legislation (P.L. 94-142) is sufficiently extensive? Does it cover all possible contingencies? What do you think it implies for teachers in decisions about the placement of exceptional children?

4. The teacher's role in mainstreaming is critical. How would you evaluate the Gickling and Theobald study? What does it mean for school systems preparing for mainstreaming? Are you aware of any changes in teachers' attitudes since the study was conducted? Why have they occurred?

5. Most warnings about hasty mainstreaming focus on teachers' attitudes. Realistically, what changes would you recommend in teacher training programs to modify existing prejudices? What should be the nature of in-service programs?

A specific example

The CET

Several states had begun mainstreaming before P.L. 94-142. In Massachusetts, a new law took effect on September 1, 1974. Called Chapter 766, it requires the state to provide a free education for all children with special needs. It also permits parents to have a voice in the educational planning for their exceptional children. If they disagree with the proposed program they have the right to appeal to the state and, eventually, to the courts. Chapter 766 also demands a careful evaluation of any youngsters with learning difficulties. To determine a child's exact needs, parents are asked to join a group of highly specialized people, called the Core Evaluation Team (CET). The Core Evaluation Team normally consists of parents, the youngster's teacher, school counselor, social worker or nurse, psychologists, a school representative, the CET chairperson, a physician, and any other specialist needed. The CET's objectives are to determine just what the child can do, identify deficiencies, and formulate an educational program.

The law states that regardless of where the children are—home, hospital, special class, regular class—if they are between 3 and 21 years old, without a high school diploma, and have special needs, the state must provide appropriate educational services. The law "calls for an atmosphere of controlled flexibility, in which differences among children will be welcomed, encouraged, and cared for" (Massachusetts State Department of Education). The educational climate should reflect the desires and needs of teachers, parents, and students, thus ensuring an appropriate learning environment for each student.

THE 766 PROCESS

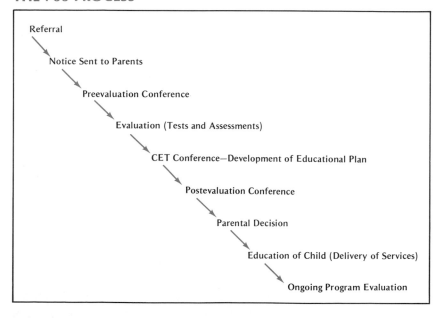

Referral

Notice Sent to Parents

Preevaluation Conference

Evaluation (Tests and Assessments)

CET Conference—Development of Educational Plan

Postevaluation Conference

Parental Decision

Education of Child (Delivery of Services)

Ongoing Program Evaluation

To illustrate precisely the workings of mainstreaming, and your involvement in placement decisions, the above sequence will be followed.

1. Even before referral, the process begins with screening, which is a brief search for those preschoolers or kindergarteners who require further testing. The initial screening involves a developmental history, physical examination, and vision, hearing, language, and motor tests. Parents receive the testing results, and if referral is necessary, parents can discuss the procedure with school

officials. The law also requires continuous screening beyond kindergarten; referral may be automatic under three conditions:

a. If, during the year, any child is failing two or more required subjects.
b. If a child will not be promoted.
c. If the school suspends a child more than five days in any quarter, permanently suspends a student, or if a pupil is absent more than 15 days without medical reason.

2. A notice must be sent to the parents no later than five days after referral for evaluation, which explains the evaluation procedure and their rights during evaluation. Parents may attend all meetings about their child's educational program, and they may bring one person to these meetings, which will be conducted in their native language. If the student is 14, or older, he or she has the right to participate.

3. The preevaluation conference is designed to permit parents to meet with some member of the Core Evaluation Team to determine why their child was referred for further evaluation. The preevaluation conference also enables CET members to acquire information that will aid them in evaluation. Consequently, there should be complete understanding between home and school about the evaluation and what specialists will participate. Since information about the home can be valuable, parents and officials may agree on a series of home visits.

4. Referral was made because someone suspected a child could have special needs. The next phase entails evaluations which may be full core or intermediate. A full core evaluation has five parts.

a. An educational history. You, or another school member, will inform the Core Evaluation Team about the child's present programs and any special services.
b. A psychological assessment. A psychologist will observe and test the child, attempting to discover not only the child's weaknesses but capabilities, and under what circumstances he or she best learns.
c. A description of classroom performance. You will also report on the child's current academic performance, and also acquire data from any other teachers the youngster may have.
d. A medical examination. Either the school doctor or the personal physician examines the child.
e. A family history. Since any pupil learns at home, as well as at school, extracurricular influences need examination. Parents obviously have extensive knowledge about how their children play with peers, their interests, their attitudes toward school and teachers, and their feelings about themselves. Usually a social

worker or school counselor with permission will visit the parents at home to accord parents and interviewers a congenial atmosphere to range over a child's background.

An intermediate evaluation may be more appropriate for some youngsters. For example, if a child can remain in a regular classroom for about 75 percent of the time with some special help, then an intermediate evaluation would suffice. As the name implies, an intermediate evaluation involves only pertinent CET members: the physician, the psychologists, or *you*.

5. The CET conference and development of an educational plan with parents' participation occurs after evaluation. If the group concludes that the child requires special help, then the educational plan must include the following:

a. A description of the child's present capabilities, and under what circumstances the child best performs (some pupils work better alone than in groups).
b. A description of any physical problems (medication may cause classroom drowsiness).
c. A description of how the child best learns (visual, auditory, other sensory channels).
d. A statement of immediate and future goals, including details about measurement programs.
e. A complete description of educational services: programs, personnel, transportation, schedules, locations (if some services are not offered in the regular classroom).

6. A written statement of the educational plan is sent to parents ten days following the CET conference. Parents then may request a postevaluation conference to clarify or dispute the plan. For example, parents may accept or refuse: any or all of the tests, any or all of the educational goals, the proposed programs, or the suggested services. Whether accepting or rejecting the plan, parents must sign and return it. If parents object to the plan, a 30-day period follows during which attempts are made to reconcile differences.

7. Within 15 days after the 30-day reconciliation period, parents must decide to accept the plan, to require an independent evaluation, or to reject the plan.

8. Upon acceptance of a mutually acceptable plan, the child immediately commences the specified program.

9. There will be continuous evaluation of the child to determine the program's effectiveness and, if necessary, to devise a new plan.

While the above description of Massachusetts Chapter 766 may seem extremely detailed, it only presents the highlights of a complex system designed to provide the fullest opportunities to ex-

HOW children with special needs are **IDENTIFIED**

LOCAL SCHOOL SYSTEMS will screen all kindergarten children to find out if any have potential learning problems.

OLDER CHILDREN will be evaluated if it's requested by parent or guardian, school personnel, court officer or family doctor, etc.

THEN... if it's decided that any child _does_ seem to need special help, a meeting will be held by concerned experts-- the **CORE EVALUATION TEAM** --to discuss how to meet those needs.

- This group includes local health, social service, education, guidance, and administrative professionals.
- PARENTS HAVE the RIGHT to be there -- with anyone else they choose (e.g., family doctor).

The Core Evaluation Team **EVALUATES A CHILD'S NEEDS** by studying the factors that influence learning abilities.

PRESENT EDUCATIONAL STATUS, including teacher's report.

Complete medical and psychological **EXAMINATION.**

Social, family, and developmental **HISTORY.**

INFORMATION on the child's self-image and how the child interacts with others.

A HOME VISIT to see child in the family setting, if appropriate, and with parents' consent.

...PLUS any other tests and studies that can help determine the child's particular problems and needs.

All this information is gathered into a REPORT ...and parents are informed of the results.

ceptional children while simultaneously carefully protecting their rights. Your involvement would be at two key points: helping to identify a child's needs by reporting his or her educational status, and working with the child and special teachers to implement the educational plan.

A secondary school program

That this legislation applies chiefly to elementary schools and is not especially relevant for secondary schools is a common misconception. Today's law applies to *both* elementary and secondary school students, 3 to 21 years old. A good example of what secondary schools expect and what they may offer exceptional students is seen in the following program at Newton North High School (Massachusetts).

Concerned about secondary school opportunities for hearing-impaired pupils, parents and educators urged implementation of quality secondary education for these students. To meet their needs a program was initiated that enrolled deaf and hearing-impaired pupils who required specialized support. Its goals were to provide hearing-impaired students with the opportunity to acquire a high school diploma, to ensure that students recognize the realities of the world of work, and to help students achieve personal, satisfying self-concepts.

Both junior and senior high school students participate in regular classes assisted by the classroom teachers and specialists. The specialists function as resource teachers, occasionally working independently with students, cooperating with the regular staff, and coordinating services when necessary. Services include tutoring, testing, counseling, and speech-hearing therapy. Parents are deeply involved: planning, conferring with teachers, and evaluating the program's services.

The junior high school program is dedicated to mastery of basic subjects—math, social studies, English, science—as well as to social integration of these students into the normal life of the school. Hearing-impaired students also have a wide choice of electives. Resource teachers often aid the regular teacher's instruction by simultaneously explaining the regular teacher's presentation. (Other resource aides teach sign language to regular staff members and students.) One early and discernible result has been the positive social and emotional development of hearing-impaired pupils.

Senior high school students have individualized programs that present a variety of learning opportunities. There are three categories of students: those who remain in the regular class and receive help outside of class; those who join classes taught by the regular and resource teacher; and those who remain in self-contained classes for the deaf. An intensive effort is also made to help these students acquire career skills, supplemented by work-study programs. Under these circumstances, hearing-impaired students learn in normal classes and begin to prepare for a productive future.

Challenges to mainstreaming

Programs similar to these are now a national phenomenon in response to P.L. 94-142. Most educators agree with the intent of the legislation—to ensure maximum opportunity for exceptional children—and many schools have frequently attempted to meet the same needs for many years. Segregation of exceptional children is ending, and the mystery surrounding special education is dis-

Some Specific Problems

sipating. Everyone must reexamine his or her view of children and become concerned about the education of *all* children.

But there are obstacles—the Massachusetts procedure is complicated. So many individuals join in the pupil's evaluation that it is often difficult to reach agreement about an educational plan. The paperwork is staggering. The Massachusetts legislation has 107 pages of regulations that schools must follow. While parents have the right to appeal, schools do not. Financial costs are enormous and have yet to be precisely calculated.

Teachers' Doubts

These are technical problems that states will solve. Yet, one major barrier remains: teachers' attitudes. Although evidence is scanty, in teachers' conferences, conventions, and meetings, the message is clear: doubt and uncertainty linger. The results of the Gickling and Theobold study will apply. Teachers believe that the

---

Mainstreaming the Secondary School Pupil

This discussion has emphasized that secondary as well as elementary teachers must prepare for mainstreaming. Gloria Stashower (1976) asks a related question: What happens when the handicapped student leaves the relatively small and sheltered environment of elementary school and enters the larger, more hectic world of secondary education? For the exceptional child, the experience merits several precautions. She describes a program in Westport, Connecticut, that resembles a typical school work-study plan in which students work in their community and receive academic credit, some money, and valuable experience. The jobs include pumping gas, cooking in the kitchen for retirement homes, and outdoor handy work.

But there is a difference: the program is for handicapped children who benefit from work experience, rapport with employers, and constant encouragement.

Placing students in jobs is not the program's sole concern since the history of exceptional children in work-study plans is not that encouraging. The same problems that plague these youngsters in school follow them to work: slow understanding, poor communication, impatience, and frustration.

Careful, thorough planning must precede any placement. Sympathetic employers, willing to try to understand a youngster's difficulty, are sought, and some even attend workshops. School supervisors maintain close contact with both student and employer. Finally, only willing students participate in the program. After application, each student is evaluated by a teacher, psychologist, and social worker who attempt to match the student with appropriate work. The program's goal is not to provide specific vocational skills, but general work skills that are vital in all jobs: punctuality, the ability to communicate and to cope with mistakes. It is an effective program that suggests that exceptional children can successfully enter the junior and senior high school mainstream.

mainstreaming goals are excellent, but they question if they can accomplish them. Hasty planning has resulted in regular teachers having 3, 4, or 5 exceptional children placed in their classes with 25 or 30 other pupils, with neither teachers nor exceptional children receiving any support. These and similar incidents—no in-service programs for teachers, lack of specialized programs—could doom mainstreaming. Teachers must cooperate fully, which they find difficult without preparation and continuous help.

The role of teachers

Ideally, mainstreaming should provide exceptional children with a continuum of educational services—from full participation in regular classes for the mildly handicapped to highly specialized services by experts. All teachers should receive support in their work with the handicapped. Unfortunately, expediency has often supplanted idealism and produced two undesirable side effects: some moderately, even severely, handicapped children have been placed in regular classes, and teachers have received neither training nor support. A small, but growing threat is the inclination of some school systems to release special-education teachers instead of utilizing them as resource personnel.

New Responsibilities

The role and responsibility of classroom teachers has sustained substantial modification because of mainstreaming. Teachers need skills previously unnecessary and not included in their training. How many current teachers needed skills to teach the mildly retarded, the physically handicapped, the emotionally disturbed, the learning disabled, the hearing and visually impaired? Also, society's changing nature—mobility, separation, divorce, financial problems—causes family tensions that produce temporary problems for normal youngsters. Teachers' duties are no longer confined to the classroom: they participate in conferences and decisions about placement; they frequently visit students who are receiving on-the-job training.

Exceptional children undoubtedly have serious anxieties about mainstreaming. Accustomed to intensive individual attention, they can easily feel overwhelmed by being one of many. Regular-class children, unfamiliar with the handicapped, may either consciously or unconsciously cause them problems: accidentally bumping a physically handicapped child, mocking a mentally retarded child. The responsibility for overcoming these difficulties and ensuring smooth integration falls on the classroom teacher.

Some Immediate Needs

Are teachers ready for these challenges? Without careful consideration of retraining procedures and modified teacher education programs, many thoughtful observers fear that exceptional children will experience a diminished education and all student learning will suffer. A recent statement from the National Advisory Council on Education Professional Development summarizes the immediate needs of classroom teachers. These include: understanding how a handicap affects learning; skill in recognizing handicaps; prescriptive teaching; skill in behavior management techniques; understanding of, and ability to respond to, the emotional needs of handicapped children; and development of a new working relationship between special and regular education.

Recommendations to Help Teachers

Projects, reflecting local and individual needs, are available for in-service training programs, and suggestions for revised teacher education curricula have been prepared. The national council specifically recommends:

1. Careful monitoring of mainstreaming conditions to safeguard exceptional children's rights while simultaneously protecting the educational opportunities of all.
2. Continued, but expanded, support of in-service training.
3. Increased opportunity for administrators, regular and special, to join in specialized programs designed to improve communication between the two disciplines.
4. Continued support of new teacher education programs and wide dissemination of those techniques that seem most promising.
5. That the National Institute of Education investigate and publicize those in-service programs that seem most promising, including a description of successful methods and materials.
6. Modification of state certification requirements to recognize existing conditions.

These are particularly thoughtful recommendations designed to furnish abilities and resources to meet expanding individual and social needs.

Teacher preparation for mainstreaming has two major emphases. One relates to changes in existing teacher education programs. Here in revised professional courses, with classroom visitation followed by student teaching in integrated classrooms, lies mainstreaming's best hope for success. But such changes take time. An immediate concern is in-service training for teachers who are now teaching exceptional children.

TEACHER EDUCATION PROGRAMS

The Deans' Projects

With the combination of social support and federal funding, mainstreaming is, and will continue to be, a reality for teachers. No longer can teacher education institutions afford the luxury of preparing their students for regular classes. There are no longer any regular classes, and this one change has radically altered teacher preparation. One of the most noteworthy responses, supported by the United States Office of Education, is known as the *Deans' Projects*. These projects, active in 31 states, Washington, D.C., and the territory of American Samoa, are intended to equip regular classroom teachers to work with exceptional pupils.

The designated colleges and universities based their projects on the needs of their regions. Reynolds (1976) states that three major classes of needs were identified:

1. Number and type of handicapped children
2. Teacher understanding and expertise
3. Number of teachers

Some colleges have reacted to intense pressure in their territory. One New York college, for example, is in a predominantly black district with a high percentage of non-English-speaking children and foster children. The most prevalent handicap is emotional disturbances. One Texas school, representing a large bilingual population, has identified its region's major handicap as language.

Although these different needs have generated various programs, the major emphasis of each is readiness to work with exceptional children. For example, one university describes its program as a "multiple-option" curriculum that prepares for a variety of occupations; that is, its students are ready to teach *all* types of handicapped youth.

The kinds of curricular changes in teacher education are interesting. Considerable emphasis is placed on interpersonal relations, which, as we have seen in the account of Westport work-study program, is essential for successful teaching of all, but especially exceptional, students. There is a strict insistence on mastery of basic instructional competencies; that is, students must *demonstrate* abilities and knowledge. The usual course in child development is merged with presentation of atypical development as seen in the following example.

Typical Development	*Atypical Development*
An overview of normal development	Behavior disorders: sensory, motor, neurological
Theories of development	Ortho-health impaired (medical implications)
The learning process	Learning disabled
Intellectual development	Mental retardation; the gifted
Piaget and cognitive development language development	Speech disorders
Personality development	Psychosocial disorders

Other courses and workshops are offered with classroom visitations leading gradually to student-teaching placement. These, and similar modifications, should enable future teachers to work well with exceptional children, not only because of increased proficiency but also because of positive attitudes toward the handicapped.

In-service programs

Still, it is today's classroom teacher who meets the handicapped child and who has immediate questions. Among the most frequent are:

How can I lessen the anxieties of both exceptional children and their classmates?

Exactly what are my obligations under mainstreaming?

How many handicapped children will be in my class?

Will I receive help in planning programs?

What is the responsibility of resource personnel?

How can I spare the time?

How can I learn more about special needs?

To answer these and numerous other questions requires planning for effective in-service programs. Voelker (1975) offers several general suggestions to aid professional growth.

1. *Classroom visitation.* Observation and demonstration by others can be invaluable. Having a skilled expert observe you, make constructive suggestions, and actively demonstrate techniques for you can substantially enhance your own expertise.

2. *Teacher demonstrations.* Administrators and supervisors can schedule visits to other schools and classrooms where master teachers offer demonstration lessons. The persuasiveness of observational learning has been amply demonstrated by Bandura and others.

3. *Meetings, institutes, and conferences.* These assemblies can be helpful if they are planned to discuss pertinent problems and permit meaningful participation.

4. *Professional library.* Since the vast special-education literature and the rapidly accumulating mainstreaming data often provide profitable suggestions, school officials should endeavor to compile bibliographies, articles, books, and government pamphlets.

5. *Curriculum and research.* Thoughtful school officials may encourage teachers to publish bulletins, to prepare curriculum alterations, and to cooperate in writing course objectives. Scholarships may be available; universities may offer course vouchers as a cour-

TABLE 13.3
Mainstreaming: Teacher Preparation

Topics	WORKSHOPS Trainers	Strategies
1. Understanding services available for exceptional children and their parents	1. A. Directors and supervisors of special education in public school systems B. Representatives from community agencies C. Parents D. Teacher Corps staff E. Principals	1. A. Presentations by specialists B. Small group discussions C. Visitations to agencies D. Reading reports prepared by agencies and school systems
2. Using community resources in regular classroom	2. A. Parents B. Principals C. Special-education professors D. Sociology professors E. Teacher Corps staff	2. A. Role playing B. Group presentations C. Community surveys D. Parent interviews E. Classroom visits
3. Instructional materials, games, learning centers, study packages, prescription writing	3. A. Instructional supervisors B. Teacher Corps staff C. Specialists in audiovisuals D. Classroom teachers E. Instructional design specialists	3. A. Materials production B. Materials exhibits C. Prescription writing

tesy for student-teacher placement; some teachers may conduct research with their classes. All of these activities promote professional growth while they also furnish information that may produce more efficient teaching and learning.

Role of the Teacher Corps

Witty (1976) summarizes a project designed to aid both preservice and in-service teachers. One of the major forces in special education and mainstreaming has been the Teacher Corps. Recently they have focused on the role of the exceptional child and attempted to help experienced and preservice teachers to develop those skills that will permit them to become sensitive to the needs of the exceptional child and to work effectively with them. They initially included many more individuals in program planning: specialists, teachers, administrators, parents, college professors, and community representatives. This was intended not only to secure needed information but also to support teachers, who would realize that they were not working alone. Detailed and realistic objectives were formulated together with activities aimed at attaining these goals.

One of the most productive activities was a series of workshops. Table 13.3 presents their format. The theme in the literature, the research, and the programs is clear: unless teachers are committed, professionally and personally, mainstreaming cannot succeed.

PROBLEMS FACING MAINSTREAMING

Truth in Labeling

Michael Scriven (1976) has written a thoughtful essay realistically assessing the advantages and disadvantages of mainstreaming. He argues strongly for integration: any isolated group is neglected; segregated education is costly; stereotyping the handicapped is common; faulty diagnoses occur frequently; exceptional children's rights are often ignored. But there are genuine problems that demand solution: mainstreaming may cause some handicapped children to be neglected; children can be cruel; all students' learning may suffer; the present system of labeling remains troublesome; and, finally, evaluation techniques are so primitive that it is almost impossible to judge the success or failure of mainstreaming.

Scriven states that educators have not honestly faced the labeling issue. Calling the handicapped "exceptional children" misrepresents them and damages those to whom the name rightly applies—the gifted. Would the community be better served if medicine labeled the sick as "exceptional with regard to health"? He reasons that juggling labels sabotages efforts to aid the handicapped, and is a slur similar to calling blacks "colored" and mature women "girls." More than semantics is involved: it suggests prejudice and can produce harmful results, for example, the neglect of the gifted.

Nevertheless, Scriven believes labeling is a necessary evil and the predictive value of handicapped categories is as good as any in the behavioral science; for example, when educable mentally retarded children reach a certain age they are unable to perform certain tasks. Kindness makes people hesitate about labeling them; but labels do not only predict, they should also communicate basic information and provide a basis for analysis. The solution lies in teaching people to use the information the label contains, and no more. Present labels are probably the best specialists can now offer, and, carefully applied, they provide useful information, permit predictions, and suggest treatment.

Attitude—students', teachers', professionals', the public's—is another issue. Classification of the handicapped is sufficiently difficult without prejudice. Do educators classify and treat by symptom or cause; that is, can they eliminate personal bias in their assessments? Rigid attitudes can cause people to view individual differences as "weird," "ugly," "queer"; this attitude can transcend any classification scheme and destroy any hope of successful treatment. As can be seen from the history of racism and sexism, assessing people on their merits can be difficult.

Finally, Scriven decries the present state of evaluation. Investigators have done a poor job of evaluating mainstreaming's benefits, the results of classification, teacher education programs, and the efficiency of special-education teachers. Critical evaluation is lacking, and until it is available, we can only question our efforts, techniques, and results.

Scriven's comments deserve thought. Whether you agree or not, they should make you realize that while we are on the verge of a great new national movement, questions remain to be answered and issues remain to be solved.

Discussion Questions

1. If your state required a Core Evaluation Team, and you were to participate, how would you prepare?

2. What was your reaction to the detailed process of identifying, evaluating, and placing a child with special needs? Do you think that all school systems would faithfully follow such a procedure? Why? Why not?

3. How do you personally react to mainstreaming? Do you believe in the concept? What do you see as its weaknesses? strengths? What kinds of help would you expect to receive?

4. Teachers' attitudes are probably the major obstacle to successful mainstreaming. What would you suggest to alter positively the attitude of experienced teachers? Are demonstrations and workshops sufficient?

5. Are you satisfied with your preparation? What would you like changed?

6. Do you agree, or disagree, with Scriven? Can you either support or attack his views specifically? His attitude toward labeling is especially interesting. Do you agree with it? Why?

Some Concluding Thoughts

The history of special education reveals a series of progressive changes—from residential schools to special classes to mainstreaming—that reflect a growing humanitarian view of exceptional children. Mainstreaming represents the culmination of centuries of neglect, scorn, concern, and, finally, love. With mainstreaming, society's relations with its children is portrayed in its finest light.

Yet, kindness, consideration, and love should not blind teachers to the harsh reality that unless they proceed cautiously, they may well damage those they are most anxious to serve. Haste may produce a dual danger. First, action forced by legislation may be ill-advised action. For example, a thread of uncertainty ran throughout this chapter: teachers remain doubtful, and, unless their fears and anxieties are allayed, mainstreaming's future is doubtful. Second, those who become obsessed with the mechanics of mainstreaming—regulations, rooms, revenues—may see it as opportunity to economize by eliminating special teachers, restricting materials, and gaining classroom space. Whether it is possible to overcome these obstacles remains to be seen.

But there are not only problems. Mainstreaming's goals are laudable. It is easy to forget that careful mainstreaming should help all pupils: regular youngsters benefit from added resources, and, if they experience temporary problems, they will have the benefit of immediate, specialized help. Mainstreaming is here; it will remain; you can make it profitable for all of your students.

Summary

- There are nine categories of exceptional children used by educators to offer guidelines for treatment. While labeling remains a problem, its elimination would probably hamper more than help.

- Historically, there have been several educational plans for exceptional children: residential schools, community schools, special classes, itinerant teachers, resource rooms, mainstreaming.

- Mainstreaming means integrating the mildly handicapped child into the regular classroom since evidence does not clearly show that isolation has been effective.

- Federal and state legislation have removed freedom of choice from local communities. Mainstreaming now has the force of government behind it.

- Teachers' attitudes toward mainstreaming, perhaps reflecting uncertainty and fear of the unknown, are ambiguous. Teachers favor its humanitarian nature, but doubt if they possess the skills to work effectively with exceptional pupils.

- Carefully planned in-service programs to help current teachers and re-designed teacher education curricula are necessary to provide instructional skills and to alleviate anxieties.

- Appropriate materials and facilities should be available to teachers for adequate instruction. The support services—special educators, psychologists, school counselors, medical personnel—also require detailed planning.

Suggested Readings

Excellent sources include both federal and state mainstreaming legislation. Most state departments of education and the U.S. Government Printing Office also offer brief documents that explain the legislation.

Cruickshank, William, and G. Orville Johnson (eds.). *Education of Exceptional Children and Youth.* Englewood Cliffs, N.J.: Prentice-Hall, 1975. An excellent overview of special education, particularly valuable for its historical analysis of the special-education movement.

Kirk, Samuel. *Educating Exceptional Children.* Boston: Houghton Mifflin, 1972. A fine source, for both its insights into exceptional children and helpful teaching suggestions.

"Mainstreaming: Origins and Implications," *Minnesota Education* 2, no. 2 (Winter 1976). Proceedings from a Deans' Projects Conference sponsored by the University of Minnesota, especially valuable because of the thoughtful comments by some of the country's leading figures in mainstreaming.

Phi Delta Kappan, LV, no. 8 (April 1974). The entire issue, devoted to special education, theory and practice, is an admirable survey of recent changes.

Part Five

The Learner and Instruction

14

The Nature of Teaching

543

Introduction

Although the learning process is the heart of educational psychology, ignoring teaching would be folly. There is no major dichotomy between the two—students teach and teachers learn—but teaching as the facilitator of learning demands separate analysis. Whether you consider teaching an art or science, the skillful manipulation of classroom stimuli and the creation of a pleasant educational atmosphere aids both you and your students.

Considerable data exist to indicate that the teaching-learning processes involve far more than the simple communication of knowledge from an infallible source to an ignorant receptor. Not only is a teacher's mastery of a subject vital for efficient transmission of knowledge, but personality also affects successful performance. Still, this is not the total explanation. Teachers interact with class members, so pupils' personalities influence any instructor's behavior. Combining these intangibles with varied environmental simuli and pupils' differences in capacities, teaching's complicated nature is readily discernible.

The view of teaching represented by passive pupils and an active teacher is no longer acceptable. For each child to learn as much as capacity permits necessitates self-activity, and an efficient means of directing such activity has come to be one of the most significant issues in any investigation of teaching. Teaching is not merely inculcating subject matter, nor conveying information, nor transmitting the experiences of a culture. It is all of these and more. Good teaching naturally results in the transmission of knowledge, but it also produces comprehension and a personal desire to continue self-improvement, to direct oneself toward a constantly deepening maturity.

Society demands that teachers know, understand, and interpret the structure of that same society to the young. Teachers must be expert in a discipline and possess some knowledge of how pupils develop and learn. They should also act as models. Still, this is not teaching. What teaching is and what distinguishes the good from the bad are the subject of this chapter. There are no positive, irrefutable rules available to guide you along a smooth road to teaching success. Any such golden list of rules is designed by the unscrupulous to ensnare the unwary. The uncompromising truth is this: recent studies of the nature of teaching contain some substantial data that, if properly and cautiously applied, may increase the competency of some teachers.

One major difficulty in translating experimental data into meaningful teaching-learning principles is that experimentation frequently involves animals. As Bugelski notes (1971), there is no consideration of past experience, the tasks (in human experimentation) are meaningless, individual differences are ignored, and it is impossible to contrast teaching techniques—teaching one rat to run a maze differs radically from *any* teaching of humans.

While direct application of laboratory results remains impractical, certain learning principles offer tentative suggestions for teaching. Berliner and Gage (1976) state that while laboratory laws of learning are untrustworthy guides to classroom practice, they have made teachers aware of what variables are important under what conditions. Jones (1967) believes that a tremendous and bewildering array of variables influences learning and confuses teachers. To reduce confusion and guide teaching, he suggests considering groups of variables that affect learning, such as characteristics of learners, nature of the material, presentation, practice and reinforcement variables, and the learning environment.

But different teachers will use these variables differently. Why? Combs et al. (1974) offer an explanation that agrees with the basic theme of this chapter. Teachers are unique personalities; this uniqueness causes them to do different things with the same material. For example, two fourth-grade teachers, using the identical course of study, create completely different learning environments and employ entirely different techniques. Yet both may be excellent teachers! It is precisely here that you must avoid value judgments: it is not the lecture or discussion method, it is not individualized instruction—it is the individual who uses these methods that determines their success or failure.

As Combs et al. note, you will remember, if you recall your own school days, that the good teachers did not behave similarly. They were unique for some reason—personality, method, values. There are no good or bad teaching methods; there are individuals who employ various methods either successfully or not. The terms "good" and "bad" are too simple. A teacher, encouraging learning, proceeds according to complex circumstances: goals, types of students, immediate conditions, and his or her own personality. The authors define efficient teachers as those who have learned to use themselves effectively and efficiently to carry out their own and society's purposes in the education of others.

You have thought and read extensively about growth and learning. Now, in your analysis of teaching, think of those theories that you found most persuasive (Bruner, Skinner, Piaget, Maslow, Erikson) and decide how *you* could most effectively apply them. How will you teach small groups? large groups? How will you handle troublesome pupils? Are your answers consistent with what you know about yourself? Remember there are no right and wrong answers. If you think that learning proceeds best by a carefully controlled sequence of small steps with constant reinforcement and little possibility of error, that technique is better for you than one entailing considerable student activity, discovery, and error. The reverse is also true.

This chapter attempts to interpret the latest findings about some of the problems that face teachers, the roles that teachers play, the characteristics of teachers that lead to fruitful interactions, and the constant pressure of variables. It then presents procedures that may improve teacher performance.

What is teaching?

The Dullest of Subjects?

Perhaps, as Barzun (1954, pg. 9) has said, education is indeed the dullest of subjects. Yet no other topic has so engaged the time, energies, and money of the American people in recent decades as this "dullest of subjects." Almost every family contacts the conflicting beliefs of various philosophies, the differing psychological interpretations of the human learning process, and the constant upheaval in the methods by which youngsters are taught.

For better or worse this involvement of the average citizens with the schools is a fact of modern education, and classroom teachers should capitalize on it. Since higher education is now an accepted and even necessary component of an individual's life, teachers are discussing educational issues with sophisticated parents. The questions asked by these parents often reflect annoyance or impatience with some of the more intangible and controversial aspects of the teaching-learning process.

Why has the school adopted a seminar for a course on the issues of nationalism? Why are lectures exclusively used in the American history course? Is the teaching machine effective for all kinds of students? These are formidable questions that have no simple answers. But it is difficult to convince parents that there are no easy explanations for the complexities of teaching and learning. The communication of knowledge appears to be a simple process. Yet, on analysis, a complicated human being must analyze and interpret intricate subject matter and then teach it so that other complicated human beings learn it meaningfully.

A COMPLEX TASK

Yet there are those who insist that there is nothing perplexing in the teaching process. They remind one of Barzun's admiral who gave him a friendly pat on the shoulder and the reassuring words,

"Any damn fool can teach naval history" (Barzun, 1954, pg. 37). This popular stereotype of the teacher ignores the complicated interaction between teacher and pupil. Barzun (1954, pg. 21) notes that there are two ways in which teachers view their responsibility:

1. They themselves tell, direct, and illustrate to aid the student in surmounting a learning obstacle.
2. They prefer to show pupils how to do it themselves.

Throughout the duration of the instructor-student interaction, there is a strong emotional commitment by both individuals. Regardless of the teaching method, regardless of the subject, and regardless of any auxilliary aids, certain intangibles exert a subtle though powerful influence upon learning and performance.

For example, studies of the human personality, although remarkably primitive and superficial, indicate that there are definite personal characteristics that will affect both teacher performance and student learning. Yet students react in an individual and often contrary manner. Some students may resent the exciting lecturer who dominates every moment of a class; others may achieve admirably under such stimulation. Some students thrive in an atmosphere where discussion is the technique; others, due to their individual personalities, are afraid to participate.

Students bring their attitudes, interests, prejudices, values, and opinions into the classroom with them. All of these influences (now designated as noncognitive variables) affect pupil performance. When you realize that these—together with the individual's inherent capacity, the difficulty of the subject, the teacher's knowledge, personality, and methods, and other environmental stimuli—all combine in the teaching-learning process, then the complicated nature of teaching is more readily appreciated.

QUALITIES OF THE TEACHER

The "Good" Teacher

Highet (1950), in his classic analysis, attempted to classify the various forces acting on the teacher by sorting them into such categories as the qualities of a good teacher, the abilities of a good teacher, and teaching methods, and then relating these to some of history's great teachers. It is refreshing to pause and consider some of Highet's criteria of the good teacher.

They must know their subject. This implies that a teacher grasps not only current material but also the core of the subject and what research is discovering at the discipline's frontiers. In an age devoted to empirical research, the expansion of knowledge is an awesome phenomenon that necessitates constant independent study by a teacher to prevent personal obsolescence.

They must like their subject and enjoy youth. To devote hours of

study beyond the demands of duty requires a commitment to a discipline and to the company of the young, both of which can be provocative masters. If a love of study and pleasure in working with youth is lacking, one should shun a teaching career.

In addition to these qualities, Highet (1950) notes that a teacher should possess certain abilities: *memory, will power,* and *kindness.* The combination of personal characteristics and capacity ultimately determines the technique selected by the individual teacher and its success in communicating knowledge to students.

A modern interpretation

Berliner and Gage (1976, pg. 5) define teaching methods as recurrent instructional processes, applicable to various subjects, and usable by more than one teacher. This formidable definition simply means that teachers engage in activities that they repeat, such as lectures and discussions, to promote student learning. What attracts youth to such a complex profession?

Becoming a Teacher

Fuller and Brown (1975) believe that the process of becoming a teacher begins early for one or a variety of reasons: satisfaction of some personal need, influence of some teacher, love of a subject, or love of youth. Early experiences as pupils probably relate to all aspects of teaching, that is, not only teaching as a career, but appropriate teacher behavior, the particular subject that will be taught, and personal rewards from teaching.

Teaching Is Intentional

McNeil and Popham (1973) state that a teacher is a person engaged in interactive behavior with one or more students for the purpose of effecting a change in those students. The teacher intends these changes, which distinguishes teaching from mere instructional material. The authors believe that a teacher is not one who engages merely in isolated activities: marking papers, sorting books, or preparing lesson plans. Parent volunteers and teacher aides frequently do these, but they are not teachers.

Teaching as a Familiar Task

Lortie (1973) believes that, since teaching is so familiar, there is a tendency for observers to see teachers' tasks as simple and straightforward. It is only as research focused on the intricacies of curriculum construction, the amazing classroom interactions, the influence of the group, and the conflicting opinions about learning that teaching was recognized as a complicated, highly personalized profession.

The reasons for teaching, the level of teaching selected (elementary or secondary), the methods employed, and the handling of interactions all coalesce to form teachers who see themselves in various roles.

TEACHERS' ROLES

Teachers perform many different tasks in many different ways; consequently, investigators have examined these behaviors attempting to obtain knowledge about the teaching process. One fruitful method has been the study of teacher roles.

Charters (1963) declares that it is the quality of expectation that makes role analysis so fascinating. Everyone lives in a distinct culture in which others expect him or her to be a definite kind of person and to behave in a definite fashion. These expectations vary from time to time, from place to place, and according to immediate conditions. For example, the expectations of a teacher's behavior are remarkably different in 1979 from what they were in 1879, or in the Soviet Union from what they are in the United States of America. Yet for a particular period of time and within definite boundaries consistent behavior is associated with occupation, status, and social class. If there is such consistency, it is reasonable to hope that more accurate dilineation of roles will provide better selection of teaching candidates and better execution of the teaching act.

Wallen and Travers (1963) identify six distinct sources of teacher roles.

1. *Patterns derived from teaching traditions.* Teachers teach as they have been taught, which is a searing indictment of teacher education. Some teacher has influenced them as a model. If educators desire to break this tradition they must make future teachers aware of who they are and why they choose as they do. As Combs et al. (1974) state, how teachers behave after they leave college largely depends on how they have learned to see themselves and their relationships to colleagues and the teaching profession itself. Future teachers must be more aware of themselves—why they choose and act as they do.

2. *Patterns derived from social learning in the teacher's background.* The development of your—any teacher's—personality largely determines your classroom behavior. Being aware of this, you can utilize methods and materials more effectively. For example, teachers who value personal freedom and exploration usually feel restricted by teaching machines and programmed instruction. Knowing the forces that helped to shape your personality can also help you to recognize any prejudices you might have. For example, you may favor students coming from your own social class.

3. *Patterns derived from philosophical traditions.* Students, impressed with their reading of Montessori, Pestalozzi, Bruner, or Skinner, resolve to teach in the same manner. Believing that it will soon be lost in the daily routine, we perhaps too easily dismiss this pattern. But students fascinated by Skinner may well be conscious of the nature and timing of reinforcement throughout their professional careers. Students fascinated by Bruner may be acutely alert to the changing modes of representation—enactive, iconic, symbolic—and attempt to match them with appropriate materials and methods.

4. *Patterns generated by the teacher's needs.* Anyone's behavior, including a teacher's, is designed to satisfy needs. Insecure teachers do not suffer questions or challenges lightly. They interpret them as personal assaults that must be speedily squelched. Their satisfaction comes from their immersion in a lecture, which enables them to play the role of the "source of all knowledge." The warm gregarious instructor who constantly engages students in dialogue may well be satisfying a need for friendship and group security. Knowing who you are enables you to identify your needs and to function more effectively in the role that satisfies both your own and student needs.

5. *Patterns generated by school and community conditions.* Community pressure frequently dictates the role you will adopt. For example, a community that is experiencing teenage turmoil may well force its school officials to harden attitudes. Accordingly, teachers must assume a greater authoritarian role in which no challenge to authority, even academic, is tolerated. You should know as much as possible about your community so that you will realize just what type of teacher behavior is expected.

6. *Patterns derived from research on learning.* Ideally, teaching should depend on learning principles taken from scientifically controlled research. While this is not so, conditions change, research improves, and you must remain professionally alive; so, continue to read scholarly journals and form your own teaching-learning connection.

Bruner and Teacher Education

Bruner (1960, pp. 88–92) examines the classroom functions of the instructor and sees three sources of teacher behavior. First, teachers are communicators of knowledge, which implies mastery of both the knowledge to be communicated and the effective methods of its communication. Second, teachers are models; they should be competent and exciting individuals who will inspire in students a love of learning. Finally, teachers are a symbol, the immediate representative of "education." In a sense, they are the embodiment of all adult society and can be particularly persuasive figures in shaping a youth's attitudes, interests, opinions, and values, let alone intellectual achievement.

In more specialized roles, teachers are often seen, sometimes reluctantly, as symbols of cultural values. And it is here that teachers often encounter resistance, since parents' education may be as great, or even greater, than the teacher's. Stephens (1967, pg. 11) rather glumly notes that at this point the teacher becomes not an exceptional scholar but one who entered teaching rather than life insurance or embalming.

Teachers also are seen as symbols of morality and character, transmitters of middle-class values. In an age when this value system is shaking throughout, teachers find themselves in an unstable and uncomfortable position. What is the ideal: self-reliance or con-

The Role of Teachers

Morris Bigge (1976), well known for his insightful comments on the interaction between learning theory and teaching, notes that there are several possible relationships between teachers and culture. Teachers may see their task as transmitting that part of their culture that the majority has designated as good, which makes teaching a highly conservative activity. In a dynamic, expanding culture, transmission of selected knowledge should be but one component of teaching; that is, cultural conservation should be linked to cultural improvement as teachers' goals. Simultaneously achieving both is difficult, but helpful in analyzing teachers' roles.

Bigge believes that teachers may have one of four different attitudes toward the goals of cultural conservation and cultural improvement.

1. Teachers may *ignore the culture,* which implies that they view it as evil. Consequently, they encourage students to disregard the culture and concentrate on self-actualization—"do your own thing." Such teachers have little interest either in cultural conservation or cultural improvement. This attitude probably reached peak popularity in the 1960s and has gradually faded.
2. Teachers may see themselves as *cultural architects.* These are the innovators who see weaknesses in the existing culture and who strive for *their* ideal. Their ideas usually arouse opposition, and they frequently turn to their students for support. The legalization of marijuana is a good example. Some teachers believe that

legalization is better than considering its use a crime. Such views cause fierce resistance, and both sides seek support.
3. Teachers may see themselves as *conservators of the culture.* These teachers believe that their principal task is to preserve traditional attitudes, values, beliefs, and knowledge. They analyze the existing culture and try to transmit its best features to a new generation. While some innovations may be beneficial, they never see themselves as active agents of change, nor do they encourage unorthodoxy, but they indoctrinate as much as the "disregarders" and the "reconstructionists."
4. Teachers may see themselves as *democratic leaders* in developing insights pertinent to amending the culture. Culture cannot be disregarded or constantly changed, nor can it remain static. Some teachers believe that they can inculcate within students the habit of studying problems in a reflective and democratic manner. They and their students can then use these techniques to correct cultural conflicts and contradictions.

Bigge offers an interesting analysis that you should consider carefully. If you believe that your task is to instigate change, but you are appointed to a conservative school in a conservative community, problems will arise if you are not willing to adapt to community pressure. Know your community.

You would enjoy Bigge's work; it is a thoughtful, well-written account of learning and teaching.

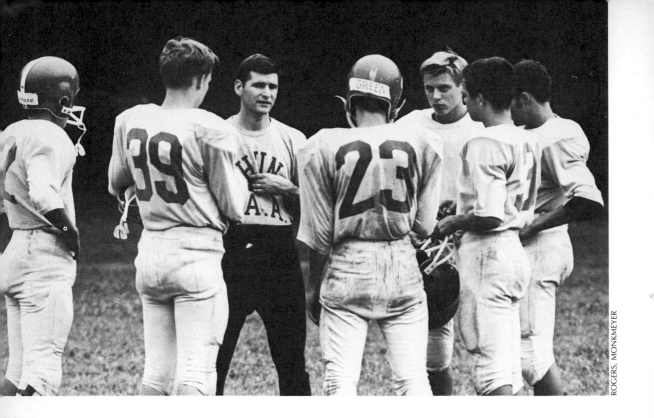

formity, independence or togetherness, individual action or group decision? Or, should teachers avoid the duties for which this role calls?

Finally, there are less complicated roles: friend of youth, member of a profession, member of a community. Different roles, different skills, different behavior coalesce in the same person—one may well question whether the task is even possible! Yet all teachers exhibit strength in some of these roles and in them they should attain maximum impact.

A related example

All too often we think of teaching as confined within the four walls of a classroom. Parents, managers, coaches, and church officials all function as teachers, frequently more effectively than formal instructors. Recently two investigators analyzed the teaching techniques of former UCLA basketball coach John Wooden, one of the most successful coaches this country has ever seen. Tharp and Gallimore (1976) state that their interest in Wooden's techniques came from a growing belief that educational psychologists depended excessively on laboratory studies and neglected proven master teachers.

A Master Teacher

They describe Wooden as a grandfatherly type who has a personal interest in and an abiding affection for his players. The

The System

bases of his system are fundamentals, discipline, hard work, self-lessness, and control. Initially, the authors expected only to find instances of reinforcement, punishment, modeling, and instructions. They quickly found that they must add two new teaching techniques: *scold reinstruction* (criticism instantly followed by "how-to-do-it right"), and the *hustle,* (verbal statements intended to intensify previous instruction).

In 15 practice sessions, the authors analyzed 2326 teaching acts, which they classified into the 11 categories seen in Table 14.1. The authors believe that their system was successful since they had to classify only 2.4 percent of Wooden's teaching acts in the miscellaneous category, "Other."

Examining the categories, note that some are more outstanding than others. Instructions in fundamentals constitute half of Wooden's teaching acts. Hustles may also serve as scolds and punishments, depending on the player. Almost all of the praises and scolds were directed at specific individuals. Wooden believes that there should be repetition to the point of automatic response.

Note the high use of scolds: 14.6 percent (including both scolds and scold reinstruction). These players were so highly motivated that little praise was necessary, which is not typical of most classrooms where more positive reinforcement may be essential. Also the players never considered Wooden's actions mean or punitive. His fairness in treating his players helped them to accept decisions they disliked. There was a discernible personal note to his use of praises or scolds; that is, the authors quickly noted that some players he mostly praised, and others he mostly scolded.

While Wooden's specific techniques have limited classroom applicability, their cognitive nature allows certain generalizations.

Some Generalizations

1. Wooden himself was a master model, clearly and sharply sketching right and wrong modes.
2. His fairness toward, and personal involvement with, his players were legendary.
3. There was mutual respect and affection on his teams.
4. His instructions were information laden, not mere empty words.

The authors state that their adaptation of scold reinstruction has already improved their teaching. They go on to conclude that while educational psychology has developed its own theory and technology, it has placed negligible emphasis on results. Perhaps the key difference between the two teaching styles (classroom or athletic) is intensity. Can, or should, we introduce more intensity into the classroom? Can youngsters use added pressure beneficially? Recall the statement that was made in the chapter on motivation: We do not need better runners; we need bigger challenges. It is a fascinating question; think about it.

TABLE 14.1
Wooden's Teaching Techniques

Code	Category	Description	Percent of Total Communications
I	Instructions	Verbal statements about what to do, or how to do it	50.3
H	Hustles	Verbal statements to activate or intensify previously instructed behavior	12.7
M+	Modeling-positive	A demonstration of how to perform	2.8
M−	Modeling-negative	A demonstration of how *not* to perform	1.6
V+	Praises	Verbal compliments, encouragements	6.9
V−	Scolds	Verbal statements of displeasure	6.6
NV+	Nonverbal reward	Nonverbal compliments or encouragements (smiles, pats, jokes)	1.2
NV−	Nonverbal punishment	This infrequent category included only scowls, gestures of despair, and temporary removal of a player from scrimmage, usually to shoot free throws by himself	Trace
W	Scold reinstruction	A combination category: a single verbal behavior which refers to a specific act, contains a clear scold, and reasserts a previously instructed behavior; for example, "How many times do I have to tell you to follow through with your head when shooting?"	8.0
O	Other	Any behavior not falling into the above categories	2.4
X	Uncodable	The behavior could not be clearly heard or seen	6.6

Source: Roland A. Tharp and Ronald Gallimore, "What a Coach Can Teach a Teacher," *Psychology Today* 9 (January 1976). Reprinted by permission of *Psychology Today.* Copyright © 1975 Ziff-Davis Publishing Company.

TEACHER CHARACTERISTICS

One final aspect of teaching deserves your attention: teacher characteristics. Can you precisely identify the attributes of the "good" and "bad" teacher? Probably not, but there are sufficient data to enable you to make some helpful generalizations.

What makes a successful teacher? No one knows. Teachers are born, some will claim; others scoff at such mystique and declare vehemently that it is possible to make a good teacher. Both assertions are faulty; education can exercise some control on teacher behavior, but undoubtedly the inherent personality of teachers will color their performance.

**Universal
Characteristics**

How do you begin to examine this issue? If you ask students what they like most in a teacher you can be fairly certain of their replies. The qualities that appear most frequently are: impartiality, helpfulness, sense of humor, equanimity. These characteristics are repeatedly reported. Older students often judge the quality of instruction: does the teacher know the subject, are methods effective, are assignments valuable or merely busy-work?

It is dangerously misleading to apply these supposedly universal characteristics to all levels of education. Good, Biddle, and Brophy (1975) remark that searching for universal characteristics that are effective in *any* context and with *all* students is a major weakness of most teacher characteristic studies. "Warmth" may be a significant characteristic in the lower grades but may cause nothing but trouble for the secondary school teacher. "Good discipline'' may be coveted at the secondary level and cause emotional problems in kindergarten. The authors believe that while there may be a few effective universal characteristics (that is, regardless of age and subject), most desirable characteristics are linked to level and material.

The teacher characteristics study

Probably the most exhaustive study of teacher behavior yet attempted is that reported by Ryans (1960) in his *Characteristics of Teachers*. The six-year study, which included 6000 teachers in 1700 schools representing 450 school systems, had several objectives:

Objectives of the Study

1. The identification of teacher behavior patterns actually observed in the classroom and any major patterns that would emerge.
2. The development of questionnaires that would appraise characteristics not apparent upon direct observation (attitudes, intelligence, educational viewpoints, and emotional stability).
3. The construction of paper-and-pencil instruments that would sample estimated teacher characteristics.
4. The comparison of numerous groups of teachers by age, sex, grade level, subject, and kind of school.

Ryans (1964) notes that one basic assumption was that particular teacher behaviors were not totally independent of each other. As they were considered to possess common elements, the investigators could sort them into a comparatively small number of groups.

It is well to emphasize the three techniques that were used to obtain data:

1. Direct observation and analysis of teacher behavior.
2. Direct inquiry, self-appraisal questionnaire.
3. Construction of the Teacher Characteristics Schedule.

Each method posed serious problems. First, what characteristics of teacher behavior belonged in the study? A decision was made to employ open-end classroom observations, reports from previous studies, and the critical-incidents technique (the traits that caused a teacher to be designated as superior or inferior). In retrospect, Ryans (1964) wonders why the behavior that people recall about teachers is usually personal or social, not concerned with the teaching-learning process. He assumes that technical competence is presumed.

Direct observation led to three patterns of a teacher's classroom behavior.

1. *Pattern X.* Warm, understanding, and friendly versus aloof, egocentric, and restricted classroom behavior.

2. *Pattern Y.* Responsible, businesslike, and systematic versus evading, unplanned, and slipshod classroom behavior.
3. *Pattern Z.* Stimulating and imaginative versus dull and routine classroom behavior.

From the paper-and-pencil instruments, several additional characteristics were identified.

1. *Characteristic R.* Favorable versus unfavorable opinions of pupils.
2. *Characteristic R_1.* Favorable versus unfavorable opinions of democratic class procedures.
3. *Characteristic Q.* Favorable versus unfavorable opinions of administrative and other school personnel.
4. *Characteristic B.* Traditional versus permissive views of education.
5. *Characteristic I.* Superior verbal understanding versus poor verbal understanding.
6. *Characteristic S.* Emotional stability versus instability.
7. *Characteristic V.* Validity of response versus invalidity of response (truthfulness in answering questions).

The TCS

Since direct observation of teacher behavior has its limitations, and any self-report inventory is open to question, a third source of data was devised. Estimates of teacher traits were made from symptoms, or correlates, of these characteristics. The final Teacher Characteristic Schedule consisted of 300 multiple-choice and checklist items that reflected personal preferences, self-judgments, personal activities, and biographical data. Three such schedules were designed: for elementary teachers, English–social studies teachers, and mathematics-science teachers. Estimates were thus available for each of the ten behaviors and characteristics.

The fourth aim of the study was to compare teacher groups classified by certain status (age, sex, grade level, experience, and type of school and community). Some interesting developments appeared: teachers who had engaged in any kind of simulated school activity were significantly more understanding, responsible, and stimulating; teachers who were over 55 compared unfavorably with younger teachers except in systematic behavior and traditional views; men who were elementary school teachers were less responsible and more permissive, while at the secondary level men showed greater emotional stability; teachers who were in large schools (17 to 50 or more teachers) scored higher on such characteristics as understanding, stimulating, favorable opinions of administration and personnel, verbal understanding, and emotional stability.

Conclusions

Summarizing the characteristics of "good" teachers, Ryans (1964) notes that the high group was generous in judgments of

Personality and Teaching Success

Sherman and Blackburn (1975) report a study of personal characteristics and college-teaching effectiveness based on the assumption that successful college teaching depends less on class management than on personality characteristics that students deem relevant. That is, it is an instructor's personal qualities that affect students' judgments.

Data were collected on 108 members of a liberal arts faculty over one and one-half years. Three separate instruments were used to evaluate faculty: the institution's evaluation (course centered, attitude), a student evaluation form (fairness, relevance), and Osgood's semantic differential (paired adjectives: logical-illogical, warm-cold). The authors collected 1500 student judgments based on these three instruments.

The results indicated that personal characteristics appear to be the cause of teacher effectiveness. That is, characteristics such as dynamic, friendly, and warm mark the effective teacher. One particularly interesting finding was when faculty were separated by discipline (biology, sociology), considerable variation appeared between personality attributes and teaching effectiveness. For example, there is a discrepancy between the humanities-arts and the science faculties. Amicability is an important characteristic for effectiveness in humanities and art, while it has little relationship to successful teaching in the sciences.

What do the authors conclude? They believe that personality characteristics, which endure and are difficult to change, are more important for effective teaching than clarity, fairness, and other behavioral attributes. These findings are significant for colleges recruiting faculty and for those faculty desiring to improve teaching: it is personal characteristics that are most significant.

others, read constantly, and exhibited wide cultural interests, such as art, music, and science. They generally were between 35 and 49, married, had achieved quite well at college, and had engaged in extracurricular activities.

One final and significant finding deserves comment. What is the relationship between pupil behavior (apathetic-alert, abstractive-responsible, uncertain-confident, dependent-initiating) and teacher behavior? A close relationship between the two appears in elementary school but not in secondary school. This outcome was confirmed by two later studies of Ryans (1961a, 1961b) in which pupil behavior was evaluated by trained observers. In one study teacher characteristics were assessed by observers; in the other a self-report inventory was used. The results were identical in both studies and agreed with the earlier data that indicated that productive pupil behavior in the elementary school was related to understanding, systematic, and stimulating teacher behavior.

TEACHERS' EXPECTANCIES

In 1968, Robert Rosenthal and Lenore Jacobson reported the results of a study that fascinated both educators and psychologists. Beginning in 1964, the authors had teachers in an elementary school administer an imposing test, The Harvard Test of Inflected Acquisition, that actually was a nonverbal IQ test. It was administered in May to youngsters who would return in the fall. Teachers were told that the test would predict which youngsters would show an academic spurt in the coming year. These would be the "intellectual bloomers." The test's supposed predictive value and the youngsters so identified were imaginary. Part of the explanation given the teachers was as follows.

Oak School

> As part of our study we are further validating a test which predicts the likelihood that a child will show an inflection point or "spurt" within the near future. This test which will be administered in your school will allow us to predict which youngsters are most likely to show an academic spurt. The top 20 percent (approximately) of the scores on these tests will probably be found at various levels of academic functioning. (Rosenthal and Jacobson, 1968, pg. 66)

In the fall, the teachers were told which youngsters had scored in the top 20 percent, and the investigators suggested that these children would probably show remarkable progress during the

A Potential Henry Higgins

year. Actually, there was no difference between them and the control group. All the youngsters were retested at the end of the school year, using the same test. The experimental group (the late bloomers) all scored higher than the control group. The investigators interpreted the results to indicate that when teachers expected more of children, the youngsters met their expectations—a self-fulfilling prophecy, or Pygmalion in the classroom.

The Results Are Challenged

The news media and general public seized upon the results and the study received enormous publicity. Uncritically accepted, the results were interpreted as heralding a breakthrough in the classroom. Many educators and investigators remained skeptical, and their skepticism was confirmed when attempts to duplicate the Rosenthal and Jacobson findings produced conflicting evidence. Other critics attacked the study's methodology. For example, Kerlinger (1973) states that Rosenthal's work has caused intense controversy. Carefully controlled sudies, in which teachers received varied information (IQ scores, no IQ scores, IQ scores inflated by 16 points, or designating some students academic bloomers) did *not* duplicate Rosenthal's findings. Kerlinger believes that these findings cast serious doubt on the Rosenthal hypothesis.

Perhaps it is safest to conclude that teachers' expectations make a difference, but not as uniformly and in a much more complex manner than originally believed. Answering his critics, Rosenthal also concluded that expectations produce effects because teachers:

1. Provide a favorable social and emotional atmosphere for the selected students.
2. Give these pupils more attention, thus furnishing carefully controlled reinforcement.
3. Spend more time with them, thus teaching them more.
4. Demand more from these children and usually receive it.

Rosenthal deduces that while teachers may not be certain how exactly their expectations affect students, they do affect them; teachers, therefore, should remain alert to this phenomenon in their assessment of pupils.

Discussion Questions

1. Do you agree that teachers are unique personalities and that these personality characteristics determine teaching success or failure? Why? Can you compile a list of "good" characteristics? Are they universal? Why? What does your answer suggest for future research?

2. Can "any damn fool teach"? Why? In your answer indicate the role of learners. Can we take "damn fools" and turn them into good teachers? Be sure you consider age, personality, and training.

3. In your present course, what role is your instructor playing? Is he or she consistent in it? Can you identify the source of the role? Ask. What role do you see yourself playing? Why?

4. Is it realistic to use coaching a sport as an example of good teaching? Why? Are there general principles that seem to apply in *any* situation and with *any* material? Specify them.

5. Examining the Ryans study, what characteristics do you feel are most important for you? Are these general or specific; that is, do they apply to all teachers, or do they relate to age, sex, or school level?

6. Should you attempt to be a "Henry Higgins"? If you accept the significance of the Pygmalion experiment what else should you consider? For example, do you apply your expectations to *all* students to the same degree?

Theories of teaching

Theories of teaching remain elusive, and Gage (1963, 1964) deplores their absence. He believes that two types of theories can evolve. The first endeavors to explain why teachers behave as they do in their roles as teachers. The second attempts to explain how the behavior of one person can influence the behavior of another.

TEACHING AND LEARNING: THEORY OR THEORIES?

Can we discuss teaching without including learning? Probably not, but we can formulate a theory of teaching as a distinct entity. There are theories of learning, completely devoid of teaching, whose main emphasis has been upon animals, but with the implied assumption that such data apply also to humans. It likewise seems possible to construct a theory of teaching that implies learning theory but remains independent of it.

For example, assume that investigators attempt to devise a theory of teaching founded upon the various roles that a teacher plays. After identifying the roles and the qualities that are typically associated with each, they are faced with the question: What processes are inherent in the student that will enable the teacher to succeed? While there may be learning without teaching, there can be no teaching without learning. Examining this statement you can see that theories of teaching must be more comprehensive than theories of learning.

In the development of a teaching theory, a point is reached when a theory of learning is necessary to complete the structure. But it remains only one aspect of the theory of teaching. Gage

(1964, pg. 269) notes that although theories of learning are vital to the understanding, prediction, and control of the learning process, they are inadequate to explain the total educational effort. Since the goal of education is to produce economical and effective learning, there is a need for more precise teaching. A teaching theory is necessary because learning theories in themselves are insufficient; that is, they are concerned solely with what happens to the learner and what he or she does. But behavioral changes in the classroom also occur because of what teachers do.

Learning Alone Is Insufficient

The most sophisticated theories of learning may offer detailed analyses about the impact of environmental stimuli upon the organism; but someone has to arrange these stimuli, and in the classroom that person is the teacher. Another theory may expound the value of discovery, but in the classroom it is the teacher who provides the materials and guides the student. It is the teacher's behavior that particularly influences behavioral changes in the learner and explains the statement that learning theories are inadequate to interpret all educational activity.

Toward a theory of teaching

What method offers the most promise in the construction of a theory of teaching? This fundamental question must be carefully weighed since its answer will undoubtedly affect the nature of the theory that is evolved. Gage (1964, pp. 273–277) suggests four types of analysis. But before he expands on each, he warns that it is highly unlikely that any one general theory can encompass the nature of teaching. There are just too many processes, behaviors, and activities. Eventually, perhaps, Gage will be proven to be overly pessimistic, but at the present level of vague groping toward some manageable structure of teaching, his warning is well taken.

Teacher Activities

The first type of analysis that he postulates is of teacher activities. Among these activities are telling, explaining, demonstrating, guiding, administrating, and so forth. If everything that teachers do in performing duties is teaching, can any one theory embrace all of these activities (Gage, 1964, pg. 275)?

Objectives

The second kind of analysis is by educational objectives: affective, psychomotor, and cognitive. Teaching is then classified by categories of objectives. When teachers guide students toward comprehension of some historical event, their behavior is related to cognitive objectives. But more than one category may be involved. For example, they may also be encouraging attitudes and interests, which belong to the affective domain. Can any one theory of teaching adequately account for all of these objectives?

Teaching Mirrors Learning

The third method of analysis holds that teaching mirrors learning, and that its components correspond to those of learning. If all

aspects of learning can be identified, then a theory of teaching naturally follows. If discovery is a key consideration in learning, then teaching must reflect the causes of discovery. What produces motivation? What kind and amount of stimuli are needed to yield the basic information from which concepts are formed?

Learning Theories

The final kind of analysis relies upon a general acceptance of learning theories. For example, conditioning, with its emphasis upon reinforcement, should imply a definite theory of teaching. If modeling is seen as the core of learning, another kind of teaching theory is inferred. For the cognitive theorist, a third type of teaching theory emerges. The difficulty is that there is no strict dichotomy among the various theories. *S-R* theorists today attempt to explain the phenomenon of insight; cognitive theorists appreciate the importance of conditioning in learning. Again, can any one theory successfully incorporate the essentials of any or all learning theories (Gage, 1964, pg. 276)?

In his presentation, Gage concludes that theories of learning will become more useful only when they are transformed into theories of teaching. Presently there is no single theory of teaching that explains the many processes by which teachers foster learning. For the foreseeable future, the most likely prediction is that several

theories of teaching will appear, each of which will correspond to a particular family of learning theories (Gage, 1964, pg. 285). Among those who have attempted to reconcile their beliefs about learning with a teaching theory are Bruner and Skinner.

BRUNER'S THEORY OF INSTRUCTION

You have previously studied Bruner's views on cognitive development, learning, and motivation. Recall that he believes learning is closely linked to structure, readiness, intuition, and motivation. In 1966, Bruner published *Toward a Theory of Instruction* in which

Prescriptive Versus Descriptive

he raised the question: Since psychology already contains theories of learning and development, why is a theory of instruction needed? His answer is that theories of learning and development are descriptive rather than prescriptive; that is, they tell us what happened after the fact. For example, from Piaget's theory we know a child of six does not have reversibility. A theory of instruction prescribes how teachers can help the child acquire it.

Bruner believes that there are four elements in any theory of instruction.

1. *The theory should specify those experiences that predispose a youngster toward learning.* What is there in the classroom or materials that will make pupils want to learn?

2. *The theory should clearly delineate the structure of any subject to aid learning.* Teachers must determine whether the subject is best presented *enactively,* that is, by emphasizing psychomotor learning; *iconically,* that is, by using images and other visuals to represent concepts; or *symbolically,* that is, by employing rules, logic, and propositions. Here the teacher acts as a decision maker: deciding whether the materials and methods are appropriate for a youngster's developmental level.

3. *The theory should specify the optimum sequence for presenting materials.* Is it always better to proceed from concrete to abstract, simple to complex, part to whole? Or is it better to present the entire structure and then fill in pieces? Since teachers must lead students through the sequence they have predetermined, instructors again act as decision makers. Your decision may have a powerful influence on the ease or difficulty with which a student learns.

4. *The theory should specify the nature and pacing of rewards and punishments.* Learning depends on knowledge of results, and the theory should indicate where, when, and under what circumstance correction and praise occur. Teachers then become actively engaged in instructing pupils to use error and to apply information correctly.

Bruner concludes that a theory of instruction must accept that a curriculum reflects the nature of knowledge, the nature of the learner, and the learning process. Perhaps a teaching theory is effective if it blurs the lines of distinction between these three. The theory should have as its ultimate goal teaching the learner to participate in the entire process of acquiring and furnishing knowledge.

SKINNER AND THE TECHNOLOGY OF TEACHING

You have already studied Skinner's views of operant conditioning and his insistence that teachers strictly control their reinforcements. Skinner's *Technology of Teaching* (1968) offers useful in-

A Perceptual Viewpoint

While Bruner is perhaps the leading proponent of perceptual psychology applied to education, you should also be familiar with the provocative thoughts of Arthur Combs. He and Donald Snygg wrote (1959) an enduring text from the perceptual viewpoint: *Individual Behavior*. Their basic premise is that all behavior, without exception, is completely determined by the perceptual field of the behaving organism. People behave according to the facts as *they* themselves see them, not as others see them.

Teaching is not merely presenting subject matter, but helping students understand the meaning of a subject so that it affects their behavior. To achieve this objective, teachers must establish an atmosphere conducive to learning. Students must be free from threat so that their perceptions are not excessively restricted to defense of self. Challenge students; do not threaten them. While accepting the dignity and integrity of students, the teacher must establish limits, which not only contributes to an accepting atmosphere, it also helps to provide structure for students. The authors believe that effective teachers use their personalities to fix limits that are helpful both for learning and the discovery of personal meaning. Consequently, teaching methods are individual matters closely related to teachers' personalities.

With this as background, the authors formulate their personal list of teaching-learning principles. Some of these are as follows.

1. Children are mainly motivated by their need for self-esteem and personal adequacy.
2. Use those techniques you have discovered, or will discover, to meet these needs.
3. You can most easily aid learning if you encourage pupils both to seek the meaning of materials and to relate it to themselves.
4. If you can manage to instill a sense of pride in pupils when they master material, learning will proceed smoothly. You must *know* your pupils to do this, and here the authors agree with Bruner when they urge that you carefully pace the work for individual children.
5. Be aware of developing attitudes; they may eventually be more important than the subject itself.

Whether or not you agree with the perceptual method, Combs, Snygg, and Bruner insist upon your personal involvement in an activity, which, in the final analysis, is intensely personal.

sights into his interpretation of teaching. Recall that Skinner believes teachers depend too heavily upon punishment and are not sufficiently aware of their use of positive reinforcement. Arguing that there are special techniques to arrange contingencies of reinforcement—the relationship between behavior and the consequences of that behavior—Skinner states that teachers now can effectively control behavior. This assumption is the basis of operant conditioning.

**Some Basic
Assumptions**

While his principles derive mainly from animal experiments, Skinner nevertheless declares that *the species of the organism makes little difference.* Here note his rationalization for applying the principles of operant conditioning to humans: experiments with pigeons, rats, dogs, monkeys, and children all have produced parallel results—the learning process appears similar for all organisms. By analyzing the effects of reinforcement and by devising procedures to manipulate reinforcement, the behavior of all organisms is brought under precise control.

The State of Teaching

But in education—where behavioral control is critical—all is chaos. Skinner then turns to one of his favorite subjects: the teaching of arithmetic. Here the responses are verbal—speaking and writing figures, words, and signs—and it is necessary to bring them under stimulus control. How do teachers accomplish this? They must use reinforcers, which traditionally have been and still

BOSTON COLLEGE PUBLIC RELATIONS

are aversive, that is, punishment. As mentioned, although yesterday's physical punishment is gone, teachers today rely excessively on sarcasm, ridicule, and low marks. So arithmetic, as most subjects, becomes mired in a maze of dislike, anxiety, and, ultimately, boredom.

50,000 Reinforcements

Another weakness in current teaching is the lack of frequent positive reinforcement. Teachers cannot reinforce each step and response, so youngsters blithely proceed in ignorance, often leaving a trail of errors behind them. For example, Skinner estimates that the first four years of arithmetic instruction could necessitate as many as 50,000 reinforcements. Most pupils are lucky to receive as many as 4000. The result is incompetent students who are not educated in the vital basic skills but in such vague achievements as "democratic citizenry," "the total personality," or "readiness for life."

Improvement is possible. Skinner (1968, pg. 199) believes that there are general characteristics of teaching that, if practiced, cultivate both teaching and learning.

1. *Define the terminal behavior.* Decide what the student should be able to do after your teaching. Proclaiming the citizen enlightened is both inadequate and unworthy; it does not describe behavior. "Knowledge" is another deceptive goal of education. Pupils—and you and I—know something when we do things; that is, we respond to stimuli differently than we did before instruction. Pupils "know" when teachers can specifically identify their behavior; that is, teachers have taught them to behave in certain ways. What they know is what they do, so teachers must objectively and concretely state their objectives.

2. *Solve the "problem of the first instance."* Once you have determined the terminal behavior (what you want students to do after teaching), you must strengthen it by reinforcement. But you cannot reinforce what does not appear. The problem of the first instance means that pupils must exhibit some aspect of the desired behavior. How can you induce it? Perhaps physically, as taking a child's hand and guiding it to form letters. Perhaps by presenting such forceful stimuli that students are forced to respond. Perhaps by having pupils imitate the teacher or some example of excellent work. Perhaps by simply telling pupils what to do and then reinforcing them when they do it. But, as Skinner notes (1968, pg. 212), learning does not occur because you have primed the behavior; it occurs only when behavior is reinforced. The above examples are only the first step in the process.

3. *Decide what you will use to prompt behavior.* One reinforcement will hardly free a response from priming stimuli. When do you stop priming pupils? If you continue too long, you are inefficient; if you stop too soon, you may cause error. Use only as much

DEMCO EDUCATIONAL CORP.

as is necessary. For example, you may wish students to be able to identify the Midwestern states, their major cities, and principal industries. You may begin by using maps and reading materials. Some cities may be near water and be port cities. Later, when students should know which cities do what, you may ask them to locate the city *without* using maps or texts. You have supplied a *prompt*, which is part of the original priming behavior.

4. *Program complex behavior.* Priming and prompting evoke the behavior to be reinforced in the presence of required stimuli. But some behavior is so complex that you cannot reinforce it as a unit. You must program it, which does not mean teaching one thing at a time as a collection of responses. What a student does halfway through a program may not be a part of the terminal behavior. Small steps are needed to insure constant reinforcement.

5. *Decide not only the proper size but the most effective sequence of steps for your program.* You must insure not only an orderly arrangement of steps but also that students are properly prepared for each step. You cannot always depend upon a subject's inherent logic. A good example is our work with Piaget. Usually students are well advised to read original sources and trace the author's work. This procedure is dangerous with Piaget because his ideas are so complex and his writing so tortuous that students, proceeding logically, may become hopelessly confused. Instructors are better advised to select basic ideas and test them before presenting the entire system. For example, you should understand the functional invariants before you plunge into the theory.

Skinner concludes that human behavior is an extremely complex subject; our teaching methods must match this complexity.

An example that reflects many of these principles is the highly structured Bereiter=Englemann program, designed to prescribe teaching procedures for disadvantaged children. The authors (1966) state that new teachers like to work with "ideas." Good teaching, however, employs much smaller and more intricate units than ideas; it involves specific information modules and specific techniques. Teaching is the interplay between information, pace, discipline, rewards, and drama as they relate to curriculum (1966, pg. 105).

Acquiring these techniques comes gradually—a motivational trick here, an attention-getting device there. The authors believe that teachers are good not because of what they are but because of what they do. Good teachers do the "right thing" because they have learned slowly—even painfully. They were not naturally proficient; they achieved proficiency through practice.

Here are some of their teaching strategies. They are intended for use in an intensive preschool program for disadvantaged children, but they have broad applicability.

1. *Do not vary your presentation methods.* Variations will confuse the culturally disadvantaged child who ordinarily experiences considerable language difficulty. Excessive variation bothers and bewilders all children who need to feel psychologically secure in the classroom. Still, youngsters, disadvantaged or not, must respond in a variety of situations and should receive school preparation. But the authors' suggestion is timely, and we should consider variation in relation to the readiness of our students.

2. *Give children sufficient time to respond.* Time has been a recurring theme in this text. You previously encountered it in Bloom's work on mastery learning and in Martin's analysis of praise. Here Bereiter and Englemann urge that the lesson's tempo be such that the youngster can respond thoughtfully.

3. *Use questions liberally.* Questions are important because they help a child attend to relevant cues. You must consider the question's difficulty: is the child capable of answering it? The value of questioning is clear from countless studies: subjects tend to re-

The Bereiter-Englemann Program

Using Praise Carefully

David Martin (1977) has recently presented some fascinating evidence about teachers' use of praise. He believes that what researchers are discovering is startling: teachers, "massively" employing praise, may actually sabotage learning. It may fix youngsters on external rewards and destroy their self-motivation. Describing Mary Budd Rowe's work at the University of Florida, Martin states that one of the most significant findings in her studies of teaching science was the "wait time" after a teacher's question. When teachers waited at least three seconds (rather than the typical one second) the students' answers were more appropriate and thoughtful. What confounded the results was praise—teachers praised different students in different ways. Praise limited persistence, lowered the students' confidence, and stifled student interaction.

Heavy praise makes pupils more dependent on extrinsic reinforcement, thus reducing any feeling of self-satisfaction that comes from learning itself. These students are accustomed to the "quick payoff" and are reluctant to involve themselves in innovative problems or complex reasoning. In one study, students of a teacher who praised excessively were compared with those of a teacher who praised minimally. The low praise schedule produced more student interaction and higher task persistence. The high praise students tended to stop frequently and seek the teacher.

Teachers praised their top and bottom students differently. For example, they would frequently praise the bottom student with less pertinence; that is, they often praised incorrect answers. This technique appears to cause inefficient problem-solving behavior. The general conclusion is that praise may be effective if judiciously used for simpler learning.

Here are some of Martin's suggestions for using praise.

1. Now that you are aware of praise's mixed blessings, listen to yourself in the classroom. If your praise is excessive, try to be silent more often and give your pupils a chance to answer. Keep quiet after asking a question.
2. Encourage students to establish their own goals and tasks. Self-motivation is more characteristic of students who work toward their own goals.
3. Confine your comments to students' responses or to the material and refrain from praising *students*.
4. Avoid generalized praise. Make your praise specific and detailed.

Martin's premise is thoughtful and provocative since we all tend to praise pupils as often as possible. Whether or not you agree, you would enjoy reading this article.

---

member more about the material on which they are questioned, and they retain it longer. The direct instructional effect of questioning is substantial (Rothkopf, 1976).

   4. *Use multiple examples.* When presenting a new concept, avoid talking too much about it. The authors advise that you "stretch" the concept; that is, if you are teaching *red* give numerous examples of different objects, sizes, shapes, all of which are different with one exception—the color red.

5. *As far as possible, prevent incorrect responses.* Helping children avoid error will help them to avoid mistake patterns. Always assume that children will repeat mistakes in similar situations and try to forestall it. Use prevention techniques.

6. *Be clear in responding to correct and incorrect answers.* If a child brings a blue crayon when asked to bring a red, do *not* praise the youngster for bringing a crayon. Youngsters cannot understand the subtle distinction. Teachers should provide nonthreatening but clear feedback. This suggestion is remarkably similar to Martin's comments about nonpertinent praise. The authors furnish several more suggestions that indicate the nature of the program: carefully controlled stimuli, judicious application of reinforcement, and the avoidance of error. The Bereiter-Englemann program is an example of behavioral principles put to action.

THEORIES AND TEACHING

The distinction between cognitive and behaviorist has been repeatedly stressed, but you should not think that you are faced with an either-or choice. Most teachers are eclectic but theoretically predisposed to one theory or the other. What can you do in your academic studies and teaching that would better enable you to adapt theory and practice to your personality?

For you to become a truly effective teacher you must skillfully apply your knowledge and transform it into effective practice. The need for self-knowledge should aid your understanding of the learning process and the means by which teaching can be more effective by relating to the individual's development (intellectual, physical, social, and emotional). There is an inevitable interaction among teacher personality, learning theory, methods, and student responses. If you understand yourself and attempt to match your unique personality to theory and to derive specific methods from this knowledge, you may well see yourself not *apart* from the learning process but actually *within* it.

Teacher know thyself

Among the millions of words that are written each year "to further the effectiveness of the teaching-learning process" very few are calculated to turn your attention inward. Some interesting answers will be forthcoming if you will stop and honestly answer the following question: "Who am I?"

Pause, reflect upon it, and move beyond the obvious replies that we all initially give to such a question. Refuse to be satisfied with the typical stereotyped replies; push instead into deeper, perhaps uncharted waters. For example, consider your role as a teacher. Who are you in the classroom? Are you a person who likes a quiet, disciplined classroom, or do you prefer the restless sounds of pupil activity?

There are no right and wrong answers to these questions, in spite of the almost unlimited praise of the "discovery" method and the almost unlimited criticism of the "telling" method. What is important in your self-analysis is your acceptance of the facts about yourself. You are a certain kind of person with definite beliefs, attitudes, opinions, strengths, and weaknesses. The more that you know about these characteristics and the manner in which they affect your classroom performance, the better teacher you will be.

It is the purpose of this section to suggest a general technique by which you can learn more about yourself and avoid many conflicts that are inherent in contradictory classroom performance. Figure 14.1 illustrates the procedure.

You can see this is a broad plan for analyzing the consistency of a teacher's classroom performance. There are innumerable other variables, ranging from the temperature of the classroom to the nature of the subject, that will influence both a teacher's and a learner's behavior. If you examine Figure 14.1 carefully, the fundamental premise is clear: your personality will largely determine your behavior and which learning theory you will find appealing, which will then affect the methods that you select to teach your subject.

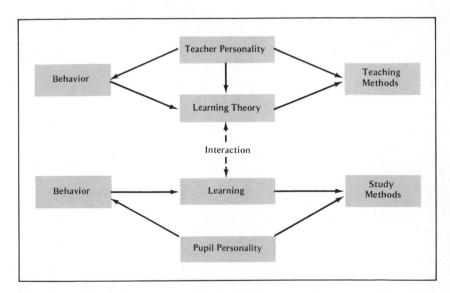

Figure 14.1 A Device for Assessing the Impact of Teacher Personality upon Classroom Performance.

BOSTON COLLEGE PUBLIC RELATIONS

**The Inherent
Assumption**

Before suggesting any specific means for analysis, several inherent assumptions in this procedure require clarification. First, there is the unmistakable belief that your personality is decisive in shaping your behavior. Are you permissive or authoritarian? Can you tolerate the hum of student energy, or do you need a quiet ordered classroom? Your personality helps to answer these questions. Second, any teacher, consciously or not, prefers a certain learning theory. You can determine your preference by defining learning to yourself. For example, if you believe that learning is essentially a cognitive process, you are probably uncomfortable with a more mechanistic interpretation of learning as a function of stimuli and responses that avoids any speculation about what occurs within the organism between S and R.

Or consider the use of error in learning. If you believe that stu-

dents should be allowed to make mistakes and then use those mistakes in solving problems, you differ from those who feel error is to be eliminated because students tend to remember their incorrect as well as correct responses. Again, the difference is between those who believe in a cognitive theory (like Bruner) and those who believe in a more behavioristic theory of learning (like Skinner).

Finally, there is the inescapable premise that methods should be determined by an instructor's personality and adherence to a learning theory. It is precisely here that inconsistency sometimes appears. A teacher may possess a personality that is comfortable with a rather mechanistic learning theory, that is, careful control of stimuli and response.

Strive for Consistency   But professional reading may generate considerable enthusiasm for the problem-solving technique, the discovery method, or the

MEDFORD, MASS. *DAILY MERCURY*

encouragement of creativity. Temporarily stimulated by reading, teachers may switch classroom techniques and urge more student activity. The result is predictable. Students are bewildered by this sudden shift from a teacher-dominated classroom to one that demands more individual initiative and learning; perhaps even discipline suffers accordingly. Consistency of classroom performance is necessary. By understanding your personality, by adapting a class of learning theories, and by adopting methods that are suitable, your teaching and learning will become more efficient.

A sense of a compatible learning theory should emerge from these attempts to achieve an insight of self. Some theories are better suited for certain personalities. In attempting to match theory with personality one conclusion clearly emerges: merely engaging in this type of search will insure a better classroom performance. Personality, learning theory, and methods should blend more harmoniously as self-awareness develops. Use your studies of personality to discover more about yourself; use your work in educational psychology to clarify your beliefs about learning; use your work in methods, student teaching, and teaching experience to make yourself a smoothly functioning professional who is able to help all kinds of students.

Match the mix

Educators and psychologists have been long fascinated by the theoretical possibility of matching students with teachers on some predetermined characteristic. Using Figure 14.1 as an example, is it possible to match pupils and instructors by personality? Those individuals who prefer classroom freedom, discovery, and the use of error would be together. Those who prefer a controlled environment would be in a different setting. The rationale would be that those who have the same preferences would work more harmoniously together. Desiring a similar learning environment, teachers and students would share similar dispositions about learning. A teacher's methods would coincide with a pupil's cognitive style and study techniques.

Should We Match?

Matching pupils and instructors remains only a theory because of limited knowledge of the human personality. Still there is considerable enthusiasm for the idea. The chief objection is itself an engrossing problem: *should* schools match pupils and instructors because of compatible views? Nonschool life provides no such match, so would providing such an artificial atmosphere not be a disservice? Would not students benefit more from occasionally working with teachers who are quite dissimilar to them?

While resolution of this question lies in the future, the effective use of personality is always present. Combs et al. (1974) state that professional teachers must both shape and discipline themselves. Being oneself, which is highly personal but never self-indulgent, is the only effective method of communication. But this is impossible without the self-awareness that we have stressed; that is, good teachers value self-disclosure tempered with self-discipline. As the authors note, good teaching is not maudlin.

A secure teacher manifests consistent behavior directed toward clear and worthy goals. Confused teachers confuse students. The authors discuss consistency as follows.

> Consistency does not lie in the repetitive character of behavior. It is a function of the stability and clarity of the individual's beliefs about what is important and worth doing. The beliefs teachers hold about what is important determine what they respond to and what methods they choose to deal with matters (Combs et al., 1974, pg. 100).

Discussion Questions

1. What do you think is the relationship between theories of teaching and learning? Do you agree with Gage's analysis? Why? What does Gage mean when he says that theories of teaching must be more inclusive than theories of learning?

2. Reread Chapters 4, 7, and 8. Now derive your own set of teaching principles from Bruner's and Skinner's work. Are you consistent with their theories? with this chapter's interpretation? How do any of your principles differ? Why?

3. Was your opinion of praise's value shaken by your reading? What was your previous belief? Will you change as a result of your reading? How can you reconcile your view with Martin's conclusions?

4. Do you think that the Bereiter and Englemann strategies are too rigid for regular classrooms? Why? How would you adapt them? Examine your answer carefully; it may reveal more than you think about your beliefs concerning learning.

5. Are you aware of any personal preference for a class of learning theories? If not, think about the question now. Can you answer it? How does your answer determine your teaching style? Comment on the need for consistency as related to both teachers' and students' needs.

Forms of instruction

Instruction can take many forms. How you teach something often is dictated by the subject matter (for example, laboratory work requires a certain teaching style), number of students (teaching an individual and teaching 75 or 100 students require different techniques), and personality needs (insecurity can pose problems in group discussions). This section focuses on individualized instruction without emphasizing technology (the subject of the next chapter), discussion methods, and the much-maligned lecture technique.

INDIVIDUALIZED INSTRUCTION

There are several interpretations of individualized instruction, which ranges from one-to-one tutoring, in which the instructor is intensely involved with a student, to the use of highly complex programs, such as Individually Guided Education (IGE) and Individually Prescribed Instruction (IPI). Glaser and Cooley (1973, pg. 847) state that it is platitudinous to say that instructional systems need to adapt to the requirements of the individual, but for schools geared to mass instruction the need is real and far from platitudinous.

Tutoring

The purest form of individualized instruction is tutoring. Ellson (1976) believes that it is incorrect to equate tutoring and individualized instruction since the latter is a broader concept that includes both individual diagnosis and group involvement. That is,

regardless of the program's individual nature, teachers work with several students. Ellson states that to qualify as tutoring the *instruction must be individualized.*

While the evidence supporting the value of tutoring is mixed (for a summary of research results and the strengths and weaknesses of the studies, see Ellson, 1976), you will want at times to work with students individually. Be sure to remember that, no matter how noble your intentions, you are an authority figure in a highly personal relationship. A student needs something from you, and how you structure this relationship affects the learning outcome. Strive for a relaxed atmosphere conducive to learning. Be **The Tutoring** certain that you and your pupil share the same expectations; for **Relationship** example, overcoming some arithmetical weakness. Explain why you are following certain procedures, returning to an academic level where the pupil is confident (for example, multiplying fractions), and what you hope to attain. Decide whether you will allow the student to make mistakes and then use them in correction, or whether you will present small steps that both instruct and eliminate the possibility of error. (Again, note the preference for a certain learning theory.) Above all, remember that there is no group in which the youngster can hide and that your mere presence can be intimidating, especially with younger pupils.

Teachers are not the only tutors. Classmates, older students, and adult volunteers also serve. Nonprofessionals require training, but once they have acquired some idea of method and use of materials, they have been quite successful in helping teachers. When students act as tutors, they improve their work and school attitudes as much as they help others.

Children Teaching Children

Peggy Lippitt (1975) comments that children teaching children is not a new idea: it is a familiar technique in large families and was often used in one-room schoolhouses. What is as important as older children helping is that they learn effective means of helping. Older children near the age of those that they are helping can talk their language and can provide excellent models for them.

There are several reasons for the growing popularity of students teaching students. It is one way of individualizing instruction; it makes older children feel useful and influential; it is an excellent motivational device; younger children like having older friends, which aids the self-concepts of both.

But in this, as in all forms of instruction, there are pitfalls.

1. Avoid exploiting the older children by always giving them the unpleasant tasks, for example, cleaning the room.
2. Be sure that the older children understand what they are doing; it is little help for the "ignorant to spread ignorance."
3. Have the older children work with younger pupils before they attempt to teach them. For example, they could act as teachers in a game.
4. Inform parents. If you are serious about this technique, then you must prepare the parents. Imagine the parents' shock should they imagine the school in the hands of the older children. Try to secure parental agreement—even cooperation, if they volunteer to participate—but if you cannot, then abandon the idea. It is doomed to failure.

Individually prescribed instruction (IPI)

A popular form of individualized instruction utilizing precise program specification is Individually Prescribed Instruction. The planning for each student's program is as painstaking as that for producing a teaching machine program. Lindvall and Bolvin (1967) explain Individually Prescribed Instruction as follows.

1. *Objectives are characterized as pupil behaviors.* Since IPI entails the extensive use of self-teaching materials, educators must devise materials that permit attainment of specific objectives.

2. *Objectives must encourage pupil progress with little unnecessary repetition.* While a logical sequence of steps is vital, the program must also provide for branching or "break points." For example, in teaching addition there are desirable spots to introduce subtraction skills.

3. *The materials must permit the students to learn from them independently without constant help from the teacher.* Since many pupils will be at different levels, the materials must allow pupils to profit from their own study. The behavioral objectives were the main guide: "What materials will enable pupils to attain this ability?"

4. *There must be a detailed diagnosis of the learner to determine existing skills and knowledge and the ideal starting point in the sequence.* As the authors note, if instruction is to be efficient and challenging, it must account for individual differences upon entering the program; it must place the learner at an appropriate level in the learning sequence, and it must accommodate the program to needs.

5. *The learner establishes a personal pace.* Most students need little teacher assistance; usually two or three teachers, with three or four teacher aides, will provide individual help. There are tests for each objective, and a test on all the unit's objectives. If pupils demonstrate sufficient mastery, then they move to the next unit. If not, additional work is provided to overcome deficiencies. Such continuous monitoring ensures that each pupil works with suitable materials.

6. *Instruction must provide opportunities for students to practice the desired behaviors.* Reading about or being told something is inadequate. Activities must allow practice in what is to be learned.

7. *Learning is enhanced through immediate feedback.* Pupils should not have to wait days to see if they are correct. The IPI procedure attempts to keep students fully and immediately informed of their progress.

8. *Success or failure in changing pupil behavior is continuously used to modify the program.* Constant monitoring of pupil programs allows constant change in the program. Material is revised depending on the feedback from pupils.

As Glaser and Cooley (1973) describe the procedure, the children get their folders at the beginning of each period. These contain information on past performance and current assignments (additional work, test). If they need help they raise their hands and teachers come to them. Children's work is immediately checked on completion and tests are administered by teachers' aides. At the end of class, the children return the folders where they are evaluated by teachers who then make new assignments.

Lindvall and Bolvin believe that these principles will achieve increasing acceptance in schools because of their individually prescribed learning tasks and the formation of curriculum into predictable teaching techniques.

Individually guided education (IGE)

For many years Herbert Klausmeier and his associates at the University of Wisconsin have been working on a new form of schooling—Individually Guided Education. It is a comprehensive design intended to achieve certain objectives through individualized instruction. But it is not individualized instruction in which students employ programmed instructional materials with little teacher assistance. Klausmeier's interpretation of individualized instruction is that in which self-instructional material is only one aspect of the program.

IGE involves:

1. Planning individual institutional programs for students.
2. Providing instructional materials (books, audiovisual materials, demonstrations) that suit individual learning styles.
3. Providing different methods of instruction: small group, large group, tutoring, independent study.
4. Matching teachers and students.

Klausmeier and Goodwin (1975, pg. 164) describe IGE as a comprehensive system of schooling that focuses on the individual not by age and not by classroom group. It is a nongraded system in which teachers work with pupils whose ages may vary as much as four years. IGE demands a new organization, team teaching, and differential staffing, as well as nongrading. There is a clear statement of objectives, assessment of pupils' readiness, constant evaluation of progress, varied teaching techniques and materials, measurement of final achievement, and, finally, a decision about future progress or remedial work. Klausmeier makes an interesting distinction between teachers in IGE and those in self-contained classrooms: the IGE teacher is engaged in all aspects of teaching-learning, such as setting goals and assessing pupils' characteristics, and in formulating instructional programs, using new material and experimenting with new techniques. Teachers have a more encompassing role.

Efforts to individualize instruction will continue and will be similar to tutoring or the elaborate programs we have just seen. Pupils can only benefit from these attempts because the spread of the principles of individualized instruction will gradually affect all teachers. Try to study some of the major programs and determine how you can adapt any attractive suggestions to your work. Remember these principles in your teaching.

1. *Be sure students understand what they are doing and why.* No matter how you phrase your objectives, be sure that they are clear to guide your teaching and provide students with a sense of direction.

2. *Be positive that your pupils can assimilate the material you are presenting.* Lack of maturity and experience are powerful obstacles to learning. Think of this physical example as a guide: forcing a 5-year-old to throw a regulation size basketball at a basket ten feet above the ground will probably cause frustration and a dislike of the game. The same is true of presenting abstract material to youngsters at a preoperational cognitive level.

3. *Understand the logic of your subject.* Know where it is more practical to divide a subject into manageable units. Know where there are opportunities to "branch," to introduce related material that will broaden learning.

4. *Adapt your instruction to the learner's pace.* While this requires effort, perhaps extra work, it will result in solid learning, enhanced motivation, and steady progress.

5. *Provide constant feedback.* Students should know as soon as possible whether they are right or wrong, what comes next, or what needs to be remedied. This demands continuous evaluation, which is a desirable legacy of individualized instruction since it encourages progress and also prevents students from falling too far behind.

THE DISCUSSION METHOD

Gall and Gall (1976) describe the discussion technique as a group of persons communicating and interacting to achieve specific objectives. Probably the critical element in successful discussion is group size. Most authorities agree that if you work with groups, keep the number to five. Below this number, group participation is limited; there is an insufficient pool of ideas. As numbers increase a few members tend to dominate discussion and others become passive participants.

If you think that you can teach some subjects better by the discussion technique, how can you organize your classroom? One way is to assign class members independent work while you lead the discussion group. Be sure that eventually all class members become group participants. You can also divide the entire class into groups with students acting as moderators. You must ensure that student leaders understand the objectives, know the material, and can lead the group.

The group

Group chemistry is complex and constantly changing. No two groups are alike. The various members' personalities are more closely linked in discussion; thus, interaction is never quite the same. While the teacher's personality is dominant in individual instruction and the lecture, there should be no total dominance in discussion; it is the exchange of ideas, as many different personalities agree, clash, search, and strive to satisfy needs, that most matters.

Kinds of Groups

Combs et al. (1974) suggest that you be certain of the kind of group you wish to form. It can be a decision group, designed to explore a problem and reach a decision, or a learning group, designed to allow participants to explore, discover, and present personal opinions. It is important to distinguish the two purposes, otherwise you have sown seeds of discord before discussion begins. Most groups you form will be learning groups.

Leadership roles

Another question relates to the role—active or passive—that you will play in the group. In almost all school situations, students expect teachers to act as leaders but, as Gall and Gall note, the discussion method is intended to encourage student participation, so you must be careful not to stifle initiative. What kind of leadership will you demonstrate? A classic leadership study by Lippitt and White (1960) had as its objective determining the effect of three kinds of leadership (democratic, authoritarian, and laissez-faire) upon group and individual behavior. It also summarized the reaction of the group and individuals when the type of leadership was changed, and it explored the relationship between various kinds of groups (family, class) and the particular social climate.

What Role?

The investigators attempted to control the personal characteristics of group members, the interrelationship pattern among the different groups, the physical setting and equipment, the activity interest and the activity content of each member, and the similarity of leadership for each group. One major concern was the personality of the leaders. Four adults with widely different personality patterns were finally selected and trained in the different leadership roles. This enabled the investigators to discover whether group reaction was caused by the leader's personality or leadership role.

The Lippitt and White Studies

The authoritarian leadership role demanded that the leader, who was to remain fairly aloof from the group, decide all policies and communicate all activities to the group one by one. The democratic leadership role had all decisions made by group discussion, wherever possible with assistance from the leader. The laissez-faire leadership role had a passive leader with all decisions left completely to the group. The leader merely supplied materials, offered advice only when asked, and avoided making any decisions. One interesting result was that individual personality characteristics were insignificant in influencing group behavior. Group members rated them solely by leadership role and not by personality. This conclusion is extremely important because it implies that regardless of teachers' personalities, they can affect class behavior if they are consistent in the type of roles selected. Obviously, personality will be a powerful force in role selection, but if there is consistency in performance (kind of role), effectiveness should increase.

Other findings showed that members under authoritarian leadership were both more dependent upon and discontented with the

leader than the other two groups. Members in the authoritarian groups were more irritable and aggressive than members of the other two groups. When the leaders deliberately arrived late, they found that members under the authoritarian leadership had initiated no work themselves, members under democratic leadership had been both active and productive, and members of laissez-faire groups had been active but not productive.

The Democratic Role

Lippitt and White conclude (1960, pg. 326) that the democratic type of adult role permitted the greatest expression of individual differences, with the laissez-faire group next in efficiency, while the authoritarian group was least effective in encouraging individual achievement. You should interpret these results cautiously since teachers cannot succeed without minimal control, which varies from person to person. But two conclusions are possible. First, the psychological atmosphere affects the kind of learning (memorization versus comprehension) and the extent of learning (retention and use of knowledge versus immediate loss of knowledge). Second, you should select the type of role, with its resultant atmosphere, that best suits your personality and allows you to function most effectively and maintain consistent behavior.

How can you evaluate the effectiveness of the discussion method? Evidence suggests that if subject matter mastery is the criterion then there is little difference between discussion and lecture. If you evaluate on other bases—creativity, complexity—discussion techniques seem superior. If you examine emotional considerations—satisfaction in school work, love of learning—the discussion method again seems more effective. Perhaps the best way to summarize these findings is to agree with Gall and Gall: generalizations should remain tentative until we have more evidence from methodologically better studies.

If you use discussion techniques, you may find these suggestions helpful.

587

1. *Be certain that you and the group members share clear and similar objectives.* Probably the greatest weakness of group discussion is that it may degenerate into mere talk—pointless and leaderless.

2. *Create a pleasant atmosphere conducive to member participation.* A threatening environment can destroy group discussion. Neither you nor any group member should dominate at the expense of others.

3. *Establish the "tone" of the group.* Immediately, but subtly, set guidelines. How much leadership will you exert? How much will you permit any one member to lead the discussion? What format will the group use? The answers to these questions are important because they set the group standards.

4. *Clearly establish your role.* Will you be an active or passive leader? If you assume an active role, then you minimize member participation, which is probably necessary in a decision group. If you are passive, how passive are you supposed to be? That is, will you answer students' questions or return them to the group? You may feel more comfortable acting as a guide: changing discussion topics, encouraging all members to participate, questioning, and summarizing.

5. *Know when to end the discussion.* Any topic has limited potential; to extend it beyond that limit is to guarantee boredom. Any group can sustain discussion for a given time; you must be alert to the limits of each group.

6. *Summarize clearly and succinctly.* Successful discussion should ensure that group members feel that their objectives were attained. Show how discussion clarified a problem, aided learning, and developed group cooperation. Leave the group with a feeling of accomplishment so that they will anticipate future discussion groups.

THE LECTURE METHOD

Lectures have been used extensively for centuries and there is little probability that their use will decrease. They have too many obvious advantages: they are economical and require no elaborate technical aids; many instructors prefer them; many students feel more secure in them; they are adaptable to multiple objectives; and they disseminate considerable information quickly. Highet describes the lecture technique as follows:

> Here the teacher talks more or less continuously to the class. The class listens, takes notes of the facts and ideas worth remembering and thinks them over later, but it does not converse with the teacher. At most, it may ask a few questions, but these are for the sake of clarification, not of discussion. The essence of this kind of teaching, and its purpose, is a steady flow of information going from the teacher to the pupils.

Most college and university courses depend on lectures; they are frequently employed in high school; even elementary school teachers utilize short lectures that last perhaps a few minutes. There are vehement supporters and detractors of this method, which, as we have noted, is about as good as any other in helping students acquire subject matter. An enthusiastic lecturer can arouse interest in a subject, communicate and interpret research results, and then relate them to other matters. Lectures are less successful with complex subjects or with material other than factual. McLeish (1976) has summarized Soviet attempts to improve lecturing; their efforts provide excellent suggestions.

1. *Do not give students conclusions, rather information and methods they can use in problem solving.* If they can read the information it should not appear in your lecture.

2. *Do not be afraid to introduce controversial topics.* Keeping your students' attention can be difficult in lectures. This is one way of overcoming the difficulty.

3. *Base your lectures on sound psychological principles that lead to concept formation.* For example, you may want to present several attributes, as well as negative examples, of a concept.

4. *Stress the relevance of your topic.* It is insufficient to present *just* facts; you must demonstrate any relationship between the material and your students' needs.

5. *Build significant questions into your lecture.* At predetermined points, stop and pose questions to your students. This is similar to the "branching" and "break points" of individualized instruction already mentioned. Never lecture for 50 or 75 minutes without a break. Your questions can both motivate students and establish the relevance of your work.

6. *Have the students use the lecture materials outside school.* Pose problems, give assignments, and encourage independent study that force students to examine the subject from a different perspective.

7. *Encourage students to ask questions.* Tell your group that you will accept questions and specify when in the lecture you will accept them. Some instructors prefer them at the end of the lecture; others will accept questions throughout the lecture. Again, it is the instructor's personality that dictates the procedure.

Memory for Lectures

Aiken, Thomas, and Shennum (1975) report a study designed to assess students' memories for lecture material. They note that during the conventional lecture students exhibit many behaviors to aid memory. They have their personal "tricks": they underline, outline, and take notes. Effective note taking can help memory of lecture material. But if note taking occurs during the actual lecture, there may be interference. The length of the lecture, the amount of information, and speed of presentation all affect memory.

The authors secured 180 subjects in an introductory psychology class and experimented with various lecture techniques. The authors presented a taped lecture, "Survival Among Sharks," at two speeds: 120 and 240 words per minute. There were high (206 information units) and low (106 information units) presentations, both of which had about the same number of words (1961–1969). In-

formation units were sentences or clauses with a single subject-verb, or subject-verb-object relationship providing new information about sharks. There were three note-taking conditions: no notes, notes taken during the lecture, notes taken during a pause in the lecture.

The authors found that spaced note taking produced better lecture learning than either of the other two conditions. High-information density and speeded speech always adversely affected recall. The authors also state that terse, or abbreviated, notes fail as retrieval cues over long intervals, while near verbatim notes produce superficial results.

The most interesting conclusion for our purpose is the finding about spaced note taking. If you use lectures, organize them so that you can stop at logical points and allow your students to take notes.

Discussion Questions

1. Have you ever had the occasion to tutor or be tutored? If so, how did you feel in the one-to-one relationship? Did the instructor make any effort to neutralize the impact of an authority figure?

2. How do you react to elaborate individualized instruction programs? Are they realistic when they involve school reorganization? What would encourage a system to undertake such a task?

3. Could you function effectively with individualized programs? It is often difficult for teachers to remain nondirective, but self-progress and self-pacing are critical to its success. How do you see *your* role in these programs?

4. Have you ever been in an excellent seminar? Why would you characterize it as excellent? Was there good group cohesion? What was the teacher's role? Was it a decision or learning group? Why?

5. Do you prefer attending lectures or seminars? Why? What do you consider a "good" lecture? How do *you* learn from it? Would you profit more from spaced note-taking lectures? Why?

Some Concluding Thoughts

This chapter described some of the chief characteristics of teaching, attempting to link learning with teaching to dramatize a smoothly functioning professional. There are as many explanations of teaching as there are of learning; the more you know of both, the more effective you will become in the classroom. While there are no satisfactory universal attributes of the "good" teacher, there are some characteristics—being accepting and warm—so obvious that they cannot be discounted. Although you probably prefer a definite teaching method—for example, discussion versus lecture—you will find yourself forced to use all techniques, so there is a compelling need to be familiar with them.

Do not allow the analysis of teaching to degenerate into a dry recital of facts; teaching is a dynamic and exciting profession that should keep one alive intellectually, socially, and emotionally.

Summary

- While there are many interpretations of teaching, analysis by roles is extremely informative.

- It is highly unlikely that any one learning theory can encompass a teaching theory; the criteria for an adequate teaching theory exceed the confines of any contemporary learning theory.

● There are certain teaching principles derived from the theories of Bruner and Skinner.

● There is a strong link between an individual's personality and classroom performance, both as to style and efficiency.

● The only pure form of individualized instruction is tutoring; other forms either involve the pupil in elaborate programs or require school reorganization.

● Successful discussion groups depend on leadership, atmosphere, clear goals, and definite agreement about the group's nature (decision or learning).

● The lecture method has been shown to be as effective as other techniques for subject matter achievement. There is constant experimentation, such as spaced note taking, to improve the lecture.

Suggested Readings

Bigge, Morris. *Learning Theories for Teachers*. New York: Harper & Row, 1976. An excellent summary of the critical relationship between teacher and learning.

Combs, Arthur and Donald Snygg. *Individual Behavior*. New York: Harper & Row, 1959. A clear description of the perceptual view of teaching and learning.

Skinner, B. F. *The Technology of Teaching*. Englewood Cliffs, N.J.: Prentice-Hall, 1968. A fine collection of essays representing Skinner's ideas on teaching.

Travers, John F. *Learning: Analysis and Application*. New York: McKay, 1972. Contains an analysis of learning, teaching, and the relationship between teaching methods and teachers' personalities.

15

Teaching and Instructional Aids

Introduction

Teaching can take many forms. Lectures, discussions, tutoring all serve a definite purpose, and each technique may achieve its objective more efficiently if teachers supplement it with one or several instructional aids. Instructional aids are just that: devices that enrich a teacher's presentation.

Instructional aids also serve definite purposes. Television and movies reach a large audience, while computers and programmed instruction further individual instruction. This chapter will concentrate on printed material, games and simulations, filmstrips and slides, motion pictures, television, programmed instruction, and computer assisted instruction.

As you read about, and perhaps use, these aids, remember that they are merely tools, actually an extension of your personality. When you lecture or lead discussions, you do so in a way that reflects your personality. You will likewise value some of these aids more than others, but know them all. There is no reason why a teacher should be unable to thread a projector, or make slides and transparencies. Learn which aids are best suited for certain purposes: select media because of their potential for achieving specific objectives. Gerlach and Ely (1971) define a medium as any person, material, or event that establishes conditions enabling the learner to acquire knowledge, skills, and attitudes. Thus, teachers, textbooks, and the total school environment are media.

These authors also believe that it is important to distinguish between materials and equipment. For example, a still picture may appear in a textbook, a slide, a filmstrip, or a bulletin board, or be used with an opaque projector. The picture is the material, and the means of displaying it—the projector or bulletin board—are the equipment. Together the material and the equipment constitute the medium.

Today, *hardware* and *software* are popular terms. Evolving from computer technology, hardware originally signified the computer and any related equipment, while software referred to the programs. Today, hardware applies to almost any machine, while software designates the material used on the machine. For example, motion pictures and projectors, overhead projectors, and videotapes are hardware, while the content is software. That is, the information in a motion picture is the software, not the film itself.

GUIDE TO SELECTION AND USAGE

To help you in selecting media that will facilitate the attainment of objectives, Gerlach and Ely offer the following guidelines.

1. *Appropriateness.* Does the medium suit the nature of the task, the developmental level of the pupils, and the objective? For example, it would be appropriate to tape a class play so that pupils identify strengths and weaknesses when they hear themselves. Elementary school pupils are familiar with tape recorders; so, it "fits" the task of helping to learn a part and achieves the specific objective of identifying and correcting mistakes.

2. *Level of sophistication.* Does the content match the students' developmental level? A bright secondary school pupil may benefit from programmed instruction that presents added depth or new challenges while the class proceeds as usual. How many times have you seen or used a filmstrip with embarassingly simple figures or dialogue? Is it better not to use it; try another medium.

3. *Cost.* Using instructional aids is expensive and you should be sure that similar material is not presented equally as well—and free—in something the school may already possess, such as textbooks, school library books, or media center materials.

4. *Availability.* Be certain that when you schedule a movie or filmstrip both material and equipment are available. This is probably a teacher's greatest source of frustration when using instructional aids. Try to arrange a school schedule so that media will be available when needed; if you use a central scheduling location, take the time each month (or week, if you have an ample supply) and arrange a definite time for the media you need.

5. *Technical quality.* Be sure that your pupils can read, hear, or distinguish the material. You do not want inferior products; *they are embarrassing and can cause discipline problems.* For example, a secondary school science teacher presented a film in which a famous French scientist was interviewed in French. The students could not understand the conversation and quickly became bored by the translation. Conditions degenerated rapidly.

These five guidelines will help you to follow the basic selection rule: the medium must help you to achieve a specific objective. If it is unavailable, of poor quality, inappropriate as to content and developmental level, then it is of dubious value in achieving any objective.

Pula and Fagone (1973) present another means of analyzing instructional aids: the communication model.

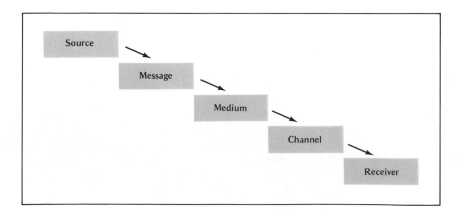

The *source* refers to the origin of information: a person, event or institution. *Message* refers to both content and packaging; *medium* shapes the message; that is, it may range from real objects to total abstraction. *Channel* means the method of communicating (magazines, tapes) and *receiver* is the learner. Examining this model, note that teachers, as the source, select the means (medium and channel) that will best approximate the learner's developmental level.

The description and evaluation of instructional aids begins with that most venerable of all tools—the printed word.

Books and printed materials

INTRODUCTION

There are several reasons for commencing our discussion of instructional aids with printed material—especially the textbook and workbook. First, it is a tried and true instrument, praised and damned over the centuries: an overwhelming obstacle for some; an endless enchantment for others. Second, it is an amazingly flexible instructional device that teachers can use for instruction, reading, illustration, reference, assignments, and enjoyment. Third, sometime in your career you will undoubtedly be on textbook selection committees. Thinking about the quality of outstanding books and how they may best be used will furnish you a sound basis for selection. Fourth, since books are with us for life, we should teach youngsters not only to respect and use them, but to appreciate them.

Approximately 30,000 books are published each year in the United States alone. Annual sales of written instructional material total about $1 billion. Rothkopf (1976, pg. 91) summarizes the phenomenon nicely:

> Whole forests die so that knowledge may pass from one generation to the next, and skill from one hand to another. From the libraries of the world and from bookshelves everywhere, the voices and hearts of both the living and the dead, some wise and some foolish, speak to those who read.

One of your tasks is to select and use those books that actually "speak" to your pupils when they read. While, unfortunately, many books at *all* educational levels are poorly written, there is *no* excuse for you to select them. Look for books whose authors tell their story in terse sentences and simple words. Avoid ponderous, academic overstatements, such as those frequently appearing in government publications.

> We respectively petition, request and entreat that due and adequate provision be made, this day and the date hereinafter subscribed, for the satisfying of these petitioners' nutritional requirements and for . . .

in the judgment of the aforesaid petitioners, constitute a sufficient supply thereof.

Translation: *Give us this day our daily bread.* Commenting on this example, Alan Otten (1976) states that it is a classic example of "peeling" the convoluted version down to plain English by eliminating legalistic jargon, redundancies, and other gobbledygook.

You may smile at this example, but undoubtedly you have encountered similar jargon. Another task is to encourage students to view books not as drudgery, but as something to be enjoyed. It is not an easy task; movies and television are colorful and vivid challengers for students' attention. But if you are successful, your pupils will have a source of lifelong pleasure.

Rothkopf believes that the single most important characteristic of written material is its stability; that is, all students using a textbook or workbook receive the same content. The book's effectiveness depends on three characteristics:

1. *Content,* which refers to completeness, accuracy, relationship to specific objectives, and amount of unrelated material.

Teaching Through Fiction

A fascinating example of books as instructional aids is *The Teaching Experience: An Introduction to Education Through Literature* (Landau et al., 1976). To convey the spirit and feeling of teaching by fiction, the authors have collected 31 selections, mainly from modern prose. For example, one study, "Luther," originally appeared in Jay Neugenborei's *Corky's Brother.* It describes how a bright ghetto pupil attracted a sympathetic English teacher. In spite of some progress, Luther eventually is committed, first to a reform school, and then to a special school for troublesome adolescents. The dialogues between the teacher and Luther reveal a touching attempt to bridge a cultural chasm.

The authors have even capitalized on the latest fad of converting books to television and present a scene from Irwin Shaw's *Rich Man, Poor Man.* Rudy Jordache's son has drawn an outrageous picture of his French teacher with the caption, "Je suis folle d'amour" (I am crazy with love). The French teacher is incensed and demands to see the father, who tries to explain the incident as typical adolescent behavior.

You would enjoy *The Teaching Experience,* not only as a sensitive insight into the nature of teaching, but as an example of books as instructional aids. For example, you may view this collection as literature; you may simply enjoy it; you may wish to use it yourself with older students; you may make assignments in it; you may use it for discussion. Here we see dramatically illustrated the flexibility of books.

2. *Representation,* which refers to clear, accurate writing and a logical organization and sequence of topics.
3. *Form,* which means the grammatical complexity and sentence length of the writing.

Rothkopf states that we are concerned with content when we inquire if a document is sufficiently complete and accurate to achieve specific objectives. We are concerned with representation and form when we determine if the writing and organization is appropriate for the students' developmental level.

Interaction

A text's writing and content no matter how admirable and appropriate cannot guarantee that a student will comprehend content. The reader must interact with the material. In Chapter 3 we discussed Richard Held's work with active and passive subjects that strongly suggested that students must actually engage environmental stimuli if learning is to occur. They cannot be mere passive recipients.

But it is difficult to specify precisely when humans are or are not interacting with the environment. That is, we may appear passive but actually be intensely active internally. The student who sits quietly through class after class, with little or no participation, and then submits a brilliant paper is always a shock and proof that activity involves inner processes.

Howe and Singer (1975) describe an experiment in which one group who expected to be tested on a scientific essay did better when they were just told to read the material than other groups who were instructed to copy and summarize it. The more active techniques were inferior to reading. Copying or summarizing may well interfere with the individual's cognitive strategies (McKeachie, 1976).

Rothkopf believes that translating written material into a useful internal representation demands skillful processing activities that are not immediately observable. Students selectively exercise their processing activities; that is, they do not use it for *everything* written in the text. To describe these processing activities, the author offers the model reproduced in Figure 15.1.

Examining the figure, you will note a similarity to the description of reading in Chapter 6: the eye stops—a fixation pause—several times per line and reads a certain number of words at each pause. Each fixation produces internal representation, which the reader then translates into usable representation. The reader can then use these results to answer questions or solve problems. The more elaborate processes of concatenation (linking ideas), elaboration (expanding the text's ideas), and rehearsal for memory enable the reader to alter and apply the resulting information. It is an interesting model that, especially if coupled with an analysis of con-

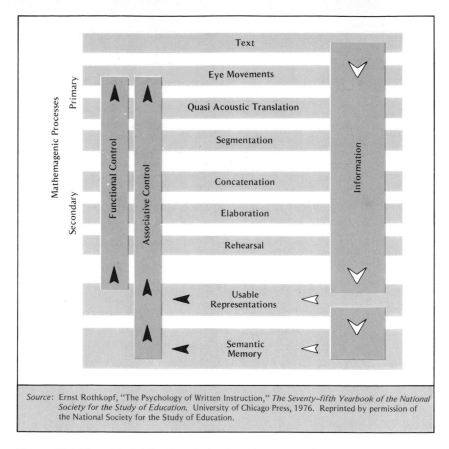

Source: Ernst Rothkopf, "The Psychology of Written Instruction," *The Seventy-fifth Yearbook of the National Society for the Study of Education.* University of Chicago Press, 1976. Reprinted by permission of the National Society for the Study of Education.

Figure 15.1 Flow Model for Translating Text into Internal Representation

tent, representation, and form, may permit teachers to determine why students do not use what they read.

SUGGESTIONS FOR USING BOOKS

Observational learning has been mentioned throughout this text. Here is a possibility for you to test these ideas. Let students see how you appreciate books—handling them, discussing them, using them, telling how television shows and movies are based on them. There is fierce competition for pupils' time; make them want to take time for books.

Here are several specific suggestions for using books in your classroom.

The Kanawha Controversy

The almost universal recognition of books' significance frequently leads to heated, if not fiery disputes. A recent incident rocked Kanawha County, West Virginia. Parker (1975) states that in spite of overcoming exploitation and hard times, and with "prosperity just around the corner," there was no peace in Kanawha County. Two factions were at odds: relatively prosperous newcomers, capitalizing on new industry in West Virginia and natives, many of whom are coal miners, relatively unconcerned with a changing America, but passionately concerned with God, family, and patriotism. The issue: textbooks.

Before 1971, a citizens' advisory committee helped select textbooks; since then teachers' committees alone made the selection: an elementary school committee, a secondary school committee, and a final recommending committee. Early in 1974, the committee recommended 324 texts and supplementary books which were displayed in the public library. There was little interest in the books.

One of the school board members challenged the content and language of certain books, and the battle lines were drawn. Tense meetings were held throughout the summer, and when school opened in the fall, 20 percent of the students failed to appear. Coal miners walked off their jobs in sympathy with the antitext protestors; Charleston's city buses were blocked, leaving 11,000 people without service. Violence flared, and the state police were sent. Citizens' review committees only increased the turmoil; the board of education building was dynamited; the December 12 school board meeting saw board members physically assaulted by protestors. Finally, one of the leaders involved in a bombing was tried and convicted, and an uneasy calm descended.

What caused the problem—parental feelings of isolation, religion, patriotism, bigotry—is not our concern. What concerns us is the tremendous importance placed on books. Never underestimate the power of the printed word.

1. *Have students use their texts.* Students seeing books unused, quickly depreciate them. Be certain they know and can use the mechanical parts of a book (table of contents, index, glossary). Since books are such flexible tools, have students use them for a variety of purposes: information and facts, pictures and general reference for a subject, comparisons.

2. *Have the students use supplementary books.* Regardless of how successfully you motivate students, there is still a feeling of work associated with texts. Try to provide fiction and complementary readings to emphasize the pleasure of reading. We have just seen a good example in *The Teaching Experience.* Biology teachers could have students read James Watson's *Double Helix,* a fascinating, in-

formative, gossipy account of the race for the discovery of DNA, a race between an English group spearheaded by James Watson and Francis Crick and a University of California group led by the famous Linus Pauling. Secondary school students in writing courses would benefit from and enjoy Brendan Gill's *Here at The New Yorker*, a witty, personal account of work at one of America's famous magazines. Try to expand your students' vision of the world of books.

3. *Be alert to reading problems.* Rothkopf's model may help you to identify where the problem occurs and, depending on your expertise, you may suggest remedial procedures or refer the pupil. Students with reading problems become adults who are unappreciative of books, thus narrowing their range of adult enjoyments.

4. *Follow the guidelines presented here to assess a book's strengths and weaknesses so that it becomes an effective tool in skilled hands.* That is, be sure that the content is satisfactory (complete, accurate, pertinent, and relevant) and that clarity and expression are apparent.

5. *If you are ever on book selection committees, proceed cautiously but objectively.* Determine that the books you select meet objective criteria (such as we have mentioned) as well as your personal approval. You must respect the community in which you teach, while suggesting change when you think it is necessary. If you find your views radically different from those of most parents, you should probably find a more compatible system. There is no right or wrong here; no "good" or "bad" values. Communities as well as individuals have philosophies, and as it is difficult to remain friendly with someone who constantly disagrees with you so it is with teachers and communities.

Finally, remember these words of Rothkopf: "Care should be taken not only that students read to learn but also that the text has been written to teach."

Games and simulations

An enduring criticism of education has been that it is grim — remember Barzun's words, "Education may indeed be the dullest of subjects." Our intent here is not to place blame on teachers, students, or institutions, but to suggest that certain techniques can be both educational and pleasant. None of our great philosophers or psychologists ever affirmed that education *must* be dull.

The current popularity of games and simulations reflects an attempt to combine learning and enjoyment. While educators have never formally endorsed play's role in development, play for play's sake has never been seriously questioned. Stamm (1976) states that

if you were to ask, "Why do children play?" you would receive an amazing variety of responses, but they would fall into three main categories:

1. Play is fun.
2. Children learn about themselves and their world through play.
3. Play permits children to cope with intense emotional reactions.

Play

Stamm provides an excellent rationale for using classroom games and simulations. If you examine children's play, you soon see that it is not a casual occurrence, but calculated to provide youngsters with knowledge about themselves and their environment. As Stamm notes, play is simply one medium through which these changes can occur.

Teachers have always attempted to brighten their students' days by devising games based on arithmetic, spelling, or geography. But it is only in the last decade that large numbers of games and simulations designed for the classroom have appeared. There are

many reasons for this growing interest: the changing role of the school from dispenser of facts to provider of meaningful experiences, the modern emphasis on active learners and discovery learning, and the availability of materials (Seidner, 1976).

PURPOSES OF GAMES AND SIMULATIONS

Rational and Emotional

While play's pleasurable aspects have been stressed, there are tangible educational advantages associated with games. Abt (1971, pg. 5) states that a game is a particular way of reviewing something. This perspective includes two components—one rational, one emotional. Any game's rational, analytic element focuses on the formal and structural characteristics that reflect life—family, school, work, politics. The emotional aspect incorporates all the chance or luck of life—what are the odds that I'll win?

Games: Serious and Otherwise

Abt then proposes a formal definition of a game: a game is an activity among two or more independent decision makers seeking to achieve their objectives in some limiting context. Games may be serious or casual and although educational games are serious, they can also be entertaining. As Abt notes, if an activity produces good educational results while offering emotional satisfaction, it is an ideal instructional aid.

The sudden surge of interest in games has occurred because educators now realize that games are effective for students of all ages since they motivate while simultaneously communicating basic facts and concepts. The representation of reality produces dramatic effects where the participants assume realistic roles, face problems, formulate strategies, make decisions, and receive instant feedback for their actions. Abt believes that serious games offer a fertile field for risk free exploration of significant intellectual and social problems. Students' role playing is excellent preparation for society's real roles.

Seidner (1976) states that there are specific goals associated with games and simulations.

1. *Communication.*   Games and simulations provide an exciting alternative to traditional techniques and encourage interaction among students of differing racial and socioeconomic status.
2. *Motivation.*   Games and simulations are frequently self-activating since students enjoy role playing, especially in situations that mirror reality.
3. *Reward structure.*   Carefully structured games permit students to attain rewards both by individual performance and as group members, resulting in learning that is better retained and transferred.

Distinctions between games and simulations

Although games and simulations are often used synonymously, there are distinctions between them since each has different objectives. For example, Stamm argues that play has multiple functions: fun, knowledge, and emotional adjustment. Games differ from play in their objectives and rules, and they may also be competitive. Games may or may not be educational; simulations are definite learning experiences.

Heyman (1975) states that simulations are learning exercises that place students in apparently real roles that force them to make real decisions. Games are fun and easily involve students in a world of quasi-fantasy. Heyman then offers some clear definitions.

1. *A game is a contest in which people agree to abide by a set of rules.*   Baseball, checkers, chess, and monopoly are good examples. Game implies fun and helps to explain their current popularity.
2. *A simulation is an imitation or simplification of some aspect of reality.*   It is an attempt to construct and use examples of reality. The training of astronauts is a good example: their mock space capsules and other training devices were called, "flight simulators."
3. *A simulation game combines the characteristics of both.*   It imitates reality but is fun; it is both enjoyable and educational. Figure 15.2 illustrates these differences.

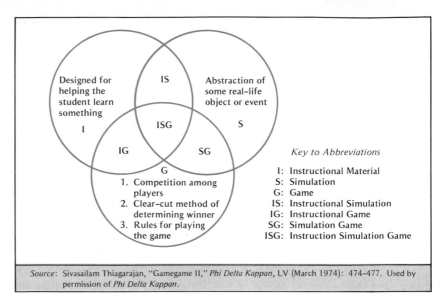

Source: Sivasailam Thiagarajan, "Gamegame II," *Phi Delta Kappan*, LV (March 1974): 474–477. Used by permission of *Phi Delta Kappan*.

Figure 15.2 Definition Diagram

USES OF SIMULATION GAMES

Practical Benefits

Abt (1971) argues that simulation games stimulate, reward, and judge intuition by pragmatic rather than dogmatic standards, and further sharpen analytic processes. Most students learn that the ideal problem-solving strategy involves both intuition and analysis. Simulation games also aid individual instruction by offering students many choices for which they must obtain information before making a decision. Both slow and advanced learners benefit from these techniques: slow learners are challenged by the game's concrete aspects; advanced learners are constantly searching for cause and effect, relationships, and applications. Simulation games are also excellent tools for encouraging acceptable social behavior. Cooperation and consideration for others are necessary.

Heyman gives several examples of popular simulation games.

1. *Democracy* is a series of eight games describing representative government. Eleven players act as a legislative group, representing their clients on specific issues. Their bills are either passed or defeated after speeches, meetings, and bargaining sessions. Students also act as lobby groups, legislative committees, and other group members. The game's object is to represent clients and to be reelected.

2. *Ghetto* gives students insight into life in a poor, inner-city neighborhood. The players are poor, with little education and heavy family responsibilities. Chance (disc, cards) dictates events over which they have no control and most of these events only make life more difficult. Players attempt to win points that make life a little easier: jobs, school, welfare, relaxation.

3. *Dangerous Parallel* is a simulation of an international crisis.

Classroom Games

It can become relatively easy for you to develop your own games and simulations. The benefits in motivation and learning justify the effort. For example, Abt (1971) describes several games intended to improve mathematical ability and application. One of these, "Equals" requires a deck of 168 cards, simply cut and comprised of 16 cards for each number, zero to nine, and 8 "wild" cards representing any number you like. There are four players, two on each team, and the goal is to be the first team to complete an equation from the cards.

Each player receives four cards and using any preferred process (addition, subtraction, multiplication, division), each team tries to combine two cards to equal two others. For example $5 - 2 = 3 \times 1$. Play shifts between teams: the first player from Team I plays one and then draws a new card; the first player from Team II does likewise, followed by the other two players. There are now two sets of cards on the table, one set from each team. With their next play each team tries to complete an equation. Abt (1971, pg. 141) gives the following example.

The first team to complete an equation wins. If the fourth player cannot complete the equation, he discards a card and draws a new card. When the partner's turn comes, he attempts the solution. The possibilities are great. For example, in our illustration, the equation could have been $5 + 2 = 6 + 1$ or $3 - 1 = 2 \times 1$.

Think about these; you can devise similar situations for most of your subjects. If you are interested in more formal games, write to these publishers requesting information:

Academic Games Associates
Johns Hopkins University
3505 North Charles Street
Baltimore, Maryland 21212

CBS Learning Center
12 Station Drive
Princeton Junction, New Jersey 08550

Interact
P.O. Box 262
Lakeside, California 92040

Science Research Associates
259 East Erie Street
Chicago, Illinois 60611

Scott Foresman and Co.
1900 East Kale Avenue
Glenview, Illinois 60025

Team I	Team II
Player A plays a 5	Player B plays a 3
Player C plays a 2	Player D plays a 1
Player A plays a 6	Player B plays a 2
Player C plays a 4	Player D plays a 2
and completes the equation	and completes the equation
$5 \times 2 = 6 + 4$	$3 + 1 = 2 \times 2$

Each of six countries has four ministers, each of whom has written material describing the crisis: one small country has attacked another and a major power is planning intervention, which will then determine how two other large countries will act. Negotiations and compromise lead to understanding of the complexities of international relations.

Like all teaching aids, there are advantages and disadvantages to simulation games. Among the advantages is the enthusiasm students display. Their involvement, activity, and sense of reality are highly motivating. Students are forced to use many devices: books, journals, newspapers, television, and slides all become pertinent resources. They also must learn to evaluate other students' views, perhaps not accepting them, but rejecting them only after careful consideration. Students thus become sensitive to others' feelings. Finally, simulation games are fun.

Among the chief disadvantages are time and numbers. Most games involve few players, which demands additional preparation for the others. They also may require more time than you are willing to allot. A related disadvantage is careful preparation. If your school system lacks funds to purchase them, you may wish to design your own. You will want to be certain that the game correlates well with subject(s) and helps to achieve objectives, which requires time and thought.

Although the disadvantages are real, overcoming them ensures a valuable learning experience. Simulation games are worthwhile teaching aids, and if you use them you will find the following suggestions helpful.

1. *Carefully consider your role.* As Heyman says: run the simulation, not the students. You become a director, a judge, permitting students to make decisions with which you may disagree, and later lead a discussion in which students express their view of why they made certain decisions based on their knowledge. Your role is nondirective; you cannot tell pupils what to do; you would destroy the game's nature and purpose. If you are uncomfortable with this role, you should avoid using simulation.

2. *If you decide to use simulation games, be selective; that is, be absolutely sure that a particular game meets your instructional objectives.* Otherwise you are wasting time. If you think of these tools as strictly noneducational, you should rely on free time to use recreational activities. Try to answer this question: Does it match the subject and suit the class's need?

3. *Know the simulation game thoroughly.* To use them well means that you must allot satisfactory time, space, and equipment. You should also know the rules *before* you ask students to use the game. Nothing is quite so deadly as a monotonous, slow progression while a teacher studies rules, trying simultaneously to tell the group. Seidner suggests assigning a few students the task of learning the game and demonstrating it to the rest of the class.

4. *Try devising your own games and simulations.* If your class is sufficiently mature, an excellent project is to design a simulation game, beginning with a game (players, rules) and moving on to more complicated simulations.

Discussion Questions

1. Using the suggestions of Gerlach and Ely concerning the selection and use of media, formulate a list of aids that would be valuable for you. Explain your choices.

2. Apply the criteria of content, representation, and form to the textbooks you are using this semester. Are they thorough and accurate, and written with a clear, concise style? Explain your answer. Now ask your various instructors why they selected certain books for their courses.

3. Textbook controversies are flaring up throughout the country almost daily. Locate an account of one of these struggles and attempt to determine causes—socioeconomic, racial-ethnic, moral-religious. What is your position?

4. Can you relate play to games and simulations? How? Do you think that your rationale is sufficient to justify their use in the classroom? Why? As an assignment for this course divide the class into groups of four or five and devise a simulation game for teaching. Follow the suggestions offered here, do additional reading, and, if your instructor permits, try it in class.

5. Do you think that the advantages of games and simulations outweigh the disadvantages? Compile your list of both, justify each item, and explain your decision.

Filmstrips and slides

Two of the most popular tools available are filmstrips and slides. Their simplicity undoubtedly explains their wide appeal. Filmstrips and slides are relatively inexpensive, and, especially with slides, teachers can construct lessons that are particularly meaningful for a group. Because of the current interest in all aspects of photography, they are also excellent motivational devices for students already possessing some knowledge of their use. If you can obtain the materials, and if you possess sufficient expertise, you can dramatically demonstrate the communication process by having them make their own slide project. The potential is enormous: learning photographic techniques; deciding why certain visuals are meaningful; determining if certain pictures relate to the work; explaining why particular photographs, for example, a post office and police station, illustrate the interdependence of community living.

FILMSTRIPS

Gillespie and Spirit (1973) describe a filmstrip as a length of 35 mm film containing a series of related still pictures called frames. The usual filmstrip contains from 30 to 50 frames; it may be either silent (with captions), or sound (packaged with a cassette possessing beeps—signals telling the operator to move to the next frame).

Pros

Gillespie and Spirit believe that teachers like filmstrips because they are relatively inexpensive—small projectors cost as little as $20 to $40, and it is possible to purchase individual viewers for as little as $15. Another appeal is the wide variety of pertinent filmstrips—the authors state that you can purchase thousands of filmstrips representing a variety of subjects and levels. They are compact, easily stored, flexible, and adaptable tools appropriate for individuals, small groups, and large groups. Teachers can do just about whatever they wish with them; that is, they may hold one frame for a lengthy period or pass over others quickly.

Cons

As with all mechanical aids, there are disadvantages. The sequence is fixed, and the lack of motion can be a detriment. Also, there is the possibility of filmstrip damage; it is easy to rip the sprocket holes. Again, the advantages far outweigh the disadvantages, and if you use them you may find the following helpful.

1. *Preview the filmstrip.* Be sure you know the content of the individual frames so that your comments match the content.

2. *Check the availability of the projector.* If you have, or have ordered, a filmstrip to complement a particular topic, be certain that you have a projector. There is nothing more frustrating, or potentially damaging to discipline, than to promise students something and then disappoint them.

3. *If your school or media center purchases filmstrips, catalog them.* Know what is accessible; if there is no school record, make your own. A good rule of thumb for all teaching procedures is to *master the routine.*

4. *Take good physical care of filmstrips.* Be careful not to tear filmstrips while using them. Store them carefully; that is, keep them in their containers, preferably in some large unit. Probably the best source of information about filmstrips is the *Index to 35 mm Educational Filmstrips*, published by R. R. Bowker and Co., 1180 Avenue of the Americas, New York, New York 10036.

SLIDES

Many of the filmstrip's characteristics, advantages, and disadvantages apply to slides. Slides are film transparencies most often contained in a two inch by two inch cardboard mount. They are more flexible than filmstrips because you can arrange them in any order you desire. They are an excellent tool because they are relatively easy to produce and can serve specific objectives. The major limitations are that slides lack captions and they are distressingly easy to disarrange.

Pula and Fagone (1973) suggest an instructional sequence for a slide-tape presentation. The subject is recycling and the general purpose is to explain, illustrate, and suggest ways that citizens can help with disposal problems. Its specific objectives are to list methods of waste disposal, to define recycling, to record the advantages of recycling, and to suggest means of participating in recycling activities. The instructional design includes both narration by the teacher and discussion.

EASTMAN KODAK COMPANY

The materials to be used include slides, slide projector, cassette tape, cassette player, overhead transparencies, and overhead projector. The budget is as follows:

3 rolls of 20-exposure Kodachrome film	$6.00
Processing	7.25
1 30-minute cassette	2.75
Total	$16.00

The 30 selected slides are then combined with the tape narration followed by group discussion. The authors believe that this sequence demonstrates the proper use of instructional materials: concern with students' learning, definite objectives, and the proper medium.

Motion pictures

There is a mystique about motion pictures that entrances us all. From youngsters captivated by *Fantasia* to sophisticated college seniors viewing *Psycho* for their film critique class, motion pictures fascinate. Educational films have attempted to capture this fascination for the classroom.

Technically, motion pictures exploit the eye's inability to distinguish between images shown in quick succession. The eye holds each image briefly, blending it with the next (Gillespie and Spirit, 1973). Gerlach and Ely (1971) describe a motion picture as a series of still pictures taken in rapid succession on either 8 mm or 16 mm film, which gives viewers the illusion of motion when activated by a motion picture projector.

Some Characteristics

Although 16 mm film size dominated usage for many years, the 8 mm or Super 8 mm is much more popular today. The 16 mm and 8 mm refer to the width of the film. While 16 mm gives a longer picture, 8 mm gives satisfactory size and clarity for the classroom. (When you go to the theater the film you view is 35 mm.) Super 8 mm is increasingly popular because the smaller sprocket holes produce larger pictures. Another great improvement is the use of cartridges, which eliminate any complicated threading.

Gillespie and Spirit argue that, since our youth spend considerable time watching television and movies, we should strive for greater visual literacy. Teachers using film should know the medium's potential and good and bad techniques. The authors believe that the better students can "think" visually the better they

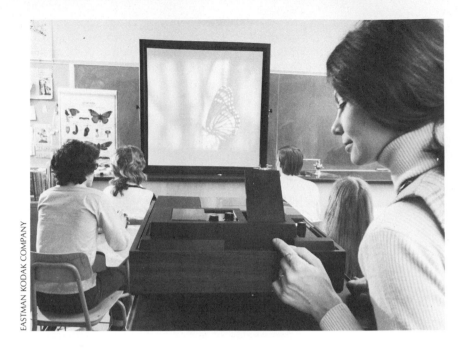

EASTMAN KODAK COMPANY

can evaluate a director's selection of scenes, the effects of different kind of shots, and the relationship among camera, subject, and viewer.

EDUCATIONAL FILM USE

Sol Worth (1974) has written an unusually thoughtful essay on educational film. Believing that research into film use has almost halted since 1950, Worth traces the history of its use since 1918 in grade schools and high schools, slowly spreading into colleges in the 1930s, but not acquiring widespread popularity until the 1960s. Now most school systems have media directors who help teachers to use film, and even to design and develop their own.

Worth criticizes three major perspectives in film analysis. Using Rudolf Arnheim's cognitive perspective (1957, 1969) that visual experience is the basis of thinking, Worth argues that Arnheim underestimates language's role in the thought process. He briefly presents the work of Gene Youngblood (1970) who believes that not only is reality perceived by the eyes but people manifest their consciousness through film. That is, it is the medium that orders what is seen; thus, film becomes the source of reality. Worth refutes this belief by asserting that humans discover personal consciousness through film, or any art, only because art exists within a human-ordered universe.

Film and Reality

Discussing the rationale for educational film, Worth is puzzled by teachers' use of films. If it is only to avoid boredom or to avoid reading, why not try something else other than movies? Arguing that film communicates and instructs, Worth believes that teachers must understand how film produces images and transmits meaning to use this process to *educate*.

Film as Communication

Interpreting film images is a complex, intentional act requiring skill, knowledge, and creative ability. It requires planning, photographing, and editing. The viewer then must decode it to derive meaning, which results in film communication. If film communication is the goal, certain questions need answering. How can a film convey implications? How can the film force viewers to make inferences? Is it similar to linguistic communication? Do different cultures use different codes? Can filmmakers learn to make meaningful statements in film that will still hold their audience?

Classroom films

Worth believes that there are two major uses of classroom film. Teaching through film, with which most of you are familiar, has emphasized film as a preferred method, easy to use, and instantly accepted by students. The current use of film to simplify the school's custodial function has raised doubts about its ability to achieve most educational goals.

Teaching *about* film attempts to help students understand the techniques and "language" of film. Even this raises an unanswerable question: Is film viewing the best way to encourage aesthetic awareness? Films alter attitudes and values, but how this happens remains a mystery. If you agree that understanding the thought process demands an understanding of the many symbolic modes by which you relate to the environment, then you should also agree that education involves more than verbal knowledge. Worth turns to Piaget's notion of forming cognitive structures as a parallel to filmmaking. Filmmaking structures reality because it depicts a set of images on film that someone structured by organizing the images into a meaningful sequence. The author believes that the cognitive structures that enable us to draw implications and inferences—to act on reality—are similar to the filmmaker's means of structuring reality. It is an interesting comparison; if we discover how the filmmaker structures the images captured on film, do we discover more about how we as humans form cognitive structures?

Since all teachers use films, guidelines are helpful.

1. *Films are instructional aids, not mere entertainment.* Be sure that the picture's theme supplements your work. In selecting films, check both content and visual appeal; one without the other is of little value.

2. *Preview your films.* One of life's more embarrassing moments comes when the film differs from your expectations: the silent movie when you expected sound, the use of a translator, outdated clothes, or completely irrelevant theme. It may even cause discipline problems.

3. *Avoid using films for custodial purposes.* Assuming that you accept film's educational value, select those that meet specific objectives. If you desire only entertainment—which may be perfectly acceptable at certain times—then be sure that students understand this.

4. *Use your films skillfully.* Provide your pupils with prior information about the film's contents, stressing those scenes that you consider most significant, and follow-up with a discussion of content and any implications and inferences they can draw.

5. *Teaching through films can also be used to teach about films.* When you preview a film make notes about effective scenes—why did they more effectively achieve a purpose than other scenes? Does the film itself tell you something about the filmmaker? Would some other communication mode have been better? Why? Does the film help us to organize our visual work, thus facilitating thinking and communicating? How?

Television

Children like watching television; adults also enjoy it. It has become a major part of our lifestyle. In 1972, the Office of the Surgeon General of the United States offered valuable insights into viewing habits and television's effect on behavior, including clues to its potential aid as a teaching tool.

Television shows are now a favorite subject of children's conversation, with about one-half of the viewing children saying they were frightened by what they had seen. Children study while watching television. Television viewing is used to reward good behavior; deprivation is used as punishment. It is a potent force. Can we make it equally as potent in the classroom?

TELEVISION AS A TEACHER

Like it or not, television is a teacher and our task is to channel it properly for educational objectives. Brightly (1976) argues that television has tenure and daily presents models that teach about sex identity, race, occupations, violence, good and evil, and consumption habits. These models appear in commercial television. Public television, often called educational television, has presented such outstanding series as "Zoom" and "Sesame Street." The Agency for Instructional Television is making a national effort to

Public Television

COURTESY OF THE CHILDREN'S TELEVISION WORKSHOP

develop series in mental health, values, and careers. Recent efforts by public television have been superb: "Nova," "The Adams Chronicles," "Jenny."

Can it have a similar classroom impact? Can television become an effective teaching aid? Schramm (1962) concludes, after investigating 393 studies, that students can learn efficiently from instructional television. He observes that schools and colleges can effectively teach almost any subject by television. The conclusion from these studies is inescapable that average students can learn as much from a television class as from typical classroom methods. Some students will learn more, others less, but the general inference is that there is no sufficient difference between the two methods.

What content can television convey?

Cognitive Information

Leifer (1976) states that the earliest and still most prevalent use of television is to convey cognitive information. Many programs are available for traditional subjects, but recently there has been a

trend to produce programs for more highly specialized audiences—blacks, inner-city children, Hispanic pupils. Schramm's
study shows, and many others confirm, that television is an effective communicator of information. Leifer then raises a pertinent
question for potential viewers: Do your instructional goals suggest
dynamic visual images, verbal interaction, individualized instruction, or unusual materials? Your answer to these questions should
help you decide which would be more effective—teacher or television.

Implicit Teaching

While there have been attempts to present social and emotional
content, these efforts have not been as concentrated. Leifer states
that perhaps equally as important is the implicit curriculum of the
program. How are the male and female roles portrayed? How are
minorities treated? Are there subtle social messages in the film?
Since such content influences viewers' social behavior, teachers
should be as sensitive to the unintended messages as to the intellectual information and evaluate a film's value by *both* criteria.

TELEVISION AND LEARNING

Garry and Kingsley (1970) suggest that teachers can greatly
broaden their use of instructional television by teaching complex
as well as simple material. Television can help to develop concepts,
solve problems, and teach creative thinking. It need not be passive

A Glossary of Terms

Before discussing specific uses of educational television, you may want to clarify some terms. Gerlach and Ely (1971) define television as an electronic system for transmitting still and moving pictures with accompanying sound through wire and space. Light and sound are converted into electrical waves and then reconverted into visible light rays and audible sound. Most commercial and some educational television programs are transmitted through the atmosphere. Instructional television—used in schools—is called closed circuit; that is, the picture and sound are transmitted directly to receivers by cable or microwaves.

Gillespie and Spirit (1973) offer a helpful glossary.

Closed Circuit Television (CCTV). Cable or microwave convey signals directly from broadcaster to receiver.

Community Antenna Television (CATV). Called cable television, it is a closed circuit system with a master antenna distributing signals within a particular area.

Open Circuit Television (OCTV). Signals are transmitted through the atmosphere to the receiver's antenna. Commercial channels and PBS use this system.

Instructional Television (ITV). Programs originate within a school system, or a school, and are transmitted through closed circuit television.

Educational Television (ETV). These programs are usually more elaborate and reach a wider audience than ITV. They mainly use an open circuit and may frequently reach several states simultaneously.

These authors believe that television is a superb teaching tool whose "high intensity" can efficiently convey information as well as shape attitudes.

instruction since research shows it is possible to produce programs that demand viewer responses and practice to obtain reinforcement. Attempts are now being made to provide interaction between viewer and television content *without* a teacher's intervention.

Nevertheless, most learning from television is still passive, which again suggests the importance of observational learning. Individuals learn by watching and listening to others, and investigators have gathered substantial evidence that clearly suggests that viewers can learn cognitive content, aggression, social behavior, and racial and sex role attitudes from television.

Observational Learning

Leifer (1976) also states that content variables—not only the message—affect learning. Among such variables are carefully structured content, simple material, and the use of repetition (as amply demonstrated on "Sesame Street"). Other influential variables are the portrayal of positive or negative consequences, characters who are similar to the viewers, and situations that are familiar. Size of the picture seems inconsequential, while color may be significant.

Content Variables

What Viewers Like

From studies of "Sesame Street's" success, investigators have concluded that young children like to see other children, animals, short self-contained segments, change, slapstick, anything familiar, and animation. They *dislike* watching adults, anything abstract, and talking. Older children and adolescents have interests similar to adults: action, humor, some familiarity, and characters with whom they can identify. These viewer characteristics can help you to select from available programs, or even design your own if you have the facilities.

Do It Yourself

Pula and Fagone (1973) believe that designing your personal program has become more feasible with low-cost cameras, video tape recorders, and classroom receivers. There is a tremendous range of materials that you could use in your production: posters, charts, diagrams, flat pictures, slides, transparencies, and the pupils as models. While your group presents a play, another student could videotape it. Using the appropriate television camera, the images were recorded on the video tape recorder. The youngsters

Classroom in the Sky

Walter Hendrickson (1975) describes one of the most ingenious and fascinating uses of educational television yet proposed. On May 29, 1974, the citizens of Alaska, Colorado, Idaho, Montana, New Mexico, Utah, Wyoming, Arizona, and Nevada eagerly anticipated the launching of Applications Technology Satellite–6 (ATS-6). The ATS-6 is designed to improve the health and learning of people in the scattered and isolated regions of these areas. For many of these people, English is only a poor second language; the primary language may be Spanish, Eskimo, or an American Indian language.

The ATS-6 was launched by a Titan III-3 rocket, still one of the most powerful in our arsenal. Educational programs are beamed up to it. Some programs are from the Public Broadcasting System; most are specially designed instructional programs broadcast in three languages; the viewer can pick the suitable sound track. Courses in reading instruction and career education are made for teachers; junior and senior high school students receive occupational training. Since medical services are a problem, considerable basic science and medical information are broadcast.

The ATS-6 is ultimately destined to perform the same function for India. Ground controllers will redirect it and the Indian government will assume complete control of all programming. Meanwhile a twin of the ATS-6, the ATS-G will maintain the same task for the United States. Here we see an amazing accomplishment—the integration of two advanced and sophisticated technologies to serve the needy.

can then watch their own performance, and you have a permanent record that you can use for many purposes.

If you decide to use either educational or instructional television, you may find the following suggestions helpful.

1. *Be sure that the program's content is appropriate.* Assessing appropriateness demands more than correlation of subject material to television program. Is the developmental level suitable? Does the program match the students' characteristics that we previously described? The evidence is clear that students learn best from people like themselves and from familiar situations.

2. *Since much of television viewing depends on passive or observational learning, be certain that the program itself is motivating.* There is little excuse today for using dull, boring programs. The effective use of color and effective models can make television viewing both profitable and entertaining.

3. *Be sure the television program serves specific instructional goals.* What do you want this program to do? Do the content and method of presentation meet your expectations?

4. *Help facilitate the learning.* Introduce the program and tell your students to watch for specific happenings. During the program call attention to pertinent parts. Stress those sections you want students to remember. Your comments may well affect later performance.

Discussion Questions

1. Several of the suggestions for using filmstrips, slides, movies, and television are quite similar. Group these and decide which are the most important. For example, previewing is critical for all of these aids. Why? How can you present content more meaningfully?

2. Discuss Worth's analysis of Arnheim's and Youngblood's views of visual experience. Do you agree with his interpretation of personal consciousness as existing within a prior, human-ordered universe?

3. Did Worth's explanation of film as communication help you to understand better how to *use* film? Does a knowledge of filmmaking help you to understand the thought process? Do you agree with Worth's conclusions concerning the parallel between Piaget's work and filmmaking?

4. Tremendous controversy, especially about violence, surrounds commercial television. Do you think that television, with what you know about observational learning, can sufficiently convey cognitive content, shape attitudes, and actually cause antisocial behavior? Be specific and furnish as many examples as possible.

5. How realistic is it to attempt to match what we know about viewer characteristics with instructional and educational television? (Be sure you can distinguish the terms.) Do you believe that it can better be done with school-produced rather than commercial programs? Link your answer to Leifer's comments about "implicit teaching."

Programmed instruction

Seeing or learning the expression "educational technology," you usually think of teaching machines. While teaching machines and other forms of automated instruction have dominated discussion of teaching aids, especially since 1954 (Skinner, 1954), there now are an amazing variety of tools that teachers have at their disposal. The discoveries of an age of technological revolution have provided education with startling new resources.

Lumsdaine (1964) believes that there is a sharp distinction between two different concepts of educational technology. First, there is the educational technology that has provided instrumentation for instructional purposes. The physical sciences have furnished such equipment as silent and sound motion picture projectors, tape recorders, closed circuit television, teaching machines, and computer-based teaching systems.

Educational Technology

Second, educational technology refers to technology as the *application of an underlying science,* such as the relationship of medicine to the biological sciences. Basic to educational technology is the science of communication, cybernetics, and perceptual theory. Lumsdaine (1964) suggests that this second interpretation of educational technology is but one aspect of a broader "psychotechnology," which refers to the application of the principles of psychology to human behavior. This version of technology includes more than education. It also encompasses such activities as psychotherapy, personnel selection, and "human engineering."

Gerlach and Ely (1971) define programmed instruction as the use of programmed materials to achieve educational objectives. Some programs are designed for teaching machines which are devices that present a program. The machine controls students' use of material, thus preventing them from looking ahead and reviewing. But most programmed instruction today occurs through programmed textbooks.

BACKGROUND OF AUTOINSTRUCTION

Although the forerunner of the teaching machine originated over a century ago, the initial appearance of the term in educational literature was in 1925, when Pressey demonstrated an instrument to the 1925 annual meeting of the American Psychological Association. Bugelski (1964) disputes his claim, arguing that Pressey's original device was not a teaching machine but a testing machine.

The Original Machine

Pressey (1964) admits that his primary intention was to score objective tests and that self-instruction was a comparatively limited secondary factor. But the machine contained the notion of autoinstruction. The 1925 instrument supplied a question with four possible answers; for each answer there was a separate key. If the student pressed the correct key, the next question was presented. If the answer was incorrect, the original question remained until the student pressed the right key. A count was made of all attempts, thus providing students with knowledge of their programs.

Its Popularity Restricted

Basically, Pressey's device was a testing and not a teaching machine. Note that students merely select what they think is the correct answer. They do not construct any response. Still it had the advantage of immediate reinforcement: students knew instantly whether they were right or wrong. But Pressey's "industrial revolution" in education was not forthcoming for another 30 years. He (1964) mentions that, primarily, educators were not ready for the abrupt break with tradition that the machines implied. But the financial collapse of 1929 also affected the reaction of educators.

There was no money for innovation, and educators were not kindly disposed toward anything mechanical that would further their unemployment rate.

In 1954, Skinner revived interest in self-instructional techniques. Applying his studies of conditioning with animals to humans, Skinner reasoned that reinforcement in the classroom is not only necessary; it must be immediate. This is an almost impossible task for the teacher, given the number of needed reinforcements and the number of pupils. Students must avoid mistakes, since mistakes once made are often learned and repeated. So each step must be sufficiently easy to insure success. Thus any type of multiple-choice item is undesirable. It is too simple for learners to make a mistake. They must construct their responses.

A further extension of programming is seen in Norman Crowder's work (1959). Students use a text that seems to be an ordinary text. Actually, the book is "scrambled" since it employs the notion of branching. The pages in this scrambled book are numbered consecutively but are not read in the usual sequence. The top part of each page presents a substantial amount of material (unlike Skinner's simple frame), while the lower half supplies several possible answers, each followed by a page number that is indicated. If the answer is incorrect, the student is reprimanded by a scolding remark and sent to another branch to review the necessary material; if it is correct, the pupil is sent to more advanced material.

Striking advances have been made in the refinement of these techniques, yet Pressey (1964) raises some thoughtful problems. Most of the evidence favoring autoinstruction has come from a learning theory devoted to animal experimentation. But humans can learn without making overt responses (simply by reading) and they can learn from their mistakes. Autoinstruction can be more valuable than it now appears. One method would be by adjunct autoinstruction, which would aid all other media of instruction (Pressey, 1964, pg. 368). The student would use a normal text book, television, and the like, and then, at suitable intervals, autoinstructional multiple-choice items would be inserted. The concept of self-instruction is thus enormously broadened: the organization of the subject is preserved, while evaluation, review, and knowledge of results are all possible.

THE PROBLEM OF REINFORCEMENT

A major task for the teacher is reinforcing a pupil's response. An instructor must decide what responses are to be rewarded, the kind of reinforcement to use, and the timing of reinforcements.

One of the most interesting stories about Skinner is the supposed explanation of his interest in education. Invited to visit the fourth grade in which his child was studying, Skinner was shocked at the learning conditions he witnessed. It seemed apparent to him that

An Example of Programming

Skinner (1968) makes a basic assumption with which you may or may not agree. He believes that although most behavioral knowledge comes from studying lower organisms, the data apply equally well to humans since the concern is to isolate the variables that control learning. Contingencies of reinforcement control behavior, and this knowledge can improve human learning if applied to teaching machines. A good example is seen in the following program.

Sentence to Be Completed	Word to Be Supplied
1. The important parts of a flashlight are the battery and the bulb. When we "turn on" a flashlight, we close a switch which connects the battery with the — — —.	bulb
2. When we turn on a flashlight, an electric current flows through the fine wire in the — — — and causes it to grow hot.	bulb
3. When the hot wire glows brightly, we say that it gives off or sends out heat and — — —.	light
4. The fine wire in the bulb is called a filament. The bulb "lights up" when the filament is heated by the passage of a(n) — — — current.	electric
5. When a weak battery produces little current, the fine wire, or — — —, does not get very hot.	filament
6. A filament which is *less* hot sends out or gives off — — — light.	less
7. "Emit" means "send out." The amount of light sent out, or "emitted," by a filament depends on how — — — the filament is.	hot
8. The higher the temperature of the filament, the — — — the light emitted by it.	brighter, stronger
9. If a flashlight battery is weak, the — — — in the bulb may still glow, but with only a dull red color.	filament
10. The light from a very hot filament is colored yellow or white. The light from a filament which is not very hot is colored — — —.	red
11. A blacksmith or other metal worker sometimes makes sure that a bar of iron is heated to a "cherry red" before hammering it into shape. He uses the — — — of the light emitted by the bar to tell how hot it is.	color
12. Both the color and the amount of light depend on the — — — of the emitting filament or bar.	temperature
13. An object which emits light because it is hot is called incandescent. A flashlight bulb is an incandescent source of — — —.	light

Source: B. F. Skinner, *The Technology of Teaching*, © 1968, pg. 45. Reprinted by permission of Prentice-Hall, Inc., Englewood Cliffs, New Jersey.

These frames are designed to teach students about the emission of light from an incandescent source. Skinner suggests that you cover the right-hand column and try it yourself to get the "feel" of it. For example, note how items two and four illustrate the practice of introducing new material into the familiar. He states that programmed material can produce more than facts and terms. Beginning with common items, such as flashlight and candles, the student combines the familiar with a few new facts resulting in a deeper understanding of the subject.

the teacher, no matter how capable, was unable to reinforce pupils' responses, and thus encourage meaningful and permanent learning. Teachers need some kind of mechanical help.

The classroom atmosphere should furnish conditions that encourage the desired behavior. That is, motivation, proper materials, meaningful goals, and the like, all are needed, but these conditions alone are insufficient. The pupil must make an acceptable response, that is, be directed toward a goal to be rewarded. Once the response is made we cannot rely upon automatic feedback by the pupil. The pleasure or displeasure that students feel because of their response is itself inadequate; it may or may not accompany the response because of the potent influence of intervening variables. Reliable reinforcement must be external.

Delayed Reinforcement

Immediately, then, the issue of delayed reinforcement arises. A student does a written assignment, or takes a test, and frequently, days, or even weeks, pass before a busy teacher returns the papers. In this example, reinforcement's value is highly questionable since animal experiments have shown that the slightest delay in reinforcement causes a distintegration of behavior. You recall similar instances in your own career. You undoubtedly will remember that you "lost interest" in the assignment, and the marked paper served little, if any, use.

Occasionally, teachers realize that some external reinforcement is necessary and, in desperation, they may say to a class, "That's fine. Everyone is doing good work." Perhaps some students are doing good work, and for them the desired behavior is reinforced. But what of the pupil who is talking, pinching a neighbor, or daydreaming? Is this behavior reinforced by your comments? Unfortunately, it is. To provide immediate reinforcement, a subject must be divided into small, carefully controlled segments that permit the student to make a response that can be reinforced. The material should be designed to construct a series of steps that ultimately will produce the desired complex behavior.

THE PROGRAM

The heart of any autoinstructional device is the program. There is general agreement that programmed instruction requires certain fundamentals: frequent response, immediate reinforcement, and an individual rate of progress. Lumsdaine (1964, pg. 383) notes that Skinner introduced a new concept: any subject is an accumulation of behavior that, logically and behaviorally, can be analyzed into a series of small steps that lead to final mastery. The instructor or the investigator can continually refine the program by utilizing the learner's responses to approach an ideal learning sequence.

Lumsdaine (1964, pg. 385) states that an instructional program is a vehicle that generates a reproducible sequence of instructional events and determines specified change from an initial range of behavioral tendencies to a terminal range of behavioral tendencies. The program is presequenced and implies a presentation to the student, and is not merely material that the student passively accepts.

Types of Programs

Most programs follow one of the three basic patterns. There are those similar to Skinner's linear programming, in which each student proceeds through a series of small, controlled steps to eliminate almost any possibility of error. Here students construct their own responses. Others are similar to Crowder's searching program, in which large segments of material are presented, errors are expected, and multiple-choice items are used. There is also the program advocated by Pressey, the adjunct program used with conventional material. Today, the trend is toward a combination of the various kinds of programming; that is, a small step program may employ branching, and the use of a "pure" program is declining.

Advantages and disadvantages

Strong arguments are waged pro and con concerning programmed instruction. It presents a logical, organized amount of material to students and forces them to respond and then gives instant reinforcement. But it is not the answer to all of our questions about learning. Students tire of the technique, and their ability to solve problems and to think creatively is not stimulated. Autoinstruction is no better than the program used, and the preparation of a good program is a major project, entailing intimate knowledge of a subject and the capacity to write clearly and meaningfully.

Pressey (1964), speculating about today's stress upon reinforcement, challenges the control it has assumed in learning theory. Reinforcement alone will not explain learning. Telling youngsters that $5 \times 3 = 15$ does not insure learning. Youngsters have to be shown, and they themselves have to do as much as possible for real learning, as opposed to rote memory alone, to occur. We learn by progressive processes of cognitive integration and classification (Pressey, 1964, pg. 368). Pressey's warning should be heeded. Reinforcement is a vital part of learning, but there is no certainty that it is the sole explanation of the learning process. You should be conscious of its value, but you also must provide for self-activity under a variety of learning conditions. Here are some guidelines for using programmed instructions.

1. *The learner's goal and the steps to reach it should be clear.* There should be no vagueness about what is to be done, nor how it is to be done. Look for clearly written programs.

2. *Initially, programmed instruction's novelty will motivate students.* How long this lasts depends on the individual, but you should remain alert to the first signs of restlessness and quickly provide other material. Otherwise, the procedure loses its effectiveness and becomes an unpleasant chore.

3. *Students should participate actively.* Instead of being passive receptors of knowledge, students direct their own learning and provide their own reinforcement. Be sure that the program is appropriate, otherwise students receive little, if any, reinforcement.

4. *Carefully prepared, small steps ensure the presentation of a limited amount of material.* Study the individual frames to be certain that not too much material is presented, but still enough to challenge This is probably the best way to preserve novelty and pleasure in using programmed instruction

5. *There should be immediate reinforcement.* Students should receive constant encouragement, learning instantly if a response is correct. Consequently there is less likelihood that pupils will retain incorrect answers. Traditionally, teachers do not return tests for several days, which allows these incorrect answers to become firmly entrenched.

6. *Allow students to proceed at individual rates.* Since most subjects require considerable factual knowledge as a basis, programming ideally permits students to master these fundamentals *individually* and to continue to more advanced work as they are ready.

Computer-assisted instruction

Computers are here to stay. As more sophisticated technology reduces their mysterious aura and, perhaps more importantly, their cost, you will encounter them more frequently in schools. A knowledge of what a computer is, some historical sense of their development, and their potential school uses will help diminish any anxiety you may have about them.

WHAT IS A COMPUTER?

Gerlach and Ely (1971) define a computer as a machine specifically designed for the manipulation of coded information. It is an automatic electronic machine that performs simple and complex operations. There are two kinds.

1. *The digital computer.* These are the most common. They function with numbers expressed directly as units in a decimal or binary system: they solve problems by counting numbers; they add, subtract, multiply, and divide with lightning speed.

2. *The analog computer.* These solve problems by measuring one quantity, using some other quantity. For example, a thermometer measures temperatures by the height of liquid in a tube; your bathroom scale measures your weight by the distance a dial moves. Analog computers use the same principle.

A computer system is a complex arrangement of electronic components. Digital computer systems have five basic elements.

1. *The input* sends data and instructions into the memory by punched cards or magnetic tapes.
2. *The memory* receives the input and holds it until other parts of the computer need it.
3. *The control unit* guides the computer's operations by selecting the appropriate instructions from the memory; that is, it tells the computer to add, subtract, multiply, divide.
4. *The arithmetic unit* now performs the proper operation.
5. *The output* records and delivers the desired information.

The process appears as follows:

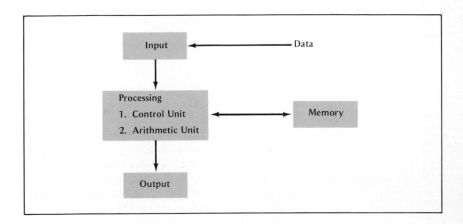

The input is usually a typewriter keyboard. At the user's request, the computer summons the appropriate program from storage, processes the request, and transmits its response back to the sender. The computer system's equipment is its hardware, while the programs are its software. The programs are elaborately

coded and their function is to "tell" the machine what to do and how to do it. One popular program language is FORTRAN (Formula Translation), which uses several basic statements like DO, GO TO, READ, WRITE, PUNCH, CALL, CONTINUE, IF. Kerlinger (1973) states that the power and flexibility of this apparently simple language cannot be exaggerated—there is almost no numerical or logical operation beyond its capability.

Speed of Operation

Kerlinger illustrates its operating speed by using the calculation of correlation coefficients: with 100 cases of two sets of one digit numbers, it would take about 20 to 30 minutes to calculate *one* correlation coefficient. He then gives an actual example. Using the responses of 296 individuals to 36 items, the means, standard deviations, 630 correlation coefficients, and several other procedures were calculated in 23 *seconds*.

WHY COMPUTERS?

Justine Baker (1975) provides an excellent account of the background of the computer movement. She states that counting has always fascinated humans. Beginning with making one-to-one correspondences between fingers and objects, more advanced calcu-

lating methods gradually appeared. The Egyptians invented simple sand calculations thousands of years ago. They made indentations in the sand that represented place values. When ten pebbles filled the right groove, they were replaced by one pebble in the center groove, and so on. The Chinese abacus and the Roman counting board also used the decimal system.

Great names in philosophy and psychology contributed to the movement. Blaise Pascal invented a primitive calculator in 1642; in 1694 Leibniz, also the creator of calculus, developed a wheel to perform all four operations ($+$, $-$, $\times$, $\div$). In the 1820s Charles Babbage designed the "Difference Engine," which calculated and printed logarithmic and astronomical tables.

But the theoretical basis for modern computer technology probably came from Alan Turing in 1936 when he wrote a paper about a machine with a read-write head and a finite symbolic alphabet. The machine would solve mathematical problems according to algorithms. The mathematician John von Neumann probably did as much as anyone to provide the theoretical basis for today's sophisticated computer.

After World War II, the computer industry boomed. As the computers reflected advancing technology, they enabled researchers to

The First Computers

move from mere mathematical purposes to decision-making procedures. In the 1950s, IBM's research center combined computer technology with Skinner's ideas of self-instruction. They connected an IBM 650 computer to a typewriter terminal as a dynamic Skinnerian teaching machine (Baker, 1975, pg. 18). The computer presented problems in typewritten form for students to solve. Self-instruction by computers had arrived.

COMPUTERS AND THE SCHOOLS

Hilgard et al. (1975) state that, with its great operating speed, a large computer can handle as many as several thousand students simultaneously, each at a different level in hundreds of curricula. For example, at each student station there is a cathode ray tube, a microfilm display device, earphones, and a typewriter keyboard. All of these are under computer control. The computer sends instructions to display an image on the microfilm projector (text, figure) and play an auditory message. Students may have to respond, which they do by operating the typewriter keyboard. The response is fed to the computer and evaluated. If it is a correct response, the computer moves to the next item; if not, the computer evaluates the type of error and then provides the appropriate remedial material.

The computer compiles a record for each student, which it checks occasionally to evaluate a student's progress and to identify

COURTESY OF IBM

any weaknesses. Consequently, constant enrichment or help is available. The authors believe that computer-assisted instruction (CAI) is the future trend. They state that CAI programs for teaching reading in the early grades is unusually successful; these youngsters substantially outperform other pupils in traditional programs. The authors believe that CAI furnishes opportunities for the maximum development of individual potential.

For example, to encourage problem-solving behavior, a teacher may program a problem into the computer. To solve it, students must supply the required logical analysis. The logic of the solution is more important than the skill of calculation. To conduct drill and practice, exercises are stored in the computer and presented on command of either teacher or student. In the tutorial method, the computer asks the student questions whose answers depend on

PLATO and TICCIT

Bunderson and Faust (1976) state that in 1971 the National Science Foundation funded two major demonstration projects: the PLATO IV Project (Programmed Logic for Automatic Teaching Operation) and TICCIT (Time-shared Interactive Computer-Controlled Information Television). Donald Bitzer at the University of Illinois was the chief developer of PLATO, which is designed to facilitate individualized instruction at the college, secondary, and elementary levels. Today's phase — PLATO IV — has a keyset for communication between student and computer and a display panel for illustrating graphic information and photographic color slides. The computer also controls related equipment: tape recorders, film projectors, audio systems, and other electronic equipment.

A fairly simple computer language — TUTOR — enables teachers to design lessons for their students. The computer will also constantly monitor and evaluate pupil progress. As Baker notes (1975), the system is so versatile it can present courses ranging from astronomy to veterinary medicine. The ultimate

goal of PLATO is to connect 4096 terminals by telephone lines to a Control Data Corporation computer. The estimated costs are comparatively low: 50 to 75 cents per hour per student. With more users, the price should drop.

In 1970 Victor Bunderson at the Institute for Computer Uses in Education at Brigham Young University joined with designers and developers from the University of Texas and the MITRE Corporation to produce TICCIT. The objective of TICCIT is to turn the teacher into a tutor-advisor, diagnostician, and problem solver. Each student terminal consists of color tv displays with sound. Unlike PLATO, TICCIT is a self-contained system; that is, the system has 128 student terminals that a college or school could purchase and distribute wherever they wish (classrooms, libraries, dormitories). The estimated cost, including hardware, CAI programs, and equipment maintenance, is less than $1 per student contact hour (Baker, 1975, pg. 23).

It is only a matter of time availability and reasonable costs before computers receive extensive educational use.

COURTESY OF IBM

The "Turtle Project"

previous replies. The computer interprets the replies and uses branching to provide appropriate learning experiences.

Understanding these basics helps you to visualize the mechanism of computer usage but gives no idea about the ingenuity of some computer projects. Baker (1975) describes the "turtle project" at the Massachusetts Institute of Technology Artificial Intelligence Laboratory. Using a computer language called LOGO, the project attempts to teach mathematics by student involvement.

Given five elements—a knowledge of LOGO, a computer, a Teletype machine (the terminal), a large, flat paper surface, and a box on wheels called a turtle (equipped with a pen)—new mathematical topics are introduced. By typing instructions youngsters can make the turtle draw a rectangle: forward 20 units, left 90°, forward 50 units, left 90°, forward 20 units, left 90°, forward 50 units. The computer controls the turtle as it follows a rectangular path, simultaneously tracing a picture of where it has been.

Baker states that educators use computers in two ways: transactional usage, which applies to administrative duties, and instructional usage, which applies to educational programs. Computers aid administrators mainly as record keepers. Tapes and discs are used to store almost limitless information about students, faculty, and other school personnel. Scheduling, financial data, library resources, and reporting to students and parents are all possibilities.

CMI

Computer-managed instruction (CMI) uses the computer as a teacher's aide. The computer grades, keeps records, and monitors progress but is not as actively involved with students as CAI. Figure 15.3 illustrates CMI.

A good way to conclude this discussion of computers is to quote Baker (1975, pg. 41):

> The computer with its attributes of speed in problem solving, virtually endless storage and retrieval capacity for enormous numbers of facts, its system of logical ordering of information, ability to make critical decisions, and ability to manage real-time systems such as space rockets and oil refineries should be part of the curriculum. It is time for administrators and educators to bring the computer into the school for the benefit of students.

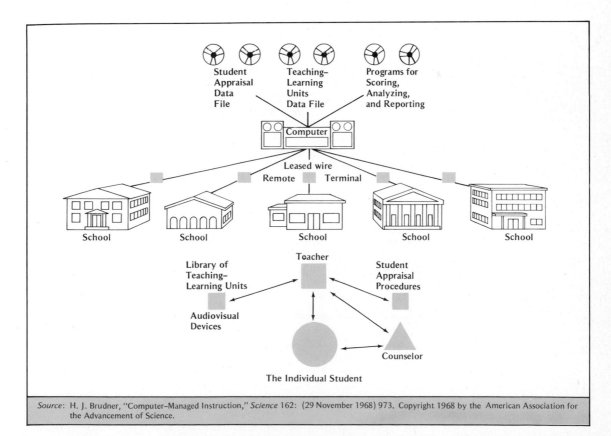

Source: H. J. Brudner, "Computer–Managed Instruction," *Science* 162: (29 November 1968) 973. Copyright 1968 by the American Association for the Advancement of Science.

Figure 15.3 Schematic Representation of a System for Computer-Managed Instruction

Discussion Questions

1. Why was Pressey's work not considered to be a teaching machine? What prevented its widespread acceptance?

2. Analyze the question of error in programmed instruction. Why is it critical? How does its acceptance in a program reflect the theorist's belief? What is Skinner's position? Do you agree?

3. What do you see as the strengths and weaknesses of programmed instruction? Does one offset the other? Do you, or would you, use programmed instruction? Why?

4. What is your reaction to computer use in schools? Are computers worth the time, money, and effort needed to make them functional? Is there a danger in education becoming too mechanized? Be sure you can distinguish CAI from CMI.

5. Think carefully before you answer this question. What do you think is a teacher's role with either or both programmed instruction and computer-assisted instruction?

Some Concluding Thoughts

As you can see from this chapter, there is an enormous array of auxiliary aids designed to help you improve your teaching. Ranging from traditional printed matter to complicated computers, your choice of instructional assistance is staggering. All of the potential aids at your disposal were not discussed. For example, overhead projectors, tapes, records, and pictures were not mentioned because you probably have considerable familiarity with them.

Perhaps the new generation of electronic calculators deserved consideration as their current availability at prices less than $20 will soon make them as necessary as flashlights or transistor radios. As the calculator technology, like that of computers, advances, more and more information will be stored on the electronic chips.

Regardless of the availability of instructional aids, remember two suggestions:

1. Be sure that you are comfortable with the tool and have complete mastery of it.
2. Be equally as sure that whatever aid you choose is appropriate for your instructional objectives.

Summary

- Teachers have a great variety of instructional aids from which to select.

● Follow carefully the guidelines suggested for selection: appropriate material, suitable for developmental level, cost, availability, and quality.

● In an age of technological advancement, it is easy to overlook the importance, flexibility, and availability of *good* printed matter.

● Certain visual aids, such as filmstrips, slides, and motion pictures, are appealing, available, suitable, and easy to use. Do not be dazzled by these admittedly enticing characteristics—*be sure the tool you select serves your instructional objectives.*

● Television usage is becoming more prevalent, which means that you must carefully preview educational television programs. If possible (time, facilities, money), involve your students in program production. It is a valuable and informative learning experience.

● Current concern with individualized instruction means that programming is here to stay. Know the procedures thoroughly so that you can determine the kind of program you want; then use it carefully to avoid boredom.

● While computers and CAI are relatively new to education they are the wave of the future and you should learn as much about them as possible.

Suggested Readings

Baker, Justine. *The Computer in the Classroom.* Bloomington, Indiana: The Phi Delta Kappa Foundation, 1975. A brief, well-written account of the computer movement, with particular emphasis on educational implications.

Gage, N. L., ed. "The Psychology of Teaching Methods." *The Seventy-fifth Yearbook of the National Society for the Study of Education.* University of Chicago Press, 1976. The entire yearbook is a fine survey of the latest data concerning teaching methods and instructional aids.

Gerlach, Vernon and Donald Ely. *Teaching and Media: A Systematic Approach.* Englewood Cliffs, N.J.: Prentice-Hall, 1971. An excellent overview of the nature and uses of instructional aids.

Gillespie, John and Diana Spirit. *Creating a School Media Program.* New York: Bowker, 1973. Summarizes many aspects of a media program and offers suggestions for appropriate selection.

Skinner, B. F. *The Technology of Teaching.* Englewood Cliffs, N.J.: Prentice-Hall, 1968. A collection of Skinner's essays on teaching that is still the basic reference for programmed instruction.

16

Classroom Management

Introduction

Many readers may believe that this is the most important chapter in the book. Managing a classroom means more than avoiding chaos; it means establishing a routine that enables learning activities to proceed smoothly. Youngsters must know what is expected of them; they must know what various signals (fire drill, assemblies, bells, whistles) mean and what they should do. Do not minimize the importance of routine: a smoothly running classroom is a major barrier to discipline problems. Teachers who give the impression of knowing what they are doing and who act decisively also give the impression of being in control.

Learning can only occur in an orderly environment. Orderly does not imply quiet or rigid. The hum and flow of youngsters engaged in meaningful activity in one classroom can be more orderly than the classroom in which you can hear a clock tick. An orderly environment is one in which everyone—teacher and students—knows what he or she is doing. So classroom management involves control, discipline, and meaningful learning.

This chapter will be extremely practical; the time has come to put your theoretical expertise to work. Your knowledge of pupils' development, your understanding of the learning process, and your utilization of instructional aids now must blend together practically. You must make them "work." Jacob Kounin, who has written a perceptive analysis of discipline and group management, states:

> The reader may even miss any expressed concern about educational objectives or philosophy of education. Even the best program requires good management techniques to get children started and moving. Your destination won't be reached if you can't get the car started and keep it moving (or stopped when necessary). And educational objectives won't be achieved if a teacher can't get children involved in the work or keep them from disturbing others (Kounin, 1970, pg. 2).

Since inexperienced teachers worry more about discipline than anything else, and since it also remains a concern for experienced teachers, discipline will be the focus of this chapter. What does desirable discipline mean? Does it reflect your personality? How does discipline relate to your other concerns? Will behavior modification techniques function effectively for you? Or do the psychoanalytically oriented influence techniques of Redl and Wattenberg seem more appropriate? If students can combine their academic work with relevant extracurricular activities, will that lessen discipline problems? If so, then career education and voluntary work programs warrant your attention. Has the teacher's new role—political, active, even radical—increased the possibility of discipline problems? Finally, what generalized, genuinely helpful suggestions emerge from these topics?

Before beginning, however, one topic demands careful consideration. Today's growing concern about children's rights directly relates to any discussion of discipline. The legal aspects of children's rights represents an expanding body of knowledge that can be only briefly outlined here. Rodham (1973) states that the Supreme Court has frequently held that the Constitution requires recognition of children's particular rights: the right to procedural protection in juvenile courts, the right to refuse to salute the flag in the public schools if it violates religious beliefs, and the right to wear a black armband protesting the Vietnam War. Yet the Supreme Court has also ruled that corporal punishment does not violate students' constitutional rights.

While the law's primary concern has been the state's limitation

Children's Rights

of parental control for the child's protection, a gradual change occurred during the compulsory schooling controversy. The question became: What is the proper social role of the school and the proper treatment of children in their schools? The precedent-setting case was *Brown* v. *Board of Education of Topeka*, 347 US483 (1954), in which the Supreme Court decided that the constitutional rights of black school children were violated by segregated education and simultaneously stressed the critical importance of public education.

Landmark Decisions

In re *Gault*, 387, US1 (1967) the Supreme Court made perhaps its most famous "child" decision concerning procedural rights in juvenile court. The decision held that children were entitled to certain due process guarantees: sufficient notice to prepare a defense, right to counsel, privilege against self-incrimination, and the right to confrontation and cross-examination. The Court, in its decision, declared that neither the Fourteenth Amendment nor the Bill of Rights applies to adults only, which prepared the way for continued advancement of the constitutional rights of children.

Since then there have been additional cases involving the due process of students in suspension hearings and disciplinary procedures. School officials can no longer plead ignorance of the constitutional rights of their students. Today's consensus is that "students do not shed their constitutional rights at the schoolhouse door."

Discipline has become a legal matter. Corporal punishment, expulsion, and suspension all symbolize failure. Often it is a consequence you cannot avoid, nor should you consider it a personal failure. There are students who are incorrigible and whose behavior is so disruptive that they must be removed for the good of the other students. But you must be aware of correct procedures: know thoroughly the guidelines that your school board has established for discipline; adhere to them strictly; consult your school administrator if you need additional help; be extremely cautious of your words and actions in such a case. Remember: children have constitutional rights.

Having sounded these warnings, you will be reassured to know that the vast majority of teachers never encounter such radical instances. The best advice is to circumvent disciplinary problems by creating a positive atmosphere and moving swiftly to prevent possible explosive situations. How to accomplish this will occupy the remainder of the chapter.

Teachers' concerns

High on any teacher's list of concerns is discipline; the more inexperienced the teacher, the greater is the concern for discipline. Fuller and Brown (1975) have identified teachers' concerns at various stages of their careers. They label the stages as survival, mastery, and consequence oriented versus change resistant. During the survival stage, teachers are primarily concerned with class control. Their goals have shifted from idealized views of students to real concern about their own ability to survive.

WHAT IS DISCIPLINE?

There can be little doubt about teachers', especially inexperienced teachers', intense concern with discipline. What is discipline? Does it have a different meaning for different people? *The American Heritage Dictionary of the English Language* offers the following definitions of discipline:

1. Training that is expected to produce a specified character or pattern of behavior, especially that which is expected to produce moral or mental development.
2. Controlled behavior resulting from such training.
3. A systematic method to obtain obedience.
4. A state of order based upon submission to rules and authority.
5. Punishment intended to correct or train.
6. A set of rules or methods.

Almost everyone can find something to accept within these interpretations, which range from the development of self-discipline (number one) to coercion (numbers four and five). Which interpretation appeals to you? Without begging the question, you would probably incorporate a little of each in your answer. Ideally, all teachers strive to inculcate self-discipline in their students. But they would also quickly admit that even punishment is occasionally necessary to safeguard the learning of all pupils. You must also build some system and order into your classroom to avoid chaos.

The Meaning of Discipline

There is probably no one tried-and-true definition of discipline. Its meaning will change with conditions and age; that is, as you establish reasonable rules to facilitate learning (as few as possible), and as pupils learn to behave according to them, discipline problems decrease. Age also introduces different meanings to discipline. Elementary school pupils need more direction and control, more structure, than do secondary students. While secondary students require less direction they also *need* a definite structure with clearly discernible boundaries. Control should be more subtle with adolescents so that they acquire that sense of "nearly equal." But when your authority is challenged and boundaries overstepped so that the learning of others is jeopardized, your reaction must be swift and decisive, *within the guidelines formulated by your school system.*

Reasonable discipline

Discipline should protect and nurture the physical, social, mental, and emotional growth of students. Rules should first protect persons and property, and *then* protect the right to participate in educational programs. Any disciplinary rules—*and their enforcement*—should be reasonable, legal, constitutional, and acceptable both to school officials and pupils (Stoops and King-Stoops, 1972). Unreasonable rules cause more trouble than they prevent; they arouse intense feeling because of their injustice and eventually serve only to challenge students.

What Is Disruption?

The authors believe that the basic guiding principle should be: what behavior interferes with the school program? Disruptive noise, fighting, deliberate and unprovoked challenges to the teacher, and truancy are behaviors that demand action. Legitimate questioning of teachers, normal noise in class movement, unusual but not provocative dress—these and similar examples seem *not* to warrant disciplinary action or rules. Remember: the fewer rules the better. If you have excessive dos and don'ts, the day becomes one long assessment of rule violations. You suffer because the more rules, the more violations. Pupils come to believe that *you* cannot maintain control. Students suffer because learning becomes secondary to the detection of rule violators. Keep your rules to a minimum but *enforce those you believe are necessary.*

National concern

Teachers and administrators are not the only ones concerned with discipline. Whiteside (1975) notes that discipline in many American schools is an incendiary issue that reaches far beyond the class-

Secondary School Discipline

De Cecco and Richards (1975) believe that America's high schools are drifting toward anarchy faster than most of us realize. Many schools, both urban and suburban, are in turmoil; rules are questioned and conflict is typical. It is estimated that school vandalism costs $500 million a year.

The authors note that schools employ two principal strategies for coping with this discord: avoidance and force. That is, officials,

teachers, and pupils either avoid conflict or attempt to crush it. Neither strategy has been successful, and reform is desperately desired. The authors believe that a partial solution may lie in negotiations among all concerned: parents, students, teachers, and administrators.

Interviewing 8500 people (8000 students) in 60 junior and senior high schools, De Cecco and Richards are convinced that the problem is institutionalized; that is, even when everyone wants solutions such organizational forces as differences in status and the secondary school's societal role inescapably produce turmoil. Some typical troubles that plague secondary schools are:

1. All rules are questioned: dress codes, classroom behavior, attendance, course content, grades, and marks.
2. Students openly defy teachers, expressing hostility by classroom disruption and school vandalism.
3. Teachers express their anger by extreme punishment or by merely going through the motions of teaching.
4. Students express their hostility toward each other by name calling, racial and ethnic slurs, and fighting.
5. Administrators express their anger toward everyone by taking sides, by enforcing rules harshly, or by secluding themselves in endless meetings in troubled times.
6. Eventually, collective action results: teachers join unions and strike; students form increasingly powerful and dangerous gangs.

Inevitable status differences in secondary schools breed conflict. Teachers have social and political power that may antagonize students. If the power boundaries are *not* clear, the struggle may be to define them. A second source of difficulty is inherent in large high schools. When students from radically

different backgrounds come together, fear, distrust, and anger easily develop. The school becomes a political socializer, which students frequently resent and resist. Thus avoidance or conflict results.

The authors argue for "conscious negotiation," which uses the basic conflict for solution. There are three steps in the process:

1. All parties state their grievances verbally, which also gives everyone the opportunity to express any anger.
2. They agree on the issues requiring negotiation.
3. They bargain so that both sides make gains and concessions.

It is important to identify precisely the parties involved; that is, occasionally it will be one individual versus another, or one group against another. If both sides in the conflict are of unequal status, a third party may be necessary. It is equally important that all parties recognize the issue causing the conflict; it may be course content or students' belief that a teacher is unfairly applying rules.

Accommodation may be difficult to achieve; anger, personal feelings, and intense commitments make any agreement painful. Settlement takes time and energy, and, as the authors note, it can be an emotional ordeal. Still the secondary school crisis demands solution, and negotiation may well be worth the effort.

---

room. Public opinion polls consistently show that discipline heads any list of citizen educational concerns. In the Eighth Annual Gallup Poll of the Public's Attitudes Towards the Public Schools, discipline again is seen as the major problem. Gallup interviewed 1549 adults, 18 and older from every region in the country and from varied communities, in their homes. Gallup believes that 1976 may have seen a turning point in the public's attitudes toward their schools.

There has been a shift toward more traditional values, and the public seems to be demanding a stricter code of conduct in the schools. Gallup states that increasing juvenile delinquency has highlighted the need for moral education, not only in the home but also in the school. These feelings are coupled with a definite demand for more basics in the curriculum.

The stricter discipline teachers favor is a complex issue. Does it mean more and more severe punishment? Who is the stricter teacher: one who believes in and uses corporal punishment, or one who scathingly humiliates students? As Whiteside notes, the more nurturant a teacher is, the more effective the punishment is. Students are especially sensitive to criticism from teachers who have offered them attention and affection.

What complicates the issue even more is that some teachers have few disciplinary problems, while others spend the day enmeshed in them. Evidence suggests that those teachers who are relaxed with students, knowledgeable in their subject, and able to communicate, and who have mastered the school's routine have the least problems. They radiate security and confidence—they are professionals. Here you may wonder how one achieves this desired state. It has much to do with understanding yourself and then acting in a manner designed to reflect your personality. Be natural; do not do anything that you find artificial; students sense this immediately. Analyze your strengths and weaknesses as an individual, and then try to capitalize on your strengths while min-

---

Problems Facing the Public Schools

Here are some specific results of Gallup's poll. Discipline leads the list of major educational problems as perceived by the nation's adults. In the eight polls, discipline has headed the list seven times. What is encouraging, however, is that the percentage of respondents noting discipline as the chief issue has *not* increased. Gallup believes that the most significant change in this poll is the increase in the number of adults who think that the schools are providing a poor curriculum.

The list of significant problems is as follows.

1. Lack of discipline
2. Integration/segregation/busing
3. Lack of proper financial support
4. Poor curriculum
5. Use of drugs
6. Difficulty of getting "good" teachers
7. Parents' lack of interest
8. Size of school classes
9. School board policies
10. Pupils' lack of interest

Gallup also asked what could be done to improve the school's quality. Answers clearly demonstrated the public's concern with curriculum and discipline. Here is the question and the percentage of respondents replying to each item. It is an interesting survey, which dramatically demonstrates the shifting values in American public opinion.

Which of these ways do you think would do most to *improve* the quality of public school education overall?

	PERCENTAGE			
	National Totals	No. Children in Schools	Public School Parents	Parochial School Parents
Devote more attention to teaching of basic skills	51	47	55	60
Enforce stricter discipline	50	47	52	64
Meet individual needs of students	42	39	47	44
Improve parent-school relations	41	43	36	47
Emphasize moral development	39	34	45	49
Emphasize career education and development of salable skills	38	39	36	37
Provide opportunities for teachers to keep up to date regarding new methods	29	27	32	29
Raise academic standards	27	28	23	38
Raise teachers' salaries	14	15	16	8
Increase amount of homework	14	12	17	21
Build new buildings	9	8	12	7
Lower age for compulsory attendance	5	4	6	1
None	1	1	*	
Don't know/no answer	4	4	2	3

*Less than 1 percent
(Totals add to more than 100 percent because of multiple answers.)

Source: George Gallup, "Eighth Annual Gallup Poll of the Public's Attitudes Toward the Public Schools," *Phi Delta Kappan* 58 (October 1976). Used by permission of *Phi Delta Kappan*.

imizing your weaknesses. (This would be an excellent time to re-read Chapter 14, concentrating especially on the personality section.)

CAUSES OF MISBEHAVIOR

There are two main causes of misbehavior: those arising from within the individual and those caused by the school. There probably is no such thing as the normal youngster; all students usually exhibit troublesome behavior during development. They are anxious, insecure, aggressive. It is only when these traits persist and become severe that they bother teachers. For most children, problems do not persist. Youngsters typically outgrow such behavior and progress to more mature stages of development.

Be alert to developmental problems and know when and where to refer them. Remember, however, that all children experience stress, and their reaction is to exhibit maladaptive behavior that relieves inner tension. Your role (shared with parents) in helping youngsters to master developmental crises is vital because the manner in which pupils meet these difficulties shapes the way that future dilemmas are faced.

You are teaching youngsters problem-solving behavior: what they learn may last a lifetime. Constant failure, punishment, and ridicule destroy confidence and produce a low self-concept. This is the worrisome elementary school pupil who becomes the sullen, rebellious secondary school student. Estimates are that about 5 percent of all school-age youngsters show serious symptoms and about 10 percent manifest milder behavioral disturbances. Thus, 85 percent of pupils proceed normally, perhaps causing teachers some anxieties with temporary maladaptive behavior (Travers, 1977, pp. 245–246).

Developmental problems

Anthony (1970) offers a brief guide to ages and problems reproduced in Table 16 1. Youngsters experience growth problems and inevitably bring them into the classroom. They usually pass quickly; if they persist, then the problem becomes serious.

TEACHING PROBLEMS

Misbehavior is caused; identifying the causes may remedy conditions and thereby modify or eliminate the troublesome behavior. Since the causes of behavior are multiple and complex, it is not always conceivable either to identify or to eliminate them. For example, unhappy home conditions may frighten a pupil, who then comes to school with building frustration and anger and becomes disruptive in the classroom. Teachers cannot eliminate nor ignore such behavior; they must deal with it promptly.

Classroom Atmosphere

The first step you should take to avoid unnecessary discipline problems is to make your classroom atmosphere inviting—relaxed yet constructive. It will not remove all of your problems, but *you* will not be the cause of difficulty. A positive environment also

TABLE 16.1
Some Developmental Problems

Ages	Problems
3 to 4 (preschool and kindergarten)	Phobias, nightmares, speech problems, masturbation, anxiety states
6 to 11 (elementary school)	School problems, school phobias, obsessive reactions, tics, depression
12 to 17 (junior and senior high school)	Identity diffusion, delinquency, acting out disorders, schizophrenia

helps youngsters with home problems; occasionally the classroom is the warmest environment that some youngsters know.

Thompson (1976) urges preventive discipline; that is, a positive learning environment allows pupils acceptable (to the school and peers) freedom and reduces drastically challenges between teachers and students. Diminishing threats and increasing tolerance lessen discipline problems. (Again, *whatever limits you impose must reflect both your personal beliefs and the school's guidelines.*)

Thompson believes that much misbehavior arises because content is irrelevant, students remain unmotivated, or teaching methods are dull. Since compulsory education forces some students to remain in school longer than they want, educators must discover ways to satisfy their needs or they will become a growing source of trouble. Career education and volunteer programs may meet their interests and wants.

Are satisfied students happy?

Realistically, everyone can be temporarily unhappy, even achieving, seemingly happy students. Jackson (1968) states that students' attitudes toward school are complicated and puzzling. Summarizing data from previous studies he demonstrates considerable negative feelings among basically satisfied students. Table 16.2 presents these results.

In Table 16.2, Study I included youngsters in the sixth through twelfth grade in a Midwestern private school. Study II was composed of students in a Midwestern public high school. Pupils in both studies responded to a checklist of 25 adjectives that best described their characteristic feelings while attending class. In both studies, satisfied students frequently used negative adjectives to describe their feelings about *typical* classroom experiences.

Note that more than half of the students in both studies felt bored, uncertain, dull, and restless. Jackson summarized student feelings nicely when he stated:

> The number of students who become ecstatic when the school bell rings and who remain that way all day is probably very small, as is the number who sit in the back of the room and grind their teeth in anger from opening exercise to dismissal. One way of interpreting the data we have reviewed so far is to suggest that most students do not feel too strongly about their classroom experience, one way or the other (Jackson, 1968, pg. 60).

As Jackson notes, students' reactions to school life are inevitably varied: most students like some aspects of school life and dislike others, and even the most satisfied pupils complain. The author believes that these feelings are unavoidable considering the inescapable clash between institutional objectives and individual de-

TABLE 16.2
Negative Adjectives Chosen by "Satisfied Students" Asked to Describe Classroom Feelings

ADJECTIVE[a]	TIMES CHOSEN			
	Boys		Girls	
	Study I (25)	Study II (34)	Study I (20)	Study II (35)
Bored	13	26	13	25
Uncertain	21	25	13	26
Dull	16	24	9	25
Restless	15	20	9	26
Inadequate	16	20	7	24
Unnoticed	5	16	4	15
Unhelped	8	16	6	17
Ignorant	13	15	3	15
Angry	4	14	4	14
Restrained	2	11	3	10
Misunderstood	5	11	2	15
Rejected	3	9	0	10

Source: Philip Jackson, *Life in the Classroom*. New York: Holt, Rinehart and Winston, 1968. Copyright © 1968 by Holt, Rinehart and Winston. Reprinted by permission of Holt, Rinehart and Winston.
[a] Adjectives have been ordered in this table on the basis of the ranking of the responses of boys in Study II.

sires. The result is occasionally a combination of frustration, unhappiness, and dissatisfaction. School's excitement, with its sharp disappointments and joys, is a colorful interlude that interrupts, rather than characterizes, the normal flow of events (Jackson, 1968, pg. 61).

Your first task in establishing a desirable classroom atmosphere is not to cause any problem yourself. While your initial reaction undoubtedly is to place all responsibility for discipline problems on students, further reflection will clearly suggest that some responsibility falls "behind the infallible side of the desk." While experience will eliminate most of these self-generated problems, to be aware of them now is to minimize their repercussions. How would you *honestly* answer the following questions?

1. *Are you unfair?* Students probably react more intensely to this issue than to any other. You must treat all students equally; this often may be difficult because some youngsters will seem to provoke you deliberately. But if you punish this youngster for disrespect, then you must punish all youngsters for disrespect. If you equivocate, a student's attitude toward you will quickly degenerate into personal resentment, with serious consequences.

2. *Are you inconsistent?* Do you react to similar conditions in a similar manner? If you scold or punish students for talking one day, then ignore them the next, you are inconsistent. If you expect students to do papers or reports carefully in October or November, and then ignore these standards in January and February, you are inconsistent. Students are bewildered; they do not know how to act; their behavior and work soon become chaotic and these conditions encourage trouble.

3. *Are you boring?* This is a blunt question that deserves a frank answer. If you maintain the same pace and procedure every day, youngsters eventually search for excitement. Break your routine; use games, stories, the playground, audiovisual techniques, discussions, lectures, group work, guests, and any relevant source or technique that will make your classroom exciting and inviting.

4. *Have you established routine?* You cannot break routine unless you have established it. Make no mistake: routine is one of your best safeguards against discipline problems. Students must know what they are to do, when they are to do it, and where they are to do it. If you betray uncertainty—ignorance about school rules, classroom procedures, location of materials, meaning of bells, function of machinery—or poor daily planning, you only invite trouble. *Master routine;* when you then break it, your students perceive change as a real treat.

5. *Do you know your subject?* Woe to the teacher who consistently cannot answer questions, who demonstrates a lesson and arrives at the wrong answer. Students quickly sense incompetence and lose respect for you.

6. *Can you control your temper?* A common mistake is to interpret all challenges personally. Some problems are personal attacks, but these are usually infrequent; most arise from the daily give and take of the classroom. If you respond spitefully, you create a sharp personal confrontation. Although it is difficult not to see misbehavior as a personal challenge, work at it; eventually your objective perspective will serve you well.

7. *Have you considered how you should best respond?* If you require considerable personal control, your disciplinary methods should focus on students' behavior, either rewarding, ignoring, or punishing it. If you are less concerned about control, you probably are more interested in a search for the causes of problems, in an understanding of the behavior. Adapt your techniques to your personality and belief; *do what you do best.*

Discussion Questions

1. This section was intended to encourage you to think about classroom discipline. How would you define it? Practically, what does it mean to you? That is, does discipline mean a quiet, controlled class with the teacher playing a dominant role? Or can it mean noise, activity, and movement?

2. Neither alternative just mentioned is better than the other. One method is better *only* for *you*. Consider why you answered as you did. Can you relate your answer to the previous discussion of teaching methods and teacher personality?

3. In spite of the current concern with children's legal rights, the U.S. Supreme Court has recently ruled that corporal punishment does not violate the constitutional rights of children. How do you interpret this decision in the light of the current social climate? Do you think it will introduce radical changes in school systems' manner of disciplining youngsters?

4. Do you believe that the "negotiation" suggestion of De Cecco and Richards has practical value? Why? The authors admit that it could "politicize" a school. Can you think of other dangers?

5. How would you interpret "reasonable discipline?" In your answer adapt your personal preferences to the reality of the school's commitment to orderly education. If your personal philosophy of discipline clashes with a school's policy, what do you recommend?

6. The discussion of sources of problems was incomplete. From your personal knowledge of children, and from reviewing the developmental section of this book, can you offer any other growth problems?

7. How do you explain satisfied students' unhappiness with school? Are some clashes inevitable, even with the best students? Can you add to the list of teacher-caused problems?

Maintaining classroom control

INTRODUCTION

Jacob Kounin (1970) has written a perceptive analysis of discipline and management techniques in the classroom. He states that his research began in an unintended classroom event. While teaching a mental hygiene course, he noticed a student reading a newspaper in the back of the room. He immediately and angrily reprimanded him. The discipline succeeded; the student's attention returned to the lecturer. But the reprimand also affected *other* class members. Attention was rigid, and a depressing silence settled on the room. This was Kounin's first experience with the "ripple effect." Punishment was not confined to one student; its effects spread to other class members. Kounin decided to study ripple effects and what he calls "desists"—a teacher's actions to stop misbehavior.

To avoid experimental contamination, Kounin and his colleagues videotaped 30 actual classrooms. They analyzed the tapes and coded teachers' desist techniques for clarity, firmness, in-

Jerkiness

withitness. When this happens you are almost compelled to attend to multiple events (overlapping). Since these teacher behaviors relate closely to managerial success they are well worth the effort.

The next topic Kounin discusses is transition smoothness. The classes he videotaped averaged 33.2 major changes in learning activities during the day. You can understand that if these are not handled smoothly chaos can result. Teachers must initiate, sustain, and terminate many activities involving many materials. If you are to maintain smooth movement, you must avoid jerkiness and slowdowns. These are teacher behaviors that abruptly introduce one activity by interrupting another: "Close your books, return to your desks, and do your arithmetic." There is no smoothness here; the youngsters are unready to interpret and act on the teacher's directions. Also avoid dangles—leaving some direction unfinished—and flip-flops—changing from one activity to another and then back again.

Slowdowns

Slowdowns occur when a teacher's behavior slows an activity's movement. There are two kinds of slowdown:

1. *Overdwelling,* when a teacher spends excessive time—beyond that which is needed for student understanding—on a talk.
2. *Fragmentation,* when a teacher has individual students do something it would be better to have the group do. For example, having children come to the reading group one by one instead of as a group.

Kounin concludes that avoiding jerkiness and slowdowns is a significant aspect of successful classroom management.

Finally, the author emphasizes that teachers are not tutors; that is, they work with groups, either the class as a whole, or subunits within the class. How can teachers keep their classes alert? Kounin observed teacher behaviors that he designated as "positive group alerting cues," such as creating suspense before calling on a pupil, and consistently calling on different pupils. "Negative group alerting cues" had teachers concentrating on only one pupil, designating a pupil to answer before asking the question, or having youngsters recite in a predetermined sequence.

> The management of classroom management skills should not be regarded as an end in itself. These techniques are, however, necessary tools. Techniques are enabling. The mastery of techniques enables one to do many different things. It makes choice possible. The possession of group management skills allows the teacher to accomplish her teaching goals—the absence of managerial skills acts as a barrier (Kounin, 1970, pg. 145).

Table 16.4 summarizes those teacher characteristics most effective for successful classroom management.

TABLE 16.4
Effective Teacher Characteristics

Teacher Characteristics	Meaning	Effective
Withitness	Knows what's going on	Yes
Overlapping	Can attend to two issues simultaneously	Yes
Transition smoothness	Handles changes well and maintains momentum	Yes
Group alertness	Keeps class "on toes"; provides challenge and variety	Yes

Behavior modification

Skinner (1973) bluntly asserts that education is in trouble. It faces problems that demand different solutions. Many of these problems are soluble by effective classroom instruction, that is, through behavior modification. Most individuals, including educators, are willing to change when scientific evidence is available to support that change. Education is presently at this stage.

AN OVERVIEW: DEFINITION OF TERMS

Stolz, Wienckowski, and Brown (1975) offer a perceptive analysis of the critical issues facing behavior modification. Noting that throughout the history of civilization people have always attempted to influence others, the authors believe that behavior modification was used long before its current interpretation and application. It is only recently that systematic attempts have been made to influence others' behavior.

The authors state that to understand behavior modification, certain terms and concepts require clarification.

1. *Behavior influence.* This occurs whenever one person exercises some control over another. It is a constant occurrence for humans, in home, school, work, or politics.

2. *Behavior modification.* When a deliberate attempt is made to apply certain principles derived from experimental research to enhance human functioning, the procedure is called behavior modification. These techniques are designed to better an individual's self-control by improving skills, abilities, and independence. One basic rule guides the total process: people are influenced by the consequence of their behavior. A critical assumption is that the current environment more directly controls behavior than an individual's early experience, internal conflicts, or personality structure.

3. *Behavior therapy.* Behavior modification and behavior therapy are often used synonymously, but behavior modification is the more general term. Behavior therapy should apply to a one-to-one client-therapist relationship. So, technically, behavior therapy is only one aspect of behavior modification.

Teachers using behavior modification attempt to influence their students' behavior by changing the environment and the way that youngsters interact with their environment, rather than by probing into backgrounds, or referring a child for medical treatment (usually drug control), or expulsion. To be successful you must clearly specify the problem behavior. What is it, precisely, that you wish a pupil to do, or not to do? Try to determine the consequences of children's behavior; that is, what do they secure by it? Then decide what *you* are going to do. Will you ignore it, hoping for extinction; or will you punish it; or will you reward some other form of behavior? Now carefully note which of your techniqes was successful and continue to adopt it for a particular student.

This may sound like nothing more than common sense, as Stolz

"That's right, a few rolls of quarters and a 747
standing by with enough fuel to Disneyland."

and his colleagues note. Parents constantly use behavior modification when they praise their children; employers offer bonuses and incentives. When systematic principles are used to control behavior, however, more than common sense is involved. Here are some behavior modification techniques.

4. *Positive reinforcement.* Positive reinforcement means, approximately, reward. It is any event following a response that increases the possibility of that response recurring. Good examples would be money, food, praise, attention, and pleasurable activities. You must be careful in using positive reinforcement with your students; what may be pleasurable (positive reinforcement) for one student may not be for another. Here is the value of knowing your students—what they like and dislike. (Review the Premack principle, explained in Chapter 7.) Positive reinforcement is a powerful tool in shaping behavior; presenting youngsters with something they like can consistently produce desirable results.

5. *Token economy.* Token economies are becoming increasingly popular in managing groups. Students, patients, group members receive tokens when they exhibit desirable behavior, collect them, and, when an accepted number are attained, exchange them for something pleasurable. For example, talkative students may receive tokens for every 15 or 20 minutes they are silent; when they have enough tokens they may trade them for extra recreation or something else they like.

6. *Shaping.* You first determine the successive steps in the desired behavior and teach them separately, reinforcing each until it is mastered. The students then move to the next phase where the procedure is repeated. Finally the total behavior is acquired by these "progressive approximations."

7. *Contingency contracting.* A teacher and student decide on a behavioral goal and what the student will receive when the goal is attained. For example, the goal may be successfully completing 20 division problems; the positive reinforcement may be an extra art period if this is the child's favorite school activity. The authors state that contracts involve an exchange—both teacher and student agree on what each will do.

8. *Aversive control.* Students maintain some undesirable behavior because the consequences are reinforcing. To eliminate the behavior an aversive stimulus (remaining after school, corporal punishment) is applied. The removal of positive reinforcement is another example of aversive control. (Recall Skinner's definition of punishment: the introduction of aversive stimuli and the withdrawal of positive reinforcement.) You have earlier read about the possible consequences of punishment's effect; but, again, use care in the selection of an aversive stimulus, and try to have students do something desirable so that you can positively reinforce them. As the authors note, "you must provide a rewarded alternative."

9. *Overcorrection.* Overcorrection combines both positive reinforcement and aversive control. For example, a girl may deliberately knock things off another pupil's desk as she moves about the room. The teacher not only has her remedy the situation (put the things back on the desk) but straighten all the other desks in the room. The positive reinforcement the girl may have received from upsetting the other is terminated, and now she must make the added effort of fixing the other desks (an aversive stimulus).

Modifying Classroom Behavior

Don Bushell (1974) states that the systematic modification of classroom behavior has been increasing since the 1960s. As one example, he describes a program for disadvantaged children, called Project Follow Through, in which considerable emphasis is placed on small group instruction. Bushell comments that shaping children's behavior requires considerable behavior and multiple consequences for the behaviors.

In their classrooms there are four adults working with 35 children. The actual teacher could be working with a reading group of six or seven children; a teaching aide could be teaching arithmetic to another six or seven youngsters; the rest could be writing or doing spelling with two helping parents. Although the parents often were on welfare and had little education, Bushell states that with training they became excellent helpers. They play an important role because they increase the students' chances of reinforcement and they also help to establish rapport between the school and community.

Curriculum materials are selected according to six criteria that help the instructors to shape behavior. These questions were:

1. Does the curriculum describe the terminal behavior?

2. Does the curriculum measure the student's entry level?
3. Does the curriculum require frequent student responding?
4. Does the curriculum contain clear criteria for correct responses?
5. Does the curriculum contain check points and prescriptions?
6. Does the curriculum accommodate individual differences?

These questions challenge curriculum makers to state their objectives behaviorally and to provide some means of determining a student's entry skills. Such materials lend themselves to token economies. Bushell describes a typical day. When the children come to school they begin small group work—reading, writing, arithmetic—and as they respond, either orally or through writing, the teachers can reinforce instantly. Correct answers and improvement produce tokens. The tokens are later exchanged for their individual privileges. The school day alternates between instructional periods and free periods during which they paint, dance, sing, or use the playground; that is, time they have earned by the accumulation of tokens. Thus the children have a freedom of choice in their school day that is most unusual.

A RATIONALE FOR BEHAVIOR MODIFICATION

Clarizio and McCoy (1976) note that, since behavior modification treats behavior, there must be justification for ignoring the *causes* of maladaptive behavior.

They offer several reasons for concentrating on the "symptoms," not the cause.

1. *Teachers are not analysts; they are not trained to explore the hidden motivation behind behavior.* Since the multiple and interactive causes of behavior elude the detection of highly trained and skilled professional counselors, busy teachers, who have neither the time, training, or experience, are less likely to detect them.

2. *Even if teachers can identify the cause of maladaptive behavior, they frequently can do little about it.* If the trouble lies in the home, a teacher's options are limited, *but the problems persist.* Consequently, teachers must focus on the child's behavior.

3. *Occasionally the causes of maladaptive behavior are discernible, and treatable, but the behavior remains.* The authors give the example of a reading problem caused by poor vision; when the physical difficulty is corrected, the reading deficiency remains.

4. *The behaviors, or symptoms, may themselves be disabling.* Children with reading problems frequently show emotional maladjustment in school. Treating one simultaneously helps the other; that is, overcoming the reading deficiency helps adjustment.

5. *Treating a misbehavior does not mean that another misbehavior automatically appears.* Many theorists and educators believe that unless the cause is removed, one symptom merely substitutes for another. To refute this belief, the authors return to reading disabilities. As the symptomatic behavior (reading difficulty) disappears, any attached emotional maladjustment usually disappears and the pupil's self-concept is considerably enhanced.

6. *Finally, and most practically and importantly, teachers can only attempt to modify the behavior.* If they succeed, they have won a notable victory, not to be belittled.

Practical suggestions

There are several widely accepted strategies for using behavior modification.

1. *Know your target.* Just what behaviors do you wish to change? Specify precisely what the behavior is and what you want it to become. Do not attempt too much. For example, some students may be unable to tolerate inattention too long; consequently, they frequently use maladaptive, disruptive behavior to secure attention. You will not immediately change that behavior for an entire day, *but you may quickly change it for a period,* and gradually extend it for an entire school day.

Making Education More Efficient

As mentioned, Skinner insists that education is in trouble. It is not enough "to free the child" or "de-school society." Education may be society's most important function, and, as its members try to ensure its continuation by transmitting it to the next generation, some carefully designed system is needed. Behavior modification has finally produced an effective technology of teaching by making three significant contributions to education (Skinner, 1973).

The first relates to teachers' assignments. Teachers have long felt that they must train minds, impart information, and foster students' interests, attitudes, appreciations, and creativity. But teachers do not manipulate minds or work with interests or attitudes. They *work with behavior* by changing students' verbal or nonverbal environment. Thus, teachers have a clearer concept of their tasks by eliminating indiscernible mental objectives.

The second contribution relates to classroom management and discipline. Why do students come to school, pay attention, study, and take tests? Skinner believes that the answer is simple: to avoid the consequences of not doing so. Most discipline problems— vandalism, truancy, disruption, and apathy— result from years of aversive control, *which still continues.* Positive reinforcement will eliminate these problems because education will provide students with positive reasons for coming to school, studying, and succeeding. It is a misunderstanding to consider such techniques as bribery. The rewards are not what is important; it is what students do to obtain the rewards that is significant.

Improvement in the design of instructional materials, many of which were discussed in the preceding chapter, is the third contribution. Skinner (1973, pg. 453) summarizes these three contributions as follows:

> The definition of objectives in behavioral terms, the design of effective classroom contingencies, and the programming of instructional materials may be all that is needed to solve many current problems in education.

2. *Know the circumstances surrounding the behavior.* When maladaptive behavior occurs, try to discover what happened immediately preceding and following it. A girl may consistently misbehave just before the reading period. She has a reading problem while her friends read smoothly and effortlessly. By being disruptive, she secures satisfaction and successfully directs attention from her difficulty. The teacher should strive for Kounin's "transition smoothness" by providing positive reinforcement *just before* the reading class, and then either ignoring (if possible) her behavior in reading or ensuring that she has some reading task that ensures positive reinforcement.

3. *Know your students so that you know what reinforces them.* While the primary reinforcers, such as food and sex, are powerful shapers of behavior, they are hardly appropriate for the classroom. Teachers must search for those things, objects, events

(recall the Premack principle) that individual students find reinforcing. For example, some students find adult attention a strong positive reinforcement; other youngsters, because of unpleasant experiences with adults, think their attention is aversive. If you use behavior modification—and everyone does, consciously or not—you *must* know your students to use reinforcers effectively. Becker (1973) believes that there are three types of reinforcers that are effective in the classroom:

a. Social reinforcers, such as physical nearness, praise, attention, smiles, and verbal behavior.
b. Activity reinforcers, such as running, playing games, drawing, singing, extra recess time, helping the librarian, field trips, and whatever else a youngster may like to do with free time.
c. Punishment, about which you have read so much.

4. *Select appropriate strategies.* Clarizio and McCoy (1976) summarize this step by urging that you select techniques that effectively encourage desirable behavior and discourage undesirable behavior. They recommend two strategies.

a. Behavior formation techniques, such as positive reinforcement and modeling, which present students with examples of desired behavior.
b. Behavior elimination techniques, such as punishment and extinction. You must decide which of these two basic strategies will best achieve the desired goal—adaptive behavior.

5. *Use feedback wisely.* Make sure that students understand the link between behavior and reinforcement. Your goal should be a gradual reduction in external reinforcement and increasing self-control.

Thoughtfully used, behavior modification techniques can help you attain a constructive classroom atmosphere.

Understanding the causes of problems

The third and final explanation of maintaining classroom control differs distinctly from Kounin's work, which focused on teachers' behavior and techniques, and behavior modification, which focused on the careful application of reinforcers. Here the search concentrates on the causes of behavior, which is quite different from behavior modification's emphasis on symptoms. Understanding a problem's cause, or causes, frequently reflects a psychoanalytic orientation. Is the misbehavior related to some early experience of the student? Is it connected to the pupil's relationship with parents? Are these underlying reasons forcing a youngster toward undesirable goals?

DISCIPLINE AND GOALS

Goal Seeking

A youngster, or an adult, is motivated toward something—a goal. Goal seeking, a frequent theme in the motivational literature, is especially important for teachers since a student seeking a goal is a joy in the classroom. Dreikurs et al. (1971) have raised several provocative issues about discipline and their discussion of goals is especially pertinent here. Their basic premise is that behavior is purposive and that correcting goals is possible, while correcting deficiencies is fantasy. They state that the force behind every human action is its goal and that all children's actions are an effort to find a place for themselves. Children are not driven through life; they seek their own goals.

Once students establish goals, their behavior manifests a certain consistency and stability which is threatened by crises and frustrations. All youngsters want attention, when they do not receive it through socially acceptable means, they try anything to obtain it. Punishment is preferable to being ignored; it reinforces one's presence. Some children feel accepted only when they do what they want, and not what they are supposed to do. The authors believe that parents and teachers who engage in a power struggle with children are eventually doomed to failure. Once a power struggle begins, youngsters want to "get even" with those who punish them. They seek revenge and the turmoil they create provides feelings of satisfaction. If children experience constant struggle and failure, they finally withdraw, desiring only to be left alone. There is no clear explanation of a child's choice of a goal, but recognizing the behavior that characterizes a particular goal should enable you to change the goal; behavior will then also change.

Discipline or punishment

The authors argue that discipline should not be considered an either-or proposition: *either* children obey instantly *or* they rule the classroom, causing chaos. Discipline does *not* mean control by punishment. The authors believe that self-discipline comes from freedom with responsibility, while forced discipline comes only from force, power, and fear. They summarize discipline's role in the classroom:

> Discipline in the classroom then means teaching the child a set of inner controls which will provide him with a pattern of behavior that is acceptable to society and which will contribute to his own welfare and progress (Dreikurs et al., 1974, pg. 24).

The classroom atmosphere must be positive, accepting, and nonthreatening. Nevertheless, children need limits and discipline means teaching them that there are certain rules that everyone must follow. Children and teachers should agree on the rules for classroom behavior, which increases their appreciation of the necessity for rules, especially when they have cooperated in formulating them. Discussing rules on borrowing, using equipment, name calling, or classroom manners is excellent training in discipline.

The authors state that both teachers and pupils need inner freedom, which results from cooperating with each other, accepting responsibility for behavior, speaking truthfully, respecting each other, and agreeing upon common behavioral rules. Here are some of their practical suggestions.

1. *Do not nag or scold.* Frequently this gives children just the attention they want.

2. *Do not ask a child to promise anything.* Children will agree to almost anything to extricate themselves from an uncomfortable situation. You just waste your time.

3. *Do not reward good behavior.* The child may only work for the reward and stop immediately. Also children expect something whenever they behave correctly. (Note the distinction from behavior modification techniques.)

4. *Avoid double standards.* What is right for the children (politeness, punctuality) is right for the teacher. (Here Dreikurs's work approximates the modeling of social learning theory.)

5. *Avoid threats and intimidation.* Children cannot learn or acquire self-discipline in a tense, hostile environment.

6. *Try to understand the purpose of misbehavior.* Why, for example, do children clown during arithmetic? Is it to get attention, or to demonstrate to peers that they are powerful, since they dare to defy adult pressure?

7. *Establish a relationship based on trust and mutual respect.* If you treat children as "nearly equal" they soon respect you and believe that you truly want to help them. Thus, they often will discuss their problem with you, which will help you devise ways to correct it.

8. *Emphasize the positive.* Refuse to take misbehavior personally and have a ripple effect permeate the classroom. Try to make *your* behavior kindly but firm.

INFLUENCE TECHNIQUES

Redl and Wattenberg (1959) have made one of the classic statements about discipline, teaching, and techniques of control. Their suggestions, called influence techniques, mirror their belief that there is a close relationship between learning and mental health. A student's mental health affects learning just as academic efficiency enables a pupil to adjust more satisfactorily. Emotional problems inevitably impair learning, although a minority of disturbed children try to compensate for their problems by overachieving academically. As the authors note, success in any phase of life is an emotional tonic.

What techniques can teachers employ to guide behavior toward desirable goals? The authors state that most teachers believe that they have little, if any, help from educational science in disciplinary matters. To be practically helpful, the authors urge you to be totally *realistic.* That is, you must accept certain administrative procedures. Will a principal support you if you send a pupil to the office? Another consideration is *your* personality. Do you think that sending a youngster to someone else for discipline is your failure and a sign of weakness to the class?

The authors suggest four categories of influence techniques:

A. Supporting self-control

The basic assumption underlying this category is that students want to do the right thing. Problems occur when they forget the rules or impulse overpowers self-control. These youngsters recover quickly if a discerning teacher, quietly mentioning their misbehavior, reinforces their self-control. Here are some supporting self-control techniques.

1. *Signals.* When a child begins to misbehave, merely shaking your head, raising a warning hand, or even just looking sometimes will stop trouble for a typically well-controlled youngster. The student regains control if the teacher acts immediately, that is, *at the beginning of trouble.* Do not hesitate; even well-controlled pupils become problems if their misbehavior goes unchecked.

2. *Proximity control.* Children begin to misbehave; the teacher simply stands by them: often your immediate presence will stifle trouble before it becomes serious. Many teachers subconsciously use this technique when they move troublesome youngsters close to them, to a front-row chair, or to an aisle where they can get to them quickly.

3. *Interest boosting.* When pupils become bored, they become restless. Occasionally going to such students and expressing interest in their work will help them renew their attention. This technique is usually successful with a well-controlled youngster who is experiencing momentary restlessness. You must know your students to be effective with this technique.

4. *Planful ignoring.* Sometimes it is better to ignore an incident if youngsters can themselves regain their poise. Be careful about this. If students interpret your behavior as weakness, you must abandon it. If you notice that well-disciplined children are becoming troublesome, you must act decisively. Only you can decide, and your decision comes from knowledge of your students.

Redl and Wattenberg state that supportive techniques have the advantage of immediately checking misbehavior, thus eliminating consideration of what to do about a serious offense. They also reinforce a child's sense of self-control. Remember, however, that these techniques are chiefly effective with those students who ordinarily behave. Do not overuse them since there is a danger that students can think you are unfair by expecting too much of them, particularly if you ignore similar behavior in more troublesome youngsters. The authors believe that these are the methods of "first choice"; that is, when they work little else is needed. If they fail, more direct efforts are necessary.

B. Situational assistance

The second class of techniques entails removing those difficulties that children themselves cannot master. You have a more active role since *you* change a program, *you* restructure the situation; that is, *you* have the responsibility of modifying the circumstances that seem to be causing the problem. These are some of the situational assistance techniques.

1. *Helping over hurdles.* Teachers can avoid many problems by providing timely assistance. Students, both elementary and secondary, must know precisely what they are doing if they are not to misbehave. First graders left to their own devices, or senior high students engaged in a project they cannot understand, are headed for trouble. Give clear directions to "help them over the hurdles."
2. *Restructuring the situation.* Change the pace of the classroom occasionally, vary the routine and shift activities so that there can be some physical release after verbal learning. Remember, however, you cannot attempt this until you establish a routine and your students realize you know what you are doing.
3. *Removing seductive objects.* You can be certain that there are some objects that attract pupils' attention, producing restlessness and problems. For example, setting up audiovisual equipment you will not use until much later will distract your pupils. Occasionally classroom projects have objects that tempt some youngsters to mischief.
4. *Anticipating planning.* The authors succinctly summarize this category's meaning: to wait for trouble to arise can be inefficient. Before a field trip, for example, tell your group what to expect and what behavior is acceptable.

Redl and Wattenberg believe that situational assistance can prevent trouble and is far better than forceful intervention. Children can learn controls without conflict. They warn, however, that solving problems this way often blinds us to the deep-seated causes of the problem and can make youngsters overly dependent. (Note the sharp distinction between Redl and Wattenberg's ideas and behavior modification.)

C. Reality and value appraisal

Helping youngsters to cope realistically with their problem is the third of the influence techniques. Although many cases of misbehavior are obscure and buried well within the personality, there still is a need for youngsters to develop a sense of cause and effect. These techniques should help students to view behavior in a different perspective.

1. *Direct appeal.* Sometimes students can improve their behavior if you show them the connection between their behavior and its consequences. Telling a student that his talking is disturbing others may help. You also must be realistic; that is, be certain that a pupil understands what his behavior is doing.

2. *Defining limits.* Children must know exactly what is expected of them. How you do this extends from posting a list of classroom rules (probably in the elementary school) to a simple yes or no at the secondary level. The fewer the rules the fewer the violations. But those you insist on, enforce. Youngsters expect limits; they want them. It provides them with security while simultaneously giving them something to test.

3. *Marginal use of interpretation.* Following their psychoanalytic beliefs, the authors state that pupils frequently act from motives they do not understand. They feel compelled to fight, disrupt, or challenge you, and are puzzled by these impulses. The authors state that helping pupils understand their motives is a long process requiring specialized treatment. They believe, nevertheless, that there are occasions when youngsters can gain control if they are given some insight into their behavior. The boy who fights in the school yard after receiving a poor test mark may avoid confrontation in future similar situations.

Redl and Wattenberg warn that, while adults may find these techniques attractive, youngsters may not respond to them because they do not share teachers' values. If students respond, these techniques are effective in establishing student control and a recognition, if not an acceptance, of the values of others.

D. Invoking the pleasure-pain principle

The final category is somewhat similar to behavior modification. What you do to children as a result of their behavior will guide their future actions. Redl and Wattenberg's interpretation of the pleasure-pain principle differs from behavior modification in that, according to the authors', teachers deliberately produce pleasant or unpleasant *feelings*. Rewards, threats, praise, and blame are all used to produce these feelings, to cause a fear of consequences, or to create inner anxiety that will help students to maintain control over their behavior. Here are some of the techniques.

1. *Rewards and promises.* If possible use positive techniques to influence behavior; they not only inform students that their actions are acceptable, they are also a powerful force in developing a satisfactory self-concept. You should be aware that pupils may work for the reward alone, circumventing intrinsic motivation. Also, be sure that all youngsters receive either a reward or a promise of one for their effort. These are not insurmountable obstacles so you should employ positive techniques as much as possible.

2. *Threats.* Pointing out undesirable consequences sometimes is the only way to have certain pupils behave properly. The authors believe that threats should be used sparingly, if at all. They may cause cheating, lying, excessive anxiety, or overt challenges by students. There is also a danger for teachers. You undoubtedly chose teaching as a career because you like young people; consequently, you may not follow through on your threat. Students see this as a sign of weakness; so, you may inadvertently cause yourself discipline problems by the careless use of threats.

3. *Praise and blame.* These techniques make people feel good or bad about themselves. Positive adult attention enhances students' self-concepts; blame may produce inner anxiety and a desire to change conduct. Praise and blame are effective only when a class respects you. Be careful not to always blame or always praise the same pupils.

4. *Punishment.* The authors define punishment as the planned infliction of an unpleasant experience to modify future behavior. It is always unpleasant and students always suffer some kind of hurt or loss. Punishment is constructive only under certain conditions: children know their behavior is wrong, the punishing person is someone the pupils respect and like, and the punishment fits the misbehavior. Otherwise, students interpret your action as revenge, which causes a lingering resentment that can only bode ill for the future. Also, time your intervention carefully; do not delay because children probably have forgotten why you are punishing them. Try to avoid mass punishment; if an entire class has misbehaved, you may have no alternative, but do not punish an entire class because you cannot identify a culprit. Enough has been said about the ramifications of punishment to cause you to apply it cautiously.

These influence techniques differ from both Kounin's suggestions for good classroom management, which are more mechanical, and behavior modification, which is only concerned with behav-

Teacher Militancy

One issue involving increasing discipline problems relates to the emerging role of contemporary teachers and students' changing perception of teachers. Teachers' demands for their rights, and their willingness to fight for them, has often, and unfortunately, cast teachers as villains. As teachers demand more money and added benefits, parents complain in front of their children, and the seeds of conflict are planted.

As Corwin notes (1975), what seems to be new about teaching is the scope and intensity of teacher militancy, which takes many forms. Teacher strikes are probably the most obvious, and, since 1967, the number of strikes has increased dramatically. Powerful teacher organizations have publicized teachers' wants and fought for their rights through collective bargaining.

Some educators believe that strikes and collective bargaining can accomplish only limited goals. Consequently, they have turned toward politics, believing that once political power is acquired, they are in a better position to seek and attain their goals. As these organizations grow, they acquire both the money and votes to become extremely influential.

These changing conditions cause students to view teachers differently. They are seen as more human, more vulnerable, more concerned with material needs, and with different interests than students may have anticipated. The aura of authority has slipped, and teachers are more susceptible to challenge. Consequently, teachers must realistically assess their role and attempt to offset any loss in prestige. One way is to ensure that performance matches demands; it is hard to argue against a highly skilled professional who demonstrates competence, compassion, *and* satisfactory results.

There is an inevitability about role change; to offset potential damage, teachers must justify these changes by the quality of their performances.

---

ior. Redl and Wattenberg argue strongly that teachers must understand the causes of misbehavior to handle it effectively. The three viewpoints are not totally distinct, and you probably will select those features from each that appeal to you and adapt them to your personality.

Discussion Questions

1. How would you explain the lack of a desist's effectiveness? You may want to include suggestions from behavior modification and influence techniques to explain your answer.

2. The teacher behaviors that Kounin found effective were actually management techniques. Why do you think they are effective? Do they reflect a teacher's personality? Can you adapt them to yourself? Can you give examples of each?

3. Be sure you understand the differences in behavior modification terminology that Stolz et al. suggest. Do you think that teachers frequently engage in behavior therapy? Should they? Consider your answer carefully.

4. Reread the punishment section in Chapter 7. If you decide to employ behavior modification techniques, both to individuals and to classes, would you ever use aversive control? How? What cautions should you observe? Give an example of both pupil misbehavior and class misbehavior and describe how you would treat each, using behavior modification techniques.

5. You must face the issue of "treating the symptom and not the cause" in behavior modification. How would you defend yourself against this charge?

6. Do you agree with Dreikurs's analysis of misbehavior? Could you suggest others, such as lack of self-discipline? Teachers are busy. Can you take the time to discover why a youngster's "attention-getting mechanism" functions in the classroom? Can you afford not to?

7. How would you evaluate Redl and Wattenberg's four categories of influence techniques? Do you agree that they are influential?

8. With what type of youngster will each work? Will signals be effective with a tough, willful teenager? Is using threats with first graders a form of overkill?

9. Whether you agree or not that teacher militancy can be a source of classroom problems, there is little doubt that teachers' roles are changing. Can you suggest other issues, related to teachers' roles, that could be a source of trouble with students?

Career education

There is a strong belief that if students are motivated then discipline problems are minimal. Both research and common sense testify to the wisdom of this belief. The problem is how to motivate all children. One attempt, called career education, tries to reconcile formal learning with familiarity with career goals and field experiences. The United States Office of Education defines career education as follows:

Career education is the total effort of public education and the community aimed at helping all individuals to become familiar with the values of a work-oriented society to integrate these values into their personal value systems, and to implement these values in their lives in such a way that work becomes possible, meaningful, and satisfying to each individual.

Career education is intended to serve pupils from kindergarten through college. For example, a first-grade class, besides their classroom work in reading or writing, may make field trips to various businesses and draw pictures of people working at different tasks. Older pupils may observe a certain occupation such as tailoring or dental hygiene, for several days. High school students may go through mock job-seeking interviews.

Not everyone is completely enthusiastic about career education. The Council for Basic Education, dedicated to liberal education, states that it makes a mockery of schooling since it is education for a job and not education for life. As jobs often become obsolete quickly, students should receive a broad liberal education that will enable them to adapt to change. Labor has also raised objections, since it fears a relaxation of child labor laws with job loss for needy adults.

The concept became popular in the early 1970s when Sidney Marland, then U.S. Commissioner of Education, gave career education top priority. Since then it has received endorsements from the U.S. Chamber of Commerce, the National Alliance of Businessmen, the National Association for the Advancement of Colored People, General Motors, and American Telephone and Telegraph, among others. Federal legislation also provided another tremendous impetus with appropriations of $15 million annually from 1974 to 1978. State legislation has provided another motive with several states now requiring their school systems to offer career education programs. Finally, initial studies tentatively indicate that youngsters in career education programs manifested better achievement in language and math than a control group.

WHAT IS CAREER EDUCATION?

In its rationale for career education, the U.S. Office of Education presents five basic components that are vital for career education.

1. *There are close interrelationships among the home, the family, the community, and the occupational society.* Each of these units has a major contribution to make to career education. For example, basic attitudes toward work are formed in the family; schools can identify those tasks that carry into future careers; and the community provides a wealth of valuable experiences that supplement basic education and aid students with career preparations.

2. *Classroom teachers should emphasize the career implication of their subjects, whenever they can.* By so doing, teachers make their subjects more meaningful and relevant, while simultaneously stressing effective job skills. Here the value of positive educational motivation can well serve the school.

3. *Every school should have a comprehensive career development program involving the cooperation and participation of both school and nonschool personnel.* Students should have a variety of experiences, both cognitive and practical, that help them to understand a working society. Such programs should also offer continuous assistance in educational and occupational choices.

4. *Some element of vocational skill training should supply students with the specific competencies necessary for, successful work.* Students should have excellent training for current and anticipated occupational openings. Note: occupational training is but one aspect of career education. Many confuse the two programs.

5. *The cooperation and involvement of public and private industry and labor is essential.* While the classroom may provide the necessary theoretical background, there must be provision for work observation, work experience, and work-study opportunities. This coordination must become the joint responsibility of formal education and the business-labor-industrial community.

Figure 16.1 illustrates how career education is an essential part of the total educational system, while encompassing vocational education as one of its components.

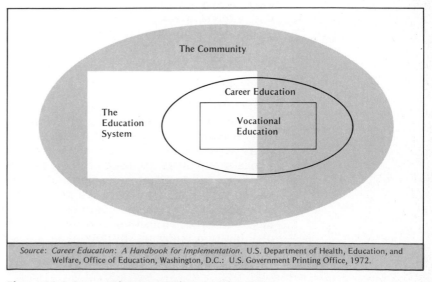

Source: *Career Education: A Handbook for Implementation.* U.S. Department of Health, Education, and Welfare, Office of Education, Washington, D.C.: U.S. Government Printing Office, 1972.

Figure 16.1 Career Education's Place in Education

Students and goals

Marland (1972) believes that two classes of students have clearly defined goals: those in college preparatory programs, and those in vocational-technical education. Most students are in neither; they are not going on to higher education nor are they preparing for particular jobs; they are "general education students." Here is where the failure rate is greatest for both students and programs. There are no real goals for either.

All education should have a clear purpose: either to prepare students to enter a job or to continue their studies. To be successful, career education must encompass the total educational spectrum from kindergarten through secondary school, and, if possible, include college and adult education. The career education curriculum should focus on jobs and work. There are more than 20,000 distinct jobs which specialists have grouped into 15 categories, such as health, manufacturing, and marketing. See Figure 16.2.

In the first six grades pupils become familiar with the cluster through instructional materials and field trips. In seventh and eighth grade, pupils explore in more detail those clusters that interest them; in ninth and tenth grade, they may concentrate on one cluster. In eleventh and twelfth grade, students investigate one career intensively. Figure 16.3 illustrates the sequence.

Note that all children receive the same career education through sixth grade (exploration of the 15 clusters). They learn, for example, that transportation occupations include aerospace, pipeline, and road and water transportation, each with hundreds of different jobs. Between seventh and ninth grade, students examine careers that interest them, followed by the acquisition of skills that will ensure successful job entry if they decide not to continue their education.

Will career education succeed?

While career education may be a concept whose time has come, it will not succeed unless policy makers (legislators, school boards) and instructors cooperate in its implementation. It may well require a reorientation of staff who resist what they conceive as a radical innovation opposed to their notion of basic education. To win their support state agencies may have to initiate carefully designed preservice and inservice programs. With the support of local administrators, these programs should impress the school's faculty that career education is a high priority item. The U.S. Office of Education suggests the following steps for implementing a career education program.

Phase I
1. Organize the appropriate interactive network of interested individuals and groups.

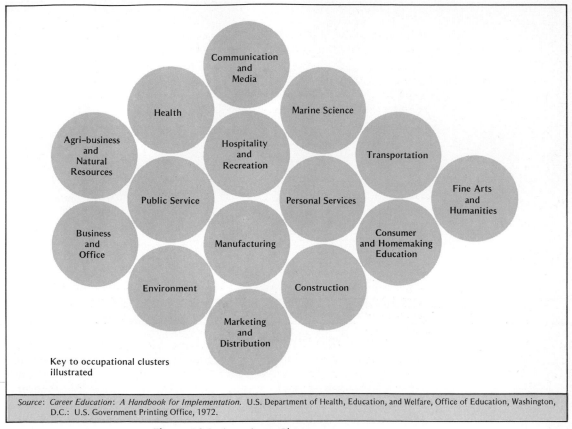

Key to occupational clusters
illustrated

Source: *Career Education*: *A Handbook for Implementation.* U.S. Department of Health, Education, and Welfare, Office of Education, Washington, D.C.: U.S. Government Printing Office, 1972.

Figure 16.2 The Fifteen Clusters

2. Promote an understanding of the concepts of career education and establish appropriate educational objectives.

Phase II

3. Study the current educational system to determine the changes necessary to turn it into a true career education system
4. Inventory and marshal all available resources.
5. Design the career education system most appropriate for your community.

Phase III

6 Gain the cooperation of all necessary organizations, institutions, and individuals.
7. Implement the system.
8. Build in an evaluative process to determine how well the system is working.

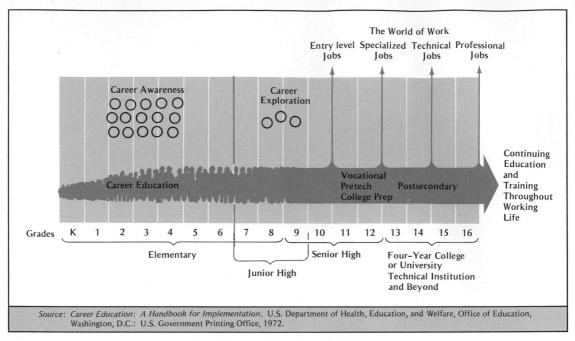

Figure 16.3 A Career Education Model

Phase IV

9. Create a feedback system to use evaluation findings to adapt and and improve career education programs.
10. Make provision for a program of maintenance to sustain early initiative and tie these activities into the interactive network.

Properly implemented, career education can help students explore their potential, aid them in their search for an adult role, and, concomitantly, further classroom motivation and reduce classroom problems.

Some Concluding Thoughts

This chapter was intended to provide practical suggestions in classroom management. Discipline is a beginning teacher's main worry and a continuous concern for any teacher. Were there some common techniques that everyone agrees are helpful? These seemed to be present on almost everyone's list (expressed in one way or another):

1. *Positive reinforcement is the ideal technique.* Everyone agrees with this principle. For whatever reason (according to behavior modification or

Volunteer Programs

Good career education programs take time to develop. One method of combining students' interest with their academic work is through volunteer programs. A relatively new and popular phenomenon, volunteer programs are primarily designed to meet the human service needs of community residents. It is a rewarding experience for secondary school students who receive the opportunity of working in hospitals, nursing homes, day-care centers, or tutoring. It is also a valuable complement to career education programs since students can select any of the 15 clusters and, through volunteer work, attain several objectives: provide needed help and services, further their occupational knowledge and skills, and make classroom subjects more practical and meaningful. Many schools offer academic credit for volunteer work, also called internships. Volunteer programs can also be a significant deterrent to discipline problems because of the student interest they generate.

You may wish to participate or even initiate such a program. Smith, Taylor, and Werblud (1976) state that a critical step in forming a volunteer program is finding satisfactory student placement in the community. Will an agency or institution use volunteers so that the student, institution, and those served all benefit? Be careful in recruiting that you match individuals with appropriate placements.

To insure quality placement, the authors urge that you consider four significant issues:

1. *Orientation.* Students should know precisely what they are to do, and why they are to do it, to reduce the dropout rate and offenses to the community.
2. *Training.* Students need to acquire knowledge and skills. As the authors note, not all volunteer placements require training. If training is needed, be sure students receive it, otherwise your program could be painfully damaged.
3. *Supervision.* Furnish direction and guidance for the volunteer. Good supervision is essential to insure that volunteers are performing adequately and to determine if an individual is temperamentally suited to the task. (Again, note the relationship between personality and performance.)
4. *Evaluation.* Provide an assessment of the volunteer's contribution. Did students achieve goals? Did the agency or institution benefit? Did their work help those who received the service?

Good volunteer programs serve students, the community, and *you*. You may be interested in learning more about this growing movement. For an excellent handbook write:

Rick Williams, Coordinator
The Korda Project
84 Eldredge Street
Newton, Mass. 02158

psychoanalytic theory), positive reinforcement facilitates learning, satisfies pupils, and minimizes discipline problems.

2. *If you must punish, do it immediately and try to have the student do something you can praise.* Do not permit punished behavior to become a

source of potential conflict between you and a student. Find *something* you can reinforce.

3. *Be alert and confident in the classroom.* This principle reflects a combination of techniques that informs students you know exactly what is happening in the classroom. When you act, act decisively. Students will respect you for it.

4. *Be consistent.* While there are many ramifications to this principle, it is best summarized as: What you do unto one, do unto all. Students detest, and quickly lose respect for, teachers who play favorites.

5. *Master routine.* You invite discipline problems when you do not know what, when, where, and why things happen in your school. Some students go one way, some another way, and chaos results. There is simply no excuse for disciplinary problems resulting from ignorance of school rules.

6. *Establish a warm and positive learning environment.* You will have some problems—everyone does—but if students sense acceptance and support, 99 of 100 will respond positively.

These are general suggestions that should be practical and helpful. Every other technique mentioned in this chapter can fit into these categories. But, above all else, remember that every teacher alive experiences disciplinary problems; they are not failures, nor are you. You are not alone. It is the way in which you treat each problem and take measures to prevent future occurrences that will determine your teaching success.

Summary

- While discipline means many things to many people, it remains a major concern of teachers.

- A lack of public school discipline leads the list of national concerns.

- Discipline problems arise from both natural growth crises and classroom conditions.

- Kounin's effective teacher behaviors—withitness, overlapping, transition smoothness, and group alertness—are helpful management techniques. Without these, there is no possibility of a smoothly running classroom.

- Behavior modification, as a science and technique, must be distinguished from behavior influence and behavior therapy.

- Focus on behavior can produce desirable change without the in-depth personality search that other theories advocate and for which most teachers are unequipped.

- A psychoanalytic analysis interprets misbehavior as the search for certain goals, which teachers can only discover through skilled and thoughtful interactions between pupil and teacher.

- Redl and Wattenberg's psychoanalytically oriented influence techniques provide helpful and practical suggestions for classroom control.

- Changing teacher roles, especially the appearance of militancy, has altered teachers' images, and perhaps made them more vulnerable to student misbehaviors.

- Of all the techniques suggested by all the theorists, positive reinforcement is probably the most effective and satisfactory to all.

Suggested Readings

Dreikurs, Rudolph, Bernice Grunwald, and Floyd Pepper. *Maintaining Sanity in the Classroom.* New York: Harper & Row, 1971. A thoughtful perspective on classroom management from a psychoanalytic viewpoint.

Jackson, Philip. *Life in the Classroom.* New York: Holt, Rinehart and Winston, 1968. A keen, realistic description of what really happens in classrooms.

Kounin, Jacob. *Discipline and Group Management in Classrooms.* New York: Holt, Rinehart and Winston, 1970. One of the best practical accounts of what teacher behaviors "work" in the classroom.

Redl, Fritz, and William Wattenberg. *Mental Hygiene in Teaching.* New York: Harcourt Brace Jovanovich, 1959. Still remains a classic; somewhere, sometime you should read this book carefully.

Skinner, B. F. *The Technology of Teaching.* Englewood Cliffs, N.J.: Prentice-Hall, 1968. Probably the best single statement by Skinner on teaching and its problems and solutions.

Appendix

Introduction to Statistical Methods in Psychology

Foster Lloyd Brown

The purpose of this appendix is to help you learn how to prescribe, compute, and interpret a few of the more commonly used statistical tools. The same data will be used throughout both to cut your learning time and to help you discover relationships between the techniques.

Sample problems are given throughout the text. The correct answers are supplied following each problem. Cover the answers until you have responded, and then see how you did.

Descriptive and inferential statistics

Statistical methods are divided into two groups: descriptive statistics, which are used to describe a situation, and inferential statistics, which are used to draw conclusions from research data. Descriptive statistical methods seldom give psychology students much difficulty and will be treated here only briefly.

DESCRIBING DISTRIBUTIONS

While many kinds of graphs are used in psychology, two are particularly common, frequency diagrams and scatter diagrams. For an example of a frequency diagram see Figure A.1. An example of a scatter diagram is given in Figure A.2.

In scatter diagrams the prior or possibly causative variable (called the independent or X variable) is plotted along the horizontal (X) axis. The later occurring or possibly caused variable (called the dependent or Y variable) is plotted on the vertical (Y) axis.

In the scatter diagram shown, Joy received a perception (X in this case) score of _____ and a reading (Y) score of _____.

6
4

Figure A.1.

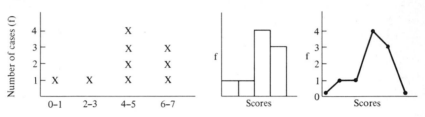

Figure A.2

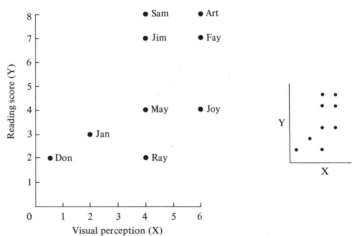

Some commonly encountered distributions are illustrated in Figure A.3. It is easy to remember which skew is negative and which is positive. Look for the long, thin tail. If it's to the left, the skew is negative; if to the right, positive.

A very difficult test would have many (low, high) _____ scores and would be skewed (negatively, positively) _____.

Figure A.3

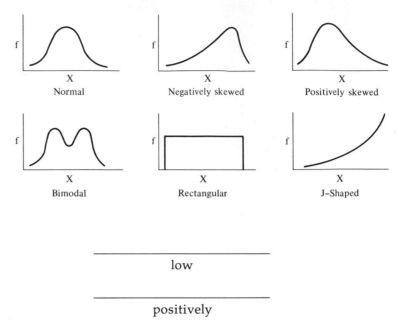

---
low

---
positively

If the scores of two very different groups are combined (such as weight lifting scores for a group of girls combined with the weight lifting scores of a weight lifting team), the result might be a _____ distribution.

---
bimodal

Measures of central tendency, such as the mean and median, measures of variability, such as the range and standard deviation, and measures of association, such as the correlation coefficient, are often used in a purely descriptive way. These applications will be considered under the heading of each measure.

RANDOM SAMPLE

Assume a set of scores for a test on visual perception given to a random sample of nine children from a large first grade:

	Scores
Don	0
Ray	4
Jan	2
May	4
Joy	6

Jim	4
Sam	4
Fay	6
Art	6

By random sample is meant that each of the first graders had an equal chance of being included in the sample. A *sample* is chosen perhaps because it is too expensive or there is not enough time to test the entire class, but the group that we really wish to know about, called the *population,* is the entire first grade.

It is often this way in the real world; the entire population about which we wish to know—all voters in a national election, all children in Headstart, all white rats, the students in a particular college, heroin addicts being maintained on methadone, cigarette smokers —is not readily measured and so a sample is studied from which one can make *inferences* about the population.

Computing the mean and the median

Given data such as the above, one might wish to find a number that represents the best estimate of the *central tendency* the visual perception scores would have shown if the entire class had taken the test. There are two major indices of central tendency: the mean (commonly called the average) and the median. A third index, the mode (most frequent score), is seldom used in psychology.

The *mean* of a set of scores is simply the sum of all the scores divided by the number of scores. This section on the mean is not so much to teach you how to compute a mean (which you can probably already do), but to introduce some symbols and a way of learning how to do more complex computations.

Using the notes and example problem, solve the practice problem.

		Example problem		
		scores		
Notes		(X)	*Practice problem*	
Sum up the scores and	Don	0	Ima	0
label the sum as ΣX.	Ray	4	Lil	2
Σ (the capital Greek	Jan	2	Dot	2
letter sigma) may be	May	4	Hal	3
read as "sum of." X	Joy	6	Sue	8
stands for scores.	Jim	4		
	Sam	4		
	Fay	6		
	Art	6	__ = __	
		ΣX = 36		

$$\frac{\Sigma X}{\quad} \qquad 15$$

N symbolizes the
number of scores. $N = 9$ $N = \underline{\hspace{1.5cm}}$

5

The mean, symbolized
by M, is the $M = \Sigma X/N$
ΣX divided by N. $= 36/9$
                               $= 4$ $M = \underline{\hspace{1.5cm}}$

3

When a few extreme scores lie at one end of a distribution (called a skewed distribution), the mean may not meaningfully reflect the central tendency of the distribution. For example, consider a hypothetical set of yearly salaries (in thousands) for a small company, the last figure being the salary of the owner.

10, 9, 9, 10, 12, 8, 12, 50

The mean salary is 15,000, but that figure would hardly communicate the real situation, say to a prospective employee. In a case like this it is generally better to use the *median*, which is computed by lining up the scores from low to high thus:

8, 9, 9, 10, 10, 12, 12, 50

and simply noting the middle score (or mean of the two middle scores in the case of even-numbered distributions).
The median for the above salaries is _____.

10

The mean, median, and mode are also used as descriptive statistics. When used to describe an existing set of scores (as contrasted to making inferences about a population), the computations are performed in just the same way as outlined above.

Variability

One common way of expressing variability is the *range*. It is computed by the formula: Range = Highest score − Lowest score. The range for the example problem on page 681 is $6 - 0 = 6$. The primary advantage of the range is the ease with which it is computed and understood. However, it is unstable because the range can be changed greatly by one extreme score. Another problem is that it tends to get bigger as the sample size gets bigger since a large sample is more likely to contain any extreme scores that may be in the population. Samples thus tend to yield estimates of the range that are *biased* in the direction of being too small.

A more useful estimate of variability is called the *standard deviation*. It is a more stable and sensitive measure than the range since it reflects the variability of every score and not just the two extreme scores at each end. Using the formula to be taught later, sample scores can be used to figure an *unbiased* estimate of a population standard deviation, that is, the estimates, over the long run, would not average too low (as with the range) or too high.

As an example to help clarify the nature of the standard deviation, assume that 100 students were to take a test that had a mean of 50 and a standard deviation of 10. Assuming these scores to be distributed in the most usual way, they might line up about as in Figure A.4.

Figure A.4

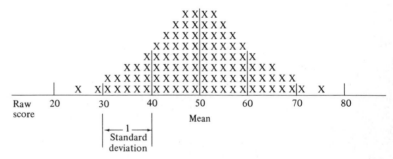

If the standard deviation were 5 instead of 10, the 100 students would be distributed more as in Figure A.5. Notice the piling up of cases about the mean and the thinning out toward the tails. In its purest form the type of bell-shaped distribution in Figures A.4 and A.5 is called a *normal distribution*. When a distribution is normal or

Figure A.5

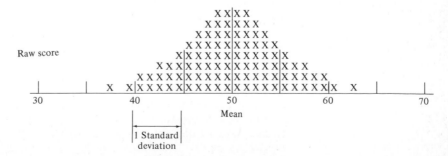

near normal the proportion of the total cases in any particular segment of the curve is rather predictable. About 68 percent of the cases lie between 1 standard deviation below the mean (called a z score of −1) and 1 standard deviation above the mean (z of +1).

Because there are 100 cases in Figures A.4 and A.5, each figure counts as 1 percent. One can see that the percent of cases lying above a z score of +1 is about _____ percent.

16

16	68	16
−1		+1

Figure A.6 offers a rather explicit view of the relationship between some types of scores and the normal distribution.

TABLE A.1

The Proportion of Cases Equalling or Exceeding Certain z Scores

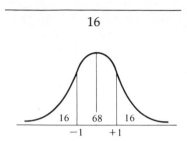

z	Proportion
0.674	.2500
1.000	.1587
1.282	.1000
1.645	.0500
1.960	.0250
2.000	.0228
2.054	.0200
2.326	.0100
2.576	.0050
3.000	.0013
3.090	.0010
3.291	.0005
3.719	.0001
4.265	.00001

One application of the standard deviation lies in the modern derivation of the Stanford Binet IQ scores which have a mean of 100 and a standard deviation of 16 (see Figure A.6). A person who is 1 standard deviation above his age group on the raw test score would be assigned an IQ score of 116 (100 + 16), 2 standard deviations above would get an IQ score of 132 [100 + (2 × 16)], ½ standard deviation below the mean would yield an IQ of 92 [100 + (−.5 × 16)], etc.

Figure A.6 Normal distribution. A crowd of 1000 persons viewed from an air-plane might look like this if each person lined up behind a sign giving his standard score on some test. *Caution:* Each type of standard score is in reference to the persons who took that particular test, so that one type of score cannot be compared directly to another. For example, an IQ score gives one's standing compared with the entire population, while an SAT score gives one's standing compared with only those who took the SAT test.

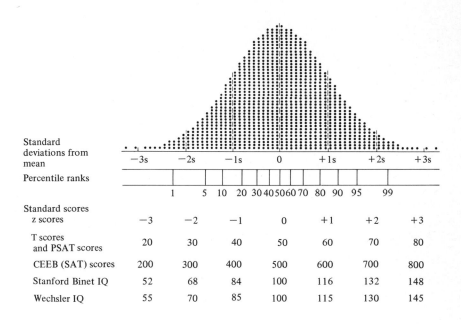

Standard deviations from mean	−3s	−2s	−1s	0	+1s	+2s	+3s
Percentile ranks		1 5 10 20 30 40 50 60 70		80 90 95		99	
Standard scores z scores	−3	−2	−1	0	+1	+2	+3
T scores and PSAT scores	20	30	40	50	60	70	80
CEEB (SAT) scores	200	300	400	500	600	700	800
Stanford Binet IQ	52	68	84	100	116	132	148
Wechsler IQ	55	70	85	100	115	130	145

How many standard deviations above the mean of his age group is a person with an IQ of 124? _____

1.5

Similarly, the mean for College Board (CEEB) scores (SAT) is arbitrarily set at 500 and the standard deviation at 100 (see Figure A.6). An SAT score of 400 indicates that a person is 1 standard deviation below the mean.

An SAT score of 700 would indicate that a person had a raw score _____ standard deviations _____ the mean.

2

---

above

As a prelude to computing the standard deviation, we shall compute a statistic that, while of little utility in itself, is an important module of each of the major techniques to follow. This statistic is the *sum of squares* (symbolized SS).

The fundamental (but in practice the slowest) formula for computing the SS is:

$$SS = \Sigma\ (X - M)^2$$

= the sum of the squared differences between each of the scores and the grand mean

For the data used in the example and practice problems on the means (p. 681), the computations run:

Example problem			*Practice problem*			
X − M	(X − M)	(X − M)²	X	M	X − M	(X − M)²
0 − 4	= −4	16	0	− 3 = ____		____
4 − 4	= 0	0				
2 − 4	= −2	4	2	− __ = ____		____
4 − 4	= 0	0				
6 − 4	= 2	4	2	− __ = ____		____
4 − 4	= 0	0				
4 − 4	= 0	0	3	− __ = ____		____
6 − 4	= 2	4				
6 − 4	= 2	4	8	− __ = ____		____
	SS = 32				SS = ____	

		−3	9
	3	−1	1
	3	−1	1
	3	0	0
	3	5	25
			36

This direct computation of the SS seems simple and fast. The rub comes with natural data where the mean is not rigged to come out as a whole number. As illustration, compute SS for the following distribution: 0, 2, 4, 6, 6, 8. The mean of these six scores is 4.33.

X	M	X − M	(X − M)²
0 − 4.33 =	____		____
2 − 4.33 =	____		____
4 − 4.33 =	____		____
6 − 4.33 =	____		____
6 − 4.33 =	____		____
8 − 4.33 =	____		____
		SS = ____	

−4.33	18.75
−2.33	5.43
−0.33	.11
1.67	2.79
1.67	2.79
3.67	13.47
	43.34

Not only does this squaring of decimal values become tedious when N is large, but the process involves two passes with a calculator or computer; the first to determine the mean, the second to compute and square differences and sum those squares. It is all a bit awkward. There is, fortunately, an algebraically equivalent formula that, while it appears more forbidding at first, is much faster and more convenient in actual practice.

This formula, to be explained shortly, for SS is:

$$SS = \Sigma X^2 - \frac{(\Sigma X)^2}{N}$$

Notes				*Example problem*			*Practice problem*
		X	X²			X	X²
Compute ΣX as	Don	0	0	Ima		0	___
before, but in	Ray	4	16	Lil		2	___
addition square	Jan	2	4	Dot		2	___
each score (X²)	May	4	16	Hal		3	___
and sum up the	Joy	6	36	Sue		8	___
squares (ΣX²).	Jim	4	16				
	Sam	4	16				
	Fay	6	36				
	Art	6	36				
	ΣX = 36				ΣX = ___		
		ΣX² = 176				ΣX² = ___	

	0
	4
	4
	9
	64
15	81

Square the ΣX. Note that $(\Sigma X)^2$ is the symbol. Do not confuse this with ΣX^2. For ΣX^2 we sum first and then square.

$(\Sigma X)^2 = 36^2$
$= 1296$

$(\Sigma X)^2 = (\_\_\_)^2$
$= \_\_\_$

15
225

Divide $(\Sigma X)^2$ by N. The result is called the correction factor (CF).	$CF = (\Sigma X)^2/N$ $= 36^2/9$ $= 1296/9$ $= 144 \quad CF = \underline{\quad}/\underline{\quad}$ $= \underline{\quad}$

225/5	45

Subtract CF from ΣX^2. The result is the corrected sum of squares (SS).	$SS = \Sigma X^2 - CF$ $= 176 - 144$ $= 32 \quad SS = \underline{\quad} - \underline{\quad}$ $= \underline{\quad}$

81 − 45
36

The "correction" the CF makes is to compensate for using raw scores rather than deviation scores (i.e., X − M). When deviation scores are used, since their mean and sum would equal 0.0, the CF drops out.

COMPUTING ESTIMATES OF THE POPULATION VARIANCE AND STANDARD DEVIATION

With the SS computed, computing estimates of population variance and population standard deviation is easy.

Notes	*Example problem*	*Practice problem*
Divide SS by (N − 1). The result is an *estimate of the population variance* (s^2).	$SS = 32$ $N = 9$ $s^2 = SS/N - 1$ $\quad = 32/8$ $\quad = 4$	$s^2 = \underline{\quad}/\underline{\quad}$ $\quad = \underline{\quad}$

36/4
9

The square root of s^2 is an *estimate of the population standard deviation* (s).	$s = \sqrt{4}$ $\quad = 2 \quad s = \sqrt{\underline{\quad}}$ $\qquad = \underline{\quad}$

$$\frac{9}{3}$$

The standard deviation is also used as a descriptive statistic for an existing set of scores. In such a case the scores on hand actually comprise the population. The symbol for the population standard deviation is σ (lower case Greek sigma). The computation differs from that for s in that the SS is divided by N instead of by $N - 1$.

For the example problem, $\sigma = \sqrt{32/9}$; for the practice problem,

$$\sigma = \sqrt{36/\underline{\quad}}$$

5

Confidence intervals

Up to this point inferential methods have been used to give the best estimate of some population value. There is a class of statistical methods directed to giving an interval within which we could feel rather confident the population value lay.

If we wished to know the mean SAT for a college and had the resources to test a random sample of students, we could determine not only that the best estimate was 525 (for example), but also that there was a 95 percent chance that the population mean was in the interval from 514 to 536 (for example).

To get some insight into this approach, consider the cases in Figure A.4 as a population. Let us now take a random sample of 4 scores, compute their mean, and plot it on the X axis.

If the first sample of scores was 40, 50, 70, and 80, place an X where its mean would be on the line below:

20 30 40 50 60 70 80

X

20 30 40 50 60 70 80

In similar manner, place an X on the line below for the means from each of these successive samples:

Sample number	Hypothetical values	Mean
1st	40, 50, 70, 80	60
2nd	40, 50, 55, 55	—
3rd	30, 35, 35, 80	—

4th	45, 45, 50, 60	—
5th	30, 35, 40, 55	—

$$
\begin{array}{c}
X\\
\overline{}\\
20\ \ 30\ \ 40\ \ 50\ \ 60\ \ 70\ \ 80
\end{array}
$$

$$
\begin{array}{c}
60\\
50\\
45\\
50\\
40\\
X\\
X\ X\ X\quad X\\
\overline{}\\
20\ \ 30\ \ 40\ \ 50\ \ 60\ \ 70\ \ 80
\end{array}
$$

Since extreme values would tend to cancel out, the distribution of means should be (less, more) _____ variable than the original distribution of single scores.

---

less

The standard deviation of these means, called the *standard error of the mean* (symbolized s_m), is easily estimated from the formula

$$
s_m = \frac{s}{\sqrt{N}}
$$

where s is the estimated standard deviation and N is the sample size. This relationship pops up in so many formulas and concepts that it may be to the behavioral scientist what $E = mc^2$ is to the physicist.

In the present example, if $s = 10$ and $N = 4$,

$$
s_m = s/\sqrt{N} = \underline{}/\sqrt{\underline{}} = \underline{}
$$

$10/\sqrt{4} = 5$

Compute s_m for the visual perception scores given earlier on p. 681.

Recall that these 9 scores had an s of 2.

$$
s_m = s/\sqrt{N} = 2/\sqrt{9} = 2/3 = .67
$$

Distribution of means

No matter what the shape of the original distribution (skewed, bimodal, rectangular, normal, etc.), a wondrous event occurs with the distribution of the means. It approaches the normal distribution. Since the mean of all the means would naturally approach the population mean, the theoretical distribution of means can be completely described.

With sample sizes equal to 4, the population mean equal to 50, and the population standard deviation equal to 10, the standard error of the means would equal _____, the mean of the means would equal _____, and the distribution would be close to _____.

5

50

normal

In short, the means would be distributed about as in Figure A.5. From the section on the normal distribution, it follows that 95 percent of the means would be within 2 standard errors of the population mean.

The experimenter does not, of course, have a large number of means. He has only his sample mean, and his need is not so much to know how sample means distribute, but how to use the values he has (M, s, and N) to get an idea of how far away the population mean is likely to be from his particular sample mean.

The following medieval spy story may help illustrate the logic

Figure A.7

behind how this is done. There was once a walled village named Gaussburg. In the very center of the village was a famous mint. Figure A.7 is a map of the village and its 100 houses. The large building marked M is the mint. Notice that about 2½ percent of the houses are beyond 2 miles upstream from the mint and about 2½ percent are beyond 2 miles downstream.

A roving band of numismatists from Würm wished to position a spy within 2 miles of the mint. Their problem was to determine how likely it was that the mint would be within 2 miles of any house chosen at random from the classified shouts of the town crier.

The map shows that 95 percent of the houses were within 2 miles of the mint.

The entire band was puzzled about how to use this information until it was realized that, conversely, the mint itself must be within 2 miles of ———— percent of the houses.

95

Feeling 95 percent confident now that the mint would be within 2 miles of any house they might randomly acquire, the numismatists finally had peace of mind. This period later came to be known as the "peace of the Würm mint spy."

In other words, 95 percent of sample means (given that the sample size is moderately large) will fall within about 2 standard errors of the population mean.

You may feel 95 percent confident that, for any particular sample mean you might gather, the population mean is not more than ———— standard errors away.

2

With small samples (below 20 or so) s (and thus s_m) starts to become erratic, so one has to cast the net somewhat further than $2s_m$ on each side of the sample mean in order to have some particular surety (as 95 percent) of capturing the population mean.

In this circumstance one computes s_m just as before, but, instead of multiplying by 2, the s_m is multiplied by a special value (t) which depends on the sample size and the probability with which one wishes to be sure of catching the population mean. For example, if one wishes to set boundaries that have a 95 percent chance of including the population mean, he could use the t table (Table A.2).

In the case of the visual perception scores, since N = 9, the t value is 2.31 (i.e., using Table A.2, N − 1 = 9 − 1 = 8, and the t value for df = 8 is 2.31). Multiplying the standard error of the mean (.67) by t (2.31) yields 1.55. The mean of the population has a 95 percent probability of being within 1.55 of the sample mean. Since the

TABLE A.2

.05 Points for the Distribution of t

N − 1	t
1	12.71
2	4.30
3	3.18
4	2.78
6	2.45
8	2.31
12	2.18
20	2.09
30	2.04
60	2.00
120	1.98
∞	1.96

sample mean is 4, the population mean has a 95 percent probability of being between 2.45 (4 − 1.55) and 5.55 (4 + 1.55). This interval from 2.45 to 5.55 is called the 95 percent confidence interval (see Figure A.8).

If for a sample of $N = 64$ the s is 16 and the mean 10, an estimate of the standard error of the mean would be _____ and the nearest t for the 95 percent would be _____. Their product is _____. The confidence interval thus extends from a lower confidence limit of 10 − _____ = _____ to an upper confidence limit of 10 + _____ = _____.

2

2.0

4

$10 - 4 = 6$

$10 + 4 = 14$

Figure A.8

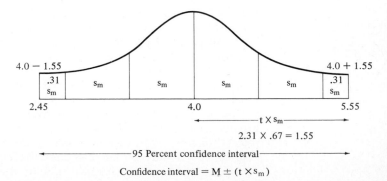

$$2.31 \times .67 = 1.55$$

95 Percent confidence interval

Confidence interval $= M \pm (t \times s_m)$

Testing statistical hypotheses

It is common in the literature of psychology to see a phrase such as, "The difference was found to be significant, at the .05 level." Significant, as used this way, does not mean important or noteworthy, but rather it means probably not due to luck and thus trustworthy. The .05 level refers to the maximum probability that the difference does not really exist in the population. In other words, if the difference between the effect of two treatments is found to be significant at the .05 level, the probability is at least .95 (19 chances out of 20) that there really is a difference in the population values and this is not just a lucky event.

Fortunately, from the standpoint of studying behavior, chance events frequently form predictable patterns. If a particular event falls outside the pattern, it can then be ascribed to nonchance.

For example, suppose that an ESP experiment is conducted in which the tester tosses a coin and concentrates on the result. A subject in the next room tries to read the mind of the experimenter. If the subject were to call 69 out of 100 tosses correctly, it would be true that he could have just been lucky. It is possible to calculate how likely this number of "hits" could occur by luck. The probability is just about (actually a little less than) 1 in 10,000 of doing this well or better when only luck is involved. If we had made a bet that only luck would be involved (such a bet is called the *null hypothesis*), the odds would be:

Probability that the null hypothesis could be correct and that only chance is involved	about 1 in 10,000 (actually c. 00009)
Probability that the null hypothesis is incorrect and should be rejected	about 9,999 in 10,000 (actually c. 99991)

It is obvious in this case that the best bet is with rejecting the null hypothesis. If the subject got 59 correct, the odds would be:

Probability null hypothesis could be correct	about 1 in 20 (actually c. 04431)
Probability null hypothesis is incorrect	about 19 in 20 (actually c. 95569)

In most research it would still be appropriate to reject the null hypothesis if the odds for it are smaller than 1 in 20 (.95), but it is customary not to reject the null hypothesis if the odds for it are greater than 1 in 20. When the kind of error where one incorrectly rejects a null hypothesis seems particularly worth avoiding, 1 chance in 100 may be used as the cutoff point. Results would then be said to be significant at the .01 level. Researchers thus lean over backward to let chance remain as the explanation for results and reject it only when the odds against it become overwhelming.

If one were using the .01 significance level and the probability that the null hypothesis could be correct was only as rare as .02, the appropriate decision would be to (fail to reject, reject) _____ the null hypothesis.

fail to reject

Analysis of variance

A psychologist might want to find out if different treatments make any difference in means. Assume that two different investigators were studying a chemical that was supposed to stimulate growth. The results of their experiments are illustrated in Figure A.9. The mean gain in the groups receiving the chemical was the same for both experiments.

The experiment having the greatest variability within groups is that of Dr. _____. The most convincing experiment that the drug would make a difference in the population is that of Dr. _____.

Aikes

Paines

Figure A.9

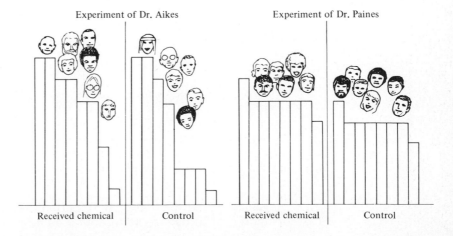

Experiment of Dr. Aikes   Experiment of Dr. Paines

Received chemical | Control   Received chemical | Control

696

INTRODUCTION TO STATISTICAL METHODS IN PSYCHOLOGY

When it is judged that a difference showing up in an experiment probably reflects a difference that would show up in the population, the experimental difference is said to be *significant*.

The difference noted in Dr. Paines experiment appears more likely to be _____.

---

significant

If we know the variability within groups, the relative amount of variability that means between groups will show by chance may be found from tables. We thus can make a hypothesis (the null hypothesis) that chance alone is the cause of any variability in means.

If the means do not behave within the bounds expected by chance, the hypothesis that chance alone is causing any variability in means (i.e., the _____) can then be (rejected, not rejected) _____.

---

null hypothesis

---

rejected

When the null hypothesis is rejected, the difference(s) among means can then be declared _____.

---

significant

High variability *between* groups tends toward (rejecting, not rejecting) _____ the _____.

---

rejecting

---

null hypothesis

High variability *within* groups tends toward (rejecting, not rejecting) _____ the _____.

---

not rejecting

---

null hypothesis

Which of the following combinations is most likely to result in a significant difference being found among the means?

	Estimate of variability between groups	Estimate of variability within groups
A	Low	Low
B	High	Low
C	Low	High
D	High	High

B

Based on the information we have just derived in the preceding problems, we can formulate an equation for the ratio between estimates of variability between groups and within groups.

$$F = \frac{\text{Estimate of variation between}}{\text{Estimate of variation within}}$$

In order to declare differences to be significant, a researcher would find the F ratio to be (high, low) ————.

---

high

The measure of variability to be used in studying F ratios is called the *variance*. Since the decisions are based on estimates of variance between and estimates of variance within, the method is appropriately called Analysis of ————.

Variance

Analysis of Variance (abbreviated ANOVA), while based on ratios of estimates of variance, is actually a tool for deciding the statistical significance of differences between ————.

---

means

Suppose that the visual perception tests (see p. 681) had been given under different conditions to different children, the matching of child to condition being random. The psychologist might now ask if it is probable that any difference in means would appear between different segments of the population if they were to be given different treatments or, equivalently, whether the different treatments caused any difference between groups in the test scores other than the fluctuation that one would expect to occur by chance or, even more simply, whether the treatments really made a difference.

The assignment of treatments might have run something like: Don and Ray were warned of dire consequences should they do badly on the test; Jan, May, and Joy comprise a sample that received neither warning nor encouragement; Jim, Sam, Fay, and Art were told only that they would probably do very well.

The visual perception data, grouped by treatment, would now look like this.

Warned		Neutral		Encouraged	
Subjects	Scores	Subjects	Scores	Subjects	Scores
Don	0	Jan	2	Jim	4
Ray	4	May	4	Sam	4
		Joy	6	Fay	6
				Art	6

Even though it is generally desirable to have the number of subjects in each treatment group be as near to equal as is convenient, notice that equality is not necessary.

For the practice problem assume that Ima and Lil receive one treatment, while Dot, Hal, and Sue receive the other. The breakdown would now be.

Treatment A		Treatment B	
Ima	0	Dot	2
Lil	2	Hal	3
		Sue	8

Don't try to fill in the answers for the next problem now. As you compute values in the next several pages, come back and fill in the blanks.

Notes		Example problem				Practice problem			
		SS	df	MS	F	SS	df	MS	F
As each value is calculated, fill in	TOTAL	32	8			—	—		
the blanks of the	BETWEEN	12 / 2	= 6.0		= 1.8	__ / __	= __	= __	
practice problem	WITHIN	20 / 6	= 3.3			__ / __	= __		
table. Correct entries will be given when the necessary calculations have been completed.									

Recall that the SS for the entire practice problem on p. 681 (TOTAL SS) was:

$$\text{Total SS} = \Sigma X^2 - \frac{(\Sigma X)^2}{N}$$
$$= 0^2 + 2^2 + 2^2 + 3^2 + 8^2 - \frac{(0+2+2+3+8)^2}{5}$$

$$= 0 + 4 + 4 + 9 + 64 - \frac{15^2}{5}$$

$$= 81 - 45 = 36$$

Notes	Example problem	Practice problem
Calculate the SS for the entire sample as before (total SS). The degrees of freedom (df) for TOTAL = N − 1.	TOTAL SS $= \Sigma X^2 - \dfrac{(\Sigma X)^2}{N}$ $= 176 - \dfrac{36^2}{9} = 32$ TOTAL df $= N - 1 = 8$	TOTAL SS = _____ TOTAL df = _____

36
4

The total SS is composed of the SS between groups and the SS within groups. Since the total SS has been calculated, it is only necessary to calculate the SS between groups. The SS within groups can then be obtained by subtraction.

Notes	Example problem	Practice problem
Sum up all scores in a cell, square this total, and divide by the number of scores in the cell. Total up this value for all cells and then subtract CF. The result is the SS between groups (SS_{bg}).	$SS_{bg} = \dfrac{(\Sigma X_1)^2}{n_1} + \dfrac{(\Sigma X_2)^2}{n_2} + \ldots - CF$ $\dfrac{(\Sigma X_1)^2}{n_1} = \dfrac{(0+4)^2}{2} = \dfrac{16}{2} = 8$ $\dfrac{(\Sigma X_2)^2}{n_2} = \dfrac{(2+4+6)^2}{3} = \dfrac{144}{3} = 48$ $\dfrac{(\Sigma X_3)^2}{n_3} = \dfrac{(4+4+6+6)^2}{4} = \dfrac{400}{4} = 100$ $SS_{bg} = 8 + 48 + 100 - 144$ $= 12$	$SS_{bg} =$ _____

13.33

With k equal to the number of groups, the df between groups (df_{bg}) is equal to k − 1.	$df_{bg} = k - 1$ $= 3 - 1$ $= 2$	$df_{bg} =$ _____

1

The SS within groups (SS_{wg}) is equal to the total SS (SS_{Tot}) minus the SS between groups (SS_{bg}).	$SS_{wg} = SS_{Tot} - SS_{bg}$ $= 32 - 12$ $= 20$	$SS_{wg} = \underline{\qquad} - \underline{\qquad}$ $= \underline{\qquad}$

$36 - 13.33$
22.67

Similarly, the degrees of freedom within groups (df_{wg}) is equal to the total df (df_{Tot}) minus the df between groups (df_{bg}).	$df_{wg} = df_{Tot} - df_{bg}$ $= 8 - 2$ $= 6$	$df_{wg} = \underline{\qquad}$

3

For each of the components of the total variance, the estimate of variance or *mean square* (MS) is equal to the SS divided by the df.

Notes	Example problem	Practice problem
For MS_{bg} divide SS_{bg} by df_{bg}.	$MS_{bg} = SS_{bg}/df_{bg}$ $= 12/2$ $= 6$	$MS_{bg} = \underline{\qquad} / \underline{\qquad}$ $= \underline{\qquad}$

$13.33/1$
13.33

For MS_{wg} divide SS_{wg} by df_{wg}.	$MS_{wg} = SS_{wg}/df_{wg}$ $= 20/6$ $= 3.33$	$MS_{wg} = \underline{\qquad} / \underline{\qquad}$ $= \underline{\qquad}$

$22.67/3$
7.56

For F divide MS_{bg} by MS_{wg}.	$F = MS_{bg}/MS_{wg}$ $= 6/3.33$ $= 1.80$	$F = \underline{\qquad} / \underline{\qquad}$ $= \underline{\qquad}$

$13.33/7.56$
1.76

The completed ANOVA table for the practice problem should now look like:

	SS	df	MS	F
TOTAL	36.00	4		
BETWEEN	13.33	1	13.33	1.76
WITHIN	22.67	3	7.56	

The calculated F can now be compared with the values in a table showing F values that cut off the most extreme 5 percent of the chance distribution (see Table A.3). To use this table merely follow across the top until the column for the df between groups is reached. For the example problem, $df_{bg} = 2$. Then follow the left hand column down to the df within groups. For the example problem, $df_{wg} = 6$. The table value is 5.14.

TABLE A.3
.05 Points for the Distribution of F

Degrees of Freedom within Groups	DEGREES OF FREEDOM BETWEEN GROUPS		
	1	2	3
1	161.4	199.5	215.7
2	18.51	19.00	19.16
3	10.13	9.55	9.28
4	7.71	6.94	6.59
6	5.99	5.14	4.76
8	5.32	4.46	4.07
12	4.75	3.88	3.49
20	4.35	3.49	3.10
30	4.17	3.32	2.92
60	4.00	3.15	2.76
120	3.92	3.07	2.68
∞	3.84	2.99	2.60

In order for us to reject the null hypothesis (that no differences exist among the means) our calculated F would have to equal or exceed (meet or beat) this table value. Since our 1.80 does not meet or beat 5.14, we cannot reject the null hypothesis. We would report, "No significant difference (.05 level) was detected among the means."

For the practice problem, our calculated F was _____, the df_{bg} was _____, df_{wg} was _____. The critical F would be _____.

1.76
1
3
10.13

Since our calculated F (fails to, does) _____ meet or beat the table F, our decision follows that we (do not have evidence to, may)

_____ reject the null hypothesis and conclude that (no evidence was found to suggest, it is most probable) _____ that the treatments make a difference in the population.

> fails to
> do not have evidence to
> no evidence was found
>   to suggest

When only two means were being compared, a technique called the t test has been much used. It involves just a bit more computation than analysis of variance and offers little in the way of advantages. If computation of a t between two independent means is called for, just compute F and take its square root. When only two groups are being compared, $t = \sqrt{F}$. The same t table (Table A.2) used in setting a confidence interval is used in the t test.

Compare the t value from Table A.2 for $N - 1 = 60$ which is _____ with the F value from Table A.3 for 1 df between (since there are two groups) and 60 df within which is _____.

> 2.00

> 4.00

Correlation coefficient

We may want to find out how well variables relate to each other. Assume that in addition to the set of scores for a test on visual perception we analyzed previously there is a second set for a test on reading skill given to the same children after three months of reading instruction. The data might be:

	Visual perception scores	Reading scores
Don	0	2
Ray	4	2
Jan	2	3
May	4	4
Joy	6	4
Jim	4	7
Sam	4	8
Fay	6	7
Art	6	8

See Figure A.2 for a scatter diagram of these scores.

A psychologist might be curious about the degree of relationship between how well an individual does on the visual perception test and how well he does later on the reading test. This relating together is called correlation. In order to correlate scores they must be paired. For example, in the data above the 0 that Don received on the visual perception test is paired with his score of 2 on the reading test. The members of the pair of scores were linked because the same person made both scores. This is probably the most common reason for pairing, but the correlation can also be studied between scores made by identical twins, husbands and wives, and so forth.

There does seem to be a tendency for those who do well on the visual perception test to also do well on the reading test. This suggests a positive correlation. Later on we will show how the degree of correlation can be expressed numerically.

If one of two paired variables can be considered the prior, causative, or more independent variable of the two, it is given the symbol X. The variable which follows the other in time or tends to be dependent on the other is symbolized as Y. However, even a high correlation does not prove a cause-effect relationship. You could predict days of high ice cream sales by measuring the softness of asphalt roads. Obviously, the soft roads do not stimulate ice cream sales and ice cream sales do not soften roads. They are apparently both dependent upon a third variable. Even when there is a cause-effect relationship, it is frequently not clear which is the cause and which is the effect. The assigning of X and Y labels is thus more a matter of convenience than of philosophical position.

In the example above, visual perception scores would be symbolized by _____ and reading scores by _____.

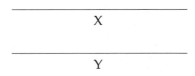

The most important measure of degree of straight-line or linear correlation is the *product moment correlation coefficient* (symbolized "r"). Values for r go all the way from +1 meaning perfect positive linear correlation (that is, if you know the value of one variable for a person, you could accurately predict that the value of the other variable for him would be the same) to −1 which signifies a perfect negative linear correlation. Values in nature usually fall somewhere between −1 and +1. A correlation of 0.0 indicates that knowing the value of one variable sheds no light at all on the value of the second.

The scatter diagrams in Figure A.10 may help give a feel for the shape of various sized correlations.

Figure A.10

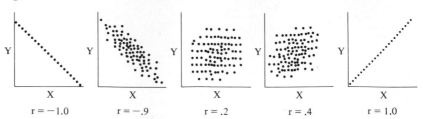

$$r=-1.0 \quad r=-.9 \quad r=.2 \quad r=.4 \quad r=1.0$$

In computing the correlation coefficient, a value similar to the SS must be found; it is the sum of products (SP). The SP involves a merger of the two variables and, just as an estimate of variance resulted when the SS was divided by $N-1$, the SP yields a covariance when divided by $N-1$ (the number of pairs minus 1).

The formula for the SP, to be explained below, is:

$$SP = \Sigma XY - \frac{(\Sigma X)\,(\Sigma Y)}{N}$$

		Example problem				*Practice problem*	
Notes	X	Y	XY		X	Y	XY
X represents the scores	$0 \times 2 =$		0		0	3	___
on the visual percep-	$4 \times 2 =$		8				
tion test. Y is the score	$2 \times 3 =$		6		2	1	___
on the reading test.	$4 \times 4 =$		16				
Each Y score is	$6 \times 4 =$		24		2	2	___
multiplied by its	$4 \times 7 =$		28				
corresponding X	$4 \times 8 =$		32		3	3	___
score. The products	$6 \times 7 =$		42				
are then summed	$6 \times 8 =$		48		8	1	___
(ΣXY).	$\Sigma X = 36$				$\Sigma X =$ ___		
		$\Sigma Y = 45$				$\Sigma Y =$ ___	
		$\Sigma XY = 204$					$\Sigma XY =$ ___

$$\begin{array}{r} 0 \\ 2 \\ 4 \\ 9 \\ \underline{8} \\ \end{array}$$

$$15 \quad 10 \quad 23$$

Notes	*Example problem*	*Practice problem*
Note the similarity of the formula for SP to that for SS. With SS it was the sum of all the X times X (i.e., itself) and then (ΣX) times (ΣX). With SP it is the sum of all the X times their respective Y and then (ΣX) times (ΣY).	$SP = \Sigma XY - (\Sigma X)(\Sigma Y)/N$ $= 204 - (36)(45)/9$ $= 204 - 180 = 24$	$SP = \underline{\quad} - \underline{\quad} / \underline{\quad}$ $= \underline{\quad}$

$$23 - (15)(10)/5$$
$$-7$$

The SS for Y (SS_y) will be needed and is computed in the same way as SS_x.

Y	Y²	Y	Y²
2	4	3	_____
2	4		
3	9	1	_____
4	16		
4	16	2	_____
7	49		
8	64	3	_____
7	49		
8	64	1	_____
45	275		

$$SS_y = \Sigma Y^2 - (\Sigma Y)^2/N$$
$$= 275 - 45^2/9$$
$$= 50$$

$SS_y = \underline{\quad} - \underline{\quad} / \underline{\quad}$
$= \underline{\quad}$

9
1
4
9
1
24
$24 - 10^2/5$
4

The formula for r is:

$$r = \frac{SP}{\sqrt{SS_x SS_y}}$$

Notes	*Example problem*	*Practice problem*
Collecting the needed statistics from previous calculations.	$SP = 24$ $SS_x = 32$ $SS_y = 50$	$SP =$ _____ (see p. 705) $SS_x =$ _____ (see p. 687) $SS_y =$ _____ (see p. 705)

$$-7$$
$$36$$
$$4$$

$$r = SP/\sqrt{SS_x SS_y}$$

$$= 24/\sqrt{(32)(50)} = \underline{\quad}/\sqrt{(\ )(\ )}$$

$$= 24/\sqrt{1600} \quad = \underline{\quad}/\sqrt{\underline{\quad}}$$

$$= 24/40 \quad\quad = \underline{\quad}/\underline{\quad}$$

$$= .60 \quad\quad\quad = \underline{\quad}$$

$$-7/\sqrt{(36)(4)}$$
$$-7/\sqrt{144}$$
$$-7/12$$
$$-.58$$

The r is also used as a descriptive statistic. In such a case, the computations are performed exactly as above.

You may wish to know if a correlation from some sample is significant. It's easy. Just enter Table A.4 with the number of pairs minus 2 (N − 2) and, in order to reject the null hypothesis of no rela-

TABLE A.4
.05 Points for the Distribution of r

N − 2 (Degrees of freedom)	r
1	.997
2	.950
3	.878
4	.811
6	.707
8	.632
12	.532
20	.423
30	.349
60	.250
120	.179

tionship in the population, your r has to be as large or larger than the table value (either in a positive or negative direction).

In the earlier calculations of r, a sample of 9 pairs of scores was found to have an r of .60. Would this indicate a probable positive correlation in the population? _____

_____

No. With $df = 9 - 2 = 7$ the r needed would be somewhere between .632 and .707. With our computed r of only .60 we cannot reject luck as the explanation for the correlation in the sample.

Finding out if frequencies are different than expected (chi square)

Analysis of variance deals with means, but sometimes a psychologist wishes to study frequencies. As an example, assume a six room house where only men were allowed in one side and only women in the other. Different drinks were served in each set of rooms so that the house plan would look like Figure A.11.

Figure A.11

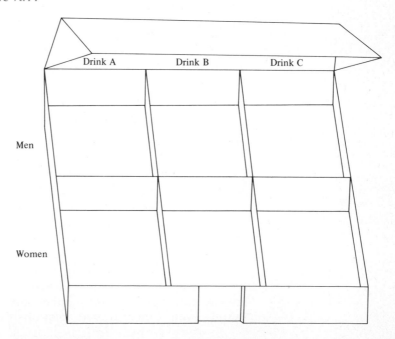

A large party is now held in the house and when it gets going well, we gently lift the roof off the house and, peering inside, we see what is illustrated in Figure A.12.

Figure A.12

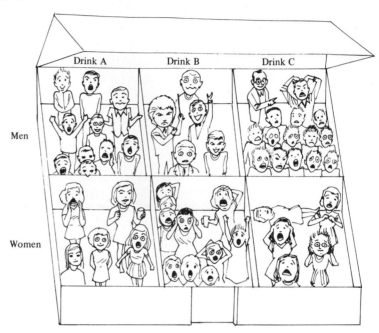

Observe the frequency in each category (room).
What is the *observed frequency* (O) in each category?

	Drink A	Drink B	Drink C
Men	_____	_____	_____
Women	_____	_____	_____

And now to find out if there is some relationship between sex and drink preferred? It looks like women might tend toward drink B and men toward drink C, but chance could cause some effect in our sample even if there was no relationship in the population.

	Drink A	Drink B	Drink C
Men	10	5	15
Women	5	10	5

It's the null hypothesis approach again. We first hypothesize that there is no relationship between sex and drink preferred.

If there were no relationship, given that 30 out of the 50 people are men (60 percent), what percent of those preferring drink C would you *expect* to be men? _____

60 percent

Since 20 persons preferred drink C and you would expect 60 percent to be men, what would be the expected frequency (E) for men preferring drink C? _____

60 percent of 20 = 12

We can summarize the separate effects by totaling around the margins. These totals are called *marginals.*

Complete the marginals for this table.

	Drink A	Drink B	Drink C	
Men	10	5	15	30
Women	5	10	5	—
	—	—	—	

15   15   20   30
                        20

The sum of the expected frequencies in one column (or line) also equals the marginal.

Since 20 persons prefer drink C and the E for men is 12, the E for women for drink C must be _____.

$$20 - 12 = 8$$

In case this intuitive approach to getting E's isn't clear to you, an alternate formula may help.

$$\text{E for any square} = \frac{\text{(Column marginal)(Row marginal)}}{\text{Grand total for all squares}}$$

For the present example,

$$\text{E men, drink B} = \frac{15 \times 30}{50} = \frac{450}{50} = 9$$

Compute the E for the remaining cells and complete this table.

E = ___ O = 10	E = ___ O = 5	E = 12 O = 15	30
E = ___ O = 5	E = ___ O = 10	E = 8 O = 5	20
15	15	20	

9	9	12
6	6	8

With O and E for each cell in hand, the final calculations are easy. For each separate cell, compute $(E = O)^2/E$.

$(E - O)^2/E = (9 - 10)^2/9$ $= -1^2/9$ $= 0.111$ _____	_____	_____
_____	_____	_____

_____

	Drink A	Drink B	Drink C
Men	0.111	1.778	0.750
Women	0.167	2.667	1.125

The sum of $(E - O)^2/E$ for all of these cells is called *chi square*. For the present problem chi square $(X^2) = 0.111 + 1.778 + 0.750 + 0.167 +$ _____ + _____ = _____ .

_____

2.667
1.125
6.598

If the observed frequencies were quite different from the expected, we would find each $(E - O)^2$ and thus $\Sigma(E - O)^2/E$ to be relatively (small, large) _____.

_____

Large

A relatively large chi square should indicate that the E's differed more from the O's than is likely by chance. As to how large a value for chi square is needed to reject the null hypothesis of no difference in the population, we again consult a table (Table A.5). To enter the table, find the degrees of freedom by multiplying the number of rows minus 1 by the number of columns minus 1. In this case it is $(3 - 1) \times (2 - 1) = 2$.

TABLE A.5
.05 Points for the Distribution of Chi Square

Degrees of freedom	Chi square
1	3.84
2	5.99
3	7.81
4	9.49
6	12.59
8	15.51
12	21.03
20	31.41
30	43.77
60	79.08
120	146.57

In the present problem, what value of chi square would we have to meet or beat in order to declare a significant (.05 level) relationship between sex and preferred drink? _____

5.99

Since our computed X^2 of 6.598 beats the critical value of 5.99, at the .05 level, we may now (reject, fail to reject) the null hypothesis of no relationship.

---

reject

Two precautions and an extension: chi square should not be used unless at least 80 percent of the E's are greater than 5. If there is only 1 degree of freedom, an adjustment is necessary. There are other applications for chi square such as testing to see if a population distribution could possibly be some particular shape. For expansion on these topics, see just about any elementary statistics text.

Some relationships

The comparisons to be made only hint at the order and elegance to be found in the study of statistics.

From Table A.1 on the normal distribution, the z value that would cut off .025 (i.e., 2½ percent) of one tail and thus a total of .05 in both tails is _____. In the t distribution (Table A.2), the .05 value for ∞ df is _____.

1.96

1.96

What is this value squared? _____. From Table A.3, what is the value of F for 1 df between and ∞ df within? _____ From Table A.5 what is the value of chi square for 1 df? _____

3.84

3.84

3.84

Critical r values can be calculated from the formula:

$$r = \sqrt{\frac{t^2}{(N-2) + t^2}}$$

From Table A.4, the critical r for N = 62 (i.e., df = 60) is _____. The 60 df value for t^2 = _____, so if the number of pairs is 62, the critical r = _____.

$$
\begin{aligned}
r &= \sqrt{t^2/(N-2) + t^2} \\
&= \sqrt{4/(62-2) + 4} \\
&= \sqrt{4/64} \\
&= \sqrt{1/16} \\
&= 1/4 = \underline{\qquad}
\end{aligned}
$$

.250   *(equation continues)*

$$\frac{\rule{3cm}{0pt}}{4}$$

$$\frac{\rule{3cm}{0pt}}{.250}$$

Bibliography

Abt, Clark. *Serious Games.* New York: Viking Press, 1971.

Ach, N. *Über die Bergriffsbildung.* Bamberg, Germany: Buchner, 1921.

Adams, James. *Conceptual Blockbusting.* San Francisco: Freeman, 1974.

Ahmann, J. Stanley. *How Much Are Our Young People Learning? The Story of the National Assessment.* Bloomington, Ind.: Phi Delta Kappa Educational Foundation, 1976.

Aiken, Edwin, Gary Thomas, and William Shennum. "Memory for a Lecture: Effects of Notes, Lecture Rate, and Informational Density." *Journal of Educational Psychology* 67 (1975): 439–444.

Allport, Gordon. *Pattern and Growth in Personality.* New York: Holt, Rinehart and Winston, 1961.

Alper, Thelma. "Achievement Motivation in College Women." *American Psychologist* 29 (1974): 194–203.

Anastasti, Anne. *Psychological Testing.* New York: Macmillan, 1976.

Angelino, H., J. Dollins, and E. V. Mech. "Trends in the Fears and Worries of School Children as Related to Socioeconomic Status and Age." *Journal of Genetic Psychology* 89 (1956): 263–276.

Anglin, Jeremy, ed. *Beyond the Information Given.* New York: Norton, 1973.

Anthony, E. James. "The Behavior Disorders of Childhood." In *Carmichael's Manual of Child Psychology,* edited by Paul Mussen. New York: Wiley, 1970.

Arnheim, Rudolf. *Film as Art.* Berkeley: University of California Press, 1957.

———. *Visual Thinking.* Berkeley: University of California Press, 1969.

Ausubel, David. *Educational Psychology: A Cognitive View.* New York: Holt, Rinehart and Winston, 1968.

Baker, Justine. *The Computer in the School.* Bloomington, Ind.: Phi Delta Kappa Educational Foundation, 1975.

Bandura, Albert. "Modeling Theory: Some Traditions, Trends, and Disputes." In *Recent Trends in Social Learning Theory,* edited by Ross Parke. New York: Academic Press, 1972.

———. *Aggression.* Englewood Cliffs, N.J.: Prentice-Hall, 1973.

Bandura, Albert, Dorothea Ross, and Sheila Ross. "Imitation of Film-Mediated Aggressive Models." *Journal of Abnormal and Social Psychology* 66 (1963): 3–11.

Bandura, Albert and Richard Walters. *Social Learning and Personality Development.* New York: Holt, Rinehart and Winston, 1963.

Barron, Frank. "The Psychology of Imagination." *Scientific American* 199 (1958): 150–166.

Barron, Frank and A. Roe. "A Predictor Committee Report." In *The Second University of Utah Research Conference on the Identification of Creative Talent,* edited by C. W. Taylor. Salt Lake City: University of Utah Press, 1958.

Bartlett, F. C. *Remembering: A Study in Experimental and Social Psychology.* London: Cambridge University Press, 1932.

Barzun, Jacques. *The Teacher in America.* Boston: Little, Brown, 1954.

Becker, Wesley. "Applications of Behavior Principles in Typical Classrooms." In *Behavior Modification in Education,* edited by Carl Thoreson. *The Seventy-second Yearbook of the National Society for the Study of Education.* University of Chicago Press, 1973.

Benjamin, Harold. *The Saber-Tooth Curriculum.* New York: McGraw-Hill, 1939.

Bereiter, Carl and Siegfried Engelmann. *Teaching Disadvantaged Children in the Preschool.* Englewood Cliffs, N.J.: Prentice-Hall, 1966.

Berelson, Bernard and Gary Steiner. *Human Behavior: An Inventory of Scientific Findings.* New York: Harcourt Brace Jovanovich, 1964.

Berliner, David and N. L. Gage. "The Psychology of Teaching Methods." In *The Seventy-fifth Yearbook of the National Society for the Study of Education,* edited by N. L. Gage. University of Chicago Press, 1976.

Bigge, Morris. *Learning Theories for Teachers.* New York: Harper & Row, 1976.

Binet, Alfred and Theophile Simon. *The Development of Intelligence in Children.* Translated by E. S. Kite. Baltimore, Md.: Williams & Wilkins, 1916.

Birch, Jack. *Mainstreaming: Educable Mentally Retarded Children in Regular Classes.* Reston, Va.: Council for Exceptional Children, 1974.

Blake, Judith. "The Changing Status of Women in Developed Countries." *Scientific American* 231 (September 1974): 136–147.

Blatt, Moshe and Lawrence Kohlberg. "Effects of Classroom Discussions Upon Children's Level of Moral Judgment." In *Recent Research in Moral Development,* edited by Lawrence Kohlberg. New York: Holt, Rinehart and Winston, 1975.

Block, James and Lorin Anderson. *Mastery Learning in Classroom Instruction.* New York: Macmillan, 1975.

Bloom, Benjamin. *Stability and Change in Human Characteristics.* New York: Wiley, 1964.

———. "An Introduction to Mastery Learning." In *Schools, Society, and Mastery Learning,* edited by James Block. New York: Holt, Rinehart and Winston, 1974.

———, ed. *Taxonomy of Educational Objectives, Handbook I: Cognitive Domain.* New York: McKay, 1956.

Bloom, Benjamin and Lois Broder. *Problem-Solving Processes of College Students.* Supplementary Educational Monograph no. 73. University of Chicago Press, 1950.

Bloom, Benjamin, J. Thomas Hastings, and George Madaus. *Handbook on Formative and Summative Evaluation of Student Learning.* New York: McGraw-Hill, 1971.

Boring, Edwin. *A History of Experimental Psychology.* Englewood Cliffs, N.J.: Prentice-Hall, 1950.

Brandhorst, Ted. "ERIC: Reminders of How It Can Help You." *Phi Delta Kappan* 58 (1977): 627–638.

Brightly, Brian. "The Effect of Television." In *The New Children,* edited by John Travers. Stamford, Conn.: Greylock Publishers, 1976.

Broadbent, D. E. "Flow of Information Within the Organism." *Journal of Verbal Learning and Verbal Behavior* 2 (1963): 34–39.

———. "The Well-Ordered Mind." *American Educational Research Journal* 3 (1966): 281–295.

Broadhurst, P. L. "Emotionality and the Yerkes-Dodson Law." *Journal of Experimental Psychology* 54 (1957): 345–352.

Brophy, Jere and Thomas Good. *Teacher-Student Relationships: Causes and Consequences.* New York: Holt, Rinehart and Winston, 1974.

Brown, Frederick. *Principles of Educational and Psychological Testing.* Hinsdale, Ill.: Dryden Press, 1970.

Brown, Roger. *A First Language: The Early Stages.* Cambridge, Mass.: Harvard University Press, 1973.

Bruininks, Robert and John Rynder. "Alternatives to Special Class Placement for Educable Mentally Retarded Children." *Focus on Exceptional Children* 3 (1971): 1–12.

Bruner, Jerome. *The Process of Education.* Cambridge, Mass.: Harvard University Press, 1960.

——. *On Knowing: Essays for the Left Hand.* Cambridge, Mass.: Harvard University Press, 1962.

——. *Toward a Theory of Instruction.* Cambridge, Mass.: Harvard University Press, 1966a.

——. "Some Elements of Discovery." In *Learning by Discovery*, edited by Lee Shulman and Evan Keisler. Skokie, Ill.: Rand McNally, 1966b.

——. *The Relevance of Education.* New York: Norton, 1971.

Bruner, Jerome, R. R. Oliver, and P. M. Greenfield. *Studies in Cognitive Growth.* New York: Wiley, 1966.

Bugelski, B. R. *The Psychology of Learning.* New York: Holt, Rinehart and Winston, 1956.

——. *The Psychology of Learning Applied to Teaching.* Indianapolis: Bobbs-Merrill, 1964, 1971.

Bunderson, C. Victor and Gerald Faust. "Programmed and Computer-Assisted Instruction." In *The Seventy-fifth Yearbook of the National Society for the Study of Education*, edited by N. L. Gage. University of Chicago Press, 1976.

Burdin, Joel. *Three Views of Competency-Based Teacher Education I.: Theory.* Bloomington, Ind.: Phi Delta Kappa Educational Foundation, 1974.

Burmeister, Lou. *Reading Strategies for Secondary School Teachers.* Reading, Mass.: Addison-Wesley, 1974.

Buros, O. K., ed. *Eighth Mental Measurements Yearbook.* Highland Park, N.J.: Gryphon Press, 1976.

Burton, William. *The Guidance of Learning Activities.* Englewood Cliffs, N.J.: Prentice-Hall, 1962.

Bushell, Don. "The Design of Classroom Contingencies." In *Behavior Modification: Applications to Education.* New York: Academic Press, 1974.

Butts, R. Freeman and Lawrence Cremin. *A History of Education in American Culture.* New York: Holt, Rinehart and Winston, 1953.

Case, Robbie. "Piaget's Theory of Child Development and Its Implications." *Phi Delta Kappan* 55 (1973): 20–25.

Chall, Jeanne. *Learning to Read: The Great Debate.* New York: McGraw-Hill, 1967.

Charters, W. W. "The Social Background of Teaching." In *Handbook of Research on Teaching*, edited by N. L. Gage. Chicago: Rand McNally, 1963.

Chauncey, Henry and John Dobbin. *Testing: Its Place in Education Today.* New York: Harper & Row, 1963.

Chomsky, Noam. *Syntactic Structures.* The Hague: Mouton, 1957.

——. *Aspects of the Theory of Syntax.* Cambridge, Mass.: The M.I.T. Press, 1965.

Christian, Chester. "Social and Psychological Implications of Bilingual Literacy." In *The Bilingual Child*, edited by Antonia Simoes, Jr. New York: Academic Press, 1976.

Clarizio, Harvey and George McCoy. *Behavior Disorders in Children.* New York: Crowell, 1976.

Clifford, M. and E. Walster. "The Effect of Physical Attractiveness on Teacher Expectations." *Sociology of Education* 46 (1973): 17–43.

Cofer, C. N. and M. A. Appley. *Motivation: Theory and Research.* New York: Wiley, 1964.

Cohen, David and Michael Ganet. "Reforming Educational Policy with Applied Research." *Harvard Educational Review* 45 (1975): 17–43.

Coleman, James C. *Abnormal Psychology and*

Modern Life. 5th ed. Chicago: Scott, Foresman, 1976.

Coleman, James S. *Equality of Educational Opportunity.* Washington, D.C.: U.S. Department of Health, Education and Welfare, Office of Education, 1966.

——. *Youth: Transition to Adulthood.* University of Chicago Press, 1974.

Combs, Arthur and Donald Snygg. *Individual Behavior.* New York: Harper & Row, 1959.

Combs, Arthur, Robert Blume, Arthur Newman, and Hannelore Wass. *The Professional Education of Teachers.* Boston: Allyn & Bacon, 1974.

Conway, Lee. "Classroom in the Sky: A Power Trip for Disadvantaged Youth." *Phi Delta Kappan* 57 (1976): 570–574.

Coolidge, J. C., M. L. Witler, E. Tessman, and S. Waldfogel. "School Phobia in Adolescence: A Manifestation of Severe Character Disturbance." *American Journal of Orthopsychiatry* 30 (1960): 599–607.

Coolidge, J. C., R. D. Brodie, and B. Feeney. "A Ten-Year Follow-up Study of Sixty-six School-Phobic Children." *American Journal of Orthopsychiatry* 34 (1964): 675–684.

Corwin, Ronald. "The New Teaching Profession." In *Teacher Education,* edited by Kevin Ryan. *The Seventy-fourth Yearbook of the National Society for the Study of Education.* University of Chicago Press, 1975.

Cratty, Bryant. *Perceptual and Motor Development in Infants and Children.* New York: Macmillan, 1970.

Cravioto, Joaquin and Else Delicardie. "Mental Performance in School Age Children." *American Journal of Disabled Children* November, 1970, 404–410.

Cressey, Marie Skodak. "Mental Retardation: Past, Present, and Future." *American Psychologist* 30 (1975): 800–808.

Cronbach, Lee. *Essentials of Psychological Testing.* New York: Harper & Row, 1970.

Crowder, Norman. "Automatic Tutoring by Means of Intrinsic Programming." In *Automatic Teaching: The State of the Art,* edited by E. Galanter. New York: Wiley, 1959.

Cruickshank, William. "The Development of Education for Exceptional Children." In *Education of Exceptional Children and Youth,* edited by William Cruickshank and G. Orville Johnson. Englewood Cliffs, N.J.: Prentice-Hall, 1975*a.*

——. "The Exceptional Child in the Schools." In *Education of Exceptional Children and Youth,* edited by William Cruickshank and G. Orville Johnson. Englewood Cliffs, N.J.: Prentice-Hall, 1975*b.*

Cruickshank, William and Henry De Young. "Educational Practices with Exceptional Children." In *Education of Exceptional Children and Youth,* edited by William Cruickshank and G. Orville Johnson. Englewood Cliffs, N.J.: Prentice-Hall, 1975.

Cruickshank, William and G. Orville Johnson, eds. *Education of Exceptional Children and Youth.* Englewood Cliffs, N.J.: Prentice-Hall, 1975.

Dacey, John. "Moral Education in Early Childhood." In *The New Children,* edited by John F. Travers. Stamford, Conn.: Greylock Publishers, 1976.

De Cecco, John and Arlene Richards. "Civil War in the High Schools." *Psychology Today* 9 (November 1975): 51–56, 120.

Denemark, George. "Human Variability and Learning: Implications for Education." In *Human Variability,* edited by Walter Waetjen. Washington, D.C.: Association for Supervision and Curriculum Development, 1961.

Dennis, Wayne. "Causes of Retardation Among Institutional Children." *Journal of Genetic Psychology* 96 (1960): 47–59.

D'Evelyn, Katherine. *Meeting Children's Emotional Needs.* Englewood Cliffs, N.J.: Prentice-Hall, 1957.

Dewey, John. *Democracy and Education.* New York: Macmillan, 1916.

——. *How We Think.* Boston: Heath, 1933.

Dion, K. "Physical Attractiveness and Evaluation of Children's Transgressions." *Journal of Personality and Social Psychology* 24 (1972): 207–213.

Dow, Peter. "MACOS: The Study of Human Behavior as One Road to Survival." *Phi Delta Kappan* 57 (1975): 79–81.

Dreikurs, Rudolf, Bernice Grunwald, and Floy Pepper. *Maintaining Sanity in the Classroom.* New York: Harper & Row, 1971.

Duncker, Karl. "On Problem Solving." Translated by Lynn S. Lees. *Psychological Monographs* 58 (1945). Whole No. 270.

Dunn, Lloyd. "Special Education for the Mildly Retarded—Is Much of It Justifiable?" *Exceptional Children* 35 (1968): 5–22.

Early, Margaret. "Important Research in Reading and Writing." *Phi Delta Kappan* 57 (1976): 298–301.

Ebel, Robert. *Measuring Educational Achievement.* Englewood Cliffs, N.J.: Prentice-Hall, 1965.

Eccles, John. "The Physiology of Imagination." *Scientific American* 199 (1958): 48, 135–142.

Eichorn, Dorothy. "Biological, Psychological, and Socio-Cultural Aspects of Adolescence and Youth." In *Youth: Transition to Adulthood,* edited by James S. Coleman. University of Chicago Press, 1974.

Elkind, David. "Giant in the Nursery—Jean Piaget." *The New York Times Magazine,* 26 May 1968.

——. "Erik Erikson's Eight Ages of Man." *The New York Times Magazine,* 5 April 1970.

Ellis, Henry C. *The Transfer of Learning.* New York: Macmillan, 1965.

Ellson, Douglas. "Tutoring." In *The Psychology of Teaching Methods,* edited by N. L. Gage. *The Seventy-fifth Yearbook of the National Society for the Study of Education.* University of Chicago Press, 1976.

Erikson, Erik. *Childhood and Society.* New York: Norton, 1950.

——. *Identity: Youth and Crisis.* New York: Norton, 1968.

Escalona, Sibylle. "Infancy: Off to a Good Start." *The New Encyclopedia of Child Care and Guidance.* New York: Doubleday, 1968.

Farb, Peter. *Word Play.* New York: Knopf, 1973.

Farina, Alfred and George Wheaton. "Development of a Taxonomy of Human Performance: The Task Characteristic Approach to Performance Prediction." In *ISAS Catalog of Selected Documents in Psychology* 3 (1973): 26–27.

Feldhusen, John. "Student Views of the Ideal Educational Psychology Course." *Educational Psychologist* 8 (1970): 7–9.

Feshbach, Seymour. "Aggression." In *Carmichael's Manual of Child Psychology,* edited by Paul Mussen. New York: Wiley, 1970.

Flavell, John. *The Developmental Psychology of Jean Piaget.* New York: Van Nostrand, 1963.

Fleishman, Edwin. "Toward a Taxonomy of Human Performance." *American Psychologist* 39 (1975): 301–313.

Fleishman, Edwin and Walter E. Hempel, Jr. "The Relation Between Abilities and Improvement with Practice in a Visual Discrimination Reaction Task." *Journal of Experimental Psychology* 49 (1955): 301–312.

Fleming, Joyce. "The State of the Apes." *Psychology Today* 7 (January 1974): 31–38, 43–46.

Flesch, Rudolf. *Why Johnny Can't Read.* New York: Harper & Row, 1955.

Frank, Lawrence. *The Fundamental Needs of the Child.* New York: National Association for Mental Health, 1952.

Frymier, Jack. *Motivation and Learning in School.* Bloomington, Ind.: Phi Delta Kappa Educational Foundation, 1974.

Fuller, F. "Concerns of Teachers: A Developmental Conceptualization." *American Educational Research Journal* 6 (1969): 207–226.

Fuller, Frances and Oliver Brown. "Becoming a Teacher." In *The Seventy-fourth Yearbook of the National Society for the Study of Education,* edited by Kevin Ryan. University of Chicago Press, 1975.

Furlong, William. "The Fun in Fun." *Psychology Today* 10 (June 1976): 35–38, 80.

Furth, Hans and Harry Wachs. *Thinking Goes to School: Piaget's Theory in Practice.* New York: Oxford University Press, 1975.

Gage, N. L. "Paradigms for Research on Teaching." In *Handbook of Research on Teaching,* edited by N. L. Gage. Chicago: Rand McNally, 1963.

——. "Theories of Teaching." In *The Sixty-third*

Yearbook of the National Study of Education, edited by Ernest R. Hilgard. University of Chicago Press, 1964.

Gagné, Robert. *Essentials of Learning for Instruction*. New York: Dryden Press, 1974.

——. "The Learning Basis of Teaching Methods." In *The Psychology of Teaching Methods*, edited by N. L. Gage. *The Seventy-fifth Yearbook of the National Society for the Study of Education*. University of Chicago Press, 1976.

——. *The Conditions of Learning*. New York: Holt, Rinehart and Winston, 1970.

Gall, Meredith and Joyce Gall. "The Discussion Method." In *The Seventy-fifth Yearbook of the National Society for the Study of Education*, edited by N. L. Gage. University of Chicago Press, 1976.

Gallagher, James. "Productive Thinking." In *Review of Child Development Research*, edited by Martin Hoffman and Lois Hoffman. New York: Russell Sage Foundation, 1964.

——. "Phenomenal Growth and New Problems Characterize Special Education." *Phi Delta Kappan* 55 (1974): 516–520.

Gallup, George. "Eighth Annual Gallup Poll of the Public's Attitudes Toward the Public Schools." *Phi Delta Kappan* 58 (1976): 187–200.

Gardner, John. *Excellence — Can We Be Equal and Excellent Too?* New York: Harper & Row, 1961.

Gardner, Lytt. "Deprivation Dwarfism." *Scientific American* 227 (July 1972): 13, 76–82.

Gerlach, Vernon and Donald Ely. *Teaching and Media: A Systematic Approach*. Englewood Cliffs, N.J.: Prentice-Hall, 1971.

Getzels, J. W. and J. T. Dillon. "The Nature of Giftedness and the Education of the Gifted." In *Second Handbook of Research on Teaching*, edited by Robert Travers. Skokie, Ill.: Rand McNally, 1973.

Ghiselin, Brewster, ed. *The Creative Process.* New York: New American Library, 1955.

Gickling, Edward and John Theobold. "Mainstreaming: Affect or Effect." *The Journal of Special Education* 9 (1975): 317–328.

Gillespie, John and Diana Spirit. *Creating a School Media Program*. New York: Bowker, 1973.

Ginsburg, Herbert and Sylvia Opper. *Piaget's Theory of Intellectual Development: An Introduction*. Englewood Cliffs, N.J.: Prentice-Hall, 1969.

Glaser, Robert. "Educational Psychology and Education." *American Psychologist* 10 (1973): 557–566.

Glaser, Robert and William Cooley. "Instrumentation for Teaching and Instructional Management." In *Second Handbook of Research on Teaching*, edited by Robert Travers. Skokie, Ill.: Rand McNally, 1973.

Goethals, George. "Adolescence: Variations on a Theme." In *Youth 1975. The Seventy-fourth Yearbook of the National Society for the Study of Education*, edited by Robert Havighurst and Philip Dreyer. University of Chicago Press, 1975.

Goethals, George and Dennis Klos. *Experiencing Youth: First Person Accounts*. Boston: Little, Brown, 1976.

Gombrich, E. H. "The Visual Image." *Scientific American* 227 (September 1972): 82–96.

Good, Thomas, Bruce Biddle, and Jere Brophy. *Teachers Make a Difference*. New York: Holt, Rinehart and Winston, 1975.

Gorman, Richard. *Discovering Piaget: A Guide for Teachers*. Columbus, Ohio: Merrill, 1972.

Gottlieb, Jay, Dorothy Gampel, and Milton Budoff. "Classroom Behavior of Retarded Children Before and After Integration into Regular Classes." *The Journal of Special Education* 9 (1975): 307–315.

Graham, Richard. "Youth and Experiential Learning." In *The Seventy-fourth Yearbook of the National Society for the Study of Education*, edited by Robert Havighurst and Philip Dreyer. University of Chicago Press, 1975.

Gray, William S. *On Their Own in Reading*. Chicago: Scott, Foresman, 1948.

Grenis, Michael. "Individualization, Grouping, Competition, and Excellence." *Phi Delta Kappan* 57 (1975): 199–200.

Guilford, J. P. "Creativity." *American Psychologist* 9 (1950): 444–454.

——. *Personality*. New York: McGraw-Hill, 1959.

——. "Intelligence: 1965 Model." *American Psychologist* 21 (1966): 20–27.

——. *The Nature of Human Intelligence*. New York: McGraw-Hill, 1967.

Guthrie, E. R. "Conditioning: A Theory of Learning in Terms of Stimulus, Response and Association." In *Forty-first Yearbook of the National Society for the Study of Education*. Part II. Bloomington, Ill.: Public School Publishing, 1942.

Hager, James. "The Educator's Role with Hyperkinetic Children." *Phi Delta Kappan* 54 (1973): 338–339.

Hall, Mary Harrington. "An Interview with Mr. Behaviorist—B. F. Skinner." *Psychology Today* 1 (September 1967): 20–23, 68–71.

Harlow, Harry, Margaret Harlow, and S. J. Suomi. "From Thought to Therapy: Lessons from a Primate Laboratory." *American Scientist* 59 (1971): 538–549.

Harris, Albert. *How to Increase Reading Ability*. New York: McKay, 1970.

Havighurst, Robert. *Developmental Tasks and Education*. New York: McKay, 1972.

Heikkinen, Henry. "A Study of Factors Influencing Student Attitudes Towards Chemistry." Unpublished Doctoral Dissertation, University of Maryland, 1973.

Held, Richard. "Plasticity of Sensory-Motor Systems." *Scientific American* 23 (September 1965): 14, 84–88.

Heller, Marc and Mary Alice White. "Rates of Teacher Verbal Approval and Disapproval to Higher and Lower Ability Classes." *Journal of Educational Psychology* 67 (1975): 796–800.

Hendrickson, Walter. "Teacher in the Sky." *Phi Delta Kappan* 56 (1975): 539–541.

Herbert, Martin. *Emotional Problems of Development in Children*. New York: Academic Press, 1974.

Hergenhahn, B. R. *Theories of Learning*. Englewood Cliffs, N.J.: Prentice-Hall, 1976.

Heron, Woodburn. "The Pathology of Boredom." *Scientific American* 196 (1957): 30, 52–56.

Heyman, Mark. *Simulation Games for the Classroom*. Bloomington, Ind.: Phi Delta Kappa Educational Foundation, 1975.

Highet, Gilbert. *The Art of Teaching*. New York: Knopf, 1950.

——. *The Immortal Profession*. New York: Weybright & Talley, 1976.

Hilgard, Ernest R. and Gordon H. Bower. *Theories of Learning*, 3rd ed. Englewood Cliffs, N.J.: Prentice-Hall, 1966.

Hilgard, Ernest, Richard Atkinson, and Rita Atkinson. *Introduction to Psychology*. New York: Harcourt Brace Jovanovich, 1975.

Horner, Matina. "Women's Will to Fail." *Psychology Today* 3 (November 1969): 36–38, 62.

Houston, W. Robert and Howard L. Jones. *Three Views of Competency-Based Teacher Education: II. University of Houston*. Bloomington, Ind.: Phi Delta Kappa Educational Foundation, 1974.

Houts, Paul. "Behind the Call for Test Reform and Abolition of the I.Q." *Phi Delta Kappan* 57 (1976): 669–673.

Howe, M. J. and L. Singer. "Presentation Variables and Students' Activities in Meaningful Learning." *British Journal of Educational Psychology* 45 (1975): 52–61.

Hull, C. L. "Quantitative Aspects of the Evolution of Concepts." *Psychological Monographs* 28 (1920): 1–86.

Hunt, J. McVicker. "Black Genes—White Environment." *Transaction* (June 1969): 12, 22.

Hydn, Holger. "Biochemical and Molecular Aspects of Learning and Memory." *Proceedings of the American Philosophical Society* 111 (1967): 326–342.

Inhelder, Barbel and Jean Piaget. *The Growth of Logical Thinking from Childhood to Adolescence*. New York: Basic Books, 1958.

Jackson, Philip. *Life in the Classroom*. New York: Holt, Rinehart and Winston, 1968.

Jenkins, R. L. "Diagnosis, Dynamics, and Treatment in Child Psychiatry." In *Diagnostic Classifications in Child Psychiatry*, edited by R. L. Jenkins and J. Cole. *Psychiatric Research Reports of the American Psychiatric Association*. Vol. 18, 1969.

Jensen, Arthur. "How Much Can We Boost I.Q. and Scholastic Achievement?" *Harvard Educational Review* 39 (Winter 1969): 1–123.

Jersild, Arthur and F. B. Holmes. *Children's Fears*. Child Development Monographs, no. 20. New York: Teachers College, Columbia University, 1935*a*.

———. "Methods of Overcoming Children's Fears." *Journal of Psychology* 1 (1935*b*): 282–283.

John-Steiner, Vera and Ellen Souberman. "Perspectives on Bilingual Education." In *Early Childhood Education*, edited by Bernard Spodek and Herbert Walberg. Berkeley, Calif.: McCutchan Publishing, 1977.

Jones, J. Charles. *Learning*. New York: Harcourt Brace Jovanovich, 1967.

Judd, William. "The Relation of Special Training to General Intelligence." *Educational Review* 36 (1908): 28–42.

Kagan, Jerome and R. Klein. "Cross-Cultural Perspectives on Early Development." *American Psychologist* 28 (1973): 947–961.

Kahn, Jack and Jean Nursten. *Unwillingly to School*. New York: Macmillan, 1964.

Kanfer, Fred. "Behavior Modification—An Overview." In *Behavior Modification in Education*, edited by Carl Thoreson. *The Seventy-second Yearbook of the National Society for the Study of Education*. University of Chicago Press, 1973.

Kean, John and Carl Personke. *The Language Arts: Teaching and Learning in the Elementary School*. New York: St. Martin's Press, 1976.

Kemp, Jerrold. *Instructional Design: A Plan for Unit and Course Development*. Belmont, Calif.: Fearon Publisher, 1971.

Keniston, Kenneth. *Youth and Dissent*. New York: Harcourt Brace Jovanovich, 1970.

Kerlinger, Fred. *Foundations of Behavioral Research*. New York: Holt, Rinehart and Winston, 1973.

Kess, Joseph. *Psycholinguistics*. New York: Wiley, 1976.

Kimble, Gregory. *Hilgard and Marquis' Conditioning and Learning*. Englewood Cliffs, N.J.: Prentice-Hall, 1961.

Kilpatrick, William. *Identity and Intimacy*. New York: Dell (Delta Books), 1975.

Kirk, Samuel. *Educating Exceptional Children*. Boston: Houghton Mifflin, 1972.

Kirp, David. "The Great Sorting Machine." *Phi Delta Kappan* 55 (1974): 521–525.

Klausmeier, Herbert, Elizabeth Ghatala, and Dorothy Frayer. *Conceptual Learning and Development*. New York: Academic Press, 1974.

Knobloch, Hilda and Benjamin Pasamanick. *Gesell and Amatruda's Developmental Diagnoses*. New York: Harper & Row, 1974.

Koch, Richard and Jean Holt Koch. "We Can Do More to Prevent the Tragedy of Retarded Children." *Psychology Today* 10 (December 1976): 88–93, 108.

Koestler, Arthur. *The Act of Creation*. New York: Macmillan, 1964.

Koffka, Kurt. *Principles of Gestalt Psychology*. New York: Harcourt Brace Jovanovich, 1935.

Köhler, Wolfgang. *Gestalt Psychology*. Rev. ed. New York: Liveright, 1947.

———. *The Task of Gestalt Psychology*. Princeton University Press, 1969.

Kohlberg, Lawrence. "The Cognitive-Developmental Approach to Moral Education." *Phi Delta Kappan* 56 (1975): 670–677.

Kolesnik, Walter. *Learning: Educational Application*. Boston: Allyn & Bacon, 1976.

Kounin, Jacob S. *Discipline and Group Management in Classrooms*. New York: Holt, Rinehart and Winston, 1970.

Krathwohl, David R., Benjamin S. Bloom, and Bertram B. Masia. *Taxonomy of Educational Objectives, Handbook II: Affective Domain*. New York: McKay, 1964.

Krech, David. "Psychoneurobiochemeducation." *Phi Delta Kappan* 50 (1969): 370–376.

Krech, David and Richard Crutchfield. *Elements of Psychology*. New York: Knopf, 1948.

Landau, Elliott, Sherrie Epstein, and Ann Stone. *The Teaching Experience: An Introduction to Education Through Literature*. Englewood Cliffs, N.J.: Prentice-Hall, 1976.

Lane, Harlan. *The Wild Boy of Aveyron*. Cambridge, Mass.: Harvard University Press, 1976.

Langer, Suzanne. *Feeling and Form: A Theory of Art*. New York: Scribner, 1953.

Lapouse, R. and M. A. Monk. "Fears and Worries in a Representative Sample of Children."

American Journal of Orthopsychiatry 29 (1959): 803–818.

Laurenz, Frances. *The Relationship Between Classroom Learning Environment and Student Attitude Toward Science.* National Science Foundation Grant, GW-6800. University of Minnesota, November 1974.

Leifer, Aimee. "Teaching with Television and Film." In *The Seventy-fifth Yearbook of the National Society for the Study of Education,* edited by N. L. Gage. University of Chicago Press, 1976.

Lenneberg, Eric. "The Biological Foundations of Language." *Hospital Practice* 2 (1967): 59–67.

Levin, Joel and Vernon Allen, eds. *Cognitive Learning in Children.* New York: Academic Press, 1976.

Levine, Seymour. "Stimulation in Infancy." *Scientific American* (May 1960): 47, 80–86.

Lewin, Kurt. *A Dynamic Theory of Personality.* New York: McGraw-Hill, 1935.

———. *Principles of Topological Psychology.* Translated by F. Heider and G. M. Heider. New York; McGraw-Hill, 1936.

———. "Field Theory and Learning." In *The Forty-first Yearbook of the National Society for the Study of Education,* Part II. Bloomington, Ill.: Public School Publishing, 1942.

Lindvall, C. M. and John Bolvin. "Programmed Instruction in the Schools: An Application of Programming Principles in Individually Prescribed Instruction." In *Programmed Instruction,* edited by Phil Lange. *The Sixty-sixth Yearbook of the National Society for the Study of Education.* University of Chicago Press, 1967.

Lippitt, Peggy. *Students Teach Students.* Bloomington, Ind.: Phi Delta Kappa Educational Foundation, 1975.

Lippitt, R. and R. K. White. "An Experimental Study of Leadership and Group Life." In *Human Development: Selected Readings,* edited by Morris Haimowitz and Natalie Haimowitz. New York: Crowell, 1960.

Lortie, Dan. "Observations on Teaching as Work." In *Second Handbook of Research on Teaching,* edited by Robert Travers. Skokie, Ill.: Rand McNally, 1973.

Luchins, A. S. and Eitl Luchins. *Rigidity of Be-* havior. Eugene: University of Oregon Press, 1959.

Lumsdaine, Arthur A. "Instruments and Media of Instruction." In *Handbook of Research on Teaching,* edited by N. L. Gage. Skokie, Ill.: Rand McNally, 1963.

———. "Educational Technology, Programmed Learning, and Instructional Science." In *The Sixty-third Yearbook of the National Society for the Study of Education.* Part I. University of Chicago Press, 1964.

Lumsdaine, Arthur A. and Robert Glaser, eds. *Teaching Machines and Programmed Learning.* Washington, D.C.: National Education Association, 1960.

Maccoby, Eleanor and Carol Jacklin. *The Psychology of Sex Differences.* Stanford University Press, 1974a.

———. "What We Know and Don't Know About Sex Differences." *Psychology Today* 16 (December 1974b): 109–112.

Maccoby, Eleanor and John Masters. "Attachment and Dependency." In *Carmichael's Manual of Child Psychology,* edited by Paul Mussen. New York: Wiley, 1970.

MacKinnon, Donald W. "The Nature and Nurture of Creative Talent." *American Psychologist* 17 (1962): 484–495.

Macmillan, Donald. "The Problem of Motivation in the Education of the Mentally Retarded." *Exceptional Children* 37 (1971): 579–586.

Mager, Robert. *Preparing Instructional Objectives.* Belmont, Calif.: Fearon Press, 1975.

Mann, Philip. *Shared Responsibility for Handicapped Students.* Miami, Fla.: Banyan Books, 1976.

Manocha, Sohan. *Malnutrition and Retarded Human Development.* Springfield, Ill.: Thomas, 1972.

Marland, Sidney. "Career Education: Every Student Headed for a Goal." *American Vocational Journal* 47 (1972): 34–38.

Marlowe, John. "Testing, Testing . . . Can You Hear Me?" *Phi Delta Kappan* 58 (1976): 256–257.

Martin, David. "Your Praise Can Smother Learning." *Learning* 5 (1977): 43–51.

Martin, Edwin. "Integration of the Handicapped Child into Regular Schools." *Minnesota Education* 2 (Winter 1976): 7–11.

Maslow, Abraham. *Motivation and Personality.* New York: Harper & Row, 1970.

McClelland, David. *The Achieving Society.* New York: Van Nostrand, 1961.

McClelland, David and D. G. Winter. *Motivating Economic Achievement.* New York: Free Press, 1969.

McGeoch, John A. and Arthur L. Irion. *The Psychology of Human Learning.* Rev. ed. New York: McKay, 1952.

McKeachie, Wilbert. "Psychology in America's Bicentennial Year." *American Psychologist* 31 (1976): 819–833.

McLeish, John. "The Lecture Method." In *The Psychology of Teaching Methods,* edited by N. L. Gage. *The Seventy-fifth Yearbook of the National Society for the Study of Education.* University of Chicago Press, 1976.

McNeil, John and W. James Popham. "The Assessment of Teacher Competence." In *Second Handbook of Research on Teaching,* edited by Robert Travers. Stokie, Ill.: Rand McNally, 1973.

Mehrens, William and Irvin Lehmann. *Standardized Tests in Education.* New York: Holt, Rinehart and Winston, 1975.

Melton, William. "Motivation and Learning." In *Encyclopedia of Educational Research,* edited by Walter S. Monroe. New York: Macmillan, 1950.

Merrill, M. D. "Psychomotor Taxonomies, Classification and Instructional Theory." In *The Psychomotor Domain,* edited by R. N. Singer. Philadelphia: Lea & Febiger, 1972.

Miller, G. A., E. Galanter, and K. H. Priban. *Plans and the Structure of Behavior.* New York: Holt, Rinehart and Winston, 1960.

Moffett, James. *Teaching: The Universe of Discourse.* Boston: Houghton Mifflin, 1968.

Molloy, Larry. "The Handicapped Child in the Everyday Classroom." *Phi Delta Kappan* 56 (1975): 377–380.

Monahan, L., D. Kuhn, and P. Shaver. "Intrapsychic Versus Cultural Explanations of the Fear of Success Motive." *Journal of Personality and Social Psychology* 29 (1974): 60–64.

Money, John and Anke Ehrhard. *Man and Woman, Boy and Girl.* Baltimore: Johns Hopkins University Press, 1972.

Moore, Shirley and Sally Kilmer. *Contemporary Preschool Education: A Program for Young Children.* New York: Wiley, 1973.

Moore, T. V. "The Process of Abstraction." *University of California Publications in Psychology* 1 (1910): 73–197.

Moriarty, Thomas. "A Nation of Willing Victims." *Psychology Today* 7 (April 1975): 43–50.

Moulton, William. "Linguistics." *Today's Education* 54 (1965): 49–53.

——. "The Study of Language and Human Communication." In *The Sixty-ninth Yearbook of the National Society for the Study of Education,* edited by Albert Marckwardt. Vol. 2. University of Chicago Press, 1970.

Murphy, Lois. *The Widening World of Childhood.* New York: Basic Books, 1962.

Murray, Edward. *Motivation and Emotion.* Englewood Cliffs, N.J.: Prentice-Hall, 1964.

Naumann, Nancy. "The Day Teacher Kept Her Mouth Shut." *Early Years* 6 (1975): 68–72.

Neale, Daniel. "A Matter of Shaping." *Phi Delta Kappan* 47 (1966): 367–379.

Nixon, John and Lawrence Locke. "Research on Teaching Physical Education." In *Second Handbook of Research on Teaching,* edited by Robert Travers. Skokie, Ill.: Rand McNally, 1973.

Olsen, Henry. "Bibliotherapy to Help Children Solve Problems." *The Elementary School Journal* (April 1975): 422–429.

Page, Ellis B. "Teacher Comments and Student Performance: A Seventy-four Classroom Experiment in School Motivation." *Journal of Educational Psychology* 49 (1958): 173–181.

Palmer, Orville. "Seven Classic Ways of Grading Dishonestly." *The English Journal* (October 1962): 464–467.

Paolitto, Diana and Richard Hersh. "Pedagogical Implications for Stimulating Moral Development in the Classroom." In *Reflections on Values Education,* edited by John Meyer. Ontario: Wilfred Laurier Press, 1976.

Parker, Franklin. *The Battle of the Books: Ka-*

nawha County. Bloomington, Ind.: The Phi Delta Kappa Educational Foundation, 1975.

Peters, Richard. "A Reply to Kohlberg." *Phi Delta Kappan* 56 (1975): 678.

Phares, E. Jerry. *Locus of Control: A Personality Determinant of Behavior.* Morristown, N.J.: General Learning Press, 1973.

Phillips, David. "Case History of a Behavior Modification Project in a Public School." In *Behavior Modification: Application to Education,* edited by Fred Keller and Emilio Ribes-Inesta. New York: Academic Press, 1974.

Phillips, John. *The Origins of Intellect: Piaget's Theory.* San Francisco: Freeman, 1975.

Piaget, Jean. *The Origins of Intelligence.* New York: International Universities Press, 1952.

——. *The Language and Thought of the Child.* New York: New American Library (Meridian Books), 1955.

——. "Development and Learning." In *Piaget Rediscovered,* edited by Richard Ripple and Verne Rockcastle. Washington, D.C.: U.S. Office of Education, National Science Foundation, 1964.

——. *Six Psychological Studies.* New York: Random House, 1967.

——. *Science of Education and the Psychology of the Child.* New York: Viking Press, 1971.

——. *The Child and Reality.* New York: Viking Press, 1973.

Piaget, Jean and Barbel Inhelder. *The Psychology of the Child.* New York: Basic Books, 1969.

Pierce, John. "Communication." *Scientific American* 227 (September 1972): 31–41.

Pines, Maya. "In Praise of Invulnerables." *APA Monitor* 6 (1975): 7.

Premack, David. "Reinforcement Theory." In *Nebraska Symposium on Motivation,* Vol. 13, edited by D. Levine. Lincoln: University of Nebraska Press, 1965.

Pressey, Sidney L. "Autoinstruction: Perspectives, Problems, Potentials." In *Sixty-third Yearbook of the National Society for the Study of Education,* Part I. University of Chicago Press, 1964.

Pula, Fred and Charles Fagone. *Multimedia Processes in Education.* Dubuque, Iowa: Kendall/Hunt Publishing, 1973.

Purpel, David and Kevin Ryan. "Moral Education: Where Sages Fear to Tread." *Phi Delta Kappan* 56 (1975): 659–662.

Reber, K. S. "On Psycholinguistic Paradigms." *Journal of Psycholinguistic Research* 2 (1973): 289–319.

Redl, Fritz. "Aggression in the Classroom." *Today's Education* 58 (1969): 30–32.

Redl, Fritz and William Wattenberg. *Mental Hygiene in Teaching.* New York: Harcourt Brace Jovanovich, 1959.

Reynolds, M. C. "A Framework for Considering Some Issues in Special Education." *Exceptional Children* 7 (1962): 367–370.

Reynolds, M. C., ed. "Mainstreaming," *Minnesota Education* 2 (Winter 1976).

Rheingold, H. L. and C. O. Eckerman. "The Infant Separates Himself from His Mother." *Science* 168 (1970): 78–83.

Rich, Jordan. "Effects of Children's Physical Attractiveness on Teachers' Evaluation." *Journal of Educational Psychology* 67 (1975): 599–609.

Robinson, H. B. and N. M. Robinson. "Mental Retardation." In *Carmichael's Manual of Child Psychology,* edited by Paul Mussen. New York: Wiley, 1970.

Rodham, Hillary. "Children Under the Law." *Harvard Educational Review* 43 (1973): 487–514.

Rogers, Carl R. *Client-Centered Therapy.* Boston: Houghton Mifflin, 1951.

——. "Toward a Theory of Creativity." In *Creativity and Its Cultivation,* edited by H. H. Anderson. New York: Harper & Row, 1959.

——. *On Becoming a Person.* Boston: Houghton Mifflin, 1961.

——. "Actualizing Tendency in Relation to 'Motives' and to Consciousness." In *Nebraska Symposium on Motivation,* edited by Marshall R. Jones. Lincoln: University of Nebraska Press, 1963.

——. *Freedom to Learn.* Columbus, Ohio. Merrill, 1969.

——. "Some New Challenges." *American Psychologist* (1973): 379–387.

——. "In Retrospect—Forty-six Years." *American Psychologist* (February 1974): 115–123.

Rose, Steven. *The Conscious Brain.* New York: Knopf, 1973.

Rosenthal, Robert and Lenore Jacobson. *Pygmalion in the Classroom.* New York: Holt, Rinehart and Winston, 1968.

Rosenzweig, Mark, Edward Bennett, and Marian Diamond. "Brain Changes in Response to Experience." *Scientific American* (February 1972): 10, 22–29.

Rosner, Benjamin and Patricia Kay. "Will the Promise of C/PBTE Be Fulfilled?" *Phi Delta Kappan* 56 (1974): 290–295.

Ross, C. E. and Julian Stanley. *Measurement in Today's Schools.* Englewood Cliffs, N.J.: Prentice-Hall, 1954.

Rothkopf, Ernst. "The Psychology of Written Instruction." In *The Seventy-fifth Yearbook of the National Society for the Study of Education.* University of Chicago Press, 1976.

Rotter, Julian B. "Generalized Expectancies for Internal Versus External Control of Reinforcement." *Psychological Monographs* 80 (1966), no. 609.

——. "External Control and Internal Control." *Psychology Today* 5 (June 1971): 37–42, 58–59.

Ruch, G. M. *The Objective or New-Type Examination.* Chicago: Scott, Foresman, 1929.

Ryans, D. G. *Characteristics of Teachers: Their Description, Comparison, and Appraisal.* Washington, D.C.: American Council on Education, 1960.

——. "Some Relationships Between Pupil Behavior and Certain Teacher Characteristics." *Journal of Educational Psychology* 52 (1961a): 82–90.

——. "Inventory Estimated Teacher Characteristics as Covariants of Observer Assessed Pupil Behavior." *Journal of Educational Psychology* 52 (1961b): 91–97.

——. "Research on Teacher Behavior in the Context of the Teacher Characteristics Study." In *Contemporary Research on Teacher Effectiveness,* edited by Bruce Biddle and William Ellena. Holt, Rinehart and Winston, 1964.

Ryder, Henry, Harry Carr, and Paul Herget. "Future Performance in Footracing." *Scientific American* 34 (June 1976): 109–119.

Sagan, Carl. *The Dragons of Eden.* New York: Random House, 1977.

Samuelson, Paul. *Economics.* New York: McGraw-Hill, 1975.

Savage, John. *Linguistics for Teachers.* Chicago: Science Research Associates, 1973.

Savage, John and Joan Jones. "Decoding and Meaning: How Different Are the Language and Cognitive Orientation?" *The New England Reading Association Journal* 9 (1973–1974): 24–28, 67–70.

Schramm, Wilbur. "Learning from Instructional Television." *Review of Educational Research* 32 (1962): 156–168.

Scott, J. P. "A Time to Learn." *Psychology Today* 2 (March 1969): 46–48, 66–67.

Scriven, Michael. "Some Issues in the Logic and Ethics of Mainstreaming." *Minnesota Education* 2 (Winter 1976) 19–22.

Seidner, Constance. "Teaching with Simulations and Games." In *The Seventy-fifth Yearbook of The National Society for the Study of Education,* edited by N. L. Gage. University of Chicago Press, 1976.

Serbin, Lisa and K. Daniel O'Leary. "How Nursery Schools Teach Girls to Shut Up." *Psychology Today* 9 (December 1975): 57–58, 102–103.

Shannon, Charles. "The Mathematical Theory of Communication." *Bell System Technical Journal* (July–October 1948).

Shepherd, M., B. Oppenheim, and S. Mitchell. *Childhood Behavior and Mental Health.* New York: Grune & Stratton, 1971.

Sherman, Barbara and Robert Blackburn. "Personal Characteristics and Teaching Effectiveness of College Faculty." *Journal of Educational Psychology* 67 (1975): 124–131.

Sigel, Irving and Rodney Cocking. *Cognitive Development from Childhood to Adolescence: A Constructive Perspective.* New York: Holt, Rinehart and Winston, 1977.

Simon, Sidney, Leland Howe, and Howard Kirchenbaum. *Values Clarification: A Handbook of Practical Strategies for Teachers and Students.* New York: Hart Publishing, 1972.

Simon, Sidney and Polly de Sherbinin. "Values Clarification: It Can Start Gently and Grow

Deep." *Phi Delta Kappan* 56 (1975): 679–683.

Skeels, Harold. *Adult Status of Children with Contrasting Early Life Experiences*. Monographs of the Society for Research in Child Development. Vol. 31, no. 3, 1966.

Skinner, B. F. *The Behavior of Organisms: An Experimental Analysis*. Englewood Cliffs, N.J.: Prentice-Hall, 1938.

——. *Walden Two*. New York: Macmillan, 1948.

——. *Science and Human Behavior*. New York: Macmillan, 1953.

——. "The Science of Learning and the Art of Teaching." *Harvard Educational Review* 25 (1954): 86–97.

——. *Verbal Behavior*. New York: Appleton-Century-Crofts, 1957.

——. "Why We Need Teaching Machines." *Harvard Educational Review* 31 (1961): 377–398.

——. *The Technology of Teaching*. Englewood Cliffs, N.J.: Prentice-Hall, 1968.

——. *Beyond Freedom and Dignity*. New York: Knopf, 1971.

——. "The Free and Happy Student." *Phi Delta Kappan* 55 (1973*a*): 13–16.

——. "Making Education More Efficient." In *Behavior Modification in Education*, edited by Carl Thoreson. *The Seventy-second Yearbook of the National Society for the Study of Education*. University of Chicago Press, 1973*b*.

——. *About Behaviorism*. New York: Knopf, 1974.

Skinner, B. F. and C. B. Ferster. *Schedules of Reinforcement*. Englewood Cliffs, N.J.: Prentice-Hall, 1957.

Smith, Debra, Rebecca Taylor, and Monica Werblud. *Make It Happen: A Guide for Developing School Volunteer Programs*. Newton, Mass.: The Korda Project, 1976.

Smith, Donald F. "Adolescent Suicide: A Problem for Teachers?" *Phi Delta Kappan* 57 (1976): 539–542.

Smith, Pamela and Glee Bentley. *Mainstreaming Mildly Handicapped Students into the Regular Classroom*. Austin, Texas: Education Service Center, 1975.

Spitz, Rene. "Hospitalism." In *The Psychoanalytic Study of the Child*, edited by O. Feni-

chel et al. New York: International Universities Press, 1945.

Stamm, Ira. "The Multiple Functions of Play." In *The New Children*, edited by John F. Travers. Stamford, Conn.: Greylock Publishers, 1976.

Stanley, Julian C. *Measurment in Today's Schools*. 4th ed. Englewood Cliffs, N.J.: Prentice-Hall, 1964.

——. "Accelerating the Educational Progress of Intellectually Gifted Youth." *Educational Psychologist* 10 (Fall 1973): 133–146.

——. "Identifying and Nurturing the Intellectually Gifted." *Phi Delta Kappan* 58 (1976): 234–237.

Stashower, Gloria. "Mainstreaming in the Work World." *American Education* 12 (1976): 9–13.

Stein, Morris L. and Shirley J. Heinze. *Creativity and the Individual*. New York: Free Press, 1960.

Stephens, J. M. *The Process of Schooling*. New York: Holt, Rinehart and Winston, 1967.

Stewart, John S. "Clarifying Values Clarification: A Critique." *Phi Delta Kappan* 56 (1975): 684–688.

Stolz, Stephanie, Louis Wienckowski, and Bertram Brown. "Behavior Modification: A Perspective on Critical Issues." *The American Psychologist* 30 (1975): 1027–1048.

Stoops, Emery and Joyce King-Stoops. *Discipline or Disaster?* Bloomington, Ind.: Phi Delta Kappa Educational Foundation, 1972.

Talbot, Nathan. *Raising Children in Modern America*. Boston: Little, Brown, 1976.

Tanner, J. M. *Growth at Adolescence*. Oxford: Blackwell Scientific Publications, 1962.

——. "Physical Growth." In *Carmichael's Manual of Child Psychology*, edited by Paul Mussen. New York: Wiley, 1970.

Tavris, Carol. "It's Tough to Nip Sexism in the Bud." *Psychology Today* 9 (December 1975): 58, 102.

Taylor, Calvin. "A Tentative Description of the Creative Individual." In *Human Variability and Learning*, edited by Walter B. Waetjen. Washington, D.C.: Association for Supervision and Curriculum Development, 1961.

Teitelbaum, Herbert and Richard Hiller. "Bilingual Education: The Legal Mandate." *Harvard Educational Review* 47 (1977): 138–170.

Terman, Lewis M. *The Measurement of Intelligence.* Boston: Houghton Mifflin, 1916.

——. *Stanford-Binet Intelligence Scale: Manual for the Third Revision. Form L-M.* Boston: Houghton Mifflin, 1960.

Terman, Lewis M. and Maud Merrill. *Measuring Intelligence.* Boston: Houghton Mifflin, 1937.

Terman, Lewis and Melita Oden. *The Gifted Child Grows Up.* Stanford University Press, 1947.

Tharp, Roland and Ronald Gallimore. "What a Coach Can Teach a Teacher." *Psychology Today* 9 (January 1976): 74–78.

Thiagarajan, Sivasilam. "Gamegame II." *Phi Delta Kappan* 55 (1974): 474–477.

Thomas, Alexander, Stella Chess, and Herbert Birch. "The Origin of Personality." *Scientific American* 223 (August 1970): 102–109.

Thompson, George. "Discipline and the High School Teacher." *The Clearing House* 49 (1976): 408–413.

Thorndike, Edward Lee. *The Principles of Teaching.* New York: Seeler, 1906.

——. *Animal Intelligence.* New York: Macmillan, 1911.

——. *The Psychology of Learning.* Vol. II. New York: Teachers College Press, 1913.

——. *Measurement of Intelligence.* New York: Columbia University Press, 1927.

——. *The Fundamentals of Learning.* New York: Teachers College Press, 1932.

Thorndike, Edward Lee and R. S. Woodworth. "The Influence of Improvement in Our Mental Function Upon the Efficiency of Other Functions." *Psychological Review* 8 (1901): 247–261, 384–395, 558–564.

Thorndike, Robert L. and Elizabeth Hagen. *Measurement and Evaluation in Psychology and Education.* 3rd ed. New York: Wiley, 1977.

Tofler, Alvin. *Future Shock.* New York: Random House, 1970.

Torrance, E. Paul. *Encouraging Creativity in the Classroom.* Dubuque, Iowa: Brown, 1970.

Travers, John F. *Learning: Analysis and Application.* New York: McKay, 1972.

——. *The Growing Child: An Introduction to Child Development.* New York: Wiley, 1977.

Travers, John F. editor. *The New Children.* Stamford, Conn.: Greylock Publishers, 1976.

Traviss, Mary P. "The Principal, Moral Education, and Staff Development." *Momentum* 4 (December 1975): 16–25.

Trezise, Robert. "Are the Gifted Coming Back?" *Phi Delta Kappan* 54 (1973): 687–688, 692.

Tyler, Ralph. *Basic Principles of Curriculum and Instruction.* University of Chicago Press, 1950.

Ulrey, Gordon. "Effects of Outdoor Education on Children's Locus of Control." Unpublished Doctoral Dissertation, Boston College, 1974.

——. "Psychological Testing of Young Children." In *The New Children,* edited by John F. Travers. Stamford, Conn.: Greylock Publishers, 1976.

Voelker, Paul. "Organization, Administration and Supervision of Special Education Programs." In *Education of Exceptional Children and Youth,* edited by William Cruickshank and G. Orville Johnson. Englewood Cliffs, N.J.: Prentice-Hall, 1975.

Vygotsky, Lev. *Thought and Language.* New York: Wiley, 1962.

Walberg, Herbert and Garry Anderson. "Classroom Climate and Individual Learning." *Journal of Educational Psychology* 59 (1968): 414–419.

Wallach, Michael. "Creativity." In *Carmichael's Manual of Child Psychology,* edited by Paul Mussen. New York: Wiley, 1970.

Wallas, G. *The Art of Thought.* New York: Harcourt Brace Jovanovich, 1926.

Wallen, Norman and Robert M. W. Travers. "Analysis and Investigation of Teaching Methods." In *Handbook of Research on Teaching,* edited by N. L. Gage. Skokie, Ill.: Rand McNally, 1963.

Watson, James. " 'I'm Just Plain Dumb!' How to Change Negative Self-Concepts in Low-Ability Children." *Today's Education: NEA Journal* 62 (1973): 26–27.

Watson, John B. "Psychology as the Behaviorist Views It." *Psychological Review* 20 (1913): 158–177.

——. *Behaviorism*. Rev. ed. New York: Norton, 1930.

Wax, Joseph. "Competition: Educational Incongruity." *Phi Delta Kappan* 57 (1975): 197–198.

Weber, George. "The Case Against Man: A Course of Study." *Phi Delta Kappan* 57 (1975): 81–82.

Wechsler, David. *The Measurement of Adult Intelligence*. Baltimore, Md.: Williams & Wilkins, 1944.

——. *Wechsler Adult Intelligence Scale*. New York: Psychological Corporation, 1955.

——. *The Measurement and Appraisal of Adult Intelligence*. 4th ed. Baltimore, Md.: Williams & Wilkins, 1958.

——. "The I.Q. Is an Intelligent Test." *New York Times Magazine* 26 June 1966.

Weidmann, Charles C. "Written Examination Procedures." *Phi Delta Kappan* 16 (1933): 78–83.

——. "Review of Essay Test Studies." *Journal of Higher Education* 12 (1941): 41–44.

Weintraub, Frederick and Alan Abeson. "New Education Policies for the Handicapped." *Phi Delta Kappan* 55 (1974): 526–530.

Wertheimer, Max. *Productive Thinking*. New York: Harper & Row, 1959.

White, Burton. *The First Three Years of Life*. Englewood Cliffs, N.J.: Prentice-Hall, 1975.

White, Sheldon. "The Learning Theory Approach." In *Carmichael's Manual of Child Psychology*, edited by Paul Mussen. Vol. I. New York: Wiley, 1970.

Whitehead, Alfred North. *The Aims of Education*. New York: New American Library, 1949.

Whiteside, Marilyn. "School Discipline: The Ongoing Crises." *The Clearing House* 49 (1975): 160–162.

Wilms, Barbara. "These Kids Are Learning to Cook and Cope." *Parents Magazine* 51 (March 1976): 40–41, 72.

Winter, Ruth. "The Long and Short of Memory." *Science Digest* 81 (1977): 36–41.

Wittrock, M. C., Carolyn Marks, and Marleen Doctorow. "Reading as a Generative Process." *Journal of Educational Psychology* 67 (1975): 484–489.

Wittrock, M. C. and Arthur Lumsdaine. "Instructional Psychology." In *Annual Review of Psychology*, edited by Mark Rosenzweig and Lyman Porter. Palo Alto, Calif.: Annual Reviews, 1977.

Witty, Elaine. "Preparing Teachers for Mainstreaming in the Department of Elementary Education." In *Shared Responsibility for Handicapped Students*, edited by Philip Mann. Miami, Fla.: Banyan Books, 1976.

Worth, Sol. "The Uses of Film." In *The Seventy-third Yearbook of the National Society for the Study of Education*, edited by David Olson. University of Chicago Press, 1974.

Wright, Lawrence. "The Bilingual Education Movement at the Crossroads." *Phi Delta Kappan* 55 (1973): 183–186.

Young, Warren. "The Enduring Mystery of Dyslexia." *Washington Star*, 28 September 1975.

Youngblood, Gene. *Expanded Cinema*. New York: Dutton, 1970.

Zintz, Miles. The Reading Process: *The Teacher and the Learner*. 2nd. ed. Dubuque, Iowa: Brown, 1975.

Name Index

Subject Index